ATHENS IN THE AGE OF ALEXANDER

THE DATED LAWS & DECREES OF 'THE LYKOURGAN ERA' 338 — 322 B.C.

ATHENS IN THE AGE OF ALEXANDER

THE DATED LAWS & DECREES OF 'THE LYKOURGAN ERA' 338 — 322 B.C.

BY

CYNTHIA J. SCHWENK

Professor of Ancient History

GEORGIA STATE UNIVERSITY

ARES PUBLISHERS INC.

CHICAGO MCMLXXXV

First Edition 1985

ARES PUBLISHERS INC.
7020 North Western Avenue
Chicago, Illinois 60645

Printed in the United States of America
International Standard Book Number:
0-89005-437-1

PREFACE

The purpose of this book is to present the dated decrees from Lykourgos's period of influence in Athens, 338/7-322/1 B.C. For the Lykourgan Era, there are over three hundred and fifty inscriptions with dates ranging from the vaguest "post 336/5" and "circa 330" to the most specific — including both the festival and civil calendar designation for the specific day of the year. Of these there are one hundred and forty-one inscriptions which are dated to a specific year in the Lykourgan Era, and these are listed in the Appendix. There are ninety-one decrees, numbered sequentially; the remaining fifty-one: treaties, ephebic lists, and dedications of bouleutai and diaitetai, are included in their proper chronological order. The ninety-one dated decrees are treated in this corpus.

I could not have done this work without access to the epigraphical material. Dr. Dina Peppa-Delmousou, Director of the Epigraphical Museum in Athens, where most of my inscriptions are housed, was most helpful during the year I initially spent examining my stones as well as during later visits to Athens. The Greek Archaeological Service also permitted me to examine stones in museums at Eleusis, the Amphiaraion, the Peiraieus, and the Akropolis.

The American School of Classical Studies in Athens offers a unique opportunity to exchange ideas and information. During my stay in Athens I was fortunate to consult a number of experienced scholars. My special thanks go to Professors Eugene Vanderpool, Judith Binder, Ronald Stroud, Kevin Clinton, Leslie Threatte, and to John Camp of the Agora Excavations.

Thanks would not be complete without acknowledging my debt to Fordyce Mitchel. From the on-the-job training in the intricacies of epigraphical study, to preparing the final manuscript he had been there — offering his wisdom and constant encouragement. I hope that in some way, this work will be an acceptable expression of my thanks.

INTRODUCTION

This work represents a pioneer effort in the presentation of epigraphical evidence: 1) all the extant dated decrees are presented in chronological order to give an epigraphical narrative of the Lykourgan era; 2) I present a complete bibliography for each decree, including work published after the appearance of the several volumes of the editio minor of *Inscriptiones Graecae* (hereafter abbreviated as *IG* II^2); 3) when physically and bureaucratically possible, I examined the stones to check for any discrepancies between the published texts and the physical remains; 4) I discuss the various restorations suggested for each degree; 5) I discuss the text of the decree, any specific problems involved, and the historical context.

It is the inclusion of all the above elements which make this presentation unique. The very novelty of the presentation, however, presents a problem in logistics: how to marshal the information into a format which is clear and concise. My solution is to separate the information concerning each decree into specific sub-headings. There can be as many as fifteen or as few as six of these sub-headings listed for a specific decree. Since the format is the same for each decree (give or take a few of the sub-headings) there follow here general comments on each sub-heading.

TITLE: The number designates the position of the decree in my Corpus. Throughout this work the symbol, #, is used to denote only the Corpus numbers and Corpus (capitalized) designates my Corpus. I have tried to make the titles as informative as possible. EM refers to the Epigraphical Museum; Ag. Inv. refers to those decrees published in *Hesperia* and housed in the Stoa of Attalos in the Agora.

PHOTO: Citations for published photos are included here. During the course of my research, I was able to obtain (with a very few exceptions) photos of those decrees with no previously published photograph from the Greek Archaeological Service for the decrees in the EM and from friends for those decrees not housed in the EM. Financial considerations have precluded inclusion of these photos here. Twenty-seven photographs, however, are included in my dissertation which covered the years 338/7 - 330/29.

EDITORS: A great number of decrees in this Corpus were found during the excavation of the Akropolis in the last century. Pittakis recorded the finds in *Ephemeris Archaiologike* by consecutive numbers, 1-4158, over the years 1837-1861. In 1855, Rangabé published a corpus of inscriptions, *Antiquités Helléniques*; his numbers are consecutive. *IG* refers to *Inscriptiones Graecae.* II is the second volume (inscriptions dated after 377 B.C.) of the editio major published by Koehler in 1877. VII, the seventh volume, deals with the inscriptions from Megara and Boiotia. II^2 is the second volume of the editio minor published by Kirchner, beginning in 1913. (Kirchner sometimes used unpublished joins, texts, and restorations supplied earlier by Velsen and Wilhelm; when this occurs, it is mentioned for the pertinent decree.) The numbers of these citations refer to corpus number, not page; journal citations include both page and corpus number, where applicable.

COLLECTIONS: Again, the numbers refer to the consecutive numbers within the specific collections, unless noted otherwise. Ditt. *Syll.* refers to Dittenberger's *Sylloge Inscriptionum Graecarum* The raised numbers are editions: first edition, 1883 and second edition, 1898; the third edition, 1915-1924, was reedited by Kirchner. Hicks refers to *A Manual of Greek Historical Inscriptions,* the second edition, 1901. Michel refers to *Recueil d'inscriptions grecques,* 1900. Tod II refers to the second volume of *Greek Historical Inscriptions*, 1948. Fuller citations are in the Bibliography at the end.

TESTIMONIA: Here I include citations from ancient authors when they are an integral part of the discussion.

SUPPLEMENTS: *SEG* refers to the *Supplementum Epigraphicum Graecum.* The first number of the citation refers to the volume; second number is that of the entry within the volume. *Bull.* is Robert's "Bulletin Epigraphique," published in *REG.* After each citation, I include in parentheses the works referred to in that citation by author.

OTHER BIBLIOGRAPHY: Since I include a separate bibliography for each decree, I have made the citations as abbreviated as possible. I always include the author, with an abbreviated form of the title of the book or journal, and, of course, the page reference. Full citations for the books and the larger, more pertinent articles can be found in the Bibliography at the end. I also include at the end a list of journals consulted with the abbreviations I have used.

The bibliographical section (editors—other bibliography) for each decree serves as a point of reference for the commentary and discussion which follow. Therefore, I include only the author's name as reference in the text (in the case of more than one work by the same author, I include what is necessary to avoid confusion).

DESCRIPTION: Included are date and place of find (when recorded) as well as any information which helps to illustrate the physical appearance of the stone.

DIMENSIONS: These are my own measurements of the stones unless noted otherwise. In the case of fragments, unless more specific measurements are included, the dimension is of the engraved surface rather than the entire stone, e.g., my measurement for the height of #12, is 0.37 m.; Kirchner recorded 0.47 m.

LETTERS: Again, the measurements are mine. The first measurement is the average height. The height of the letters usually varies, and this is indicated along with any unusual characteristics.

MAJUSCULE TEXT: This is included only when there is some discrepancy in the published text, and a majuscule text would clarify the commentary. For any inscription published in the editio major, Koehler provides a majuscule text.

EPIGRAPHICAL COMMENTARY: This is always included when there is a majuscule text or when the amount of commentary on the physical aspects of the stone is sufficient to require a separate entry. I use the following abbreviations for editors: Boe., Boeckh; Dins., Dinsmoor; Ditt., Dittenberger; Froe., Froehner; Ki., Kirchner; Koe., Koehler; Kum., Kumanudes; Mer., Meritt; Oik., Oikonomides; Osb., Osborne; Pitt., Pittakis; P.-M., Pritchett-Meritt; Pritch., Pritchett; P.-N., Pritchett-Naugebauer; Rang., Rangabé; Schw., Schweigert; Sok., Sokolowski; Tzun., Tzuntas; Ung., Unger; Vel., Velsen; Wal., Walbank; Wilh., Wilhelm.

MINUSCULE TEXT: The text is usually based on the latest published text and incorporates any new readings and/or restorations of my own. Occasionally, the minuscule text (and majuscule text, when included) is not in proper sequence: this happens when the full text takes up less than one full page but, because of the sequence, would have to be split over two pages. This is done on the assumption that one can get a better idea of the text if it is viewed in its entirety. This could not be done for all of the decrees, since some are too long for even a full page.

COMMENTARY: I note here any changes made in the text since its last publication. Anything to do with the restoration, such as stoichedon order, differences of opinion, are noted in this entry. Abbreviations of editors are the same as above (epigraphical commentary).

DISCUSSION: This is the heart of the work, and the differences in content and length reflect the diversity of the ninety-one decrees treated. In general, I discuss the content of the decree, historical references, if applicable, and any points of controversy. As for the controversies, I can do no better than quote J.A.O. Larsen from his review of Meiggs and Lewis, *A Selection of Greek Historical Inscriptions to the End of the Fifth Century B.C.* (*CP* 65[1970] 192-193):

> *With this ['the greater prominence and assertiveness of epigraphy in recent years'] has come also a considerable amount of polemics and disagreement. At least that is the impression caused by the mass of controversial literature which has passed through the hands of the reviewer and left him with the feeling that he could never have an independent opinion on some of these problems unless he gave up all other research on Greek history.*

The interpretation of the calendar is the chief point of controversy in the Lykourgan era. General background can be found in Pritchett-Neugebaur *The Calendars of Athens* and Meritt *The Athenian Year.* Information as to the enactment of decrees and laws is not so much controversial as it is incomplete. Both Rhodes in *The Athenian Boule* and DeLaix in *Probouleusis at Athens* provide up-to-date accounts of the legislative process at Athens. Henry, in *The Prescripts of Athenian Decrees* has done the same for the formulaic prescripts. (All decrees in this Corpus which record any of the enactment formula are included by Rhodes and DeLaix; any which include the formulaic prescript are included by Henry. I include citations in the bibliography for each decree only when that decree had been given fuller treatment by Rhodes or DeLaix or Henry other than inclusion in a list.)

The content of this work lends itself to a natural division: by year the decrees were published, and then, within that year, the individual entries in chronological order (the decrees which do not record the specific day of enactment are placed after the decrees with specific dates for that year). There are three decrees which do not record the archon's name but which I feel should be included. #3 is dated for historical reasons to 337; I have placed it in the year of Chairondas, 338/7, because that is where I think it belongs. #17 is dated to either 336/5 or 335/4 and #47 to either 331/30 or 330/29. For the sake of convenience, I have placed them at the end of the earlier year: #17, in the year of Pythodelos, 336/5; #47, in the year of Aristophanes, 331/30.

II^2 363 has been restored with four dates in the Lykourgan era: 324/3 (II^2 363), 326/5 (Meritt *Hesperia* 10 [1941] 49); 331/30 (Meritt

Ath. 89); and 335/4 (Meritt *TAPA* 95[1964]213-217). In such cases where a decree is restored to various years, my usual policy is to assign the decree to the year most recently restored, in this case 335/4. There are problems, however, with all of the restorations, and I prefer to place it where it best fits the historical context, namely, in 326/5 where it is designated #67. Two decrees, #20, #62, are included in this Corpus, despite the fact that more recent scholarship has placed them outside the Lykourgan Era, because Kirchner listed them as Lykourgan.

One decree, II^2 350, is not included in this Corpus, but probably should be. Kirchner tentatively placed II^2 350 in 331/30. Meritt did as well in *Hesperia* 43 (1974) 464, but in *Hesperia* 45 (1976) 173, he reneged and placed the decree in 318/7. Since Meritt, and after this manuscript was completed, Joe Breslin, in the article, "A Decree of Polyeuktos of Sphettos published in *Ancient World* 12 (1985), has argued convincingly that the mover of II^2 350, Polyeuktos, could not have proposed the decree in 318/7 because he was dead.

Atlanta, Georgia

Cynthia J. Schwenk

TABLE OF CONTENTS

Preface v
Introduction vii
Table of Contents xiii

I. The Year of Chairondas
338/7

1. *Athens honors loyal Akarnanians* *1*
2. *Athens honors two Andrians* *13*
3. *Law and instructions for repairs of Peiraius fortifications* *18*

II. The Year of Phrynichos
337/6

4. *Athens honors Alkimachos* *27*
5. *Lemnos decree* *30*
6. *Law Against Tyranny* *33*
7. *Athens bestows proxeny* *41*
8. *Decree* *47*
9. *Athens honors Chairestratos* *49*
10. *Honorary Decree* *51*
11. *Athens honors Kaliteles of Kydantidai* *55*
12. *Athens honors Asklepiodoros* *57*
13. *The Orgeones of Bendis honor the Hieropoioi* *63*
14. *Athens honors two doctors* *68*

III. The Year of Pythodelos
336/5

15. *Lykourgos proposes honors for a public benefactor* *72*
16. *Decree* *79*
17. *Law and Regulations concerning the lesser Panathenaia* *81*

IV. The Year of Euainetos
335/4

18. *Athens honors Hieropoioi, Phyleus and two other men of the Deme Oinoe* *95*

19. *Decree* *105*
20. *Decree* *106*
21. *Lykourgos proposes a law to deal with the religious reforms* *108*
22. *Decree* *126*

V. The Year of Ktesikles 334/3

23. *Demades proposes a Decree* *129*
24. *Demades proposes citizenship for Amyntor* *132*
25. *Lykourgos proposes honors for Diotimos* *134*
26. *Decree from Cholargos concerning the Thesmophoria* *136*

VI.The Year of Nikokrates 333/2

27. *Lykourgos proposes Enktesis for the Merchants of Kition* *141*
28. *Athens honors Pytheas* *146*
29. *Athens grants proxeny (?) to a Chian* *151*
30. *Decree* *157*
31. *Athens grants citizenship to Archippos* *159*
32. *The Lease of a garden by the Orgeones of the Heros Iatros (Hero Doctor)* *173*

VII. The Year of Niketes 332/1

33. *Athens grants proxeny* *177*
34. *Decree* *181*
35. *Decree* *183*
36. *Lykourgos proposes honors for a Plataian* *187*
37. *Demades proposes honors* *190*
38. *Athens honors Amphis of Andros* *192*
39. *Athens grants proxeny to an Abderite* *196*
40. *Athens bestows a gold crown upon Amphiaraos* *198*
41. *Athens honors Phanodemos* *201*
42. *Decree from the Deme Eitea* *205*
43. *Eleusis honors Philokomos* *212*

VIII. The Year of Aristophanes 331/0

44. *Athens honors an actor* *220*
45. *Athens honors Rheboulas the Odrysian* *223*
46. *Deme (?) Decree* *227*

47. *The Teithrasians honor their Councilors* 229

IX. The Year of Aristophon
330/29

48. *Lykourgos proposes honors for Eudemos of Plataia* 232
49. *Decree* 238

X. The Year of Kephisophon
329/8

50. *Athens honors Epimelitai of the Amphiaraic Games* 241
51. *Demades proposes honors for a Larisaian* 248
52. *The Orgeones of Bendis Honor their Epimeletai* 252

XI. The Year of Euthykritos
328/7

53. *Decree* 260
54. *Athens honors Androkles, Priest of Asklepios* 266
55. *Decree* 278
56. *Decree and Dedication of the Boule* 280

XII. The Year of Hegemon
327/6

57. *Athens bestows Proxeny on an Eretrian* 285
58. *Athens honors Memnon of Rhodes* 289
59. *Decree* 294
60. *Athens bestows Isotelia* 298
61. *The Tribe Aiantis honors Teleskopas* 300
62. *Decree* 305

XIII. The Year of Chremes
326/5

63. *Decree* 308
64. *Decree* 313
65. *The Tribe Pandionis honors their Choregos* 316
66. *The Deme Aixone honors two Choregoi* 319
67. *Athens honors Dionysios (of Herakleia?)* 322

XIV. The Year of Antikles
325/4

68. *Athens honors Herakleides of Salamis* 334
69. *Decree* 344
70. *The Deme Athmonon honors their Merarchs* 348

XV. The Year of Hegesias
324/3

71. *Decree* ... 355
72. *Decree* ... 356
73. *Decree* ... 358
74. *Decree* ... 360
75. *Decree* ... 363
76. *Deme Decree of Peiraieus* ... 366
77. *The Syllogeis honor Lysikles and Euthykritos* ... 370
78. *The Eikadeis honor Polyxenos* ... 376

XVI. The Year of Kephisodoros
323/2

79. *Lapyris of Kleonai helps Athens* ... 381
80. *Decree* ... 392
81. *Athens honors her ambassador to Phokis* ... 394
82. *Athens honors Theophantos* ... 401
83. *Athens honors Euphron of Sikyon* ... 407
84. *Athens honors Apollonides of Sidon* ... 418
85. *Athens grants honors* ... 426

XVII. The Year of Philokles
322/1

86. *Decree* ... 433
87. *Demades proposes honors* ... 436
88. *Athens honors the Doctor Euenor* ... 440
89. *Decree* ... 449
90. *Decree* ... 451
91. *Decree* ... 452

APPENDIX

Inscriptions of the Lykourgan Era Dated to a Specific Year ... 455
Abbreviations ... 464
Bibliography ... 469
Athenian Eponymous Archons from the Lykourgan Era 338/7 — 322/1 ... 483
Ancient Authors Cited ... 484
List of Entries by Previous or Original Publication ... 486

INDICES

I. *Inscriptions Cited* *490*

II. *Proper Names*

A: *Athenians* *495*

IIa: *Athenian names (not in Greek)* *498*

IIb: *Non-Athenians* *499*

IIc: *Incomplete Names* *500*

III. *Geographical* *500*

IIIa: *Attica* *500*

IIIb: *Non-Attica* *502*

IV. *Deities, Festivals, Sacred Sites, Religious Officials and Groups* *503*

V. *General Index* *506*

I. THE YEAR OF CHAIRONDAS, 338/7

1. *ATHENS HONORS LOYAL AKARNANIANS* EM 7138

editors: Pittakis ΕΦ. (1852/55) 1309: Rangabé (1855) 2280; Velsen Monatsber. Berl. (1856) 115-127; IG II 121; IG II^2 237 + Add. page 659.

collections: Ditt. Syll. 109; Syll.^{2} 147+Add. page 218; Syll.^{3} 259; Hicks 149; Michel 102; Tod II 178.

testimonia: Aischines Against Ktesiphon 27, 97-98; Aristotle Athenaion Politeia 43.2; Diodoros xvii 3.3.

supplements: SEG 17.24 (Stamires); 21.266 (Pritchett-Neugebauer, Meritt); 24.95 (Lambrechts, Pečírka).

other bibliography: Meier comm. ep. 98 (not seen); Reusch De diebus cont. 8 no. 118; Thumser De civium Athen. mun. 18; Schubert De Proxenia 55-58; Schaefer Dem. III 50-51; Wilamowitz Hermes 22(1887) 245 n. 2; Wilhelm Hermes 24 (1889) 331; GGA 1(1898) 221; CRAI (1900) 526 n.2; Ferguson Ath. Sec. 33, 39; Hausoullier Rev. Crit. 47(1899) 406; Dinsmoor Archons 355; Kahrstedt Staatsgebeit 291 n. 3; Pritchett-Neugebauer Cal. 40,42; Stamires Hesperia 26(1957) 243; Lambrechts Proxenie. 91, 130; Meritt Ath. 73-76; Pečírka Enktesis 49-51; Osborne BSA 67(1972) 129-158; Vestigia 17(1973) 434; ZPE 42(1981) 171-178; Henry Prescripts 38.

description: The stone, found in 1852 on the Akropolis, west of the Propylaia, is Pentelic marble. The top and bottom are broken; the sides are original, but both sides (especially the left) and the surface are badly worn.

dimensions:
H 0.54 m.
W 0.44 m. (above)
0.44 m. (below)
Th 0.115 m.

letters: 0.006 m. The round letters, Θ, Ο, Ω, are quite small, .005; largest, H, is .007. The chi, usually small, large, taking up the full space, as do K, M, Σ, Φ.

majuscule text: and next two pages.

. . . . Δ Ο Υ Α Ρ Χ Ο . . . . Ε . Α

. . . Π . . . . Ν Ε Ι Α Σ Η Ι Φ . . . .

. . . Α Μ . . Τ Ε Υ Ε Ν Θ Α Ρ Γ Η Λ . . . .

. . . Ι . . Σ Π Ρ Υ Τ Α Ν Ε Ι Α Σ Τ Ω . . . . Π Ε Ψ Η . Ι Ξ Ε Ν . . .

. . . . . Ε Ρ Χ Ι Ε Υ Σ Ε Δ Ο Ξ Ε Ν Τ . Ι . . . . Σ Ι Π Π Ο Σ . . . . . .

. . . . . . Ε Υ Σ Ε Ι Π Ε Ν Π Ε Ρ Ι Ω Ν Ο Ι Α . . . . . Ν Ε Σ Λ Ε Γ Ο Υ Σ . . . .

. . . Ω Ν Κ Α Ι Κ Α Ρ Φ Ι Ν Α Σ Ο Ι Ν Ε . Ν Ε Λ . . . . Ε Σ Δ Ε Δ Ο Χ Θ Α Ι . . .

. . . Ω Ι Ε Π Ε Ι Δ Η Φ Ο Ρ Μ Ι Ω Ν Κ Α Ι Κ Α Ρ . Ι Ν Α Σ Ο Ν Τ Ε Σ Π Α Τ Ρ Ο . .

. . . . Ο Ι Τ Ο Υ Δ Η Μ Ο Υ Τ Ο Υ Α Θ Η Ν Α Ι Ω Ν Δ Ι Α Φ Υ Λ Α Τ Τ Ο Υ Σ Ι Ν . .

. . . Ν Ο Ι Α Ν Η Ν Ο Ι Π Ρ Ο Γ Ο Ν Ο Ι Α Υ Τ Ο Ι Σ Π Α Ρ Ε Δ Ο Σ Α Ν Π Ρ Ο Σ . .

. . Η Μ Ο Ν Τ Ο Ν Α Θ Η Ν Α Ι Ω Ν Κ Α Ι Ν Υ Ν Ι Β Ο Η Θ Η Σ Α Ν Τ . . . Ε Τ Α Δ .

. . . Ε Ω Σ Σ Υ Ν Κ Α Τ Ε Τ Α Τ Τ Ο Ν Τ Ο Μ Ε Τ Α Α Θ Η Ν Α Ι Ω . Κ . . Ο Τ Ι Ο .

. Ρ Α Τ Η Γ Ο Σ Π Α Ρ Α Γ Γ Ε . Λ Ο Ι Ε Π Α Ι Ν Ε Σ Α Ι Α Υ Τ Ο . . . . . Τ Η Σ .

. . . . Κ Α Ι Σ Τ Ε Φ Α Ν Ω Σ Α Ι Ε Κ Α Τ Ε Ρ Ο Ν Α Υ Τ Ω Ν Χ Ρ Υ Σ Ω Ι Σ Τ Ε Φ .

. . I . Π Ε Ι Δ Η Δ Ε Φ Ο Ρ Μ Ι Ω Ν Α Τ Ο Ν Φ Ο Ρ Μ Ι Ω Ν Ọ Σ Κ Α Ι Κ Α Ρ . Ι Ν .
. . . . . Ν Ε Π̣ Ο Ι Ḥ Σ̣ Α Ṭ . ᵛ Α Θ Η Ν Α Ι Ο Ν Ο Δ Η Μ Ο Σ Ο Α Θ Η Ν Α Ị Ω Ν Κ .
. . Ο Υ . Ẹ Κ Ε Ι Ν Ο Υ Ε Κ . . Ν Ο Υ Σ Κ Α Ι Τ Ο Ψ Η Φ Ị Σ Μ Α Κ Α Θ Ο Η . Ο Ι Ḥ
. . Σ Ε Γ Ε Ν Ε Τ Ο Α Ν Α Γ . . . Α Π Τ Α Ι Ε Ν Α Κ Ρ Ο Π Ο Λ Ε Ι Ε Ι . . . Φ Ọ Ρ
. Ι Ω Ν . . Α . Κ Α Ρ Θ Ι . . . Κ Α Ι Τ Ο Ι Σ Ẹ Κ Γ Ο Ν Ο Ι Σ Α Υ Τ Ω Ν Κ̣ Ỵ Ρ Ι Α
. . . Ν . . . . . Ạ Ν Η Ν Ε . . . Ẹ Ν Ο Δ Η . Ο Σ Φ Ọ Ρ Μ Ι Ω Ν Ι Τ Ω Ι Π Α Π Π Ω
Ι . Υ . Ω Ν ᵛ . . Ẹ . . . Ι Δ Ε . Υ Ṭ Ο Υ . Φ Υ Λ Η . Κ Α Ι Δ Η Μ Ο Ν Κ Α Ι Φ Ρ Α
. . . . Ṇ Β Ο . . . . Τ Α Ι Ε Ι Ν Α Ι Ε Π Ạ Ị Ν Ε Σ̣ Ạ Ι Δ Ε Κ Α Ι Τ Ο Υ Σ
. . . Ọ . . . Κ . Ρ . . . . Ο Υ Σ Β Ο . Η Θ Η Σ Α Ν Τ Α Σ Μ Ε Τ Α Φ Ο Ρ Μ Ι Ω
. . . . Α . . . Ρ Φ . . . . Ε Ι Ν Α Ị Α Υ . Ο Ι Σ̣ Ε Ω Σ Α Ν Κ Ạ Τ Ε Λ Θ Ω Σ Ι
. . . . Ο . . . Ω Ν Β Ο Υ Λ Ω Ν Ṭ Α Ι Ο Ι Κ Ο Υ Σ Ι Ν Α Θ Η Ν Η
. . . . Κ . Ο Υ Κ Α Ι Δ Ι Δ Ọ Ν Α Ι Α Υ Τ Ο Υ Σ Δ Ι Κ Α .
. . . . Θ . . . Ρ Α Θ Η Ν Α Ι Ο . Κ Α Ι Τ Α Σ Ε Ι Σ Φ Ο Ρ Α Σ
. . . . Γ . . Ν . . Ṭ . . . Ε Τ Α Α Θ Η Ν Α Ι Ω̣ Ν Ε Ι Σ Φ Ε Ρ Ε Ι Ν Κ Α Ι
. . . . Ι . Υ . . . . . Ṇ Β Ο Υ Λ Η . Τ Ḥ Ṇ Α Ε Ι Β Ο Υ Λ Ε Υ Ο Υ Σ

. . . Α Ι Τ Ο . Σ Σ Τ Ρ Α Τ Η Γ Ο . Σ Ο Ι Α . Α Ε Ι Σ Τ Ρ Α Τ Η Γ Ω Σ Ι Ν Ο Π Ω Σ
. . . . . Δ Ι . . . Τ Α Ι . . . . . . Ψ . Ι . Ε Τ Ο Δ Ε Τ Ο Ψ Η Φ Ι Σ Μ Α Ε Ν Σ Τ
. . . . Λ Ι Θ Ι Ν . Ι Τ Ο . . . . . . Α Τ Ε . Τ . Σ Β Ο Υ Λ Η Σ Κ Α Ι Σ Τ Η Σ Α Ι
. . . Κ Ρ Ο Π Ο . . Ι Α Ν Α Γ . . . Α Ι Δ Ε Κ . Ι Τ Α Ο Ν Ο Μ Α Τ Α Τ Ω Ν Α Κ Α Ρ
. . . Ω Ν Ε Ι Σ Τ Η Ν Α Υ Τ Η . . . . Λ Η Ν Υ Π Ο Γ Ρ Α Ψ Α Ν Τ Α Τ Α Σ Π Ο Λ Ε Ι
. . . Σ Α Κ Α Ρ Ν Α Ν . . . . Κ . . Τ Ο Σ Ε Σ Τ Ι Ν ΕΙΣ Δ Ε Τ Η Ν Α Ν Α
. . . Φ . Ν Τ Η Σ Σ Τ Η . . . . Ι Τ Ο Ν Τ Α Μ Ι Α Ν Τ Ο Υ Δ Η Μ Ο Υ Τ Ω Ι
. . . . Τ . . . . Ρ . . . Ο Ν Τ Α Δ Ρ Α Χ Μ Α Σ Ε Κ ΤΩΝ Κ Α Τ
. . . . Τ . . . . . Μ . .

(in wreath) (in wreath)

Φ Ο Ρ Μ Ι Ω Ν Α   Κ Α Ρ Φ Ι Ν Α Ν

Ο Δ Η Μ Ο Σ   Ο Δ Η Μ Ο Σ

epigraphical commentary: As can be seen from the underlining, many letters seen by previous editors (Pečírka as well for lines 24-28) are no longer visible on the stone. And yet, by examining the stone in direct sunlight, I was able to see a number of letters which were bracketed in previous texts; and Osborne (ZPE) has seen more letters at the end of the text. These additons will be noted where they occur. All dots are mine, unless noted otherwise.

1 end There is no stone where Kirchner recorded a "preserved" epsilon and alpha, nor is there any indication that the break is new. Pečírka, 49, noted this, and traced the error back to Koe. This "Schoenheitsfehler" (Pečírka) suggests that the stone had not been examined between Velsen (1856) and Pečírka (1966). (But cf. lines 7, 26, 27 below.)

3 st. 18 Λ new reading, seen by Vel.

7 st. 19 Ṇ dotted also by Ki. in Syll.[3].

8 st. 26 Ị new reading.

10 st. 8 N dotted in Syll.[3], now can not be read.

20 st. 14 E new reading.

24 st. 21 Ị new reading.

25 st. 9 Λ reported by Vel. and Koe. (maj. text). Although there are some scratches, there is no letter in this stoichos; cf. Pečírka 51.

26 st. 26 I new reading (also printed by Schubert).

28 st. 15 Ṭ new reading.

30 st. 19 Σ new reading.

31 st. 7 I new reading.

32 st. 8,9 ỊṆ new reading.

35 st. 32 EI in one stoichos.

36 beg underlined letters were seen by Ki. Osborne read: Γ.ΑΦ̣ṆΤΗΣΣ̣ΤΗ, but did not read Ị in st.21 (my new

reading).

37 st. 28 Δ new reading, also seen by Osborne, who read much more at the beginning than Ki. (shown in text) or me: Γ.ΑΜΜΑΤΕΙΤ....9....Ρ..ΚΟΝΤΑΔΡΑΧΜΑΣ.

st. 37,38 ΤΩΝ in two stoichoi; Ω new reading, seen by Vel., Osb. (who places nu and kappa in one stoichos).

38 st. 24 T, st. 29 M are printed in II^2 237 and are included here for the sake of defining the problem. As noted in my 1977 dissertation: "The T is in fact imaginary beneath the well preserved omicron. M is only apparent in the photograph; it is 1/3 again too wide; its long hastae flare whereas those of other mus are vertical; is is engraved squarely on the first leaf left of the knot of the right wreath; and it is to the left of the proper stoichos. In other words, it is nothing more than two scratches on the stone. I suggest a shortened ending line ... or, if the restoration must be kept, introducing another line at the left of the two wreaths. This, as well as the fact that the names of other Akarnanians were to be inscribed on the stele, may explain the unusual unsymmetrical placement of the wreaths." Osborne's agreement as to the non-existence of tau and mu and his new readings at the beginning of line 38: ..ΗΦΙΖ..Τ confirms my suggestion.

40 in left wreath: Μ, Σ new readings, also seen by Osb., who read all of the letters in both lines of both wreaths.

minuscule text: next three pages.

commentary: The text is based on Kirchner's. It is inscribed in stoichedon order, 41 letters to the line. The order is violated by crowding in lines 35 and 37, and perhaps in line 26. Vacats occur in lines 16 and 21; in line 23, the vacat is probably a rasura. There are substantial changes in lines 1 and 2; from line 36 on I have recorded Osborne's new readings and restorations. I have removed the brackets from letters read by me. The restorations are Velsen's unless noted otherwise.

1 Πανδιονίδος: Koe. (cf. #2, II^2 238). Vel. restored [--ίδος ε.ά/της] since the prytany could be either the ninth or the tenth. Reusch's restoration of the day of the month and prytany (cf. line 3) necessitated the use of the tenth prytany.

stoich. 41

[Ἐπὶ Χαιρώ̣ν]δου ἄρχο[ντος ἐπὶ τῆς Πανδιονίδος δεκά]-
[της] π[ρυτα]νείας, ἧι Φ[ίλιππος Ἀντιφήμου Εἰρεσίδης]
[ἐγρ]αμ[μά]τευεν, Θαργηλ[ιῶνος δευτέραι φθίνοντος, ἕ]-
[κτη]ι [τῆ]ς πρυτανείας· τῶ[ν προέδρων ἐ]πεψή[φ]ιζεν ...
..5.. Ἐρχιεὺς· ἔδοξεν τ[ῶ]ι [δήμωι· Ἡγή]σιππος [Ἡγησίο]-
[υ Σουνι]εὺς εἶπεν· περὶ ὧν οἱ Ἀ[καρνᾶ]νες λέγουσ[ιν Φο]-
[ρμί]ων καὶ Καρφίνας οἱ νέ[ο]ν ἐλ[θόντ]ες, δεδόχθαι [τῶι]
[δήμ]ωι, ἐπειδὴ Φορμίων καὶ Καρ[φ]ίνας ὄντες πατρό[θε]-
[ν φίλ]οι τοῦ δήμου τοῦ Ἀθηναίων διαφυλάττουσιν [τὴ]-
[ν εὔ]νοιαν ἣν οἱ πρόγονοι αὐτοῖς παρέδοσαν πρὸς [τὸ]-
[ν δ]ῆμον τὸν Ἀθηναίων καὶ νυνὶ βοηθήσαντ[ες μ]ετὰ δ[υ]-
[νάμ]εως συνκατετάττοντο μετὰ Ἀθηναίω[ν] κ[αθ]ότι ὁ [σ]-
[τ]ρατηγὸς παραγγέ[λ]λοι, ἐπαινέσαι αὐτο[ὺς ἀρε]τῆς [ἕ]-
[νεκα] καὶ στεφανῶσαι ἑκάτερον αὐτῶν χρυσῶι στεφ[ά]-

[νω]ι· [ἐ]πειδὴ δὲ Φορ[μ]ίωνα τὸν Φορμίωνος καὶ Καρ[φ]ίν[α]
[πάππο]ν ἐποιήσατο ᵛ Ἀθηναῖον ὁ δῆμος ὁ Ἀθηναίων κ[α]-
[ὶ τ]οῦ[ς] ἐκείνου ἐκ[γό]νους καὶ τὸ ψήφισμα καθ' ὃ ἡ [π]οίη-
[σι]ς ἐγένετο, ἀναγ[έγρ]απται ἐν ἀκροπόλει, εἶ[ναι] Φορ-
[μ]ίων[ι κ]α[ὶ] Καρφί[ναι] καὶ τοῖς ἐκγόνοις αὐτῶν κυρία-
[ν τὴ]ν [δωρει]ὰν ἣν ἔ[δωκ]εν ὁ δῆ[μ]ος Φορμίωνι τῶι πάππω-
ι [α]ὐ[τ]ῶν ᵛ [ἐλ]ε[σθα]ι δὲ [α]ὐτοῦ[ς] φυλὴ[ν] καὶ δῆμον καὶ φρα-
[τρίαν ἧς ἂ]ν βο[ύλων]ται εἶναι. ἐπαινέσαι δὲ καὶ τοὺς
[ἄλλ]ο[υς Ἀ]κ[α]ρ[νᾶνας τ]οὺς βο[ι]ηθήσαντας μετὰ Φορμίω-
[νος κ]α[ὶ Κα]ρφ[ίνα καὶ] εἶναι αὐ[τ]οῖς, ἕως ἂν κατέλθωσι-
[ν ἔγκτησιν ὧν ἂν] ο[ἰκι]ῶν βούλωνται οἰκοῦσιν Ἀθήνη-
[σι ἀτελέσι τõ μετοι]κ[ί]ου καὶ διδόναι αὐτοὺς δίκα[ς]
[καὶ λαμβάνειν κα]θ[άπε]ρ Ἀ̣θηναῖο[ι] καὶ τὰς εἰσφορὰς
[ἐὰν τινες] γ[ίγ]ν[ων]τ[αι μ]ετὰ Ἀθηναίων εἰσφέρειν καὶ
[ἐπιμελεῖσθα]ι [α]ὐ[τῶν τὴ]ν βουλὴ[ν] τὴν ἀεὶ βουλεύους-

[αν κ]αὶ το[ὺ]ς στρατηγο[ὺ]ς οἳ ἂ[ν] ἀεὶ στρατηγῶσιν, ὅπως
[ἂν μὴ ἀ]δι[κῶν]ται. [ἀναγρά]ψ[α]ι [δ]ὲ τόδε τὸ ψήφισμα ἐν στ-
[ήληι] λιθίν[η]ι τὸ[ν γραμμ]ατέ[α] τ[ῆ]ς βουλῆς καὶ στῆσαι
[ἐν ἀ]κροπό[λε]ι. ἀναγ[ραψ]αι δὲ κ[α]ὶ τὰ ὀνόματα τῶν Ἀκαρ-
[νάν]ων εἰς τὴν αὐτὴ[ν στή]λην ὑπογράψαντα τὰς πόλει-
[ς τῆ]ς Ἀκαρναν[ίας ὧν εἰς ἕ]κ[ας]τός ἐστιν. εἰς δὲ τὴν ἀνα-
γ̣[ρ]αφὴ]ν τῆς στή[λης δοῦνα]ι τὸν ταμίαν τοῦ δήμου τῶι
γ̣[ρ]α̣μμα̣τ̣ε̣ῖ τ[ῆς βουλῆς τ]ρ[ια]κοντα δραχμὰς ἐκ τῶν κατ-
[ὰ ψ]η̣φίς[μα]τ̣[α ἀ]- in wreath in wreath
[ναλις]κ̣[ομέ]- Φορμίωνα Καρφίναν
[νων τῶι δήμωι.] ὁ δῆμος ὁ δῆμος

2 name of secretary: Stamires. Φίλιπποϲ 'Αντιφῶντοϲ Εἰτεαῖοϲ Ferguson on the basis of II^2 587 line 3.

3 date: Reusch, on the basis of Aisch. III.27. Ki., Add. 659, as well as Syll.^{3} and Hicks, P.-N., Tod, accept Hausoullier's restoration: θαργηλ[ιῶνοϲ τετράδι φθίνον-ταϲ, τρ/ίτη]ι [τῆ]ϲ πρυτανείαϲ. Reusch's restoration assumes 36 days for the tenth prytany; Hausoullier changed it to conform to Aristotle's "rule" that there are 36 days in the first four prytanies, 35 days in the last six. Although Hausoullier's restoration conforms to Aristotle, it implies that there were two meetings of the ekklesia (the first, from Aisch.; the second, from this decree) separated by only one day. I follow Meritt, 75, who prefers Reusch's original restoration by adopting a more flexible approach to Aristotle's "rule". (See #15, II^2 328, for a fuller discussion of Aristotle's "rule.") If, however, Aristotle must be followed to the letter and Reusch's restoration is therefore not acceptable, there are other alternatives. By assuming that 338/7 is intercalary, Mer. provides two restorations which separate the meetings by a wider interval. Another possibility, not considered since Vel., is to put the conciliar date in the ninth prytany, with tribe Hippothontis, and make the corresponding festival date earlier in Thargelion. Henry notes that "the earliest example in which both the name and day of the month are given appears to be ii^2 237," this decree.

5/6 name of proposer: PA 6351. APF.

18 mid ἀναγ[έγρ]απται: Koe. ἀνάγ[ει σ]τῆσαι Vel. Tau (st. 20) is certain.

23 mid βο[ι]ηθήσανταϲ: wrongly attributed to Koe. by Ki. Actually, Koe. shows a space between the omicron and the eta in the majuscule text, and makes no note on βοηθήσανταϲ in the minuscule text.

26 beg restoration: Wilh., CRAI. [σιν ἀτελέσιν μετοι]κ[ί]ου Vel.; [σι ἀτελέσι τοῦ μετοι]κ[ί]ου Tod, who mistakenly notes that Vel.'s restoration is one letter too short, and fails to note that his own restoration is still one letter too long. None of these three restorations is quite satisfactory: Vel. adds the nu-movable before a consonant; Wilh. omits the nu-movable before a vowel and uses τõ for τοῦ (although τοῦ is used consistently on the rest of the stone). Pečírka suggests that

τοῦ could have been written in two spaces, referring to the εἰς in line 35 and the τῶν in line 37. (But these two cases of crowding which occur in the last five lines probably reflect an effort to finish the text in a smaller space.) The only entirely satisfactory restoration would require 18 letters in a space meant for 16. A final possibility, [σιν ἀτελέσι μετοι]κ[ί]ου, omits τοῦ and assumes a vacat. Vacats, as Vel. pointed out, occur in lines 16, 21, and 23, although the last is perhaps a rasura (Tod).

27 beg restoration: Schubert. [καὶ δέχεσθαι ἐξ ἴσ]ο[υ π]αρ' Ἀθηναίο[υ] Michel; [καὶ τυγχάνειν ἴσ]ο[υ π]αρ' Ἀθηναίο[υ] Vel.;]ο[.π]αρ' Koe. These earlier restorations are negated by Schubert's reading of theta in st. 15 which I confirm as certain, instead of Vel.'s omicron. On the other hand, because of the dissappearance of so many other letters since Vel.'s day, his traces of alpha in st. 18 should not be ignored.

28 beg restoration: Thumser, on the basis of II^2 2498 line 7. [ὁπόσαι ἂν] γ[ίγ]ν[ωνται Vel.

36-40 restoration: Ki. placed the end of the restored formula in line 38; I shortened line 38 and added a line 39. Osborne caculated that a maximum of 11 letters was possible to the left of the wreaths and therefore extended the end of the formula over 3 lines. He also includes in his text for lines 35-42 (ZPE, 172) [nomina] for lines 41 and 42 to indicate the beginning of a list of the other Akarnanians.

This decree honors two Akarnanians, Phormion and Karphinas. They are commended, crowned with gold crowns, and given citizenship, an honor previously held by their grandfather, Phormion. They have their choice of tribe, deme, and phratry. (Osborne, in Vestigia, implies that this decree includes a phratry restriction, but in BSA includes it with those with no restrictions. See #31 [II^2 336] for a discussion of this constitutional change.)

Also honored are an undesignated number of Akarnanians who had helped the Athenians, while serving under

Phormion and Karphinas. These Akarnanians are praised, granted enktesis (the right to acquire and own property; in this case, only houses, not land), exemption from the metic's tax, and equality with citizens in court and in paying special taxes. They are to be put under the care of the Boule and of the generals.

The grants to the Akarnanians are unusual in that they are given only until such time as the Akarnanians return home. This restriction in regard to enktesis, and the further clarification, that the houses are to be acquired by choice, has no parallel. (Pečírka, 51; cf. Wilhelm Hermes, who considers the addition of "according to their own choice" a way to get around the usual legal restrictions of enktesis.) Under the year 335/4, in connection with the death of Philip, Diodoros (17.3.3) mentions Akarnanians who had been exiled because of Philip. This event has been associated with Philip's activities soon after Chaironeia; this fits the date of our decree, and it explains the decree's unusual provisions mentioned above, which show that the Akarnanian exiles temporarily residing in Athens were above metic status. (Cf. Wilhelm and Schubert.)

The "help" provided by the Akarnanians has been associated with the battle of Chaironeia, in spite of the fact that there is no direct evidence. The indirect evidence, however (Aischines and Diodoros), and the information from this decree strongly suggests that: 1) a contingent of Akarnanians, led by Phormion and Karphinas, fought alongside Athens at Chaironeia; 2) these Akarnanians were subsequently exiled by Philip; 3) Athens showed her gratitude by allowing them to reside in Athens.

2. *ATHENS HONORS TWO ANDRIANS* EM 7062, 7061, 7061[a]

photo: 'OJ 10(1907) 33.

editors: Fr. A Pittakis EΦ. (1856/61) 3834; IG II^2 122.
Fr. B Drerup Musée Belge 9(1905) p. 391.
Fr. A+B+C Wilhelm 'OJ 10(1907) p.32; IG II^{2}238.

collection: Michel, Suppl. I, 1466.

testimonia: Lykourgos Against Leokrates 42.

supplement: SEG 17.25 (Stamires).

other bibliography: Stamires Hesperia 26(1957) 243.

description: The three fragments are Pentelic marble. Fr. A was found on the Akropolis, east of the Erechtheion, in 1860. The provenance of the other fragments is unknown. Most of the right side of Fr. B is preserved, as are the rough-picked backs of Fr. A and Fr. B. The broken lower part of a cymation tops Fr. A. The rest of the edges and back of Fr. C are broken.

dimensions:

Fr. A	Fr. B+C
H 0.19 m.	H 0.56 m.
W 0.245 m.	W 0.368 m.
Th 0.108 m.	Th 0.12 m.

letters: 0.007 m. The first two lines are 0.011 m. Very few alphas have cross bars.

minuscule text: and next page.

stoich. 24

Fr. A [Δρακο]ντίδου
[Ἡγηcί]ου Ἀνδρίων.
[Ἐπὶ Χαιρ]ώνδου ἄρχοντοc̣ ἐπὶ [τ]-
[ῆc Πανδι]ọντίδοc δεκάτηc π̣ρ[υτ]-
[ανείαc ἧι] Φί[λ]ιπποc Ἀντιφ[ήμο]-
[υ Εἰρεcίδηc] ἐγ̣ραμμ̣άτευε̣[ν...]
- - - - - - - - - -
- - - - - - - - - -

Fr. C .... ἐπαι[νέcαι μὲν αὐτοὺc κα]- Fr. B
[ὶ cτ]εφανῶcαι α[ὐτῶν ἑκάτερον θ]-
[αλλ]οῦ cτεφάνωι ἀνδραγ[αθίαc]
[ἕν]εκα καὶ εὐνοίαc τῆc περ<ὶ> τὸ[ν]
[δῆ]μον τὸν Ἀθηναίων· εἶναι δὲ κ-
[αὶ] προξένουc καὶ εὐεργέταc τ-
[ο]ῦ δήμου τοῦ Ἀθηναίων καὶ αὐτ-
[οὺ]c καὶ ἐκγόνουc Δρακοντίδη-
[ν Ἀ]μφοτέρου καὶ Ἡγηcίαν Στηc-
[αγόρ]ου καὶ εἶναι αὐτοῖc ἂν το-
[υ δέωνται πρ]όcοδον πρὸc τε τὴ-
[ν βουλὴν κα]ὶ πρὸc τὸν δῆμον τὸ-
[ν Ἀθηναίων] πρώτοιc μετὰ τὰ ἱε-
[ρά· ἀναγράψ]αι δὲ τόδε τὸ ψήφιc-
[μα τὸν γραμ]ματέα τῆc βουλῆc ε-
[ἰc ἀκρόπολι]ν εἰc cτήλην λιθί-
[νην· εἰc δὲ τὴ]ν ἀναγραφὴν τῆc c-
[τήληc δοῦνα]ι τὸν ταμίαν : ΔΔ : δρ-
[αχμὰc ἐκ τῶν] κατὰ ψηφίcματα ἀ-
[ναλιcκομέν]ων τῶι δήμωι· καλέ-
[cαι δὲ αὐτοὺc] ἐπὶ ξένια εἰc τὸ
[πρυτανεῖον] εἰc αὔ<ρ>ιον.

[in wreath]	in wreath
[ἡ Βουλή]	[ὁ Δῆμ]οc

epigraphical commentary: I have based this text on Kirchner's, with alterations in Fr. A, lines 5/6, Fr. B+C, lines 4, 22, and the addition of the restored wreath. In this instance, the underlined letters distinguish Fr. C from Fr. B. All dots are mine. The text is inscribed in stoichedon order, restored to 24 letters to the line. Although there is no violation of the stoichedon order on the stone, the letters in the vertical lines do not fall directly under one another, nor has the stonecutter left the same distance between horizontal lines, e.g.,in Fr. B+C, the distance between lines 5 and 6 is c. 0.010 m.; between lines 6 and 7, c. 0.015 m. In comparison with the preserved right edge on Fr.B, the horizontal lines slant down to the right. For an honorary decree, the appearance of this stele does not measure up even to the usual standard of the Lykourgan period.

The top and upper right-hand corner of a wreath (signifying the honorary crown) remain 0.025 m. beneath the last line of the text. This wreath is as far to the right as possible; there is ample room for Wilhelm's restoration of a second wreath to the left.

Fr. A

1,2 Michel notes that these lines are not in stoichedon order. The letters are larger, but they have been cut in stoichedon order, i.e.; the letters of line 2 are directly beneath those of line 1.

3,5 Koe.'s majuscule text is correct, but an error in printing in the minuscule text left lines 3 and 5 with only 23 letters. This was noted by Ki, and corrected.

5 Pittakis read all of ΦΙΛΙΠΠΟΣ; I can not read the second iota.

Fr. B+C

3 st. 19 Γ̣ new reading.

4 end ΠΕΡΙ ΤΟ[Ν] Ki.; ΠΕΡΤ̣Ο̣ on stone.

22 end ΑΥΡΙΟΝ Ki.; ΑΥΨΙΟΝ on stone.

commentary: Koehler restored Fr. A, except lines 1 and 2; Drerup restored Fr. B, except Wilhelm's changes in line 2 (see below); Wilhelm restored Fr. A, lines 1 and 2, Fr. C, and the wreaths below the text.

Fr. A

5/6 name of secretary: Stamires. Although the name fits in #1, here it is one letter too long. Stamires suggests two letters in one stoichos, but that does not occur anywhere else on the stone. The stonecutter does have a tendency to skip letters: epig. comm., line 22. I suggest he missed a letter. Dropping the upsilon at the end of the patronymic is common earlier and still attestable in Lykourgan times. This does not occur in the other two patronymics below, but in this case, without the upsilon, the patronymic would just fit the end of line 5.

Fr. B+C
2 end: Wilhelm. Drerup's ἕκαστον is still possible. Although Wilh.'s restoration is more correct grammatically, it requires a 25 letter line. With the new reading in line 4, this line is the only instance of stoichedon violation. Again, as in line 6 above, I suggest the stonecutter left out a letter. The stoichedon order may be untidy, but I think the stonecutter managed to engrave 24 letters to the line.

10 ἅν = ἐάν; Ki., with reference to Meisterhans, 256. When Wilh. published the 3 fragments, he noted that this decree provides another example of the use of ἅν (Meisterhans records only 6 instances of the use of ἅν from the 5th to the 3rd centuries). Although 3 of the 6 examples occur in this period on #68 (II^2 360–325/4), in lines 49, 63, 69, the other omitted letters on this stone suggest that here the omission of the epsilon may have been accidental.

This decree records honors given to Drakontides and Hegesias of Andros. Each man is praised and crowned with an olive crown because of his uprightness and good will to the Athenian people. The men and their descendents are also honored with the status of proxenos (friend of Athens) and euergetes (benefactor). They are given prosodos (leave to approach or speak) to the Boule and Demos first after the sacred business (see Robert AE [1965] 45, for this definition). The secretary is to be given 20 drachmai to inscribe this decree on a stone stele on the Akropolis. The two Andrians are also invited to dine in the prytaneion the next day.

The missing part of this inscription probably provided information concerning the day the decree was passed and the reasons for honoring Drakontides and Hegesias. In the fifth century, Andros had been a tributary member of the Delian League, and in the fourth, a member of the Second Athenian League (II^2 43 line 112). Athens placed a protective garrison on Andros in 356 during the Social War (II^2 123), and the Treasurers of Athena list a crown with which the Andrians had crowned the Athenian demos in 348/7 (II^2 1441 lines 12-13). Although Andros fell under Macedonian control some time after Chaironeia, there is no doubt that down to that point the Andrians were loyal to Athens. Lykourgos (Leokrates 42), notes that immediately after Chaironeia Athens sought aid from men of Andros, Keos, Troizen, and Epidauros. This inscription proves that at least two men from Andros did something to aid the Athenians, possibly by helping to secure the grain supply.

The orators (Lykourgos, cited above; Aischines III. 24), give the impression that a general panic occurred after the defeat at Chaironeia. It is tempting to associate this decree with #1 and to suggest that after the situation in Athens had stablized there was a general show of gratitude to Athens's friends or former allies. The physical evidence of the stone, i.e.: poor letter-cutting and placement, suggests that so much legislation was passed that less competent workmen were called in to handle the overflow. The granting of honors to specific individuals would allow Athens to maintain diplomatic relations with other states without violating any limitations imposed by Philip's Hellenic League.

3. *LAW AND INSTRUCTIONS FOR REPAIRS OF PEIRAIEUS FORTIFICATIONS* Peiraieus Museum

photo: Kirchner Imagines Plate 29 no. 62 (lines 13-46); Maier Mauerbau. Plate 7.

editors: Dragatsis AE (1900) 91-102; Foucart Journ. Sav. (1902) 177-193, 233-245 (lines 1-47); Frickenhaus Mauern (1905) 14-29 (lines 48-113); IG II^2 244; Maier Mauerbau. (1959) 36-48 no. 10.

collection: Michel 1465 (lines 1-46); 1515.

testimonia: Aischines Against Ktesiphon 27, 236; Demosthenes On The Crown 248; Against Timokrates 20-23; Lykourgos Against Leokrates 44.

supplement: SEG 19.57 (Kirchner Imagines, Maier, Scranton HLB).

other bibliography: Lattermann Bauinschr. 39f.; Wilhelm Beitr. 232, 233 n. 3; Davis AJA 34(1930) 14, 19; Säflund Opus. Arch. 1(1935) 98 n. 2; Scranton Walls 118-119; HLB 19(1960) 166, 169; Cawkwell JHS 83(1963) 66 n. 109; Rhodes Boule 20 n. 4, 123, 125, 220, 238, 276, 280; DeLaix Proboul. 67, 135-136, 142; Stroud Hesperia 43(1974) 162; cf. Maier for fuller bibliography.

description: The stone is grey marble. It was found in Mounichia west of the theater. When I saw it (1973) it was standing upside down in the darkest room of the "old" Peiraieus Museum. The left side, top, and back, which is smooth, are preserved. The right side and bottom are broken. Between lines 46 and 47 (indicated by a short black line under the first four letters of line 46) someone began a preliminary cut for breaking the stele in two -- probably in antiquity.

dimensions:
H 0.80 m.
W 0.54 m.
Th 0.125 m. (above)
0.13 m. (below)

letters: 0.005 m. Smallest, O, X, are sometimes .003; largest, Φ, is .008. The letters are not uniform, some, M, Σ, are incised at different angles.

minuscule text: next four pages.

[θ] ε̣ [ο ῑ]
[Κηφισοφῶν Κεφαλίωνος] Ἀφιδναῖος εἶπεν· ἀγαθῆι τύχηι τοῦ [δήμου τοῦ Ἀθηναίων· ὅπως ἂν.........42..........]
[.......17........ κα]ὶ τὰ περὶ τὴν Ἠτιώνειαν καὶ τὸν ἄλλο[ν Πειραιᾶ ....55..........]
.......17........ δὲ καὶ τὰ ἔλλοιπα τῶν λιθίνων τειχῶν μ..........63..........
[......14...... ἐπ]ισκευασθῶσιν, ἐπισκευαζηται δὲ καὶ τὰ [μακρὰ τειχη..........53..........]
......14......α̣ δεδόχθαι τοῖς νομοθέταις τοὺς μὲν ἀρχι[τέκτονας τοὺς παρὰ τῆς πόλεως μισθοφοροῦντας καὶ ἄλλον τὸμ βουλόμενον εἰ]-
[σενεγκεῖν συγγρα]φὰς συγγράψαντας καθ' ἕκαστον τῶν ἔργων [.........27.........παραδιδόναι τοῖς πρυτάνεσι καὶ τῶι γραμμα]-
[τεῖ, τοὺς δὲ πρυτάν]εις καὶ τὸγ γραμματέα παραλαβόντας ἐκτ[ιθέναι ἐν τῶι βουλευτηρίωι ....39......... κ]-
[αὶ προγράφειν ἕδρ?]αν αὐτὸ καθ' αὐτό περὶ τούτων, τὴν δὲ βουλὴν ....62..........
[.....12...... ὁπ]οίας δ' ἂν χειροτονήσει ἡ βουλή, κατὰ ταύτα[ς ....62..........]
.......16....... ταλάντων ἔργα σὺν τῶι ἐπὶ Φυλὴν διδομέ[νωι, ...60..........]
[...9.... οἰκοδο]μηθῆι τὰ τείχη. ὅπως δ' ἂν καὶ χρήματα εἰς τὰ [ἔργα ....58..........]
[...8.... κατὰ τὸ]ν ἐνιαυτὸν ἕκαστον ἐκ τοῦ προτέρου νόμο ει ....62..........
......15.......ν τοῦ διαμέσου χώματος ἀρξάμενον ἀπὸ τοῦ ....62..........
......14...... καὶ μὴ ἀνήλωται εἰς τὰ τείχη. ὑπάρχειν δὲ κα[ὶ ....61..........]
[...9.... πεντη]κοντάρχους, ἐπειδὴ οὐ γίγνεται ἡ αἵρεσις α ....62..........
......14...... τὰς ὑπηρεσίας παρὰ τὸ ἐς Σάμωι ἐκ τοῦ ἐνιαυ[τοῦ ....59..........]
[.....12...... το]ῦ δανεισθέντος ἐκ τῶν τειχοποιικῶν ταλάντο[υ ....60..........]
......15....... ἐλλείπηι εἰς τὰ δέκα τάλαντα, μερίζειν τοὺ[ς ....60..........]

......14...... εἰσφέρειν δὲ καὶ τοὺς μετοίκους τὸ ἕκτον μέ[ρος ....58..........................]
......13...... τὰ ὑπάρχοντα χρήματα ἐν τῶιδε τῶι νόμωι τειχ[οποιικά· καὶ γίγνεσθαι τὴν μὲν πρώτην καταβολὴν ἐπὶ τῆς πρώτης πρυτανεία]-
[ς, τὴν δὲ δευτέρα]ν ἐπὶ τῆς πέμπτης, τὴν δὲ τρίτην [ἐ]πὶ τῆς ἐνάτης· δ[......................51...................... τοὺς ἡιρημ]-
[ένους ἐπὶ τὴν ἐπ]ιμέλειαν τῶν τειχῶν καὶ τὸν ἀντιγραφέα τὰ ἀνα[λισκόμενα ....51......................]
[...6... ἐπὶ τῆς ἐ]νάτης πρυτανείας πρὸ τῆς καταβολῆς. ὅπως δ' ἂν τ ....60..........................
[....8.... λε]λογισμένων τῶγ χρημάτων εἰδότες καταβάλλωσιν ο[ἱ μέτοικοι ....51......................]
[... τοὺς τ]αμίας καὶ τοὺς ἐπιμελητὰς τῶμ μετοικικῶν [σ]υμμοριῶ[ν ....50...................... βουλῆς ἕδρ]-
[αν πρὸ τ]ῆς καταβολῆς τῶγ χρημάτων μίαν ἡμέραν περὶ τοῦ λογισμ[οῦ ....39.................. ἐπιμελεῖσθαι ὅπως ἂν ἡ]
[ἕδρ]ạ [γ]ένηται ἢ ὀφείλειν ἕκαστον τῶμ προέδρων ἑκατὸν δραχμὰς [ἱερὰς τῆι Ἀθηναίαι· χειροτονῆσαι δὲ τὸν δῆμον αὐτίκα μάλα ἐπιστάτας δύο]
[ἄνδ]ρας ἐξ Ἀθηναίων ἁπάντων, οἵτινες ἐπιμελήσονται τῶν ἔργων [τῶν εἰς τὰ μακρὰ τείχη καὶ εἰς τὰ περὶ τὴν Ἠτιώνειαν καὶ τὸν ἄλλον Πειραιᾶ,]
[ὅπ]ως ἂν ἐξεργάζωνται οἱ μισθωσάμενοι κατὰ τὸν ἐνιαυτὸν ἕκασ[τον ....48...................... διδόναι δὲ]
[ἑκ]ατέρωι αὐτῶν τρεῖς ὀβολοὺς τῆς ἡμέρας ἐκ τῶν τειχοποιικῶν, τοὺ[ς δὲ θεσμοθέτας ....19........ διδόναι τοῖς τειχοποιοῖς καὶ το]-
[ῖ]ς ἡιρημένοις ἐπὶ τὰ τείχη ἡγεμονίαν δικαστηρίου ὅταμ παραγ[ίγνηταί τι παρὰ τὰς συγγραφὰς καὶ τὴν μίσθωσιν· ὅταν δὲ οἱ μισθωσάμενοι μ]-
ὴ ἐξεργάζωνται, εἶναι κατ' αὐτῶν τὰς αὐτὰς τιμωρίας καθάπερ περ[ὶ ....23.......... ἐπιμελεῖσθαι δὲ τοὺς ἐπὶ τὰ τείχη ἡιρημένο]-
υς μετὰ τῶν τειχοποιῶν καὶ τῶν ταμιῶν καὶ τῶμ μακρῶν τειχῶν καὶ [τῶμ περὶ τὴν Ἠτιώνειαν καὶ τὸν ἄλλον Πειραιᾶ, ὅπως οἱ μισθωσάμενοι ἐξερ]-
[γ]άζωνται τὰ ἔργα καὶ εἴ τινες τῶμ μισθωσαμένων ἢ ἐγγυησαμένων ἀ[πειθοῦσιν? ....42...................... εἰσάγει]-
[ν] τούτους εἰς τὸ δικαστήριον. τὴν δὲ βουλὴν τὴν ἀεὶ βουλεύουσαν ε ....58..........................
ν μίαν ἡμέραν τῆς πρυτανείας ἑκάστης βουλῆς ἕδραν περὶ τῶν τειχ[οποιικῶν ....49...................... τ]-
ους ἡιρημένους καὶ τοὺς ταμίας τῆς θεõ καὶ τοὺς τειχοποιούς. ὅτα[ν δὲ συντελεσθῆι δόκιμον τέλος ἔχον κατὰ τὰς συγγραφὰς ἕκαστον τῶν ἔρ]-
γων διδόναι εἰς ἀνάθημα τῆι μὲν βουλῆι πεντακοσίας τοῖς δ[ὲ τειχοποιοῖς καὶ τοῖς ἀρχιτέκτοσι τριακοσίας. μερίσαι δὲ τοὺς ταμί]-

ας ἐκ τῶν τειχοποι̣ι̣κῶν χρημάτων ὅπως δ' ἂν καὶ οἱ λιμένες κλείωνται [κλείθροις ὡς ἀσφαλεστάτοις εἰσενεγκεῖν τοὺς ἀρχιτέκτονας τοὺς πα]-
ρὰ τῆς πόλεως μισθοφοροῦντας καὶ ἄλλον τὸμ βουλόμενον συγγραφὰ[ς συγγράψαντας ....37.......... τῆι βουλ]-
ῆι τῶν συγγραφῶν χειροτονῆσαι καθ' ἅστινας ἂν δοκῆι αὐτῆι ἐγδιδό[ναι τὰ ἔργα ....31.......... τοὺς δὲ ἡιρημένους ἐ]-
πὶ τὴν ἐπιμέλειαν τῶν τειχῶν ἐπιμελεῖσθαι καὶ τούτων τῶν ἔργων ὅ[πως ἂν ἐξεργάζωνται οἱ μισθωσάμενοι, λαμβάνοντες ὀβολὸν(?) ..6.. παρ]-
[ὰ] τῆς πόλεως, τὸ δὲ ἀργύριον εἶναι εἰς ταῦ[τ]α ἐκ τῶν χρημάτων τῶν τει[χοποιικῶν. ἀποδιδόναι δὲ τὸ ἀργύριον τοὺς τειχοποιοὺς μετὰ τῶν
[ι]ροτονημένων ὑπὸ τοῦ δήμο τοῖς μισθωσαμένοις τὰ ἔργα λαμβάνον[τας ἐκ τῶν τειχοποιικῶν (34 litt.) Διοτ(?)]- κεχε]-
[ι]μος Τιμωνίδο Ἁλαιεύς, Φιλόδημος Αὐτοκλέους Ἐροιάδης· Διόδωρος [patr. dem., nomen patr. dem. ἀρχιτέκτονες].

[Σ]υ̣γγραφαὶ τοῦ τείχους τοῦ Μουνιχ-
[ί]ασι. οἱ μισθωσάμενοι τὰς τομὰς τῶ-
ν λίθων ἐπὶ τὰ τείχη τεμοῦσιν πέτ-
ρας ὁπόθεν ἂν ἕκαστος μισθώσηται
ι ὁμαλοὺς καὶ ὑγιοὺς καὶ πελεκήσ-
ουσιν ὀρθοὺς πανταχῆι καὶ εὐγων-
ίους πρὸς τὰ μέτρα ἃ ἂν μισθώσηται
ι ἕκαστος καὶ πρὸς τοὺς ἀναγραφέ-
ας οὓς ἂν οἱ τὴν ἐργασίαν μισθωσά-
μενοι κελεύωσιν, καὶ κομιοῦσι πρ-
ὸς τὸ ἔργον ἄγοντες ὁποίους ἂν κε-
λεύωσι πρώτους οἱ τὴν ἐργασίαν μ-
[ι]σθωσάμενοι, καὶ καθαιρήσονται

ποιῶν τὰ μέτωπα τῶν κλιμακτήρω[ν] st. 27
λεῖα καὶ ὀρθὰ καὶ ἐξαμησάμενο(ς) [τ]-
ὴν λατύπην τὴν ἐγκεχωμένην ἐκ [τõ]
στρογγύλο πύργο ἅπασαν, πληρώσ[α]-
ς τὸμ πύργον λίθοις μὴ ἐλάττοσι[ν]
ἢ δίποσιν, ἐὰμ μή που ἀνάγκη ἦι θε[ι]-
ναι ἐλάττω πρὸς τὸ χωρίον, τὸ δ̣ὲ̣ [ὕψ]-
ος ἴσους τῶι στοίχωι τῶι ἔξωθ[εν, σ]-
υντιθεὶς ἁρμόττοντας πρὸς [ἀλλή]-
λους πανταχῆι, ποιῶν τοὺς ἁ[ρμοὺς]
τοῦ πληρώματος τούτο ἀπότ[ους. λί]-
θοις δὲ χρῆσθαι εἰς τὸ πλήρω[μα το]-
ῖς ὑπάρχουσιν ἐν τῆι Μουνιχ[ίαι, π]-

πρὸϲ τὸ ἔργον τὸν λίθον ἕκαϲτον ο-
ὗ ἂν οἱ τὴν ἐργαϲίαν μιϲθωϲάμενο-
ι κελεύωϲιν, οὗ ἂν ἧι ζεύγει πρόϲο-
δοϲ· ἐὰν δέ τιϲ τῶν λίθων ἔχει τι κρ-
οιὸν μὴ μεῖζον ἢ ἡμιποδίου, ὃ μὴ ἔϲτ-
[αι φ]ανερὸν κειμένου τοῦ λίθου, ἔϲ-
[ται δό]κιμοϲ. τέμνειν δὲ καὶ κομίζ-
[ειν τοὺϲ λίθο]υϲ πρὸϲ τὸ ἔργον τοὺ-
[ϲ ἄνδραϲ ὡϲ ἂν ἕκ]αϲτοϲ μιϲθώϲητα-
[ι ἱκανοὺϲ κατὰ τὴ]ν̣ ἡμέραν ἑκάϲτη-
[ν ἐπιμελουμένουϲ] ὅπωϲ ἂν κομίζω-
[νται οἱ λίθοι ἐν τ]οῖϲ χρόνοιϲ τοῖ-
[ϲ γεγραμμένοιϲ, ἄρχε]ιν δ̣ὲ τοῦ κομ-
[ίζειν τοὺϲ λίθουϲ τὴν] δ̣εκάτην ἡμ-
[έραν ἀφ' ἧϲ ἂν ἡμέραϲ παρα]λάβηι τὰ
[μέτρα ......14...... γ]έ̣νηται π-
.........21.........αμενοι
[.........21.........μ]άλακη
..........24..........η εν
...........26...........Ι

λὴν ὁπόϲοι ἂν ἐπιϲημανθῶϲιν [χρή]-
ϲιμοι ὄντεϲ εἰϲ τὴν οἰκοδομ[ίαν τ]-
ῶν νεωρίων, καὶ ἐπικόπτειν τ[ὰ πλη]-
ρώματα ὀρθὰ κατὰ κεφαλὴν πρ[ὸϲ τὸ]-
ν τοῖχον τοῦ πύργου τὸν ἔξω ἐ[φ' ἑκά]-
ϲτηϲ τῆϲ ἐφόδου. ταῦτα οἱ μιϲ[θωϲά]-
μενοι ἀποδώϲουϲιν πεποιημ[ένα ἅ]-
παντα ὀρθὰ καὶ ἁρμόττοντα πα[ντα]-
χῆι καὶ πρὸϲ τὴν ἔντορνον ϲτρ[ογγ]-
ύλα καὶ τὰϲ προϲαγωγὰϲ ὁμοία[ϲ κύ]-
κλωι ὅπωϲ ἂν ἧι ὀρθὰ τὰ μεταπύ[ργι]-
α καὶ οἱ πύργοι ἁπανταχῆι καὶ α[ἱ κ]-
λίμακεϲ, παρεχόμενοι αὐτοὶ αὐ̣[το]-
ῖϲ καὶ τοῖϲ λιθοτόμοιϲ ἀναγρα[φέ]-
αϲ καὶ τἆλλα πάντα ὧν ἂν δέωντα[ι ε]-
ἰϲ τὸ ἔργον· τοὺϲ λίθουϲ τοὺϲ εἰ[ϲ τ]-
ὸ πλήρωμα τῶι πύργωι προϲάξετ[αι]
αὐτὸϲ αὐτῶι ἅπανταϲ ὅϲων ἂν [δέητ]-
αι. ἀποδώϲουϲιν ταῦτα ἅπαν[τα πεπ]-
οιημένα κατὰ τὰ γεγραμμέ[να ....]
.¯Κ..^Ι̣Κ..Ρ̣....Ν̣Ι̣Τ̣ΩΙ...6...

epigraphical commentary: The text is Kirchner's. Maier's more recent text is less accurate with regard to the number of restored spaces in the stoichedon order. Indeed, Maier is dubious about using a line of 111 letters in lines 2-46, although he includes the restorations of Frickenhaus and Wilhelm which require a line of this length. Foucart had restored on the basis of a stoichedon line of 83 letters for lines 2-46 and 3 columns below, but Frickenhaus, estimating that the epsilon of ΘEOI in line 1 stands above the 36th stoichos of line 2, established a line of 111 stoichoi (for lines 2-46) and 4 columns below; he was followed by Wilhelm and Kirchner and, since Maier offers only doubts and no alternatives, I have used Kirchner's text. It differs only in that lines 2-46 are printed in single rather than double lines. The illusion produced by the corpus text, that there is more vertical distance between the lines in the upper half of the inscription is false; the lines in the columns below are spaced the same as the lines above.

This commentary, which is not based on autopsy, is confined to noting 1) differences between Kirchner's text which is reproduced and the newer one of Maier, and 2) the violations in the stoichedon order (shown by braces in the text). Maier notes violations by line only; unless noted also by Kirchner, it is impossible to pinpoint the stoichos in which the crowding occurs.

1-4 Maier could not read: E in line 1; line 2 st. 20-23; line 3 st. 20-22; line 4 st. 18-22.

10 st. 15 O Maier.

17 Maier notes crowding in an unidentified stoichos; not noted by Ki.

18 st. 40 II.

31 st. 7 ΩI.
st. 46 II.

33 st. 105 "33 fin. item in HIPHMENOY litt. 1 et 2." Ki.; since there are unrestored stoichoi in this line, I do not know why Ki. included this violation.

39 st. 22 HI.

40 st. 15 II Maier.

43 st. 7 M Maier.

59 st. 1 Ị Maier.

72 st. 20 A Maier.

75 st. 21 E Maier.

81 st. 26 N Maier.

82 st. 26 T Maier.

110 st. 24 Δ̣ Maier.

113 TH.Ḳ..ΩỊḲ..P̣..Ḳ.ṆỊṬΩII..^{5}.. Maier.

commentary: Maier's new supplements to and deletions from Kirchner's text are noted below.

4 end: M[ουνιχίασιν?--] Maier.

5 end : [μακρὰ τεῖχη --] Maier.

8 end/9 beg: Maier does not restore.

22 end: I assume the omission of brackets in Ki.'s text is a printing error; Ki. attributed the restoration to Dragatsis.

28 end: [---δὲ τὸν δῆμον----δύο] Maier.

31 end: [---τειχοποιοῖc?---] Maier.

39 end: [---ἀρχιτέκτοσι?---] Maier.

46 end: [---ἀρχιτέκτονες?] Maier.

76 end: [---οἱ μισθωσ]άμενοι Maier.

The Julian year has been established for the date of this law on the basis of historical considerations (full discussions in both Foucart and Frickenhaus). The problem is, 338/7 or 337/6 ? Lykourgos, Demosthenes and Aischines all mention wall-building or wall-repairing activities following Chaironeia. Only in Aischines III.27 is a specific date mentioned: in the year of Chairondas (338/7), on the last day but one of Thargelion (i.e., 337), Demosthenes moved that the ekklesia meet on the second and third of Skirophorion to choose superintendents and treasurers for work on the walls. Kirchner dates this law to the second half of 337, i.e., the year of Phrynichos (337/6). He is followed by Tod II p. 243, Scranton and Maier; Säfflund considers 337 a *terminus post quem*; and Cawkwell wants to place this law earlier, in the period of Euboulos. Kirchner refers to Frickenhaus for a discussion of the date, but neither Frickenhaus nor Foucart venture to name the archon in whose year the legislation was passed. I can see only two reasons for Kirchner's choice of the year of Phrynichos. First, because Kirchner assumed that Demosthenes must have moved the legislation resulting from the meetings of Skirophorion, while this law is moved by Kephisophon. But Aischines does not say who moved the legislation of Skirophorion and Kirchner fails to consider the possibility that Kephisophon and Demosthenes were cooperating in this matter. The second reason is that the presence of the nomothetai suggested to him that the legislation took place in the first prytany of the new year following the meetings in the last prytany of the previous year (on the basis of Demosthenes XXIV.20-23). But we now know that nomothetai could be called at any time in the year and not just in the first prytany, so this hypothetical argument is no longer valid (see #6 below).

Thus there seems to be no overwhelming reason for placing this law in 337/6 rather than 338/7, the only sure date in the literary evidence. I believe this law resulted from the appointment of nomothetai which was called for in Skirophorion, the last month of the year of Chairondas, but the vague date of 337, i.e., either the last month of the year of Chairondas or early in the first half of the year of Phrynichos, is more suited to the present state of evidence.

Both Foucart and Frickenhaus discuss the actual content of this inscription. Maier's more recent discussion summarizes its various elements. The opening formula, like those of other fourth century laws, is that of a regular decree of the Demos: it begins with ΘΕΟΙ, followed by a very short prescript (only the mover), a short motive statement, transition formula, then the text; the law ends with a postscript. Below the law, in the same size letters, but in columns of 27 letters to the line, which preserve the stoichedon order of the lines above, are instructions for a single part of the construction in Mounichia. Publication of the law and technical specifications together is unusual; Maier notes only one other instance, the building decree of 307/6 (II^2 463 + Hesperia 9 [1940] 66 no. 9; but see also #21, II^2 333).

The text, lines 6-44, can also be divided into sections: 1) planning and outline (lines 6-10); 2) financial matters (lines 11-28); 3) supervision (lines 28-31); 4) penalties and judicial settlements (lines 31-38); 5) drawing up of the votive offerings at the end of the work (lines 38-40); 6) building for harbor moles (lines 40-44). Only the fifth element is singular; the other sections conform to the usual procedure in building legislation.

II. THE YEAR OF PHRYNICHOS, 337/6

4. *ATHENS HONORS ALKIMACHOS* EM 7063

photo: Svoronos Ε Θ. ΜΟΥΣ. Plate 216 no. 5.

editors: Pittakis ΕΦ. (1837/39) 240; Rangabê (1855) 412; IG II 123; IG II^2 239.

collections: Hicks 152; Svoronos ΕΘ. ΜΟΥΣ. 441; Tod II 180.

testimonia: Arrian Anabasis I.18.1, VI.28.4; Harpokration s.v. "Alkimachos."

supplement: SEG 21.267 (Schweigert, Pritchett-Neugebauer, Oikonomides, Meritt).

other bibliography: Sauppe De proxenis 14; Reusch De dieb. cont. 8 no. 123; Schaefer Dem. III^2 32 n. 2; Wilhelm ÖJ 11 (1908) 91; Binneboessel Studien 56; Schweigert Hesperia 9(1940) 327; Pritchett-Neugebauer Cal. 42; Oikonomides ΠΛΑΤΩΝ 8(1956) 112-114; Meritt Ath. 76; Osborne BSA 67(1972) 158; Mikalson Year 99, 190; Henry Prescripts 38 n. 28.

description: This stone was found on the Akropolis in 1838. The marble is Pentelic; all sides are broken. Only a bit of drapery (identified as a seated Athena) remains from the relief above the decree.

dimensions:
H 0.31 m. (entire)
0.10 m. (below cymation)
W 0.21 m.
0.15 m. (below cymation)
Th 0.114 m.

letters: 0.008 m. First two lines, .009. The alphas do not have cross bars.

minuscule text: next page.

commentary: The text is Kirchner's. The E of ΘΕΟΙ, on the fillet above the cymation, is now covered by the painted ed. maj. number; it can still be read from an angle. Both dots are mine. The decree is in stoichedon order, restored by Koehler to 26 letters. Restorations are Koehler's unless noted below.

[Θ] ε [ο ί] stoich. 26
'Α λ κ ί μ α [χ ο c].
['Ε]πὶ Φρυνί[χου ἄρχοντος ἐπὶ τῆς 'Α]-
[κ]αμαντίδ̣[ος ἕκτης πρυτανείας, ἧ]-
[ι] χ̣αιρέc[τρατος 'Αμεινίου 'Αχαρν]-
[εὺ]c ἐγρα[μμάτευεν· Γαμηλιῶνος δ]-
[εκάτ]ηι ? - - - - - - - - - - - - -

2 alternate restorations: 'Αλκίμα[χος ἐποίησεν] Pittakis; 'Αλκίμα[χος ἐγραμμάτευε] Rang.; 'Αλκιμά[χωι, 'Αντιπάτρωι?] Hicks; 'Αλκιμά[χωι Προξενία?] Tod, who also offers four more alternatives; 'Αλκιμά[χου Πελλαίου] Oik.

6/7 date: Reusch, used by Ki.; Koe. did not venture to restore the month or the day. [--Γαμηλιῶνος ἑ/βδόμ]ηι [ἱσταμένου---] Schw. on the assumption that #5 (Hesperia 9[1940] 325-327 no. 35) and this decree were passed on the same day. Although Schw.'s restoration is accepted by P.-N., and Tod, Oik., and Mer. carry the comparison between #5 and this decree even further by including the day of the prytany from #5, the 7th of any month is always dedicated to Apollo (Mikalson, 90; see #35 [II^2 420] for a fuller discussion of Mikalson's work). Since Schw.'s restoration is not the only possibility, it is preferable to separate #4 and #5 and, in the case of this decree, go back to Reusch's earlier suggestion.

All that is left of the decree proper is the date, and very little of that. Above the text is the usual ΘΕΟΙ. The next line, ΑΛΚΙΜΑ[--, has invited a number of restorations (see commentary, line 2). Pittakis mistook Alkimachos as a sculptor and Rangabê assumed the decree was headed by the secretary's name, a formula common earlier in the century, but not in the Lykourgan period; subsequent restorations have been made to link this

Alkimachos with the one mentioned by Harpokration, who quoted from Hypereides' speech Against Demades to the effect that Alkimachos and Antipater were made Athenians and proxenoi (presumably on Demades' motion). Citizenship and proxeny, however, were not granted together at this time. To explain this implicit error in Harpokration, Sauppe proposed to emend the text; Schaefer's solution was to identify the present decree as the one which granted Alkimachos his proxeny and II^2 391 as the one which recorded his citizenship (II^2 391, though passed during the oligarchy between 321 and 318, reaffirms the politeia which had been granted to one Alkimachos, son of Al[kim]achos [Apolloni]ates in the archonship of [Niko]krates, 333/2); finally, Wilhelm resolved the dilemma of Harpokration's text by suggesting that one man became proxenos, the other a citizen; he also identified the Alkimachos of this text with Alkimachos, son of Agathokles of Pella mentioned by Arrian (VI.28.4) This would make Schaeffer's hypothesis untenable.

Since Wilhelm, the Alkimachos of Harpokration, that of Arrian and that of this decree have been considered as one and the same man; it is a reasonable assumption. The difficulty is that this stone provides only the name; it does not even confirm that the decree is honorary, although this is highly probable (Osborne also acknowledges the possibility that this decree is a grant of citizenship). It is equally possible that the Alkimachos of this decree is identical with the Alkimachos of II^2 391, or an Alkimachos otherwise unknown from either literary or epigraphical sources.

Demades moved three other decrees in 337/6 (#5, #7 [II^2 240], #8 [II^2 241]) and Tod, relying on the possible connection between Harpokration and this decree, suggests that Demades may also have been the mover of this decree. Oikonomides agrees, noting that this would give Demades a total of four decrees in the year of Phrynichos; this is probably a minimum rather than a maximum for so active a politician.

337/6

5. *LEMNOS DECREE* Ag. Inv. I 5234, I 2409

photo: Hesperia 9(1940) 326.

editor: Schweigert Hesperia 9(1940) 325-327 no. 35.

other bibliography: Pritchett-Neugebauer Cal. 42; Oikonomides ΠΛΑΤΩΝ 8(1956) 112; Meritt Ath. 76; Mikalson Year 99, 190.

description: The two fragments are Pentelic marble with only the rough-picked back and inscribed surface preserved. They were found in the Agora excavation: Fr. A, 1938; Fr. B, 1935.

dimensions:		letters: 0.005 m.
Fr. A	Fr. B	Smallest, such as
H 0.10 m.	H 0.21 m.	Ω, are .004; lar-
W 0.10 m.	W 0.071 m.	gest, such as B,
Th 0.08 m.	Th 0.081 m.	are .007.

minuscule text: stoich. 39

Fr. A vacat

[Ἐπὶ Φ]ρυνι̣χ̣ο̣[υ ἄρχοντος ἐπὶ τῆς ....10.... ὀγδό]-
[ης π]ρ̣υταν̣ε̣[ίας ἧι Χαιρέστρατος Ἀμεινίου Ἀχαρν]-
[εὺ]ς̣ ἐγραμ̣μ̣[άτευεν· Ἐλαφηβολιῶνος ὀγδόηι ἐπὶ δέ]-
[κα], πέμπτ̣[ηι τῆς πρυτανείας· τῶν προέδρων ἐπεψήφ]-
[ι]ζ̣εν Ἐργ[.........20.........· ἔδοξεν τῶι δήμ]-
[ωι· Δ]ημάδ̣[ης Δημέου Παιανιεὺς εἶπεν· περὶ ὧν οἱ θε]
[σμο]θ̣έτα[ι λέγουσι ....24..........]
[....]ς̣α[...............33...............]

Fr. B

[- - - - - -]ωι̣ ευτ[...7....]
[- - - - ἐν] Λ̣ῆμνω[ι..6...]
[- - - - - - -]τον[...8.....]
[- - - - - - - β]ο̲υλῆι [...8....]
[- - - - - -]τ̣ῆ̣ν ε[...8....]
[- - - - - -]υντω̣[...7..]
[- - - - - - τ]ῆι βο[υλῆι ...]
[- - - - τῆ]ι̲ βουλῆ̣[ι ....]
[- - - - - -]μη περ̣[..5..]
[- - - - - - χρ]ηματί[cαι ..]
[- - - - ἐν Λ]ῆ̣μνωι κ[..5..]
[- - - -]ουc τοὺc [....]
[- - - -]τὸμ βαcι[λέα·]
[- - - -] ἕκαcτ[..5..]
[- - - -] δὲ τοὺc [....]
[- - - π]α̣ραγεγρ[αμμέ]-
[ν- - - - - - κ]α̣ὶ ὁ γραφ[....]
[- - - - - -]ένου καὶ [....]
[- - - - - -θ]εcμοθετ[....]
[- - - - - -]ιν εἰc̣ τ̣[....]

epigraphical commentary: The text is based on Schweigert's, with the exception of the date (see below). Since 1940, more letters have become obscure; they are dotted. The two underlined letters, Fr. B, lines 12, 16 are now unreadable. The stoichedon order, restored to 39 letters to the line, is violated twice, lines 12, 13. Dots are mine; Schweigert also dotted the letters in lines 1-6, 8 of Fr. A; line 17 of Fr. B.

Fr. B
10 st. 28 Although only part of the surface of this stoichos remains, Λ can be read and there is no evidence of a cross bar for alpha or delta.

12 st. 30 HI in one stoichos.

13 st. 30 HN in one stoichos.

commentary: When Schweigert published this decree, he restored the date on the assumption that it and #4 were passed on the same day, 7th of Gamelion, 5th day of the 6th prytany. His restoration for lines 1-4 reads:

> [Ἐπι Φ]ρυνι̣χο̣[υ ἄρχοντος ἐπὶ τῆς Ἀκαμαντίδος ἕκτ]-
> [ης π]ρ̣υταν̣ε̣[ίας ἧι Χαιρέστρατος Ἀμεινιου Ἀχαρν]-
> [εὺ]ς̣ ἐγραμ̣μ̣[άτευεν· Γαμηλιῶνος ἑβδόμηι ἱσταμέν]-
> [ου], πέμτ̣[ηι τῆς πρυτανείας· των προέδρων ἐπεψηφ]-

Mikalson, however, has pointed out that the 7th day of the month is always devoted to Apollo (90). Of four possible restorations which fit the letters on the stone, I offer the only restoration which requires no exceptions and allows for a balanced distribution of full and hollow months. The equation is: Elaphebolion [18] = Prytany [VIII] 5 = 254th day. There are three possibilities for the tribe which held the 8th prytany: Kekropis, Erechtheis, or Antiochis.

Fr. A
6/7 Schweigert prefers θεσμοθέται over the possible [ἀγονο]θέτα[ι] based on line 27.

21 Probable reference to Philip, since Lemnos was one of the few possessions left to Athens after Chaironeia. (Schweigert, with reference to Glotz-Roussel-Cohen Histoire Grecque IV, 1, p. 196; Schaefer Dem. III^2 28.)

This stone gives the unsubstantial information that probably on the fifth day of the eighth prytany, the eighteenth day of Elaphebolion, Demades moved some type of legislation. Oikonomides' article is concerned with literary and epigraphical evidence for the decrees moved by Demades; for Demades' activities in this year, see #4; for the entire Lykourgan Era, #23 (Hesperia 9 [1940] 339-340).

On the basis of Fr. B, lines 10 and 19, Schweigert suggests that the decree is concerned with a report or recommendation of the thesmothetai concerning Lemnos, "but no continuous sense can be achieved in the text of Fragment B" (327).

337/6

6. *LAW AGAINST TYRANNY* Ag. Inv. I 6524

photos: Hesperia 21(1952) Plates 89, 90; Hesperia 22 (1953) Plate 20a; JHS 73(1953) Plate 1 no. 1; ΠΟΛΕΜΩΝ 6 (1956/7) Symmeikta 29, 33; Hausmann Gr. Weihreliefs 43, 44.

editor: Meritt Hesperia 21(1952) 355-359 no. 5.

collection: Pouilloux Choix 121-124 no. 32.

testimonia: Andokides On the Mysteries 80, 96; Deinarchos Against Demosthenes 62-63; Demosthenes Third Olynthiac 10, On the Crown 132-134; Lykourgos Against Leokrates 52-53, 127; Plutarch Demosthenes 14.4, Phokion 16.1-3.

supplements: SEG 12.87 (Meritt Hesperia 1952); 15.95 (Wycherly, Robert Bull. 1956); 17.26 (Oikonomides); 18.12 (Ostwald, Sealey, Hausmann); 24.96 (Pouilloux, Braccesi).
Bull. (1954) no. 76 (Meritt Hesperia 1952, 1953, Thompson); (1956) no. 88 (Wycherly); (1958) no. 198 (Ostwald, Oikonomides); (1959) no. 129 (Sealey).

other bibliography: Vanderpool Archaeology 3(1950) 34-37; New York Times May 26, 1952; Kougeas ΝΕΑ ΕΣΤΙΑ 62 (1952) 836-839; Thompson Hesperia 22(1953) 51-53; Meritt Hesperia 22(1953) 129; Cook JHS 75(1953) 111; Larsen CP 49(1954) 1-14; Ostwald TAPA 86(1955) 103-128; Wycherly JHS 75(1955) 118-121; Oikonomides ΠΟΛΕΜΩΝ 6(1956/7) Symmeikta 28-36; Conomis Hellenika 16 (1958) 6-13; Sealey AJP 79(1958) 71-73; Hausmann Gr. Weih. 43-44; Meritt Ath. 77; Braccesi Epigraphica 27 (1965) 110-126; Rhodes Boule 28 n. 2; 32 n. 1, 51 n. 3, 138 n. 6, 276; DeLaix Proboul. 67, 136, 171; Stroud Hesperia 43(1974) 151-188.

description: This stele is a rarity for the Lykourgan period--it is complete and requires no restoration.

Below the pediment, traces of a painted egg and dart design remain on the molding. The relief probably represents Democracy crowning the Demos (Cook describes Demos as old and careworn). The marble is white (Meritt adds: Pentelic?). The cutting above the first line of text probably represents an attempt, already in antiquity, to sever the relief from the rest of the stele. Perhaps the abandonment of the project reflects upon the quality of the sculptured relief; it was not worth the effort. (Cf. #42, a decree from Eitea, for another example.)

dimensions: letters: 0.005 m.

H 1.57 m.
W 0.41 m. (above)
0.43 m. (below)
Th c. 0.10 m. (above)
0.12 m. (below)

minuscule text: next page

epigraphical commentary: The text is inscribed in stoichedon order, 36 letters to the line. There is one violation: at the beginning of line 15 IEIN is inscribed in 5 spaces. The stonecutter omitted the cross bars for alphas in lines: 10 st. 12; 12 st. 27; 13 st. 35; 18 st. 30; 21 st. 13; 26 st. 36; 27 st. 35. In line 11 st. 2, the letter on the stone is iota; in line 13 st. 4, the letter is nu.

I include below Meritt's translation with two changes: in line 11 of the text, for ὅσιος I prefer <u>innocent</u>; Meritt had <u>blameless</u>; for lines 24-26 I offer the simplified "set one of them by that entrance into the Areios Pagos where one goes into the Bouleuterion." Meritt's original translation of lines 24-26 read "set one of them by the entrance into the Areopagos, that entrance, namely, near where one goes into the Bouleuterion," and in <u>Hesperia</u> 1953, Thompson suggested "set one of them by the entrance, the one into the Areopagos, the one into the Bouleuterion, as one goes in." The sense of the phrase (whether in simplified or complex translation) is difficult to ascertain because the meeting place of the Council of the Areios Pagos at the time of Lykourgos is underdetermined. Thompson's translation allowed him to suggest the Old Bouleuterion; in 1977, I followed Vanderpool's suggestion that the Council met, not on the exposed peak of the Areios Pagos, but under the protection of its northern cliff in the area now covered by the massive rock fall. More recently, John Camp, of the Agora

stoich. 36

Ἐπὶ Φρυνίχου ἄρχοντος ἐπὶ τῆς Λεωντίδος ἐν-
άτης πρυτανείας ἧι Χαιρέστρατος Ἀμεινίου
Ἀχαρνεὺς ἐγραμμάτευεν· τῶν προέδρων ἐπεψή-
φιζεν Μενέστρατος Αἰξωνεύς· Εὐκράτης Ἀριc-
τοτίμου Πειραιεὺς εἶπεν· ἀγαθῆι τύχηι τοῦ δ-
ήμου τοῦ Ἀθηναίων· δεδόχθαι τοῖς νομοθέται-
c· ἐάν τις ἐπαναστῆι τῶι δήμωι ἐπὶ τυραννίδι
ἢ τὴν τυραννίδα συνκαταστήσηι ἢ τὸν δῆμον τ-
ὸν Ἀθηναίων ἢ τὴν δημοκρατίαν τὴν Ἀθήνησιν
καταλύσηι, ὃς ἂν τὸν τούτων τι ποιήσαντα ἀπο-
κτείνηι ὅσιος ἔστω· μὴ ἐξεῖναι δὲ τῶν βουλευ-
τῶν τῶν τῆς βουλῆς τῆς ἐξ Ἀρείου Πάγου καταλ-
ελυ<μ>ένου τοῦ δήμου ἢ τῆς δημοκρατίας τῆς Ἀθ-
ήνησιν ἀνιέναι εἰς Ἄρειον Πάγον μηδὲ συνκα-
θίζειν ἐν τῶι συνεδρίωι μηδὲ βουλεύειν μη-
δὲ περὶ ἑνός· ἐὰν δέ τις τοῦ δήμου ἢ τῆς δημοκρ-
ατίας καταλελυμένων τῶν Ἀθήνησιν ἀνίηι τῶ-
ν βουλευτῶν τῶν ἐξ Ἀρείου Πάγου εἰς Ἄρειον Π-
άγον ἢ συνκαθίζηι ἐν τῶι συνεδρίωι ἢ βολεύη-
ι περί τινος ἄτιμος ἔστω καὶ αὐτὸς καὶ γένος
τὸ ἐξ ἐκείνου καὶ ἡ οὐσία δημοσία ἔστω αὐτοῦ
καὶ τῆς θεοῦ τὸ ἐπιδέκατον· ἀναγράψαι δὲ τὸν
δε τὸν νόμον ἐν στήλαις λιθίναις δυοῖν τὸν γ-
ραμματέα τῆς βουλῆς καὶ στῆσαι τὴμ μὲν ἐπὶ τ-
ῆς εἰσόδου τῆς εἰς Ἄρειον Πάγοṿ τῆς εἰς τὸ βο-
υλευτήριον εἰσιόντι, τὴν δὲ ἐν τῆι ἐκκλησία-
ι· εἰς δὲ τὴν ἀναγραφὴν τῶν στηλῶν τὸν ταμίαν
δοῦναι τοῦ δήμου : ΔΔ : δραχμὰς ἐκ τῶν κατὰ ψη-
φίσματα ἀναλισκομένων τῶι δήμωι vacat

vacat

Excavations, has suggested that there had been steps below the east end of the Hephaisteion (which faces the Agora) and that these steps provided a place for the Council to meet. Camp's suggestion seems reasonable: it keeps the Council in the open air; the steps could be reached by going by the entrance to the Bouleuterion; one would have to "go up" (lines 14 and 17) to sit on the steps; and it does not contradict any of the three suggested translations for lines 24-26.

translation: In the archonship of Phrynichos, in the ninth prytany of Leontis for which Chairestratos, son of Ameinias, of Acharnai, was secretary; Menestratos of Aixone, of the proedroi, put the question to a vote; Eukrates, son of Aristotimos, of Peiraieus, made the motion: with Good Fortune of the Demos of the Athenians, be it resolved by the Nomothetai: If anyone rise up against the Demos for tyranny or join in establishing the tyranny or overthrow the Demos of the Athenians or the democracy in Athens, whoever kills him who does any of these things shall be innocent. It shall not be permitted for anyone of the Councillors of the Council from the Areios Pagos --if the Demos or the democracy in Athens has been overthrown--to go up into the Areios Pagos or sit in the Council or deliberate about anything. If anyone--the Demos or the democracy in Athens overthrown--of the Councillors of the Areios Pagos goes up into the Areios Pagos or sits in Council or deliberates about anything, both he and his progeny shall be deprived of civil rights and his substance shall be confiscated and a tenth given to the Goddess. The secretary of the Council shall inscribe this law on two stelai of stone and set one of them by that entrance into the Areios Pagos where one goes into the Bouleuterion, and the other in the Ekklesia. For the inscribing of the stelai the treasurer of the Demos shall give 20 drachmai from the moneys expendable by the Demos according to decrees.

commentary: Meritt's full commentary with his original publication obviates the necessity of repeating it here. There are, however, two points: 1) the motive behind this legislation; and 2) presence of the nomothetai. Both have become the focal points of subsequent discussion and will be treated below.

There is no direct reference to the Law of Eukrates in the literary sources. But there is information which has been used to shed light on this decree: Deinarchos (I.62-63) says that Demosthenes proposed a decree extending the powers of the Council of the Areios Pagos (date: Ostwald--before 344; Sealey--340/39); in the Antiphon affair the Council reversed the decision of the court and condemned him to death (Plutarch Demosthenes 14.4; Demosthenes 18.132-134); the Council replaced Aischines with Hypereides as representative to the Amphiktiony (Demosthenes 18.132-134); and, after Chaironeia, it replaced Charidemos with Phokion as general of the countryside (Plutarch Phokion 16.1-3); it also condemned those who fled the country in its hour of peril (Lykourgos I.52-53; Deinarchos I.62-63).

Ostwald places this decree in its legal context by reviewing tyranny legislation back to Drakon. For the motive behind the decree, he follows Larsen, who sees the Law of Eukrates as "the reaction against the usurpation of the Areopagus on the part of what genuine democratic spirit still survived" (9). Sealey carries this line of thought a step further by suggesting that this "attack" on the Council of the Areios Pagos is in effect aimed at Demosthenes (73; it would be almost an immediate reaction since Sealey places Demosthenes' decree granting more power to the Council in 340/39, with the events described in the rest of the primary evidence falling between then and the date of this decree).

Oikonomides also reviews previous tyranny legislation, but arrives at a different solution. He emphasizes the presence of the nomothetai and concludes from their presence that there must have been previous legislation which the Law of Eukrates is to supersede. Oikonomides, 35, suggests a law enacted after the return of the democrats from Phyle in 403, which determined when the Council should meet and which also provided severe penalties to any member who refused to take part in the meetings. Oikonomides' interpretation of Demosthenes 23.20-23 is the usual one, but the "new" law on Athenian silver coinage (date 375), published by Stroud in _Hesperia_, seems almost nonchalant in its consideration of former legislation. Lines 55-56 (Stroud's translation) read: "If there is any decree recorded anywhere on a stele contrary to this present law, let the Secretary of the Boule tear it down." The passage in Demosthenes has been interpreted to imply that first, an old law had to be considered and rejected, and then nomothetai were appointed to make a revision; the new coinage law, however, implies that a new law is legislated to fit new developments, and then any contrary decrees are struck off the books. Apparently there existed no previous _law_ on accepting Athenian silver as legal tender; had there been such a law, we may assume that the former rules would have been followed.

Until a full-scale study is done on the nomothetai (both Stroud, 162, and Rhodes, 50 note 5, stress the need), it seems unwise to base an interpretation on the "duties" or procedure of the nomothetai. The same caution should be observed as to when the nomothetai could be called. Demosthenes, in his speech, _On the Crown_ 20-23, is our sole authority for the 11th day of the first prytany as the only time the nomothetai could be called. Sealey has considered the Law of Eukrates as "unusual" because it was not enacted earlier in the year (71, citing the above passage from Demosthenes), and he emphasizes this point to confirm his suspicion of "an extraordinary situation--and political intrigue." And yet, I have argued that #3 was enacted after the first prytany (cf. discussion for #3 and below). And Demosthenes, himself, in the Third Olynthiac 10, suggests calling the nomothetai to repeal old laws; the historical context is most likely shortly before the fall of Olynthos, autumn 348, long after the first prytany. Although Sealey argues that this "excited demand" does not prove that the board of nomothetai could be established at any time, Rhodes (51) rightly stresses that "the few inscribed νόμοι surviving from the fourth century show that νομοθεσία could occur at any time during the year." To Rhodes's evidence, Table H, page 276, we can now add the Law on Silver Coinage and note that II^2 222 has been brought down into the Lykourgan period by Osborne BSA 67 (1972) 133 note 15, following Johnson (I have given II^2 222 a more specific date--see addendum to #31 [II^2 336]).

If Demosthenes' speech On the Crown had not survived, the functions and responsibilities of the nomothetai would have been interpretated from the epigraphical evidence. First, the nomothetai are involved with finances (Foucart in Journ Sav. 1902, noted this connection in his discussion of #3). Maier noted that the presence of the nomothetai in #3 is unusual, but it would not be so if appropriations for the wall repairs were made in haste, after the yearly appropriations had been made. The same applies to the new law on silver coinage of 375; the newly appointed Dokimastai are to be paid by the Apodektai (from current revenues) until the next year begins, but after that time they will be paid from the same sources as the mint workers. This confirms that nomothetai were required to give authority for new or unusual appropriations after the yearly ones had been set. "Finance seems the clearest example of a topic which ought to have been dealt with by nomos." (Rhodes, 50; cf. DeLaix, 141.) Second, the nomothetai could be called at any time during the year. The Law of Eukrates is unique among fourth century nomoi surviving on stone in that it does not deal with finance; but it provides definite evidence that the nomothetai could act at a time other than the first prytany--the date is carved on stone. For some reason, in the ninth prytany of 337/6, Eukrates felt that it was necessary to define the duties and responsibilities, in regard to tyranny, of the Council of the Areios Pagos. Eukrates also wanted his proposal to have the force of a law--not just a decree, so a board of nomothetai was established.

None of these assumptions contradicts Demosthenes's statement; rather they complement it. At the beginning of the year, there would be discussion about whether the nomothetai were needed, but they could also be called at any time they were needed.

The primary evidence recorded at the beginning of this discussion shows only that after Demosthenes' decree (Deinarchos I.62-63) the Council of the Areios Pagos did play a larger role in the affairs of the state. When the Council is mentioned in speeches of this period, it is used as an example of justice and wise patriotism toward the city of Athens. Rather than an attack on the Council, the Law of Eukrates gives tacit acceptance of its new responsibilities and acknowledges the need to revive the laws accordingly. The purpose of this law is to prevent the Council or any of its members from giving (or being forced to give) legal sanction in case of tyranny, as Thompson stated when the discovery of the stele was first announced (New York Times). It could even be argued that the Law of Eukrates was designed to protect this stronger Council from being forced to legitimize a tyrant or to comply with his orders. In 337/6, neither the Council nor any of its members, neither Demosthenes nor anyone else in the "Lykourgan Coalition" was aiming at tyranny; that tyranny (the subversion of the Demos and demokratia in any form) might be imposed from outside was the only fear. What Philip did in the various Greek states counted for more than the "paper" safeguards to existing constitutions in his Hellenic League.

337/6

7. *ATHENS BESTOWS PROXENY* EM 7154

editors: Pittakis ΕΦ. (1840/42) 1043, 1049; Rangabé (1855) 413; Velsen Rh. Mus. 11(1857) 598; IG II 124; IG II^2 240.

collections: Syll. 110; Syll.^{2} 148; Syll.^{3} 262; Hicks 153; Michel 103; Nachmanson 38; Tod II 181.

other bibliography: Pritchett-Neugebauer Cal. 43; Oikonomides ΠΛΑΤΩΝ 8(1956) 114-115; Meritt Ath. 77; Mitchel Lyk. 176-180; Heisserer ZPE 41(1981) 216-218.

description: The stone, found on the Akropolis in 1840, lost and found again in 1842 (according to Pittakis), is Pentelic marble. The left side is original, but worn and partly broken away. All other sides are broken; the back is rough-picked and probably original. The surface is pitted and very worn. In the upper right hand corner, the beginning of a cymation can be seen. Otherwise, there are no clues as to the nature of the decoration on this stele.

dimensions: letters: 0.007 m.
H 0.57 m.
W 0.37 m.
Th 0.11 m.

majuscule text:

Θ̲ Ε Ο
. . Ι Φ Ρ Υ Ν Ι Χ Ο Υ Α Ρ Χ Ο Ν Τ Ο Σ̣ . . .
. . Ι Ο Ν̣ Ι Δ Ο Σ Δ̣ Ε Κ Α Τ Η Σ Π Ρ Υ . Α̣ .
. Χ Α Ι̣ Ρ . . Τ Ρ Α Τ Ο Σ Α Μ̣ Ε Ι Ν Ι Ο̣ . .
Υ Σ Ε̣ . . . . . Α Τ Ε Υ Ε Ν Τ Ω Ν̣ Π Ρ Ο Ε .
. Ψ Η . . . . Ν̣ Α̣ Ν Τ Ι Φ Α Ν Η Σ Ε Υ Ω Ν .
. Η̣ . . . . . . Η̣ Μ Ε Ο Υ Π Α Ι Α Ν Ι Ε Υ .
. . . Θ̣ . . . Υ Χ Η Ι̲ . Ο Υ Δ Η Μ Ο Υ Τ Ο .
. . . . . . Ο Χ̣ . Α̣ Ι̣ Τ Ω Ι Δ Η Μ Ω Ι Ε̣ Π .
. . . . . Σ̣ . . . . . . ∩̲ . Α̣ Ν̣ Δ Ρ Ο Ν . Ν̣ .
. . Ο̲ . . .̄ Ν̲ Δ Η Μ Ο Ν Τ̣ Ο Ν̣ Α Θ Η Ν Α̣ Ι .
. . Α̲ . Ε Π Ι Μ Ε̣ Λ Ε Ι Τ̲ Α̲ Ι Α Θ Η Ν Α Ι .
. . . . Ο Υ̣ . Ε Ν Ω Ν̣ Ω Σ̣ Φ Ι Λ Ι Π Π Ο Ν .
. . . Α̲ Θ Ο Ν Ο̣ Τ̣ Ι Δ Υ̣ . . . Α Ι Α Θ̲ Η̣ Ν .
. . Α̣ . Ι Λ Ι Π Π Ο Υ Ε̣ . . . Ι̣ Π Ρ Ο̲ Ξ Ε .
. . Ε̣ . Γ . Τ Η Ν Τ . Υ . . . Ο Υ Τ̣ Ο Υ Α Θ
. . Υ Τ Ο Ν Κ̣ Α Ι Ε Κ̣ Γ Ο Ν̣ Ο Υ Σ Α Υ Τ Ο .
. . Ε̣ Λ Ε̣ Ι Σ Θ Α Ι Α̲̣ Υ̣ Τ̣ Ο Υ̣ Τ Η Ν Β Ο̣ Υ̣ .
. . Υ̣ Σ Σ Τ Ρ Α Τ Η Γ Ο Υ Σ Ο Τ Ο Υ Α Ν Δ .
. . Γ̣ . Α Ψ̣ Α̲̣ Ι̣ Δ Ε Τ Η Ν Π Ρ Ο Ξ Ε Ν Ι Α̣ .
. . . . Λ Ι Θ̣ Ι Ν Η Ν Κ̣ Α Ι Σ Τ Η Σ Α Ι . .
. . . . Α . Ο Ν Κ Α̣ . Α̣ Π Ρ Υ Τ Α Ν Ε Ι . .
. . . . Ε Ι Ε̲ Ι Σ . Ε Τ Η Ν Α Ν Α Γ Ρ Α̣ . .
. . Λ Η Σ . . Τ Ω Ο Τ Α Μ Ι Α Σ Τ Ρ Ι Α . .
. . . Α Σ Κ̲ Α Τ̲ Α Τ Ο Ν̲ Ν Ο Μ Ο Ν

epigraphical commentary: A number of letters read by previous editors must now be underlined; yet, I have read many letters bracketed by Koehler and Kirchner and Heisserer has reconsidered the letters in lines 9-10. Those new readings will be noted below. With the exception of st. 6 and st. 21, line 10, all dots are mine.

3 st. 21 new reading; st. 20, 21 Tʹ Vel.

4 st. 2 new reading; st. 7 Σ Vel.; st. 16, 17 new readings, also seen by Vel.

5 st. 1, 3 new readings, also seen by Vel.; st. 7 M Vel.

6 st. 3, 9 new readings; st. 6, 7 ¯Γ Vel.

7 st. 9 new reading; st. 2-10 H.Λ...ΣΔ..M Vel.

8 st. 5, 7 H, T Vel.

9 st. 2, 6 Vel. read Ω, Δ.
st. 8 new reading, also seen by Vel.
st. 20 new reading, bracketed by Heisserer, who notes that Walbank read Ẹ for st. 22.

10 ...[Σ̣].Σ̣[Ṭ]...Ị O.ANΔPOṂẸNỌ..$\overset{5}{.}$.. Heisserer, who could not read Σ̣ and Ṭ read by Wal. (per ep.) and thus bracketed them. Vel. read Θ̣ in st. 6 (which Heisserer rejects) and Σ in st. 13 (which helps Heisserer's argument; see comm. below). In st. 19 I read nu; since neither mu nor nu is very well cut, this letter could be mu.

11 st. 13, 20 new readings; st. 4 Σ̣ Vel.

13 st. 6 new reading.

14 st. 11-13 ΔOY Vel.

16 st. 4, 6, 11 P, –, O Vel.

17 st. 2 A Vel.

18 st. 3, 18 new readings.

19 st. 3 new reading.

21 st. 3, 4 HN Vel.

23 st. 20 new reading, also seen by Vel.

24 st. 7 O Vel.

25 st. 5 new reading, also seen by Vel.

minuscule text:

θ ε ο [ί] stoich. 27

[Ἐπ]ὶ Φρυνίχου ἄρχοντοϲ [ἐπὶ τῆϲ Πα]-
[νδ]ιονίδοϲ δεκάτηϲ πρυ[τ]α̣[νείαϲ ἧ]-
[ι] Χαιρ[έϲ]τρατοϲ Ἀμεινίο[υ Ἀχαρνε]-
ὺϲ ἐ̣[γραμμ]άτευεν· τῶν προέ[δρων ἐπ]-
[ε]ψή̣[φιζε]ν Ἀ̣ντιφάνηϲ Εὐων[υμεὺϲ· v]
[Δ]η[μάδηϲ Δ]η̣μέου Παιανιεὺ[ϲ εἶπεν·]
[ἀγα]θ[ῆι τ]ύχηι [τ]οῦ δήμου το[ῦ Ἀθηνα]-
[ίων δεδ]όχ̣[θ]αι τῶι δήμωι, ἐ̣π[ειδὴ ..]
..^{5}..Σ̣....Ι̣Ο̣.ΑΝΔΡΟΜ̣Ε̣ΝΟ̣..^{5}..
[πρ]ὸ[ϲ τὸ]ν δῆμον τ̣ὸν Ἀθηνα̣ί[ων νῦν δ]-
[ὲ κ]α[ὶ] ἐπιμελεῖται Ἀθηναί[ων τῶν ἀ]-
[φικν]ου̣[μ]ένων ὡϲ Φίλιππον [πράττω]-
[ν ἀγ]αθὸν ὅτι δύ[νατ]αι Ἀθην[αίοιϲ π]-
[αρ]ὰ [Φ]ιλίππου, ε[ἶνα]ι πρόξε[νον καὶ]
[εὐ]ε[ρ]γ[έ]την τ[ο]ῦ [δήμ]ου τοῦ Ἀθ[ηναίω]-
[ν α]ὐτὸν καὶ εκγόνουϲ αὐτο[ῦ καὶ ἐπ]-
[ιμ]ε̣λεῖϲθαι αὐτοῦ τὴν βου[λὴν καὶ]
[το]ὺϲ ϲτρατηγοὺϲ ὅτου ἂν δ[έηται. ἀ]-
[να]γ[ρ]άψαι δὲ τὴν προξενία[ν εἰϲ ϲτ]-
[ήλην] λιθίνην καὶ ϲτῆϲαι [τὸν γραμ]-
[ματέ]α [τ]ὸν κα[τ]ὰ πρυτανεί[αν ἐν ἀκρ]-
[οπόλ]ει· εἰϲ [δ]ὲ τὴν ἀναγρα̣[φὴν τῆϲ ϲ]-
[τή]ληϲ [δό]τω ὁ ταμίαϲ τριά[κοντα δρ]-
[αχμ]ὰϲ κατὰ τὸν νόμον. vacat

commentary: The text incorporates new readings noted above. The restorations are Velsen's, unless noted below. The stoichedon order of 27 letters to the line is violated only once: line 6 has 26 letters. Since the stoichedon order on the stone for line 6 is correct, I have restored the vacat at the end of the line. In his discussion of lines 9-12, Heisserer has noted that "the stoichedon arrangement occasionally is untidy" (217) in order to provide enough space for the name and ethnic of the honorand in line 10. Although Heisserer's restoration is discussed below, I note here that although the letters are untidily cut, the stoichedon order is maintained throughout (with exception noted above); there is no instance of crowding.

9 end-10: I have left this section unrestored (as did Koe. and Ki.), but have included letters read by Heisserer and Wal. as well as earlier editors (see ep. com. above). [ἀ̣ν/ὴρ ἀγα]θ[ὸc Σϖσ]οc 'Ανδρο[μέ]ν[ουc--] Vel.; εὖ/νουc ἐ̣σ]τι ...]ο[. 'Α]νδρον[ί]κ̣[ου ....] Hiller; εὖ/εργετ]ε̣[ι....]ο̣['Α]νδρομ[έ]ν[ουc Μ̣ακ/εδ]ώ̣[ν] Wilh.; [..-/.....11.....]δρο[ν .]ν[...6...] Koe. Heisserer's restoration is a combination of the beginning of Hiller's, the end of Vel.'s, and a suggestion for the ethnic: [ἐ̣]π[ειδὴ εὖ/νουc̣ ἐ]c̣[τὶ 2-3]ιο[c] 'Ανδρομέ̣ν̣ο̣[υc Χῖοc] (ὀ̣r 'Ἀ̣ν̣δ̣ρομέ̣ν̣ο̣[υc Κρῆc] with ten 5 or 6 letter names offered). As is evident from the number of restorations offered it is impossible to know where the reason for the honor stops and the name of the honorand begins. Although Heisserer does offer three 5 letter possibilities for the name, he must presume crowding at the end of the line to fit in even the shortest ethnic (see above, comm.). Another possibility, which does not help to identify the honorand, but would ease the crowding in line 10, is that the name of the honorand--name, patronymic, ethnic or perhaps only name and ethnic--was inscribed above the extant text; either on the fillet above the cymation (see description) or within a pediment which was already separated from its stele in antiquity (II^2 113, #60, preserves the name of the honorand in its pediment). If the name were recorded elsewhere, then lines 9-10 could have recorded: a longer reason for the honor with only the honorand's name or the honorand's name and patronymic with one or more vacats at the end of line 10. I.e., the possibilities are too numerous to record Heisserer's or any other editor's restorations for this line.

11/12 end: Henry (per ep. to Heisserer) 'Αθηναί[ων ἐ̣σ-τί/ν καί Vel.; Koe., Ki. did not restore.

13/14 end: Koe. Φί̣λιππον [καὶ ποε/ῖ ἀγ]αθό̣ν Vel.

14/15 end: Koe. αἶοις κ/ατ]ά̣ Vel.

This decree honors a man who helped Athenian envoys to Philip, doing what he could to secure favorable treatment from the king. The Demos grants this man (and his descendents) proxeny and the title of <u>euergetes</u> (benefactor) and puts him under the care of the Boule and the generals.

Only traces of the name of the man honored remain in line 10. Various restorations are recorded in the commentary above; Heisserer suggests that the man came from a minor Greek state, and Schaefer (<u>Dem.</u> III^2 33) suggests that he should be identified as the Antipater who is mentioned along with Alkimachos by Harpokration (cf. #4 above). Since none of these identifications fit the preserved letters and traces on the stone, I prefer to leave the line unrestored

There need be little doubt, on the other hand, that the man was in fact either a Macedonian or some other friend of Philip; and no doubt at all that the mover was Demades. Thus we have here the strongest epigraphical evidence (stronger than #4, where the mover's name is only a probable conjecture and #5 or #8 [II^2 241], where the purpose of the decrees is pure guesswork) in support of the literary tradition which says that Demades promoted Macedonian honors and interests at Athens in return for monetary awards (cf. Oikonomides; a list of all Demades' decrees in this Corpus can be found in discussion, #23). We should not, however, lose sight of the historical context of 337/6; Demades had been one of the chief negotiators of the peace and alliance with Philip, and he if anyone should have known who had proved helpful in securing more favorable terms for the Athenians. This decree, then, (and the others) may express genuine gratitude for past help and have an eye more on future influence at court for Athens than on personal monetary gain. (cf. Mitchel 176-180, esp. 177). Demades' decree concerning Lemnos, #5, the possession of which had been confirmed to Athens by Philip's generosity, shows that final settlements were still being arranged in 337/6 and that Demades had a hand in it.

337/6

8. *DECREE* EM 7066, 7066[a]

editors: Fr. A IG II 127.
Fr. A+B IG II^2 241.

other bibliography: Wilhelm ʹOJ 1(1898) Beibl. 45; Pritchett-Neugebauer Cal. 43; Oikonomides ΠΛΑΤΩΝ 8(1956) 115; Meritt Ath. 77.

description: The two non-contiguous fragments are Pentelic marble. The right side of Fr. A, although damaged, is original; all other sides are broken. When found, Fr. B confirmed Koehler's restoration of Fr. A; it is now illegible.

dimensions:

Fr. A	Fr. B
H 0.20 m.	H 0.20 m.
W 0.156 m.	W 0.14 m.
Th 0.13 m.	Th 0.14 m.

letters: 0.008 m. Smallest, X, is .005; Ω, usually small, is .007. The letters are square.

minuscule text: next page.

commentary: The text includes new readings in line 6 st. 22, and 7 st. 23. The dots are mine. The stoichedon order is restored to 28 letters; there are no violations. Wilhelm noted that the fragments went together, supplied the name of the chairman of the proedroi, and validated Koehler's restoration of the entire text.

stoich. 28

[Θ ε ο] ί

Fr. B Fr. A

[Ἐπὶ Φρυνίχου] ἄρχ[οντος ἐπ]ὶ τῆς Παν-
[διονίδος δεκ]άτη[ς πρυτα]νείας, ἧι Χ-
[αιρέστρατο]ς Ἀμει[νίου] Ạχαρνεὺς ἐ-
[γραμμάτευε]ν· τῶν π[ροέδ]ρ̣ων ἐπεψήφ-
[ιζεν Ἀντιφά]νης Εὐω[νυμεὺς]· Δημάδη-
[ς Δημέου Παι]ανιεὺς [εἶπεν·] ἀγαθῆι τ-
[ύχηι τοῦ δή]μου τ[οῦ Ἀθηναίω]ν̣ δεδόχ-
[θαι τῶι δήμ]ωι - - - - -

The only information this inscription supplies is that Demades moved a decree when Phrynichos was archon, in the tenth prytany. The specific date is not recorded; however, this decree and #7 record the same chairman of the proedroi, an office picked by lot each day and which could be held just once a year. Therefore #7 and #8 were passed on the same day. I have not placed them at the end of the year, after the decrees with specific month or prytany dates, because they can be placed in a more specific chronological order in this particular year. Numbers 7-12 were all passed in the 10th prytany. #7 and #8, however, do not show the same chairman of the proedroi as #9, passed on the 22nd day of the prytany; nor #10, #11, #12, passed on the 35th day of the prytany. Since the 22nd and 35th days were probably the last two assemblies of the 10th prytany, it is reasonable to assume that #7 and this decree were passed at one of the two earlier regular sessions of this prytany.

Demades' legislative activities are discussed above, #7. The fact that #7 bestowed honors on someone at Philip's court may suggest, but by no means proves, that this decree had the same or a similar purpose.

337/6

9. *ATHENS HONORS CHAIRESTRATOS* EM 12893

photo: Hesperia 7(1938) 293, figure 21.

editor: Schweigert Hesperia 7(1938) 292-294 no. 19.

supplement: Bull. (1939) no. 59 (Schweigert).

other bibliography: Schweigert Hesperia 9(1940) 342; Pritchett-Neugebauer Cal. 42; Meritt Hesperia 21(1952) 357; Ath. 77.

description: The stone, found in 1937 in the Agora excavations, is Pentelic marble. It is broken all around except for the right side.

dimensions:
H 0.22 m.
W 0.115 m.
Th 0.07 m.

letters: 0.006 m. Smallest, Ω, is .005; largest, Φ, is .009; other large letters, N, Σ, Y, are .007.

minuscule text: next page.

commentary: The text is based on Schweigert's establishment of a stoichedon order of 40 letters to the line and very full restoration. All dots are Schweigert's, except under the mu in line 11 st. 36; the two underlined letters, line 18 st. 35, line 20 st. 38, are now unreadable. Other changes are noted below.

6 The vacat on the surface of the stone uses 7 stoichoi, which, added to the 5 stoichoi for εἶπεν, makes 12. Therefore, the proposer's name can occupy no more than 28 letters; not 29 as in Schw.'s text.

11 st. 36 [M] Schw. There is enough of the mu left on the surface of the stone to dot rather than bracket this letter.

15 st. 39, 40 Α̣ Ρ̣ Schw. These letters do not need dots.

stoich. 40

[Ἐπὶ Φρυνίχου ἄρχοντος ἐπὶ τῆς Πανδιονίδος δ]ε̣κά-
[της πρυτανείας· Χαιρέστρατος Ἀχαρνεὺς ἐγρ]α̣μμά-
[τευεν· Σκιροφοριῶνος ἕκτηι ἐπὶ δέκα, δευτέρ]αι κ[α]-
[ὶ εἰκοστῆι τῆς πρυτανείας· τῶν προέδρων ἐπ]ε̣ψήφ̣[ι]-
[ζεν ....20......... ἔδοξεν τῶι δή]μω[ι] vvv
[- - - - - not more than 28 letters - - - εἶπεν] vacat
[ἐπειδὴ Χαιρέστρατος ὁ γραμματεὺς ὁ κατ]ὰ πρυταν-
[είαν ἐν παντὶ καιρῶι καλῶς καὶ φιλοτίμω]ς ἄρχει τ-
[ὴν ἀρχὴν αὐτοῦ καὶ ἡ βουλὴ ἐπήινεσέ τε καὶ] ἐστεφά-
[νωσεν αὐτὸν ......15...... εὐνοίας ἕν]εκα δεδ-
[όχθαι τῶι δήμωι ἐπαινέσαι Χαιρέστρατον] Ἀ̣μ̣ε̣ινί-
[ου Ἀχαρνέα δικαιοσύνης ἕνεκα καὶ στεφαν]ῶ̣σαι αὐ-
[τὸν χρυσῶι στεφάνωι ἐπειδὰν τὰς εὐθύνας] δῶι δόξ-
[αντ' ἄρξαι τὴν ἀρχὴν δικαίως καὶ κατὰ τοὺς] νόμους
[...............34...............]εντοαρ
[...............34...............]ην τὴν π̣
[...............34...............]ε ἐν ἔι.
[...............34...............]γ̲ραφε.
[.............28.............ἀναγράψα]ι δὲ [τ]-
[όδε τὸ ψήφισμα τὸν γραμματέα τὸν κατὰ πρυταν]ε̣[ία]-
[ν ἐν στήληι λιθίνηι κτλ.]

This decree honors Chairestratos, son of Ameinias, of the deme Acharnai, who was grammateus kata prytaneion for the year 337/6. Chairestratos is honored with a crown (gold?) for performing his duties as secretary justly and correctly and according to the laws. Since these honors are voted while Chairestratos is still secretary, the necessary stipulation, "when he has passed his euthynai (audit at the end of one's year in office)" is included (cf. #18, II^2 330+445). Meritt, (Hesperia 357), sees "according to the laws" a significant addition for the secretary who held office in the year that the Law of Eukrates (#6), with its emphasis on the democratic process, was passed.

Schweigert's restoration requires the omission of ᾗι before and the patronymic after, the secretary's name. These omissions also occur in #10 (II^2 242, restored by Boeckh) and #12 (II^2 276, completely restored by Schweigert). I note that in #11 (II^2 243), passed on the same day as #10 and #12, there is room for the relative pronoun, and that all three of Schweigert's examples of the omission occur in restoration.

The date is straightforward: the 16th of Skirophorion, 22nd day of the 10th prytany. (Cf. Pritchett-Neugebauer; Meritt Ath.)

337/6

10. *HONORARY DECREE* EM 7064

photo: Svoronos ΕΘ. ΜΟΥΣ. Plate 217 no. 4.

editors: Pittakis ΕΦ. (1852/53) 1305; Rangabé (1855) 414; IG II 125; IG II^2 242.

other bibliography: Boeckh Epigr. chronol. Studien 15; Unger Philol. 39(1880) 522; Svoronos ΕΘ. ΜΟΥΣ. 667 no. 442; Binneboessel Studien 57; Suesserott Plastik 274 no. 168; Pritchett-Neugebauer Cal. 43; Meritt Ath. 77; Henry Prescripts 38 n. 27, 42, 45 n. 62.

description: The stone is Pentelic marble; it was found in 1836, west of the Parthenon. The left side of the inscription, the cymation and the relief are preserved; all other sides are broken. Only the bottom half of a standing draped figure remains from the relief which topped this stele.

dimensions:
H 0.38 m. (entire)
0.195 m. (below cymation)
W 0.20 m. (cymation)
0.14 m. (below)
Th 0.13 m

letters: 0.006 m. The Φ is low in the line; K is almost square.

majuscule text:

Ε

. Π Ι·Φ Ρ Υ Ν Ι̲ Χ̲ . Υ

. Ο Σ Δ Ε̲ Κ Α Τ̣ . . .

Χ̣ Α Ρ Ν̲ Ε̣ Υ̣ Σ Ε̲ Γ̣ . .

Ν Ε Ι . Α Ι Ν Ε̣ . . .

Π̲ Ρ Υ Τ Α Ν Ε Ι̣ . . .

Θ̲ Υ Κ Ρ Α Τ Η Σ . . .

Ε Ι Δ Ο Υ Μ Υ . . . .

. Α Ρ Χ̲ Ο̣ Ν̣ Ο̲ . . . .

. Ν Ο . . . .

. Α Γ Γ Ε̲ . Λ . . . .

. Ν Τ Ο̣ . Δ̲ Ε̲ . . . .

. Ε Σ Μ Ο̣ Θ̲ . . . . .

. Σ Ι . Λ̲ Τ̲ . . . . .

Ε Δ Ε Ο Ν̲ Τ̣ Ο̲ . . . .

Σ Θ Α Ι Τ . . . . . .

. Σ Τ Ο Ν̣ . . . . . .

epigraphical commentary: Letters which can not now be read are underlined. Kirchner dotted letters in line 9 st. 6 and line 13 st. 5; all other dots are mine.

5 st. 4 K Velsen.

12 st. 5 N Velsen.

14 st. 1-6 ΥΣΙΝΑΥ Velsen.

16 st. 6 Y Velsen

minuscule text: stoich. 33

[Θ] ε [ο ῖ]
[Ἐπὶ Φρυνίχ[ο]υ [ἄρχοντοϲ ἐπὶ τῆϲ Πανδιονί]-
[δ]οϲ δεκάτ[ηϲ πρυτανείαϲ· Χαιρέϲτρατοϲ Ἀ]-
χαρνεὺϲ ἐγ[ραμμάτευεν· Σκιροφοριῶνοϲ ἕ]-
νει [κ]αὶ νέ]αι, πέμπτηι καὶ τριακοϲτῆι τῆϲ]
πρυτανεί[αϲ. τῶν προέδρων ἐπεψήφιζεν Εὐ]-
θυκράτηϲ [Ἀφιδναῖοϲ· Διόφαντοϲ Φραϲικλ]-
είδου Μυ[ρρινούϲιοϲ εἶπεν· ἐπειδὴ ..5..]
.αρχον̣ο - - - - - - - - -
.νο - - - - - - - - - - -
.αγγε[λ]λ - - - - - - - - -
.ν τὸ[ν] δὲ - - - - - - - - -
[θ]εϲμο̣θ[ετ - - - - - - - - -]
.ϲι. Λ Τ - - - - - - - - -
ἐδέοντο [- - - - - - - - - ἐψηφί]-
ϲθαι τ[ῆι βουλῆι προϲαγαγεῖν ..8.. ε]-
[ἰ]ϲ τὸν [δῆμον - - - - - - - - -]

commentary: I have changed the numbering to include the epsilon of [Θ]Ε[ΟΙ] as the first line. Boeckh established the stoichedon order of 33 letters to the line when he restored the prescript, lines 1 through the middle of line 7; Koehler supplied the name of the proposer, lines 7/8, from #12 (II^2 276); the restorations, lines 8-14, are Velsen's; lines 15/16, 17, Kirchner's.

3 mid: Only Koehler restored ἧι before the secretary's name. Since this violates the stoichedon order, Kirchner omitted the pronoun as Boeckh had done. (Cf. #9; Unger printed the prescript from Koehler's text, but noted that the pronoun should be omitted.) Henry (42), who includes this prescript in his discussion of "secretary without patronymic" notes in note 54: "It is not possible to accomodate the patronymic by the expedient of omitting the preceding πρυτανείαϲ from the lacuna; for Ἀμεινίου occupies only 8 letter spaces" If, however, ἧι and the patronymic were restored, the 2 words would occupy the 10

spaces left by the omission of prytaneias.

All that remains in this decree is the restored date: when Phrynichos was archon, when the tribe Pandionis held the 10th prytany, Chairestratos of the deme Acharnai was secretary; the 29th day of Skirophorion, 35th day of the prytany; the chairman of the proedroi, Euthykrates of the deme Aphidna, put the vote to the people; Diophantos, son of Phrasikleides, of the deme Myrrinous, was the proposer.

After the prescript, there are just too few letters on the stone to give any indication of the nature of this decree. However, the decree is probably honorary, and the presence of th[esmoth]etai in line 13 suggests some connection with #5. (Perhaps honors to the thesmothetai for their participation in the Lemnos settlement?)

It is worth notice that of the eleven certain decrees which survive from the year of Phrynichos, six decrees are from the last, 10th, prytany. #7 concerns honors voted for a Macedonian and #8, passed on the same day and proposed by the same man, Demades, suggests similar circumstances. #9 honors the secretary of the year, #11 (II^2 243) records honors to an Athenian, reason unknown, and this decree, although the content is lost, does mention thesmothetai, Athenian officials. Perhaps #10 and #11, definitely #9, represent the usual end-of-the-year business of passing decrees in honor of annual office holders whose terms were coming to an end.

#9 was passed on the 22nd day of the last prytany. #10, #11, and #12 (II^2 276) were passed during what must have been the last ekklesia of the year (the 35th day is either the last or the next to last day of 337/6, Meritt, 77f.). #12 honors Asklepiodoros (probably a metic) on his own petition. Apparently he felt that his accomplishments merited recognition, and this was his last chance in the year of Phrynichos to receive it.

337/6

11. *ATHENS HONORS KALITELES OF KYDANTIDAI*

EM 7065

editors: Pittakis *EΦ*. (1852/55) 1303: Rangabé (1855) 2277; Beulé *L'acropole* (1862) 340; *IG* II 126; *IG* II^2 243.

other bibliography: Koehler *Hermes* 5(1871) 15; Gilbert *Neue Jahrb*. 1(1880) 537; Miller *De decr*. 53 n. 3; Pritchett-Neugebauer *Cal*. 43; Meritt *Ath*. 77; Rhodes *Boule* 43 n. 6, 64 n. 8, 243, 249; DeLaix *Proboul*. 117, 141; Henry *Prescripts* 38 n. 28, 45-46.

description: The stone is Pentelic marble, found in 1852, near the Propylaia. Most of the left side is preserved; all other sides are broken. The bottom left part of a wreath which must have been in the middle of the stele, remains above the text.

dimensions:
H 0.30 m.
W 0.19 m.
Th 0.103 m.

letters: 0.008 m. Some A's do not have cross bars; the letters are very similar to those of #4.

minuscule text: next page.

commentary: I have dotted a few letters which are now unclear and added the fragment of the wreath. The stoichedon order of 29 letters to the line was established by Koehler who is also responsible for the restorations. The change in word order in lines 5/6 (the Boule is always mentioned first; cf. Rhodes 64 n. 8, 249), is noted by Kirchner; discussed by Gilbert and Miller; and, more recently, by Henry (45-46), who notes of this mistake: "Whether or not this completely unnerved our mason is hard to tell: it certainly did not improve his spelling" (with reference to omissions in lines 7, 8, 11). All agree it was the error of a careless mason. The use of a single consonant in Μυρ(ρ)ινοῦσιοϲ, line 7, and in Καλ(λ)ιτέληϲ, line 8 makes plausible the restoration ἐκ(κ)λησίαι, line 11: noted first by Koehler in *Hermes*.

stoich. 29

[Ἐπὶ] Φρυνίχου ἄρ[χοντοϲ ἐπὶ τῆϲ Πανδ]-
[ι]ονίδοϲ δεκάτη[ϲ πρυτανείαϲ ἧι Χαι]-
ρέϲτρατοϲ Ἀμει[νίου Ἀχαρνεὺϲ ἐγρα]-
μμάτευεν· τῶν πρ[οέδρων ἐπεψήφιζεν]
Εὐθυκράτηϲ Ἀφι[δναῖοϲ· ἔδοξεν τῶι δ]-
ήμωι καὶ τε͂ι βου[λε͂ι· Διόφαντοϲ Φραϲ]-
ικλείδου Μυριν[ούϲιοϲ εἶπεν· περὶ ὧ]-
ν Καλιτέληϲ λέγ[ει ὅτι ὁ δῆμοϲ ἐψηφί]-
ϲατο αὐτῶι προβ[ούλευμα, ἐψηφίϲθαι]
τῆι βουλε͂ι τοὺϲ [μὲν προέδρουϲ χρημ]-
[α]τίϲαι περὶ αὐτ[οῦ ἐν τῆι πρώτηι ἐκλ]-
[ηϲ]ίαι, γνώμην δὲ [ξυμβάλλεϲθαι τῆϲ β]-
[ου]λ̣ῆϲ εἰϲ τὸν δῆ[μον, ὅτι δοκεῖ τῆι βο]-
[υλῆ]ι ἐπαινέϲαι [μὲν Καλιτέλην ....]
....ουϲ Κυδ̣α̣ν[τίδην]

The prescript of this decree indicates only that it was passed in the 10th prytany, but the inclusion of the name of the chairman of the proedroi allows the specific date to be determined, since #10 and #12, which have the full date, also have the same chairman. Diophantos, son of Phrasikleides, of the deme Myrrhinous, moved both this decree and #10 (PA 4435; APF).

The presence of the wreath indicates that Kaliteles was honored with a crown; the reason, however, and whether he received other honors can not be determined, since the extant portion of this decree deals only with the procedure followed before the decree was passed. See Rhodes, 65, and DeLaix, 117 note 20, for the commissioning of a probouleuma by the ekklesia.

12. *ATHENS HONORS ASKLEPIODOROS* EM 2743

editor: Kirchner IG II^2 276, from Wilhelm's text.

supplement: Bull. (1944) no. 65 (Schweigert).

other bibliography: Schweigert Hesperia 9(1940) 342; Meritt Hesperia 21(1952) 357; Lewis Hesperia 37(1968) 377; Rhodes Boule 43, 72-73, 250, 261; DeLaix Proboul. 120, 134, 138, 140.

description: The stone is Pentelic marble; provenance is unknown. The stone is broken at top and bottom; the right side, part of the left side, and the rough-picked back are preserved.

dimensions:
H 0.37 m.
W 0.44 m.
Th 0.17 m.

letters: 0.0065 m. Smallest, A, Δ, K, O, are .006; largest, Y, is .009.

majuscule text: next two pages.

epigraphical commentary: Letters read by Wilhelm but now unreadable are underlined. I have read three letters bracketed by Wilhelm: N line 6 st. 7; N line 27 st. 31; E line 28 st. 2. All dots are mine. The text is inscribed in stoichedon order, 31 letters to the line; lines 18, 19, 20, give the first stoichos on the left; line 27 (and Wilhelm's no longer legible rho in line 12) give the last stoichos on the right. In the text of II^2 276 the first 5 lines (my lines 5-9) are shifted one space to the left of their proper stoichoi. (See commentary for changes in restoration.) Kirchner is responsible for the edition of II^2 276, but he used Wilhelm's notes. Therefore it is impossible to know to whom this error should be attributed. (For a similar occurrence, see #21, II^2 333.)

On the stone, st. 12, lines 6-10 read vertically K, O, Δ, Λ, H, whereas in II^2 276, lines 6-10 read P, T, Ω, E, H.

minuscule text: after majuscule text.

commentary: The text incorporates both Schweigert's restoration of the prescript, lines 1-4, based on his

. . . . . . Σ Π̲ Ρ̲ Υ̲ Τ̲ Λ̣ . . . .
. . . . . . Ν . . . . Κ Ρ Α Τ̲ Η̲ . . . .
. . . . Ο Τ Α Μ Ι Ο Σ̣ Ε̲ . . . .
. . . . Δ Ω̣ Ρ Ο Σ̣ . . Λ̲ Υ̲ . . . .
. . . . Υ Λ Ε Ι Ε Ν Ν Ο Μ Α̣ Ι̲ . . . .
. . . . Τ Ω Ι Δ Η Μ Ω Ι Ε Π Ε Ι Δ̲ Η̲ . . . Λ̣ Η Π Ι . . .
. . . . Α Γ Α Θ Ο Σ Ε Γ Ε Ν Ε Τ Ο Μ̲ . . . Μ Ε Ν Ο Σ̣ Π̲ .
. . . . . . Π̣ Ο Λ Ε Μ Ι Ο Υ Σ Π . . . Ν Ε̲ . . Τ̲ Η Σ Τ Ρ Ι Η Ρ̲
. . . . . . Χ Α Ρ Η Τ Ο Σ Τ Ο Υ Α Ι Ξ Ω Ν̣ . . Σ̣ Ε Π Α Ι Ν Ε .
. . . . . . Ν Κ Α Ι Σ Τ Ε Φ Α Ν Ω Σ Α Ι Θ Α̣ . Λ Ο Υ Σ Τ Ε Φ .
. . . . . Δ Ρ̣ Α Γ Α Θ Ι Α Σ Ε Ν Ε Κ Α Κ Α Ι Κ Α Λ Ε Σ Α̣ Ι Ε .
. . . . . Α̲ Ε Ι Σ Τ Ο Π Ρ Υ Τ Α Ν Ε Ι Ο Ν Ε Ι Σ Α Υ Ρ Ι Ο Ν .
. . Α̲ Ι Δ Ε Α Υ Τ Ω Ι Κ Α Ι̲ Ι̲ Σ Ο Τ Ε Λ̲ Ε Ι Α Ν Κ Α Ι Ε Κ Γ .
Ν̣ Ο Ι Σ Ο Ι Κ Ο Υ Ν Τ Ι̣ Α̲ Θ̲ Η̣ Ν Η Σ Ι Ν Κ Α Θ Α Π Ε Ρ Τ Ο̲ Ι̲ .
Α̣ Λ̣ Λ Ο Ι Σ Ι Σ Ο Τ Ε Λ̲ Ε̣ Σ̣ Ι̣ Ν Ο Π Ω Σ Α Ν Ε Ι . Ω̣ Σ Ι Ν̣ Π .

ΝΤΕΣΟΣΟΙΑΝΣΤΡΑΤ̣ΕΥΩΝΤΑΙΜΕΤΑΘΗΝΑ.
.ΝΟΤΙΤΙΜΑΙΟΔΗΜΟΣΤΟΥΣΑΝΔΡΑΣΤΟΥΣ.
.ΑΘΟΥΣΤΟΔΕΨΗΦΙΣΜΑΤΟΔΕΑΝΑΓΡΑΨΑΣ̣.
..ΑΜΜΑ̲Τ̲Ε̲ΥΣΕΝΣΤΗΛΕΙΛΙΘΙΝΕ̲Ι̣ΣΤΗΣΑ.
.Ε̣ΝΑΚ̲....ΛΕΙΕΙΣΔΕΤΗΝΑΝΑΓ̣ΡΑΦΗΝΔ̣.
.Ω̣ΟΤΑ̲....ΤΟΥΔΗΜΟΥΕΙΚΟΣΙΔΡΑΧΜΑΣ̲.
.ΤΩΝΚ̣....ΗΦΙΣΜΑΤΑΑΝΑΛΙΣΚΟΜΕΝΩΝ.
.ΙΔΗΜΩΙ v ΚΗΦΙΣΟΦΩΝΚΑΛΛΙΒΙΟΥΠΑΙΑΝ̣
.Ε̣Υ̣ΣΕΙ̲ΠΕΝΤΑΜΕΝΑΛΛΑΚΑΘΑΠΕΡΤΕΙΒΟ̣.
............Σ̣ΚΛΗ̣Π̲Ι̲Ο̲Δ̣Ω̲ΡΟΣ̣ΑΝΗΡ̲ΑΓ.
.........................ΟΝΑ...

[Ἐπὶ Φρυνίχου ἄρχοντοc ἐπὶ τῆc Πανδιο]-
[νίδοc δεκάτηc πρυτανείαc· Χαιρέcτρα]- stoich. 31
[τοc Ἀχαρνεὺc ἐγραμμάτευε· Σκιροφορι]-
[ῶνοc ἕνει καὶ νέαι, πέμπτηι καὶ τριακο]-
[cτῆι τῆ]c πρυτα[νείαc· τῶν προέδρων ἐπε]-
[ψήφιζε]ν [Εὔθυ]κράτη[c Ἀφιδναῖοc ..5..]
[....10.... Π]οτάμιοc ε[ἶπεν· περὶ ὧν ἔδ]-
[οξε Ἀcκληπιό]δωροc [Πο]λυ.....11.....
[... ἐν τεῖ βο]υλεῖ ἔννομα ἱ[κετεύειν· ἐψ]-
[ηφίcθαι] τῶι δήμωι· ἐπειδὴ [Ἀcκ]ληπι[όδω]-
[ροc ἀνὴρ] ἀγαθὸc ἐγένετο μ[αχό]μενοc π[ρ]-
[ὸc τοὺc] πολεμίουc π[λέω]ν ἐ[πὶ] τῆc τριήρ-
[ουc τῆc] Χάρητοc τοῦ Αἰξων[έω]c, ἐπαινέ[c]-
[αι αὐτὸ]ν καὶ cτεφανῶcαι θα[λ]λοῦ cτεφ[ά]-
[νωι ἀν]δραγαθίαc ἕνεκα καὶ καλέcαι ἐ[π]-
[ὶ ξένι]α εἰc τὸ πρυτανεῖον εἰc αὔριον· [ε]-
[ἶν]αι δὲ αὐτῶι καὶ ἰcοτέλειαν καὶ ἐκγ[ό]-
νοιc οἰκοῦντι Ἀθήνηcιν καθάπερ τοῖ[c]
ἄλλοιc ἰcοτελέcιν, ὅπωc ἂν εἰ[δ]ῶcιν π[ά]-
ντεc ὅcοι ἂν cτρατεύωνται μετ' Ἀθηνα[ί]-
[ω]ν ὅτι τιμᾶι ὁ δῆμοc τοὺc ἄνδραc τοὺc [ἀ]-
[γ]αθούc· τὸ δὲ ψήφιcμα τόδε ἀναγράψαc [ὁ]
[γρ]αμματεὺc ἐν cτήλει λιθίνει cτηcά[τ]-
[ω] ἐν ἀκ[ροπό]λει· εἰc δὲ τὴν ἀναγραφὴν δ[ό]-
[τ]ω ὁ τα[μίαc] τοῦ δήμου εἴκοcι δραχμὰc [ἐ]-
[κ] τῶν κ[ατὰ ψ]ηφίcματα ἀναλιcκομένων [τ]-
[ῶ]ι δήμωι· v Κηφιcοφῶν Καλλιβίου Παιαν̣-
[ι]ε̣ὺc εἶπεν· τὰ μὲν ἄλλα καθάπερ τεῖ βο[υ]-
[λεῖ· ἐπειδὴ δὲ Ἀ]cκληπιόδωροc ἀνὴρ ἀγ[α]-
[θὸc - - - - - - - - - - - - -]ονα ...

recognition of the chairman of the proedroi in line 6 (same chairman as #10, #11) and Wilhelm's restoration of the rest of the text. The slight changes in lines 1-9 were made to conform to the stoichedon order on the stone.

1-9 The shift of these lines one stoichos to the right to compensate for the error in II^2 276 (and subsequently in Schweigert's prescript) requires the omission of Wilhelm's vacat at the end of line 9, but leaves an extra stoichos to be added somewhere in the first 4 lines of Schwigert's restoration. Since Schweigert's restoration requires a number of omissions, the problem is to decide where to put the extra stoichos. Although Schweigert cites examples from 337/6 (see discussion, #9) for omitting the relative pronoun before and the patronymic after the secretary's name in the text of this inscription, there is no example in this year for the omission of the nu-movable at the end of ἐγραμμάτευεν nor for the omission of the final upsilon in the archon's name. With the extra letter space, one of these exceptions can be eliminated; I have added the upsilon at the end of the archon's name.

6 beg. The new reading, N, supports Schweigert's restoration of the chairman's name.

8 'Ασκληπιό]δωρος [Πο]λυ----: Wilhelm connects the man honored in this decree with Φίλων 'Ασκληπιοδώρου ἰσοτελής, II^2 7879.

13 Χάρης Αἰξωνεύς: PA 15294; APF.

27 Κηφισοφῶν Καλλιβίου Παιανιεύς PA 8417; APF under PA 3773.

This decree honors Asklepiodoros, on his own petition (see #10 for possible reason). He is praised and granted an olive crown for fighting against the enemy while sailing on the ship of Chares of Aixone. The more tangible honor is the grant of isotelia (the right to pay taxes as citizens do, rather than the special tax on resident aliens) to Asklepiodoros and his descendants, as long as they live in Athens (Rhodes, 43 note 6, notes that Asklepiodoros was probably a metic). Twenty drachmai are appropriated to have the stele set up on the Akropolis. The stone breaks off at the beginning of a rider proposed by Kephisophon, son of Kallibios, of the deme Paiania.

The text of II^2 276 was dated ante 336/5 and Kirchner suggested ca. 342, noting that II^2 1622, line 751, records Chares as trierarch in 342/1. Actually II^2 1622 shows that Chares was <u>syntrierarch</u> in that year, and, since his name is fifth in a list of six syntrierarchs for the ship Amphritite, this could hardly be called "Chares' ship." The trierarchy implied in the present inscription probably occured later and so accords well with Schweigert's restoration of the later date. Davies, though apparently unaware of Schweigert's restoration which places the present decree in 337/6, assumed that Chares' trierarchy followed his syntrierarchy. II^2 417 (dated by Kirchner, post 330), a list of men who paid the <u>eutaxia</u> liturgy, records in line 26: Χά[ρ]ηϲ Ω...ΟΥ Αἰ-ξων[έωϲ] and so attests to Chares' activity in the late 330's. The new reading (used also by Davies) is Lewis's <u>Hesperia</u> 377. Lewis also provides a more specific date (not included by Davies): one or two years <u>before</u> 331/30, which would bring Chares' <u>eutaxia</u> even closer to the trierarchy of the present decree.

Just above Davies's entry for the Chares of this decree is the entry for Chares, the well known general, Χάρηϲ Θεοχάρουϲ 'Αγγελῆθεν with the appropriate testimonia. Davies, however, confuses the two men in his discussion of Kephisophon, the proposer of the rider to this decree (<u>PA</u> 8417, <u>PA</u> 3773 D, p. 149 in Davies). He is right to note Kephisophon's connection with Chares the general (Aisch. II.73) but errs when he mentions Chares the trierarch of this decree (with Kirchner's date, 342) as further evidence for the connection. (Davies seems arbitrary in his use of recent material: he does not mention Schweigert's 1940 article; he uses only part of the new information in Lewis's article, 1968.)

Davies places Kephisophon's activities in and before the 340's, although none of the literary or epigraphical evidence (even with Davies's incorrect dates) excludes Kephisophon from being active in the 330's. Davies discounts the identification of this Kephisophon with the one mentioned by Deinarchos (I.45) as one of the politicians convicted in the Harpalos affair, 324. He does so on the basis of II^2 7062, the gravestone of a Kephisophon Paianieus dated by Kirchner to the mid fourth century. However, the vague "med s. IV," based on letter forms, especially in the case of a grave monument, must be the least desirable form of establishing or discounting a date.

From the standpoint of the prosopography of the two Athenians mentioned in this decree, there can be no objection to a date of 337/6. Epigraphically, my new reading of nu in line 6 helps confirm Schweigert's restoration of the prescript, and the correction of the stoichedon order allows for the removal of one of the two irregularities in it.

337/6

13. *THE ORGEONES OF BENDIS HONOR THE HIEROPOIOI* Peiraieus Museum

editor: Kirchner IG II^2 1255, using Wilhelm's text.

other bibliography: Wilhelm ÖJ 5(1902) 132; Ferguson

HThR 37(1944) 61-140 (especially 95-107); Hesperia Supplement 8 (1949) 130-163 (especially 155).

description: The inscription was found in the Peiraieus; I found it (in 1973) on the floor of the old Peiraieus Museum beneath two other inscriptions, covered with dust. It is white marble; the medium-picked top and upper right side are preserved; the back, which is very roughly picked, may be original; the other sides are broken. A molding remains above the cymation.

dimensions:
H 0.41 m. (entire)
0.31 m. (below cymation)
W 0.27 m.
Th 0.07 m.

letters: 0.007 m. Smallest, Δ, is .005; largest, Φ, is .010; the N and H are narrow whereas Π is almost square; bottom bars of Ω meet: Ω.

majuscule text:

Ρ Γ Ε Ω Σ Ι Ο Λ Υ Μ Π Ι Ο Δ Ω

Ε Ι Π Ε Ν Ε Π Ε Ι Δ Η Ο Ι Ι Ε

. Φ Ρ Υ Ν Ι Χ Ο Υ Α Ρ Χ Ο Ν Τ

. Λ Η Θ Η Σ Α Γ Κ Α Ι Φ Ι Λ .

. Μ Π Η Σ Κ Α Ι Τ Η Σ Κ Ρ Ε Α̣

. Α Λ Λ Ω Ν Π Α Ν Τ Ω Ν Ε Ψ̲ .

. Ε Ω Σ Ι Ε Π Α Ι Ν Ε Σ Α̣ . .

. Α Ν Ω Σ Α Ι Χ Ρ Υ Σ Ω Ι̣ . .

. Α̣ Κ Ω Σ Ι Ω Ν Δ Ρ Α . . . .

. . Σ Θ Ε Ν Ο Υ Σ Κ Υ . . . .

. . Ν Α Υ Σ Ι Ν Ι Κ Ο . . . .

. . . Ν Η Ν Μ Ο Σ Χ̣ . . . . .

. . . Σ Ε Ν Ε Κ Α Τ . . . . .

. . . . Γ Ρ Α Ψ Α̣ . . . . . .

. . . . Λ Ε Ι Λ . . . .

. . . . . Ω Ι Τ . . . .

. . . . . Α̣ Λ Λ̲ . . . .

epigraphical commentary: The dot in line 7 is Kirchner's; the rest are mine. The two underlined letters printed as certain in II^2 1255 are no longer legible. There are three new readings.

4 st. 8 (min.-st. 19) The N read by Wilhelm is a certain Γ on the stone.

5 st. 15 (min.-st. 26) Ạ new reading.

9 st. 2 (min.-st. 13) Ạ new reading.

minuscule text:

stoich. 26

[Ἔδοξεν τοῖc ὀ]ργεῶcι· Ὀλυμπιόδω-
[ροc ....8....] εἶπεν· ἐπειδὴ οἱ ἱε-
[ροποιοὶ οἱ ἐπὶ] Φρυνίχου ἄρχοντ-
[οc καλῶc ἐπεμε]λήθηcαγ καὶ φιλ[ο]-
[τίμωc τῆc τε πο]μπῆc καὶ τῆc κρεα̣-
[νομίαc καὶ τῶν] ἄλλων πάντων· ἐψ[η]-
[φίcθαι τοῖc ὀργ]εῶcι ἐπαινέcα̣[ι α]-
[ὐτοὺc καὶ cτεφ]ανῶcαι χρυcῶι [cτ]-
[εφάνωι ἀπὸ τρι]α̣κοcίων δρα[χμῶν]
[Ἀντιφάνην Ἀντι]cθένουc Κυ[θήρρ]-
[ιον, Ναυcίφιλον] Ναυcινίκο[υ Κεφ]-
[αλῆθεν, Ἀριcτομέ]νην Μοcχ..5..
[..5..φιλοτιμία]c ἕνεκα τ[ῆc εἰc]
[τοὺc ὀργεῶναc. ἀνα]γράψα[ι δὲ τὸδ]-
[ε τὸ ψήφιcμα ἐν cτή]λει λ[ιθίνει κ]-
[αὶ cτῆcαι ἐν τῶι ἱερ]ῶι τ[ῆc Βενδῖ]-
[δοc τὸν γραμματέα Θ]άλλ[ον – –]

commentary: The text is based on Kirchner's; I have changed one letter and taken two out of brackets (see above). All restorations are Wilhelm's, except line 16/17, restored by Kirchner. The stoichedon order is 26 letters to the line and is violated nowhere on the stone, although Wilhelm's restoration requires 27 letters in either line 7 or 8.

10 [’Αντιφάνην ’Αντι]σθένουc Κυ[θήρριον]: *PA* 1237; *APF* under *PA* 1194.

11 [Ναυσίφιλον] Ναυσινίκο[υ Κεφαλῆθεν]: *PA* 10601; no *APF*.

16/17 τ[ῆc Βενδῖδοc]: restored by Kirchner as the only diety whose name will fit the space left by Wilhelm's restoration of the secretary, Thallos.

17 Θ[άλλ]ον: restored by Wilhelm. Ferguson, *HThR* 98 note 43, has added further support in that this Thallos could be the father of Stephanos, honored when epimelites by the orgeones of Bendis, II^2 1324 (redated to late 4th-early 3rd century by Dow *HThR* 30[1937] 197 note 54); the connection is made by assuming that both are descendants of Stephanos, son of Thallos, mentioned by Lysias, 19.46 (*PA* 12883). *APF* 12883 has [Θ]άλλο[c], refering to this text. However, no one has seen the omicron and even the second lambda can not now be read.

This decree records honors awarded to the *hieropoioi* (religious officials) by the *orgeones* (sacrificing associates) of the cult of Bendis. Antiphanes, son of Antisthenes, of the deme Kytheros; Nausiphilos, son of Nausinikos, of the deme Kephale; and Aristomenes, son of Mosch--- are awarded a gold crown worth 300 drachmai for the good and zealous care they had taken for the procession, distribution of the sacrifices, and all their other duties. The secretary, Thallos, is to set up the stele in the sanctuary of Bendis.

The text of this decree does not provide the usual evidence for distinguishing between an Athenian association or one of Thracian metics, that is, the Athenian association is designated by an olive wreath or by meeting on the 2nd day of the month; Thracian, by an oak wreath or meeting on the 8th day of the month (Wilhelm, 132). The fact that the officials are Athenian citizens does not offer any conclusive proof as to the nature of this association. Only if these hieropoioi are the officials of this specific association of the orgeones of Bendis, elected by their associates, could the association be securely designated as one of citizens. And that fact can not be determined since the hieropoioi of this decree could just as well be a subcommittee of the state board of ten hieropioi selected annually by lot to officiate at all state religious festivals (Arist. AP 54.6). In this case, the hieropoioi would naturally be citizens and, in turn, the association could be composed of either Athenians or metics.

Ferguson argues for the identification of these hieropoioi as the state officials who had carried out duties for the orgeones of the Athenian (citizen) association. He notes, inconclusively, that the crown is to be gold, rather than olive or oak (HThR 99 note 43; he makes no comment about the small amount, only 300 drachmai, for three men) and that the Bendideia was an official state festival (Hesperia 55; in which the members of both the citizen and metic associations participated). Ferguson's argument that a citizen association would be more likely to call in state officials is even less convincing. Although the practice of honoring officials, both public and private, is a typically Athenian practice, we should remember that part of Lykourgos's overall program was the consideration of foreign cults (cf. #27 [II^2 337] and another decree concerned with Bendis, #52 [II^2 1256]). This practice served two purposes: it would contribute something extra to the general religious revitalization; it would make living in Athens (or more correctly, the Peiraieus) more agreeable for metics.

14. *ATHENS HONORS TWO DOCTORS (?)* EM 7170, 5321

photo: *Hesperia* 28(1959) Plate 75.

editors: Fr. A *IG* II Add. 159b p. 424; *IG* II^2 304.
Fr. B *IG* II^2 604.
Fr. A+B Hubbe *Hesperia* 28(1959) 169-171 no. 1; Peek *AM* 67(1942) 6 no. 3 and Mitsos *Hesperia* 16(1947) 264 no. 16, announced the new join but offered no new text.

supplements: *SEG* 18.11 (Mitsos, Hubbe, Pritchett-Meritt). *Bull.* (1960) no. 132 (Hubbe).

other bibliography: Pritchett-Meritt *Chron.* 75; Cohn-Haft *Physicians* 76-77 no. 2.

description: A stele of Pentelic marble with bottom, Fr. B, preserved. Fragment A, composed of 2 joined pieces, was found between the Theater of Dionysos and the Odeion of Herodes Atticus. The find-spot of Fragment B is unknown. The two are now joined and stand in the Epigraphical Museum.

dimensions:
H 0.82 m.
W 0.424 m. (above)
0.215 m. (below-stone)
0.427 m. (below-restored)
Th 0.093 m. (above)
0.11 m. (below)

letters: 0.007 m. Smallest, O, X, some Ω's are .005; largest, B, P, Σ, are .009. As noted by Ki., circle of phi is flattened at the bottom: Φ, the middle hastae of mu are the same height as the outer hastae: M .

minuscule text: next page.

commentary: The text is based on Hubbe's (he included the join of II^2 304 and II^2 604 which had been noted by Peek and Mitsos). I have changed the numbering to include Hubbe's restored first line. Hubbe dotted letters in line 2 and underlined 2 letters read by Koehler. The letter on the stone in line 9 st. 10 is Π.

Fragment A consists of the text, with a stoichedon order of 30 letters to the line, and 3 of the 4 wreaths: the two in line 16 and the right-hand wreath in line 17. Hubbe restored lines 1 and 2; the rest of the text is

Koehler's restoration.

stoich. 30

Fr. A

[......13...... τὴν εὔνοιαν ἐνδεικν]-
ὑ̣μενοι̣ ἣ̣[ν ἐcχήκαcιν πρὸc τὴν πόλιν κ]-
αὶ νῦν καὶ ἐν τῶ[ι ἔμπροcθεν χρόνωι κα]-
ὶ αὐτοὶ καὶ οἱ πρ[ό]γον[οι αὐτῶν· δεδόχθ]-
αι τῶι δήμωι ἐπα[ι]νέcαι αὐτο[ὺc εὐνοί]-
αc ἕνεκα καὶ φιλ[ο]τιμίαc τῆc εἰ[c τὸν δ]-
ῆμον τὸν Ἀθηναί[ω]ν καὶ cτεφανῶcα[ι ἑκ]-
άτερον αὐτῶν χρ[υ]cῶι cτεφάνωι ἀπὸ X δ-
ραχμῶν· ἀνα<γ>ράψ[α]ι δὲ τόδε τὸ ψήφιcμα
ἐν cτήληι λιθίν[ηι] τὸν γραμματέα τῆc
βουλῆc καὶ cτῆc[αι] ἐν τῶι Ἀcκληπιείω-
ι τῶι ἐν ἄcτει· εἰc̲ δὲ τὴν ἀναγραφὴν τῆ-
c cτήληc δοῦναι [τ]ὸν ταμίαν τοῦ δήμου
𐅄 δραχμὰc ἐκ τῶν κ̲ατὰ ψηφίcματα ἀναλ-
ιcκομένων τῶι δήμωι. vacat

in wreath ὁ δῆμοc | in wreath ὁ δῆμοc

Fr. B in wreath ἡ βουλή | in wreath ἡ βουλή

ἐπ[ὶ ἱερέωc]
Θεοφά[νουc - - - -]
Ἀχ[αρνέωc]

vacat 0.14

Fragment B includes the left-hand wreath in line 17, and lines 18-20. Hubbe restored line 18; and uses

Kirchner's restoration in lines 19 and 20.

1/2: Hubbe bases his restoration on: II^2 483 lines 19-20; II^2 522 lines 3-4; and II^2 641 lines 17-19.

16-17: The presence of the two wreaths with Demos and two wreaths with Boule indicates that two men were honored.

18-20: Kirchner, in II^2 604, had restored ʽΕπ -- Θεοφά-[νους] ʼΑχ[αρνεύς] as the name, patronymic and demotic of a man who had been honored in the decree which he rightly judged to be missing above the wreath. The name he got from a gravestone, II^2 5804 (cf. PA 7077); it should be noted, however, that the name he referred to as Θεοφάνης on II^2 5804 is actually Θειοφάνης on the stone.

After II^2 604 had been joined to II^2 304, both Mitsos and Peek assumed that the three lines recorded the name, patronymic, and demotic of one of the two men honored in the decree above, but the centering of lines 18-20 on the stone rules out the placement of the two men's names side by side. The alternative of placing the second man's name below the first is ruled out by a vacat of 0.14 m. between line 20 and the preserved bottom of the stele. Hubbe solves the problem with a new interpretation, restoring lines 18-20 as a dating formula: the name of the priest of Asklepios, followed by his patronymic and demotic. This also allows the decree to be dated since, after 356/5, the priests of Asklepios were appointed annually according to cyclical tribal rotation (Pritchett-Meritt 74). Hubbe then goes by Kirchner's date for II^2 304, between 352/1 and 336/5, and finds only one year available for a priest from the tribe Oineis: 337/6. (Hubbe 171; see Pritchett-Meritt, 75, for the chronological table of priests of Asklepios.)

The beginning of this decree is lost; the text begins with the end of the Boule's pronouncement concerning the two men honored. The Demos awards a crown worth a thousand drachmai to each man for his goodwill and zealous conduct toward the people of Athens. The decree ends with the usual provisions for engraving and setting up the stele, in this case, in the Asklepieion.

Kirchner records that Wilamowitz, in an unpublished communication, identified the men as physicians, presumably because the stele was to be set up in the Asklepieion. Cohn-Haft points out that there is no internal evidence for this identification but nevertheless includes this document in his book, 76f. no. 2.

The possibility that these men were physicians, coupled with the fact that this is the year following the battle of Chaironeia, suggests further that these men may have been active in treating the wounded of that battle. We do not have the dating formula of this decree, and its place in this Corpus in no way implies that it belongs chronologically with the end-of-the-year honorary decrees from the tenth prytany which immediately precede it here. That the decree belongs to one of the earlier prytanies of Phrynichos's year is a possibility which should be kept in mind.

III. THE YEAR OF PYTHODELOS, 336/5

15. *LYKOURGOS PROPOSES HONORS FOR A PUBLIC BENEFACTOR* EM 7175

editors: Pittakis Ἐφ. (1852/55) 1428; Rangabé (1855) 530; IG II 180; IG II^2 328.

supplement: SEG 21.268 (Pritchett-Neugebauer, Meritt).

other bibliography: Reusch Hermes 15(1880) 338; Unger Att. Arch. 669; Wilhelm Hermes 24(1889) 138; Dinsmoor Archons 356; Pritchett-Neugebauer Cal. 43; Meritt Ath. 11-15, 78; Pritchett CP 63(1968) 53-54; Rhodes Boule 1-30, 250, 269; DeLaix Proboul. 118, 145-172.

description: Fragment of Hymettan marble; the right side and a bit of the molding on top are preserved. The left side and bottom are broken.

dimensions:	letters: 0.007 m. Smallest, Δ, O,
H 0.30 m.	are .006; largest, H, Φ, Ψ, are
W 0.11 m.	.009. E and Σ vary in height;
Th 0.12 m.	thetas have no central dot.

minuscule text: next page.

commentary: Restorations and establishment of the stoichedon order of 28 letters to the line are Koehler's. Exceptions are noted below. All dots are mine. Line 2 st. 28 and line 17 st. 25 can not now be read. The stoicheson order is not violated on the stone, although the restoration requires 29 letters in line 9.

1 archon: Reusch, accepted by Ung., Wilh., Ki.; Koe. did not restore an archon and placed this decree in the 320's.

2, 4/5 date: Reusch, accepted by Ki., Dins., P.-N., Mer. [--- δευτέρας πρυτ]ανείας -----[-- Μεταγειτνιῶνος τετ]ράδι Reusch (as an alternate).

stoich. 28

[᾿Επὶ Πυθοδήλου ἄρχοντοϲ ἐπ]ὶ τῆϲ ᾿Α̣[κ]-
[αμαντίδοϲ τετάρτηϲ πρυτ]ανείαϲ ἧ-
[ι ....19......... ἐ]γραμμάτ-
[ευεν· Μαιμακτηριῶνοϲ τετ]ράδι φθί-
[νοντοϲ, ὀγδόει καὶ εἰκοϲτ]εῖ τῆϲ πρ-
[υτανείαϲ· τῶν προέδρων ἐπ]ε̣ψ̣ήφιζε̣-
[ν ....19......... ἔ]δοξεν τῆ-
[ι βολῆι καὶ τῶι δήμωι· Λυκο]ῦργοϲ Λυ-
[κόφρονοϲ Βουτάδηϲ εἶπε· περ]ὶ ὧν λέγ̣-
[ει ..5..ϲ, δεδόχθαι τῆι βουλ]ῆι τοῦ-
ϲ προέδρουϲ οἳ ἂν λάχωϲιν πρ]οεδρε-
[ύειν εἰϲ τὴν πρώτην ἐκκληϲί]αν προ-
[ϲαγαγεῖν αὐτὸν εἰϲ τὸν δῆμ]ον καὶ [χ]-
[ρηματίϲαι, γνώμην δὲ ξυμβ]άλλεϲθα-
[ι τῆϲ βουλῆϲ εἰϲ τὸν δῆμον] ὅτι δοκε̣-
[ῖ τῆι βουλῆι, ἐπειδὴ ..5..]ϲ̣ Εὔπορ.
..........22..........ΙΠΓ...

5 ὀγδόει καὶ εἰκοστ]εῖ: P.-N., Mer. μιᾶι καὶ τριακοστ]εῖ Reusch, Ki.; ἑβδόμει καὶ δεκάτ]ει Reusch (to go with alternate above); ἐνάτει καὶ εἰκοστ]εῖ Dins.

11/12 restoration: Ki. Although Koe.'s majuscule text includes both lines on the stone, his minuscule text omits any restoration between προέδρουϲ (line 11) and εἰϲ τὴν (line 12). Ki. did not acknowledge the restoration in his aparatus criticus, but it must be his; scholarship between the major and minor editions of the corpus deals only with the date.

14 mid ξυμβ]άλλ: Ki., συμβ]άλλ Koe. Although the use of xi in ξύν had become obsolete by the 4th c., the xi was kept for this particular formulaic expression (s.v. σύν, Liddell and Scott page 1690).

This decree begins with the usual dating formula, then records the legislative procedure prior to the vote in the assembly, but the stone breaks off at the beginning of the actual proposal. The name of the man honored is restored as: ..5..ς, son of Εὐπορ--, deme or nationality unknown. All three elements of the text must be discussed.

The most recent scholarship concerning the calendar (Pritchett-Neugebauer, 43, and Meritt, 10-15) is in agreement about the restoration of the date on which this decree was passed: the 28th day of the 4th prytany (conciliar date), held by the tribe Akamantis; the 4th day before the end of the 5th month, Maimakterion (festival date). There is, however, disagreement as to the specific day within the year, for the festival date as well as the conciliar date.

The "festival year" was the normal year of twelve lunar months of 29 1/2 days each; it was regulated by the archon and was used for dating religious festivals. In practice, this would normally lead to an alternation of "full," 30-day, and "hollow," 29-day, months. Since the lunar year was short (only 354 days) in relation to the solar year of 365 days, it was adjusted every third year or so, usually by the intercalation of a second Poseideion (VI) in the middle of the year (during the winter) and this resulted in an intercalary year of 384 days. (See Pritchett *CP* for discussion of the use of Poseideion.) For the festival year, the disagreement involves the count of days for the last decade of the month. For Pritchett, the 4th day before the end of the month must *always* be the 27th, whether the month is full or hollow (see chart, *Cal.* 30/31; reproduced in #29 [II^2 339a] discussion). For Meritt, the 4th day before the end of the month can be either the 26th or the 27th, depending upon whether the month is hollow or full (see chart, Ath. 45; also #29, II^2 339a, for a fuller discussion of the count of days with a reproduction of Meritt's chart as well).

The "conciliar year," on the other hand, reflected the artificial political divisions into ten tribal prytanies, each one of which acted as executive committee of the Boule for a tenth of the year, that is, of the festival year of 354 days. Aristotle (AP 43.2) says that for such an ordinary year, the first four prytanies held office for 36 days and the remaining six for 35. There are two problems with Aristotle's statement. First, it falls in the latter half of the Athenaion Politeia which he calls the "constitution as it is now," that is, in the Lykourgan period which was one of considerable constitutional reform. It is not certain therefore which of his statements should be assumed to have a broader chronological application. More important with regard to his statement about the lengths of prytanies is the question whether he meant it to be absolute, rigid and invariable; and furthermore, whether he meant it to be applied as well to the longer intercalary year (with the necessary adjustments, 4x39 + 6x38 = 384). There is no ambiguity in the text, and Pritchett-Neugebauer have taken it as an absolute, invariable "rule" for both ordinary and intercalary years. Meritt, on the other hand, argues for some flexibility; that the "rule" was actually the "norm," to be followed in general but not rigidly. In this work I follow the latter point of view.

The restored date in the present text (as well as the earlier restorations; see commentary) requires an intercalary year, i.e., one in which a second Poseideion was added to adjust the ordinary 12 month lunar cycle to the seasonal, solar year. Therefore the conciliar year is one in which the prytanies are assumed to be 39 or 38 days in length, and the dating equation can be worked out with these two facts in mind.

Pritchett-Neugebauer adhere strictly to the application of Aristotle's "rule," and their "rule" concerning the count of days producing the equation: [Maimakterion] (V) 27 = Prytany [IV] [28] = 145th day of the year. Meritt objects to this equation because it requires 4 full (30-day) and 2 hollow (29-day) months for the 6 months (inclusive) from Maimakterion (V) to Elaphebolion (IX), including, of course, a second, intercalary Poseideion (VI); and then a sequence of 3 hollow months in a row at the end of the year to account for the other two calendar equations from this year. (See #18, II^2 330+445, which was set up in 335/4, but contains two decrees from 336/5.)

Meritt's equation, [Maimakterion] 26 = Prytany [IV 28] = 144th day, by making Maimakterion hollow, evens out the hollow and full months, but breaks Aristotle's "rule" since the third prytany could have had only 38 days. It should be kept in mind, however, that in this specific case, an intercalary year, it is not Aristotle's "rule" that is broken, but rather a modern hypothesis. See Meritt, pages 14 following, for his table showing the relationship between the conciliar and festival years.

As for the earlier restorations; Dinsmoor's 29th day of the 4th prytany requires 3 full months out of the first four; Reusch's 31st day of the 4th prytany (accepted by Kirchner) could not equal the 27th day of Maimakterion even if all the first five months of the year had been full. To equate the day of the prytany to day of the month and have at least one hollow month in the first five would involve breaking Aristotle's "rule" to a greater extent than does Meritt's proposal. Reusch's alternate restoration, because it is so early in the year, neither breaks Aristotle's "rule" nor gives an abnormal full and hollow sequence: [Metageitnion 27] = Prytany [II] 17 = 56th day.

In this specific case, the differences of opinion do not affect the restoration of the date on the decree. Both Pritchett-Neugebauer and Meritt agree on the date as restored in the text above. The determination of the _day_ of the year depends on whether one prefers, as Pritchett-Neugebauer do, a strict adherence to the hypothetical Aristotelian rule concerning the length of prytanies, in spite of the fact that this makes for a highly irregular sequence of full and hollow months through the year and leaves it with only 383 days instead of the cannonical 384; or, with Meritt, to approach Aristotle's "rule" (and the count of days) with more flexibility to attain a full 384-day year with a regular sequence of alternating full and hollow lunar months, documented for this intercalary year of 336/5 by the Babylonians (Parker & Dubberstein, _Babylonian Chronology_, 35-36; cited by Meritt, 12).

After the dating formula comes the usual notification that: the chairman of the proedroi (his name is lost) put the motion to the vote; it is decreed by the Boule and the Demos; Lykourgos, son of Lykophron, of the deme Boutadai was the proposer. There follows the legislative process: in this instance, the honorand petitioned the Boule, the Boule deliberated and then bade the proedros who would be alloted to preside to introduce him in the first (following) meeting of the ekklesia and to bring this gnome (motion) of the Boule to a vote (cf. #11 for a similar action).

The duties of the Boule and its subdivisions are most recently discussed by Rhodes, 1-30, and DeLaix, 145-172. This decree shows the usual procedure of introducing proposed legislation first to the Boule and then to the ekklesia in the form of probouleuma, although Rhodes's tables (244-268) show that it is not spelled out in this way in the majority of the decrees surviving from this period. There are, however, a number of contemporary instances, mainly honorary decrees, in which the Demos initiates legislation without a probouleuma. Because of the honorary nature (i.e. not absolutely vital to the welfare of the state) of these "aprobouleutic" measures, DeLaix (137f.) sees no contradiction to Aristotle's statement (AP 45.4) that such procedure was forbidden.

The fact that the present decree is probouleutic, and that the actual procedure followed is recorded on the stone, points to an honorand of some importance (cf. DeLaix, 138). More telling is the name of the proposer: Lykourgos. Including the present one, Lykourgos moved six decrees included in this Corpus: #21 (II^2 333) concerns a law regulating religious functions; #25 (II^2 414a) honors one of the generals; #27 (II^2 337) grants enktesis to the Kitians; #36 (II^2 345) honors a man from Plataia (like the present decree, only the prescript and beginning of a proposal are preserved); #48 (II^2 351+624) honors Eudemos of Plataia who, by his contributions, made the new stadium possible.

In addition, the content of #53 (II^2 452) is lost, but has]νος Βουτά[δης on the stone; II^2 1623, lines 276-308, records a decree proposed by Lykourgos to protect commerce from pirates--the general, Diotimos, who was given the job, is probably the man honored in #25 (see Schweigert Hesperia 9 [1940] 341; Mitchel Lyk. Ath. 194 note 122); and II^2 1672 which deals with the building program at Eleusis, refers to two decrees moved by Lykourgos, one of the Boule, line 302, one of the Demos, line 303 (add Camp's publication in Hesperia 43(1974) no. 3, 322-324). All these decrees, and others we know from the literary tradition, concern important matters and they show the many ways in which Lykourgos tried to revitalize Athens (cf. Mitchel Lyk. Ath.) The fact that Lykourgos apparently moved this decree in the Boule suggests that he was a member of that body in the year of Pythodelos, but this assumption is unnecessary if we assume rather that Lykourgos, because of his extraordinary office, as financial administrator for the quadrennium, had the right of prosodos in the Boule (for prosodos, see #2).

It is unfortunate that the name of the man honored in this decree is lost; more unfortunate still that we do not know what he did that prompted Lykourgos himself to propose the honors.

336/5

16. *DECREE* Ag. Inv. I 4899

photo: Hesperia 26(1957) Plate 52.

editor: Meritt Hesperia 26(1957) 207-208 no. 54.

supplement: SEG 17.27 (Meritt).

description: A fragment of Pentelic marble, broken on all sides (Meritt notes the rough back may be original), found on the north slope of the Akropolis. Above the first line is a trace of molding; below the last line is a rebate (for later use--Meritt).

dimensions:	letters:
H 0.12 m. 0.055 m. (surface) W 0.07 m. Th 0.10 m.	0.007 m. Smallest, Δ, Θ, O, are .004; E, T, Y, are .008. Theta has no central dot; eta is very wide: ⊢⊣.

minuscule text:

non stoich.

[Ἐπὶ Πυ]θοδή[λου ἄρχοντος ἐπὶ τῆς - - - -]
[- - - -]ς πρυτ[ανείας ἧι - - - $\underline{19}$ - - - -]
[ἐγραμ]μάτευ[εν· - - - - -ῶνος- - - - - -]
[- - -]ι καὶ εἰ[κοστεῖ τῆς πρυτανείας - -]
[- -]

commentary: The restorations are Meritt's. The letters are poorly inscribed and non-stoichedon.

2 secretary's name: the number of letters for the name of the secretary is known from #15.

This small fragment offers only the beginning of the dating formula, and even that is heavily restored. The non-stoichedon order is unusual for a decree of the Lykourgan period. Other non-stoichedon inscriptions are: #22 (II^2 331), 335/4, #26 (II^2 1184) 334/3; #46 (II^2 1181) 331/30; #56 (AE [1917] 40-48 no. 92) 328/7; #69 (II^2 361) 325/4; #76 (II^2 1176+) 324/3; #77 (II^2 1257) 324/3; #80 (II^2 366) 323/2. Wilhelm (followed by Kirchner) suggested that II^2 366 had been set up privately; this explanation may also apply to the present decree.

17. *LAW AND REGULATIONS CONCERNING THE LESSER PANATHENAIA* Ag. Inv. I 5477, EM 7153

photo: Fr. A Hesperia 28(1959) Plate 43.

editors: Fr. A Lewis Hesperia 28(1959) 239-247.
Fr. B Pittakis EΦ. (1840/42) 1064; Rangabé (1885) 814; IG II 163; IG II² 334.

collections: Ussing Inscr. page 45; Michaelis Parthenon 332; Ditt. Syll. 380, Syll.² 634, Syll.³ 271; Le Bas Voyage 401; Michel 679; Prott-Ziehen II 1.29; Pleket Epigraphica I 25; Sokolowski Lois 33.

supplements: SEG 18.13 (Lewis, Robert Bull. and Hellenica); 21.269 (Syll.³, Pleket); 25.65 (Sokolowski).
Bull. (1960) no. 131 (Lewis); (1961) no. 278 (Robert Hellenica).

other bibliography: Michaelis AM 2(1877) 18 n. 7; Doerpfeld AM 12(1887) 50, 51; Ziehen Rh. Mus. 51(1896) 212; Mommsen Feste 119; Hausoullier Rev. Crit. 50(1900) 25; Pfuhl Pompis 4; Deubner Att. Feste 24-26; Herington Athena 31; Robert Hellenica 11/12(1960) 189-203; Rhodes Boule 98, 129, 134, 250, 276, 278; DeLaix Proboul. 67, 134, 140-142.

description: Both fragments are Pentelic marble. Fr. A was brought in from the vicinity of Evangelistria Street, May 27, 1938; Fr. B was found in 1846 in the Propylaia. Although there is no physical join, Lewis's association and placement of the two fragments has not been questioned. Only part of the double molding at the top of Fr. A is preserved; of Fr. B, only the right side.

dimensions:
Fr. A
H 0.30 m.
W 0.27 m.
Th 0.106 m.
Fr. B
H 0.326 m.
W 0.39 m.
Th 0.13 m.

letters: 0.005 m. Smallest, Δ, O, T, are .0045; largest, P, Σ, are .006. In Fr. A, the letters in line 2 average .009; although only the bottom right 1/4 of the omicron of ΘEOI remains, it was larger than the omicrons in line 2.

minuscule text: Fr. A, next two pages.

stoich. 42

[Θ ε] ο [ί]
['Επὶ ....ca. 9.... ἄ]ρχοντος
.......16........c.4.. 'Αριστόνικος 'Αρι[στοτέλο]-
[υς Μαραθώνιος εἶπ]εν· τύχηι ἀγαθῆι τοῦ δήμου [τοῦ 'Αθη]-
[ναίων, ὅπως ἂν τῆι] 'Αθηνᾶι ἡ θυσία ὡς καλλίστ[η ἧι Πανα]-
[θηναίοις τοῖς μ]ικροῖς καὶ πρόσοδος ὡς πλεί[στη γέν]-
[ηται ἱεροποιο]ῖς, δεδόχθαι τοῖς νομοθέτ[α]ι[ς· τὴν μὲν]
[Νέαν μισθοῦτω]σαν δέκα ἡμέραις πρότερον ν...7...
[οἱ πωληταὶ δέκ]<α> ἔτη κατὰ δικληρίαν τῶι τὸ π[λεῖστον]
[διδόντι τῶι πρ]οτέρωι ἔτει ἢ ὧι ἂν ἡ ΔΑ.ΑΝΤΙ...7...
[....10.... μι]σθωταῖς ἐγγυητὰς λαμβάνου[σι. τοὺς δ]-
[ὲ πωλητὰς τὴ]ν πεντηκοστὴν πωλεῖν τὴν ἐν τῆ[ι Νέαι χω]-
[ρὶς τῶν ἄλλω]ν. τοὺς δὲ πρυτάνεις προγράφει[ν βουλῆς]
[ἕδραν εἰς τὴ]ν μίσθωσιν τῆς Νέας διαρρήδην [καὶ τῆς π]-

[εντηκοcτῆc] τὴν πρᾶcιν τῆc ἐν τῆι Νέαι χωρὶ[c ..6...]
[..6... ἡ πρό]cοδοc γένηται δυοῖν ταλάντο[ιν ..6...]
[....9.... τ]ῶν κτημάτων τῶν ἐν τῆι Νέα[ι] κ....9....
....10.....ρχειν τῆι Ἀθηνᾶι. τοῦτο ......13......
[...7... Παν]αθηναίων τῶν μικρῶν τ[....9.... οἱ δὲ ἀ]-
[ποδέκται με]ρ̣ιζόντων αὐτὸ εἰc ταῦ[τα τοῖc ἱεροποιο]-
[ῖc ....9....]ον δ' εἶναι καὶ τὸμ προ.......14.......
.....11.....αι μιcθοῦν καθὸ [illegible].......16........
.....11.....ι̲. τὸν δὲ ταμίαν ....19.........
......12......οντατης.^.........20..........
......13......^- - - - - - - - - - - - - - - - -

commentary: Fragment A The text is based on Lewis's, who made the restorations based on the stoichedon order of 42 letters to the line from Fr. B. I have underlined letters read by Lewis which I could not read. All dots are Lewis's; I agree with his reading of unclear letters. The horizontal position of the text can not be fixed precisely, since both sides are broken. There is more of the stone, however preserved beyond the written surface on the right side. According to Lewis's calculations, this requires that at least 5 letters be restored beyond the last preserved letter. Centering of line 2 is ruled out by this need to restore at least 5 letters on the right; even combined with the shortest archon's name in the time span Lewis is working with, 336-330, the line would be too far to the left. By beginning line 2 near the left-hand edge and adding on the right one more restored letter to the five required, Lewis can restore the archons: Φρυνῖχου (337/6); Πυθοδῆλου (336/5); Εὐαινέτου (335/4); Νικήτου (332/1). Lewis prefers to follow the majority of previous editors for Fr. B so has restored space for the archons of 336/5 or 335/4. But the <u>circa</u> 9 should be a reminder that at least four dates are possible for this inscription.

Lewis has commented at length on this new fragment. The chief difficulty for restoration lies in the interpretation of ἡ Νέα, lines 7-18. Lewis identifies it with νειός or νεός (agricultural land resting from cereal planting) to be leased and help finance the Lesser Panathenaia. This ignores the fact that the word for agricultural land is always masculine. Robert, in <u>Hellenica</u>, takes the obvious interpretation--"new land" (νέα χώρα) and identifies the Nea as Oropos, given to Athens by Philip in 338/7. This new identification eliminates not all, but many of the problems encountered by Lewis, especially in respect to the πεντηκοστῆ, line 12, which can now be interpreted in its usual sense, i.e.; an import-export tax (in this case, levied at the borders of Oropos), rather than the produce tax suggested by Lewis.

Sokolowski follows Robert; some of his restorations (see below) are based on the identification of the Nea as Oropos.

2 archon: Πυθοδῆλου or Εὐαινέτου Lewis.

3 st. 17: Although Lewis makes it clear that this sigma is uncertain, Sok. does not dot this letter.

4 dots: Sok. prints none for this line.

6/7 alternate restoration: πλεῖ[στη ἐγλ/εχθῆι τοῖς θεο]ῖς Sok.

9 δικληρίαν: Lewis notes that this is the first instance of this word in Greek, and that it must mean "in two sections." Robert, Hellenica p. 197 note 6, can qualify the new term: it refers to the Nea in its entirety, both the part possessed by the Demos as a whole (the source of income for the lesser Panathenaia) and the part which had been alloted to the ten tribes. See Hypereides, In Defense of Euxenippos 16, for explanation of the allotment to the ten tribes.

8/9 alternate restoration: ν[..4.. οι π/ωληταὶ εἰς δέκ](α) Sok.; Ν[εμεσίων]? Lewis (see above). The alpha, <α> in line 9, has no crossbar. Lewis is reluctant to assume a mistake in cutting, but in Fr. B, line 22 st. 24 and line 34 st. 25, the crossbars are also omitted in definite alphas. Also four thetas do not have center dots: Fr. A line 19; Fr. B lines 10, 12, 28. Therefore there should be no hesitation in reading alpha here.

9/10 alternate restoration: π[ρόσοδα σ/υνθέντι τῶι πρ]οτέρωι Sok.

10/11 alternate restoration: ΔΑ.ΑΝΤΙ[μισθωθῆ/ι καὶ ἄλλοις μι]σθωταῖς (text), ἢ λᾶ[ς] ἀντι[μισθωθῆ/ι ? (commentary) Sok.

13/14 alternate restoration: προγράφει[ν ἐν στήλ/αιν δυοῖν τῆ]ν Sok. Woodward's suggestion, προγράφει[ν ἐν τῆι β/ουλῆι καὶ τῆ]ν, is recorded by Lewis.

15/16 alternate restoration: χωρὶ[ς ἑκάστην / ὅταν δὲ ἡ πρό]σοδος Sok. Finley in Lewis suggests: χωρὶ[ς τῶν ἄλλ/ων. ἐὰν δὲ πρό]σοδος; Woodward in Lewis suggests: χωρι[σθεῖσαν / ὅπως ἂν ἡ πρό]σοδος.

16/17 alternate restoration: ταλάντο[ιν ..(6)../..(7).. ἐκ τ]ῶν Sok. Both Finley and Lewis offer the same restoration for this line: ταλάντο[ιν κατὰ ἐν/ιαυτὸν ἀπὸ τ]ῶν.

17/18 alternate restoration: Νέαι κ[αὶ τῆς πεντ/ηκοστῆς ὑπά]ρχειν Sok., following Finley in Lewis's commentary; Woodward in Lewis suggests κ[αὶ τῆς ..4../... ὥστε ὑπά]ρχειν. Note that Sok. does not bracket the iota in ΝΕΑ[Ι].

18/19 alternate restoration: τοῦτο [ἀναλῶσαι εἰϲ τὴ/ν θυσίαν Παν]αθηναίων Sok.

20 st. 11: Sok. does not dot the rho.

21 beg: [ῖϲ διαλογισμ]όν Sok.
end: προ[τέρων προσόδων·] Sok.

22 alternate restoration: κ]αὶ μισθοῦν καθότ[ι Sok.

minuscule text: Fr. B, and next two pages.

- - - - - - - - - - - - - - - ι..
[- - - - - - - - - - - - - - - ὅπωϲ ἂν εὐ]ϲ̣[εβ]ῶϲ κα-
[ὶ - - - - - - - - - - - - - - -] κ̣α̣τ' ἐνιαυτὸν κ-
[αι πέμπηται ἡ πομπὴ π]α̣ρ̣ε̣ϲ̣κευ̣[αϲμ]ε̣νη ὡϲ ἄριϲτα τῆι 'Α-
[θηνᾶι καθ' ἕκαϲτο]ν τὸν ἐνιαυτὸν ὑπὲρ τοῦ δήμου τοῦ 'Α-
[θηναίων καὶ τἆλ]λα ὅϲα δεῖ διοικῆται περὶ τὴν ἑορτὴ-
[ν τὴν ἀγομένην τ]ῆι θεῶι καλῶϲ ὑπὸ τῶν ἱεροποιῶν εἰϲ
[τὸν ἀεὶ χρόνον, ἐ]ψηφίϲθαι τῶι δήμωι, τ̣ὰ μὲν ἄλλα καθά-
[περ τῆι βουλῆι, θ]ύειν δὲ τοὺϲ ἱεροποιοὺϲ τὰϲ μὲν δύο
[θυϲίαϲ τήν τε τῆ͜ι] 'Αθηνᾶι τῆι 'Υγιείαι καὶ τὴν ἐν τῶι ἀρ-
[χαίωι νεῶι θυο]μένην καθάπερ πρότερον καὶ νείμαντ-
[αϲ τοῖϲ πρυτάν]εϲιν πέντε μερίδαϲ καὶ τοῖϲ ἐννέα ἄρ-
[χουϲιν τρεῖϲ] κ̣αὶ ταμίαιϲ τῆϲ θεοῦ μίαν καὶ τοῖϲ ἱερ-
[οποιοῖϲ μίαν] κ̣αὶ τοῖϲ ϲτ[ρα]τ̣ηγοῖϲ καὶ τοῖϲ ταξιάρχ-
[οιϲ τρεῖϲ καὶ τ]οῖϲ πομπ[εῦϲι]ν τοῖϲ 'Αθηναίοιϲ καὶ τα-

[ῖς κανηφόροι]ς κατὰ <τὰ> εἰώ[θότα], τ̣ὰ δὲ ἄλλα κρέα Ἀθηναίο-
[ις μερίζειν· ἀ]πὸ δὲ τῶν τε̣[τταρ]άκοντα μνῶν καὶ τῆς μι-
[ᾶς τῶν ἐκ τῆς μ]ισθώσεως τῆ̣ς ν̣έας βοωνήσαντες οἱ ἱερ-
[οποιοὶ μετὰ τ]ῶν βοωνῶν πέμψαντες τὴν πομπὴν τῆι θε-
[ῶι θύοντων τα]ύτας τὰς βοῦς ἁπάσας ἐπὶ τῶι βωμῶι τῆς
[Ἀθηνᾶς τῶι με]γάλωι, μίαν δὲ ἐπὶ τῶι τῆς Νίκης προκρί-
[ναντες ἐκ τῶν] καλλιστευουσῶν βοῶν, καὶ θύσαντες τῆ-
[ι Ἀθηνᾶι τῆι] Π̣ολιάδι καὶ τῆι Ἀθηνᾶι τῆι Νίκηι ἁπασῶ-
[ν τῶν βοῶν τῶ]ν ἀπὸ τῶν τετταράκοντα μνῶν καὶ μιᾶς ἑω-
[νημένων νε]μ̣όντων τὰ κρέα τῶι δήμωι τῶι Ἀθηναίων ἐν
[Κεραμεικῶ]ι καθάπερ ἐν ταῖ̣ς ἄλλαις κρεανομίαις· ἀ[π]-
[ονέμειν δὲ] τὰς μερίδας εἰς τὸν δῆμον ἕκαστον κατὰ [τ]-
[οὺς πέμπον]τας ὁπόσους ἂν παρέχηι ὁ δῆμος ἕκαστος· [ε]-
[ἰς δὲ τὰ μι]σθώματα τῆς πομπῆς καὶ τὸ μαγειρικὸν κα[ὶ]
[κόσμησιν] τοῦ βωμοῦ τοῦ μεγάλου καὶ τἆλλα ὅσα προς-

...⁸.... εἶσθαι περὶ τὴν ἑορτὴν καὶ εἰς παννυχίδα
[διδόναι] :𐅄: δραχμάς· τοὺς δὲ ἱεροποιοὺς τοὺς διοι[κ]-
[οῦντας τ]ὰ Παναθήναια τὰ κατ' ἐνιαυτὸν ποεῖν τὴν πα[ν]-
[νυχίδα] ὡς καλλίστην τῆι θεῶι καὶ τὴν πομπὴν πέμπε̣[ι]-
[ν ἅμα ἡ]λίωι ἀνιόντι, ζημιοῦντας τὸν μὴ πειθαρχο[ῦντ]-
[α ταῖς ἐκ] τῶν νόμων ζημίαις̣· ἐλέσθαι δὲ τὸν δῆμ[ον ...]
[........¹⁸........ ἄ]ν̣[δ]ρας ἐξ Ἀθηναίων ἀπ[άντων ο]-
[ἵτινες - - - - - - - - - - - - - - -]

commentary: Fragment B Koehler established the stoichedon order of 42 letters to the line and is responsible for the restorations unless noted below. All dots are mine. I have changed the letter in line 31 st. 9 to conform to the reading on the stone. Line 9 has 43 letters; Koehler suggested that the τῆι in the restoration used only two stoichoi. Errors in cutting are noted in commentary for Fr. A, lines 8/9.

3 πέμπηται: Hausoullier; τελεσθῆι Michel.

9 beg.: Rang; this almost certain restoration is one letter too long. Perhaps τῆι was carved in two stoichoi: THI.

9/10 ἐν τῶι ἀρ/[χαίωι νεῶι θυο]μένην: Ussing, followed by Doerpfeld, Mommson, Michel, Ki.; Ki. in Ditt. Syll.[3] adds a question mark; 'Αρ/[είωι Πάγωι Rang. followed by Michaelis; ἀρ/[χαίωι ἱερῶι; Zeihen 'Αρ/[χηγέτιδος θυο]μένην Sok. (See discussion below.)

12 τρεῖς: Rang.; πέντε Michel.

14 τρεῖς: Michaelis.

25/26 alternate restoration: ἀ[π/οδιδόναι δὲ] Rang.; ἀ[π/οφοῦναι δὲ] Ditt. Syll.[2], followed by Michel; ἀ[π/οδιδόντες] τὰς Zeihen.

26/27 [τ/οὺς πέμπον]τας: Blass, in Ditt. Syll.[2]; [ἄ/νδρα νέμον]τας Rang., Michel.

29/30 alternate restoration: προσ[ή/κει προνο]εῖσθαι Ditt. Syll.[2]. Ki. did not include this restoration in his text because Vel. (noted by Koe. in II[2] 163) had noted an omega, line 30 st. 8. Sok. takes st. 8 out of brackets, reads it as a dotted omicron, and thus includes Ditt.'s restoration in his text.

31 st. 9: Π Ki. All previous editors and Sok. have the correct reading. I assume this was a mistake in the printing of II[2] 334.

35 st. 22: Rang., Ussing and Ki. read a clear sigma. The other editors, including Koe. and Sok., prefer to bracket this letter. I have left the letter out of brackets, but believe it should be dotted.

It is unfortunate that such an important document from the Lykourgan era survives only in two broken fragments. Even so, II^2 334 and the newer fragment published in Hesperia have provided scholars with material for understanding the religious, economic, and political aspects of the Lykourgan administration. That all of these aspects can be found in one inscription reflects Lykourgos's all-encompassing interest in the welfare of Athens; see Mitchel Lyk. 197f.

Since the literature on this inscription is extensive, I will attempt only a general discussion of the content including the more significant problems.

Fragment A begins with the common heading, ΘΕΟΙ. The next line would give the date if the archon's name were not lost. Although a Lykourgan date has always been accepted, the dates assigned by editors have varied. For example: Kirchner, noting the similarity of letter styles, proposed that II^2 334 and #21 (II^2 333) were cut by the same mason, and so assigned II^2 334 to c. 335/4 (the date of #21 is 335/4); Sokolowski, with no explanation for his exclusion of 336/5, prints both Fr. A and Fr. B with date, 335/4-330/29; Koehler is perhaps the most honest--he dates II 163 "Lykourgan." As mentioned in the commentary, the discovery of the new fragment enabled Lewis to narrow the possibilities but "336/5 or 335/4" is still misleading since it implies only two alternatives. I agree with Lewis in preferring an earlier date, which becomes more probable if one accepts, as I do, Robert's identification of the Nea as Oropos, acquired in the settlement following Chaironeia as a result of either Philip's magnanimity or his attempt to place a bone of contention between the Athenians and their erstwhile Boiotian allies. At any rate, it is unlikely that Lykourgos would wait very long before establishing how Athens would exploit such a valuable acquisition. In fact, Lewis's restoration does not exclude the archon of 337/6 and by 330 (the date usually assigned to Hypereides' Defense of Euxenippos) one of the "mountains" of Oropos, which had been assigned to the ten tribes in pairs, was the subject of a legal action which had probably been growing for some time.

The proposer of this law, Aristonikos, son of Aristoteles, of the deme Marathon, is well-known (PA 2028; see Lewis also for testimonia). He was sentenced to death, along with Demosthenes, Hypereides, Eukrates (the mover of #6), and other lesser known persons on Demades' motion after the Lamian War, 332/1.

The Greater Panathenaia was held every four years; Athena received a new peplos at this time. For the Lykourgan period, the dates are: 338/7, 334/3, 330/29, 326/5, 322/1. This law, however, concerns the Lesser Panathenaia, held annually in the three years between the more elaborate festival. In order that the sacrifices be as beautiful as possible and the revenues be as great as possible, the nomothetai resolved to use the revenues from the Nea (see #6 for discussion of the nomothetai; also, Lewis, 246f.)

I have discussed the two identifications of the Nea above: Lewis's identification presumes that the revenue was to come from leasing of the land, the pentekoste would then be a 2% tax on the produce; Robert's identification, which I accept, requires that the revenues come from the farming out of the pentekoste, the import-export tax. The poletai, or Sellers, were Athenian officials who let out taxes and other state properties such as silver mines to the highest bidders, and so they fit either interpretation. The rest of the text records the procedures involved; the alternate restorations and suggestions I have recorded in the commentary, as well as Lewis's more detailed comments, show that the specific meaning remains unclear.

Concerning Fr. A, Lewis notes, 246, that the "concept of making sure that there are specific funds for a specific purpose seems quite new in Athenian public finance." His explanation rests on the date of the Panathenaia: toward the end of the first prytany (28th Hekatombaion), when the large demands on the revenue at the beginning of the prytany might leave too little left to finance the festival in the proper manner.

The text between Fr. A, the law, and Fr. B, the decree of the Demos, is lost. It probably recorded a probouleuma of the Boule, since lines 16 and 17 of Fr. B presuppose information as to the specific amount of money apportioned which can not have been in the law. (Lewis, 239; see #15 for discussion of the probouleutic process.) Assuming a lost probouleuma between the two fragments would make Fr. B an amendment of the Demos, rather than an aprobouleumatic measure. Lewis remarks that the combination of a law and decree on the same stone is "unparalled," but see #3 for the "unusual" publication of law and building specifications on the same stele and #21 (II^2 333) for law and specifications together; Lewis explains this singularity by noting the permanent nature of the provisions of the decree.

The decree of the Demos, Fr. B, records regulations for the festival. The regulations recorded on the stone appear to be an expansion, in detail, of the provisions made by the Boule (lines 7/8; DeLaix 134). First there is to be one sacrifice to Athena Hygieia (Health) and one in the AP----. The restoration of the beginning of line 10 remains a problem. The possibilities (recorded in Greek in the commentary, line 9/10, above) are: 1) "in the old temple." This is the majority opinion, but, as Dittenberger pointed out, Syll.[2], sacrifices were not performed inside temples. 2) "in the old hieron (sacred area)." Ziehen's suggestion allows an outside sacrifice, but it is one letter too long and is unattested in any document. 3) "on the Areios Pagos." This location is completely out of context as Herington, 31 note 4, points out. 4) "in the [sanctuary of] Archegetis (Founder of the City)," Sokolowski, 66. But there is no more evidence for a place associated with Athena in this guise on the Akropolis than there is for a place called the "old hieron" (number 2 above). And it is rather unfair of Sokolowski to point out that Ziehen's restoration is unattested when his own suggestion presupposes another sanctuary which is equally unattested. Since the restoration of the "old temple" occupies the correct number of letters and could refer to the location of the "new" Erechtheion, within which we know from Pausanias (I.26.5) there were three altars, I have retained that restoration in this text.

Wherever it took place, the meat from this sacrifice is to be alloted to state officials: the prytaneis, five parts; the nine archons, three parts; the treasurers of Athena, one part; the hieropoioi, one part; the strategoi (generals) and the taxiarchs (commanders of tribal contingents), three parts; the parade marshals and kanephoroi (maidens who carry baskets in the procession), according to custom; the rest was to be distributed to the Athenian citizenry.

The main sacrifice, however, is to be at the Great Altar of Athena Polias, composed of as many cattle as the 41 minai from the rent of the Nea can buy. Although one of these cows, the most beautiful, is reserved for the altar of Athena Nike, all the meat from these combined sacrifices goes down to the Kerameikos to be distributed to the Demos, "as in other meat distributions."

A sum of fifty drachmai is allotted for such things as parade costs, the cooking, the decoration of the Great Altar and other things appropriate to the festival and accompanying Pannychis (Night Celebration; see Deubner, 24). The fragment ends with special instructions to the hieropoioi responsible for the Lesser Panathenaia. They are to celebrate the Pannychis as beautifully as possible and see that the procession begins with the rising of the sun; they should penalize misbehavers with penalties provided in the laws.

I have noted the significance of this inscription for the Lykourgan period. In the wider historical and religious context it is the one Lykourgan document which provides scholars with the most information about the most important festival in Athens: the annual procession and sacrifices dedicated to the patron goddess of the city--Athena.

IV. THE YEAR OF EUAINETOS, 335/4

18. *ATHENS HONORS HIEROPOIOI, PHYLEUS AND TWO OTHER MEN OF THE DEME OINOE* EM 7136, 7218

editors: Fr. D Pittakis Eφ. (1856/61) 4023; IG II 219; IG II^2 445.
Fr. B+C Tsuntas Eφ. (1885) pages 131-142.
Fr. A+B+C Koehler IG II 5.128b (from Lolling's minuscule text); IG II^2 330.
Fr. A+B+C+D Wilhelm Att. Urk. V(1942) 147-148.

supplement: Bull. (1942) no. 32 (Wilhelm Att. Urk. V).

other bibliography: Koehler AM 7(1882) 102-108; Schoell Sitz. Ak. München. (1886) 83-139, esp. 114-115; Wilhelm Hermes 24(1889) 136-139; Ferguson Ath. Sec. 37; Pritchett-Neugebauer Cal. 43, 44; Meritt Ath. 11-15, 78-79; GRBS 17 (1976) 152, Rhodes Boule 28, 43, 50, 73, 101, 129-130, 227, 243, 250, 261, 276; DeLaix Proboul. 67, 117-118, 119, 120-123, 140, 141-142; Henry Prescripts 37 n. 23,24, 38-39, 43, 107; Hansen ZPE 30(1978) 151, 156.

description: All four fragments were found on the Akropolis; they now stand as a reconstructed stele in the Epigraphical Museum. Part of the top molding survives in Fr. A; Fr. B and Fr. C preserve the left-hand edge; Fr. D, which records the bottom right wreath, preserves the right-hand edge.

dimensions:
H 1.16 m.
W 0.47 m.
Th 0.145 m.

letters: 0.005 m. Smallest, Ω, is .003; other small letters, Λ, M, O, X, are .004; largest, Φ, is .007; other large letters, B, Π, P, are .0055. Letters in wreath, Fr. D, are 0.10.

minuscule text: next two pages.

epigraphical commentary: I record one new reading: epsilon in line 17 st. 11. I have underlined a number of letters which I could not read and dotted letters

Fr. A [Ἐπὶ Ε]ὐαινέτου ἄρχο[ντος ἐπὶ τῆς ..6...ΐδος τρίτης πρυτ]-
[ανε]ίας, ἧι Πρόξενος Π[υλαγόρου Ἀχερδούσιος ἐγραμμάτευ]-
[εν]· ἕνηι καὶ νέαι, ἑβδό[μηι καὶ δεκάτηι τῆς πρυτανείας· ἐκκ]-
[λη]σία· τῶν προέδρων ἐ̣[πεψήφιζεν ....18........ ἔδ]-
[οξ]εν τῶι δήμωι· Θεόδω̣[ρος Ἀντιφάνου Ἀλωπεκῆθεν εἶπεν· ἐπ]-
[ε]ιδὴ Φυλεὺς χειροτ[ονηθεὶς ἱεροποιεῖν τῆι τε βουλῆι κα]-
[ὶ] τῶι δήμωι ἐπὶ Πυθο[δήλου ἄρχοντος τὴν ἀρχήν, ἐφ' ἣν ἐχειρ]-
[οτ]ονήθη, ἦρξεν καλ[ῶς καὶ κατὰ τοὺς νόμους καὶ ὑπὸ τῶν πρυ]-
[τα]νειῶν πασῶν ἐστ[εφανώθη .....12....., ἐπηινέθη δὲ κα]-
[ὶ ὑπὸ τῆς β]ουλῆς [καὶ τοῦ δήμου ....22.........]
...10.... Γ[..............29.............. κατὰ τὸ]-
Fr. B [ν ν]όμον κα̣[ὶ ....31............... δεδόχθ]-
[αι] τῶι δήμω̣ι ἐ[παινέσαι τὸν ἱεροποιὸν τῆς βουλῆς καὶ τοῦ]
[δή]μου τὸν ἐπὶ [Πυθοδήλου ἄρχοντος Φυλέα Παυσανίου Οἰνα]-
[ῖο]ν καὶ στεφαν̣[ῶσαι χρυσῶι στεφάνωι ἀπὸ Χ δραχμῶν· τὸ δὲ ἀ]-
[ρ]γύριον τὸ εἰ[ς τὸ]ν στ̣ε̣φ̣[ανον προδανεῖσαι τὸν ταμίαν τοῦ]
[δ]ήμου ἐκ τῶν ε[ἰς τ]ὰ κατὰ ψηφ[ίσματα ἀναλισκομένων τῶι δή]-
[μ]ω̣ι̣· ὅπως δ' ἂν ὁ τ̣[α]μ̣ίας ἀπολάβ[ηι τὸ ἀργύριον τὸ εἰρημένον,]
[τ]ο̣ὺ̣ς προέδρους, οἳ ἂν λάχ̣ωσι[ν πρῶτον προεδρεύειν εἰς το]-
[ὺ]ς νομοθέτας προσνομ̣οθετῆ[σαι περὶ τοῦ ἀναλώματος ὅπως]
[ἂ]ν καὶ οἱ ἄλλοι οἱ καθιστάμ̣ε[νοι ἱεροποιοὶ φιλοτιμῶντα]-
ι̣ πρός τε τὴν βουλὴν καὶ τὸν δ[ῆμον ἄρχειν κατὰ τοὺς νόμου]-
ς̣ καὶ εἶναι χρήσιμοι̣ τῶι δήμ[ωι τῶι Ἀθηναίων· ἀναγράψαι δ]-
ὲ̣ τόδε τὸ ψήφισμα̣ τὸν γραμμα[τέα τὸν κατὰ πρυτανείαν ἐν σ]-
τ̣ήληι λιθίνηι καὶ τὸ τῆ̣ς̣ βου̣[λῆς ὃ εἶπε Ἀγασίας καὶ τὸ τοῦ]
δήμου ὃ εἶπεν Ἱπποχάρης καὶ [στῆσαι ἐν ἀκροπόλει, εἰς δὲ τ]-
ὴν ἀναγραφὴν τῆς στήλης δοῦ̣[ναι τὸν ταμίαν τοῦ δήμου .. δ]-
ρ̣α̣χ̣μὰς ἐκ τῶν κατὰ ψηφίσμα[τα ἀναλισκομένων τῶι δήμωι].
[Ἐπ]ὶ Πυθοδήλου ἄρχοντος [ἐπὶ τῆς ...ηΐδος ἐνάτης πρυτανεί]-
[ας], τετράδι ἐπὶ δέκα, δευτ[έραι τῆς πρυτανείας· βουλὴ ἐν βουλ]-
[ευτ]ηρίωι· τῶν προέδρων ἐπε[ψήφιζε ....20........ ·]
[ἔδ]ο̣ξεν τῆι βουλῆι· Ἀγασ̣ί[ας Χαιριγένους Ἰκαριεύς? εἶπεν· ἐπ]-
[ειδ]ὴ Φυλεὺς Παυσανίου Ο[ἰναῖος χειροτονηθεὶς ἱεροποιεῖ]-
[ν τῆι] βουλῆι καὶ τῶι δήμω[ι τὴν ἀρχὴν ἄρχει δικαίως καὶ κατὰ]
[τοὺς ν]όμους καὶ αἱ πρυτα[νεῖαι αἱ ἀεὶ καθήκουσαι αὐτὸν ἐπη]-
[ινέκα]σ̣ι καὶ ἐστεφανώκα[σι· ὅπως ἂν οὖν ἐφάμιλλον ἦι καὶ τοῖς]
[ἄλλοις] ἱ̣ο̣[ῖς] λαγχάν[ουσι ....28..........]

Fr. C ....16.......Δ[...............27............... δεδό]-
[χθαι τῆι βουλῆι, ἐ]παιν[έσαι Φυλέα Παυσανίου Οἰναῖον ἀρετῆ]-
[ς ἕνεκα καὶ δικαι]ο̣σύνης [τῆς εἰς τὴν βουλὴν καὶ τὸν δῆμον τὸ]-
[ν Ἀθην]α̣ίων̣ [κ]α̣ὶ στεφανῶ̣σα[ι αὐτὸν χρυσῶι στεφάνωι ἀπὸ Χ δρα]-
[χμῶ]ν, ἐπειδὰν τὰς εὐθύ̣νας [δῶι· ὅπως, δ' ἂν καὶ ὁ δῆμος αὐτὸν τιμ]-
[ῆσ]η̣ι, τοὺς προέδρους οἳ ἂν λ[άχωσι προεδρεύειν εἰς τὴν πρῶτ]-
[ην] ἐκκλησίαν, χρηματίσαι π[ερὶ αὐτοῦ, γνώμην δὲ ξυμβάλλεσθ]-
[αι] τῆς βουλῆς εἰς τὸν δῆμο[ν ὅτι δοκεῖ τῆι βουλῆι, εἶναι αὐτῶ]-
[ι ε]ὑρέσθαι παρὰ τοῦ δήμου ἀγ[αθὸν ὅτι ἂν δύνηται].
[Ἐπ]ὶ Πυθοδήλου ἄρχοντος ἐπ[ὶ τῆς ..6...ίδος δεκάτης πρυτα]-
[ν]ε̣ίας, ἕνει καὶ νέαι, ἑβδόμη̣[ι καὶ τριακοστῆι τῆς πρυτανεία]-
[ς]· ἐ̣κκλησία· τῶν προέδρων ἐ̣πε[ψήφιζε ....19........]
ἔ̣δοξεν τῆι βουλῆι καὶ τῶ̣ι δ[ήμωι· Ἱπποχάρης ....9.... Ἀλωπ]-
ε̣κῆθεν εἶπεν· περὶ ὧν Φυλε[ὺς χειροτονηθεὶς ὑπὸ τῆς βουλῆς]
κα[ὶ] τοῦ δ[ή]μου καὶ οἱ συν[άρχοντες ἱεροποιοὶ λέγουσιν Παυσ]-
ανίας καὶ Χαρίδημος, δε[δόχθαι τῆι βουλῆι τοὺς προέδρους ο]-
ἳ ἂν λάχωσι προ[εδρ]εύε̣[ι]ν [εἰς τὴν πρώτην ἐκκλησίαν, προσαγα]-
γεῖν αὐτοὺς πρ̣[ὸς τὸν δῆμον καὶ χρηματίσαι, γνώμην δὲ ξυμβά]-
[λ]λεσθαι τῆς β̣[ουλῆς εἰς τὸν δῆμον ὅτι δοκεῖ τῆι βουλῆι, ἐπαι]-
[νέ]σαι Φυλέα Π[αυσανίου Οἰναῖον ἀρετῆς ἕνεκα καὶ δικαιοσύ]-
[νης κ]αὶ στεφαν[ῶσαι χρυσῶι στεφάνωι, ἐπειδὰν τὰς εὐθύνας δ]-
[ῶι· ἐπα]ινέσαι δὲ [καὶ τοὺς συνάρχοντας ἱεροποιοὺς Παυσανί]-
[αν καὶ Χ]αρίδημον Ο[ἰ]να[ίους, ὅτι δικαίως καὶ κατὰ τοὺς νόμου]-
[ς ἄρχουσ]ι τὴν ἀρχὴν κα̣[ὶ στεφανῶσαι ἀμφοτέρους χρυσῶι στε]-
[φάνωι ἀ]πὸ : Χ : δραχμῶν· τὸ [δὲ ἀργύριον τὸ εἰς τοὺς στεφάνους πρ]-
[οδανεῖ]σαι μὲν τὸν τα[μίαν τοῦ δήμου ....19........]
[..5.., τὸν] δ[ὲ] ταμίαν ἀ[πολαβεῖν - - - - - - - - - -]
....11....ον ἀπο -

[in wreath]
[Φυλεὺς Οἰναῖον]
[ἡ βουλή]

[in wreath]
[Φυλεὺς Οἰναῖον]
[ἡ βουλὴ καὶ ὁ δῆμος]

[in wreath]
[Παυσανίας Οἰναῖον]
[ἡ βουλὴ καὶ ὁ δῆμος]

Fr. D
in wreath
[Χαρίδημος] Οἰναῖον
[ἡ βουλὴ κ]αὶ ὁ δῆμος

recorded by Kirchner and previous editors which are too unclear to be certain readings (Kirchner did not dot any letters). A few thetas do not have central dots: line 5 st. 13; line 9 st. 6; line 20 st. 7. The alpha has no cross bar in line 20 st. 10. Many of the upsilons resemble taus: line 10 st. 10; line 14 st. 5; line 17 st. 5; line 26 st. 5; line 30 st. 19; line 33 st. 9; line 35 st. 18; line 40 st. 17; line 42 st. 16, 18; line 46 st. 21; line 52 st. 6; line 55 st. 6.

commentary: The stoichedon line of 46 letters was established for lines 12-28 of the first decree (I) of 335/4 (Fr. B), by Tsuntas; it must be violated for Wilhelm's restoration in line 20 (see below). Although he did offer restorations, Tsuntas did not specify the number of letters for the two other decrees of 336/5 (Fr. C); he just noted that the length should be two or three letters longer. Wilhelm improved upon Tsuntas's text and established a stoichedon line of 48 letters for both decrees (II, III). There is a violation in line 36 (see below).

Although previous editors have labeled the 3 decrees on this stele A, B, C, I prefer to follow Henry who uses Roman numerals to distinguish the 3 decrees. This avoids any confusion with the fragments, which are designated by letters. With the exceptions noted below, the restorations for Fr. A and Fr. D are Koehler's; Fr. B and Fr. C, Tsuntas.

1 ...^{6}..ίδοc: Mer. Ki. restored 'Αντιοχίδοc, for he assumed that this decree and #22, II^2 331, (which preserves the tribe in prytany) were passed on the same day. But an unpublished inscription (dating formula recorded in Meritt *Ath.* 80; reproduced in #22) shows that the tribe Antiochis held the tenth, not the third, prytany.

2 secretary: Wilh., patronymic and demotic supplied from a bouletai list, II^2 1700, line 213 (*AM* 29[1904] 244).

5 proposer: Wilh. identified him as a bouleutes in the following year, 334/3 (II^2 1750 line 61).

11 end-13 end: Koe.

14/15 demotic: Wilh. identified this hieropoios with Phyleus, son of Pausanias, of the deme Oinoe who proposed honors for Herakleides in 330/29 (II^2 360V, #68); see *PA* 15045.

15 amount: Koe.

16 προδανεῖσαι: Koe. παραδιδόναι Schoell; στέφανον νῦν μὲν δότω ὁ ταμίας το/ῦ] Tsun.

18 τὸ εἰρημένον: Wilh.

20 περὶ τοῦ ἀναλώματος: Wilh.

21 ἱεροποιοί: Koe.

22/23 Wilh.

27 amount ΔΔ: Tsun. Koe., Ki., Wilh. leave unrestored.

32 'Αγασί[ας Χαιριγένους 'Ικαριεύς: Ki., by relating this man to PA 15227, Χαιριγένης 'Αγασίους 'Ικαριεύς, cleruch in the fourth century.

33/34 χειροτονηθεὶς ἱεροποιεῖ/ν Koe.

34 τὴν ἀρχὴν ἄρχει δικαίως: Wilh.

35 end: Koe. πρυτα[νεῖαι αὐτὸν φιλοτιμίας ἕνεκα Tsun.

36 end: Wilh. ἐστεφανῶκα[σιν Tsun. Wilh. omitted the nu-movable and suggested crowding of the last two letters, iota and sigma, into one stoichos. I suggest as more likely the crowding of ηι into one stoichos; the omicron and iota of τοῖς are less probable, but possible.

39 demotic: Wilh.

41 amount: Koe.

42 end: Wilh. [δῶι· ἵνα δὲ καὶ ὁ δῆμος αὐτὸν τιμ]- Tsun.

47 δεκάτης: Wilh.

51 end: Lolling. Φυλ[εὺς Οἰναῖος....9....λέγουσιν Wilh.

52 end ἱεροποιοί: Ki.

57 demotic: Wilh.

59 end ἱεροποιούς: Ki.

60/61 Wilh.

62-64 Koe. τ[ὸ δὲ ἀργύριον τὸ εἰς τὸν στέφανον τοῦ τὸ/ν μερί]σαι μὲν τὸν τα[μίαν τῶν στρατιωτικῶν τῶι ταμίαι τοῦ δ/ήμου, τὸν] δ[ὲ] ταμίαν δ[οῦναι Schoell, on the basis that the outlay should come from another fund. But Ki. notes that the money is for <u>three</u> crowns (at least--see below ll. 66-69), and Schoell's restoration allows for only one. Also, the letter, line 64 st. 17, is a clear alpha rather than the delta in Schoell's text.

66-69 name: When Wilh. added this fragment, he noted that the name in this lower right hand wreath should be Pausanias or Charidemos since the name Phyleus is too short to be symmetrical. He did not, however, venture to restore the other crowns required by the decrees. I have done so on the assumption that Phyleus received two crowns, one from the Boule (II line 41) and one from the Boule and Demos (I line 15); Phyleus's colleagues, Charidemos and Pausanias, each received one crown from the Boule and Demos (III lines 59-62).

My measurements confirm that the width of the restored stele is correct: the 23 extant letters in lines 26-28 are exactly half of the restored stoichedon order of 46 letters to the line; the 23 letters measure 0.23 cm.; the width of the restored stele at that point is 0.47 cm.; therefore, the original width may have been a centimeter less than restored, but, in any case, the stele was not wide enough to accommodate three wreaths side by side (the width of the incomplete wreath is already 0.20 cm.).

Although the stele allows for just two wreaths side by side, there is no reason to deny the probability that the original stele was taller than its plaster restoration. In fact, the decrees confirm at least three crowns which require two rows of crowns. Two crowns for Phyleus make the stele more symmetrical and, I think, confirm the correct interpretation of the relationship between the three decrees. (See discussion below.)

The arrangement does not have to be as I have offered, as long as Fr. D is on the right side of the stele, and does not have Phyleus as the restored honoree (see Wilhelm's comment above).

This stele records three decrees which honor certain hieropoioi of 336/5. The first, #18I, a decree of the Demos passed in 335/4, awards a gold crown to Phyleus, son of Pausanias, of the deme Oinoe, and proposes to constitute a board of nomothetes to appropriate money for awards to other hieropoioi. It finally orders the engraving on the same stele with the present decree two decrees of the preceding year, one (#18II), a decree of the Boule moved by Agasias honoring Phyleus alone, and the other (#18III), a decree of the Boule and the Demos moved by Hippochares honoring both Phyleus and his fellow hieropoioi and fellow demesmen, Pausanias and Charidemos. Henry (43) suggests that Decrees II and III were not originially intended for publication; the fact that III was published, however, makes it the first document to record the type of meeting--ἐκκλεσία (line 49; see also Henry, 38-39). For discussion of the dates in 336/5, see Meritt, Ath. 11-15, 78-79, GRBS, and #15 above; as was the case in #15, the restoration does not change, only the interpretation of the count of days.

#18II is a decree of the Boule enacted in the ninth prytany of the preceding year. It honors Phyleus with a gold crown to be awarded after he passes his euthynai, an annual auditing of accounts of each man who has held office for the year. The omission of this clause allowed Aischines to prosecute Ktesiphon, who had proposed honors for Demosthenes while Demosthenes still held office (Aisch. Ktes. 9-12; see also Rhodes, 15). II ends with an open clause which allows for further benefits if the Demos sees fit. (Rhodes, Table L, page 281, labels such clauses "allo agathon.")

III is a decree of the Boule and the Demos from the tenth prytany of 336/5, which either confirms the gold crown voted by the Boule alone or (as I consider more likely) confers another crown by the Boule and the Demos together and then goes on to confer the same honor upon each of his two colleagues in office: Pausanias and Charidemos, both from the same deme as Phyleus. Again, there is the restriction that Phyleus must first pass his audit [restored], but apparently this did not apply to his colleagues.

Decree I was enacted about four months later, in the third prytany of 335/4. It acknowledges the two earlier decrees (although it does not name, it may refer obliquely to Phyleus's two colleagues, οἱ ἄλλοι οἱ καθιστάμε[νοι ἱεροποιοί]) and provides for the publication of all three. Apparently the annual appropriations did not provide for this expenditure, since the presence of the nomothetai is required for appropriations for the crowns and for special funds for similar use in the future. It appears that such honors for this particular purpose were without precedent. If this was indeed a new procedure (as it certainly was a new expenditure of public funds) it is not without parallel in the Lykourgan period and conforms well with the program for civic and religious revitalization.

Rhodes (50) discusses this decree in relation to two others of the Lykourgan period, II^2 222 (new date, mid 330's, from Osborne, <u>BSA</u> 67[1972] 133 note 15; for a more specific date see addendum to #31) and #50, IG VII 4254. In these decrees the presence of the nomothetai guarantees an "unexpected" expenditure (solved in #50 by a transfer of funds). I have argued in #3 that this is why a <u>law</u> was required for the repair of the Peiraieus fortification rather than a decree. (See also #6 for discussion of nomothesia; Hansen, 156, for this decree.)

There remains the question of the office which was held by Phyleus. Koehler (<u>AM</u> 102-108), followed by

Kirchner, identified the hieropoios and his two synarchontes, line 52, as three of the συλλογεῖς τοῦ δήμου. The fact that the syllogeis were known to have certain religious functions led Koehler to restore ἱεροποιός and ἱεροποιεῖν throughout the inscription. Not a single letter of either word is preserved on the stone. Although the restoration is on the whole convincing, there is no evidence that the syllogeis were called hieropoioi when they performed religious duties (see #77 where 2 syllogeis perform religious duties but are still called "syllogeis").

Rhodes (129f.) has re-examined the evidence for the syllogeis: they were certainly a thirty-man board composed of three bouleutai from each tribe, and it is likely that they played a part in convening meetings; the epigraphical evidence confirms their connection with certain religious duties. Rhodes, in citing the epigraphical sources for syllogeis (II^2 1257 [#77], II^2 1425, II^2 1749, II^2 2821), also notes (130) Koehler's assumption that the three men honored in II^2 330, these decrees, constituted a tribal contingent of this board, but rejects it: "how even Athenian laxity could describe the tribal contingent of a bouleutic sub-committee as χειροτ[ονηθέντες ἱεροποιεῖν τῆι τε] Βουλῆι καὶ τῶι δήμωι [elected to perform religious duties for the Boule and the Demos] I do not understand."

Rhodes is right in rejecting Koehler's hypothesis. His reason, however, is wrong, because it is based on a misrepresentation of the evidence of II^2 330. He implies --by printing the plural χειροτ[ονηθέντες, whereas only the singular appears or is restored on the stone and always applies only to Phyleus--that all three men were elected to perform their duties and concludes: "the office was elective, and almost certainly triumviral, but that seems to be all we can say about it." If this is true of the syllogeis (as it probably is) it proves that Phyleus and his colleagues were not members of that board. Phyleus alone was elected (restored on the basis of line 6, χειροτ[ονηθείς --]) and he alone had to render his euthynai. Although his colleagues are called synarchontes and are said to perform an arche, it is likely that Phyleus was not only chief of his board but also that he was the only one of the three who handled public moneys. The others may have been co-opted (with the approval of the Boule) by the person elected, or perhaps appointed (καθιστάμενοι, line 21). The fact that one of the synarchontes, Pausanias, must be a close relative--father, brother, or first cousin--suggests that Phyleus played some part in their appointment.

The office and functions performed by Phyleus and his synarchontes cannot be defined precisely. However, I have retained Koehler's restoration of hieropoioi, and suggest that this three-man board provided for and/or performed certain sacred rites or procedures for the sessions of the Boule and the meetings of the Ekklesia. This could not be the board of ten hieropoioi for all of Athens (cf. #13): this board was selected by lot (Aristotle AP 54.6-7); Phyleus, obviously the head of his board, was elected. But, as Rhodes notes (130) "clearly there were large numbers of hieropoioi in Athens."

However many hieropoioi there were in Athens, the three men honored in this decree performed their duties so generously and well that first the Boule and then the Demos felt it necessary to honor them, even though this meant calling for the nomothetes to insure that the necessary funds were available.

335/4

19. *DECREE* Ag. Inv. I 3960

photo: <u>Hesperia</u> 9(1940) page 237.

editor: Schweigert <u>Hesperia</u> 9(1940) 327/8 no. 36.

other bibiliography: Meritt <u>Ath.</u> 79/80.

description: The fragment is Pentelic marble. Only the rough-picked back and molding on top are preserved. It was found in April, 1936, during excavations in the Agora.

dimensions:
H 0.285 m.
W 0.36 m.
Th 0.148 m.

letters: 0.008 m. Smallest, O, is .005; largest, Σ, Y, are .010.

minuscule text:

stoich. 26

[Ἐπὶ Εὐα]ι̣νέτου ἄρχοντος ἐπὶ τῆ[ϲ]
[Ἀκαμαν]τ̣ίδος πέμπτης πρυτανε[ί]-
[αϲ ἧι Πρόξ]ενοϲ Π[υλα]γόρου Ἀχερ[δ]-
[ούϲιοϲ ἐ]γραμμάτ̣[ευ]ε̣ν· Ποϲειδε[ῶ]-
[νοϲ ἑνδεκ]ά̣τει· τῶ[ν π]ροέδρων ἐ[πε]-
[ψήφιζε Νι]κοκλ[ῆϲ] Ῥαμνούϲιοϲ. vv

vacat

.....9.....Ṇ.... Παιανιε[ὺϲ εἶπ]-
[εν· ......12......]εν .....10.....
.....11..... π[ρό]τ[ερον ...7...]

commentary: The text records Schweigert's restorations for a stoichedon order of 26 letters to the line. As Schweigert notes, and the photograph shows, the inscribed surface is difficult to read. I have underlined letters I could not read, and, because of the condition of the stone, I will only note here that I think I can read the sigma of Nikokles in line 6 st. 14, and an omicron in line 8 st. 17. The vacat between lines 6 and 7 is 0.015 m.

Schweigert relates the Nikokles of this inscription to a man of the same name who was father of an ephebe in 128/7 B.C., Hesperia 4 (1935) no. 37 line 168.

All that remains of this decree is the dating formula. It was passed in the fifth prytany on the eleventh day of Poseideion (or the twelfth, Meritt). Since the day within the prytany is omitted, this decee offers no information about the correspondence between conciliar and festival year for 335/4.

335/4

20. *DECREE* EM 7072

editors: Koehler IG II 132; IG II^2 332.

other bibliography: Reusch Hermes 15(1880) 337; Unger Att. Arch 670; Pritchett-Neugebauer Cal. 44-45; Meritt Ath. 82.

description: This fragment of Pentelic marble was found on the Akropolis. The left side and two feet (which were part of the relief above the decree) remain; other sides are broken.

dimensions:
H 0.30 m. (surface)
0.41 m. (entire)
W 0.10 m.
Th 0.16 m.

letters: 0.011 m. Smallest, O, is .008; largest, Σ, is 012. The letter size is quite large for the Lykourgan Era.

minuscule text: next page.

commentary: The text is Kirchner's. I offer no changes in the reading of the stone. Only the fragmentary heading remains on the stone, and the dating formula is heavily restored.

stoich. 26

῾Επ[ὶ Εὐαινέτου ἄρχοντος ἐπὶ τῆc]
῾Ερ[εχθηΐδοc ὀγδοΐηc πρυτανεΐα]-
c ἧ[ι Πρόξενοc ᾿Αχερ ἐγραμμάτευε]-
ν· ᾿Ε[λαφηβολιῶνοc δεκάτηι ὑcτέρ]-
αι, ἑ[νδεκάτηι τῆc πρυτανεΐαc· τῶ]-
ν πρ[οέδρων ἐπεψήφιζεν ᾿Αριcτοκ]-
ράτ[ηc ....9.... ἔδοξεν τῆι βου]-
λῆι [καὶ τῶι δήμωι .....12.....]
ΔΙΟ - - - - - - - - - - - - - - -
ΙΟΣ - - - - - - - - - - - - - - -

This decree may have "no probative value for the calendar" (Pritchett-Neugebauer, 45; seconded by Meritt); however, for general information, the dates assigned to it are as follows:

1) Koehler did not offer a date.

2) Reusch used a number of criteria to offer a dating formula for either 336/5 or 333/2; he preferred 336/5.

3) Unger suggested 335/4, the year of Euainetos; Kirchner, in II^2 333, used Unger's date and added an abbreviated form of the name of the secretary of that year.

4) Pritchett-Neugebauer offer for 353/2 (st. 25):

῾Επ[ὶ Θουδήμου ἄρχοντος ἐπὶ τῆc]
῾Ερ[εχθηΐδοc ..6... πρυτανεΐα]-
c ἧ[ι Φιλοκήδηc Δωροθέου Παλλη]-
νε[ὺc ἐγραμμάτευεν· δευτέραι κ]-
αὶ ε[ἰκοcτῆι τῆc πρυτανεΐαc· τῶ]-
ν πρ[οέδρων ἐπεψήφιζεν ..6...]-
ρατ[ηc ....8.... ἔδοξεν τῆι βου]-
λῆι [καὶ τῶι δήμωι ....11....]

There are problems in each of the previous restorations. I have not discussed them in detail because I agree with Pritchett-Neugebauer who move this inscription out of the Lykourgan period and into the middle of the fourth century, when larger letters were more common.

335/4

21. *LYKOURGOS PROPOSES A LAW TO DEAL WITH THE RELIGIOUS REFORMS* EM 7148+7151, 7150+7147, 7077 7149, [2459-unpublished Fr. G]

photo: Kirchner Imagines Plate 29 (Fr. A+B, lines 4-12).

editors: Fr. A Pittakis EΦ. (1837/39) 289, (1852/55) 2674; Rangabé (1855) 492.
Fr. B Pittakis EΦ. (1837/39) 973; Rangabé (1855) 521.
Fr. C Koehler Hermes 1(1886) 312-322, based on transcript of Kumanudes.
Fr. A+B, C+D Koehler II 162.
Fr. E Bournouf Rev. Arch. 28(1874) 316 no. 6.
Fr. C+E Koehler II Add. 162 page 411.
Fr. A+B, C+E, F, D Kirchner, II^2 333, using Wilhelm's transcript and restorations for C+E, F. (Wilhelm announced the association of C+E with the new fragment, F, in Beitr., but did not publish a full text at that time.)

testimonia: [Plutarch] Lives of the Ten Orators 852b.

supplements: SEG 15.96 (Woodward); 16.53 (Tréheux, Wycherly); 21.271 (Pritchett-Neugebauer, Meritt).

other bibliography: Schoell Sitz. Ak. München. (1886) 120; Koerte AM 18(1893) 256 n. 1; Foucart Journ. Sav. (1902) 186; Wilhelm Beitr. 292; Pritchett-Neugebauer Cal. 44; Tréheux BCH 80(1956) 469; Woodward Hesperia 25(1956) 106; Wycherly Ath. Ag. III (1957) 79 n. 209, Meritt Ath. 80; Clement AJA 69(1965) 193; Linders Studies 56 n. 36, 74-75; Petropoulou GRBS 22(1981) 39-68.

description: The six published fragments were found on the Akropolis; they are Hymettan marble. The seventh fragment, G, and its provenance are still to be published by Dr. Peppas Delmousou, but it too probably came from the Akropolis. Fragments A+B, C+E, and D+G are physically joined, whereas Fr.F, which is associated with Fr. C+E, is still separate. The only preserved edge is the right-hand side of Fr.F. The backs of the two thickest fragments, C and F, are smooth in contrast to the usual rough-picked finish for a stele recording a decree and are probably original. Two other laws of the Lykourgan period (#3 and #17) were published on large stelai but were comparatively thin (0.13 m.) in comparison with this inscription (0.16 m.); but #3 does have a smooth back like #21.

dimensions:
- Fr. A+B
  - H 0.22 m.
  - W 0.42 m.
  - Th 0.13 m.
- Fr. C+E
  - H 0.29 m.
  - W 0.36 m.
  - Th 0.16 m. (C)
  - 0.10 m. (E)
- Fr. F
  - H 0.25 m.
  - W 0.21 m.
  - Th 0.16 m.
- Fr. D+G
  - H 0.175 m.
  - W 0.130 m.
  - Th 0.036 m.

letters: 0.005 m. Smallest, Δ, Λ, O, are .004; largest, P, Σ, are .006. The letter size (smaller than the usual .007 m. for decrees) is another common physical characteristic of the laws of the Lykourgan period: the letters on this stone and #17, both .005, could have been cut by the same mason, as Kirchner suggested (see #17); letters in #3 and #6 are also .005.

majuscule text: next two pages.

epigraphical commentary: I have included the majuscule text in order to show my new readings and to clarify the difficulties found in the texts of Kirchner and Koehler. The underscored letters set off by a line (Fr.C, lines 1-4) were seen only by Kumanudes; apparently this part was broken off after that time. A second line shows where Fr.C and Fr.E meet, and a third line traces the join between Fr.D and Fr.G. Underscoring signifies those letters which I could not read. (For Fr. A+B, C+E, the underlined letters were read by Koehler and Kirchner unless otherwise noted below; for Fr.E, the letters were read by Wilhelm and Kirchner.) All dots are mine.

The stoichedon order is violated twice on the stone; in line 22 of Fr. C+E: in C, five letters (NOTOY) are crowded into four stoichoi (st. 16-19); in E, eight letters (ΘEONIEPO) occupy six stoichoi (st. 27-32). Koehler

Fragment A

...............ΛΗΣΤΟΝΔΕ
......ΠΟ̣ΜΠΕΑ̣ΜΗΔΕΚΑΤΕΝΕΙΓΚΑ
....ΥΔΗΜΟΣΙΟΥΟΠΩΣΑΝΟΔΗΜΟΣΙ̣
....ΕΝΕΓΚΑΣΩΝΚΑΙΛΑΒΟΥΣΩΝΜΗ
..Α̣ΡΑΤΟΝΔΕΤΟΝΝΟΜΟΝΟΦΕΙΛΕΤΩ......Χ̣Μ Fragment B
.Η̣ΝΕΙΗΟΙΔΗΜΟΣΙΟΙΟΙΕΝΤΗΙΑΚΡ.....ΙΔΙ̣Α̣Ι̣
Τ̣ΟΝΔΕΤΟΝΝΟΜΟΝΜΑΣΤΙΓΟΥΣΘΩΕΚΑ̣...ΣΑΥΤΩΝ
Ι̣ΟΝΑΝΑΤΙΘΕΝΑΙΤΑΑΝΑΘΗΜΑΤΑΧΡΥ..Η̣ΑΡΓ.ΡΑΠΟΗ̣
ΣΙΟΥΣΜΙΑΜΜΕΝΔΩΡΕΑΝΩΝΛΑΜΒΑΝ..ΑΡΑΤΟΥΔΗΜΟΥΑΝ
ΤΙΘΕΝΑΙΧΡΥΣΑΗΑΡΓΥΡΑΚΑΙΕΑΝ....ΣΑΛΛΟΙΛΑΒΩΣΙΠ̣
.ΡΟΥΝΤΟΝΔΕΝΟΜΟΝΤΟΝΔΕΚΑΙΤ....ΡΙΤΗΣΕΞΕΤ̣ΑΣΕΩΣΤΩ̣
.ΕΙΚΑΙΣΤΗΣΑΙΕΝΑΚΡΟΠΟΛΗΙΕ̣..ΔΕΤΗΝΑΝΑΓΡΑΦΗΝΜΕΡΙ

0.04

.........ΤΗΣΣΚΙΡΟΦΟΡ.......ΤΗΙΙΣΤΑΜΕΝΟΥΝΟΜΟ
...........ΓΟΣΛΥΚΟΦΡ.......Τ̣ΑΔΗΣΕΙΠΕΝΟΠΩΣΑ̣Ν̣
............ΦΟΡΗΣΟΙΑ........ΙΤΑΚΑΝ̣ΑΚΑΙΤΑΛΛΑ
.............Ε̣ΙΣΙΔΙΑ.........ΑΤΟΙΣΜΗΔΕΚΑΘ
..............ΘΕΩΡΙΑ..........Κ̣ΕΛΕΥΟΥΣ
................ΝΑΠ...............Λ̣ΣΕ̣
.................ΙΑ̣

Fragment D

....ΙΑΚΙ̣
....ΑΝΤΩΝ
..Χ̣ΘΕΙΣΑΠΟ
...ΑΛΛΟΤΙΗΔ
...ΑΓΕΙΚΑΙΤΗ
..ΥΚΟΣΜΟΥΣΤΕΦΑ
..ΙΥΠΑΡΧΟΝΤΩΝΤ
..Η̣ΝΕΒΔΟΜΗΚΟΝΤ
...ΓΡΑΨΑΙΤΟΝ
....Α̣ΣΠΟΗΣΑΣ
.....Ν̣ΔΕΤΟΝ
......ΙΝΤΟΜΙ
......Χ̣ΕΙΝΔ
.......ΘΕΟ
.......Α̣Ι

Fragment C

.........I
........._I
.........ΛΙ.....ΩΚΟΣ
.........ΑΚ.=ΑΓΕΙΤΟΥ
.........ΕΠΕΙΔΗΔΕΚΤΟΥ.........ΛΙ Fragment F
.........ΝΤΑΤΟΥΤΩΝΤΩΝΧΡΗ.........ΕΚΑΝ
.........ΟΔΕΔΑΝΕΙΣΜΕΝΑΕΞΑ.........ΜΠΕΑ
.........ΙΑΤΑΜΕΓΑΛΑΜΕΡΙΖΕΣΘ.........ΛΕΙΟ.ΕΝΔΕ
.........ΛΑΚΤΙΚΟΝΕΙΣΤΑΠΡΟΔΕΔ.........ΕΚΤΗΣ.ΙΟΙ¦Π
.........ΝΤΟΝΚΑΝΗΦΟΡΙΚΟΝΟΠΩΣΑ.........ΟΝΚΑΙΤΑΜΙΕΥ
.........ΑΙΠΕΝΤΗΚΟΝΤΑΑΙΓΙΔ.ΣΚΑ.........ΙΤΩΙΣΩΤΗΡ.¦
.........ΕΝΤΕΤΟΥΕΝΙΑΥΤΟΥΕΚΑΣΤΟ.........Ο:ΚΑΙΤΟΥΤΩΝΤΟΥ
.........ΩΝΤΟΥΔΙΟΣΤΟΥΣΩΤΗΡΟΣΠΟ.........ΙΤΟΥΕΝΙΑΥΤΟΥΕΚΑΣ
.........ΑΙΤΟΥΣΑΥΤΟΥΣΜΕΤΑΤΩΝΕΠΙ.........ΩΝΧΡΗΜΑΤΩΝΤΟΙΝΘΕΟΙΝ
.......ΙΤΩΙΔΙΙΤΩΙΟΛΥΜΠΙΩΙ::ΚΟΣΜ.........ΤΟΥΣΜΕΤΑΤΩΝΤΟΥ..ΜΕ
......ΑΤΟΥΤΑΜΙΟΥΤΟΥΔΗΜΟΥΕΚΤΩΝΙ.........ΚΑΙΤΩ.ΔΙΟΝΥΣΩΙΚΟΣΜΟΝ
....ΥΕΝΙΑΥΤΟΥΕΝΤΗΙΤΕΤΡΑΕΤΙΑΙΕΚ.........ΣΑΙΤΗΙΑΘΗΝΑΙΤΗΙΙΤΩΝΗ
...ΜΟΥΣΕΚΤΗΣΑΠΑΡΧΗΣΤΗΣΑΠΟΤΩΝΤΕ.........ΟΝΙΑ.ΤΟΥΤΟΤΟΤΕΛΟΣΕΜ
..Ο.ΣΑΣΘΑΙΔΕΚΑΙΤΗΙΑΓΑΘΗΙΤΥΧΗΙΚ.......Σ.........ΩΝΤΗΣΑΓΑΘΗΣΤΥΧΗΣΜΕ
...ΣΤΑΤΩΝΤΟΥΙΕΡΟΥΤΗΣΑΓΑΘΗΣΤΥΧΗΣΠΟ....ΘΑ.........ΟΥΣΙ.ΙΔΙΚΑΙΤΟ
...ΟΙΣΚΑΙΤΩΙΑΜΦΙΑΡΑΩΙΚΑΙΤΩ.ΑΣΚΛΗΠΙΩ.ΚΕΚ.........ΟΣΟΥΕΠΙΓΡΑ
....ΟΣΜΟΝΕΚΑΣΤΟΝΟΤΟΥΑΝΗΙΤΩΝΘΕΩΝΙΕΡΟΣΚΑΙΤΟΣΤ.........ΟΥΤΟΥΠΟΤΟΥ
.ΙΟ.ΣΤΩΝΘΕΩΝΤΟΑΡΓΥΡΙΟΝ.ΟΕΚΤΟΥΔΕΡΜΑΤΙΚΟΥΓ.........Π..ΤΗΣΠΕΡΙΔΕ
.ΤΩΝΙΕΡΩΝΤΗΣΑΡΤΕΜΙΔΟ..ΗΣΒΡΑΥΡΩΝΙΑΣΚΑΙΤΩΙ.........ΛΕΛ.ΟΥΣΚΑΙΕΠΕ
.ΕΟΝΕΙΛΩΟΝΚΑΙΑΜΕΙΝΟΝ.ΩΙΔΗΜΩΙΤΩΙΑΘΗΝΑΙΩΝ.........Ε.ΟΥΣΤΗΙΑΡΤΕ
.ΣΚΑΙΚΑΛΛΙΟΥΣΗΕΩΝΤΙΩΣΠΕΡΝΥΝΕΧΕΙΕΠΕΡΕΣΘΑ.........ΟΥΑΝΠΚΕ
.ΤΑΜΙΚΡΑ.ΣΤΑΜΕΝΑΚΑΙΟΣΑΜΗΕΜΠΑΡΑΔΟΣΕΙΕΣΤΙ.........ΩΙΤΩΙΔΗ
Σ.ΟΥΣΙΕΡΟΥΣΤΗΙΔΗΜΗΤΡ.ΚΑΙΤΗΙΚΟΡΗΙΜΕΙΖΟ.........ΧΕΙΕΠΕΡ
...ΕΡΙΤΩΝΕΝΤΟΙΣΑΛΛΟΙΣΙΕΡΟΙΣΤΩΝΚΑΤΑΜΙ.........ΡΓΥΡΙ
...Ο.ΤΟΙ..ΟΝ.......ΤΑΚΑΤΑΤΑΥΤΑΤΟΝΑ.........ΚΟΣΜ
.......ΟΥ...........Ε.ΖΟΥΣΚΑΙΚ.........ΩΝΙΕΡ
.........................ΣΙΩΙ Fragment E
..........................Ο

did not show this crowding in his majuscule text. There is no violation in line 23 as Kirchner recorded; the disturbance in his text was caused by the omission of TO (st. 13, 14). Since I have changed some restorations in Fr.C+E,F to comply with the correct letter order on the stone, possible instances of stoichedon violation for that part of the text will be discussed below in the commentary.

Fr. A+B

2 st. 25, 26 (min.-st. 56,57): Ki. dotted the KA.

5 st. 32, 33 (min.-st. 63,64): X̣M new readings; .Δ Ki.

8 st. 21-27 (min.-st. 52-58): MATAXPỴ Koe.; MATATAXPY Ki.

9 st. 29 (min.-st. 60): only Ki. printed the alpha here.

14 st. 37, 42,43 (min.-st. 68,73,74): N, ẠṆ new readings; ΠΕ.ΟΠΩΣΑΙΓ Koe.; ΠΕ.ΟΠΩΣΛΙ (ΛΙ = α̃ν) Ki.

15 st. 34 (min.-st.65): Ṇ new reading.

Fr.C+E,F

It is for these fragments that the majuscule text is necessary. The stoichedon order of the letters is incorrect in Ki.'s minuscule text (he does not provide a majuscule text) in four places; one of the errors (lines 23ff.) in II^2 333 was carried over from Koe.'s majuscule texts for Fr. C (II 162) and Fr. E (II Add. 162).

In Ki.'s text for Fr. C, the letters in lines 1-10 are one stoichos closer to the left-hand side than they should be; at the beginning of line 10, NTO (st. 14-16) is above IΠΕ (line 11 st. 14-16) on the stone; NTO would be above ΑΙΠ (st. 13-15) in Ki.'s text.

In Ki.'s text for Fr. C+E (and Koe.'s majuscule text for Fr. C), the letters in lines 23-33 are one stoichos closer to Fr. F than they should be: near the beginning of line 23, ΤΩΝ (st. 6-8) is below ΣΜΟ (line 22 st. 6-8) on the stone; ΤΩΝ would be below ΜΟΝ (st. 7-9) in Ki.'s text.

In Ki.'s text for Fr. E, the letters in lines 30-33 are six stoichoi closer to Fr. F than they should be; in the middle of line 30, ΤΑΚ (st. 21-23) is below ΣΙΕ (line 29 st. 21-23) on the stone; ΤΑΚ would be below ΣΤΩ (line 29 st. 27-29) in Ki.'s text.

In Ki.'s text for Fr. F, the letters in lines 30 and 31 are one stoichos closer to the right-hand side than they should be: at the end of line 30, ΚΟΣ (st. 73-75) is below ΓΥΡ (line 29 st. 73-75) on the stone; ΚΟΣ would be below ΥΡΙ (line 29 st. 74-76) in Ki.'s text.

In this Corpus, the text of Fr. C+E,F in II^2 333 is the most serious example of problems arising from Ki.'s use of Wilh.'s notes and transcript (see #12 for another). I have designated the text of II^2 333 as Ki.'s chiefly for convenience, but it should be kept in mind that the text of Fr. C+E.F is based on Wilh.'s association of the three fragments and on his restorations with a line of eighty-two letters. Below, in the commentary, I note the restorations attributed to Wilhelm by Kirchner, but it is impossible to know how the errors in the stoichedon order crept into the text of II^2 333.

All of the letters in lines 5-7 of Fr. F are new readings; most of the letters in lines 8-12 are also new readings, and the ones seen by Ki. are recorded immediately below for comparison.

8 st. 60-64 (min.-st. 65-69): ΣΙΛ.Ε Ki.

9 st. 60-62 (min.-st. 65-67): ΚΙΝ Ki.

10 st. 61-66 (min.-st. 66-71): ΚΑΤ \^Μ Ki.

11 st. 61-68 (min.-st. 66-73): Τ..Ι .Ω.Ρ Ki.

12 st. 61-67 (min.-st. 66-72): :ΚΑΙΤΟΥ Ki.

13 st. 11 (min.-st. 60): Ω new reading.
st. 60 (min.-st. 65): Ι new reading.

14 st. 58-60 (min.-st. 63-65): ΩΝΧ new readings.
st. 76 (min.-st. 81): Ν̣ new reading.

16 st. 58-61 (min.-st. 63-66): Κ̣Α̣ΙΤ new readings.

17 st. 58-61 (min.-st. 63-66): Σ̣ΑΙΤ̣ new readings.

18 st. 59-61 (min.-st. 64-66): ΟΝΙ new readings.
st. 77 (min.-st. 82) Μ̣ new reading.

19 st. 39 (min.-st. 44): I could not read Koe.'s sigma, but it does fit in the restoration as the sigma of τοῦς.

20 st. 32, 38,39 (min.-st. 37, 43,44): Π̣, ΘΑ new

readings; I, ΟΦ Koe., Ki.
st. 63, 69 (min.-st. 68, 74): Ο, Δ new readings; Ε, Ω Ki. The definite delta can be seen in the photograph.

21 st. 66 (min.-st. 71): Σ̣ new reading; I Ki.

24 st. 61-63 (min.-st. 66-68): Λ̣ΕΛ̣ new readings.
st. 65-67 (min.-st. 70-72): ΟΥΣ new readings.

25 st. 62 (min.-st. 67): E̲ new reading.
st. 64-66 (min.-st. 69-71): ΟΥΣ new readings.

26 st. 14 (min.-st. 19): N new reading.
st. 67-73 (min.-st. 72-78): ΟΥΑ̣̲ΝΙΠ̣ΚΕ new readings; ΟΥΛΗ.ΚΕ Ki.

29 st. 36 (min.-st. 41): Ι̣̲ new reading.

31 st. 8,9 (min. 13, 14) ΟΥ in st. 7, 8, according to Ki.'s text. At the end of the line Fr. F, Ki. reads ΩΠΙΕ.

Fr. D+G
Fr. G and its join to Fr. D are still to be published by Dr. Delmousou. All dots are mine.

11 st. 6: I Koe., Ki.

12 st. 12: I Koe., Ki., is more likely the left-hand hasta of an eta.

13 st. 7 The chi does not need a dot.

minuscule text: next three pages.

commentary: I have underlined letters read by previous editors which are no longer legible. All the dots are mine and are carried over from the majuscule text; new readings are included.

Restorations for Fr. A+B, and Fr. D, are Koehler's, with exceptions noted below. When Wilhelm added Fr. F to the right of Fr. C+E he was able to restore full lines across the gap and to establish the 82-letter line. His new restorations include: the middle of line 13; before Fr. F. line 14; middle of line 15; middle of line 16; beginning, line 17; all of line 18; beginning and middle (after Fr. E) of line 22; middle (after Fr. E) of line 23; all of line 25; all of line 28; all of line 29.

Fr. A+B stoich. 82

.......45.......λης, τὸν δὲ ....29.......
.......37....... πομπέα μηδὲ κατενειγκα ....25.......
[.......33....... το]ῦ δημοσίου ὅπως ἂν ὁ δῆμος .Ι.......24.......
.......35....... ἐνεγκασῶν καὶ λαβουσῶν μη.......25.......
[.......32....... π]αρὰ τόνδε τὸν νόμον ὀφειλέτω [..δρα]χμ[ας ....16.......]
.......32.......ηνειη οἱ δημόσιοι οἱ ἐν τῆι ἀκρ[οπόλη]ι διαι.......15.......
[.......27....... παρὰ] τόνδε τὸν νόμον, μαστιγούσθω ἕκα[στο]ς αὐτῶν ....15.......
.......31.......ιον ἀνατιθέναι τὰ ἀναθήματα χρυ[σᾶ] ἢ ἀργ[υ]ρᾶ ποη.......12.......
[.......23....... τοὺς δημο]σίους μίαμ μὲν δωρεὰν ὧν λαμβάν[ει πα]ρὰ τοῦ δήμου ἂν.......10.......
[.......28....... ἀνα]τιθέναι χρυσᾶ ἢ ἀργυρᾶ καὶ ἐὰν [τινε]ς ἄλλοι λάβωσι π[αρὰ τοῦ δήμ]-
[ου ....26....... ἀργυ]ροῦν· τὸν δὲ νόμον τόνδε καὶ τ[ὸν πε]ρὶ τῆς ἐξετάσεως τῶ[ν ...6...]
[.......19....... ἐν στήληι λιθίν]ει καὶ στῆσαι ἐν ἀκροπόληι, ε[ἰς] δὲ τὴν ἀναγραφὴν μερί[σαι....]

0.04

['Επὶ Εὐαινέτου ἄρχοντος ἐπὶ τῆς 'Αντιοχίδος δεκά]της· Σκιροφορ[ιῶνος ἕκ[τηι ἱσταμένου· νομο[θετῶν ἕδρ]-
[α· τῶν προέδρων ἐπεψήφιζεν ....14....... Λυκοῦρ]γος Λυκόφρ[ονος Βου]τάδης εἶπεν· ὅπως ἂν ....8.......
[.......41....... αμ]φορῆς οἱ ἀ[ργυροῖ κα]ὶ τὰ κανᾶ καὶ τἄλλα ....8....
.......44....... εἰσὶ δια....9....ατοις μηδὲ καθ.......10.......
.......45....... θεωρία ....10.... κελεύους[ι ....12.......]
.......47.......ΝΑΠ.......15.......ΛΣΕ.......14.......
.......48.......ΙΑ.......32.......

Fr. C+E, F [I]

[_I]

.........22..........ΛΙ[..5..ΩΚΟ]Σ
.........22..........ΑΚ[._ΑΓΕΙΤΟ]Χ
.........21......... ἐπειδὴ δ'ἐκτοῦ ....32..............ΛΙ......15.......
[......15....... τὰ παρό]ντα τούτων τῶν χρη[μάτων ....24...........]ΕΚΑΝ.....13......
[........18........ πρ]οδεδανειcμένα εξα[..........26............ πο]μπέα ......14......
[....12..... Παναθήνα]ια τὰ μεγάλα μερίζεcθ[αι ....23............]λει ὅ[θ]εν δὲ ....10....
.........19........ λακτικὸν εἰc τὰ προδεδ[ανειcμένα ....16.......] ἐκ τῆc .ΙΟΙΙΠ...8....
[....13..... κόcμο]ν τὸν κανηφορικὸν ὅπωc ἄ[ν ....24..........]ον καὶ ταμιευ........
........17.......αι πεντήκοντα αἰγίδ[α]c κα[ὶ ....21......... τῶι Δι]ὶ τῶι Σωτηρ[ὶ] Ι:..5..
[......16........ π[έντε τοῦ ἐνιαυτοῦ ἑκάcτο[υ ....25...........]ο : καὶ τούτων του..4..
......15.......ων τοῦ Διὸc τοῦ Σωτῆροc πο[ήcαcθαι ....21.........]ι τοῦ ἐνιαυτοῦ ἑκάc[το]-
[υ.....13......]αι τοὺc αὐτοὺc μετὰ τῶν ἐπι[cτατῶν .....12..... ἐκ τῶν ἱερ]ῶν χρημάτων τοῖν θεοῖν .
....12......ι τῶι Διὶ τῶι Ὀλυμπίωι :: κόcμ[ον ....25...........] τοὺc μετὰ τῶν τοῦ [τε]μέ[ν]-
[ουc ..5.. μετ]ὰ τοῦ ταμίου τοῦ δήμου ἐκ τῶν ἱ[ερῶν χρημάτων ..4.. ποήcαcθαι δὲ] καὶ τῶ[ι] Διονύcωι κόcμου
[ἑκάcτου το]ῦ ἐνιαυτοῦ ἐν τῆι τετραετίαι ἐκ [τῶν ἱερῶν χρημάτων .....11.....]cαι τῆι Ἀθηνᾶι τῆι Ἰτωνῆ-
[ι τοὺc κόc]μουc ἐκ τῆc ἀπαρχῆc τῆc ἀπὸ τῶν τε[μενῶν ....23..........]ονια . τοῦτο τὸ τέλοc ἐμ
[..6... π]ο[ή]cαcθαι δὲ καὶ τῆι Ἀγαθῆι Τύχηι κ[όcμον τοὺ]c [ταμίαc τῶν ἱερῶν χρημάτ]ων τῆc Ἀγαθῆc Τύχηc με-
[τὰ τῶν ἐπι]cτατῶν τοῦ ἱεροῦ τῆc Ἀγαθῆc Τύχηc πο[ήcαc]θα[ι δὲ καὶ ....17.......]ουcι.ιδι καὶ το[ῖc]
[ἄλλοιc θε]οῖc καὶ τῶι Ἀμφιαράωι καὶ τῶ[ι] Ἀcκληπιῶ[ι] κεκ..........25...........οcου ἐπιγρά[ψαι]
[δὲ ἐπὶ τὸ κ]όcμον ἕκαcτον ὅτου ἂν ἦι τῶν θεῶν ἱερὸc καὶ τὸ cτ[..........24..........]ουτο ὑπὸ τοῦ [δήμ]-
[ου ..4..]ιο[ι]c τῶν θεῶν τὸ ἀργύριον [τ]ὸ ἐκ τοῦ δερματικοῦ γ[ιγνόμενον ....12......]π..τηc περὶ δὲ ..4.
...6.. τῶν ἱερῶν τῆc Ἀρτέμιδο[c τ]ῆc Βραυρωνίαc καὶ τῶι ....20..........λελ.ουc καὶ ἐπε[ρέcθ]-

[αι τὸν θ]εόν, εἰ λῶον καὶ ἄμεινον [τ]ῶι δήμωι τῶι Ἀθηναίων [ποηcαμένωι τοὺc κόcμουc ἱ]ε̣[ρ]ουc τῆι Ἀρτέ[μιδι]
[μείζου]c καὶ καλλίουc ἢ ἐῶντι ὥcπερ νῦν ἔχει· ἐπερέcθα[ι δὲ καὶ ....21..........]ΟΥΑΝΠΚΕ...4.
[.. τὰ κα]τ̣ὰ̣ μικρὰ [ἱ]cτάμενα καὶ ὅc̣α μὴ ἐμ παραδόcει ἐcτι̣[ν εἰ λῶον καὶ ἄμεινον τῶι ποηcαμέν]ωι τῶι δή̣[μωι τ]-
[ουc κό]c̣[μ]ο̣υc ἱεροὺc τῆι Δήμητρ[ι] καὶ τῆι Κόρηι μείζο[νας καὶ καλλίονας ἢ ἐῶντι ὥcπερ νῦν ἔ]χει· ἐ̣π̣ερ[έcθ]-
[αι δὲ καὶ π]ε̣ρ̣ὶ τῶν ἐν τοῖc ἄλλοι̣c ἱεροῖc τῶν κατὰ μι̣[κρὰ ἱcταμένων ....22.......... ἀ]ργυρι̣.-
....8...Ο̣.Τ̣ΟΙ..Ο̣Ν̣....8....τα κατὰ ταυτὰ τὸν Λ̣..................37...................κοcμ[ο]-
.....12.....Ο̣Υ̣[....11..... μ]ε[ί]ζουc καὶ κ[αλλίουc ἢ ἐῶντι ὥcπερ νῦν ἔχει· .....13..... ἐκ τ]ῶν ἱερ̣-
[ῶν χρημάτων ? ....22..........]ΣΙΩΙ̣...................46..........................
...............33...............Ο̣

Fr. D
...ιακι̣
...αντων
.χ̣θειc ἀπὸ
..ἄλλο τι ηδ
..αγει καὶ τη
ο]υ κόcμου cτεφα
.ι ὑπαρχόντων τ
.η̣ν ἑβδομήκοντ[α
..γράψαι τὸν
...αc ποῆ̣cαc[θαι
.. τὸ]ν̣ δὲ τὸν
..5.. ιντομη̣
. ὑπάρ]χ̣ειν δ[ὲ
..6.. θεο
...6...α̣ι

Otherwise, the restorations for Fr. C+E are Koe.'s; I assume other restorations in Fr. F are Ki's; exceptions are noted below.

Fr. A+B

When Ki. used Wilh.'s 82-letter line for the text of Fr. A+B, he allowed 9 letters for the tribe in prytany, in line 13. Since then, the tribe has been established as Antiochis, which requires 10 letters. Therefore, in the two lines which are restored to the end (10 and 13), the last letter must go on the next line, i.e.: in line 10, Ki. has δημο]-; in line 13, Ki. has εδρα]. I keep Ki's restoration of 'Επὶ Εὐαινέτου (also restored in #18, #19, and [20] [II^2 332, but now assigned to 353/2]); 'Επ' Εὐαινέτου is restored for #22 and the unpublished fragment, EM 13067 (recorded by Meritt, Ath. 80, and included with #22; Clement. 193, prefers ἐπ' for this decree).

6 ἀκρ[οπόλη]ι: Schwenk, cf. line 12. ἀκρ[οπόλε]ι Koe., Ki.

9 middle: there are only 3 spaces between the two fragments. I suggest that the EI of λαμβάν[ει occupy one stoichos.

11/12 possible restoration: τ[ῶν ἱερῶν χρημάτων ?] Tréheux.

13 tribe in prytany: Meritt, from unpublished inscription, Ath. 80.

13/14 νομο[θέτων: Foucart; the rest of the restoration is Schoell's (νομο[θέται Schoell).

16 alternate reading: fortasse εἰς ἴδια Koe.

Fr. C+E,F

Since the stoichedon order is off in Ki.'s text, some of the restorations must be changed to conform to the stone with Wilh.'s 82-letter line. In most cases, where there is difficulty, the same restorations can be kept with a few slight changes. The text and restorations are mine for lines 7-11, Fr. F, and other places where I have read more letters (see majuscule text).

20 mid πọ[ήσασ]θα[ι δὲ καὶ: Schwenk. ιο..4..οφ Koe., Ki.
end: The new readings of omicron in st. 68 and delta

in st. 74 rule out Ki's 'Ελε]υσι[ν]ίωι.; although delta could be alpha (st. 74), the omicron still rules out Petropoulou's ['Ε]λευσινίαι (61 note 73).

22 mid: καὶ τὸ στ[Koe. καὶ τὸς τ[αμίας Ki. Perhaps Ki. made this restoration to provide an example on the stone of τὸς for τοὺς which he restored in line 25; this is no longer necessary (see below).

24/26 restoration: in a letter to Koe. (II.5 page 296), Foucart suggested for these lines: ἐπερέσθαι τὸν θε]ὸν εἰ λῷον καὶ ἄμεινον [τ]ῶι δήμωι τῶι 'Αθηναίων [--- μείζου]ς καὶ καλλίους <ἢ> ἐῶντι ὥσπερ νῦν ἔχει· ἐπερέσθα[ι Ki. attributes lines 25/26 to Foucart with no mention of the differences between Foucart's restoration and the text of II² 333: at the end of line 24, Ki. has ἐπερέσσ?] at the beginning of line 26, Ki. has μείζονα]ς. I assume that these changes, as well as the use of τὸς for τοὺς (middle of line 25), attributed to Wilh. by Ki., were made in order to conform to the stoichedon order. The correct order, however allows for Foucart's original restoration which is more acceptable: ἐπερέσθα[ι is on the stone, line 26--with only one sigma; the suffix for μείζους is more consistent with the use of καλλίους and is the more common form for these comparatives in this period (see Meisterhans, 151 no. 17; my restoration, line 31; but see also, line 28); τὸς for τοὺς is found nowhere on the stone and only in Ki.'s restoration, line 22, which I reject.

26 end: when Woodward offered the new restoration for line 27, beg., he also conjectured [τάδε παρέλαβον οἱ ταμίαι χρυσᾶ] to indicate the sense of his restoration. The letters preserved at the end of line 26, however make this conjecture impossible (as indeed do the letters printed by Ki.).

27 beg: Woodward. ...7... Koe., Ki.
mid: τῶι Schwenk. ἐστ[ίν, εἰ λῶιον καὶ ἄμεινον ποιησαμένωι Ki., with λῶιον noted as an exception. λῷον, the usual form does occur on the stone, line 25; the added iota in ποιησαμένωι occurs nowhere on the stone nor elsewhere in restoration. With the extra letter space from the error in the stoichedon order, and the removal of the two iotas, τῶι can be included in the restoration.

28 beg: [τοὺς κό]σ[μ]ους Ki. In the text of II² 333 there are 9 letter spaces between the last letter on the

stone in line 27 and the first letter in line 28. There are, in fact, only 8 letter spaces. I suggest crowding of the omega and iota at the end of line 27: δ[ήμωι τ]-. See also my restoration, Fr. A+B, line 9 middle.

mid: [- καλλίονας -] Schwenk. [- καλλίους -] Ki. To fit the corrected stoichedon order, Ki.'s longer version of the comparative, μεί<u>ζονος</u>, must be retained, and the extra letter space allows its companion to be restored with the same suffix: καλλ<u>ίονος</u>.

end: ἐπερ[έσσ] Ki. Again, the correct stoichedon order allows for the usual spelling of this verb.

29 mid: Woodward. κατὰ μ[ικρὸν παραδιδομένων Koe.; κατὰ μ[έρος Ki. My reading of dotted iota, st. 41, substantiates Woodward's restoration.

30 mid: Schwenk, from new readings.

31 mid: Schwenk, cf. line 26.

31/32: restoration: Schwenk. cf. lines 16, 17.

Fr. D+G

Woodward restored the end of line 10. Other additions to the reading of Fr.D are a result of its join to the new fragment, G.

"When chosen by the Demos, [Lykourgos] brought together large sums of money on the Akropolis, providing adornment for the Goddess, solid gold Nikai (Victories), processional vessels of both gold and silver, and gold ornaments for one hundred <u>kanephoroi</u> (basket carriers)." This passage from the third decree included at the end of Pseudo-Plutarch, <u>Lives of the Ten Orators</u> 852b, has been associated with Lykourgos's law concerning religious affairs ever since Koehler published and added Fr. C. Pseudo-Plutarch tells <u>what</u> Lykourgos did, this law shows in part <u>how</u> he did it, i.e., by paying careful attention to small details and making sure, by means of a law, that the sacred monies (anything, such as votives, dedicated to a God) are accounted for and used correctly. Thus, the character of Lykourgos's program, implied already in #17, where Lewis sees the concept of alloting special funds for specific purposes as an innovation, is manifest in this more general legislation.

Much has been written about this inscription, but no one has gone into what it actually says. The reason is that so much of the text is lost that it can not be made to yield much coherent information. Here follows an account, however disjointed, of what the text includes and what it seems to deal with.

The text of Fr. A+B is very sketchy and, if we assume the same 82-letter line as in Fr. C+E,F, there is no way of knowing whether what is left of one line has any connection with the preceding or succeeding line. One notes: a procession, something connected with the Demos, somethings brought and received, a fine for violating the law; minor officials (probably public slaves) on the Akropolis, flogging for law violators; setting up dedications of gold or silver and a gift someone received from the Demos. Line 10 mentions the setting up of gold or silver [dedications] and makes some provisions in case any others receive similar [gold or] silver [gifts] from the Demos. This decree ends by prescribing that both the following law and the one concerned with <u>exetasis</u> (examination) [of certain things, perhaps sacrifices or dedications or perhaps the sacred monies], should be [inscribed] on a stone stele and set up on the Akropolis and that the [tamias of the Demos?] should appropriate funds for the engraving. The following restoration of lines 10 end-11 beg. is one stoichos too long, but would not be if the eta and iota of στῄληι are crowded into one stoichos (see line 22, Fr. C+E); it is given exempli gratia: τῶ̣[ν ἱερῶν ἀ/ναγράψαι τὸν γραμματέα ἐν στήληι λιθίν]ει κτλ. Tréheux (comm. lines 11/12) suggests that the inclusion of the law concerning the exetasis is the reason for "formal peculiarities" found in Lykourgan inventories.

After the vacat, what is definitely a law--νομο-[θετῶν ἕδρ/α--begins with the usual prescript for a decree (minus name of secretary and day in prytany): when Euainetos was archon, when the tribe Antiochis held the 10th prytany, the 6th day of Skirophorion; the nomothetai were in session (note that this is <u>not</u> the beginning of the year; see discussion of nomothesia in #3 and #6); the name of the chairman of the proedroi is lost, but Lykourgos, son of Lykophron, of the deme Boutadai, was the proposer. The date of this inscription was established by Koehler: he reasoned that since 334/3 is the year in which the reorganization of the sacred monies began to show up in the inventories (II^2 1496), the law initiating the reorganization must precede the inventories; he decided 335/4 would be most appropriate, perhaps because of Lykourgos's reputation for getting things done quickly. From the rest of Fr. A+B only a reference to silver amphoras, baskets and other [processional] vessels (πομπ-ε<ῖ>α ?--the iota is omitted on the stone, line 2, Fr. A+B; line 7, Fr. F) can be gleaned.

There is no way to be sure where Fr. C+E,F should be placed. It could be the continuation of the law proposed by Lykourgos; or it could be the law concerned with the exetasis, the publication of which was ordered in Fr. A+B. In any case, this fragment does deal with more specific details and so provides still another example of a law combined with detailed specifications on the same stele; this weighs against Lewis's opinion that such a combination is "unusual" (see discussions, #3 and #17).

At the beginning of Fr. C+E,F we find a sum of money or perhaps a surplus (if [τα περιό]ντα is read for Ki.'s παρό?]ντα) from some fund or other which may have been appropriated ahead of time for some religious purpose, perhaps for a procession suggested by the restoration at the end of line 7. This may be connected with the appropriations for the Greater Panathenaia which appears in line 8. "Money let out ahead of time" is mentioned twice (lines 7 and 9), then, in line 10, the kanephoric ornamentation, followed by a purpose clause.

Lines 11-33 deal with specific Gods and Goddesses. Zeus the Saviour is treated first, lines 11-14. Connected with him are 50 goatskins; [he is also to receive at least] five of something each year. Line 13 records something to be made [and dedicated?] each year; then a Board is to take some action in company with the <u>epistatai</u> (overseers) with regard to the sacred monies of the Two Gods (perhaps Goddesses). If καὶ ποήσασθα]ι (vel sim.) is restored at the beginning of line 15, we have an ornament (or better, ornaments, if we restore κόσμ̣[ους and assume the 2 double interpuncts were painted over with a numeral) made for Olympian Zeus by a Board in cooperation with men [in charge of] the precinct and the Treasurer of the Demos out of the sacred monies; in line 16 there is an ornament for Dionysos also from sacred monies but designated "each 12-month period in the 3-year period;" there follow ornaments for Itonian Athena, paid for by the first fruits from (the rent of) her precincts; lines 19/20 provide that the Treasurers of the sacred monies of the goddess Good Fortune along with the overseers of her sanctuary have some ornament made for her;

then some other [Board should do the same?] for the other gods and for Amphiaraos and Asklepios (Petropoulou, 61, notes that Amphiaraos is in Oropos, not at some hypothetical location in Athens); lines 21/22 order someone to inscribe on each ornament and (each garment, if one reads τὸ στ̣[όλισμα ἕκαστον ? --]) the name of the god to whom it belongs; line 23 mentions the money generated from the hides (of the sacrificial victims) and 24, the sanctuaries of Brauronian Artemis; then "the god" (probably Apollo) is to be asked whether it would be more profitable and better for the Demos of the Athenians to make the ornaments sacred to Artemis (line 25) bigger and better or leave them just as they are; to ask further about the small objects and all that are not included in the *paradosis* (the annual handing over of accounts), whether it would be more profitable and better for the Demos to have ornaments sacred to Demeter and Kore (line 28) made from these, bigger and better or to leave them just as they are; and finally to ask about the small objects in the other sanctuaries and again the question (line 31) whether things should be made bigger and better or left as they are.

The melting down of gold objects is recorded in II^2 1596 B 200ff., and Woodward (106) suggests that our lines 27-29 refer to the same activity. Linders (56) notes that ὅσα μὴ ἐμ παραδόσει ἐστιν line 27) must refer to objects which had been kept apart by the temple staff and so were not included in the formal paradosis; she also suggests that these objects were probably defective (or perhaps damaged). The melting down of many small and defective dedications would have provided precious metal for making one new and larger adornment for the Goddess.

If the bulk of the votive offerings to Artemis Brauronia were kept in Brauron, as Linders (73) argues, then the objects to be melted down could be said to have been "brought together on the Akropolis" (Ps.-Plutarch). The two sets of officials required in each case in which payment comes ἐκ τῶν ἱερῶν χρημάτων would be one way to assure that appropriations go where they are intended, and any money coming in, such as from the sale of hides (line 23), is also carefully watched. Fr. D+G is so small that it gives no information. As in the case of Fr. C+E,F, its placement is not certain.

I have discussed Lykourgos's general program above (see especially #15). All of the decrees and laws treated in this Corpus reflect that program in some way. This law, however, moved by Lykourgos himself, is perhaps the epitome of his overall program in that it touches upon and brings together the religious, patriotic, financial and military aspects of it. The religious aspect is, of course, the attention paid to Athens' tutelary dieties, who protect Athens and her citizens and govern all phases of public and private life and whose worship and festivals bind the Athenians not only to the gods but to the state and to one another. By restoring sanctuaries and providing for regular and impressive festivals in honor of the gods, Lykourgos hoped not only to gain the favor of Heaven and revive faith but also to enhance the other aspects of his program.

The economic aspect is also important. Through the consolidation and reorganization of dedications and the careful husbanding of the Gods' income not only were the sanctuaries and festivals given a sound funding independent of the secular fiscus, but at the same time Athens acquired a sounder economic base just as she had in the times of Perikles; although no mention of it survives on the stone, there was very likely a provision for the restoration of the Golden Nikai which had given their gold "for the cause" in the last days of the Peloponnesian War (cf. Mitchel TAPA 93[1962] 214). This leads directly into the military aspect which rests on the economic--just as Perikles' gold and ivory Athena Parthenos and the Golden Nikai were not only religious dedications but were also to be used in case of emergency, so the large sums of money and the gold and silver objects, which Lykourgos's law caused to be housed on the Akropolis and preserved in other sanctuaries, constituted a reserve which could be used in the event of war. Another connection, of course, between the military and religious aspects is the religious indoctrination of the ephebes who, as they assumed their first civic obligations, swore the Ephebic Oath in the sanctuary of the goddess Aglauros and were taken around to the sanctuaries of the other gods and spent at least part of their time in training in participating in the religious festivals as an elite corps.

335/4

22. *DECREE* EM 7411

editors: Velsen in IG II 342; IG II^2 331.

supplement: SEG 21.270 (Pritchett-Neugebauer, Meritt).

other bibliography: Pritchett-Neugebauer Cal. 44-45; Meritt Ath. 81; Henry Prescripts 37 n. 23.

description: This fragment of Pentelic marble was found on the Akropolis. Kirchner's restoration assumes that the stone was broken on all sides; Meritt's restoration presumes that the right side is original. Examination of the stone as well as the crowding of the omicron at the end of line 2, which suggest that the stone cutter had reached the right edge too quickly, supports Meritt's view. A stoichedon order is not maintained on this stone.

dimensions:	letters: 0.007 m. Smallest, O X, are .006; largest, P, Σ, are .009.
H 0.145 m.	
W 0.065 m.	
Th 0.09 m.	

minuscule text:

non stoich.

[Ἐπ' Εὐαινέτου ἄρχοντος ἐπὶ τῆς Ἀντιο]χίδος
[δεκάτης πρυτανείας ἧι Πρόξενος Πυ]λαγόρο
[Ἀχερδούσιος ἐγραμμάτευεν· ἕνηι] καὶ νέα[ι,]
[πέμπτηι καὶ τριακοστῆι τῆς πρυταν]είας·
[ἐκκλησία· τῶν προέδρων ἐπεψήφιζεν ——]χ̣ος vacat
- ΛΗ
- - - - - - - - - - - - - - - - - - - Φ
- - - - - - - - - - - - - - - - - - - Ρ

commentary: The text is based on Meritt's opinion that the right side is original. Koehler restored only the tribe in prytany, Antiochis, line 1, and the day of the month, last, 29th, line 3 (this presumes a hollow month); Kirchner then restored the rest of the date on the basis of this decree being passed on the same day as #18 (II^2 330+445): the 17th day of the third prytany, 29th day of the month (the name of the month is omitted here as in #18; for Kichner's date, it would be Boedromion).

A new inscription, EM 13067, to be published in its entirety by Stamires, however, shows that Kirchner's date is impossible. I include on the following page Meritt's publication (Ath. 80; SEG 21.272) of the dating formula of EM 13067.

This decree shows that the tribe Antiochis held the 10th prytany rather than the third. Therefore the restoration is Kirchner's with Meritt's change from 3rd to 10th prytany (to conform to the new inscription) and the subsequent change in the date in the prytany. The day of the month remains the same, the last, but the month must be full so that the date will be the 30th (the name of the month is still omitted; in this case it would be Skirophorion; Henry notes that this omission is "particularly characteristic in the case of the last day of the month").

EM 13067

[Θ] ε ο [ί]
[Ἐπ' Εὐαιν]έτου ἄρχοντος ἐπὶ [τῆϲ]
[Ἀντι]οχίδοϲ δεκάτηϲ πρυτα[νεί]-
[αϲ ἧι] Πρόξενοϲ Πυλαγόρου [Ἀχερ]-
δοῦϲ]ιοϲ ἐγραμμάτευεν· Σ[κιροφ]-
[ορι]ῶνοϲ ὀγδόηι ἐπὶ δέκα, [τ]ρ̣[ίτη]-
[ι κ]αὶ εἰκοϲτῆι τῆϲ πρυταν[είαϲ·]
κτλ.

I agree with Meritt's omission of the final upsilon restored by Kirchner at the end of line 2; the omission is based on the assumption that the right-hand edge is worn, but original (see description above) and thus that there was no room for another letter. I have also added the letters in lines 7 and 8, which are on the stone (and can be seen on the photograph) but have not been included in either of the two previous publications. The non-stoichedon arrangement is unusual for this period, there are only 9 of these decrees in this Corpus (see #16).

Again an inscription which tells us nothing but the date; that, at least, is fairly secure. The name of the secretary of the Boule for 335/4 is partially on the stone and fits easily into the restoration. The dating formula has most of the usual elements; only the name of the month is omitted. Meritt's restoration of the 35th day in the prytany assigns the assembly which passed this decree to the very last day of the year of Euainetos.

V. THE YEAR OF KTESIKLES, 334/3

23. *DEMADES PROPOSES A DECREE* EM 7152, 12773

photo: Fr. A Hesperia 9(1940) 339.
Fr. B Hesperia 4(1935) 170.

editors: Fr. A Koehler IG II 5.163b; IG II^2 335; Schweigert Hesperia 9(1940) 339-340; Oikonomides ΠΛΑΤΩΝ 8(1956) 115 no. 6.
Fr. B Broneer Hesperia 4(1935) 169-170 no. 32.
Fr. A+B When he republished Fr. A, Schweigert associated the two fragments, but did not republish Fr. B.

supplements: SEG 21.274 (Broneer, Schweigert, Pritchett-Neugebauer, Oikonomides, Meritt).
Bull. (1944) no. 65 (Schweigert; also for #24, #25).

other bibliography: Leonardos ΑΔ 1(1915) 211 (noted by Kirchner in Addenda to II^2 335); Pritchett-Neugebauer Cal. 46; Meritt Ath. 83.

description: The fragments are Pentelic marble. For Fr. A, Koehler just noted excripsi in arce; Fr. B was found in the eastern part of the north slope of the Akropolis. The locations indicate that the stele was originally set up on the Akropolis. There are no preserved sides on either fragment.

dimensions:
Fr. A
H 0.235 m.
W 0.18 m.
Th 0.11 m.
Fr. B
H 0.08 m.
W 0.05 m.
Th 0.06 m.

letters: 0.009 m. Smallest, Ω, is .007; largest, A, E, H, K, Σ, T, Y, are .010. Schweigert has noted the similarity between the letter forms of this decree and those of #24 and #25.

minuscule text: next page.

stoich. 21

Fr. A [θε]οῖ

[Ἐ]π̣ὶ Κτηϲικ[λέουϲ ἄρχοντο]-

[ϲ] ἐπὶ τῆϲ Ἀκα̣[μαντίδοϲ ἐνά]-

[τ]ηϲ πρυτανε[ίαϲ ἧι Μνηϲίφ]-

[ι]λοϲ Μνήϲ[ω]ν[οϲ Φαληρεὺϲ ἐ]-

[γ]ραμμάτευε[ν· Μουνιχιῶνο]-

[ϲ] ἕκτηι μετ' [εἰκάδαϲ· ἐκκλη]-

[ϲ]ία· τῶν πρ[οέδρων ἐπεψήφι]-

[ζ]ε̣ν Δημο[κρ...ϲ Παιανιεύ]-

ϲ· ἔ]δοξεν̣ [τῶι δήμωι· Δημάδη]-

[ϲ Δ]η̣μ̣έο̣[υ Παιανιεὺϲ εἶπεν].

Fr. B - - - - - - - - Α̣Ν - - - - - - - -

- - - - - - - - ΦΙΑ̣ - - - - - - - -

- - - - - - - - ΚΑ̣ - - - - - - - -

- - - - - - - Ι̣Π - - - - - - - -

commentary: The text for Fr. A is based on Schweigert's restorations. The dots in line 10 st. 7 and line 11 st. 6 are mine. The rest are Schweigert's; they result from his new readings: line 1 st. 3, 4; line 2 st. 10; line 9 st. 2; line 10 st. 7 (he did not dot this letter); line 11 st. 3, 4, 6 (Koehler read only the epsilon, st. 5; Kirchner read epsilon in st. 4). Oikonomides agrees with Schweigert's new readings in line 2 (but does not dot the alpha) and line 11 (but he dots the omicron, as I do); otherwise his readings are the same as Koehler's and Kirchner's. Schweigert's addition of ΘΕ]ΟΙ, based on the certain reading of omicron iota on the stone, makes eleven lines of text rather than the ten in II^2 335.

Restorations and the stoichedon order of 21 letters to the line were made by Koehler. Schweigert has added Leonardos's restoration for lines 10 and 11. Schweigert was able to date #24 and #25 to the same day as this decree on the basis of the chairman of the proedroi; the restoration in lines 9/10 is a composite of the name from all three decrees. Meritt is responsible for providing the number of the prytany (lines 3/4) and the month (lines 6/7), used by Schweigert for his text. I have used Broneer's text (the only one) for Fr. B.

3/4 number of prytany: Mer. τρί/τ]ηc Koe., Ki.

5 demotic: Schw. Koe., Ki., left blanks.

6/7 month: Mer. [Βοηδρομιῶνο]/c Koe., Ki. Since Mounichion is one letter shorter than Boedromion, Schweigert was able to add the nu-movable to ἐγραμμάτευεν.

9 chairman of the proedroi: Schw. Δημο[σθένηc Παινιεύ/c Leonardos.

Besides the usual dating formula, the only information this fragment provides is that the name of the proposer was Demades. (See #4, #5, #7, #8, and the next decree, #24 [II^2 405], #51 [II^2 353], #87 [II^2 372], all moved by Demades.) As I have noted in the commentary, Schweigert's identification of the chairman of the proedroi is identical for this decree, #24, and #25 (II^2 414a). It is the present decree, with ἐ]πὶ Κτησικ[λέουc, which allowed Schweigert to date #24 and #25 to this year, 334/3.

I list only three inscriptions under the year 334/3. The impression, however, that this was a lean year for epigraphists is incorrect. One stele, #31 (II^2 336), was probably set up in 333/2, but it includes a decree of 334/3. The other epigraphical documents for this year take forms other than decrees: II^2 1493, 1494, 1495, an accounting by the Treasurers of Athena and other officials, is an obvious result of the law for reform, #21, moved by Lykourgos the year before. Fordyce Mitchel confirms the restoration of Demades of Paiania as the Military Treasurer, lines 12, 16, of II^2 1493 (<u>TAPA</u> 93[1962]

219 and corrigenda, AJA 70[1966] 66); 334/3 was another busy year for Demades. II^2 1750 is a prytany list; it records the fifty men who were bouletai from the tribe Antiochis for this year. And Hesperia 29(1960) 39-40 no. 49, is a choregic dedication.

Perhaps most noteworthy is that the year of Ktesiphon marks the beginning of the long tradition of dedications and honorary decrees connected with the Athenian ephebeia. In addition to the two long-known dedications of this year (II^2 1156 and 1189) Mitchel has added II^2 2970, formerly dated to 315/14 (Hesperia 33[1964] 349-351) and AE (1965) 134-136, an honorary tribal decree formerly dated to 361/60 (ZPE 19 [1975] 233-243).

334/3

24. *DEMADES PROPOSES CITIZENSHIP FOR AMYNTOR* EM 7190

editors: Lolling in Kirchhoff's "Inscriften von der Akropolis" Sitz. Ak. Berlin (1887) 1068 no. 7 (majuscule text); Wilhelm Hermes 24 (1889) 144; IG II 5.193b; IG II^2 405; Schweigert Hesperia 9(1940) 340 (new lines 1-10); Oikonomides ΠΛΑΤΩΝ 8(1956) 116 no. 9 (although Oikonomides used Schweigert's restorations for #23, his text for this decree is the same as II^2 405).

supplement: SEG 21.275 (Schweigert, Oikonomides, Meritt).

other bibliography: Pritchett-Neugebauer Cal. 46 n. 22; Meritt Ath. 83; Osborne BSA 66(1971) 305-306 n. 56; BSA 67(1972) 130 n. 4, 132-3, 136, 150 n. 84, 156; Vestigia 17(1973) 434.

description: The fragment is Pentelic marble; it was found on the Akropolis. Only the right side is preserved.

dimensions:
H 0.36 m.
W 0.245 m.
Th 0.118 m.

letters: 0.010 m. Smallest, T, Ω, are .008; largest, Φ, is .013

minuscule text:

stoich. 19

[Ἐπὶ Κτηϲικλέουϲ ἄρχον]-
[τοϲ ἐπὶ τῆϲ Ἀκαμαντίδο]-
[ϲ ἐνάτηϲ πρυτανείαϲ ἧι]
[Μνηϲίφιλοϲ Μνήϲωνοϲ Φ]-
[αληρεὺϲ ἐγραμμάτευεν·]
[Μουνιχιῶνο]ϲ̣̲ ἕ̣̲[κτ]η̣[ι μετ']
[εἰκάδαϲ· ἐ]κ̣κλ[ηϲ]ία· τῶ[ν π]-
[ροέδρων ἐ]πεψήφ̣ιζεν Δ[η]-
[μοκρ...ϲ Π]αια[ν]ιεὺϲ· ἔδ̲-
[οξεν τῶι δήμ]ωι· Δημάδηϲ
[Δημέου Πα]ι[α]ν̲ιεὺϲ εἶπε-
[ν· ἐπαινέϲαι] Ἀμύντορα, [ἐ]-
[πειδὴ εὔνοι]αν ἐνδείκν̣-
[υται περὶ Ἀθ]ηναί̣ουϲ, εἶ̲-
[ναι δ' Ἀμύντορ]α Δ[ημ]η̣τ̣ρίο-
[υ Ἀθηναῖον α]ὐτὸν καὶ ἐκ-
[γόνουϲ αὐτο]ῦ καὶ εἶναι
[αὐτῶι γράψα]ϲθαι φυλῆϲ
[καὶ δήμου κα]ὶ φρατρίαϲ
[ἧϲ ἂν βούλητ]αι, ὧν οἱ νόμ̣-
[οι λέγουϲιν·] τὸν δὲ γ[ραμ]-
[ματέα - - - - - -]

commentary: The text is a composite of II^2 405 and Schweigert's six new lines. The dotted letters of line 6 are new readings by Schweigert; Wilhelm saw one vertical stroke of the eta in st. 15, which neither Koehler nor Kirchner recorded. All other dots and the underlinings are mine. I read two letters previously in brackets: line 11 st. 9; line 13 st. 19.

14 περί: Koe. πρὸς Wilh.

This decree records a grant of citizenship proposed by Demades and awarded to Amyntor, son of Demetrios, and his descendants. Amyntor is to be enrolled in whichever tribe, deme, and phratry he chooses, but according to the laws (see #3 for the introduction of this new restriction and discussion of Osborne's recent scholarship). This honor is granted because Amyntor had shown eunoia (good will) to the Athenians. Amyntor's nationality and what he did for the Athenians is lost. The appearance of Demades as proposer does not require that Amyntor be Macedonian or have Macedonian connections; Demades' career was less stereotyped than most previous scholars have assumed; cf. Mitchel TAPA 93(1962) 213-229; also #51 (II^2 353).

This decree, #23 (also moved by Demades), and #25 (II^2 414a) were all enacted on the same day, according to Schweigert. All three decrees are missing the day within the prytany, so that a calendar equation can not be determined (see Meritt, 83; Pritchett-Neugebauer, 46, record "ca. 290th day" for #23).

334/3

25. *LYKOURGOS PROPOSES HONORS FOR DIOTIMOS*

EM 7177

photo: Hesperia 9(1940) 341.

editors: Koehler IG II Add. 180b; IG II^2 414a (as the first fragment of II^2 414, composed of 4 fragments); Schweigert Hesperia 9(1940) 340-341. In publishing #85 Schweigert (Hesperia 9[1940] no. 42) used Fr. B and Fr. C of II^2 414 and joined Fr. D to II^2 285, so that Fr. A, the present decree, now stands alone.

testimonia: [Plutarch] Lives of the Ten Orators 844a; IG II^2 1623 lines 276-308.

supplement: SEG 21.276 (Schweigert, Mitchel, Meritt).

other bibliography: Pritchett-Neugebauer Cal. 46 n. 22; Meritt Ath. 83; Mitchel TAPA 93(1962) 213-229; Lyk. 194 n. 122.

description: The fragment is Pentelic marble; it was found between the theater of Dionysos and the Odeion of Herodes Atticus. Only the left side of the fragment is preserved.

dimensions:	letters: 0.007 m. Smallest,
H 0.13 m.	O, Ω, are .006; largest, P,
W 0.107 m.	Σ, Y, are .009.
Th 0.076 m.	

minuscule text:

stoich. 21

[Ἐπὶ Κτηcικλέουc ἄρχοντο]-
[c ἐπὶ τῆc Ἀκαμαντίδοc ἐνά]-
[τηc πρυτανείαc ἧι Μνηcίφ]-
[ιλοc Μνήcωνοc Φαλη: ἐγραμ]-
[μάτευεν· Μουνιχιῶνοc ἕκτ]-
[ηι μετ' εἰκάδαc· ἐκκληcία· τ]-
[ῶν προέδρων ἐπεψήφιζεν Δ]-
ημοκ[ρ...c Παιανιεὺc· ἔδο]-
ξεν τῶ[ι δήμωι· Λυκοῦργοc Λ]-
υκόφρο[νοc Βουτάδηc εἶπε]-
ν· περὶ ὧ[ν Διότιμοc ὁ cτρατ]-
ηγὸc λέ[γει· ἐπειδὴ ἀποφαί]-
νει κρ̣[.......13....... γέγ]-
ονεν.........17.........
αι.........19.........

commentary: Lines 1-6 are Schweigert's new restorations based on #23. Schweigert also restored: the demotic of the secretary, line 8; the name of the general, line 11; end of lines 12 and 13. Lines 8-15 (1-9 in II^2 414a) are

Koehler's restoration with the exception of Schweigert's changes. The rho, line 13 st. 5, is dotted by all three editors. I leave the nu, line 14 st. 4, undotted as Koehler does; Kirchner omitted it; Schweigert dotted it.

7 restoration: Ki.(?) This line appears in Ki.'s text, but it is not numbered; it does not appear in Koe.'s text.

7/8 proedros: Schw. Δ/ημοκ[ρᾶτης Ki.

The testimonia furnish the key to Schweigert's new restorations. Ps-Plutarch notes that Lykourgos proposed a decree to honor Diotimos in 334/3; II^2 1623, a naval list of 334/3 records a decree proposed by Lykourgos (lines 276-285) in 335/4, which provided that the general, Diotimos, be sent with two swift ships against the pirates. This information supports Schweigert's restoration of both the date and the general, Diotimos. Schweigert (341) proposes that the present decree is the one described by Ps-Plutarch, that it was the direct result of the decree moved by Lykourgos the previous year, and that Diotimos was honored because he brought the naval expedition to a "successful conclusion." The policy of keeping the seas safe from pirates is very much in keeping with Lykourgos's program (cf. Mitchel Lyk.) and implies that this service was recognized by Philip and the Hellenic League as part of Athens's responsibility.

334/3

26. *DECREE FROM CHOLARGOS CONCERNING THE THESMOPHORIA* Paris, Louvre MND 957

photo: Michon Mém. acad. des inscr. 13(1913) Plate 13.

editors: Michon Mém. acad. des inscr. 13(1913) 1-24; IG II^2 1184.

supplement: Bull. (1942) 32 (Wilhelm).

testimonia: Isaios III.80; VIII.19,20.

other bibliography: Wilhelm Att. Urk. V 156-157.

description: The inscription is in Paris; I have not seen it. Michon notes only that: the inscription came from Athens; it is marble; only the bottom part of the stele remains. From the photograph, it would seem that both sides and the bottom are original; nothing is said of the condition of the back. Dimensions are Michon's.

dimensions:
H 0.50 m.
W 0.255 m.
Th 0.04 to 0.06 m.

letters: Michon does not include letter height; Ki. only notes that letters correspond to middle of 4th century. The photo shows that the letters vary in size and are poorly cut.

minuscule text: next page.

commentary: The text is based on Kirchner's. He read three letters bracketed by Michon: A - last letter, line 9; I - last letter, line 18; Λ - 4th letter, line 25. The text is well-preserved; the few supplements are Michon's. For line 4, he notes that the use of the genitive τῆϲ ἱερείαϲ instead of the dative, τῆι ἱερείαι, must be stone cutter's error.

This inscription records the end of a decree which dealt with the organization of the festival, the Thesmophoria (presumably on the local level; see Michon, 5-6, 20) for the deme Cholargos. Even without lines 1 and 2, which indicate the end of a previous section, there are indications in the extant text that there was more information above: in lines 23/4, the publication of the decree is to be carried out by τοὺϲ ἐπὶ Κτηϲικλέουϲ ἄρχοντοϲ--the officials in question were probably mentioned above (Kirchner suggests τοὺϲ ταμίαϲ). Even though prescripts for deme decrees are more abbreviated than for decrees of the Boule and Demos, there is usually some sort of preamble at the beginning of the text (cf. #42, ΑΔ 25[1970] 204-214; #47, Hesperia 31[1962] no. 3).

non stoich.

\- - - - - - - - τοὺϲ ἱε[ρ]-
[ο]μνήμοναϲ.
τὰϲ δὲ ἀρχούϲαϲ κοινεῖ ἀμφοτ-
έραϲ διδόναι τῆϲ ἱερείαϲ εἰϲ
τὴν ἑορτὴν καὶ τὴν ἐπιμέλεια-
ν τῶν Θεϲμοφορίων ἡμιεκτεῖον
κριθῶν, ἡμιεκτεῖον πυρῶν, ἡμι-
εκτέον ἀλφίτων, ἡμιεκτέον ἀλ-
[ε]ύρων, ἰϲχάδων ἡμιεκτέον, χοᾶ̣
οἴνου, ἡμίχουν ἐλαίου, δύο κοτ-
ύλαϲ μέλιτοϲ, ϲηϲάμων λευκῶν χοί-
νικα, μελάνων χοίνικα, [μ]ήκωνοϲ
χοίνικα, τυροῦ δύο τροφαλίδαϲ μὴ
ἔλαττον ἢ ϲτατηρια[ί]αν ἑκατέραν
καὶ ϲκόρδων δύο ϲτατῆραϲ καὶ δᾶιδ-
[α] μὴ ἐλάττονοϲ ἢ δυεῖν ὀβολοῖν καὶ
ἀργυρίου ⊦⊦⊦⊦ δραχμάϲ· ταῦτα δὲ δι-
δόναι τὰϲ ἀρχούϲαϲ· ὅπωϲ δ'ἂν γί[[γι]]-
γνηται ὑπὲρ τοῦ δήμου τοῦ Χολαργέω-
ν κατὰ τὰ γράμματα εἰϲϲτὸν ἅπα-
ντα χρόνον, ϲτῆϲαι ϲτήλην καὶ ἀν[α]-
γράψαι τόδε τὸ ψήφιϲμα ἐν ϲτήλε[ι]
λιθίνει ἐν τῶι Πυθίωι τοὺϲ ἐπὶ Κτηϲι-
[κ]λέ[ο]υϲ ἄρχοντοϲ· ὅ τι δ'ἂν ἀναλῶϲ-
ωϲι λ[ογ]ίϲαϲθαι Χολαργεῦϲιν.

vacat

The part which remains deals with the responsibilities of the archousai, the two women chosen to preside over the festival. As Michon notes (4–6) Isaios shows that the honor of being chosen one of the archousai for the Thesmophoria brought with it a liturgy funded by the woman's husband. This decree indicates what that liturgy entailed.

Both archousai are bidden by the priestess (Michon, 5–6, identifies her as the priestess of Demeter at Eleusis) to provide for the festival and the organization of the Thesmophoria: a half-hecteus (1/6 of a medimna) each of barley, wheat, barley groats, wheat meal, and dried figs; then a chous (measure of capacity) of wine, a half-chous of olive oil; two kotyles (small vessal, 12 Kotyle = 1 chous) of honey; one choinix (dry measure) each, of white sesame seeds, black sesame seeds, and poppy seeds; two fresh cheeses, each no less than a stater; 2 staters of garlic; a torch no less than 2 obols; and in silver, four drachmai.

Michon goes into great detail about the various foods and how they might be used. One certain aspect is that this decree confirms that wine was consumed at the Thesmophoria. Michon (9) had noted that some scholars have thought that wine was prohibited due to the connection with Demeter. As to the measurements, he decided that for the cheese, a stater refers to monetary value, whereas for the garlic, it refers to weight (15). Kirchner's opinion, that both references in the text are to weight, seems more reasonable.

The decree ends with the instructions for publication: "in order that this decree of the deme Cholargos endure, the officials in charge during the archonship of

Ktesikles are to have a stele engraved with the text and set it up in the Pythion;" the expenses are to be covered by the citizens of Cholargos.

As Michon has noted, this decree sheds a bit more light on the workings of the Thesmophoria, even if it is on the local level. Of the decrees included in this Corpus, it is the only one which deals both with the local level and the actual responsibilities of participants in a festival, in this case, the archousai.

There are eight deme decrees dated to a specific year in the Lykourgan Era: this decree, #26; a decree from Eitea, #42 (ΑΔ 25[1970] 204-214); #43 (REG 91[1978] 289-306) from Eleusis; a decree found at Sounion, probably from the ancient deme, Sounion, #46 (II^2 1181); a decree from Teithras, #47 (Hesperia 31[1962] no. 3); a decree from Aixone, #66 (II^2 1198); a decree from Athmonon, #70 (II^2 1203); and a decree from the Peiraieus, #76 (II^2 1176). Only this decree and #46 are not cut in stoichedon order (but see #16 for a list of decrees which are non-stoichedon in this Corpus). All of the deme decrees, however, do seem to reflect in some way that they are deme publications and not the record of a decree of the Boule and Demos of Athens.

VI. THE YEAR OF NIKOKRATES, 333/2

27. *LYKOURGOS PROPOSES ENKTESIS FOR THE MERCHANTS OF KITION* EM 7173

editors: Foucart Des Assoc. Relig. 187-189 (majuscule text); IG II 168; IG II^2 337.

collections: Ditt. Syll.^{2} 551; Syll.^{3} 280; Michel 104; Prott-Ziehen II 30; Tod II 189; Sokolowski Lois 66-68.

supplements: SEG 24.98 (Ditt.^{3}, Tod, Pečírka); 25.67 (Urdahl, Sokolowski).

other bibliography: Koehler Hermes 5(1871) 351; Gilbert Neue Jahrb. (1879) 231; (1880) 535; Lenz Das Synedrion 46-50; Miller De decr. 30; Dow AJA 66(1962) 363; Pečírka Enktesis 59-61; Urdahl Symb. Oslo. 43(1968) 55; Rhodes Boule 59, 67-68, 73; DeLaix Proboul. 119-120; Mitchel Lyk. 194-195; Henry Prescripts 38 n. 28, 43.

description: The stele of Pentelic marble was found in the Peiraieus in 1870. A more specific find spot has never been recorded. With the exception of a chip off the upper left hand corner and a few smaller chips, the stele is complete.

dimensions:
H 1.075 m.
W 0.279 m. (above)
0.325 m. (below)
Th 0.09 m. (above)
0.10 m. (below)

letters: 0.007 m. Smallest, Ω, is .0045; largest, Φ, Ψ, are .010.

minuscule text: next page.

epigraphical commentary: Kirchner read all the letters as clear, I have dotted letters which are now unclear. The stoichedon order of 20 letters to the line is nowhere violated.

Since the stone is intact, there are no serious problems in reading. There are, however, as Foucart and

Tod have noted, discrepancies in spelling: ἐνποροι (line 33) and ἐμπόροις (line 39); Κιτιέων (line 40) and Κιτιεί-ων (line 21); τῆι βουλεῖ (lines 6/7, 19); ο for ου (line 31 st. 15); ει for ε (line 10 st. 2, 3, line 21 st. 5, 6, line 22 st. 1, 2); ει for ηι (line 3 st. 12, 13, line 7 st. 4, 5, line 19 st. 19, 20, line 25 st. 7, 8). Foucart suggested that the irregularities are not just engraver's errors, but indicate a still uncertain orthography. The likelihood that this stele was set up on private initiative (see below) may also account for the inconsistencies in spelling.

stoich. 20

[Θ] ε ο ί

Ἐπὶ Νικοκράτους ἄρχοντ-
ος ἐπὶ τῆς Α̣ἰγεῖδος πρώτ-
ης πρυτανείας· τῶν προέδ-
ρων ἐπεψ̣ήφιζεν Θεόφιλο-
ς Φηγούσιος· ἔδοξεν τῆι β-
ουλεῖ· Ἀ̣ντίδοτος Ἀπολλο-
δώρου Συπαλήττιος εἶπε-
ν· περὶ ὧ̣ν̣ λέγουσιν οἱ Κιτ-
ιεῖς περὶ τῆς ἱδρύσεως
τῆι Ἀφροδίτηι τοῦ ἱεροῦ,
ἐψηφίσθαι τε̣ῖ̣ βουλεῖ το-
ὺς προέδρου̣ς̣ οἳ ἂν λάχωσ-
ι προεδρεύειν εἰς τὴν πρ-
ώτην ἐκκλησίαν προσαγα-
γεῖν αὐτοὺς κα̣ὶ̣ χρηματί-
σαι, γνώμην δὲ ξυνβάλλεσ-
θαι τῆς βουλῆς εἰς τὸν δῆ-
μον ὅτι δοκεῖ τῆι βουλεῖ
ἀκούσαντα τὸν δῆμον τῶν
Κιτιείων περὶ τῆς ἱδρύσ-

ειωϲ τοῦ ἱεροῦ καὶ ἄλλου
Ἀθηναίων τοῦ βουλομένο-
υ βουλεύϲαϲθαι ὅτι ἂν αὐ-
τῶι δοκεῖ ἄριϲτον εἶναι.
Ἐπὶ Νικοκράτουϲ ἄρχοντ-
οϲ ἐπὶ τῆϲ Πανδιονίδοϲ δ-
ευτέραϲ πρυτανείαϲ· τῶν
προέδρων ἐπεψήφιζεν Φα-
νόϲτρατοϲ Φιλαίδηϲ· ἔδο-
ξεν τῶι δήμωι· Λυκοῦργοϲ Λ-
υκόφρονοϲ Βουτάδηϲ εἶπ-
εν· περὶ ὧν οἱ ἔνποροι οἱ Κ-
ιτιεῖϲ ἔδοξαν ἔννομα ἱκ-
ετεύειν αἰτοῦντεϲ τὸν δ-
ῆμον χωρίου ἔνκτηϲιν ἐν
ὧι ἱδρύϲονται ἱερὸν Ἀφρ-
οδίτηϲ, δεδόχθαι τῶι δήμ-
ωι δοῦναι τοῖϲ ἐμπόροιϲ
τῶν Κιτιέων ἔνκτηϲι[ν] χ[ω]-
ρίου ἐν ὧι ἱδρύϲονται τὸ
ἱερὸν τῆϲ Ἀφροδίτηϲ καθ-
άπερ καὶ οἱ Αἰγύπτιοι τὸ
τῆϲ Ἴϲιδοϲ ἱερὸν ἵδρυντ-
αι.

This stele records two decrees concerned with a grant of enktesis (see #1) enabling the merchants of Kition in Kypros to establish a sanctuary to their Aphrodite (Ourania) in the Peiraieus. The abbreviated formula for this special grant and the lack of the usual provisions for publication of the decree have suggested to scholars concerned with this aspect that the stele was commissioned privately by the merchants of Kition (Koehler Hermes, II^2 337, Ditt.[3], Tod, Pečírka, and now Henry) and set up at the site of the sanctuary in the Peiraieus.

The first decree was passed by the Boule in the first prytany of Nikokrates' archonship. The request by the merchants of Kition is acknowledged, and, rather than issue a definite recommendation, the Boule decided that discussion among the Kitians and any Athenian who wishes should occur at the first meeting of the ekklesia, at which time the Demos will decide what would be best. Rhodes notes this first decree as the "clearest instance" of an open probouleuma (59 note 3; see Table G, 271, for other examples) and Delaix agrees that the matter is to be referred to the ekklesia without specific recommendation (119/120). Neither Rhodes's nor DeLaix's interpretations carry the negative connotation suggested by Sokolowski (68), viz., that the Boule had not reached a favorable opinion.

The second decree was passed by the Demos in the second prytany on the motion of Lykourgos. This decree actually grants the enktesis to the merchants of Kition. Pečírka points out the conditions in the decree: the privilege of owning land is for the specific purpose of establishing the sanctuary to Aphrodite (60).

Pečírka also discusses at length the reference in the last lines of the decree: that the Kitians are to set up their sanctuary just as the Egyptians had set one up to Isis. A Lykourgos nicknamed Ibis is mentioned by Aristophanes in the Birds. Although the matter is incapable of proof, this Lykourgos is usually identified as

Lykourgos's grandfather who was put to death by the Thirty Tyrants. Koehler, starting from this identification, suggested that Lykourgos the grandfather actually proposed a grant of enktesis to resident Egyptians for the establishment of a sanctuary to Isis (Hermes 352; followed by Tod, Ditt.) whose worship in Athens would then be dated to the late fifth century; thus Lykourgos would be following in his grandfather's footsteps. Pečírka, however, notes the chronological difficulties involved in Koehler's interpretation and prefers a more sober view: that although Lykourgos may indeed have inherited from his grandfather an interest in Egypt, neither man would necessarily have been specifically involved in a grant of enktesis to Egyptians (61; following Dow HThR [1937] 184f.). Mitchel makes the more likely assumption that Lykourgos here is referring not to a motion made by his grandfather in the distant past but to a precedent set more recently by himself (194). This would remove the necessity of hypothesizing an otherwise unattested fifth century sanctuary of Isis at Athens.

This decree moved by Lykourgos is typical of his overall program; he would not have needed an ancestral precedent to take an interest in the religious well-being of a group of metics in the Peiraieus, be they Egyptians or Kitians. His interest in native Athenian cults has already been noted (#21), but the present text adds a new dimension of which Athens could justly be proud: the open-minded acceptance of foreign cults for the welfare of the numerous resident-aliens, and these in turn formed an important (if not the most important) element in the Athenian economy. The Egyptians and Kypriotes were particularly important for the importation of grain.

Finally there is the building of the new sanctuary itself (with the creation of jobs) and, considering the probable prosperity of the Kitian community, the further adornment of the Peiraieus.

333/2

28. *ATHENS HONORS PYTHEAS* Oropos 246

editors: Leonardos *ΕΦ.* (1889) 28, pages 15-16; *IG* VII 3499; Foucart *REG* 6(1893) 1-7; *IG* II^2 338.

collections: Ditt. *Syll.*^{2} 580; *Syll.*^{3} 281; Michel 105.

testimonia: Aristotle *Athenaion Politeia* 43.

supplement: Bull. (1974) no. 95 (Koerner).

other bibliography: Pritchett-Neugebauer *Cal.* 46; Meritt *Ath.* 48-51; Mitchel *TAPA* 93(1962) 220-221; *Lyk.* 174 note 34; Rhodes *Boule* 16 n. 1, 68 n. 3, 237, 261, 272; DeLaix *Proboul.* 121, 123, 140, 141; Koerner *APF* 22-23(1974) 190-191; Pritchett *CSCA* 9(1976) 188-189.

description: This stele of white marble was found in the area of the temple of Amphiaraos. It is now on a wall in the museum at the Amphiaraion at Oropos. The pediment has a few chips, but the first decree is intact. The stone is broken at the bottom, just at the beginning of a second decree.

dimensions:
H 0.51 m. (entire)
0.40 m. (below pediment)
W 0.414 m.
Th 0.085 m.

letters: 0.006 m.
Smallest. O, is .004;
largest, Φ, is .008.
H, M, N, are narrow;
K is square.

minuscule text: next page.

commentary: The stoichedon order is 35 letters to the line. It is violated once: in line 2, A and I use just one stoichos (29th). There are 4 new readings, all in line 34: Β̣ st. 21; Λ̣ st. 24; Ρ̣ st. 29; Ν̣ st. 35. Also recorded is the space between the two decrees. Restorations in line 32 and the beginning of line 33 are Dittenberger's; Koehler restored the rest of line 33 and line

34. Koerner has established that αὐτόθι (line 17) refers to there--the sanctuaries of Ammon and Amphiarios, where Pythias did his work--rather than here--in Athens where the decree was passed; Robert agrees.

stoich. 35

Θ ε ο ί

Ἐπὶ Νικοκράτουϲ ἄρχοντοϲ ἐπὶ τῆϲ Αἰγηιδοϲ
πρώτηϲ πρυτανείαϲ, ἧι Ἀρχέλαϲ Χαιρίου Παλ-
ληνεὺϲ ἐγραμμάτευεν· Μεταγειτνιῶνοϲ. ἐνά-
τηι ἱϲταμένου, ἐνάτηι καὶ τριακοϲτῆι τῆϲ v
πρυτανείαϲ· τῶν προέδρων ἐπεψήφιζεν Νικί-
αϲ Θημακειεύϲ· ἔδοξεν τῶι δήμωι· Χαιριωνίδ-
ηϲ Λυϲανίου Φλυεὺϲ εἶπεν· περὶ ὧν ὁ δῆμοϲ πρ-
οϲέταξεν τῆι βουλῆι προβουλεύϲαϲαν ἐξεν-
ειγκε̃ν περὶ Πυθέου καθότι τιμηθήϲεται ὑπ-
ὸ τοῦ δήμου, τύχηι ἀγαθῆι δεδόχθαι τῶι δήμω-
ι, ἐπειδὴ Πυθέαϲ αἱρεθεὶϲ ἐπὶ τὰϲ κρήναϲ τῶ-
ν τε ἄλλων τῶν ἐν τῆι ἀρχῆι ἐπιμελεῖται καλ-
ῶϲ καὶ φιλοτίμωϲ καὶ νῦν τήν τε πρὸϲ τῶι τοῦ
Ἄμμωνοϲ ἱερῶι κρήνηγ καινὴν ἐξωικοδόμηκ-
εν καὶ τὴν ἐν Ἀμφιαράου κρήνην κατεϲκεύακ-
εν καὶ τῆϲ τοῦ ὕδατοϲ ἀγωγῆϲ καὶ τῶν ὑπονόμ-
ων ἐπιμεμέληται αὐτόθι, ἐπαινέϲαι Πυθέαν
Σωϲιδήμου Ἀλωπεκῆθεν, ἐπειδὰν τὰϲ εὐθύνα-
ϲ δῶι καὶ ϲτεφανῶϲαι αὐτὸν χρυϲῶι ϲτεφάνω-
ι ἀπὸ :Χ: δραχμῶν ἀρετῆϲ ἕνεκα καὶ δικαιοϲ-
ύνηϲ τῆϲ περὶ τὴν ἐπιμέλειαν τῶν κρηνῶν, ὅπ-
ωϲ ἂν καὶ οἱ ἄλλοι οἱ ἀεὶ χειροτονούμενοι ἐ-
πὶ τὰϲ κρήναϲ φιλοτιμῶνται ἕκαϲτοι εἰϲ τὸ-
ν δῆμον. ἀναγράψαι δὲ τόδε τὸ ψήφιϲμα καὶ τὸ

τῆϲ βουλῆϲ εἰϲ ϲτήλαϲ v λιθίναϲ δύο τὸν γρα-
μματέα τὸν κατὰ πρυτανείαν καὶ ϲτῆϲαι μία-
ν μὲν ἐν τῶι τοῦ Ἄμμωνοϲ ἱερῶι, μίαν δὲ ἐν Ἀνφ-
ιαράου, εἰϲ δὲ τὴν ἀναγραφὴν τῶν ϲτηλῶν δότ-
ω ὁ ταμίαϲ τοῦ δήμου : ΔΔ : δραχμὰϲ ἑκατέραϲ
τῆϲ ϲτήληϲ ἐκ τῶν εἰϲ τὰ κατὰ ψηφίϲματα ἀνα-
λιϲκομένων τῶι δήμωι.

0.010

[Ἔδοξεν τῆι βουλῆι· ὀγ]δόηι καὶ τριακοϲτῆι:
[τῆϲ πρυτανείαϲ· βουλὴ ἐν] β̣[ου]λ̣[ευτη]ρ̣ίωι· τῶ̣ν̣
[προέδρων ἐπεψήφιζεν - - - - - - - - - - - - - -]

Originally this stele contained at least two decrees. The first is a decree of the Demos, passed on the 9th day of Metageitnion, the 39th day of the first prytany. Since in this decree mention is made of the Demos's request for a probouleuma, what remains of the second decree--a very abbreviated dating formula, the 38th day of the prytany and the mention of the Bouleuterion--has always been considered to be the beginning of the Boule's probouleuma, passed on the day before the meeting of the Ekklesia.

The decree honors Pytheas, son of Sosidemos of the deme Alopeke, in his capacity as epimeletes (overseer, commissioner) of the fountains (or springs). Since Pytheas performed his duties well and patriotically he is to be honored with a gold crown worth a thousand drachmai, provided he passes his euthynai at the end of his term of office. (See #9, #18, for other examples of this protection clause.) Along with the regular duties of the office, Pytheas also constructed a fountain at the sanctuary of Ammon and restored the fountain and waterworks at the sanctuary of Amphiaraos. This explains why two stelai are to be set up: one in the sanctuary of Ammon; the other at the Amphiaraion.

The date, the 39th day of the first prytany, shows that the year of Nikokrates was intercalary. (See above, #15, for discussion of the calendar.) Foucart (3) and Pritchett-Neugebauer (46) have discussed the calendar in respect to this decree and contend that it confirms Aristotle's information (_Ath_. _Pol_. 43.2) that the extra four days, left after dividing the days of the year among the ten prytanies, were added to the first four prytanies of the year. Meritt (84/5) has noted however, that this decree confirms only that the _first_ prytany held 39 days; the decree does not help to establish the number of days for the subsequent prytanies (Pritchett _CSCA_, mentions this decree in his discussion of #29 [II^2 339]).

The office, epimeletes of the fountains, which Pytheas held is mentioned by Aristotle (_Ath_. _Pol_. 43) in connection with two other offices, that of military treasurer and that of the directors of the theoric fund, which had the same peculiarities: they were elective (rather than alloted) and the terms of office did not begin and end with the civil year, but rather lasted from Panathenaia to Panathenaia. This decree supports both descriptions: line 11 shows that Pytheas was elected to his office and the 39th day of the first prytany is much too early for Pytheas to have accomplished all the work for which he is honored if he had only taken office with the beginning of the civil year. It is more reasonable to assume that Pytheas took office at the Greater

Panathenaia of 334/3, on the 28th day of Hekatombaion of the year of Ktesikles.

When Pytheas _ended_ his term as epimeletes of the fountains is another question. Mitchel, in his discussion and reinterpretation of II^2 1493, 1494, 1495, interprets Aristotle to mean that the three offices were quadrennial, from Greater Panathenaia to Greater Panathenaia, and offers substantial proof that when Demades held the office of military treasurer it was a four year term, from Hekatombaion 28 of 334/3 to Hekatombaion 28 of 330/29 (_TAPA_ 220f., correction in _Lyk_. 174 note 34). Rhodes, on the other hand, devotes a special note (D, 235-240) to the directors of the theoric fund, the third office mentioned by Aristotle, and uses this decree as the most substantial proof that the three offices were annual: if the office was quadrennial, then Pytheas would have to wait three more years before he received the honors granted in this decree of 333/2 (237). Although he prefers an annual term, Rhodes admits that the problem is still unresolved and suggests that, if indeed the term were quadrennial, there may nevertheless have been an annual audit and thus Pytheas could expect to receive his honors shortly. This suggestion may solve the problem since it conforms to the fifth century practice of the Treasurers of Athena and other boards for which we have evidence and allows for the four-year term of office.

The mention of a sanctuary of Ammon is interesting. A contemporary inventory of the Treasurers of Athena (II^2 1496 lines 96-97) records an offering to Ammon by the _strategoi_ (generals) of 333/2. Foucart (6-7) suggests that the Athenian interest in Ammon was not therefore flattery to the Macedonian king, but rather an Athenian search for an oracle not under Macedonian influence, such as Delphi and Dodona were by this time.

This decree honoring Pytheas is the first of a number of dated inscriptions from the Lykourgan era found at the Amphiaraion. Whereas #17 suggests that the Athenians were already making use of the revenues from Oropos, which Philip had bestowed on them after Chaironeia, this decree shows that they took the responsibility as well as the revenues and were taking care of Amphiaraos and his sanctuary in Oropos.

333/2

29. *ATHENS GRANTS PROXENY (?) TO A CHIAN* EM 7160

photos: Lambrechts Prox. Plate 12; Meritt Ath. Figure 1 (also on dust jacket); Pritchett AACS Plate 21 (photo of latex squeeze of lines 6, 7).

editors: Pitakis EΦ. (1840/42) 464; IG II 169; IG II^2 339a.

collection: Michel 1467.

supplements: SEG 16.54 (Pritchett-Neugebauer, Lewis, Daux, Binneboessel); 21.277 (Meritt Ath., Pritchett AACS); 26.75 (Meritt Mnemosyne, Pritchett CSCA).
Bull. (1958) 189 (Lewis).

other bibliography: Usener Rh. Mus. 34(1879) 391; Wilhelm Att. Urk. I 481 Binneboessel Studien 81; Meritt Hesperia 4(1935) 532; Ath. 48-50; GRBS 17 (1976) 147-152; AJP 95(1974) 272-277; Mnemosyne 30(1977) 229-230; Daux Fouilles Delphes III 3.2; Pritchett-Neugebauer Cal. 48; Lewis BSA 50(1955) 27; Lambrechts Prox. 40-41, 136, 157; Pritchett AACS 276-277; CSCA 9(1976) 188-191; Clement AJA 69(1965) 193; McGregor Phoenix 20(1966) 217; Samuel Chron. 60 n. 1; Henry Prescripts 36 n. 18; Mikalson Year 8-9, 40, 44; Walsh ZPE 41(1981) 107-124.

description: This fragment of Pentelic marble was found in the precinct of Artemis Brauronia on the Akropolis in

1840. It is broken on all sides. Remains of sculpture--an amphora and head and chest of a sphinx--show that the stele was originally topped by a relief. The first line is on the fillet of the cymation.

Wilhelm, in Att. Urk. I, of 1911, associated this fragment with an unedited fragment of the same stoichedon order, 25 letters to the line. (Michel, in 1900, included both fragments under 1467--he must have had advance notice.) The association continued into the second edition of the corpus as II^2 339a+b. The two fragments were separated in 1947 by Pritchett-Neugebauer, 48 note 27, on the basis of two different checker patterns. This dissociation has cleared up the incongruity of a man from Pydna (339b) being honored on a stele topped with a characteristically Chian symbol, a sphinx with amphora (339a). Only the top fragment can be dated; 339b must be left to fend for itself.

dimensions:
H 0.23 m. (entire)
0.135 m. (below relief)
0.092 m. (below cymation)
W 0.125 m.
Th 0.11 m.

letters: 0.012 m. on fillet; 0.007 m. in text. Smallest, Δ, O, Π, T, are .006; largest, P, Σ, Y, are .008.

minuscule text:

stoich. 25

[Προξ]ενία Α̣ι
[Ἐπὶ Νι]κοκράτου[c ἄρχοντοc ἐπὶ]
[τῆc Παν]διονίδ[οc δευτέραc πρυ]-
[τανεί]αc ἧι ἐγρ[αμμάτευεν Ἀρχέ]-
[λαc Χα]ι[ρ]ίου Πα[λληνεὺc· Μεταγε]-
[ιτνιῶ]νοc ἕκτ[ηι φθίνοντοc, πέμ]-
[πτηι κα]ὶ δε̣[κάτηι τῆc πρυτανεί]-
[αc - - - - - - - - - -]

commentary: The text includes new readings in line 1 (see below). In line 7 st. 9, Pritchett-Neugebauer and Meritt read a definite epsilon; I prefer to dot this letter. The stoichedon order is 25 letters to the line. Only in Pritchett-Neugebauer's first restoration for line 6 (see below) would the order be violated. Restorations are Koehler's, except lines 5 and 6, restored by Usener.

1 restoration: [Ξ]ένια ᾽Αρ[τέμιδι] Pitt.; [Προξ]ενία ᾽Α[---] Koe.; [Προξ]ενία Λ[ύκωι Πυτναίωι] Wilh. Since the two fragments are now separated and the name and ethnic came from II^2 339b, the end of the line can not now be restored. The fifth letter can be printed as a dotted alpha, which was the reading before Wilh., and in the sixth letter space the reading of either an iota or the left hand hasta of another letter can be taken out of brackets. Enough of this sixth letter survives to show that it could not be an upsilon; this can be seen in the published photographs and has been noted by both Pritchett and Lewis. The restoration of [Προξ]ενία is retained because it does fit: based on my measurements, the restoration of four letters at the beginning of line 1 requires 8 cm.; the restoration of five letters at the beginning of line 2 also requires 8 cm. The word occurs, however, only in the now separated II^2 339b.

3 prytany: Koe. restored the second prytany here on the basis of the second decree of II^2 337, line 27 (#27).

4/5 secretary: Koe. in II.5 page 51, from II^2 338 (#28).

5-7 date: as noted above, Usener; followed by Mer., Clement. [Μεταγειτνιῶ]νος ἕκτ[ηι μετ' εἰκάδας· ἐνάτηι καὶ] δ[εκάτηι τῆς πρυτανείας] Koe.; [Μεταγειτνιῶ]νος ἕκτ[ηι μετ' εἰκάδας v ἕκτηι κα]ὶ δε[κάτηι τῆς πρυτανείας] P.-N. 46, (adopted by Samuel) or [Μεταγειτνιῶ]νος ἕκτ[ηι ἐπὶ δέκα· ἐκκλησία κυρ]ία ἐ[ν, page 48. In CSCA, Pritchett offers 5 other possibilities (including Koe.'s); even more, depending on the use of vacats.

Once the "false" information has been removed along with II^2 339b, this decree yields very little information on its own. To judge from the restored heading ([Προξ]-ενία) and the fragmentary relief (Sphinx and amphora) the subject matter of the decree was probably honors and the grant of proxeny for one or more Chians. It was passed early in the archonship of Nikokrates, but efforts to reach a more precise date and to restore the dating formula have provoked many pages of controversy (Henry notes as well that the verb precedes the name of the secretary, an unusual order).

The controversy revolves around the count of days in the last decade of the month. (For previous discussion of the calendar, see #15.) There is no problem with a full month of 30 days; the usual designation and alternatives are set down in this chart (based on Pritchett-Neugebauer, pp. 30f.

1. νουμηνία
2. δευτέρα ἱϲταμένου
3. τρίτη "
4. τετρὰϲ "
5. πέμπτη "
6. ἕκτη "
7. ἑβδόμη "
8. ὀγδόη "
9. ἐνάτη "
10. δεκάτη "
11. ἑνδεκάτη
12. δωδεκάτη
13. τρίτη ἐπὶ δέκα
14. τετρὰϲ " "
15. πέμπτη " "
16. ἕκτη " "
17. ἑβδόμη ἐπὶ δέκα
18. ὀγδόη " "
19. ἐνάτη " "
20. εἰκοϲτή, δεκάτη προτέρα
21. δεκάτη φθίνοντοϲ, δεκάτη ὑϲτέρα
22. ἐνάτη φθίνοντοϲ, ἐνάτη μετ' εἰκάδαϲ
23. ὀγδόη " , ὀγδόη " "
24. ἑβδόμη " , ἑβδόμη " "
25. ἕκτη " , ἕκτη " "
26. πέμπτη " , πέμπτη " "
27. τετρὰϲ " , τετρὰϲ " "
28. τρίτη " , τρίτη " "
29. (full month) δευτέρα φθίνοντοϲ, δευτέρα μετ' εἰκάδαϲ
29. (hollow month) ἕνη καὶ νέα
30. (full) ἕνη καὶ νέα

Note that the last decade is counted backward from the last day of the month, which is designated ἕνη καὶ νέα. There are a few inscriptions in the Lykourgan period, such as #23, which designate these days with an ordinal number plus μετ' εἰκάδαϲ (after the 20th), but much the more common designation is an ordinal plus φθίνοντοϲ (of the waning [month]). Meritt notes (Ath. 46 note 6) that, although the designations δεκάτη προτέρα (for the 20th) and δεκάτη ὑστέρα (for the 21st) can not be excluded as possibilities, they are usually associated with the use of the μετ' εἰκάδαϲ formula and therefore more common in the later Hellenistic period (see #59 for an example of δεκάτει μετ' εικάδαϲ).

The problem is what to do with a hollow month of 29 days. Since it is known from #28 that Hekatombaion was full with 30 days, it has never been questioned that Metageitnion of this year was hollow with 29 days. Pritchett-Neugebauer, Pritchett (in his later articles) and Mikalson, contend that the omitted day for a hollow month was δευτέρα φθίνοντος, the last day but one. This is based on literary evidence--chiefly scholia--and the assumption that the Athenians determined their festival calendar by actual monthly observation of the new moon and thus would not know before the end of the month whether it would be hollow or full. Meritt, on the other hand, following different scholia and the assumption that the Athenians knew the length of the month at least by the 20th, believes that the omitted day was more likely the 21st or 22nd; in any case, not δευτέρα φθίνοντος. J. A. Walsh, in his article, "The Omitted Date in the Athenian Hollow Month," supports Meritt's opinion. Indeed, Walsh's examination of previous scholarship, and his investigation into the significance not only of the Solonian calendar reforms but also the term used to designate a 29-day month, "hollow," point to the definitive conclusion "that δεκάτη/ἐνάτη φθῖνοντος was the omitted date in the Athenian hollow month," (124) thus rendering any subsequent argument concerning this specific calendar "problem" pointless. I include the chart, based on Meritt, *Ath.* p. 45, on the next page for clarification.

The restored text used here as #29 gives, according to Meritt's count, the calendar equation: Metageitnion [2]4 = Prytany [II] 1[5] = 54th day. For Pritchett, however, the designation ἕκτηι φθίνοντος must always be the 25th day with the result that for this year Metageitnion

25 would be the 55th day; but to make the 15th day of the second prytany the 55th day would mean that the first prytany had lasted 40 days, something which is highly improbable (indeed impossible; see now Meritt <u>GRBS</u>). So Pritchett-Neugebauer offered two alternate restorations (subsequently, Pritchett added more; see commentary above).

Every Month	Every Month
1. νουμηνία	11. ἐνδεκάτη
2. δευτέρα ἱϲταμένου	12. δωδεκάτη
3. τρίτη ἱϲταμένου	13. τρίτη ἐπὶ δέκα
4. τετρὰϲ ἱϲταμένου	14. τετρὰϲ ἐπὶ δέκα
5. πέμπτη ἱϲταμένου	15. πέμπτη ἐπὶ δέκα
6. ἕκτη ἱϲταμένου	16. ἕκτη ἐπὶ δέκα
7. ἑβδόμη ἱϲταμένου	17. ἑβδόμη ἐπὶ δέκα
8. ὀγδόη ἱϲταμένου	18. ὀγδόη ἐπὶ δέκα
9. ἐνάτη ἱϲταμένου	19. ἐνάτη ἐπὶ δέκα
10. δεκάτη ἱϲταμένου	20. εἰκοϲτή

Full Month	Hollow Month
21. δεκάτη φθίνοντοϲ	21. ἐνάτη φθίνοντοϲ
22. ἐνάτη φθίνοντοϲ	22. ὀγδόη φθίνοντοϲ
23. ὀγδόη φθίνοντοϲ	23. ἑβδόμη φθίνοντοϲ
24. ἑβδόμη φθίνοντοϲ	24. ἕκτη φθίνοντοϲ
25. ἑκτη φθίνοντοϲ	25. πέμπτη φθίνοντοϲ
26. πέμπτη φθίνοντοϲ	26. τετρὰϲ φθίνοντοϲ
27. τετρὰϲ φθίνοντοϲ	27. τρίτη φθίνοντοϲ
28. τρίτη φθίνοντοϲ	28. δευτέρα φθίνοντοϲ
29. δευτέρα φθίνοντοϲ	29. ἕνη καὶ νέα
30. ἕνη καὶ νέα	

The first one (46) allows for a first prytany of 39 days: Metageitnion [2]5 = Prytany [II] 1[6] = 55th day, but the drawback is that a vacat must be assumed even with the rare μετ' εἰκάδαϲ formula and indeed there would be two vacats if the more common φθίνοντοϲ were used. Pritchett-Neugebauer's second restoration (48) assumes an incomplete calendar equation, giving only the festival date, Metageitnion 16, but this requires reading a dotted alpha (line 7 st. 8) where a sure delta had not been questioned previously (Pitt., Koe., Ki., Mer.). Delta was reconfirmed by Clement in 1965 and McGregor in 1966 and by my own recent examination of the stone.

Since neither Pritchett-Neugebauer's restorations, nor Pritchett's later restorations, hold up under cross-examination, (in fact, they are unnecessary since they were devised to accommodate the ommission of the date δευτέρα φθῖνοντος in a hollow month), I have kept the one first proposed by Usener and followed by Kirchner, Meritt, Clement, and McGregor; it fits best the letters on the stone and the stoichedon order.

The relief emerges as the most unequivocal aspect of this fragment. It has been discussed by Wilhelm, Binneboessel, Daux, Lewis, and Lambrechts, and all have agreed that a Chian symbol is portrayed. The sphinx and amphora appear on coins and a few other stone reliefs. And, as Lewis points out, the dissociation of II^{2} 339a from II^{2} 339b simplifies matters for those who tried to reconcile a man from Pydna with a Chian symbol.

333/2

30. *DECREE* [Lost]

photo: none; Pittakis *EΦ.* (1840/42) 378 has a sketch.

editors: Pittakis *EΦ.* (1840/42) 378; Rangabê (1855) 532; *IG* II 492; *IG* II^{2} 340.

other bibliography: Reusch *Hermes* 15(1880) 341; Unger *Att. Arch.* 675; Wilhelm *EΦ.* (1890) 203; Pritchett-Neugebauer *Cal.* 46; Meritt *Ath.* 84.

description: This fragment, now lost, was found on the Akropolis in 1840. Aside from Pittakis's sketch, there is no description, except that it was Pentelic marble. It may have remained on the Akropolis, but it is not included in a fairly recent compilation of the inscriptions which are still there.

dimensions: not recorded. letters: not recorded.

minuscule text:

stoich. 23

[Ἐπὶ Νικοκράτουϲ ἄρχοντοϲ ἐ]-
[πὶ τῆϲ ..5..ίδοϲ τετάρτηϲ π]-
[ρυτανείαϲ, ἧι Ἀρχέ]λαϲ Χαι[ρί]-
[ου Παλληνεὺϲ ἐγρ]αμμάτευ[εν]·
[Μαιμακτηριῶνοϲ] ἐνδεκάτ[ηι],
[δωδεκάτηι τῆϲ πρ]υτανεία[ϲ· ἐ]-
[κκληϲία κυρία· τῶν] προέδρ[ων]
[ἐπεψήφιζε Νικοκρ]άτηϲ Φλ[υε]-
[ὺϲ· ἔδοξεν τῆι βουλῆ]ι καὶ τ[ῶι]
[δήμωι - - - - - -]ερ...

commentary: The text is based on Kirchner's. The stoichedon order of 23 letters to the line was established by Koehler's restoration of ἐκκλησία κυρία in lines 6/7. Reusch, followed by Unger, restored the date in lines 5/6, which established the year as intercalary; both suggested the year of Hegemon, 327/6. After #28 was found, Wilhelm was able to restore the name of the secretary for the year 333/2, lines 1-4. Wilhelm also changed the date of the prytany from the 12th to the 11th (which also fits); but Kirchner returned to Reusch's date and also restored the name of the chairman of the proedroi; lines 8/9, on the possible connection with PA 10922.

Only the calendar equation remains on this decree of the Boule and the Demos. Both Pritchett-Neugebauer and Meritt agree on this equation: [Maimakterion] 11 = Prytany [IV 12] = 129th day.

31. *ATHENS GRANTS CITIZENSHIP TO ARCHIPPOS*
EM 7237, 7237[a]

editors: Fr. A Pittakis ΕΦ. (1837/39) 27; (1852/55) 2019.
Fr. B Pittakis ΕΦ. (1837/39) 211.
Fr. A+B Rangabé (1855) 426, 427; IG II 230; IG II[2] 336 + Add. page 659.

supplements: SEG 15.97 (Wilhelm Att. Urk., Pouilloux); 21. 273 (Schweigert, Pritchett-Neugebauer, Meritt Ath., Mitchel); 21.278 (Dow); 28.50 (Hansen).
Bull. (1942) no. 32 (Wilhelm).

other bibliography: Buermann Jahrb. Suppl. 10(1878/9) 354-355; Reusch De diebus cont. 12; Schoell Stiz. Ak. Münch. (1886) 123 note 2; Unger Att. Arch. 677; Wilhelm Arch. Epig. Mitt. 15(1892) 6; CRAI (1900) 529; Mélanges Nicole 602; AM 39(1914) 266; Att. Urk. V 103-106; Johnson CP 9(1914) 425; Leonardos ΑΔ (1916) 219; Schweigert Hesperia 9(1940) 341; Pritchett-Meritt Chron. 6-7; Pritchett-Neugebauer Cal. 45-46; Pouilloux Thasos I 197; Meritt Ath. 82; Hesperia 32(1963) 434-435; Mitchel TAPA 93 (1962) 227-229; Dow HSCP 67 (1963) 43, 87-88; Hesperia 32(1963) 341-342; Osborne BSA 66(1971) 304, 305/6 n. 56, 61, 308 n. 69, 325 n. 6; BSA 67(1972) 130-158; Vestigia 434; Anc. Soc. 7(1976) 108; Rhodes Boule 68, 73; DeLaix Proboul. 123, 133; Henry Prescripts 38 n. 27, 39, 42-43, 46 n. 65, 66, 107; Hansen ZPE 30(1978) 151-157.

description: The two fragments of white marble were found on the Akropolis. Since Rangabé's association of the two, they have always been treated as part of one stele. In Fr. A, the upper part of the left side is preserved, as well as the lower part of the relief. The cymation is 0.05 m.; the side molding of the frame of the relief is 0.03 m. Fr. B is broken on all sides. Both fragments have rough-picked backs.

dimensions:
Fr. A
H 0.44 m. (entire)
0.337 m. (below cymation)
W 0.22 m.
Th 0.13 m.

letters; 0.006 m. Smallest, Ω, is .005; largest, Σ, Φ, Ψ, are .010. The ends are splayed in many of the letters which have open straight strokes.

Fr. B
H 0.38 m.
W 0.225 m.
Th 0.133 m.

minuscule text: next two pages.

epigraphical commentary: I have renumbered the text to include the restored first two lines in Fr. A and the restored first line of Fr. B. All dots are mine in Fr. A; in Fr. B, Kirchner dotted letters in line 13 st. 17, line 15 st. 18, line 20 st. 5, line 21 st. 16, line 23 st. 13, and the 11th letter in line 5 which he reads as nu; the rest are mine. Underlined are those letters which are no longer legible. In turn, for Fr. B, there are a few new readings noted below.

Fr. B

3 st. 15, 16 Π̣Π̣ new readings.

4 st. 7 Ạ new reading.

5 st. 9-11 ιΩΙ Wilh. AM. TO]Ṇ Ki.

7 st. 5 Ḥ Dow. N Leonardos.

11 st. 15 Γ̣ Vel.; N Rangabé.

12 st. 15-17 ΞΕΝ Ki. ΣΣΜ Vel.; ΕΣ. Rangabé.

13 st. 17 Ẹ Ki., Rangabé. O Vel.

18 st. 15 O new reading.
st. 12-18 ΚΑΙΕΠΑΙ Vel.

19 st. 13-17 ΟΙΕΩΝ new reading. ΟΟΕΟΥ Vel.

22 st. 13-16 N..O new reading. ΗΣ.Μ Vel.

24 st. 13 Ọ new reading.
st. 13-16 ΟΥ.Ο Vel.

29 st. 8-11 Θ.Λ. new reading. ʳ... Koe.; ΩΙΛ'|/ Vel. The theta, st. 8, can be seen clearly on the photograph (lower left hand corner).

stoich. 31

Fr. A [Ἐπὶ Κτηcικλέουc ἄρχοντοc ἐπὶ τῆc]
[.ι.ηΐδοc τετάρτηc πρυτανείαc]
ἧι Μνηcι̲φιλοc Μνήcω[νοc Φαλη ἐγραμμά]-
τευεν· Μα̣ιμακτηριῶ̣ν[οc ἐνδεκάτηι, μιᾶ]-
ι καὶ εἰκοcτεῖ τῆc π[ρυτανείαc· ἐκκληc]-
ία κυρία̣· τῶν προέδρω̣[ν ἐπεψήφιζεν ...]-
όθεοc̣ Κυδα· ἔδοξεν τῶ̣[ι δήμωι ....8.....]
δφρονοc Λακι : εἶπεν· [περὶ ὧν Ἄρχιπποc λ]-
έγει καὶ ἡ βολὴ προε[βούλευcεν περὶ αὐ]-
τοῦ, ἐψηφίcθαι τῶι̣ δ̲[ήμωι ἐπαινέcαι μὲ]-
ν Ἄρχιππον τὸν Ἀρχι.......15.......
ὅτι ἀνὴρ ἀγαθόc ἐcτ[ιν περὶ τὴν πόλιν τ]-
ὴν Ἀθηναίων καὶ νῦν [καὶ ἐν τῶι ἔμπροcθ]-
εν χρόνωι καὶ ποεῖ [ὅτι δύναται ἀγαθόν]·
cτεφανῶcαι δὲ Ἄρ[χιππον χρυcῶι cτεφά]-
νωι ἀπὸ : Χ : δραχμῶ[ν φιλοτιμίαc ἕνεκεν τ]-
ῆc εἰc Ἀθηναίο[υc· ἐπειδὴ δὲ καὶ ὁ πατὴρ]
α̣ὐτοῦ Ἀθηνα[ίων φίλοc ἦν καὶ ἔδωκεν αὐ]-
[τ]ῶι ὁ δῆμο[c τὴν πολιτείαν, εἶναι καὶ αὐ]-
[τ]ὸν Ἄρ̣[χ]ιπ[πον καὶ τοὺc ἐκγόνουc Ἀθηνα]-
[ίο]υ̲c̲ καὶ [φυλὴν καὶ δῆμον καὶ φρατρίαν]
ἑλέcθα[ι ὧν ἂν βούληται εἶναι· τοὺc δὲ π]-
[ρ]υτάνε̣[ιc τοὺc τῆc .ι.ηιδοc δοῦναι πε]-
[ρ]ὶ αὐτ[οῦ τὴν ψῆφον εἰc τὴν πρώτην ἐκκλ]-
[η]cία[ν καὶ τοὺc θεcμοθέταc εἰcαγαγεῖ]-
[ν] αὐ[τῶι τὴν δοκιμαcίαν - - - - - -]
- - - - - - - - - - - - - - - - - - -

Fr. B [- - - - - - - - - - - - ἐκ τῶν κα]-
[τὰ ψηφίσμα]τ̲α ἀνα[λισκομένων τῶι δήμω]-
[ι· καλέσαι] δὲ Ἄρχιπ̣π̣[ον ἐπὶ δεῖπνον εἰς]
[τὸ πρυτ]α̣νεῖον εἰς [αὔριον].
[εἶναι δ' αὐτ]ῶ̣ι φρατρίας γενέσθαι πλ[ὴ]ν
[ὧν οἱ νόμοι ἀπαγορεύουσιν].

[Ἐλαφ]ηβολιῶνος ἕνε[ι καὶ νέαι, ἕκτει κα]-
[ὶ εἰκ]οστεῖ τῆς πρυτ[ανείας ἧι Ἀρχέλας]
[Παλλ]η̣νεὺς ἐγραμμά[τευεν· ἐκκλησία· τῶ]-
[ν προ]ε̣δρων ἐπεψήφι̣[ζεν .....12....]
..5..ς· συνπρόεδρ̣ο̣[ι· ......14......]
..5.., Θυμοχάρης Τ̣ε[ιθράσιος, ...7...]
[Κυδαθ]ηναιεύς, Εὔ̣ξεν ......14......
..5..ος Κεφαλῆθεν, Ε̣......14......
[... Ἐλ]ευσίνιος, Νικι......14......
..5..ης Ἀρι̲στάρχου Φ̣[...7... εἶπεν· π]-
[ερὶ ὧν] ἔδοξεν Ἀρχ̣ιππ[ος ἐν τῶι δήμωι ἔν]-
[νομα] ι̲κετεύειν, ἐπειδ̣[ὴ .....12.....]
[... Ἀ]ρχιππος κα[ὶ ὁ] πάπ[πος ....10....]
[.. ἀδ]ελφο[ὶ] καὶ οἱ ΕΩΝ ......14......]
....υ̣σιν ἐπί τε [το]ῦ [πολέμου τοῦ πρὸς Λ]-
[ακεδ]αιμονίους ..π̣......15......
.... Ἀθηναίων Ν ..Ο......15......
[.. Εὔφ]ριλλος ετ̣.......18.......
..5..ν τοῦ δήμο̣[υ ....17.......]
...6... Ἀθηναι.......19.......
[.... Ἀρ]χίππω[ι - - - - - - - -]
...7... τὴν ε - - - - - - - - - -
[.... προ]γόνω[ν - - - - - - - -]
...7...Θ.Λ - - - - - - - - -

commentary: The stoichedon order is 31 letters to the line. Kirchner notes 32 letters for Fr. B, line 2 but there are only 31. In Fr. A, Velsen suggested that the first two lines of the dating formula had been on the cymation and that they would not conform to the stoichedon order of the text below. The first two lines were probably 28 and 26 letters long. Fr. B, line 5, has 53 letters crowded into the normal 31 letter line.

Koehler restored the prytany as the 4th, τετάρτης, on the basis of the position of Maimakterion as the 5th month in the festival calendar in Fr. A, line 2. Restorations in Fr. A, lines 9, 16, 20, 21; Fr. B, lines 11, 18, 28, are also Koehler's. The other restoration are Velsen's unless noted below.

Fr. A
1/2 in cymation: The year 334/3 with archon Ktesikles is known from the secretary, line 3, who also appears in #23, firmly dated to 334/3 (Koe. II 5 p. 64).

The tribe in prytany must be either Aigeis or Oineis, based on a new restoration for line 21, Mitchel (228). Schoell's restoration of Hippothontis in line 2 was based on Vel.'s restoration of that tribe in line 21. Mitchel has shown that Hippothontis could not have held the 4th prytany in 334/3. (He designates the 6th prytany for Hippothontis in TAPA but has corrected this to the 8th prytany, AJA 70[1966] 66.)

3 secretary's demotic: Schweigert used his restoration of an abbreviated demotic here to restore the same to #25 and date it also to 334/3.

4/5 date: Reusch.

16 end: Koe. [ν ἀνδραγαθίας ἕνεκα τ] Wilh. Arch. Epig. Mitt.

17 end: Buermann.

18 end: Buermann.

19 beg and τὴν πολιτεῖαν: Buermann. Rest of line restored by Wilh. Arch. Epig. Mitt.

22 mid: ἧς Johnson. ὧν Vel.

23 end: Mitchel. [τῆς Ἱπποθωντίδος δοῦναι πε]- Vel.

Fr. B
5 beg.: αὐτ]ῶι Wilh. *AM* αὐτό]ν̣ Ki. Osborne (*BSA* 1972, p. 142) follows Wilh.'s restoration and adds three new readings: the tau (dotted) where Wilh. read a horizontal hasta, but only in majuscule letters (see ep. com.); the certain reading of eta in πλ[ῆ]ν; the omega (dotted) of [ῶ̣ν.

7/8 secretary: Dow, *Hesperia*. [Κικυ]ννεύς Leonardos, based on reading of nu in the 5th stoichos (see above). This decree (III) was dated by Kirchner to "non ante 318/7" because of the presence of all the symproedroi rather than just the chairman. It was later brought up to 320/19 (Pritchett-Meritt 6-7), but still remained 14 years after the first decree. Dow noted that the restoration of the secretary of 333/2 fits the stoichedon order and brought the first listing of symproedroi to the year 333/2 (note also Henry, 107).

16 restoration: Wilh. *CRAI*.

17 beg: Wilh. *CRAI*.

20 end: Wilh. *Mél. Nicole*.

23 beg: Wilh. *Mél. Nicole*.

Before discussing the context of the text, the relationship of the two fragments and of the at least two decrees to one another demands some explanation. Fr. A, topped as it is with a relief and cymation, obviously comes first, and it records a decree of the year 334/3, when Ktesikles was archon and Mnesiphilos was secretary. It breaks off before the end of the first decree. Then comes Fr. B, the first four lines of which are the end of a decree and have the formulae which deal 1) with the appropriation of money for the publication and 2) with the invitation to dine on the morrow in the Prytaneion. At first it might seem that Fr. B must follow Fr. A very closely and be the end of the first decree. At line 6, however, begins a new decree with a very abbreviated dating formula in an unusual sequence; it has only the date by month, the day of the prytany, and the name of the secretary, followed by the names of all the _symproedroi_ (presiding board) instead of the name of the _epistates_ (presiding officer) alone. Such an abbreviated formula forces us to recognize that the immediately preceding decree had a more complete dating formula including the names of the archon and of the prytanizing tribe. It becomes immediately obvious, therefore, that the first four lines of Fr. B can not be the end of the first decree on Fr. A, for in the first place, the name of the secretary, Mnesiphilos, fits neither the stoichedon order nor the surviving letters on the stone and, secondly, the year of the second decree on Fr.B is intercalary whereas 334/3 was ordinary. It is therefore necessary to recognize in the first four lines of Fr. B not the end of the first decree on Fr. A, but the end of yet another decree now lost which came between the first and what now must be called the third which begins on line 5 of Fr.B.

All this was seen by Dow (_Hesperia_) who then proceeded to restore the name of the secretary of 333/2, [Ἀρχέλας Παλλ]ηνεῦς in Fr. B, lines 6/7 (Decree III), and to show the close temporal sequence between Archippos's first grant of citizenship in 334/3 and the subsequent decrees concerning him and his family in the following year. Decree II with which Fr. B begins was also of the year of Nikokrates; since it contains the publication formula for the whole stele, all three decrees are presented here under 333/2 in spite of the fact that Decree I was passed (but not published) in the preceding year. (Because Henry, 46, is concerned with the unusual arrangement of the prescript of II^2 336III, he follows Dow. Osborne, BSA [1971] 305/6 n. 56, records Dow's explanation but still admits the possibility that lines 1-4 on Fr. B record the end of Decree I, begun on Fr. A.)

Confirmation of Dow's thesis is furnished by Meritt (Hesperia) who shows that the calendar equation of Fr. B, lines 5 and 6, "is precisely correct for the 295th day in the intercalary year of Nikokrates." The festival date is the last day of Elaphebolion which in an intercalary year would be the tenth month. Meritt assumed for this calculation an "untampered" alternation of full and hollow months, i.e. (5x30) + (5x29) = 295. For the conciliar calendar he assumed three 39-day prytanies followed by four 38-day ones to which he added the 26th day of the eighth prytany, i.e. (3x39)+(4x38)+26 = 295. If, however, the first four prytanies were of 39 days, it would be the 296th day of the conciliar calendar and one would have to assume, as did Meritt (Ath. 85), that the months alternated full and hollow for the first nine months, but that Elaphebolion had an extra day--and this too, would yield the 296th day of the festival calendar. Both equations are possible and either one supports the dating of II^2 336III in 333/2; the choice depends on one's calendrical priorities.

All three decrees deal with a certain Archippos. The first decree (I), on Fr. A, is the most complete and so gives the most information. It was passed in the year of Ktesikles, 334/3, by the Demos on the 11th day of Maimakterion, the 21st day of the 4th prytany. Because he has been a good man with regard to the Athenian polis both now and in the past and does whatever good he can, Archippos is awarded a gold crown worth a thousand drachmai because of his zeal towards the Athenians. And since his father also was a friend to the Athenians and they had given him citizenship, Archippos and his descendants are to be granted citizenship, and allowed to pick the phyle, deme, and phratry of his choice. The last lines, heavily restored, refer to the required "second vote" to be taken at the next meeting of the ekklesia and, perhaps, instructions for the thesmothetes to administer the dokimasia (examination). Wilhelm, in AM, doubted this restoration, lines 23-24, contending that in 334/3, dokimasia for citizenship was not used. Osborne, who has more recently studied citizenship grants, designates 318 for the first such use of dokimasia (Anc. Soc.; cf. BSA 1971).

What is left of the text of the second decree (II) at the beginning of Fr. B, has been included above. Line 5 adds a qualification to Archippos's range of choices: he can choose any phratry except those forbidden by the laws. Since this was crowded into the space which had been left between Decrees II and III and this space is noticeably larger (0.18 m.) than the normal vertical checker (an average ranging somewhere between 0.0125 and 0.0138 m.), it must be an addendum to the lost second decree, added after the third decree was inscribed. Its constitutional significance will be discussed below.

The third decree (III) was passed by the Demos on the last day of Elaphebolion, 29th or 30th day (see above), on the 26th day of the 8th prytany, in the year of Nikokrates. Rhodes (73) lists II^2 336 (III) as passed by the Demos, but notes that it is restored, and that τῆι βολῆι would fit the stoichedon order just as well, but that this spelling is unlikely this late in the fourth century (but see ἡ βολή in Fr. A, line 9).

After the abbreviated dating formula comes the long list of symproedroi, lines 9-14. The rest of Decree III is sparsely restored, but seems to be concerned with more information as to the ways in which Archippos's grandfather and most likely his grandfather's brothers helped the Athenians in the war against Sparta. Wilhelm has offered a fuller restoration (<u>Att. Urk.</u> V 104) which adds Archippos's father, Athenian descendants, and a great uncle Hipparchos, but leaves unclear their relation to the "war against Sparta." (Wilhelm had already noted [<u>Mél. Nicole</u>] that Euphrillos was a good Thasian name; for the restoration below, he added that Euphrillos could be the father or son of [Π]α[γ]χ[άρη]ς Εὔφρ[ίλ]λο, II^2 33 line 19.) Also, line 18 requres 32 letters, my reading precludes ἔκγονοι at the end of line 19, and τῶι δήμωι at the end of line 22.

Fr. B

[ἔν]-
[νομα] ἱκετεύειν, ἐπειδ[ὴ ὁ πατὴρ ὁ Ἀρχίπ]-
[που Ἄ]ρχιππος κα[ὶ ὁ] πάπ[πος Ἄρχιππος καὶ]
[οἱ ἀδ]ελφο[ὶ] καὶ [οἱ ἔκγονοι Ἀθηναῖοι ὑπ]-
[άρχο]υσιν ἐπί τε [το]ῦ [πολέμου τοῦ πρὸς Λ]-
[ακεδ]αιμονίους [Ἵπ]π[αρχος ὁ πρόθειος α]-
[ὐτοῦ] Ἀθηναίων [τῶι δήμωι χρήσιμος ἦν? κ]-
[αὶ Εὔφ]ριλλος

Even though Wilhelm's restoration cannot be accepted, there is no strong reason to reject his association of the Archippos of this inscription with the men in II^2 24 and II^2 25, Archippos and Hipparchos, Thasians who were honored (II^2 24) and then granted citizenship (II^2 25) just before the King's Peace of 387/6 which ended the Corinthian War (first noted in Wilhelm's article in <u>Mél.</u>

Nicole). Both the first and the third decrees refer to Archippos's ancestors and mention that they acted well towards Athens. The Archippos of II^2 336 could easily be a Thasian, whose family already had strong ties with Athens. Now that Philip had deprived the Athenians of their mainland "possessions" in the Thraceward area, Thasos may have gained a new strategic importance for them.

The documents in this Corpus are important because they show an Athens still concerned with rewarding foreigners who had proven themselves helpful in diplomacy or commerce or sympathetic with Athenian policy, or an Athens offering refuge on a basis of equality to some who had lost out at home because of pro-Athenian (or anti-Macedonian) attitudes; this inscription is no exception. Of greater interest in this particular case, however, are the hints of constitutional change in Lykourgan Athens itself.

The first of these changes is the addition of a restrictive formula to the grant of citizenship: in Decree I, lines 19/20, Archippos (and his descendants) is to choose the tribe, deme, and phratry whichever one he wants; in the addendum stuck in at the end of Decree II (Fr. B, line 5) Archippos is to become (a member) of (whatever) phratry (he wants) except those forbidden by the laws. Since this addendum is directly after Decree II, and the physical evidence shows that it was inscribed after Decree III, it is reasonable to assume that it is an addition to Decree II. Since, furthermore, there was a vacat between Decrees II and III (where the addendum is now inscribed), there was probably a similar vacat between Decrees I and II, and that would be the obvious place for an addendum to Decree I. Therefore the introduction of this new restriction must have occurred between the 4th prytany of 334/3 (Decree I) and the 8th prytany of 333/2 (Decree III). And by accepting Fr. B line 5 as an addendum to Decree II, an even more specific date for the introduction of a restrictive clause can be determined. #24 (II^2 405), dated to the 9th prytany of 334/3, and so earlier than Decree III, also shows a restrictive clause, ὧν οἱ νόμοι λέγουσιν (i.e., choose a phratry from <u>those which the laws prescribe</u>). Thus there is a five-prytany period between Decree I of the 4th prytany (without restriction) and #24 of the 9th prytany with the first surviving restrictive clause, and these two documents bracket the time in 334/3 when the Athenians first passed laws prescribing which phratries a new citizen could choose. Osborne, in his article in 1971 (<u>BSA</u> 305/6 note 56), drew the same chronological conclusions, but only <u>if</u> Fr. B line 5 were to belong to Decree II. By 1972, he notes (but gives no reasons) that "the probabilities slightly favor" viewing Fr. B line 5 as an addendum to Decree I and so dates the introduction of the restriction sometime between 338/7 (citing #1, the last previous grant of citizenship without a restrictive clause) and the 4th prytany of 334/3, Decree I (<u>BSA</u> 135; in <u>Vestigia</u>, Osborne states only that the changes occured "firmly in the Lykourgan period"). Since, as has been shown (see above), the "probabilities" favor the suggestion that Fr. B line 5 is an addendum to the decree which it directly follows on the stone, the more specific time period in 334/ must be favored as the time the Athenians began to restrict new citizens as to phratry choice.

Decree II of this inscription remains the first to use the clause, πλὴν ὧν οἱ νόμοι ἀπαγορεύουσιν, the more common form until 319, when the general κατὰ τὸν νόμον is first used (Osborne BSA 1972 p. 136). Is this an indication that ὧν οἱ νόμοι λέγουσιν had become inadequate? It certainly would have been easier to cram this shorter clause into the vacat between Decrees II and III; yet the stonecutter inscribed the longer πλ[ὴ]ν [ὧν οἱ νόμοι ἀπαγορεύσιν], and this, in turn, implies a substantive change (especially if ὧν οἱ νόμοι λέγουσιν was in the text of Decree II and the addendum was in fact a corrigendum).

Whatever the form of the clause, there is no doubt that it restricts the choice of phratry. Osborne agrees (BSA [1972] 142/3), and notes that line 5 of Fr. B of this inscription insures that the restriction concerns the phratry alone (note 56). This restriction may imply that a large number of foreigners were being received into the civic ranks (see Dow HSCP; Osborne BSA [1972] 139, also suggests more frequency of grants), but this is not evident from the comparatively small number of grants of citizenship preserved from the Lykourgan period; or the implication may be that certain phratries were concerned not with quantity, but quality, and wanted nothing to do with any foreigner. There is no way to know whether the laws referred to in these clauses were distributive in fact or rather restrictive and exclusionary. In any case, it is not surprising to note that the phratry (representing the socio-religious aspect of citizenship) was in Lykourgan Athens still of at least equal importance with the tribe and deme (the secular and political) in the creation of new citizens.

The clause concerning the second vote for a grant of citizenship is not new in 334/3 (Osborne dates the first appearance to 369/8, BSA [1972] 138). The formula, however, as it appears in Fr. A, lines 22-25 of Decree I--τοὺς δὲ πρυτάνεις ... δοῦναι περὶ αὐτοῦ τὴν ψῆφον εἰς τὴν πρώτην ἐκκλησίαν--becomes the standard form of expression from 334/3 onwards (Osborne, 149).

Another stark contrast between Decree I and Decree III appears in the prescripts where (I) has the usual τῶν προέδρων ἐπεψήφιζεν ...όθεος Κυδα(θηναιεύς), i.e. the epistates alone put the motion to the vote, but (III) includes the whole board of symproedroi: τῶν προέδρων ἐπεψήφιζεν ....17.......ς· συμπρόεδροι ------. Again, the change is emphasized by the fact that both forms appear on the same stone and suggests that the custom (not law) first appeared in 333, one of several minor changes designed to involve more people in the workings of the government so as to share both the responsibilities and the honors and thus to increase interest, patriotism, and zeal (cf. Mitchel Lyk. 202).

ADDENDUM

If it is agreed that the clause ὧν οἱ νόμοι λέγουσιν is correctly dated between prytany 4 and prytany 9 of 334/3 and that it was extremely short-lived and soon (by prytany 8, 333/2) superseded by πλὴν ὧν οἱ νόμοι ἀπαγορεύουσιν, then the only other decree using the shorter expression (II^2 222) which has already been dated roughly to the mid-thirties by Osborne (BSA [1972] 133 note 15), probably should be given a more precise date: after prytany 4 (334/3), close to prytany 9 (334/3), and before prytany 8 (333/2). It is not included in this Corpus because it is impossible to prove that Fr. B, line 5 goes with Decree II, and in any case, II^2 222 would still not be dated to a specific year. (Hansen's article is concerned with the function of the proedroi of the nomothetai; he does not discuss the date of II^2 222.)

32. *THE LEASE OF A GARDEN BY THE ORGEONES OF THE HEROS IATROS (HERO DOCTOR)* EM 13051

photo: ΠΡΑΓ. ΑΚΑΔ. ΑΘ. page 10.

editors: Vallindas & Pantazopoulos ΠΡΑΓ. ΑΚΑΔ. ΑΘ. 13 fasc. 2(1948) 5-23.

collections: Pleket Epigraphica I 43; Behrend Att. Pacht. 38; Nouveau Choix 27.

supplements: SEG 24.203 (Vallindas-Pantazopoulos, Papagiannopoulos-Palaios, Robert).
Bull. (1950) no. 72a (Vallindas-Pantazopoulos, Papagiannopoulos-Palaios).

other bibliography: Lord AJA 3(1899) 44-53; Papagiannopoulos-Palaios ΠΟΛΕΜΟΝ 3(1947/48) 128; Travlos Dictionary 573.

description: The five fragments of white marble, now joined and set in plaster to form a stele, were found on Euripidou Street in Athens and published in 1948. Although the editors give the thickness as 0.05 m., it is impossible now to measure since the back of the stele is all plaster. Some molding remains at the top; the sides are preserved but, again, they are encased in plaster.

dimensions:
H 0.47 m.
W 0.238 m.(above)
0.254 m.(below)
Th 0.05 m.

letters: 0.006 m. Smallest, A, O, X, are .005; largest, Φ, is .010; P is .008. Horizontal hastae of E are slanted: Ɛ . Many letters seem to have been struck twice: Σ, T, Λ.

minuscule text: next page.

commentary: The text includes the bracketing of epsilon and iota in the heading (editors read all the letters) and inclusion of 2 dots in line 29 st. 15 (which editors read as a vacat). The stoichedon order is 17 letters to the line, except in line 6 where the last two letters, ΣΙ are in the 17th stoichos, and in line 22 where there is a vacat at the end of the line. Angular brackets denote errors in the cutting on the stone: line 16 st. 16 is N; line 20 st. 1 is I, st. 16 is Λ; line 22 st. 9 is O;

Θ [ε] ο [ί] stoich. 17

Κατὰ τ[άδ]ε ἐμίϲθωϲεν Χάροψ [Φ]αληρεὺϲ καὶ ο-ὶ ὀργ[εῶ]νεϲ τοῦ ἥρωιο τὸν [κῆπ]ον Θραϲυβούλ-ωι Ἀ[λωπε]κῆθεν εἴκοϲι̣ δ̣ραχ[μῶν] τοῦ ἐνιαυτõ ε̣κάϲτου ἔτη τριάκον-τ̣α· ἀποδιδόναι δὲ τὴν μίϲθωϲιν ἐ[ν] τῶι Θαργ-ηλιῶνι· ἐνοι[κ]οδομεῖ-ϲθαι δὲ Θραϲ[ύ]βουλον ἐάν τι βούληται τοῖϲ αὐτοῦ τέλ[ε]ϲιν ἐν τῶι χωρίωι τῶι ἔξω τοῦ ὀχ-ετοῦ· ἐπειδὰν δὲ ἐξ<ή>κ-ει ὁ χρόνοϲ τῆϲ μιϲθώ-ϲεωϲ ἀπιέναι Θραϲύβ-ουλον λαβόντα τὸν κέ-<ρ>αμον καὶ τὰ ξύλα κ<α>ὶ τὰ θυρώματα, ἐὰμ μή τι αὐτὸν πεί<θ>ει Χάροψ v καὶ οἱ ὀργεῶνεϲ· ϲτῆϲ-αι δὲ ϲτήλην Θραϲύβο-υλον ἐν τῶι ἱερῶι ἀντ-ίγραφα τῶνδε τῶν ϲυν-θηκῶν. Χρόνοϲ· ἄρχει Ν-ικοκράτηϲ ἄρχων. Χρῆ-ϲ<θ>αι δὲ τῶι ἱερῶι : κα-θ̣αρῶι. vacat

line 29 st. 2 is O. Restorations and corrections are those of Vallindas and Pantazopoulos.

This inscription is a departure from the usual fare of honorary decrees. It is concerned with the lease of land by the orgeones of the cult of the Heros Iatros (see #13 for discussion of orgeones). Although the hero's identity is not mentioned on the stone, Papagiannopoulos-Palaios, following Pantazopoulos, has noted that the find spot of #32 is very close to the find spot of II^2 839 and II^2 840, which do deal specifically with the Heros Iatros; thus there is a strong probability that all three came from the same sanctuary (128). The editors of _Nouveau Choix_ (150) place the sanctuary about 500 meters to the northeast of the Agora near the corner of Euripidou and Athenas Streets.

The terms are straightforward. The lesee, Thrasyboulos of the deme Alopeke, is to pay 20 drachmai each year in the month of Thargelion for the duration of 30 years. It has been noted that the sum of 20 drachmai is quite small; also this is the first instance of a lease for 30 years (Robert, 148; _Nouveau Choix_ 150-151). Then there is a provision that Thrasyboulos may make any sort of construction he wishes, at his own expense, as long as it is done beyond the water main. _Nouveau Choix_ (150) notes that two ancient mains running northeast-southwest have been partially excavated just south of Euripidou Street and suggests that the area of the sanctuary in which Thrasyboulos is allowed to build is _north_ of the main (151). When the lease is ended, Thrasyboulos is allowed to take with him the tiles, woodwork, and doors, unless the orgeones have been able to persuade Thrasyboulos (to leave them). It is Thrasyboulos's duty to set up the terms of the contract on a stone stele in the sanctuary. The lease begins in the archonship of Nikokrates. Thrasyboulos is to keep the sanctuary clean.

A lease of 306/5 with similar terms, but with more detail, was published by Lord, *AJA* 3(1899); it is now II^2 2499. *Nouveau Choix* mentions other leases and goes into more detail concerning the specific terms of this lease and its relation to others.

VII. THE YEAR OF NIKETES, 332/1

33. *ATHENS GRANTS PROXENY* EM 7209

editors: Pittakis EΦ. (1840/42) 950; Rangabê (1855) 520; IG II 210; IG II^2 344.

supplements: SEG 3.84 (Kirchner); 12.88 (Koumanoudes-Oikonomides); 21.279 (Meritt Ath., Hesperia).

other bibliography: Ditmar Coron. 80-82; Schweigert Hesperia 8(1939) 33-34; Pritchett-Neugebauer Cal. 48-49; Koumanoudes-Oikonomides ΠΟΛΕΜΩΝ 5(1952/5) 27; Lambrechts Prox. 60, 157; Meritt Ath. 86; Hesperia 32 (1963) 426; Walbank ZPE 48(1982) 264-266.

description: This fragment of Pentelic marble was found west of the Erechtheion in 1839. Walbank points out that the left side is preserved; the photograph confirms that observation (see Plate 19 of my dissertation). The other sides are broken. Although the back is rough-picked, it is impossible to tell if it is original. The condition of the stone is bad. For many of the letters I have underlined as unreadable, there is just no surface left on the stone--perhaps the result of making squeezes.

dimensions:
- H 0.185 m.
- W 0.27 m.
- Th 0.168 m.

letters: 0.007 m. Smallest, Δ, Ο, Ω, are .005; largest, Υ, Φ, Ψ, are .010.

minuscule text: next page.

commentary: As noted above, the surface is gone for many of the letters read previously. These letters are underlined; all dots are mine.

Restorations, lines 15-25, and the stoichedon order of 23 letters to the line are Velsen's. Dittmar noted the duplication of the otherwise unknown phrase ἐπα[ινέσαι αὐ/τὸν κ]αὶ ε[ῖ]ναι αὐτὸν in lines 2/3 of II 210 (lines 15/16 of #33, this decree) and ἐπαινέσαι α[ὐτὸν καὶ εἶναι αὐτὸν] in line 11 of II 183 (#82, II^2 368) as well as the fact that the rest of II 210 (lines 3-12) and the rest of the first decree of #82 (lines 11-18) were worded identically (with the exception of the amount for setting up the stone: this decree has 3 stoichoi for the amount, ΔΔ[Δ]; #82 has only 2 stoichoi, [ΔΔ]).

stoich. 23

[προξενία ....15.......]
[Ἐπὶ Νικήτου ἄρχοντοϲ ἐπὶ τῆ]-
[ϲ ...ντίδοϲ δευτέραϲ πρυτα]-
[νείαϲ, ἧι Ἀριϲτόνουϲ Ἀριϲτό]-
[νου Ἀναγυράϲιοϲ ἐγραμμάτε]-
[υεν· βοηδρομιῶνοϲ ἐνάτει ἱϲ]-
[ταμένου, δευτέραι καὶ τριακ]-
[οϲτῆι τῆϲ πρυτανείαϲ· ἐκκλη]-
[ϲία κυρία· τῶν προέδρων, ἐπεψ]-
[ήφιξεν ....14....... Πολ]-
[ύευκτοϲ Σωϲτράτου Σφήττιο]-
[ϲ εἶπεν· ἐπειδὴ .....11.....]
[..........22.......... ἐ]-
[νδείκνυτα]ι τὴν [εὔνοιαν πρὸ]-
[ϲ Ἀ]θηνα[ίο]υς ἐπα[ινέϲαι αὐτὸ]-
[ν κ]α̣ὶ ε[ἶ]ν̣α̣ι αὐτὸν [πρόξενον κ]-
[αὶ] ε̣ὐ̣ε̣ρ̣γέτην̣ τοῦ δ̣[ήμου τοῦ Ἀ]-
[θην]αίων̣· ἀν̣αγ̣ράψαι [δὲ τὸ ψήφ]-
[ιϲμα] α̣[ὐ]τ̣ῶι̣ τὸν γραμμ[ατέα τὸ]-
[ν κατ]ὰ̣ πρυτ̣ανεῖαν κα[ὶ ϲτῆϲα]-
[ι ἐν ἀ]κροπόλει, εἰϲ δὲ [τὴν ἀνα]-
[γρ]α[φ]ὴ̣ν τῆϲ ϲτήληϲ δοῦ[ναι τὸ]-
[ν] ταμ[μ]ίαν τοῦ δήμου ΔΔ[Δ δραχμ]-
[ὰ]ϲ̣ ἐκ τῶν κατὰ ψηφίϲμ[ατα ἀνα]-
[λι]ϲκ̣ο̣μένω̣[ν]· vacat

He concluded that the same decree honoring the same person was inscribed on the 2 separate stelai. Confirmation for that conclusion came from the fact that a word for word restoration of the first 10 lines from #82 above line 1 of II 210 fit exactly the stoichedon order of 23 letters to the line. Kirchner followed Dittmar so that the first line on the stone (and II 210) is the 14th line in the text of II^2 344 as well as the text presented here. (Walbank consistently equates line 16 rather than line 15 with the 2nd line on the stone; this is presumably a typo.)

Walbank's observation that the left side of the stone is original means that the first two restored letters in each line must be shifted to the end of the preceeding line (calculations are in his note 7, page 265). He includes the text of lines 12-15 (265):

[..5.. εἶπεν· ἐπειδὴ ...7....]
[..........22.......... ἐ]-
[νδεῖκνυτα]ι τὴν [εὔνοιαν πρὸ]-
[ϲ Ἀ]θηνα[ῖο]υϲ, ἐπα[ινέϲαι κτλ.]

(15 [ρὸϲ Ἀ]θηνα[ῖο]υϲ, ἐπα[ινέϲαι αὐ]- Ditt., Ki.)

Since this corrected text allows for only 29 letters for the full name of the honorand in this decree rather than the 31 letters required for the honorand in #82 (lines 9/10), Walbank concludes that the man honored in this decree "is therefore not the same man as the honorand of <u>IG</u> II 368" (265). It must be noted, however, that a length of 29 stoichoi for the full name of the honorand in this decree is required <u>only</u> if the honorand's ethnic contains 9 letters: Dittmar was able to equate the 2 decrees even though this one has 23 letters to the line and #82 has 33 letters to the line because for this decree, the combination of 31 stoichoi for the full name in lines 12-14 (31 stoichoi from lines 9/10 of #82) and 18 stoichoi for the name and ethnic in lines 1/2 (18 stoichoi from line 1 of #82) with the rest of the restorations of lines 1-10 from #82 fit exactly a stoichedon order of 23 letters to the line. In other words, the beginning of the full name of the honorand in this decree occurs in st. 17 of line 12 only because in lines 1/2 above, 9 stoichoi were allotted for the ethnic of the honorand. The dissociation of the honorands of #33 and #82 means that since the length of the ethnic is unknown, we cannot ascertain the length of the full name either. If, therefore, Dittmar's restoration is retained, the placement of the beginning of the preamble, 'Ἐπὶ Νικήτου, etc., must be arbitrary. I have chosen the beginning of line 2 (in fact, without the necessity to make this text conform exactly to that of #82, the first line is superfluous). Dittmar (and Kirchner) placed it in the 4th stoichos to allow for the name and patronymic of the honorand of #82:

[Προξενία Θεοφάντου ..6....]
[... ἐπὶ Νικήτου κτλ.]

(Contrary to Walbank's statement, page 264, there is no vacat in st. 3, line 2 of II^2 344; both Kirchner and Dittmar required all 9 stoichoi to coincide with the 9 stoichoi for the ethnic in #82.)

"The identical wording of lines 1-12 [sic] of IG II 344 and of lines 10-18 of IG II 368 still leaves a strong supposition that these two decrees were both passed on the same day at the same assembly" (Walbank, 265; lines 1-12 on the stone equal lines 10-18 of #82; for II^2 344 it would be lines 14-25). I present a text which includes Dittmar's restoration with the caveat that, despite the duplication of lines 14-25 of #33 and lines 10-18 of #82, without the specific length of the honorand's name to anchor the beginning and end of that restoration, the argument for dating this decree to 332/1 (let alone a specific date within that year) becomes tenuous. Another anchor to confirm Dittmar's restoration was the same number of stoichoi for the mover. Meritt had restored the demotic of the mover, lines 11/12, based on Schweigert's restoration of the same in line 8 of #82: [Σφήττιος εἶπεν ᵛ]. Although it does not now confirm Dittmar's restoration, if we can assume that Polyeuktos proposed honors to two men in 332/1, then his entire name should be restored. Since the name of the honorand is now unknown, Meritt's restoration of the vacat is not necessary (*Hesperia*, the restoration of the vacat does not shorten the name of the honorand to 30 stoichoi, as Walbank states, 265; it is to compensate for the fact that the demotic in #82 should be 9 stoichoi).

As the text now stands we have a straightforward honorary decree, passed on the 32nd day of the second prytany, the 9th day of Boedromion. The proposer, Polyeuktos, son of Sostratos, of the deme Sphettos, proposed #67 (II^2 363), which belongs in 326/5, and II^2 350, which

Kirchner dates to the Lykourgan period, but the latest scholarship has placed in 318/7 (Meritt Hesperia 45[1976] 173). 131b Even without the date, lines 14-25 tell us that a foreigner is to be honored with proxeny and the title benefactor of the Demos because he has shown good will to the Athenians. Thirty drachmai are appropriated for engraving and setting the stele up on the Akropolis.

With the dissociation of the honorand of this decree with the honorand of #82, any further information is lost. We can assume, however, that if this decree was passed in 332/1, it was set up in that year. That assumption applies to any decree passed in 332/1, including the decree honoring Theophantos recorded as the first decree of #82. The implications of that assumption will be discussed in #82.

332/1

34. *DECREE* Ag. Inv. I 830

photo: Hesperia 5(1936) page 414.

editor: Meritt Hesperia 5(1936) 413-414 no. 11.

other bibliography: Pritchett-Neugebauer Cal. 49; Meritt Ath. 86.

description: This fragment of Pentelic marble was found in the Agora in 1933. Only the right side is preserved, including the cymation and part of the pediment. The iota of the heading, ΘΕΟΙ, is engraved on the fillet.

dimensions:
H 0.175 m. (entire)
0.095 m. (below pediment)
W 0.122 m.
Th 0.095 m..

letters: 0.006 m. Smallest, Ο, Ω, are .004; largest, Σ, is .008.

minuscule text: next page.

commentary: Restorations are Meritt's. The stoichedon

order is 31 letters to the line; it is disturbed only once, with a preserved vacat in st. 27, line 7.

stoich. 31

[Θ ε ο] ί
[Ἐπὶ Νικήτου ἄρχοντοϲ ἐπὶ τῆϲ] Κεκροπί-
[δοϲ πέμπτηϲ πρυτανείαϲ ἧι Ἀρ]ιϲτόνου-
[ϲ Ἀριϲτόνου Ἀναγυράϲιοϲ ἐγρ]αμμάτε[υ]-
[εν· Ποϲιδεῶνοϲ ἐνδεκάτει, πέμπ]τει καὶ
[δεκάτει τῆϲ πρυτανείαϲ· τῶν πρ]οέδρων
[ἐπεψήφιζεν name 16 demotic] v ἔδ[οξ]-
[εν τῶι δήμωι - - - - - - - - - -]

All that remains of this decree is the heavily restored dating formula. This decree provides, however, an excellent example of the reasoning which allows an epigraphist to restore the date when so little is left on the stone. The inscription is assigned to the year of Niketes from the name of the secretary in line 3; that restoration gives a stoichedon order of 31 letters which in turn shows that the prytany must be either the 5th, 7th, or 10th, and that the date by prytany, lines 5/6, must be between the 13th and 19th; for the year of Niketes such dates in the 7th and 10th prytanies require corresponding dates in Anthesterion and Skirophorion; these months do not fit the stoichedon order in line 5; the 5th prytany, with corresponding month, Posideon, does fit (Meritt, Hesperia 414, paraphrased).

The resulting equation is [Posideon 11] = Prytany [V 15] = 158th day. Pritchett-Neugebauer agree with the restoration, but count the day as the 159th. The discrepancy of one day occurs because Pritchett-Neugebauer, following strictly the so-called "rule" of Aristotle, have made all of the first four prytanies contain 36 days. Meritt, however, believes that for this year it was the first three and the tenth prytanies which were of 36 days. Unger was the first to note that the last prytany of the year had to have 36 days. The same one-day discrepancy occurs also for #35-#41 from this year. (See #15 for discussion of the calendar and #28 for a more specific discussion of the division of the year into prytanies.)

332/1

35. *DECREE* EM 7633

editors: Lolling AΔ (1889) 12 page 94; IG 5.493b; IG II^2 420; Dow Hesperia 32(1963) 347-348; Meritt AJP 85(1964) 304-306.

supplements: SEG 21.322 (Dow, Meritt AJP); 22.93 (Meritt AJP).

other bibliography: Mikalson Year 29-31, 190; Meritt GRBS 17(1976) 147 note 2; Hansen GRBS 18(1977) 43-70.

description: The small fragment of Pentelic marble was found on the Akropolis. All sides are broken except a small part of the right side and the lower right-hand part of a pediment. The back is rough-picked.

dimensions:
H 0.24 m.(with pediment)
0.11 m.(below pediment)
W 0.165 m.
Th 0.088 m.

letters: 0.006 m. Smallest letter, O, is .004; largest, H, I, K, N, Σ, are .008. The letters were carved in a slipshod manner.

minuscule text: next page.

epigraphical commentary: The text is based on Meritt's alternate restoration for II^2 420 (AJP 305). His reading of omega, line 4 st. 37, is reaffirmed; the rho in line 4 st. 44, read by Dow without a dot, should be dotted, as by Meritt. Dow dotted a rho, line 5 st. 38 ; only the circular part of the letter remains; it is lower than the rho 3 stoichoi to the right but could be similar to the one in line 4 st. 40; or it could be theta. In line 7 st. 39, Meritt read two sigmas, st. 41, 42, clearly. Only the upper stroke of the first sigma is visible and is here dotted, following Dow. The second sigma, in st. 42, can not now be read on the stone and is here underlined.

stoich. 47

[Ἐπὶ Νικήτου ἄρχοντος ἐπὶ τῆς ...ντίδος ἕκ]της πρυτανεία-
[ς ἧι Ἀριστόνους Ἀριστόνου Ἀναγυράσιος ἐγρ]αμμάτευεν: [Γα]-
τετράδι ἐπὶ δέκα, τρίτει καὶ δεκάτ]ει
[μηλιῶνος ὀγδόει ἐπὶ δέκα, ἐβδόμει καὶ δεκάτ]ει τῆς πρυτ[αν]-
ὀγδόει φθίνοντος, μιᾶι καὶ εἰκοστ]ει
[είας, ἐκκλησία στρατηγῶν παραγγειλάντων, τ]ῶ̣μ προε̣δρ[ων ε]-
[πεψήφιζεν .....¹².... ἔδοξεν τῶι δήμωι, Εὐ]θ̣υκράτ[ης ..]
[- - - - - ca. 16 - - εἶπεν, ἐπειδὴ - - ca. 10 - - Θ]ε̣ομνή[στου]-
[- - - - - - - - - - - - κτλ. - - - - - - - - - - - -]Σ̣Σ[..⁵..]

[Ἐπὶ Νικήτου ἄρχοντος ἐπὶ τῆς ....ίδος πρώ]της πρυτανεία-
[ς ἧι Ἀριστόνους Ἀριστόνου Ἀναγυράσιος ἐγρ]αμμάτευεν: [·Εκ]-
[ατομβαιῶνος ἕκτει ἐπὶ δέκα, ἕκτει καὶ δεκάτ]ει τῆς πρυτ[αν]-
[είας, ἐκκλησία στρατηγῶν παραγγειλάντων, τ]ῶ̣μ προέδ̣ρ[ων ἐ]-

commentary: The stoichedon order is 47 letters to the line; Dow suggested ca. 50 letters; Kirchner, following Lolling and Koehler, noted only that the text was stoichedon. Meritt discussed the problem of restoration in his article; the archon's name must be short, the secretary's name must be long, and in line 4, the designation of the ekklesia must fill 23 stoichoi. Meritt found that the year 332/1 fulfills the first two requirements and that στρατηγῶν παραγγειλάντων (using II^2 911 for a near parallel) fits line 4. Another possiblity is ἀπὸ βουλῆc ἐκκλησία κυρία σύγκλητοc (305). I include below the minuscule text Meritt's first choice for the restored date. The equation, Prytany [I] [16] = Hekatombaion [16] = 16th day, had not been challenged until Mikalson noted that Hekatombaion 16 is the day for the Synoikia festival. Since Meritt also offered three alternate restorations for the 6th prytany, month Gamelion (AJP), and he himself has noted the importance of taking festival days into account (GRBS), there can be no objection to offering the text above.

In line 1 there are only two possibilities for tribe in prytany: Αἰαντῖδοc or Λεωντῖδοc. None of the three dates in Gamelion conflicts with a known festival day.

Kirchner provided the skeleton for the dating formula; Lolling, followed by Meritt (AJP), restored Εὐ]ρυκρά-τ[ηc in line 5, but Εὐ]θ̣υκράτ[ηc is epigraphically possible and prosopographically far more likely. Lolling offered two restorations for line 6: the one used in the text; and Δι]ομνή[στου, which is now impossible because of the new reading of dotted episilon, st. 39.

Dow's restoration was based on the reading of συ]μπροέδρ[οι in line 4 (which the dotted omega in st. 37 renders impossible). Thus he assumed that the text from line 4 on should be restored as a list of names of the men who were symproedroi on that day. As noted under #31, the dating of the third decree to 333/2 marks the beginning of the custom of listing the symproedroi in decrees, but it was not a hard and fast rule, and the new reading in st. 37 precludes their being restored here.

Only Meritt's restoration of this decree gives a semi-specific date: either the 14th, 18th or 22nd of Gamelion; the 13th, 17th or 21st day of the 6th prytany. Koehler, following Lolling, suggested a date in the third century; Kirchner dated II^2 420 "post a. 336/5"; Dow suggested 330-308/7. From the general appearance and letter style, however, there is no reason not to place this decree in the Lykourgan era. Meritt's restoration had not been challenged until Mikalson, and since Mikalson objects only to the specific day, Hekatombaion 16, the assignment of this decree to 332/1, the year of Niketes (a short archon name, long secretary's name, see commentary above), the month Gamelion, the 6th prytany, stands firm, even though the specific day cannot be pinned down.

Meritt's original restoration for the 16th of Hekatombaion allowed him to offer some justification for the restoration of the ekklesia as the one called by the generals, a designation which is not found on stone until much later. "A meeting of the assembly on the sixteenth, so soon after the normal first meeting of the year on the eleventh, may seem odd, though less so if the generals requested it" (*AJP* 305). The three alternate restorations (used in the minuscule text above), offered in response to this concern, make the extraordinary aspect weaker (the 11th of other months does not *have* to be a meeting day), and we are left with accepting the restoration of a meeting called by the generals because it fits the stone (see also Meritt's alternate designation for the ekklesia meeting in the commentary above). In any case, Hansen has recently challenged the generally accepted view that, in addition to the regular four meetings per prytany, extraordinary sessions could be called whenever the situation demanded it. He concludes (44) that, although it was certainly possible to summon the assembly in a special way, there was no meeting in addition to the regular four. Thus a meeting specially summoned by the generals in any prytany would have taken the place of one of the four regular sessions.

Mikalson lists seven decrees from the Lykourgan era, whose accepted restoration give a date which conflicts with a known festival day. For the first four, #4, #5, this decree, #35, and #48 (II^2 351) either there had already been alternate restorations offered (as for this decree) or one can be suggested (as for #5). One decree, II^2 363 (#67) is a special case. There are two, however, II^2 353 (#51) and II^2 359 (#63) which can not be changed and so provide two exceptions in the Lykourgan era to Mikalson's rule that the Athenians did not have meetings of the ekklesia on festival days.

332/1

36. *LYKOURGOS PROPOSES HONORS FOR A PLATAIAN* EM 7168, 7167

photo: Fr. A Svoronos ΕΘ. ΜΟΥΣ. Plate 216.4.

editors: Fr. A Pittakis ΕΦ. (1856/61) 3412.
Fr. B Pittakis ΕΦ. (1856/61) 3534.
Fr. A+B IG II 173; IG II^2 345.

other bibliography: Reusch De diebus cont. 10; Unger Att. Arch. 425; Wilhelm UDA 218; Binneboessel Studien 14 no. 60; Pritchett-Neugebauer Cal. 49; Meritt Ath. 86; Mikalson Year 124-126, 130-131; Henry Prescripts 39.

description: Both fragments of Pentelic marble were found on the Akropolis in 1858. For Fr. A, the left side and lower part of the relief are preserved; the back is not preserved. The right side and only the cymation below the relief of Fr. B are preserved; some of the back of Fr. B has a flat finish.

dimensions:
Fr. A
H 0.215 m. (entire)
0.09 m. (below cymation)
W 0.17 m.

letters: 0.007 m.
Smallest, Κ, Λ, Ο, are .005; largest, Φ, Ψ, are .009.

Th 0.088 m.
Fr. B
H 0.42 m. (entire)
0.32 m. (below cymation)
W 0.145 m.
Th 0.35 m.

minuscule text: next page.

commentary: The text is based on Kirchner's. With the exception of line 16 st. 21, all dots are mine. The underlined letters can not now be read. Other changes include three new readings: Σ line 22 st. 25; Χ line 23 st. 25; Λ line 24 st. 24. (Since these new readings occur in the same stoichoi and in the same order as the 3 underlined letters, lines 20, 21, 22, they may reflect a printing error carried over from the editio major to the text of II^2 345.)

Koehler established the stoichedon order of 30 letters to the line and made the restorations. Exceptions are noted below.

7 beg [Διονύσου]: Reusch. [Πειραιεῖ] Koe.

14 end: Wilamowitz (in II^2 345). παρέ[χει]ν Koe.

15 end: Wilh.

This is the first of four decrees, #36, #37, #38, #39, passed on the same day in the year of Niketes: the 7th day of the 8th prytany, held by Antiochis; the 19th day of Elaphebolion (the day is the 255th, Meritt; 256th, Pritchett-Neugebauer; see #34 for discrepancy). Reusch's restoration, line 7, of the theater of Dionysos was accepted by Wilhelm and Kirchner; line 6 of #39 confirms that meeting place (Henry confirms that this marks the first restored mention of venue). The meeting of the ekklesia was shortly after the festival of Dionysos (cf. Mikalson, 124-126), and as Schweigert notes (26), a time when many illustrious foreigners would be present, a time for the Demos to vote many honors.

stoich. 30

Fr. A

Θεοί   Fr. B

'Επὶ Νικήτου ἄρ[χοντος ἐ]πὶ τῆς 'Αντιοχ-
ίδος ὀγδόης π[ρυτανεία]ς ἧι 'Αριςτόνο-
υς 'Αριςτόνο[υ 'Αναγυράςι]ος ἐγραμ[μά]τ-
ευεν· 'Ελαφη̣[βολιῶνος ἐν]ά̣τηι ἐπὶ δέ[κ]α,
ἑβδόμ[ηι τῆς πρυτανείας]· ἐκκληςία [ἐ]ν
[Διονύςου· τῶν προέδρων ἐ]πεψήφιζε[ν] Ν-
[ικόςτρατος Κόπρειος· ἔδ]οξεν τῶι δήμ-
[ωι· Λυκοῦργος Λυκόφρονο]ς Βουτάδης ε-
[ἶπεν· ἐπειδὴ .....10.....]ήμου Πλα[τ]αι-
[εὺς πρότερόν τε ἐπηγγεί]λατο τ̣[ῶ]ι [δ]ήμ-
[ωι ....18........]ς γίγνητ̣[α]ι
.........20..........α̣ι ἀργυ[ρί]ου
.........20..........ο παρέ[σχε]ν τ-
.........20..........ν καὶ [νῦν ἐ]πι-
[........18........ το]ῦ̣ ςτ[ρατη]γ̣οῦ
- - - - - - - - ΛΣ..5..ΙΙΙ
- - - - - - - - ΙΣ....ΝΤΟ
- - - - - - - - - Θ..5..ΛΝ
- - - - - - - - - - Σ̱..ΥΕΠ
- - - - - - - - - - Χ̱.. ΑΙ
- - - - - - - - - - Λ̱Σ..ΙΕΠ
- - - - - - - - - - - Χ..ΙΕΛ
- - - - - - - - - - - Λ..6...

In #36, #38, #39, none of the men honored is an Athenian; in #37, not enough can be read to prove that the man honored is a foreigner, but it is likely since Demades made the motion (his possible connections with Macedonia have been discussed in #7).

At any rate, the man honored in this decree is a Plataian. His name and patronymic are lost, as are the motive for granting honors and the honors received. Money is mentioned (line 13) and also a general (line 16), but there is not enough left on the stone to provide any connected information. The fact, however, that Lykourgos was the proposer supports the assumption that, whoever the Plataian was and whatever he had done, his contribution was such that Lykourgos wished to add his personal endorsement. (See #15 for other decrees moved by Lykourgos.)

332/1

37. *DEMADES PROPOSES HONORS* EM 7164

editors: Pittakis ΕΦ. (1852/55) 1963, (1856/61) 2682; Rangabé (1855) 428; IG II 174; IG II^2 346.

other bibliography: Pritchett-Neugebauer Cal. 49; Oikonomides ΠΛΑΤΩΝ 8(1956) 115; Meritt Ath. 87; DeLaix Proboul. 137.

description: This fragment of Pentelic marble was found on the Akropolis in 1842. Only the right side and back are preserved.

dimensions:	letters: 0.006 m. Smallest, Δ, T,
H 0.235 m.	Ω, are .005; largest, Γ, P, Y,
W 0.225 m.	are .007. Alphas do not have
Th 0.11 m.	cross bars.

minuscule text: next page.

commentary: I have dotted a few letters and underlined those letters which are no longer legible but which Kirchner saw. There are four new readings: Σ line 14 st. 17; N line 15 st. 23; Velsen also read the Δ line 10 st. 23, and N line 16 st. 17. The stoichedon order is 25 letters to the line; a vacat, however, must occur in the restoration at the end of line 5 or the beginning of line 6, and there must be crowding of two letters into one space either at the end of line 6 or the beginning of line 7. On the assumption that the stonecutter intentionally ended the first two lines of the second decree with complete words, a vacat has been added at the end of line 5, and it is suggested that iota was inscribed in the space between epsilon and alpha in the 23rd and 24th stoichoi of line 6. (Such crowding is not unusual, and Kirchner must have assumed it here, but it is not indicated in his text.)

stoich. 25

[- - - - - - - - - - ἐκ]
[τῶν κατὰ ψηφίcματ]α ἀ[ναλιcκομ]-
[ένων τῶι δήμωι· κα]λέcαι δ[ὲ καὶ α]-
[ὐτὸν ἐπὶ ξένια] ε[ἰ]c τὸ πρυ[τανεῖ]-
[ον εἰc αὔριον].
[Ἐπὶ Νικήτου] ἄρχ[ο]ντοc ἐπ[ὶ τῆc v]
[Ἀντιοχίδοc] ὀγδόηc πρυτα[ν]ε[ίαc],
[ἧι Ἀριcτό]νουc Ἀριcτόνου Ἀν[αγ]-
[υράcιοc ἐ]γραμμάτευεν· Ἐλαφ[ηβ]-
[ολιῶνοc ἐν]άτηι ἐπὶ δέκα, ἐ[β]δόμ-
[ηι τῆc πρυτα]νείαc· τῶν προ[έ]δ[ρω]-
[ν ἐπεψήφιζε]ν Νικόcτρατοc Κ[όπ]-
[ρειοc· ἔδοξε]ν τῶι δ[ήμ]ωι· Δημά[δη]-
[c Δημέου Παια]νιεὺc εἶπεν· [ἐπει]-
[δὴ .....9.....]ο[c] Ἀριcτήιδ[ου ..]-
[...7... διατε]λεῖ εὔνουc [ὤ]ν τ[ῶ]-
[ι δήμωι τῶι Ἀθηναί]ων καὶ υ....
........17........ι καὶ ..Ε.
..........19..........ΣΤ..Τ.

All restorations are Koehler's. He used Velsen's text and restorations.

This is the second of four decrees passed on the same day in the year of Niketes (see #36 for date and location of the meeting). The proposer is another illustrious Athenian, Demades, son of Demeas, of the deme Paiania (see #7, #23, for discussion of Demades).

As to the man honored, only his father's name, Aristeides, is known. Since he had been well-disposed toward the Athenian people, and probably had other good works to his credit, this son of Aristeides was to be voted honors which are lost. Lines 1-4, however, contain the end of another decree which was inscribed above the one moved by Demades. Since it can be assumed that that decree also concerned the son of Aristeides, we know that he was entertained in the prytaneion. DeLaix (137 n. 71) provides a long list of decrees for which "no telltale signs of an underlying probouleuma may be conclusively demonstrated," but the examples of #18 and especially #27 suggest that lines 1-4 of this inscription are the end of a decree recording an action in the Boule, i.e., representing a so-called open-ended probouleuma which would introduce the honorand to the ekklesia and invite him to dinner in the prytaneion, but otherwise leave the specific benefits up to the People.

332/1

38. *ATHENS HONORS AMPHIS OF ANDROS* EM 7155

photo: Svoronos ΕΘ. ΜΟΥΣ Plate 215.1.

editors: Fr. A Kumanudes ΑΘΗΝΑΙΟΝ 6(1877) 131 no. 6.
Fr. A+B Wilhelm AM 15(1890) 219-222; IG II 5.173b.
Fr. A+B+C IG II^2 347 (Fr. C from Wilhelm's transcription; he noted the addition of Fr. C in UDA, but did not provide a text.)

collection: Michel 1468.

supplement: _SEG_ 14.55 (Lewis).

other bibliography: Wilhelm _RM_ 56(1901) 582; _Berl. phil. Woch._ 22(1902) 1098; _UDA_ 218; Binneboessel _Studien_ 14 no. 61; Pritchett-Neugebauer _Cal._ 49; Lewis _BSA_ 49(1954) 37; Lambrechts _Prox._ 100, 157; Meritt _Ath._ 87; Osborne _BSA_ 67(1972) 158.

description: The two fragments, A+B, are of Pentelic marble; they are now joined with plaster. Fr. B is actually three smaller fragments, apparently joined since they were found. Fr. A was found in the Asklepieion; the find spot of Fr. B was not recorded. All sides are broken. The lower part of the relief remains above the text. It shows the feet of two male figures who apparently were clad in _himatia_ and faced each other. Binneboessel (14) suggests that since the figure on the right is much larger, he is a god. Since the text says that Amphis is to receive a crown, perhaps the relief represents a god crowning him (cf. II^2 367, #81, for an almost exact parallel). Apparently only Wilhelm saw Fr. C; it has no number in the Epigraphical Museum. An examination of the stone and of the arrangement of the letters might lead one to question the restoration [τῶι δήμωι] in what may have been a vacat (cf. #1, #39 [_Hesperia_ 8(1939) no. 6]).

dimensions:
- H 0.575 m. (entire)
- 0.40 m. (below relief)
- W 0.26 m.
- Th 0.125 m.

letters: 0.007 m. Smallest, O, is .005; largest, B, Σ, Y, are .009.

minuscule text: next page.

commentary: The text is based on Kirchner's. The underlined letters are no longer legible; all dots are mine. There are two changes. In line 11, the 19th letter is mu, Ἄμφις; Ἄνφιν is also on the stone, line 16. In line 14, the parentheses around the iota of τῶι have been removed; it is not omitted, as indicated in previous texts, but shares st. 16 with the omega. Two other discrepancies should be noted: the omicron, line 8 st. 12 has a central dot as if a theta; in line 10 st. 17, the tau looks very much like a rho.

stoich. 22

Fr. A Fr. B

[ʼΕπὶ Ν]ικήτου ἄρχοντοϲ [ἐπὶ τ]-
[ῆϲ ʼΑν]τιοχίδοϲ ὀγδοίη[ϲ πρυ]-
[τανεί]αϲ, ἧι ʼΑριϲτόνου[ϲ ʼΑρι]-
[ϲτόν]ου ʼΑναγυράϲιοϲ ἐ[γραμ]-
[μάτε]υεν· ʼΕλαφηβολιῶν[οϲ ἐν]-
[άτει] ἐπὶ δέκα, ἑβδόμει τ[ῆϲ π]-
[ρυτα]ν̲είαϲ· τῶν προέδρω[ν ἐπ]-
[εψήφ]ι̲ζεν [Ν]ικόϲτρατοϲ [Κόπ]-
[ρειο]ϲ· ἔδο[ξ]εν τῶι δήμωι· [ʼΑρι]-
[ϲτόξ]ε̲νοϲ [Κη]φιϲοδότου̲ ...
[...ε]ὺϲ εἶπεν̲· [ἐ]πει̲δὴ ῞Αμφιϲ Δι...
[... ῞Α]ν̲δ̣ριοϲ διατελεῖ ἐ[πιε]-
[ικῆϲ ὢ]ν τῶι δήμωι τῶι ʼΑθ[ηνα]-
[ίων κα]ὶ̲ νῦν καὶ ἐν τῶι̲ παρ[εληλ]-
[λυθό]τι χρόνωι, δεδόχθαι̲ [τῶι]
[δήμωι] ἐπαινέϲαι ῞Ανφι̲ν̣ [Δι.]
..5.. ῞Ανδριον̣ καὶ ϲτεφ[ανῶ]-
[ϲαι κι]τ̲του̲ [ϲτε]φάνωι ἀρ̣[ετῆ]-
[ϲ ἕνεκα καὶ δικ]αιοϲύν[ηϲ· εἶ]-
[ναι δὲ αὐτὸν πρ]όξενον̣ [καὶ ε]-
[ὐεργέτην τοῦ] δ̣ήμου τ̣[οῦ ʼΑθη]-
[ναίων καὶ ἐκγό]ν̣ο̣[υϲ ..6..]
- - - - - - - - - - - -
- - - - - - - - - - - -

Fr. C

δρα[χμὰϲ] ἐκ τῶν κατ[ὰ ψηφίϲμ]-
ατα ἀναλιϲκομέν[ω]ν [τῶι δήμ]-
[ωι].

The stoichedon order is 22 letters to the line, established by Wilhelm. All three violations are on the stone. In line 11, the 15 letters, from the first epsilon of εἶπεν to the iota of Ἄμφιϲ, use only 10 stoichoi; Wilhelm suggests that εἶπεν had been omitted originally. Line 14 has 23 letters due to the new reading of iota with the omega in st. 16. Line 15 has 23 letters; theta and alpha occupy st. 18.

Restorations are Wilhelm's. Koehler added the name of the proposer, Ἀριστόξ]ενοϲ, lines 9/10. The restoration for lines 12/13, ἐ[πιεικῆϲ] is Lewis's; Wilhelm, followed by Kirchner, had offered ε[ὔνουϲ ὢν {ὢ]ν}.

This is the third of four decrees passed on the same day; the date is discussed in #36. And, so far, this decree offers the most information; since Amphis of Andros has maintained a generous attitude toward the Demos both now and in the past time, he is to be honored with a crown of ivy because of his goodness and justice; and he and his descendants are to be granted proxeny and called benefactors of the Athenians.

The ivy crown denotes a dramatist. In his first publication of this decree (Fr. A+B in AM), Wilhelm identified the man honored as the Amphis, who is known from Souidas as a poet of middle comedy; and in his review of Kirchner's Prosopographia Attica (Berl. phil. Woch.) Wilhelm would add this inscription as evidence for PA 785 (Osborne also makes this connection). There is a problem in that Souidas identifies Amphis as an Athenian while the decree calls him an Andrian; the name, furthermore, is non-Athenian. A possible solution is that Amphis, who is here voted proxenos and euergetes, may later have received a grant of citizenship.

39. *ATHENS GRANTS PROXENY TO AN ABDERITE* Ag. Inv. I 3364

photo: Hesperia 8(1939) page 26.

editor: Schweigert Hesperia 8(1939) 26-27 no. 6.

other bibliography: Pritchett-Neugebauer Cal. 49; Lambrechts Prox. 51, 57, 134, 157; Meritt Ath. 87.

description: The five small fragments of Pentelic marble (now joined) were found in the debris of the demolished Church of Christ in 1936. All sides are broken.

dimensions:
H 0.345 m.
W 0.11 m.
Th 0.052 m.

letters: 0.007 m. Smallest, Δ, Λ, M, are .006; largest, Σ, is .009.

minuscule text: next page.

commentary: The text is based on Schweigert's. There are no changes, except to show that the sigma and iota in line 9 occupy one stoichos, st. 5. Schweigert restored the stoichedon order to 29 letters to the line. It is violated twice: in line 7, the restoration required 30 letters; in line 9 is the violation on the stone, noted already.

Restorations are Schweigert's. His restoration of the mover, Euboios, son of Kratistoleos, of the deme Anagyrous, lines 8/9, is tentative (PA 5313, Davies, APF, calls the restoration "exceedingly uncertain"); Schweigert has restored line 19 as having dropped out of the text; he credits Meritt with the restoration of the ethnic of the man honored, lines 9/10, and 14.

This is the last of four decrees passed on the same day, discussed in #36. The man honored is the son of Onomarchos, from Abdera. The reason(s) for the honors is lost, but the stone does reveal that the son of Onomarchos (and his descendants) is to receive a gold crown, to be granted proxeny and called benefactor of the Demos. The decree ends with the usual formula for publication of the stele--with the unusual omission of who is to be responsible, the secretary kata prytaneian. Schweigert's restoration of this entire line of exactly 29 letters in an inscription of the same stoichedon order has an important implication for the carving of decrees.

stoich. 29

[᾿Επὶ Νικήτου ἄρχοντος ἐπὶ τῆc ᾿Αντιο]-
[χίδοc ὀγδόηc πρυτανείαc ἧι ᾿Αριcτό]-
[νο]υ̣[c ᾿Αριcτόνου ᾿Αναγυράcιοc ἐγραμ]-
[μά]τευ[ε]ν· ᾿Ε[λαφηβολιῶνοc ἐνάτηι ἐπὶ]
[δέ]κα ἑβδό[μηι τῆc πρυτανείαc· ἐκκλη]-
[cία] ἐν Διο[νύcου· τῶν προέδρων ἐπεψή]-
[φιζ]εν Ν[ι]κ[όcτρατοc Κόπρειοc ἔδοξεν]
[τῶι δ]ήμ̣ωι· Ε[ὔβοιοc Κρατιcτόλεω ᾿Ανα]-
[γυρ(?)]άcιοc εἶ[πεν· ἐπειδὴ ....9.... ὁ ᾿Α]-
[βδη]ρίτηc ....21..........
...ε προα..........21..........
... τῶι δ[ήμωι ....15....... δεδ]-
[όχθαι] τῶ[ι δήμωι ἐπαινέcαι ...7...]
.ν ᾿Ον̣[ο]μά[ρχου ᾿Αβδηρίτην καὶ cτεφαν]-
[ῶc]αι χρυc[ῶι cτεφάνωι· εἶναι δ' αὐτὸν]
[κ]αὶ πρόξε[νον καὶ εὐεργέτην τοῦ δήμ]-
[ο]υ τοῦ ᾿Αθη[ναίων αὐτὸν καὶ ἐκγόνουc]
[α]ὐτοῦ· ἀνα[γράψαι δὲ τόδε τὸ ψήφιcμα]
<τὸν γραμματέα τὸν κατὰ πρυτανείαν>
[ἐ]ν cτήληι [λιθίνηι καὶ cτῆcαι ἐν ἀκρ]-
[ο]π̣όλει, εἰ[c δὲ τὴν ἀναγραφὴν τῆc cτή]-
[λη]c δοῦνα[ι τὸν ταμίαν τοῦ δήμου ΔΔΔ]
[δρ]α̣χμὰc ἐ[κ τῶν κατὰ ψηφίcματα ἀναλ]-
[ιc]κομένων [τῶι δήμωι].

vacat

Unless the stonecutter was working from a copy already

blocked out in stoichedon order of 29 letters, it is hard to imagine how such a perfect lapsus oculi could have taken place. Since only the lefthand vertical hasta of the final nu of line 24 survives on the stone and there is no surface at all at the right, it is impossible to comment on the appropriateness of the restoration [τῶι δήμωι] (cf. #38).

332/1

40. *ATHENS BESTOWS A GOLD CROWN UPON AMPHIARAOS* Oropos 245

editors: Leonardos ΕΦ. 3(1891) 79-84 no. 36; IG VII 4252.

other bibliography: Pritchett-Neugebauer Cal. 49; Meritt Ath. 87-88.

description: This stele of Pentelic marble was found whole in a drain in the Amphiaraion. It is topped by a pediment, and the back is rough-picked.

dimensions:

H 0.78 m. (entire)
0.68 m. (below pediment)
W 0.30 m. (pediment)
0.285 m. (below pediment)
0.32 m. (below)
Th 0.08 m.

letters: 0.005 m. Smallest, X, is .003; A, O, Ω, are .004; largest, Ψ, is .008.

minuscule text: next page.

commentary: There is no need for restorations in this text; the stoichedon order is 27 letters to the line. Between lines 34 and 35, the eta of τήν was left out; a bracketed eta at the end of line 34 in the IG text is incorrect: the eta can not be restored because it was never there. In line 37 the brackets have been removed from around the alpha, st. 15; although the IG text shows the alpha, it unnecessarily brackets the sigma, st. 13. In short, every letter that was ever engraved on the stone can still be read.

stoich. 27

Θεοί

Ἐπὶ Νικήτου ἄρχοντοϲ, ἐπὶ τῆϲ Ἐρε-χθηΐδοϲ ἐνάτηϲ πρυτανείαϲ, ἧι Ἀρι-ϲτόνουϲ Ἀριϲτόνου Ἀναγυράϲιοϲ ἐγραμμάτευεν, ἑνδεκάτηι, τρίτηι καὶ εἰκοϲτῆι τῆϲ πρυτανείαϲ· ἐκκ-ληϲία κυρία· τῶν προέδρων ἐπεψήφ-ιζεν Ἐπιχάρηϲ Ἀγνούϲιοϲ. Ἔδοξεν τῶι δήμωι, Φανόδημοϲ Διύλλου Θυμ-αιτάδηϲ εἶπεν· ἀγαθῆι τύχηι τοῦ δ-ήμου τοῦ Ἀθηναίων, ἐπειδὴ ὁ θεὸϲ καλῶϲ ἐπιμελεῖται τῶν ἀφικνουμ-ένων Ἀθηναίων καὶ τῶν ἄλλων εἰϲ τ-ὸ ἱερὸν ἐφ' ὑγιείαι καὶ ϲωτηρίαι π-άντων τῶν ἐν τῆι χώραι ϲτεφανῶϲα-ι τὸν Ἀμφιάραον χρυϲῶι ϲτεφάνωι ἀπὸ :Χ: δραχμῶν καὶ ἀνειπεῖν τὸν κήρυκα τοῦ δήμου ὅτι ϲτεφανοῖ ὁ δ-ῆμοϲ ὁ Ἀθηναίων τὸν Ἀμφιάραον χρ-υϲῶι ϲτεφάνωι ἀπὸ :Χ: δραχμῶν, τὸ δὲ ἀργύριον τὸ εἰϲ τὸν ϲτέφανον δ-οῦναι τὸν ταμίαν τῶν ϲτρατιωτικ-ῶν καὶ παραδοῦναι τὸν ϲτέφανον π-οηϲάμενον τοῖϲ ἐπιμεληταῖϲ ἀνα-θεῖναι εἰϲ τὸ ἱερόν, τοὺϲ δὲ ἐπιμε-λητὰϲ ἀνειπόνταϲ τὰ ἐψηφιϲμένα τῶι δήμωι ἐν τῶι ἱερῶι ἀναθεῖναι τὸν ϲτέφανον τῶι θεῶι ἐφ' ὑγιείαι καὶ ϲωτηρίαι τοῦ δήμου τοῦ Ἀθηνα-

ίων καὶ παίδων καὶ γυναικῶν καὶ τ-
ῶν ἐν τῆι χώραι πάντων, ἀναγράψαι
δὲ τόδε τὸ ψήφιcμα ἐν cτήληι λιθί-
νει καὶ cτῆcαι ἐν τῶι ἱερῶι τὸν κα-
τὰ πρυτανείαν γραμματέα, εἰc δὲ τ-
<ῆ>ν ἀναγραφὴν τῆc cτήληc δοῦναι τὸ-
ν ταμίαν τοῦ δήμου :ΔΔ: δραχμὰc ἐ-
κ τῶν κατὰ ψηφίcματα ἀναλιcκομέ-
νων τῶι δήμωι.

This decree and the next one, #41, were found together at the Amphiaraion. They were passed on the 23rd day of the 9th prytany held by the tribe Erechtheis, the 11th day of Thargelion. The name of the month is omitted in this decree but appears in #41. The proposer, Phanodemos, son of Diyllos, of the deme Thymaitadai, is himself the recipient of honors in #41.

Phanodemos proposes: with good fortune to the Athenian Demos! Since the god (Amphiaraos) takes good care of those Athenians and all others in the land who come to the sanctuary for health and protection, Amphiaraos should be crowned with a gold crown worth a thousand drachmai. And the herald of the Demos is to announce that the Athenian Demos is responsible for that fact. The Treasurer of the Military Fund is to furnish the money for the crown, and, once he has had the crown made, he is to hand it over to the epimeletai (of the sanctuary); the epimeletai are to proclaim in the sanctuary the decrees passed by the Demos and place the crown on (the head of) the god for the good health and safety of the Athenian Demos and of the children, women and everyone in the land. Then follows the usual publication formula and twenty drachmai are appropriated for the purpose.

This decree and the next show again that the Athenians considered their recent acquisition of Oropos and its sanctuary of Amphiaraios an integral part of their religious and political life. For the identity of Phanodemos, see the following decree.

332/1

41. *ATHENS HONORS PHANODEMOS* Oropos 243

editors: Leonardos <u>EΦ.</u> 3(1891) 82-85 no. 37; <u>IG</u> VII 4253.

collection: Ditt. <u>Syll.</u>[3] 287.

testimonia: Jacoby <u>Fr. Gr. Hist.</u> III B 325.

other bibliography: Pritchett-Neugebauer <u>Cal.</u> 49; Meritt <u>Ath.</u> 88; Rhodes <u>Boule</u> 77, 243, 250; DeLaix <u>Proboul.</u> 120.

description: This stele of white marble was found with #40 in a drain at the Amphiaraion. Except for the corners of the pediment, which are broken, the stele is complete.

dimensions:
H 0.695 m. (entire)
0.568 m. (below pediment)
W 0.33 m. (above)
0.307 m. (below)
Th 0.08 m.

letters: 0.005 m. Smallest, Δ, O, X, are .004; largest, Φ, is .009.

minuscule text: and next page.

stoich. 30

Θεοι

Ἐπὶ Νικήτου ἄρχοντος, ἐπὶ τῆς Ἐρεχθη-
ΐδος ἐνάτης πρυτανείας, ἧι Ἀριστόνο-
υς Ἀριστόνου Ἀναγυράσιος ἐγραμμάτ-

ευεν, Θαργηλιῶνοϲ ἑνδεκάτει, τρίτηι καὶ εἰκοϲτῆι τῆϲ πρυτανείαϲ, ἐκκληϲία κυρία· τῶν προέδρων ἐπεψήφιζεν Ἐπιχάρηϲ Ἁγνούϲιοϲ. Ἔδοξεν τῶι δήμωι: Δημήτριοϲ Εὐκτήμονοϲ Ἀφιδναῖοϲ εἶπεν· ἐπειδὴ Φανόδημοϲ Θυμαιτάδηϲ καλῶϲ καὶ φιλοτίμωϲ νενομοθέτηκεν περὶ τὸ ἱερὸν τοῦ Ἀμφιαράου, ὅπωϲ ἂν ἥ τε πεντετηρὶϲ ὡϲ καλλίϲτη γίγνηται καὶ αἱ ἄλλαι θυϲίαι τοῖϲ θεοῖϲ τοῖϲ ἐν τῶι ἱερῶι τοῦ Ἀμφιαράου, καὶ πόρουϲ πεπόρικεν εἰϲ ταῦτα καὶ εἰϲ τὴν καταϲκευὴν τοῦ ἱεροῦ, δεδόχθαι τῆι βουλῆι τοὺϲ προέδρουϲ οἳ ἂν λάχωϲιν προεδρεύειν εἰϲ τὴν πρώτην ἐκκληϲίαν προϲαγαγεῖν Φανόδημον πρὸϲ τὸν δῆμον καὶ χρηματίϲαι, γνώμην δὲ ξυμβάλλεϲθαι τῆϲ βουλῆϲ εἰϲ τὸν δῆμον ὅτι δοκεῖ τῆι βουλῆι ἐπαινέϲαι Φανόδημον Διύλλου Θυμαιτάδην φιλοτιμίαϲ ἕνεκα τῆϲ πρὸϲ τὸν θεὸν καὶ τὸ ἱερὸν τοῦ Ἀμφιαράου καὶ ϲτεφανῶϲαι χρυϲῶι ϲτεφάνωι ἀπὸ :Χ: δραχμῶν, ἀναγράψαι δὲ τόδε τὸ ψήφιϲμα ἐν ϲτήληι λιθίνει τὸγ γραμματέα τὸν κατὰ πρυτανείαν καὶ ϲτῆϲαι ἐν τῶι ἱερῶι τοῦ Ἀμφιαράου, εἰϲ δὲ τὴν ἀναγραφὴν τῆϲ ϲτήληϲ δοῦναι τὸν ταμίαν τοῦ δήμου :ΔΔ: δραχμὰϲ ἐκ τῶν κατὰ ψηφίϲματα ἀναλιϲκομένων τῶι δήμωι.

commentary: No restorations are required for this text. The stoichedon order is 30 letters to the line. There are 29 letters in line 8; st. 30 has 2 dots as punctuation. There are 31 letters in line 33 with omega and iota occupying st. 30.

This decree was passed on the same day as #40. It was moved by Demetrios, son of Euktemon, of the deme Aphidna. The man honored is Phanodemos, son of Diyllos, of the deme Thymaitadai. Phanodemos is to be honored because he had not only shown care and zeal in carrying out his duties as special nomothete for the sanctuary of Amphiaraos so that the newly created quadrennial festival for Amphiaraos would be the best possible (as well as the sacrifices to the other gods who shared the sanctuary), but also had provided resources for the festival and sacrifices as well as for the general repair of the sanctuary. Here follows a probouleuma passed by the Boule in the preceding (8th) prytany which directs the proedroi who are allotted to preside at the first meeting of the ekklesia (in the next, i.e. ninth, prytany) to introduce Phanodemos to the Demos and to bring to a vote the Boule's motion to praise him for his zeal for the god and for the sanctuary and to crown him with a gold crown worth a thousand drachmai. The text ends with the usual instructions and appropriation for the inscribing and setting up of the stele.

This decree is unusual in that it was apparently enacted by the Demos alone, ἔδοξεν τῶι δήμωι (line 8), yet further down on the stone it includes not only the resolution formula of the Boule, δεδόχθαι τῆι βουλῆι (line 17), but also the probouleumatic formula (lines 17-23). The usual procedure, when the formal probouleuma is inscribed, is that the decree would then be recorded as enacted by both bodies: ἔδοξεν τῆι βουλῆι καὶ τῶι δήμωι. Rhodes (77f.) list fifteen decrees in which this discrepancy occurs and concludes that, since the decrees are scattered chronologically from 339/8 to 100/99, such irregularities do not indicate a specific type of legislation, but are merely examples of "secretarial carelessness." DeLaix's complicated explanation of the peculiarity is pointless since he apparently has overlooked the presence of the probouleumatic formula as well as the actual opinion (γνώμη) of the Boule lower on the stone (120).

Phanodemos is the famous Atthidographer and author of an Atthis of at least nine books (cf. Jacoby; PA 14033, not in APF). Even before his concern with the festival and sanctuary of Amphiaraos we find him both as honorand and as mover of decrees passed in 343/2 (II^2 223 A+B) and his name is recorded on the base of a dedication by the Boule to Hephaistos. His advice to the Boule, for which he is honored, probably had something to do with this dedication.

Phanodemos's interest in the Amphiaraia did not end with his legislative recommendations reflected in #40 and #41. He returned three years later as chairman (his name is listed first) of a board of ten epimeletai elected to supervise the "Greater Amphiaraia" which he had been instrumental in setting up. Among the Ten were Lykourgos himself and Demades, as well as several well-known figures of Lykourgan Athens (see #50, VII 4254, for fuller discussion). And in the next year (328/7) his name appears first in a list of others who contributed to a private dedication of 24 bouleutai (#56, AE (1917) 40-48 no. 92). Several of the same group of epimeletai and contributors are responsible for a nearly contemporary Athenian dedication to Apollo from Delphi (Syll.[3] 296) on which Phanodemos's name is again first. This was on the occasion of a Pythaïs, a sacred procession from Athens to Delphi which the Athenians made at irregular intervals whenever it was indicated by lightning flashing over Harma on Mt. Parnes. J. Bosquet has suggested (BCH 88 [1964] 655-675) that the main Athenian dedication on this occasion was none other than the famous Akanthos Column; his identification of the three maidens, however, as the daughters of Kekrops is less certain (accepted by Mitchel Lyk. 206, but withdrawn per. litt.).

Phanodemos's role as single nomothetes is unusual for the fourth century when a board of 50 is the usual number, appointed from a panel of jurors. The singularity of his office probably indicates that he was a recognized expert. Such an expert on Athens's mythical and cultic history was obviously a kingpin in Lykourgos's program for religious reform and revitalization. In fact, Jacoby is inclined to call Phanodemos Lykourgos's "minister of public worship and education" (Comm. p. 172). No mere armchair historian, Phanodemos may have been commander of the island of Ikos during the war against Philip, in 340 (Jacoby, idem.).

332/1

42. *DECREE FROM THE DEME EITEA* Rhamnous Apotheke 11

photo: ΑΔ 25(1970) Plates 70, 71.

editors: Kaloyeropoulou ΑΔ 25(1970) 204-214; 265-267; Bicknell Historia 27(1978) 369-374 reproduces Kalouyeropoulou's text.

supplement: Bull. (1972) no. 152 (Kaloyeropulou,

Vanderpool).

other bibliography: Vanderpool AΔ 25(1970) 215-216.

description: Since this stone was not available for examination, the description is based on that of Kaloyeropoulou and on the published photograph. Three fragments of Pentelic marble, found accidentally in October, 1961, at the south end of the village of Grammatiko in Attika, are now joined. The resulting stele consists of a curved upper terminal, a relief, and then the text of 22 lines. The back is rough-picked.

The curved terminal at the top is an unusual adornment for a decree (cf. Kaloyeropoulou's discussion, 204 note 3); the shape is more commonly associated with grave monuments. Noting that the terminals of grave monuments of this type were usually painted, Kaloyeropoulou suggests that this stele was treated the same way, although no trace of paint remains.

Below the upper terminal the stele has been cut back both at the sides (creating a taper) and on the obverse. There is no transitional cymation. At the top of this recessed surface, directly below the terminal and between it and the relief, the four letters of the prescript, ΘE-OI are spaced out evenly over the entire width of the stele. The shallow relief is sunk into the surface, leaving a reserved frame at the sides, while the prescript occupies the top of the frame and the text begins at the bottom.

The relief has two figures: on the left, facing right in the typical posture of adoration before a divinity, is the small figure of a bearded man wearing a himation; on the right is a larger female figure whose head intrudes slightly into the upper frame of the relief; she is facing left and extends her right arm which holds a wreath above the man's head. The male figure is Hippokles, who is honored in the decree below (line 11), and the female figure is Basile, the goddess in whose sanctuary the stele is to be set up (lines 18/19). Kaloyeropoulou devotes pages 210-214 to a detailed study of the relief, dating it on artistic grounds to 340-330 B.C., a discussion interesting in itself but unnecessary if the archon's name is correctly restored in line 17.

The text of the decree begins below the relief. Although the vertical stoichoi are not strictly parallel, the decree was engraved in stoichedon order which is nowhere violated on the preserved part of the stone. There is a deep cut across the entire width of the stele below line 4, which completely obliterates line 5 and parts of lines 4 and 6. As Kaloyeropoulou notes, the attempt to sever the stele for the sake of the relief as a work of art was probably begun and abandoned in antiquity. Compare #6 for a similar occurence where it is also noted that perhaps the quality of the relief was not worth the effort. The stele is broken on the right side, below line 10, and at the bottom.

dimensions:

H 0.67 m. (entire)	letters: 0.006 m.
0.49 m. (relief + text)	Smaller, Ω, is .005;
W 0.265 m. (above)	Largest, E, K,
0.275 m. (below)	are .006.
Th 0.047 m.	

majuscule text: next page.

epigraphical commentary: The majuscule text is based on the photograph. Two new readings are recorded: the lower half of a vertical stroke, line 6 st. 11; an iota, line 16 st. 2. There is a discrepancy in line 6 of Kaloyeropoulou's text; her restoration shows only 5 letters between the mu, st. 4, and the pi, st. 12, whereas there are 7 letter spaces on the stone. The right-hand margin is uneven because the dots indicate letter spaces only where letters have been restored in Kaoyeropoulou's text.

There is something very obviously anomalous about the text as it stands. Lines 2 through 12 were surely inscribed with a stoichedon order of 24 letters per line. A vacat is an easy restoration in the last stoichos of line 3 after Hippokles' name, and the restoration of lines 4 and 5 which gives only 23 letters to line 4 is anything but certain except for the general sense, e.g. the word εὔνους is characteristic for foreigners, not fellow demesmen. If we accept then that the text was stoich. 24 through line 12, we find a diminuation to 23 letters in line 13 (a sure restoration) and 22 letters in line 14 (equally sure). Line 15 apparently shrinks to 21 letters, but this is not necessary if a vacat is restored to mark the end of the honorary decree before the publication clause. If these modifications of the text are acceptable we have a text which begins with stoich. 24 (through line 12), has one transitional line of stoich. 23 (line 13), and runs to the end with stoich. 22 (lines 14-21).

Such a text, in which the variation in length of line makes a regular pattern, is much easier to explain than one in which the preserved part is invariable stoichedon but the restored lines are arbitrary lengths. Going beyond Kaloyeropoulou's identification of the monument as a grave stele, one may conjecture that it had been rejected as a funerary stele because of some slight damage to its righthand edge, beginning just below the present break.

Θ E O I
Τ Ι Μ Ο Κ Ρ Α Τ Η Σ Τ Ι Μ Ο Κ Λ Ε Ο Υ Σ Ε Ι Τ Ε
. Ι Ο Σ Ε Ι Π Ε Ν Ε Π Ε Ι Δ Η Ι Π Π Ο Κ Λ Η Σ
. . . . Ο Υ Σ Ε̣ Ι̣ Τ̣ Ε̣ . . . .
. . . .
Ι Δ Η Μ . . . . . ι Π Ο Ε Ι Ο Τ Ι Α Ν Δ Υ . .
Τ Α Ι Α Γ Α Θ Ο Ν Τ Ο Υ Σ Δ Η Μ Ο Τ Α Σ Κ Α Ι .
Υ Ν Κ Α Ι Ε Ν Τ Ω Ι Π Α Ρ Ε Λ Η Λ Υ Θ Ο Τ Ι Χ Ρ
Ο Ν Ω Ι Κ Α Ι Λ Ο Γ Ω Ι Κ Α Ι Ε Ρ Γ Ω Ι Δ Ε Δ Ο
Χ Θ Α Ι Τ Ο Ι Σ Δ Η Μ Ο Τ Α Ι Σ Ε Π Α Ι Ν Ε Σ Α
Ι Ι Π Π Ο Κ Λ Ε Α Δ Η Μ Ο Κ Λ Ε Ο Υ Σ Ε Ι Τ . .
Ι Ο Ν Κ Α Ι Σ Τ Ε Φ Α Ν Ω Σ Α Ι Χ Ρ . . . . . .
Ε Φ Α Ν Ω Ι Α Π Ο 𐅄 Δ Ρ Α Χ Μ . . . .
. Ν Ε Κ Α Κ Α Ι Δ Ι Κ Α Ι Ο . . . .
. . . . Ο Υ Σ Δ Η Μ Ο Τ Α Σ . . . .
. Ι . . . . . Ε Τ Ο Ψ Η Φ̣ . . . .
Μ Ι Α Ν Τ̣ . . Ε̣ . Ι Ν̣ Ι . . . .
Τ Ο Σ Κ Α Ι Σ Τ Η . . . .
Σ Ι Λ Η Σ Ι Ε Ρ Ω Ι . . . .
Ν Η Ι Κ Α Ι Λ Ο Γ Ι . . . .
. Ο Τ Α Ι Σ Ο Τ Ι . . . .
. . . vacat

VACAT

The treasurer of the tiny deme of Eitea, which sometimes sent two representatives to the Boule, and sometimes only one (see Vanderpool), on finding the deme's treasury depleted by the gold crown worth 500 drachmai, may have sought to relieve his fellow demesmen of further expense by buying a rejected sepulchral stone and hiring an apprentice (surely no more than a journeyman) mason to carve a modest relief and engrave the decree. This interpretation would explain why the text gets narrower toward the bottom whereas Kaloyeropoulou indicates that the stele's taper would cause it to become wider.

minuscule text: next page.

commentary: With the exception of a query in line 5, the supplement in the middle of line 6 and the vacats suggested at the end of line 3 and the middle of line 15, all restorations are Kaloyeropoulou's. They are for the most part convincing, and she includes in her commentary many corroborating parallels from other decrees.

6 δῆμ[ωι καὶ ε]ὖ̣ ποεῖ: Schwenk. δῆμ[ωι καὶ] ποεῖ Kaloyeropoulou, followed by Bicknell. Kaloyeropoulou's restoration is too short by 2 letters for the stoichedon pattern, which she nowhere mentions and perhaps did not notice. My restoration is supported by the new reading (from the photograph) of a dotted upsilon in st. 11 and by parallels in II^2 493.17, 467.17 and 1193.27 (the last two restored but reasonably certain).

The format of this inscription is typical for a deme decree (cf. #26 for list of dated ones in Lykourgan era). The proposer, Timokrates, son of Timokles, of the deme Eitea, moves that Hippokles be honored because he was benevolent and useful in carrying out duties for the Demos, doing well by word and deeds, whatever good he could for his fellow demesmen both now and in the past. He is honored with a gold crown worth 500 drachmai. The Treasurer for the year is to have the stele engraved and set up in the sanctuary of Basile and charge the expense to the demesmen. The date comes, almost accidentally, from the designation of the local treasurer as the one serving when Niketes was archon. There is no dating formula such as is a regular feature of decrees passed by the Boule and Demos in Athens, and on the whole legislation in the local demes was less formal in every way.

stoich. 24 (2-12)
23 (13)
22 (14-21)

Θ ε ο ί

[relief]

Τιμοκράτηc Τιμοκλέουc Εἰτε-
[α]ῖοc εἶπεν: ἐπειδὴ Ἱπποκλῆc v
[Δημοκλέ]ουc Ε̣ἰ̣τ̣ε̣[αῖοc εὔνου]-
[c? ὢν καὶ χρήcιμοc διατελεῖ τῶ]-
ι δήμ[ωι καὶ ε]ὖ̣ ποεῖ ὅ, τι ἂν δύ[νη]-
ται ἀγαθὸν τοὺc δημότac καὶ [ν]-
ῦν καὶ ἐν τῶι παρεληλυθότι χρ-
όνωι καὶ λόγωι καὶ ἔργωι, δεδό-
χθαι τοῖc δημόταιc ἐπαινέcα-
ι Ἱπποκλέα Δημοκλέουc Εἰτ[εα]-
ῖον καὶ cτεφανῶcαι χρ[υcῶι cτ]-
εφάνωι ἀπὸ 𐅅 δραχμ[ῶν ἀρετῆc]
[ἕ]νεκα καὶ δικαιο[cύνηc τῆc]
[εἰc τ]οὺc δημόταc [v ἀναγράψ]-
[α]ι [δὲ τόδ]ε τὸ ψήφ[ιcμα τὸν τα]-
μίαν τ̣[ὸν] ἐ̣[π]ὶ̣ Ν̣ι[κήτου ἄρχον]-
τοc καὶ cτῆ[cαι ἐν τῶι τῆc βα]-
cίληc ἱερῶι [ἐν cτήληι λιθί]-
νηι καὶ λογί[cαcθαι τοῖc δη]-
[μ]όταιc ὅ, τι [ἂν ἀνάλωμα γένη]-
[ται]. vacat

vacat

The two men mentioned in this decree are not otherwise known in Attic prosopography. Kaloyeropoulou, however, identifies Hippokles as the father of a woman, Samakion, whose name appears on a grave monument dated "post med. s. IV" (II^2 6007). She also suggests that Timokrates may be a descendant of Timokles Eiteaios, Treasurer of the Gods in 424/3 and 423/2 (I^2 242.114; I^2 243.122; I^2 324.36; PA 13733, not in APF). If this association is accepted, then Timokles, the Treasurer of the Gods, must be dissociated from [.$\overset{4}{..}$..κρ]ᾰτηϲ Τιμο[κλέ-ουϲ Εἰτεαί]ου, one of the heroes of Phyle in 403 B.C. (Hesperia 10 [1941] 288 no. 78.37), for he is listed under the tribe Akamantis, whereas Timokrates, the proposer of this decree, comes from the deme Eitea which belongs to the tribe Antiochis (see Vanderpool, and below; there is no problem, however, if Bicknell's designation of Akamantid Eitea is correct).

Kaloyeropulou noted that the restoration of Basile as the goddess in whose sanctuary the stele is to be set up is the only one possible. This chthonic goddess is known to have been worshipped in two other locations: with Neleus and Kodros in Athens; with Echelos and Kephisos in New Phaleron (more exact locations on page 209). Eitea can now be included as a third location; it holds the distinction of being the only sanctuary which Basile has all to herself.

It was previously known that there were two small demes with the name Eitea, one in the tribe Akamantis, the other in Antiochis, but the location of neither was established. Now, with the discovery of this decree, one of the demes can be located exactly: at the modern village of Grammatiko, eight kilometers north of the plain of Marathon, six kilometers inland from Rhamnous. Vanderpool has shown, moreover, that this deme, Eitea, belongs to the inland trittys of the tribe (X) Antiochis, and must be the neighbor of another small deme, Semachidai, of the same tribe and trittys in an area known as Epakria in northeastern Attika north of Mt. Pentelikon (215f.; but see Bicknell). Such a decree as this shows civic activity on the local level operating in the Lykourgan period, but is by no means peculiar to that period.

332/1

43. *ELEUSIS HONORS PHILOKOMOS* Eleusis Museum

editors: Coumanoudis & Gofas <u>REG</u> 91 (1978) 289-306.

description: Since I have not seen this stone I base the description and dimensions given below on that of the editors. The stele is Pentelic marble, preserved except for a small "cassure" (break or crack--it is impossible to know without a photograph) in the upper part. There is a bas-relief consisting of a two-handled urn on a stand surrounded by an olive wreath in the middle of the stele. The stele was found in Eleusis, January 7, 1970, during an excavation of a house's foundation; the stone had been used in the wall of a house built later than the Roman period. Coumanoudis was able to remove a clay crust without damaging the surface. The stele was transported to the Eleusis Museum.

dimensions:
H 0.93 m.
W 0.398 m. (above)
0.452 m. (below)
Th 0.08 m. (above)
0.11 m. (below)

letters: 0.006 m. (line 1).
0.008 m. (lines 2-17).
0.006 m. (lines 18-53).

minuscule text: next three pages.

commentary: The text, including all restorations, is from <u>REG</u>. The first decree has larger letters and a stoichedon order of 36 letters to the line; the second

stoich. 35 (2–17)
43 (18–53)

Θ [ε ο] ι
Ἐπιγένηϲ εἶπεν· τύχηι ἀγαθῆι τῶν δημοτῶν· v
ἐπειδὴ Φιλόκωμοϲ εἰϲηγήϲατο τοῖϲ δημότα-
ιϲ π[ερὶ τ]ῆϲ Ἄκριδοϲ ἀποδόϲθαι τῶι θεῶι τὴν
λιθ[οτομ]ίαν, ὅπωϲ ἂν ἡ θυϲία γίγνηται ὡϲ καλ-
λίϲτ̣η, [καὶ ἐώ]ν̣ηται παρὰ τῶν δημοτῶν Μοιροκ-
λῆϲ [εἰϲ] π̣ε̣ν̣[τ]ε ἔτη τριῶν ἡμιμν[αί]ων τοῦ ἐνι[α]-
υτοῦ καὶ ἑκατὸν δραχμὰϲ ἐπέ[δωκ]εν εἰϲ τὰ Ἡ̣[ρ]-
[ά]κ̣[λ]εια· [δε]δό[χ]θαι Ἐλευϲινίο[ιϲ]· ἐ̣π̣αινέϲαι [Φ]-
ιλόκωμον Φαλανθίδου καὶ [ϲτ]εφανῶ<ϲα>ι χρ[υ]-
[ϲ]ῶ̣ι ϲτεφάν̣ωι ἀρετῆϲ ἕνεκα κα[ὶ] ε̣ὐνοίαϲ τῆ[ϲ]
εἰϲ τοὺϲ δημότα̣ϲ, εἰϲ δὲ τὸν ϲτέφανον τὸ [ἀργ-]
ύριον δοῦναι Φιλοκώμωι ἐναντίον τῶν δημ[ο]-
τῶν ἑκατὸν δραχμὰϲ Μοιροκλέα, ἐπαινέϲαι δ-
ὲ Μοιροκλέα Εὐδυδήμου, ὅτι τοῖϲ δημόταιϲ ἐ-
πιμελεῖται, ὅπωϲ ἂν ἦι πρόϲοδοϲ ὡϲ πλείϲτη,
καὶ ϲτεφανῶϲαι θαλλοῦ ϲτεφάνωι. vacat
[relief]

Φιλόκ̣ω[μ]ος Φαλανθίδου Ἐλευσίνιος εἶπεν· τύχηι ἀγαθ-
ῆι τῶν δημοτῶν· ὅπως ἂν τῶι Ἡρακλεῖ τῶι ἐν Ἄκριδι πρόσ-
οδος ἦ̣ι ὡ̣ς πλείστη κ̣αὶ ἡ θυσία θύηται ὡς καλλίστη, ἐψη-
φίσθαι τοῖς δημόταις· τὰς λιθοτομίας τὰς Ἐλευσῖνι, ἐ-
π̣[ειδὴ .....]Ι̣ΩΝ εἰσὶν ἱερ̣αὶ τοῦ Ἡρακλέως τοῦ ἐν Ἄκρι-
δι, μ[ισ]θοῦν τὸν δήμαρχον ἐν τῆι ἀγορᾶι τῶν δημοτῶν τῶ-
ι τὸ π[λεῖσ]τον διδόντ[ι]· τὸν δὲ μισθωσάμενον ἀποδιδόν-
αι τὴν μίσθωσιν τὴν μὲν ἐπὶ Νικήτου ἄρχοντος ἐν ὧι ἂν
χ̣ρόν̣[ωι] τοὺς δημότας πε[ί]θει, πρὸ τῆς θυσίας, μετὰ δὲ Νι-
κήτην ἄρχοντα εἰς τὸν Μεταγειτνιῶνα μῆνα ταῖς ἀρχα-
ιρεσίαις, ὅταν οἱ δημόται ἀγοράζωσιν ἐν τῶι Θησείωι·
ἐγγυητὰ[ς] τ̣[ε] καταστησάτω ὁ μισθωσάμενος δύο ἄνδρας
[ὁμουμέν]ους ἦ̣ μὴν ἀποδώσειν τὴν μίσθωσιν πᾶσαν ἐν τῶ-
ι χρό[νω]ι τῶι εἰρημένωι· τὸν δὲ δήμαρχον λαβόντα τοῦτ-
ο τὸ ἀργύριον παρέχειν εἰς τὴν ἑ̣ορτὴν τοῦ Ἡρακλέως τ-
ο[ῦ ἐν Ἄκ]ριδι· διαχειροτονῆσαι δὲ αὐτ̣ίκα μάλα τοὺς δη-
μότας ἐὰν τε εἰς ἐνιαυτὸν δοκεῖ μισθοῦν, ἐὰν τε εἰς πλ-
έω χρόνον, ὁπότερα δ' ἂν δοκεῖ, ταῦτα κύρια εἶναι καὶ μι-

cθοῦν πρὸc ταῦτα τὸν δήμαρχον· μὴ ἐξέcτω δὲ εἰπεῖν μη-
θένα τοῦτο τὸ ἀργύριον ὡc δεῖ ἄλλοθί που τρέψαι ἢ εἰc
τὴν θυcίαν τοῦ Ἡρακλέωc, μηδὲ τοῖc ἱερομνήμοcιν ἐπι-
ψηφίcαι, μηδὲ τῶι δημάρχωι· ἐὰν δέ τιc ἢ εἴπει ἢ ἐπιψηφ-
ίcει παρὰ τόδε τὸ ψήφιcμα, ὀφειλέτω τῶι θεῶι τὸ διπλά-
cιον ἢ ὅcον ἂν εἴπει ἢ ἐπιψηφίcει· καὶ ὁ εὔθυνοc καὶ ὁ c-
υνήγοροc ἐπάναγκεc αὐτῶν καταγιγνωcκόντων τοῦτο
τὸ ἀργύριον ἢ αὐτοὶ ὀφειλόντωcαν· ἀναγράψαι δὲ τόδε
τὸ ψήφιcμα τὸν δήμαρχον ἐν cτήλει λιθίνει καὶ cτῆcα-
ι ἐν τῶι ἱερῶι τοῦ Ἡρακλέωc τοῦ ἐν Ἄκριδι, ὅπωc ἂν τὰ ἐψ-
ηφιcμένα ὑπὸ τῶν δημοτῶν κύρια εἶ εἰc τὸν ἀεὶ χρόνον
ḳ[αὶ μ]ὴ καταλύηται· cυνεπιμεληθῆναι δὲ τῆc cτήληc ὅπ-
ωc ἂν cταθεῖ ἐν τῶι ἱερῶι τὸν ἱερέα τοῦ Ἡρακλέωc Ἀν[τ]ι-
φά[ν]ην πρὸ τῆc θυcίαc τῆc ἐπὶ Νικήτου ἄρχοντοc· εἰc δὲ
τὴν ἀναγραφὴν τῆc cτήληc δοῦναι τὸν δήμαρχον δέκα .˙.
[δ]ραχṃ[ὰc ἐ]κ τῆc τοῦ θεọῦ προcόδου. Κύριον δὲ εἶναι τόδ-
[ε τὸ ψ]ήφιcμα ἀπὸ Νικήτου ἄρχοντοc, ἀφ' ἧc ἂν ἡμέραc οἱ δ-
ημόται ψηφίcωνται. vacat

decree, with smaller letters has a stoichedon order of 43 letters to the line. The editors give a dimension of 0.04 m. between the lines in the first decree--this must be a misprint--0.004 m. is more appropriate and they do give a space of 0.003 between the lines in the second decree. Although it is not stated, I would assume that the letter sizes and number of stoichoi balance out and that the side margin would be about the same for both (as in #88).

The stone cutter made one error at the end of line 10: the stone reads [ΣΤ]ΕΦΑΝΩΙΧΡ[Υ].

For lines 21/22, the editors restore only ἐπ[ειδὴ .....]ỊΩN, noting that the restoration of an adverbial expression would be appropriate, but that, whatever the restoration, it should convey the idea that the quarry has always belonged to Herakles on Akris. They also note the restoration offered separately in letters from G. Daux and Ph. Gautier: ἐπ[εὶ ἐκ προγό]νων. The editors, however, stick with the reading of iota in st. 11, line 10, rather than the dotted nu read by Daux from a photograph.

This stele records two decrees of the deme Eleusis (see #26 for a list of other deme decrees in this Corpus). The first, Decree I, lines 2-17, was passed in the archonship of Niketes, 332/1; the second Decree II, lines 18-53, records the deliberations which led to Decree I, which it therefore preceded in time. Thus it is appropriate to discuss Decree II first.

Decree II records a proposal made by Philokomos, son of Phanthides, of the deme Eleusis. In order to raise the income for Herakles on Akris so that his sacrifice be as beautiful as possible, Philokomos proposes that the stone quarries in Eleusis which belong (have always belonged?; see commentary, lines 21/22) to the sanctuary of Herakles on Akris be leased by the Demarch (archon of deme), in an assembly of the demesmen, to the highest bidder. And that the bidder, subject to the approval of the demesmen, is to pay his rent before the sacrifice, after Niketes is archon, in Metageitnion when the demesmen assemble in the Theseion to elect officials. Two men should be appointed to provide surety that the money will be paid at that time. The Demarch, when he receives the money, is to use it for the festival of Herakles on Akris. The demesmen are to vote by hand whether the lease should be for one year or longer, and whichever length they authorize, the Demarch is to abide by their decision. There follow safeguards that the money not be diverted to other uses and that no decree be allowed to negate this one.

In order to insure permanency, the Demarch is to have a stone stele engraved and set up in the sanctuary of Herakles on Akris and Antiphanes, the priest of Herakles on Akris, is to help him so that the stele is set up before the sacrifice in the year of Niketes. Ten drachmai are authorized from the revenues of Herakles on Akris to defray the cost of the stele. The decree becomes valid in the archonship of Niketes, on the day when the motion is passed.

Decree I records the consequences. The lease is established at 3 half minas (150 drachmai) per year for five years. The lessor, Moirokles, son of Eudydemos, has not only paid the rent, but also contributed 100 drachmai to the festival, which will be used for a gold crown to honor Philokomos for his virtue and good will to the demesmen. Moirokles is to receive an olive crown.

Coumanoudis and Gofas discuss various aspects of this decree, including a prosopographical commentary and a topographical commentary--suggesting that an unnamed hill above the Telesterion in Eleusis may be the Akris of this inscription. They conclude with a ten-page "Commentaire juridique" which includes: a detailed discussion of politics and officials on the deme level; how revenues were obtained; and a specific discussion of the procedures recorded in this inscription in comparison with practices used elsewhere in Attica and Greece.

What is more pertinent to this Corpus, however, is how this inscription fits into the context of the Lykourgan Era and more specifically, the religious reforms initiated at this time. There are, of course, the statewide reforms which were given the force of law: in 336/5, #17 dealt with the Lesser Panathenaia; in 335/4, #21, Lykourgos himself proposed much more comprehensive reforms. But on a local level, there was activity as well: in 334/3, the deme Cholargos published regulations for their local Thesmophoria (#26); in 333/2, the orgeones of Heros Iatros leased a garden--presumably to enhance the revenues and thus their worship (#32). Toward the end of 333/2, comes Decree II of this inscription; and, after Metageitnion, in the year of Niketes, 332/1, Decree I (the sense from Decree II is that Niketes has been elected archon but has not taken over the office yet--the editors, p. 296, note the probability that Decree II was passed "tout pres du dêbut de L'archontat de Nikètes, dêjà designê"; Decree I, on the other hand, must have been passed in 332/1, although it does not record Niketes' name: the rent was to be paid in Metageitnion in the year of Niketes and that had been done).

Therefore, by 332/1 (soon after the meeting in Metageitnion, the second month?), we have one instance of reforms which mirror on the deme level what Lykourgos in #21 had done on the state level. First there is the attention to detail--making sure that the revenue got to the right place at the right time--with two men to act as surety and all done in the presence of the demesmen. Second, there is the outcome of this painstaking procedure: that all revenue generated be put to use making the sacrifice and festival for Herakles on Akris "as beautiful as possible." The connection can not be fortuitous: "Lykourgos's example of straightening out all the state cults must have excited the private demes and orgeones to get into the act! (F. W. Mitchel, _per ep._).

VIII. THE YEAR OF ARISTOPHANES, 331/0

44. *ATHENS HONORS AN ACTOR* EM 7322

photo: Ghiron-Bistagne Acteurs page 79.

editors: Kumanudes ΑΘΗΝΑΙΟΝ 5(1876) 184-185; IG II Add. 208b; IG II^2 348; Ghiron-Bistagne Acteurs 78-79.

supplements: SEG 21.282 (Pritchett-Neugebauer, Meritt Ath.); 23.54 (Meritt TAPA); 26.76 (Ghiron-Bistagne).

other bibliography: Reusch De diebus cont. 123; Wilhelm UDA 218-220; Pschor Berl. phil. Woch. (1910) 253; Pritchett-Neugebauer Cal. 49; Meritt Ath. 90-91; Hesperia 30 (1961) 49; TAPA 95(1964) 217; Henry Prescripts 34, 37 n. 24, 42 n. 53, 45 n. 62.

description: This fragment of Pentelic marble was found between the theaters of Dionysos and Herodes Atticus, on the south slope of the Akropolis. The lower left-hand corner of a pediment, with cymation and fillet, and the left side are preserved; the rest is broken. Some of the original back may be preserved.

dimensions:
H 0.19 m. (entire)
0.07 m. (below cymation)
W 0.13 m.
Th 0.11 m.

letters: 0.005 m. Smallest, O, is .003; largest, E, K, N, are .006. Letters are a bit larger in the pediment.

minuscule text: next page.

epigraphical commentary: The text is based on Kirchner's. With the exception of epsilon, line 7 st. 8, all dots are mine; the one underlined letter is now illegible. Lines 1-4 are not in stoichedon order. Line 5 is alone on the fillet. The few alternate readings are below.

2 5th. letter, E: Ki. / Koe.; Kumanudes read nothing.

[Ἐπὶ Ἀριϲτοφάνουϲ]
[ἄρχοντοϲ ἐπὶ τῆϲ Ἀκα]-
μα̣[ντίδοϲ ὀγδόηϲ, ἐνάτηι]
ἐπὶ δέ[κα, ἕκτηι τῆϲ πρυτανείαϲ]·
ἐκκληϲί[α ἐν Διονύϲου· τῶν προέδρων]
ἐπεψήφιζ[εν ....22..........]
vacat 0.015
Ν̣ικόϲτρατοϲ Λ[- - - - - - - - ἐγραμμάτευεν]
vacat 0.045 stoich. 29
Φιλέαϲ Ἀν[τιγένου Παιονίδηϲ εἶπεν·]
ἐπειδὴ Πε̣.........21..........
ὁ ὑποκρ[ιτὴϲ τοῖϲ τε Διονυϲίοιϲ ὑπεκ]-
[ρ]ίνατ[ο φιλοτίμωϲ ἔν τε τοῖϲ ἄλλοιϲ]
[ἐ]ϲτί[ν ἀνὴρ ἀγαθὸϲ περὶ Ἀθηναίουϲ·]
ε̣ψη̣[φίϲθαι - - - - - - - - - - - -]

5 12th letter, A: Kumanudes. For the restoration of the secretary, later retracted, Mer. read Α̣.

7 st. 8 Ε̣: not read by Kumanudes, Koe., or Wilh.

11 st. 1 E: Kumanudes, Ki. ¯ Koe.

commentary: Lines 1-6, which occupy the pediment, and line 7, on the fillet, are not in stoichedon order. The stoichedon order for lines 8-13 is 29 letters to the line, but the restorations show violations in line 8 (30 letters) and line 10 (28 letters).

Restorations are Wilhelm's. Reusch had restored on the basis of a full dating formula in the pediment, making the MA in line 3 part of the month, Maimakterion, and the name in line 7 the person honored. Wilhelm calculated the width of the stele at 0.328 m. and the height of the pediment, 0.085 m., which makes a full dating formula within the pediment impossible. His restoration makes the MA in line 3 part of the tribe in prytany, Akamantis and requires the omission of the month (see #22, #40, for similar omission); the name of the secretary appears on the fillet as line 7. The name of the mover, line 8, Wilhelm restored from II^2 410, line 29 and the full name in the first crown; II^2 410 (dated ca. 330) honors various priests and a board of hieropoioi which had been active in conducting the Dionysia.

Of the years in this period for which the secretary is unknown, Wilhelm chose the year of Aristophanes (331/30) whose name is the only one which would fit his dimensions for the pediment. Proceeding from that point, he noted that lines 10/11 refer to an actor. That led him to restore the place of meeting of the ekklesia as the theater of Dionysos, line 5. Wilhelm considered that 17 Elaphebolion was an appropriate day for a meeting ἐν Διονύσου because it would be after the City Dionysia (cf. Mikalson Year 137); but did not restore the specific dates. Pschor, using #36 as an example of a meeting in the theater of Dionysos on 19 Elaphebolion, restored the dates as Elaphebolion 19, 6th day of the prytany.

For the name of the secretary, Meritt (Ath. 90) suggested the composite name Νικόστρατος Ἀρχέλεω ἐκ Μυρρινούττης taken from this decree and II^2 363, which he had restored for the year 331/30. Henry, who records lines 1-8, includes Meritt's restoration and notes that the "interesting and unusual prescript" does "give considerable prominence to the name of the secretary" (34). Meritt later abandoned the composite name and transferred II^2 363 to the year 335/4 (TAPA 217), but that restoration too has its anomalies and does not fit the historical circumstances referred to in the text. (It has been given the number #67 and placed in 326/5, using the second of the four restorations which Meritt has offered.)

Although Kirchner included the first 2 lines, he did not number them so that his line 1 is line 3 in this text. I prefer to number the first two restored lines in this text (Henry does the same; p. 34).

Most of the scholarship on #44 concerns the date. Meritt's formula for the date is: <Elaphebolion> 1[9] = Prytany [VIII 6] = 255th day. Pritchett-Neugebauer offer 1[9] or 1[8] for the day of the month since the exact relationship of full to hollow months is not known for this year.

Wilhelm's observation that the decree concerned an actor made the restoration possible by association with the festival of Dionysos. Who the actor was, however, what he did to deserve the honors and which honors he received are all lost. Considering the prominence of actors in the diplomatic relations betwen Athens and other states (especially Macedon) earlier in the decade, we would like to know more about this decree. Referring to II^2 657, Ghiron-Bistagne notes the political influence that the actor Philippides had with Lysimachos later in this century. He then notes that the actor Neoptolemos was known to have had political influence with Philip, and then makes a very tentative association with the actor of this decree.

331/30

45. *ATHENS HONORS RHEBOULAS THE ODRYSIAN*

NM 1476

photos: Svoronos ΕΘ. ΜΟΥΣ. Plate 106.2; Speier RM 47 (1932) Plate 28.3 (part of relief); Süsserott Plastik Plate 9.1 (all of relief and first line of text).

editors: Kumanudes ΑΘΗΝΑΙΟΝ 5(1876) 102-103; IG II Add. 175b; IG II^2 349.

collections: Michel 1469; Hicks 160; Tod II 193.

testimonia: Aischines Against Ktesiphon 164-167; Curtius X 1.45; Deinarchos Against Demosthenes 34-36; Demosthenes Against Aristokrates 118; Diodoros xvii 62-63; Plutarch Demosthenes 24.1.

other bibliography: Schaefer Dem. III^2 183; Wilhelm Hermes 23(1888) 462 n. 2; Hoeck Hermes 26(1891) 89-116; Swoboda "Seuthes III" RE 2022; Binneboessel Studien 14 no. 62; Speier RM 47(1932) 62-69; Süsserott Plastik, 20, 28, 61-65, 86, 175, 179; Pritchett-Neugebauer Cal. 49-50; Meritt Ath. 91; Badian Hermes 95(1967) 191-192; Borza CP 66(1971) 230-235; CP 67(1972) 233-245; Rhodes Boule 69 n. 2, 250.

description: The four fragments of Pentelic marble were found between the theaters of Dionysos and Herodes Atticus. They are now joined and set into a plaster stele which stands in the National Museum. The fragmentary text is topped by a fragmentary relief: Athena, the torso of a man, and six horses' hoofs remain. The first two lines are on the fillet of the cymation.

dimensions:	letters: 0.006 m. Smallest, O, is .005; largest, Σ, is .009. Letters in line 3 are a bit larger; letters in lines 9-12 are c. .001 m. smaller.
H 0.69 m.(entire)	
0.323 m.(below cymation)	
W 0.46 m. (relief)	
0.40 m. (below relief)	
Th 0.13 m.	

minuscule text:

῾Ρηβοῦλαϲ Σεῦθου:ὑὸϲ Κότυοϲ ἀδελφὸϲ ᾿Ανγελ[ῆθεν].
Θ ε ο [ί]
᾿Επὶ ᾿Αριϲτοφάνουϲ ἄρχοντοϲ
ἐπὶ τῆϲ Κε[κ]ρ̣οπίδοϲ δεκάτηϲ πρυτα- stoich. 28
ν̣είαϲ· Σκ[ιρ]οφοριῶνοϲ δεκάτηι ἱϲ[τ]-
α̣μένου, [ἕκτ]ει καὶ δεκάτει τῆϲ πρυ[τ]-
ανεία[ϲ· τῶν] προέ̣δρων ἐπεψή[φι]ζ̣ε̣ [Δω]-
ρόθε[οϲ ᾿Αλ]α̣ιεὺϲ· vacat
᾿Εδοξεν [τῆι βουλ]ῆι καὶ τῶι δήμωι· Νόθ[ιπποϲ Λυϲίου Διο]-
μειεὺ[ϲ εἶπε· π]ερὶ ὧν ὁ δῆμοϲ πρό̣[τερον ἐψήφιϲται ἐπὶ]
[τῆϲ - -ίδο]ϲ πρυτανείαϲ τ̣[οὺϲ προέδρουϲ οἳ ἂν λάχ]-
[ωϲιν ἐν τῶι δήμ]ωι προεδ̲̣[ρεύειν - - - - - - -]

commentary: The text is based on Kirchner's. All dots are mine; one letter is underlined, line 12, which now can not be read. The first three lines are heading and are non-stoichedon. Koehler restored the stoichedon order as 28 letters to the line for lines 4-8. Although Kirchner designated the rest of the text as non-stoichedon, Koehler's majuscule text and my own examination of the stone confirm that the letters in lines 9-12 are in fact cut in stoichedon order. It is the restorations that give these lines uneven lengths: line 9 is 43 letters; line 10, 42 letters; lines 11 and 12 are not restored to full length.

Restorations are Koehler's with the exception of the demotic at the end of line 1, suggested by Hiller von Gaertringen (Koehler had ἄνγελ[ος]); and the name of the mover in line 9, supplied by Wilhelm from PA 11131.

This decree is concerned with Rheboulas, son of Seuthes and brother of Kotys. Rheboulas and Kotys had previously been honored with citizenship (Demosthenes 23.118); their deme is Angele. They are from the ruling family of the Odrysians, a tribe in Thrace. The decree was passed on the 16th day of the 10th (last) prytany, 10th day of Skirophorion in the year of Aristophanes, about June of 330 (both Pritchett-Neugebauer and Meritt agree on the day of the year: 335th day).

This decree of the Boule and the Demos is a consideration of a matter which the Demos alone had voted on earlier, perhaps directing it to the Boule for a probouleuma. Its purpose is unknown, but it has always been assumed to be of an honorary nature. The earlier decree, though "over-condensed" and recording only a sanction by the Demos, is designated probouleumatic by Rhodes (250); he offers in note 2, page 69, an expansion of the formula, line 11, to bring the decree into accord with the usual procedure, but not, unfortunately, with what is on the stone. The procedure as well as the content remains an enigma.

What this decree does show, if it is indeed honorary, is that Athens was trying to stay on good terms with the Odrysians in 330, a very volatile time within the Lykourgan era. The year had seen Antipater face down Memnon (Alexander's rebellious governor in Thrace) and crush the attempt of Agis III to throw off Macedonian domination. Athens narrowly avoided sharing in the Spartan misfortune, and it may be that the Odrysians had supported Memnon in the north. Chronologically the pacification of Memnon (and his Thracian allies?) preceded the defeat of Agis, and this in turn preceded the defeat of Dareios at Gaugamela (Curtius VI 1.21; Badian; Borza). Since Gaugamela was fought in late September, 331, the defeat of Agis came nearly a year before the passage of this decree in favor of Rheboulas, which can not therefore be associated with any rebellion of Seuthes III in cooperation with Memnon as described by Tod. Perhaps the decree in favor of Rheboulas is an example of Athens's maintaining good diplomatic relations in a general way with no specific intent, or the obvious emphasis on Rheboulas's status as a citizen by the prominent placing of his demotic in the heading may be taken to indicate that he was coming to take up residence in the city because he was an exile from his native land or for some other reason. Henry's suggestion that this decree may have been set up privately--the name of the secretary is omitted and the isolation of the enactment formula is old-fashioned(44)--would support the suggestion that Rheboulas was in Athens. The offering of refuge to political exiles is something else of which the Athenians of this period were justly proud.

The date of #45 is close to that of the famous process "On the Crown" which finally, after six years, was brought to trial, shortly after Agis's defeat. One of Aischines' attacks on Demosthenes (3.164-167) portrays three recent events as lost opportunities for Athens due to Demosthenes' inaction. If Seuthes' rebellion had also occurred at this time, it is surprising that

Aischines did not include it, too, in the list of Demosthenes' cowardly mistakes. It would have strengthened his argument that Athens had passed up favorable situations, and in turn, that Demosthenes' part in the events was even more traitorous. Deinarchos (1.34-36) also speaks of Demosthenes' lost opportunities without mentioning the Odrysians. Again, the conclusion must be made that this decree, #45 has no visible connection with an Odrysian uprising in this year.

331/30

46. *DEME (?) DECREE* EM 4218, 4218[a]

editor: Kirchner IG II^2 1181.

other bibliography: Traill Pol. Org. 41, 45.

description: The marble fragment consists of two pieces, now joined. The only adornment is a simple fillet on top (see dimensions below). The right side (what is left of it) is original. The surface on the top is smooth-finished and now bears "ΣΟΥΝ ΡΑΜΝΟΥΣ" in paint, either to show find spot or perhaps where the stone was housed at some time. Kirchner records only that the stone was found at Sounion.

dimensions:
- H 0.07 m. (text)
- 0.13 m. (entire)
- W 0.09 m. (text)
- 0.28 m. (fillet)
- Th 0.025 m. (text)
- 0.73 m. (fillet)

letters: 0.005 m. Although most of the letters are obscure, most are .005; a few omicrons are .004.

minuscule text: next page.

commentary: Text and restorations are Kirchner's. The restoration of the demotic for Tharrias is based on Kirchner's identification of him as a prytanis in 341/40, PA 6590.

non stoich.

vacat

- - - - - - - - - -ς ὁ ἐπὶ Ἀριστοφάνους ἄρχον-
[τος - - - - - - - - -]τωι̣ Θαρρίας Θαρριάδου
[Ἐρχιεὺς - - - - - - -] ε̣̈θ̣υ̣εν ἐφ' ὑγιείαι καὶ σωτη-
[ρίαι - - - - - - - - - - -]νίδο[.... τ]οῦ δήμου
- - - - - - - - - - - - - - - - - - Ε̣Κ̣Α̣...

Kirchner uses the designation "Decretum Suniensium" for this inscription and II^{2} 1180. But, whereas II^{2} 1180 records references to the deme Sounion (lines 3, 13/14) and has a specific find spot (used by Traill, 45, as evidence for the location of the deme), there is no internal epigraphical evidence to prove that this inscription, II^{2} 1181, is a deme decree, let alone that it came from the ancient deme of Sounion; nor does the vague "Sunii" allow for a strong argument based on geographical proximity. The indirect evidence does, indeed, point to a deme decree: placement of the archon's name as a modifier for an official; the absence of any dating formula; the non-stoichedon format; a find-spot outside of Athens. (See #26 for a list of deme decrees in this Corpus.) It must be noted, however, that, although this inscription is fragmentary, the "official" of the year of Aristophanes could be a religious functionary (ὑγείαι καὶ σωτηρίαι ?) and that, if Kirchner's identification of Tharrias is correct, the only person mentioned on stone comes from a deme, Erchia, which is neither in the same tribe as Sounion, nor is it geographically close (Traill, 41, 45, and maps at rear).

47. *THE TEITHRASIANS HONOR THEIR COUNCILORS*
EM 13336

photo: Hesperia 31(1962) Plate 118.

editor: Vanderpool Hesperia 31(1962) 401-403 no. 3.

collection: Meritt & Traill Councillors 45.

supplements: SEG 21.520 (Vanderpool Hesperia 1962). Bull. (1964) no. 163 (Vanderpool Hesperia 1962); (1967) no. 226 (Vanderpool Hesperia 1966).

other bibliography: Vanderpool Hesperia 35(1966) 281-282.

description: This fragment of Pentelic marble was found in the village of Pikermi in Attika. Only the right side is preserved; the right corner of the pediment above is broken away.

dimensions:
H 0.55 m. (entire)
0.46 m. (below pediment)
W 0.11 m.
Th 0.07 m.

letters: 0.007 m. Smallest, Δ, Ω, are .005; largest, Φ, is .010. Individual letters vary as to size.

minuscule text: next page.

commentary: The text is based on Vanderpool's. I have taken one letter out of brackets, line 19 st. 12 (Meritt & Traill also see the iota). Letters in st. 10 in lines 3, 5, 6, 7, 8, are faintly visible, but not enough to warrant removal of the brackets.

The restorations are Vanderpool's. The stoichedon order of 16 letters to the line is established by the restorations in lines 1 and 17-20.

This decree comes from the deme Teithras, located at Pikermi. Only the beginning of the archon's name is preserved, and there is no fuller dating formula, as is usual in a decree of a local deme (cf. #42; #26 for list of deme decrees). The archon's name could be restored as either Ἀριστοφάνους] or Ἀριστ[οφῶντος], the year either 331/30 or 330/29. (It should be kept in mind that, since the archon's name defines the year in which the bouleutes held office, this decree could have been set up after those bouleutes' term in office--330/29 or 329/8; see #70.)

stoich. 16

[Ἔδοξεν Τειθ]ραcῖοι
[c ....8.... ε]ἶπεν cτ-
[εφανῶcαι το]ὺc βουλ-
[ευτὰc τοὺc ἐ]π' Ἀριcτ-
[οφ..5.. ἄρχ]οντοc χ-
[ρυcῶι cτεφά]νωι ἕκα-
[cτον αὐτῶν ἐ]πειδὴ κ-
[αλῶc καὶ φιλ]οτίμωc
[ἐπεμελήθηc]αν τῶν θ-
[υcιῶν καὶ τῶ]ν ἄλλων
[ὅcα ἐκέλευc]αν οἱ δη-
[μόται· οἵδε β]ουλευτ-
[αὶ ἐγένοντο] Βλέπυρ-
[οc Φυλεΐδου], Μαντικ-
[λῆc ...7...]άνηc Ἀν-
[....10....ι]νιάδη-
[c....9....ο]υ· ἀναγ-
[ράψαι δὲ τόδε] τὸ ψήφ-
[ιcμα ἐν cτήλη]ι λιθί-
[νηι καὶ cτῆcα]ι ἐν τῶ-
[ι- - - - - - - - -] vacat

The decree records honors granted to the four men who served in the Boule from Teithras. Each is to be honored with a gold crown since he carried out the sacrifices and other duties of his office well and zealously. Vanderpool notes that two preserved lists of bouleutai show that four is the usual number from Teithras. He was able to restore the name and patronymic of only the first man listed, Βλέπυρ[ος Φυλεΐδου]; he was Curator of the Naval Yards in 349/8 (II^2 1620 lines 45/46), and is the orator in another decree found at Pikermi, published in _AM_ 49(1924) 1-13. Since his publication of this decree, Vanderpool has published a grave stele, dated to the fourth century, which records a Μαντ[c. 5] Τειθρ[ασιος] (_Hesperia_ 1966); he notes that the grave stele should probably be connected with the family of Mantikles, the councilor honored in this decree, if not the councilor himself.

IX. THE YEAR OF ARISTOPHON, 330/29

48. *LYKOURGOS PROPOSES HONORS FOR EUDEMOS OF PLATAIA* EM 7196, 292

editors: EM 7196 Pittakis *EΦ.* (1856/61) 3453; Velsen *Arch. Zeit.* 17(1859) Anzeiger 69-72; *IG* II 176; *IG* II^2 351.
EM 292 *IG* II^2 624.
[Wilhelm saw that II^2 624 fit in the upper right hand corner of II^2 351 which had already been mounted in a plaster base. The join was made and noted in the Addenda to the first volume of *IG* II^2, page 660.]

collections: Ditt. *Syll.*^{2} 151; *Syll.*^{3} 288; Michel 109; Hicks 161; Tod II 198; Pouilloux *Choix* 6.

supplements: *SEG* 21.283 (*Syll.*^{3}, Pritchett-Neugebauer, Tod, Pouilloux, Meritt, Pritchett *AACS*); 24.99 (Pečírka).

other bibliography: Curtius *Philol.* 24(1865) 273; Unger *Philol.* 38(1879) 426; *Att. Arch.* 672; Wilhelm *GGA* 1(1898) 221; *EΦ.* (1905) 216; *ÖJ* 10(1907) 34; Dinsmoor *Archons* 370; Pickard-Cambridge *Dionysos* 137; Pritchett-Neugebauer *Cal.* 50; Woodward *JHS* 68(1948) 161; Meritt *Ath.* 91-94; Dow *AJA* 66(1962) 356; Pritchett *AACS* 323; Pečírka *Enktesis* 68-70; Mikalson *Year* 154/5; 190/91; Henry *Prescripts* 35 n. 10, 36 n. 17, 46-47

description: This stele of Pentelic marble was found on the Akropolis, east of the Propylaia. The smaller fragment was found on the northern slope of Arkropolis. Although the sides and surface are chipped and worn, only the upper left hand surface is missing; the addition of the small fragment to that corner has confirmed the earlier restorations.

The stele tapers toward the top (see dimensions below). The sides, however, are asymmetrical; the right side is practically perpendicular to the floor and all of the taper is on the left side. The letters are in stoichedon order, but they follow the taper of the stele rather than a true vertical. The left margin widens only slightly: the width of 10 stoichoi in line 11 is 0.135 m. while the width in line 39 is 0.14 m. The final letters on the right are more true to the vertical because they are parallel to the right side. (Dow discusses this stele and provides a sketch in his article, AJA; cf. also, Pečírka, page 68.)

dimensions:
H 0.96 m.
W 0.34 m. (above)
0.354 m. (below)
Th 0.218 m. (above)
0.24 m. (below)

letters: 0.006 m. Smallest, Μ, Π, Ω, are .005; largest, Σ, Υ, are .007.

minuscule text: stoich. 19-24

[Εὐδῆμ]ου Πλαται[έως].
[Ἐπὶ Ἀριστ]οφῶντος ἄρχοντο[ς]
[ἐ]π̣[ὶ τῆς] Λ̣εωντίδος ἐνάτη[ς] π̣[ρυ]-
ταν[εία]ς ἧι Ἀντίδωρος Ἀντι[νου]
Παι[ανι]εὺς ἐγραμμάτευεν· ἐ[ν]-
[δ]εκά[τ]ηι Θαργηλιῶνος. ἐνάτη[ι]
[κ]αὶ δ[ε]κάτηι τῆς πρυτανείας·
[τ]ῶν π[ρ]οέδρων ἐπεψήφιζεν Ἀν̣[τι]-
φάνη[ς] Εὐωνυμ̣εύς· ἔδοξεν τῶι̣
[δήμωι]· Λυκοῦργος Λ̣υκόφρονος
[Βουτά]δης εἶπεν· ἐπειδὴ̣ vacat
[Εὔδημ]ος πρότερόν τε ἐπη[γ]γ[εί]-
[λατο τ]ῶι δήμωι ἐπιδ̣ώσειν [εἰ]ς̣
[τὸν π]όλεμον εἴ τ[ι] δέ[οι]το [ΧΧΧ]Χ̣
[δ]ραχμὰς καὶ νῦν [ἐπ]ι[δέδ]ω[κεν]
εἰς τὴν ποίησιν τοῦ στ̣αδ[ί]ου
καὶ τοῦ θεάτρου τ̣οῦ Παν̣αθη[ναι]-
κοῦ χίλια ζεύγη καὶ τα̣ῦτα
πέπομφεν ἅπαντα̣ π[ρὸ Π]αναθη-

ναίων καθὰ ὑπέc[χετο, δ]εδόχθ[αι]
τῶι δήμωι ἐπαι[νέcαι Ε]ὔδημ[ον]
[Φι]λούργου Πλατα[ιέα] καὶ c[τε]-
φανῶcαι αὐτὸν θαλλõ cτεφ[άνωι]
εὐνοίαc ἕνεκα τῆc εἰc τὸν
δῆμον τὸν Ἀθηναίων καὶ εἶν[αι]
αὐτὸν ἐν τοῖc εὐεργέταιc το[ῦ]
δήμου τοῦ Ἀθηναίων [α]ὐτὸν καὶ
ἐκγόνουc καὶ ε[ἶν]α[ι] αὐτῶι vacat
ἔνκτηcιν γῆc καὶ οἰκίαc καὶ
cτρατεύεcθαι αὐτὸν τὰc vacat
cτρατιὰc καὶ τὰc εἰcφορὰc vacat
εἰcφέρειν μετὰ Ἀθηναίων. vacat
ἀναγράψαι δὲ τόδε τὸ ψήφιcμα
τὸν γραμματέα τῆc βουλῆc καὶ
cτῆcαι ἐν ἀκροπόλει, εἰ[c] δ[ὲ] τ[ὴν]
ἀναγραφὴν τῆc cτήλη[c δοῦ]να[ι]
τὸν ταμίαν τοῦ δήμ[ο]υ [-----]
δραχμὰc ἐκ τῶν εἰc τὰ κα[τὰ ψη]-
φίcματα ἀναλιcκομέν[ων τῶι]
δήμωι.

vacat 0.40

epigraphical commentary: The text is based on Kirchner's; lines 3-9 are from the new text printed for those lines in the Addenda, page 660, which noted the addition of II^2 624. There is no vacat between lines 22 and 23 as shown in Kirchner's text and it has been removed. Although the letters are in stoichedon order, the stonecutter usually ended the line with a full word or at least the end of a syllable so that the length of the lines vary from 19 to 25 letters. Pečírka has observed that there is room for only 24 stoichoi to the line. Using line 35 as an example (where the last iota shares the 18th stoichos with epsilon and so effects a restored line of 25 letters in only 24 stoichoi), he assumes that of the other four lines restored to a length of 25 letters (i.e. 17, 20, 23) the final iota shared the 24th stoichos with the letter preceding; in line 4, either the iota shared the 21st stoichos with tau or tau, iota, and nu occupied the 21st and 22nd stoichoi. This crowding is indicated in my text.

Only line 8 remains a problem; the restoration in the Addenda, even allowing for a "crowded" iota, still leaves a line of 25 letters. When II^2 624 was added, the fragment showed that the names of the chairman of the proedroi ended in -phanes (line 9) and Kirchner (or Wilhelm?) restored the name Aristophanes. There are, however, variant readings of the first two letters of the name at the end of line 8: Pittakis read AN; Velsen, ANI; Koehler, ΛH; Kirchner, in II^2 351, AP; in Addenda, AP. The discrepancies in both the reading of the letters on the stone and the length of the line have convinced me that Kirchner's restoration must be rejected. Pečírka's suggestion, Antiphanes, is preferable (see commentary below).

All dots are mine. Underlined letters are those which can not now be read because the surface of the stone has deteriorated. Since Velsen read more letters than Koehler or Kirchner, the problem may be one of too much "squeezing." In the small fragment, the two underlined letters can not be read because of the plaster mounting. There are 5 new readings: N line 13 st. 21; I line 27 st. 24; Δ line 33 st. 10; O line 35 st. 12; Y line 37 st. 17. Brackets have also been removed from letters which were read by Velsen: in line 29, 2 iotas, st. 16, 18; N line 39 st. 18.

commentary: The restorations are Koehler's, with the exception of Pečírka's restoration of 'Αν[τι]φάνηc, lines 8/9. (Kirchner, in Add. p. 660, has Ἀρ[ιστο]φάνηc, in II^2 351 'Αρ[...7...]; Koehler has [Δη/..5..]; Velsen, Ἀν[τι/φάνηc?]; Pittakis, 'Αν[τί/δωροc].) If Pečírka's restoration is correct, then, for the Lykourgan era, Antiphanes would be the first man to have served as chairman of the proedroi twice (cf. #7, #8; Henry, 47 n. 70, accepts Pečírka's restoration).

Everyone is agreed that 330/29 was intercalary, but the date as it appears on the stone can be reconciled with neither an ordinary nor intercalary year, nor yet with the date of the following decree #49 (II^2 352). Unger (followed by Kirchner, Dinsmoor, Pritchett-Neugebauer) proposed that the error was in the prytany date: that rather than ενάτηι καὶ δεκάτηι, the 19th (lines 6/7), the day was in fact ενάτηι καὶ εικοστῆι, the 29th day. Thus 330/29 would be intercalary, the equation: Thargelion 11 = Prytany IX <2>9 = 337th day, and that is perfectly acceptable.

The problem arises when this date is placed next to that of #49, where the equation reads: Thargelion 14 = Prytany IX 3[2] = 240th day. To avoid meetings of the ekklesia only three days apart, Meritt has suggested that the error lay in the festival date and has proposed (for this decree): Thargelion <1> = Prytany IX 19 = 327th day. Henry, who reproduces lines 1-11 (46-47), follows Meritt's suggestion for the equation, but makes the day the 326th (with no explanation); he lists this decree (incorrectly) with those in which the name of the epistates precedes the secretary (36 n. 17). Pritchett, on the other hand, is reluctant to see a meeting of the ekklesia on the first day of the month, which was always a sacred day in Athens (AACS 323 n. 40). Pritchett's opinion is reinforced by Mikalson's study which shows that there is not a single meeting of the ekklesia on the the first day of any month. Therefore Meritt's emendation of the festival calendar must be rejected (see #35 for other restorations considered doubtful by Mikalson). And, in fact, the 11th day of the month was "clearly a regular meeting day" (Mikalson 184; but see II^2 363, #67, for an exception in Anthesterion).

In accepting the date on the stone, the 11th of Thargelion, for #48, we must face squarely the anomaly of another meeting of the ekklesia on the third day thereafter, the 14th, a date which is also on stone (#49). Perhaps the anomaly is less than Meritt thought; he objects to two meetings so close together when there is "no indication that either one was in any way exceptional" (93; see also #35, discussion), but #49 is in fact exceptional to the extent that it was a kyria ekklesia (primary meeting of the ekklesia), and its agenda was to a large extent cut and dried, requiring relatively little preparation on the part of the Boule. A quick examination of decrees with the designation kyria ekklesia shows first, that they could be anytime in the prytany; second, that slightly more than half occur after the 17th day of the prytany, as #48 does (Pryt. IX 32). The kyria ekklesia so late in the prytany, therefore, creates no problem and the "crowding" of two ekklesiai into four days should not prevent the acceptance of what is on the stone and surely amended and restored. Finally it should be noted that there is no way these two equations can be made to conform to Aristotle's so-called "rule" (cf. #15).

This decree, moved by Lykourgos himself honors Eudemos of Plataia for his many and varied services to Athens. Eudemos had formerly offered to contribute four thousand drachmai for the war, if it should be needed, and he had just provided a thousand yoke of animals for the construction of the Stadium and the Panathenaic _theatron_ and had brought them before the Panathenaia just as he had promised. He and his descendants are honored with the title _euergetes_ (benefactor) of the Athenian people; he is granted _enktesis_ (right of ownership) of both land and house.

Pečirka (70) notes that there is no mention of Eudemos's descendants in connection with the grant of enktesis, but it seems unreasonable that his heirs should be forced to sell the house and land and not be allowed to inherit; it is better to assume that they were able to exercise _de facto_ Eudemos's right of enktesis.

There are two other points of controversy about this decree. The first is the reference to "the war." Dittenberger, followed by Hicks, wanted to see an immediate danger of war and have Eudemos's offer refer to events of 330. Tod (280) feels that the contrast πρότερόν τε ... καὶ νῦν, lines 12, 15, refers to a longer interval of time and suggests the war which ended with Chaironeia. This is closer to the mark, but the phrase "if it be needed" shows that it was not that part of the war which preceded Chaironeia when the money certainly was needed, but to the short period of frantic preparations made by the Athenians after Chaironeia and before the unexpectedly generous terms offered by Philip caused the Athenians to make peace and thus made Eudemos's generosity unnecessary. The situation in 330 has been discussed in #45, and in my opinion the "crisis" or "lost opportunity" occurred mostly in the speeches of Aischines and Deinarchos and is in any case, therefore, inappropriate.

The second point is the reference to τὸ θέατρον τὸ Παναθηναικόν. The suggestion has been made that the stonecutter erred and should have engraved τοῦ σταδίου Παναθηναικοῦ καὶ τοῦ θεάτρου (Curtius, followed by Dittenberger) to show that Eudemos contributed money both for the Panathenaic stadium and for the theater of Dionysos (Lykourgos was epistates for both projects). The more likely explanation, however, is that the stonecutter did not make a mistake and that _theatron_ refers to the closed, theater-like end of the Panathenaic stadium which required more material and work than did the simple retaining walls along the long sides. Again, the text offers corroboration: Eudemos got it all together _before the Panathenaia_ just as he had promised. There is no mention of the Dionysia.

Eudemos's actual status in Athens is a _non liquet_, but see Pečírka (70) for a full bibliography and useful discussion.

330/29

49. *DECREE* EM 7161

editors: Pittakis _ΕΦ._ (1852/55) 1407; _ΕΦ._ (1856/61) 2699 notes Rangabé's repetition; Rangabé (1855) 424, 2308; _IG_ II 177; _IG_ II^2 352.

other bibliography: Pritchett-Neugebauer _Cal._ 50; Meritt _Ath._ 92-94; (see #48 for bibliography on the date of #48 and #49 which must be discussed together).

description: This small fragment of Pentelic marble was found north of the Parthenon on the Akropolis in 1842. It is broken on all sides.

dimensions:	letters: 0.010 m. Smallest, H, Ω, are .009; largest, A, Π, P, Σ, Φ, are .011. Letters are quite large and well-defined. Ω, usually smallest letter, is as large as most of the other letters.
H 0.28 m.	
W 0.255 m.	
Th 0.135 m.	

minuscule text:

[Θ] ε [ο ί] stoich. 20

vacat 0.04

[Ἐπὶ Ἀριϲτ]οφῶντ[οϲ ἄρχον]-
[τοϲ ἐπὶ τ]ῆϲ Λεων[τίδοϲ ἐν]-
[άτηϲ πρυ]τανεία[ϲ, ἧι Ἀντί]-
[δωροϲ Ἀν]τίνου Πα[ιανιεὺ]-
[ϲ ἐγραμμ]άτευεν· Θα[ργηλι]-
[ῶνοϲ τε]τράδι ἐπὶ δ[έκα, δε]-
[υτέραι] καὶ τριακοϲ[τῆι τ]-
[ῆϲ πρυτα]ν̣είαϲ· ἐκκλη[ϲία]
[κυρία· τῶν προ]έ[δρων] ἐ[πεψ]-
[ήφιζε --------------]

commentary: The text is based on Kirchner's. The one dotted letter is mine. Restorations are Koehler's. The stoichedon order is 20 letters to the line.

This decree was passed on the 32nd day of the 9th prytany, held by the tribe Leontis; the 14th day of Thargelion. The dates of this decree and #48 have been discussed in the commentary for #48, although there is some disagreement about the date of #48, the date for this decree has always been accepted as correct. One piece of information which this decree provides is that in the 9th prytany of the year of Aristophon, the kyria ekklesia was not the first meeting of the prytany as one might assume from Aristotle AP 43.4-6; it was probably at least the third (see also, #48).

X. THE YEAR OF KEPHISOPHON, 329/8

50. *ATHENS HONORS EPIMELITAI OF THE AMPHIARAIC GAMES* Oropos 252

editors: Leonardos *ΕΦ.* (1891) 86-91 no. 38; *IG* VII 4254.

collections: Ditt. *Syll.*^{2} 639; *Syll.*^{3} 298; Michel 108; Pouilloux *Choix* 2.

other bibliography: Pritchett-Neugebauer *Cal.* 50; Lewis *BSA* 50(1955) 27-36 no. 29; Oikonomides *ΠΛΑΤΩΝ* 8(1956) 108; Charitonides *Hesperia* 30(1961) 30-57; Meritt *Ath.* 94; Mitchel *TAPA* 93(1962) 226 n. 39; *Lyk.* 165-214; Rhodes *Boule* 28 n. 3, 50 n. 1, 73 n. 3, 101 n. 4, 129 n. 7, 261, 276; Hansen *ZPE* (1978) 156.

description: The two fragments of white marble were found next to #40 and #41 in a drain at the Amphiaraion. The fragments are now joined and form a stele which stands in the museum. The stele is topped by a pediment similar to #41.

dimensions:
- H 0.84 m. (entire)
- 0.685 m. (below pediment)
- W 0.356 m. (pediment)
- 0.334 m. (above)
- 0.354 m. (below)
- Th 0.06 m.

letters: 0.006 m. Smallest, Ω, is .004; largest, Σ, Ψ, are .007. Φ looks like ϕ.

minuscule text: next page.

commentary: The text is based on Pouilloux's. The alpha, line 43 st. 1, bracketed by all editors, can be dotted. The double points, lines 24-31, which appear on the stone and in both of Leonardos's texts and Dittenberger's majuscule text have been added; Pouilloux has commas. Angular brackets denote omissions. The restorations are Leonardos's. The end of line 5 was erased; the double brackets denote that erasure.

The stoichedon order is 27 letters to the line. It is not violated on the stone although the addition of Pyanopsion at the end of line 5 gives a line of 28 letters.

θεοί stoich. 27

Ἐπὶ Κηφιϲοφῶντοϲ ἄρχοντοϲ, ἐπὶ τ- ῆϲ Ἱπποθωντίδοϲ τρίτηϲ πρυτανε- ίαϲ, ἧι Σωϲτρατίδηϲ Ἐχφάντου Εὐπ- υρίδηϲ ἐγραμμάτευεν, [[Πυανοψιῶνοϲ]] ἕκτει ἐπὶ δέκα, τρίτει καὶ τριακο- ϲτεῖ τῆϲ πρυτανείαϲ· ἐκκληϲία· τῶ- μ προέδρων ἐπεψήφιϲζεν Δημοχάρ- ηϲ Φλυεύϲ· ἔδοξεν τῶι δήμωι· Δημοϲ- θένηϲ Δημοκλέουϲ Λαμπτρεὺϲ εἶπ- εν· ἐπειδὴ οἱ χειροτονηθέντεϲ ὑπ- ὸ τοῦ δήμου ἐπὶ τὴν ἐπιμέλειαν το- ῦ ἀγῶνοϲ καὶ τῶν ἄλλων τῶν περὶ τὴ- ν ἑορτὴν τοῦ Ἀμφιαράου καλῶϲ καὶ φιλοτίμωϲ ἐπεμελήθηϲαν τῆϲ τε π- ομπῆϲ τῶι Ἀμφιαράωι καὶ τοῦ ἀγῶν- οϲ τοῦ γυμνικοῦ καὶ ἱππικοῦ καὶ τ- ῆϲ ἀποβάϲεωϲ καὶ τῶν ἄλλων πάντω- ν τῶν περὶ τὴν πανήγυριν ὧν αὐτοῖ- ϲ προϲέταξεν ὁ δῆμοϲ, δεδόχθαι τῶ- ι δήμωι, ἐπαινέϲαι τοὺϲ αἱρεθέντ- αϲ, Φανόδημον Διύλλου Θυμαιτάδη- ν<:> Λυκοῦργον Λυκόφρονοϲ Βουτάδη- ν: Δημάδην Δημέου Παιανιέα: Σώφιλ- ον Ἀριϲτοτέλουϲ Φυλάϲιον: Θραϲυ- λέοντα Θεοφῶντοϲ Ἀχαρνέα: Ἐπιτέ-

λην Σωινόμου Περγασῆθεν: Νικήρα-
τον Νικίου Κυδαντίδην: Ἐπιχάρην
Ἀγωνοχάρους Παιανιέα: Θυμοχάρη-
ν Φαίδρου Σφήττιον: Κηφιcοφῶντα
Λυcιφῶντος Χολαργέ(α): δικαιοcύνη-
c ἕνεκα καὶ φιλοτιμίαc τῆc πρὸc τ-
ὸν θεὸν καὶ τὸν δῆμον τῶν Ἀθηναίω-
ν, καὶ cτεφανῶcαι αὐτοὺc χρυcῶι c-
τεφάνωι ἀπὸ : Χ : δραχμῶν· δοῦναι δὲ α-
ὐτοῖc καὶ εἰc θυcίαν καὶ ἀνάθημα
Η : δραχμάc· τὸ δὲ ἀργύριον τ<ὸ> εἰc τή-
ν θυcίαν προδανεῖcαι τὸν ταμίαν
τοῦ δήμου· ἐν δὲ τοῖc πρώτοιc νομο-
θέταιc προcνομοθετῆcαι τῶι ταμ-
[ί]αι· 'δοῦναι δὲ καὶ τὰc τριάκοντα δ-
[ρ]αχμὰc τὸν ταμίαν τοῦ δήμου τοῖc
αἱρεθεῖcιν ἐπὶ τὸν ἀγῶνα, ἃc εἴρη-
ται διδόναι ἐν τῶι νόμωι τῶι αἱρε-
θέντι ἐπὶ τὴν εὐταξίαν'· ἀναγράψα-
ι δὲ τόδε τὸ ψήφιcμα τὸγ γραμματέ-
α τῆc βουλῆc καὶ cτῆcαι ἐν τῶι ἱερ-
ῶι τοῦ Ἀμφιαράου· εἰc δὲ τὴν ἀναγρ-
αφὴν τῆc cτήληc δοῦναι τὸν ταμία-
ν τοῦ δήμου : ΔΔΔ : δραχμὰc ἐκ τῶν κατ-
ὰ ψηφίcματα μεριζομένων τῶι δήμ-
ωι.

This decree honors the ten men elected by the Demos to serve as epimeletai for the games and other rites at the Amphiaraion. The decree was passed by the Demos when

Kephisophon was archon, 329/8, the 33rd day of the third prytany, held by Hippothontis, the 16th day of Pyanopsion. Sostratides, son of Echphantos of the deme Eupyridai, was secretary; the chairman of the proedroi was Demochares of the deme Phlya; Demosthenes, son of Demokles of the deme Lamptrai (not the famous orator as Tarn assumed; cf. Mitchel TAPA, Lewis 36 n. 47), made the motion.

The men are honored because they carried out all of their duties well and zealously (Pouilloux, 27, elaborates on the specific duties), as indeed could be expected from such an illustrious gathering. The list (and presumably the board itself) is headed by Phanodemos, son of Diyllos, of the deme Thumaitadai (PA 14033; no APF). We know of Phanodemos already from #40, in which he proposed honors to Amphiaraos, and #41 of the same year, 322/1, in which he in turn was honored for his work at the Amphiaraion. Lykourgos, son of Lykophron, of the deme Boutadai, needs no introduction (PA 9251; APF; see Mitchel Lyk. 11-13). A short discussion of the specific decrees moved by Lykourgos can be found in #15. Demades, son of Demeos, of the deme Paiania, is also a major figure in this period (PA 3263; APF; see Mitchel TAPA which confirms that Demades was Military Treasurer in 334/3; Lyk. 14-18). He was the most prolific orator of this period (at least from the extant documents; see Rhodes, 269). Oikonomides' article, 105-125, includes all of the decrees attributed to Demades (but see Charitonides, 44 n. 19, for correction).

Sophilos, son of Aristoteles, of the deme Phyle, and Thrasyleon, son of Theophon, of the deme Acharnai (PA 7329; no APF), are otherwise unattested. Epiteles, son of Soinomos, of the deme Pergase (PA 4955, 4963; no APF), was involved as well in other sanctuaries. In 323/2, he proposed #79 (II^2 365) which deals with the Nemean games; in 327/6 (date from Daux BCH 78[1954] 375/6) he was honored with proxeny by the Delphians; he is listed as *naopoios* at Delphi a number of times in the twenties (see Lewis, 35).

Nikeratos, son of Nikias, of the deme Kydantidai, is the last known descendant of Nikias, the fifth century general (PA 10742; APF 10808; see Lewis 30/31). Davies, pp. 406 f., gives an up-to-date account of Nikeratos's liturgies. They were numerous, as befits a member of this wealthy family. As with Sophilos and Thrasyleon, Epichares, son of Agonochares, of the deme Paiania, appears only on this board (PA 4999; no APF); II^2 7020 appears to be his father's grave stone.

With the exception of this decree, the rest of the known career of Thymochares, son of Phaidros, of the deme Sphettos (PA 7412; no APF), occurs later, in the teens (Lewis, 35, suggests that Thymochares was in his thirties when he served on this board). Last but not least is Kephisophon, son of Lysiphon, of the deme Cholargos (PA 8419; no APF), perhaps best known as the mover of the decree of 325 which authorized the founding of a colony on the Adriatic (II^2 1629 lines 165-232; Tod II 200; see also Lewis, 33; Mitchel *Lyk*. 33). Kephisophon's son, Lysiphon, served as bouleutes either in 336/5, according to Charitonides (*Hesperia* p. 52, line 300, p. 56) or earlier, before 341, according to Larsen (CP 57[1962] 104). Two of Lysiphon's fellow board members from this decree, #50, were also fellow bouleutai: Demades (*Hesperia* p. 43 line 144) and Epiteles (*Hesperia* p. 38 line 42).

Nikeratos and Kephisophon also appear on II^2 2409. Lewis has now joined II^2 2409 to II^2 1924, a list of diaitetai dated to 330/29. Since Athenians were liable for this duty only in their 60th year, when their military obligations were over, the age of the two men can be determined. It was this new certain information about two of the men that prompted Lewis's discussion of the present decree, #50; *Syll.*[3] 296, a contemporary dedication to Apollo which lists the ten men who conducted the Pythais; and #56 (*AE* [1917] 40-48 no. 92) a dedication of the boule and honorary decree from the Amphiaraion which lists ten men who contributed to the dedication along with those in the Boule. *Syll.*[3] 296 has always been discussed in relation to the present decree (cf. #41); the two lists share Phanodemos, Demades, Lykourgos, and Nikeratos. But it is the addition of the third list, #56, which shares Phanodemos, Demades and Kephisophon with #50, which provides "a fair cross-section of the governing party under Lycurgus" (Lewis 35; Charitonides provides a chart). From that premise, Lewis goes on to note "the high average age of those whose age is ascertainable" and concludes that "experience and wealth are the chief passports to power in this period" (35). This observation substantiates the general view that the fourth century, and in particular Lykourgan Athens, was tending toward a more moderate democracy (cf. Mitchel *Lyk.* 173f.). However, Lewis's further observation, that it was easier for Lykourgos to cooperate with Demades and Thymochares than with Demosthenes and Hypereides (36), is not convincing since it is based chiefly on the absence of the two men from all three lists.

Although the presence of these ten men is the usual focal point for a discussion of this decree, this decree should also be considered in any discussion of nomothesia. After listing the men, the decree continues: because of their justice and zeal the men are to be honored with a gold crown worth a thousand drachmai and to be given one hundred drachmai for the sacrifice and dedication. But the treasurer of the Demos is to advance (προδανεῖσαι, line 38) the silver for the sacrifice and pay to the elected epimeletai of the games the 30 drachmai which had been earmarked for the official elected for the eutaxia (discipline; lines 41-45) at the next sitting of the nomothetai. Hansen's opinion, that the commissioning of the nomothetai by the ekklesia is exceptional, has been noted in #18. Rhodes (especially 50 n. 1) sees this as a commissioning of the nomothetai for the purpose of an unexpected new expenditure, but actually all the decree shows is that there is to be a transfer of funds (which also needs the approval of the nomothetai, albeit fairly casually). There is no way to know where the other 70 drachmai are to come from to make 100, or if the 30 drachmai are to be in addition (perhaps to pay for the stele?) to the 100 drachmai advanced by the treasurer of the Demos (the money may be coming from a fund set up at the request of the Demos in #18). The exact details remain vague. However, the combination of new or transferred expenditures and the almost casual calling in of the nomothetai, "the next time the nomothetai sit," rather than at the first of the year is significant (cf. #3, #6).

The decree ends with the publication formula: the secretary is to be given 30 drachmai to have the stele inscribed and set up in the Amphiaraion.

The importance of Oropos and the Amphiaraion to Athens has been noted above, #17, #28, #40, #41. This decree adds another dimension: some very important Athenians felt that this new acquisition was important enough to contribute their time and probably money (cf. #56)

329/8

51. *DEMADES PROPOSES HONORS FOR A LARISAIAN*

EM 7195

editors: Pittakis Εφ. (1840/42) 941; (1852/55) 2041 (after stone was cleaned); Rangabé (1855) 419; Koehler & Velsen IG II 178; IG II^2 353.

other bibliography: Unger Att. Arch. 672; Deubner Att. Feste 35-36; Pritchett-Neugebauer Cal. 50-51; Oikonomides ΠΛΑΤΩΝ 8(1956) 116; Meritt Ath. 94-95; Mikalson Year 78, 191; Habicht AM 97(1982) 171-184.

description: This fragment of Pentelic marble was found in 1839 north of the Akropolis. The left-hand side, which shows small chisel marks, and the rough-cut back are preserved; the other sides are broken.

The fragment now stands in a plaster base in the Epigraphical Museum. Since the original width (approximately 0.48 m.) is not restored, the appearance of the stele is misleading: rather than tall and slender, the original fragment, given the preserved height of 0.67 m., would have been short and stocky. Thus it is probable that the orginal stele was taller than preserved. But whether the lost height was above, in the form of a pediment or relief or another decree; or below, or both, can not be determined.

There is no abrupt change in the surface of the stone. Because of later reuse, most likely as a threshhold, the letters begin to be faint from line 8 on so that after line 15, there is no formal vacat, the letters have simply been worn away.

dimensions:
H 0.67 m.
W 0.255 m.
Th 0.122 m.

letters: 0.008 m. Smallest, O, is .007; largest, Y, is .010. The letters are cut poorly and inconsistently.

minuscule text:

stoich. 23

[Ἐπὶ] Κηφισο[φῶντος ἄρχοντος]
[ἐπ]ὶ τῆς Αἰγε[ῖδος τετάρτης π]-
[ρ]υτανείας, ἧι [Σωστρατίδης Ἐ]-
[χ]φ[ά]ντου Εὐπυ[ρίδης ἐγραμμά]-
[τευ]εν· Πυανοψ[ιῶνος ἕνηι καὶ]
[νέα]ι, ἑνδεκά[τηι τῆς πρυτανε]-
[ί]α[ς]· τῶν προέ[δρων ἐπεψήφιζε]
...ππος Ὠαθ[εν· ἔδοξεν τῶι δή]-
μωι· Δημάδης [Δημέου Παιανιε]-
[ὺ]ς εἶπεν· ἐπειδ[ὴ ....10....]
[. Χ]οίρου Λαρισ[αῖος ...7...]
...7... ///Υ///ΕΙ[....10.... τ]-
[οῦ δήμ]ο[υ τ]οῦ Ἀθ[ηναίων ..5..]
....9....ΙΓΟ....11....
....10....Σ....12....

epigraphical commentary: The text is based on Kirchner's. All dots are mine. Various readings are recorded below.

2 end Γ: Velsen, Schwenk. ‾ Koe.; Γ Ki.

8 beg ...ΠΠΟΣ: Premerstein in II^2 353. ΩΣ.ΠΠΟΣ Rang.; _.ΠΠΟΣ Vel.; Σ.ΠΠΟΣ Koe.

11 beg ΟΙΡΟΥ: Koe., Ki. ΓΟΙΡΟΥ Vel.

12 ///Υ///ΕΙ: Ki. ΣΙ...ΟΥΕ Vel.; ʹΙ...ΟΥʽΕΙ Koe.

commentary: Restorations are Velsen's and Koehler's. They established the stoichedon order of 23 letters to the line; it is violated neither on the stone nor in restoration. Koehler, in II 5 p. 296, added the secretary's name from #50. Kirchner's suggestion of either Ἔφιππος or Δάιππος as the chairman of the proedroi, line 8, denies the earlier readings of sigma in st. 2. In line

11, Koehler restored the patronymic as Κοῖρου; Hiller suggested the Χοῖρου, used by Kirchner; Oikonomides follows Kirchner.

This decree is in some ways more frustrating than those which have only the date preserved. There is more information than just the date: the restoration of Demades, the son of Demeas, of the deme Paiania, as the proposer has never been questioned; nor has the restoration of a man from Larisa as the subject of the decree. Although there is no confirmation on the stone, either from the text or the presence of a wreath, the identification of the decree as honorary has been assumed as well; in fact, Oikonomides boldly assumes that the honor was that of proxeny. And this decree confirms the fact that Demades did not restrict his activities to proposing honors for Macedonians only (cf. #24), although this fact is tempered by the close relationship between Thessaly and the Macedonian king at this time. The information is incomplete, however, and, as with the other extant decrees proposed by Demades, provokes questions which can not be answered and speculation which can not be substantiated (#4, #7, #24 are incomplete in some way; #5, #8, #23, #87 [II^2 372] give only the date).

The date is straightforward and there is no controversy over the restoration: the 11th day of the 4th prytany held by the tribe Aigeis; the last day of Pyanopsion. There is, however, a difference of opinion about the count of days. Pritchett-Neugebauer follow Aristotle's "rule" that the first 4 prytanies (in an ordinary year) held 36 days. Therefore the 11th day of the 4th prytany would be the 119th day of the civil year (36×3+11 = 119). The 119th day of the festival year requires not only that

Pyanopsion be full, but also that only one of the first four months of the year 329/8 would be hollow: Pyanopsion (IV) 30 = Prytany [IV] 11 = 119th day (see #15 for discussion of calendar). Meritt's equation, which allows for a more natural alternation of full and hollow months, is based on a 35-day 3rd prytany (36×2+35+11 = 118) and a hollow Pyanopsion: Pyanopsion [29] = Prytany [IV] 11 = 118th day. As has been noted above, #15, I prefer Meritt's more flexible approach; Unger, who did not have the advantage of using Aristotle's Athenaion Politeia, also assumed that the day was the 118th.

Whether Pyanopsion is hollow or full in 329/8, the designation, ἕνηι καὶ νέα remains. Mikalson, (78), notes that the Chalkeia was celebrated on this same day, ἕνηι καὶ νέα Πυανοψιῶνος, and he therefore includes II^2 353 in his list of 34 decrees which "can now with some certainty be regarded as incorrect" (190-193). This decree, II^2 353, however, is not a fragmentary text. The only other possible restoration in line 5/6--given that the year is ordinary, the month (Pyanopsion, line 5) and day in prytany (11th, line 6) are on the stone--is δευτέρα φῖνοντος which is too long by six stoichoi. It must be conceded, therefore, that an ekklesia could be held the same day as the Chalkeia.

Mikalson's list of 34 "doubtful" restorations includes seven Lykourgan decrees: #4, #5, #35, #48, #63 (II^2 359), #67 (II^2 363), and this decree, #51. For the first four, Mikalson's objection has been noted and alternate restorations can be found. This decree, #51, and #63, however, must remain exceptions to the normal practise of not holding meetings of the ekklesia on a festival day. There is just too much on the stone to allow for an alternate restoration (see #67 for a discussion of its specific problems). The specific festivities which coincide with the date of #63 can be shown to coexist well with a meeting of the ekklesia (ep. com. #63). Although the evidence for the Chalkeia is scarce, Deubner notes first the ancient sources, Souidas and Harpokration, who say that while this festival was celebrated by the whole Demos in earlier times, in later times the participants were only the artisans and craftsmen (35); and second, that the character of the festival was simple (schlichten, 36). Whatever form the Chalkeia took, it must be accepted that at least in 329/8, a meeting of the ekklesia and the celebration of the Chalkeia both occured on the last day of Pyanopsion. (Habicht, 177, points out that in the middle of the second century, B.C., the Chalkeia was much more than "simple" and suggests that Lykourgos was responsible for this revitalization. Given Lykourgos's interest in religious matters, this suggestion is tempting. That a meeting of the ekklesia did coincide with the Chalkeia in 329/8, makes the suggestion less attractive.)

329/8

52. *THE ORGEONES OF BENDIS HONOR THEIR EPIMELETAI* Copenhagen, Ny Carlsberg Glyptothek 1043a

photos: entire fragment: Hartwig Bendis figure 1, p. 5; Trendelenburg "Bendis" Plate 1; Nilsson "Bendis" figure 1, page 171; Bodnar Archaeology 26(1973) page 275.
relief: Hartwig Bendis Plate 1; Arndt Glyptotèque Plate 88; Lippold Glyptothek Plate 15; Speier RM 47(1932) Plate 28; Süsserott Plastik Plate 9.

editors: Koehler IG II.5 Add. 573b. page 298 (from a photograph); Hartwig Bendis 1-12; Trendelenburg "Bendis" 1-15; IG II^2 1256.

collections: Ditt. Syll.[2] 724; Syll.[3] 1095; Michel 980.

supplement: Bull. (1942) no. 44a (Nilsson).

other bibliography: JDAI 10(1895) Anzeiger 20; Wilhelm OJ 5 (1902) 131-133; Foucart "Bendis" 95-102; Arndt Glyptotèque 132; Binneboessel Studien 15 no. 66; Speier RM 47(1932) 62, 69/70, 93; Süsserot Plastik 218; Nilsson "Bendis in Athen" From Collection of Ny Carlsberg Glyptotek III (1942) 169-188 and reprint with addendum in Opuscula selecta Vol. III (1960) p. 80; Ferguson HThR 37 (1944) 95-107; Hesperia Supplement 8(1949) 130-163 (especially 150-154); Daux BCH 88(1964) 433-441; Pečírka Enktesis 122-130; Bodnar Archaeology 26(1973) 271-277.

description: I did not examine this stele which is in Copenhagen. There are, however, a number of good photographs available; in Nilsson's reproduction, even the individual letters can be read clearly. The bottom and lower right hand side of the stele are broken. Below the text there are two wreaths; only 2/3 of the right wreath remains because of the break. The stele is topped with a relief which is framed on the sides by antae, above by molding, and below by the fillet and cymation which separate it from the text. The upper right hand corner is broken; the frame and a bit of the background of the relief are lost. The relief itself consists of four major figures. To the left is a pair of bearded, robed men, obviously mortals--they are only about 2/3 the full height of the relief. The other two figures, a male (center right) and female (right), are the height of the relief--obviously divine beings. And in the upper left hand corner, above the heads of the men, is an inset with the upper halves of five figures carved in low relief.

There is general agreement over the identity of the major figures. The two smaller figures are assumed to be Euphys and Dexios, the two men honored in the text below. The large female figure (right) is Bendis. The attributes--Phrygian tiara, animal skin around her waist, spear in left hand, bowl in right--are correct (cf. Ferguson HThR, 102; Foucart, 96-98). This identification was made by Trendelenburg and has never been disputed

There is disagreement as to the identification of Bendis's male companion, the bearded figure leaning on a staff (center right). He looks like Asklepios and, in fact, is identified as such by Trendelenburg, Hartwig, Koehler, Dittenberger, Binneboessel, Speier, Nilsson, and Bodnar. This identification, however, had already been questioned by Wilhelm (131) who noted that Bendis is paired with a certain Deloptes in line 15 of II^2 1324 (see also Foucart 98), and that a Samian inscription (*AM* 25 [1900] 72) which honors the "hero" Deloptes shows an "Asklepios-like" figure. Ferguson strongly accepted Wilhelm's identification, but his argument has been undermined. First, the majority opinion refutes his statement that the figure is "ordinarily identified as Deloptes" (*Hesperia* 150 n. 52). Second, his clincher, a relief, *SEG* 3.759, which he and others saw as representing Bendis and Deloptes, has now been definitively identified as representing Hades and Dionysos (see Daux for full bibliography; at first glance the middle figure in *SEG* 3.759 seems to be the twin of the Bendis in this inscription until one notes, from Daux's excellent plates, that "she" has curls rather than the Phrygian tiara and carries a thrysis rather than a spear and a kantharos rather than a plate or bowl). In spite of the fact that Ferguson's "strong" argument is weakened, I agree with Ferguson's minority opinion. If the figure were Asklepios, it should be expected that his name or at least some acknowledgement of his presence appear in the text.

The five figures in the inset have always been identified as Hermes, the three nymphs, and Pan. There is, however, a descrepancy in the most recent studies concerned with the relief. Nilsson (169) lists *six* figures: "Hermes, drei Nymphen, Pan und der Achelooskopf." Ferguson (*Hesperia* 150 n. 52) confuses the issue further by noting the *two* Nymphs in Nilsson's description. This brings the total back down to five, but makes the identification of the separate figures impossible. Bodnar's identification (275) of the figure farthest to the left as the river god Acheloös, *rather* than Pan is possible--they seem to have similar attributes and the figure in question is completely obscured by shadow in Bodnar's photograph. Since this problem of a discrepancy as to the number of figures arose, I have been assured, both through photographs and record of first hand observation (with thanks to John Fischer) that there are only five figures in the inset. It is difficult to believe that Nilsson, who was most likely to have seen the actual stone, would have made such an error. Considering the similarities in iconography of Acheloös and Pan, of which Nilsson certainly would have been aware, the most likely explanation for this dilemna is printing error: rather than the word "und" in the quotation cited above, the word should have been "oder." I.e, "Hermes, drei Nymphen, Pan *oder* der Achelooskopf" (Nilsson, 169).

It is the inset with the usual identifications which led Hartwig (11) and then Nilsson (169/70) to identify the large bearded figure as Asklepios, on the premise that geographical proximity of the sanctuaries in the Peiraieus--Asklepieion, Nymphaion, Bendideion--bred familiarity. I still think that Asklepios would have been acknowledged in the text. Geographical proximity, however, may be why these particular five dieties were chosen as spectators; line 18 of II^2 1283 does provide evidence that the Nymphaion was next to the Bendidion (cf. Wilhelm *ÖJ*, the initial publication of II^2 1283, Ferguson, *Hesperia* 150 n. 52).

dimensions: Kirchner gives only the height and width of the stele; the other measurements are from Trendelenburg's publication.

H 0.82 m. (entire) letters: 0.007 m.
0.35 m. (relief)
W 0.45 m. (relief)
0.35 m. (below)

minuscule text:

stoich. 31

Θ ε ο ί
Φιλοκράτηϲ vv εἶπεν· ἐπειδὴ Εὔφυηϲ κα-
ὶ Δέξιοϲ γενόμενοι ἐπιμεληταὶ τοῦ ἱε-
ροῦ ἐπὶ Κηφιϲοφῶντοϲ ἄρχοντοϲ καλῶϲ
καὶ φιλοτίμωϲ ἐπεμελήθηϲαν καὶ ἀξίω-
ϲ τῆϲ θεοῦ καὶ τῶν ὀργεώνων, δεδόχθαι τ-
οῖϲ ὀργεῶϲιν, ϲτεφανῶϲαι Εὔφυη καὶ Δέ-
ξιον δικαιοϲύνηϲ καὶ ἐπιμελείαϲ ἕνε-
κα χρυϲῶι ϲτεφάνωι ἑκάτερον ἀπὸ : Η : δρα-
χμῶν καὶ ἀναγράψαι τόδε τὸ ψήφιϲμα ἐν
ϲτήλει λιθίνει καὶ ϲτῆϲαι ἐν τῶι ἱερ[ῶ]-
ι τῆϲ θεοῦ.

[two wreaths]

commentary: The text is based on Kirchner's. Koehler read less letters, but he was using a photograph. Kirchner's text, with only one letter restored (line 11 st. 31), can be confirmed by Nilsson's photograph. The stoichedon order is 31 letters to the line.

This decree honors two men, Euphys and Dexios, who handled their duties as epimeletai zealously, well, and worthily both toward the Goddess and their fellow orgeones. On the motion of Philokrates, the orgeones decided that Euphys and Dexios each be granted a gold crown worth 100 drachmai. The stele is to be set up in the sanctuary of the Goddess.

Although her name is not mentioned in the text, there is no doubt that the Goddess in question is Bendis. The iconography is correct (see above); there is also the famous passage in literature which implies that, at least in the Peiraieus, "the Goddess" refers to Bendis. Plato's _Republic_ opens with Sokrates on his way to the Peiraieus to check out the inauguration of a procession for "the Goddess"; she is later identified as Bendis (_Republic_ 354A; cf. Trendelenburg, 13; Ferguson _HThR_ 96/7).

The text does not identify the association of orgeones as Athenian or Thracian (see #13 for the criteria; cf. Ferguson _HThR_ 98). Ferguson has pointed out, however, that the presence of inscribed _olive_ wreaths rather than oak is a very strong indication that the orgeones are Athenians (_Hesperia_ 152 note 62). And if the orgeones are Athenians, then their epimeletai, Euphys and Dexios, must also be Athenians, not slaves as the absence of their demotics suggested to Dittenberger in _Syll._^{2} 724 (cf. Wilhelm, 134; Foucart, 99).

As is evident from the bibliography above, Bendis in Athens has been the subject of a number of studies.

Nilsson's and Ferguson's recent studies are the most complete, since they both include the fifth century inscription published by Pappadakis which first appeared in 1941 (_AE_ [1937] 808-823; _SEG_ X 64b). Pečírka's study of II^2 1283 led him to a discusson of _SEG_ X 64b and, from there, the inauguration of the cult of Bendis in Athens. He in turn relies chiefly on Nilsson and Ferguson, but disagrees with them about their interpretation (following Pappadakis) of _SEG_ X 64b as the specific document which records the inauguration of Bendis as the object of an official state cult around 430 (129; the new inscription is more correctly dated to c. 413/2; cf. Raubitschek, _SEG_).

Since these more general studies are available, a discussion of the cult of Bendis would be redundant. The fact, however, that a foreign goddess _was_ worshipped in Athens--was, indeed, the object of an official state cult--does deserve more attention. Foucart (95) pointed out the incongruity: that a foreign goddess should be worshipped in a city-state which had never been enthusiastic about new gods and even less enthusiastic about "barbarian" ones. His answer to the enigma was that the Athenians had acted upon an oracle from Dodona (100; line 6 of II^2 1283).

Although Foucart gives the obvious immediate reason for the inauguration of the cult of Bendis in Athens, it is Nilsson who explains why the Athenians would have bothered to solicit and/or accept the oracle in the first place. When marshaling the epigraphical and literary evidence for the cult, Nilsson noted that it fell into three distinct periods: late fifth century, the Lykourgan era, and third century (170-174). He noted further that the first two periods coincided with diplomatic activity between Athens and Thrace, more specifically, Odrysia. He cites the evidence for Athens's relations with Sitalkes during the Peloponnesian War (178/9; see also Ferguson HThR 104), and cites #45, honors to Rheboulas the Odrysian (196), as evidence for a similar tie in the Lykourgan era (181). The conclusion is obvious: first the inauguration and then the subsequent revitalization of the cult of Bendis in Athens were chiefly due to political considerations (Nilsson, 183).

Nilsson stresses this point, especially for the Lykourgan era, which contains the largest amount of solid epigraphical evidence. In 337/6 orgeones of Bendis honored their epimeletai, #13. II^2 1496A line 86 shows for 334/3 an appropriation of 457 drachmai for the Bendideia, which Nilsson considers to be relatively high (175). There is this decree, #52, of 329/8, and Nilsson dates a relief in the British Museum, which commemorates the torch race (part of the Bendideia), to a bit earlier than #52 (175, figure 3; see also Bodnar, 275). Ferguson (153) believes that II^2 1361, a law for regulation of the cult, is probably Lykourgan (cf. Nilsson, 172) and suggests it may be dated a "little before" II^2 1324, a dedication which has now been moved up to the late 4th or early 3rd century by Dow (HThR [1937] 197 note 54). There is, as well, the relief, SEG 3.759, found in Euboia and described above in the description; and the relief carved in a quarry wall on Paros which Bodnar has associated with Bendis and dated to the Lykourgan era.

One major purpose of this Corpus is to show, from the epigraphical evidence, the various facets of the Lykourgan program. #15 provides a general discussion, while #17, #21, and #27 show more specifically that although Lykourgos would never overlook the political advantages of a situation, religious considerations were important as well. And the Bendis inscriptions listed above should be seen in this larger context.

The inauguration of a religious cult for political expediency fit well into the earlier Periklean scheme (cf. Herington Athena). Political motivation also explains the absence of evidence of the cult between the end of the Peloponnesian War and the Lykourgan era: as Nilsson notes (180), diplomatic relations with Thrace were strained. Also, there would not be much religious vitality in a cult established for political reasons. Political considerations obviously played a part in the renewed interest in Bendis in the Lykourgan era. There is evidence, however, of a continuation of interest in Bendis into the third century (Nilsson, 173/4), even after Athens had been defeated in the Lamian War. There is no adequate political explanation for this continued interest. Perhaps the explanation lies in Lykourgos himself: that he had managed, whether deliberately or inadvertently, to rejuvenate the cult of Bendis with more vitality than it had when it was inaugurated, probably under the influence of Perikles.

XI. THE YEAR OF EUTHYKRITOS, 328/7

53. *DECREE* EM 7246

photo: Pritchett AACS Plate 22b (incomplete).

editors: Pittakis EΦ. (1856/61) 3539; Koehler (& Velsen) IG II 236; IG II[2] 452; Meritt Ath. p. 96.

supplements: SEG 14.56 (Meritt AJP, Pritchett-Meritt); 21.284 (Meritt Ath., Pritchett-Neugebauer, Pritchett AACS, Dow); 23.55 (Meritt TAPA, Woodhead); 24.100 (McGregor); 25.68 (Pritchett Phoenix).

other bibliography: Reusch De diebus cont. 14; Schmidt Gr. Chron. 576; Sundwall Schaltzyklos 17; Meritt AJP 59 (1938) 499; TAPA 95(1964) 217-21; Pritchett-Meritt Chron. 2; Pritchett-Neugebauer Cal. 51; Klaffenbach Gnomen 21 (1949) 135; Lewis BSA 49(1954) 49; Dow Hesperia 32(1963) 348/50; Pritchett AACS 281-3; Phoenix 23(1969) 169/70; Clement AJA 69(1965) 194; McGregor Phoenix 20(1966) 217; Woodhead Mnemosyne 19(1966) 90.

description: This fragment of Pentelic marble was found north of the Parthenon. It is broken on all sides, the back may be original.

dimensions:
H 0.26 m.
W 0.20 m.
Th 0.105 m.

letters: 0.006 m. Smallest, O, is .004; largest, Φ, is .010; Letters in line 1 seem slightly larger. Size of specific letters in text are not always the same. Letters are poorly cut, e.g., in line 4, maj. text: E, st. 1, Δ, st. 6.

majuscule text: next page.

epigraphical commentary: The reading of line 4 is very controversial; I include only those strokes which appear to be part of a letter. The letters are poorly cut, and although the letters in the text (after line 1) lie below each other in a stoichedon pattern, the alignment is not precise, nor are vertical and horizontal lines of letters perpendicular; i.e., the printed majuscule text is much neater than the actual stone.

Τ Ο Υ   Α Ρ   Χ Ο Ν Τ Ο Σ̣

Ο Σ Ε Κ Τ Η Σ Π Ρ Υ Τ̣ Α ^ Ε

Ο Υ Α Γ Ν Ο Υ Σ Ι Ο̣ Σ̣ . Γ̣ Ρ̣

Ε Ι Ε Π Ι Α Ε Κ Α̣ \ | . / Ͱ

Ι Α Σ Ε Κ Κ Λ Η̣ . . . . . .

Ν Π Α Μ Φ Ι Λ Ο̣ Σ̣ Φ . . . .

. Α̣ Λ Α Ι Ε Υ Σ̣ Θ . . . . .

. . Ε Ι Δ Η Σ Α . . . . . .

. Ε Λ Ι Τ Ε Υ Σ Γ̣ . . . . .

. Α̣ Ι Ο Σ Β Ο Υ Λ . . . . .

. . Ν Ο Σ Β Ο Υ Τ / . . . .

. . ′Σ Ε Π Ι Μ Ε̣ . . . . .

. . . . Σ Γ Ε Λ . . . . . .

2 st. 13 ^: read as clear N by all others. The diagonal stroke goes only halfway, however, and a stroke (or scratch) to the right makes the letter appear to be a mu. In fact, a mu can be read clearly in the photo in Pritch. *AACS* Plate 22. Since the letter must be nu, no one has ever questioned this reading.

4 st. 9-14 for the sake of clarity, I present the various readings, noting that only Pitt., Koe., Dow, presented a majuscule reading.

AA/|/\\|	Pitt.; whose text is not stoichedon.
A.|.||′	Koe.
A.|..|	Vel.
A.E.ΠT	Schmidt.
A.\\..K	Sundwall.
A.E...	Ki., following Reusch and Schmidt.
A.NATE	Mer. *AJP*; P.-M. *Chron.*
A.|\/..̣.	P.-N.
AMIAIK	Mer. *Ath.*
A1|/Γ̣r	Stamires, in Pritch. *AACS*.

AMI.IK Dow.
AṂIẠİḲ McGregor, from photo.

st. 10 What is on the stone is a short diagonal line in the lower right corner of the "stoichos". It is clear enough to preclude the restoration, even in brackets, of any letter which does not have a diagonal stroke, such as Π (Ki.) or E (Mer. AJP; see comm. below).

st. 11 There is a definite vertical stroke in this stoichos. Although P.-N. (and others) are correct in noting that the stroke is to the left of the middle of the "stoichos," the fact that the stoichedon order is not precise, that the letters are poorly cut, and that there is no indication of any other stroke to the right of the sure vertical stroke makes iota a definite possibility.

st. 12 I can not read any trace of a letter.

st. 13 What appears to be only part of a stroke could be iota.

st. 14 The vertical stroke is definite; I could feel the diagonal stroke with my fingernail.

5 st. 8 Ḥ I Vel.

6 st. 9 Σ̣ new reading.

7 st. 2 Ạ new reading.
st. 3-7 ΛΑΙΕΥ ΛΟΙΕΥ Vel.
st. 9 Θ new reading; all others read O.

8 st. 2-9 .ΕΙΔΗΣΑ ΛΕΙΔΗΣΑ Mer.; .ΕΙΔΗΚΛ Vel.

9 st. 9 Γ̣ Vel., Schwenk; Π Koe., Ki., Mer. There is no sign of the right vertical stroke; the surface there is worn.

11 st. 10 / A Koe. + Vel., Ki., Mer.

12 st. 3-9 ΄ΣΕΠΙΜΕ̣΄ .ΣΕΠΙΜ Vel.; ^ΣΕΠΙΜ^ Koe. Ki., Mer.; .ΣΕΠΙΜΕ Dow, noting that traces of round letters in st. 3 and 9 are spurious. Dow also notes that the letter in st. 3 could be upsilon, thus supporting my reading.

13 st. 5-8 ΣΓΕΛ ΣΓΕ/ Vel.; ΣΓΕ/ Koe., Ki., Mer.; ΣΓΕ/ Dow.

minuscule text: next page.

commentary: The text incorporates my readings from the stone (see above). The stoichedon order of 36 letter spaces was established by Koehler's restorations; it has not been questioned, although Meritt's restorations, which I basically follow, require a vacat in lines 2 and 11, a double vacat in line 10 and the omission of nu-movable at the beginning of line 4. The basic restorations also go back to Koehler; changes and additions are noted below.

stoich. 36

[Ἐπὶ Εὐθυκρί]του ἄρχοντοϲ̣

[ἐπὶ τῆϲ Ἀκαμαντίδ]οϲ ἕκτηϲ πρυτ̣α̣νε[ίαϲ v ἧι Π]-
[υθόδηλοϲ Πυθοδήλ]ου Ἁγνούϲιο̣ϲ̣ [ἐ]γ̣ρ̣[αμμάτευ]-
[ε· Γαμηλιῶνοϲ ὀγδό]ει ἐπὶ δέκα̣, μ̣ι[ᾶ]ι̣ κ̣[αὶ τριακ]-
[οϲτεῖ τῆϲ πρυτανε]ίαϲ· ἐκκλη̣[ϲία κυρία· τῶν πρ]-
[οέδρων ἐπεψήφιζε]ν Πάμφιλο̣ϲ̣ Φ[ηγούϲιοϲ· ϲυμ]-
[πρόεδροι ....8....] Ἁ̣λαιεύ̣ϲ, Θ.....12.....
[......14...... Χολλ]είδηϲ, Α.....13.....
[......15...... Μ]ελιτεύϲ, Γ̣.....12.....
[.....13..... Οἰν]α̣ῖοϲ, Βοῦλ[ιϲ Θοραιεύϲ vv]
[Λυκοῦργοϲ v? Λυκόφρο]νοϲ Βουτά̣[δηϲ εἶπεν· ...]
.......17.......ΣΕΠΙΜΕ̣.....12.....
........19........ΣΠΕΛ......13......

1 archon: Mer. AJP. [Ἐπὶ Θεοφρᾶσ]του Vel. + Koe., Ki. (313/2).

2/3 secretary: Mer. AJP, on basis of #54, line 4; #56, line 35.

4/5 date: Mer. Ath. (note that this date does require the unusual omission of nu-movable). Mer., in AJP, also offered: [εν· Γαμηλιῶνος ἕκτ]ει ἐπὶ δέκα, [ἐ]νάτε[ι καὶ εἰκ/οστεῖ. [εν· Γαμηλιῶνος ἕκτ]ει ἐπὶ δέκα, [μ]ι[ᾶ]ι κ[αὶ τριακ/οστῆι Vel. + Koe.; [εν· Γαμηλιῶνος ἕκτ]ει ἐπὶ δέκα, [π]έ[μπτει καὶ δε/κάτει Reusch, Schmidt, Ki.; [ε· Γαμηλιῶνος ἐνάτ]ει ἐπὶ δέκα, [μ]ι[ᾶι] καὶ εἰκοσ/τεῖ Sundwall, note text would be 2 stoichoi too short; [εν· Γαμηλιῶνος ἕκτ]ει ἐπὶ δέκα, [πέμπτει καὶ δε/κάτει P.-N.

10 Βοῦλ[ις Θοραιεύς: Lewis, based on #56, line 17.

11 mover: M.-P. Chron. Lewis's restoration for line 10 and the restoration here of Lykourgos means that there would be three vacats between what is on the stone in lines 10 and 11. Mer.'s text in Ath. includes two vacats at the end of line 10; he notes only in a footnote, however, that "the first 16 letters in the name of Lykourgos occupied seventeen letter-spaces."

Koehler, with Velsen, included this decree in the editio major of the Corpus as II 236. At that time it was assumed that the listing of the names of those who served as symproedroi was limited only to the years 318/7 -308/7 (see #31, II^2 336, for symproedroi). And the only year within that time span which would fit a secretary from the deme Hagnous, tribe Akamantis, within the tribal cycle for secretaries was the year of the archon Theophrastos, 313/2. Koehler's restoration of the date (presumably to best fit what he saw on the stone), however, required that the year 313/2 be intercalary: [Gamelion] 1[6] = Prytany VI [31]. This restoration presented an anomaly, as Koehler noted, because the preceeding year, 314/3, had already been shown to be intercalary. Kirchner accepted the year but, in order to resolve the anomaly, combined Velsen's readings and Premerstein's consideration of the stone with the restorations offered by Reusch and Schmidt to produce for the text of II^2 452, lines 4/5: [Gamelion] 1[6] = Prytany VI [15], a date for an ordinary year.

Next Meritt (AJP), acting on the information supplied by Dow (subsequently published in Hesperia) that the listing of symproedroi did not exclude a date earlier than 318/7, went back to the Lykourgan era and found the year of Euthykritos, 328/7, to be the only other year available for a secretary from the tribe Akamantis. His restoration in AJP (1938) was: [Gamelion] 1[6] = Prytany VI [29], in an intercalary year. Although Pritchett accepted the year and presumably the new restored date as well in Chronology (1940); he and Meritt added the restoration of Lykourgos as mover at this time), he has subsequently denied any restoration which makes 328/7 an intercalary year because he considers the next year, 327/6, to be intercalary. In Cal. (1947), he returned to Kirchner's restoration; in AACS (1963), he suggested a restoration based on Stamires's readings or perhaps a date after 315.

With the exception of Pritchett, and Klaffenbach, who would not make a decision, the other epigraphists who have considered this decree since 1938, have accepted the date of 328/7 and most have agreed with Meritt's subsequent restoration in Ath. (1961; despite the difficulties mentioned in the commentary and especially noted by Dow): [Gamelion] 1[8] = Prytany VI [3]1 = 225th day of an intercalary year. It must be noted, however, as I have done in the epigraphical commentary, that any restoration at the end of line 4 can only be tentative and thus does not prove that the year is intercalary. The restoration of a date for the other decree with a calendar formula from this year, #54 (II^2 354) can also be contrived to give an intercalary or ordinary year. The decrees with a dating formula from 327/6 (see discussion, #57) also do not offer positive proof as to the nature of that year.

What can be accepted is that this decree was published in 328/7; the reason for placing it after 318/7 no longer exists. Indeed, another outcome of Dow's article was to show that the inclusion of the secretary's name, as in this decree, was not usual in the time of Demetrios of Phaleron. Meritt's restoration of the name and patronymic of the secretary from #54 with confirmation of the secretary's full name in #56; Pritchett and Meritt's identification of the mover as the Lykourgos; and Lewis's identification of the last symproedros, again based on #56, all confirm that this decree is from the Lykourgan era.

This is a quick summary of the citations in the bibliography listed above; they are all concerned with the "calendar problem" because all that remains on this stone is the prescript with the date. A lot of words have been expended to "prove" a specific restoration which in turn "proves" whether this year is intercalary or ordinary. I have chosen Meritt's restoration because MI[A]I seems to fit best what remains at the end of line 4.

See #15 for a list of certain and possible decrees moved by Lykourgos. Because of the extra vacat necessary to restore Lykourgos's name in this decree, it remains only a possibility. As to the content of this decree, there is nothing; only a possibility that if Dow's and my reading of the right diagonal of upsilon in st. 18, line 12 is correct, then the decree may have dealt with epimeletes.

328/7

54. *ATHENS HONORS ANDROKLES, PRIEST OF ASKLEPIOS* EM 7162, 251

photos: Wilhelm UDA 232; Hesperia 28(1959) Plate 35; Pritchett AACS 22a (line 5).

editors: Fr. A Kumanudes ΑΘΗΝΑΙΟΝ 6(1878) 134/5; Wilhelm Hermes 24(1889) 140-2 no. xvi; IG II 5.178b.

Fr. A+B Wilhelm *UDA* 230/4; *IG* II [2] 354; Hubbe *Hesperia* 28(1959) 171-4 no. 2.

supplements: *SEG* 18.14 (Meritt *AJP*, Hubbe); 21.285 (*Syll.* [3], Pritchett-Neugebauer, Meritt *Ath.*, Pritchett); 23.56 (Meritt *TAPA*).
Bull. (1960) no. 132 (Hubbe).

collections: Michel 1470; Ditt. *Syll.* [3] 299.

other bibliography: Reusch *Hermes* 15(1880) 341; Meritt *AJP* 59(1938) 499; *Ath.* 96/7; *TAPA* 95(1964) 217-221; Pritchett-Neugebauer *Cal.* 51/2; Pritchett *AACS* 279-281; Pickard-Cambridge *Festivals* 69/70; Rhodes *Boule* 16 n. 1; DeLaix *Proboul.* 123/4, 140/41; Henry *Prescripts* 36 n. 16, 37 n. 23, 47.

description: The two fragments of Pentelic marble are now joined. Fr. A was found between the theaters of Dionysos and Herodes Atticus (Asklepieion ?). Fr. B was found in the Pelargikon. Half of a pediment which topped the stele is preserved at the top of Fr. A. The lower left side (Fr. B) and the upper right side (Fr. A) as well as the rough-picked back are preserved.

dimensions:
H 0.687 m.(entire)
0.515 m.(text)
W 0.406 m.
Th 0.118 m.

letters: 0.006 m. Smallest, A, Δ, are .004; largest, Φ, is .009. B, P, Σ, T, Y, are .007; A, E, Ω, are .005. Some alphas have no cross bar.

majuscule text: next three pages.

epigraphical commentary: The text is inscribed in stoichedon order; there is no violation on the stone. Hubbe was able to add a number of new readings, some clearly, some with dots. With the exception of E in line 20 st. 23 and P, line 37 st. 16, I agree with the new readings, although I do not think that any of these letters are clear enough to be printed without dots. I note below where Hubbe dotted his new readings. Otherwise all dots are mine.

5 st. 34 Γ Kumanudes, Reusch, Koe., Lolling (in Wilh. *Hermes*), Pritch. *AACS*; Π̣ P.-N., Mer. *TAPA*, noting pi must be dotted because it could be gamma, also that it can not be epsilon; Π Mer. *Ath.*; Ẹ Mer. *AJP*. There is really no disagreement as to what appears on the stone. The

disagreement is about what the letter can <u>not</u> be.

Fr. A

I

. . . . ΧΟΝΤΟΣΙΕΡΕΙΩΣΔΕΑΝΔΡΟ

. . . . Ε̣ΩΝΕΠΙΤΗΣΑΝΤΙΟΧΙΔΟΣΟΓ

. . . . ΣΗΙΠΥΘΟΔΗΛΟΣΠΥΘΟΔΗΛΟΥ

. . . . ΜΜΑΤΕΥΕΝΕΝΗΙΚΑΙΝΕΙΑΙΓ̣

. . . . ΙΤΗΣΠΡΥΤΑΝΕΙΑΣΕΚΚΛΗΣ

. . . . ΠΕΨΗΦΙΣΕΝΕ̣ΠΙΓΕΝΗΣΕΡΟ

. . . . Ω̣ΙΔΗΜΩΙΠΡΟΚΛΕΙΔΗΣΠΑΝΤΑ

. . . . ΜΕΩΝΕΙΠΕΝΑΓΑΘΗΙΤΥΧΗΙ:

. . . . ΜΩΙ̣ΤΑΜΕΝΑΓΑΘΑΔΕΧΕΣΘΑΙ

. . . . ΕΡΕΥΣΓΕΓΟΝΕΝΑΙΕΚΤΩΝΙΕ

. . . . Ω̣ΝΕΠΕΙΔΗΔΕΑΝΔΡΟΚΛΗΣΙΕ̣Ρ

Fr. B . . . . Ν̣Τ̣ . . . . ΚΛΗΠΙΩΙΕΠΙΜΕΛΕΙΤΑΙΤΟ .

ΤΕΙΕΡΟΥΚΑΙ . . . ΑΛΛΩΝΩΝΑΥΤΩΙΟΙΝΟΜΟΙΠΡ

ΟΣΤΑΤΤΟΥΣΙΝΚ̣ . . ΩΣΚΑΙΕΥΣΕ̣ΒΩ̣ΣΚΑΙΟΙΛΑΧ̣

ΟΝΤΕΣΕΠΙΜΕΛΗΤ . ΙΤΗΣΕΥΚΟΣΜΙΑΣΤΗΣΠΕΡ .

ΤΟΘΕΑΤΡΟΝΑΠΕΦΗ . . ΝΑΥΤΟΝΕΝΤΩΙΔΗΜΩ . . .

ΗΣΙΜΟΝΓΕΓΟΝΕΝΑΙΑ̣.Τ̣ΟΙΣΠΕΡΙΤΗΝΕΠ....
ΕΙΑΝΤΟΥΘΕΑΤΡΟΥΕΠΑΙ̣Ν̣.Σ̣.ΙΑΝΔΡΟΚ.....
ΕΙΝΙΟΥΕΚΚΕΡΑΜΕΩΝΤΟΝΙΕΡ.Α̣ΤΟΥΑ......
ΟΥΚΑΙΣΤΕΦΑΝΩΣΑΙΑΥΤΟΝΕΠ...Α̣ΝΤ̣......
ΝΑΣΔΩΙΧΡΥΣΩΙΣΤΕΦΑΝΩΙΑΠΟ:Χ̣........
ΡΕΤΗΣΕΝΕΚΑΚΑΙΔΙΚΑΙΟΣΥΝΗΣΚΑ........
ΑΥΤΩΙΤΟΝΤΑΜΙΑΝΤΟΥΔΗΜΟΥ:ΔΔΔ........
ΕΙΣΘΥΣΙΑΝΕΚΤΩΝΕΙΣΤΑΚΑΤΑΨΗΦΙΣΜ̣.....
ΑΛΙΣΚΟΜΕΝΩΝΤΩΙΔΗΜΩΙΤΟΝΔΕΓΡΑΜΜ̣.....
ΤΟΝΚΑΤΑΠΡΥΤΑΝΕΙΑΝΑΝΑΓΡΑΨΑΙΤΟΔ̣.....
ΦΙΣΜΑΕΝΣΤΗΛΗΙΛΙΘΙΝΗΙΚΑΙΣΤΗΣΑΙΕ̣....
ΙΕΡΩΙΤΟΥΑΣΚΛΗΠΙΟΥΕΙΣΔΕΤΗΝΑΝΑΓΡ....
Τ̣ΗΣΣΤΗΛΗΣΔΟΥΝΑΙΤΟΝΤΑΜΙΑΝΤΟΥΔΗΜ̣....
.Δ:ΔΡΑΧΜΑΣΟΘΕΝΟΙΝΟΜΟΙΚΕΛΕΥΟΥΣΙ̣....

0.015

ΕΥΕΤΙΩ̣ΝΑΥΤΟΚΛΕΙΔΟΥΣΦΗΤΤΙΟΣΕΙΠ.....
.ΝΟΙΕΡΕΥΣΤΟΥΑΣΚΛΗΠΙΟΥΤΟΥΕΝΑΣΤΕ̣....
.ΙΠΕΡΙΤΩΝΙΕΡΩΝΩΝΕΘΥΕΝΤΩΙΑΣΚΛΗΠ̣....

. . Ι Τ Ο Ι Σ Α Λ Λ Ο Ι Σ Θ Ε Ο Ι Σ̣ Τ Ο Ι Σ Μ Ε Τ Α Υ Τ Ο Υ̣ . . . .
. . Τ̣ . . . . Σ̣ Θ̣ Α Ι . . Ι Β Ο Υ Λ Η Ι Τ Ο Υ Σ . . . . .
. . . . Δ Ρ Ε Υ Ε Ι Ν Ε Ν Τ Ω . . . . .
. . . . Α̣ Ν Π Ρ Ο Σ Α Γ Α Γ . . . . .
. . . . Χ̣ Ρ Η Μ Α Τ Ι Σ Α . . . . .
. . . . Λ Λ Ε Σ Θ Α Ι Τ Η̣ . . . .
. . . . Τ Η Ι Β Ο Υ Λ . . . . .
. . . . Ν Α Α Π Α Γ Γ . . . . .
. . . . Ι Ε Ρ Ο Ι Σ Ε̣ . . . . .
. . . . Α Ι Τ Ο Υ . . . . . .

The reason for this disagreement (naturally) is the calendar restoration. That will be treated in the commentary below. I note here, however, that I initially read this letter as epsilon. Despite the fact that the stone is eroded here, I could see and feel a bottom stroke. In addition, epsilons are small in this inscription, .005 m.; the height of this letter measures .005.

8 st. 13 Ω̣ new reading; Hubbe also dotted.

11 st. 13 Ω̣ Kumanudes also showed this letter as unclear; Koe. shows only half of it.

13 st. 8,9 ṆṬ new reading; Hubbe also dotted.

18 st. 16, 18 Ạ, Ṭ new readings; Hubbe read clearly.

19 st. 21 Σ̣ new reading; Hubbe read clearly.

20 st. 23 Hubbe read E.
24 Ạ new reading; Hubbe read clearly.
28 Kumanudes read Λ; I note above that many alphas do not have cross bars.

25 st. 29 Ṃ new reading; Hubbe read clearly.

26 st. 29 Ṃ new reading; Hubbe read clearly.

33 st. 30 Ẹ new reading; Hubbe read clearly.

34 st. 30 Π̣ new reading; Hubbe read clearly.

35 st. 30 Ỵ new reading; Hubbe also dotted.

36 st. 3 Ṭ new reading; Hubbe also dotted.
13, 14 Σ̣Θ̣ new readings; Hubbe read clearly.

37 st. 16 Hubbe read Ρ̣.

40 st. 30 Ḥ new reading; Hubbe read clearly.

43 st. 29 Ẹ new reading; Hubbe also dotted.

minuscule text: next two pages.

commentary: The text is based on Hubbe's. The restorations for Fr. A are Koehler's with the exceptions noted below. Koehler's restorations for lines 14 and 15 were confirmed by Wilhelm's publication of Fr. A+B. The restorations for Fr. B are Wilhelm's (used by Kirchner for II[2] 354) with exceptions noted below.

stoich. 34

Fr. A [Θ ε] ο ί
[Ἐπ' Εὐθυκρίτου ἄρ]χοντοϲ ἱερέωϲ δὲ Ἀνδρο-
[κλέουϲ ἐκ Κεραμ]έων ἐπὶ τῆϲ Ἀντιοχίδοϲ ὀγ-
[δόηϲ πρυτανεία]ϲ ἧι Πυθόδηλοϲ Πυθοδήλου
[Ἁγνούϲιοϲ ἐγρα]μμάτευεν· ἕνηι καὶ νέαι Γ
[.....13.....]ηι τῆϲ πρυτανείαϲ· ἐκκληϲ-
[ία· τῶν προέδρων] ἐπεψήφιϲεν Ἐπιγένηϲ Ἐρο-
[ιάδηϲ· ἔδοξεν τ]ῶ̣ι δήμωι· Προκλείδηϲ Παντα-
[λέοντοϲ ἐκ Κερα]μέων εἶπεν· ἀγαθῆι τύχηι:
[δεδόχθαι τῶι δή]μωι τὰ μὲν ἀγαθὰ δέχεϲθαι
[ἃ ἀπαγγέλλει ὁ ἱ]ερεὺϲ γεγονέναι ἐκ τῶν ἱε-
[ρῶν τῶν τυθέντ]ων· ἐπειδὴ δὲ Ἀνδροκλῆϲ ἱερ-
Fr. B [εὺϲ λαχὼ]ν̣ τ̣[ῶι Ἀϲ]κληπιῶι ἐπιμελεῖται το[ῦ]
τε ἱεροῦ καὶ [τῶν] ἄλλων ὧν αὐτῶι οἱ νόμοι πρ-
οϲτάττουϲιν κ[αλ]ῶϲ καὶ εὐϲεβῶϲ καὶ οἱ λαχ-
όντεϲ ἐπιμελητ[α]ὶ τῆϲ εὐκοϲμίαϲ τῆϲ περ[ὶ]
τὸ θέατρον ἀπέφη[να]ν αὐτὸν ἐν τῶι δήμω[ι χρ]-
ήϲιμον γεγονέναι α[ὐ]τοῖϲ περὶ τὴν ἐπ[ιμέλ]-
ειαν τοῦ θεάτρου· ἐπαιν[έ]ϲ[α]ι Ἀνδροκ[λέα Κλ]-
εινίου ἐκ Κεραμέων τὸν ἱερέα τοῦ Ἀ[ϲκληπι]-
οῦ καὶ ϲτεφανῶϲαι αὐτὸν ἐπ[ειδ]ὰν τ[ὰϲ εὐθύ]-
ναϲ δῶι χρυϲῶι ϲτεφάνωι ἀπὸ : Χ : [δραχμῶν ἀ]-
ρετῆϲ ἕνεκα καὶ δικαιοϲύνηϲ κα[ὶ δοῦναι v]
αὐτῶι τὸν ταμίαν τοῦ δήμου : ΔΔΔ [: δραχμὰϲ]
εἰϲ θυϲίαν ἐκ τῶν εἰϲ τὰ κατὰ ψηφίϲμ[ατα ἀν]-
αλιϲκομένων τῶι δήμωι· τὸν δὲ γραμμ[ατέα]

τὸν κατὰ πρυτανεῖαν ἀναγράψαι τόδ[ε τὸ ψή]-
φιcμα ἐν cτήληι λιθίνηι καὶ cτῆcαι ἐ[ν τῶι]
ἱερῶι τοῦ Ἀcκληπιοῦ· εἰc δὲ τὴν ἀναγρ[αφὴν]
τῆc cτήληc δοῦναι τὸν ταμίαν τοῦ δήμ[ου : Δ]
[Δ]Δ: δραχμὰc ὅθεν οἱ νόμοι κελεύουcι[ν. vvv]

vacat 0.015

Εὐετίων Αὐτοκλείδου Σφήττιοc εἶπ[ε· περὶ]
[ὧ]ν ὁ ἱερεὺc τοῦ Ἀcκληπιοῦ τοῦ ἐν ἄcτε[ι λέγ]-
[ε]ι περὶ τῶν ἱερῶν ὧν ἔθυεν τῶι Ἀcκληπ[ιῶι v]
[καὶ] τοῖc ἄλλοιc θεοῖc τοῖc μετ' αὐτοῦ· [ἀγαθ]-
[ῆι] τ̣[ύχηι ἐψηφί]cθαι [τῆ]ι βουλῆι τοὺc [προέδ]-
[ρουc οἳ ἂν λάχωcι π]ρ̣[οε]δρεύειν ἐν τῶ[ι δήμωι]
[εἰc τὴν πρώτην ἐκκληcί]αν προcαγαγ[εῖν τὸν]
[ἱερέα πρὸc τὸν δῆμον καὶ] χρηματίcα[ι αὐτῶι]
[ἐν ἱεροῖc, γνώμην δὲ ξυμβά]λλεcθαι τῆ[c βου]-
[λῆc εἰc τὸν δῆμον ὅτι δοκεῖ] τῆι βουλ[ῆι τὰ μ]-
[ὲν ἀγαθὰ δέχεcθαι τὸν δῆμο]ν ἃ ἀπαγγ[έλλει]
[ὁ ἱερεὺc γεγονέναι ἐν τοῖc] ἱεροῖc ἐ̣[φ' ὑγιεί]-
[αι καὶ cωτηρίαι τῆc βουλῆc κ]αὶ τοῦ [δήμου.]
[- -]

The stoichedon order of 34 letters to the line, established by Reusch when he restored the archon's name, is confirmed by Fr. B, and is not violated on the stone. Restorations in lines 23 and 34 require a vacat at the end of the line; line 31 requires 3 vacats. These vacats are noted in Hubbe's text; he did not note that there is an unused letter space at the end of line 44--I have. After line 37, the stonecutter seems to have been less strict in keeping to the stoichedon order. Wilhelm's (and Kirchner) restoration (recorded below) required violations only in line 38 (33 stoichoi) and line 40 (32 stoichoi), but only at the expense of the correct placement of the letters on the stone; i.e., to conform to the letters on the stone, the restoration of the beginning of line 38 requires two letters in one stoichos and 2 vacats (not one) at the end of the line. Although Hubbe's restorations require more violations, they do conform to the placement of the extant letters on the stone. For clarity, I have marked where 2 letter are assumed to have occupied one stoichos at the ends of lines 37, 38, 39, 43.

The restorations for lines 5/6 (below) deal with the day of the prytany and if any of the restorations could be deemed certain, then the nature of the year could be determined (for the problem of establishing whether 328/7 is ordinary or intercalary see discussion, #53). Since I have noted in the epigraphical commentary above, however, that the one letter (line 5 st. 34) upon which all the restorations rely is uncertain, I agree with Hubbe by printing what does remain of the letter and offering no restoration. On the other hand, I do not think epsilon is excluded as a possibility and therefore prefer Meritt's AJP restoration (for an intercalary year) as the one which offers the least calendrical problems.

With the exception of Kumanudes' restoration (and Pritchett's inclusion of it as possible in AACS) all the other restorations assume that the stone cutter omitted the month, Elaphebolion. The term, προτέραι, is used by Wilhelm, Velsen, Kirchner and Meritt (Ath.). The date on the stone, ἕνηι καὶ νέαι, designates the last day of the month, in this case, Elaphebolion. Προτέραι would designate the first "last day" of the month, in fact, the second to the last day of the month. Pritchett (AACS) notes that the designation, προτέραι, should only be used for the last month of the year, Skirophorion. Although there is not enough evidence to prove when προτέραι could be used, I note that neither Wilhelm, Velsen, Kirchner, not Meritt (Ath.) had any qualms about using this designation for Elaphebolion.

2 archon: Reusch.

3 demotic: Kumanudes.

3/4 prytany: Reusch.

5 secretary's demotic: Mer. AJP from #56 line 35.

5/6: Γ[αμηλιῶνος, ἕκτ]ηι Kum. (requires a vacat; Γ[κτηι καὶ καὶ εἰκοστ]ῆι, Γ[νάτηι καὶ δεκάτ]ηι Reusch, who obviously thought epsilon was possible; [προτέραι, εἰκοστ]ῆι Vel., Ki., following Wilh. Hermes; ἕ[κτηι καὶ εἰκοστ]ῆι Mer. AJP; π[έμπτει καὶ δεκάτ]ηι P.-N. Cal., Pritch.

AACS; π[ροτέραι <πέμπτει καὶ> εἰκοστ]ῆι Mer. Ath., with pi dotted in TAPA.

9 patronymic and demotic of mover: Ki. PA 12200.

32 end: εἶπεν· περὶ Wilh. UDA; would require 2 letters in 1 stoichos.

37/38: τῶ[ι δήμω/ι εἰς - - Wilh. Hermes.

38/39: προσαγαγ[εῖν /αὐτὸν πρὸς τὸν δῆμον καὶ Wilh. Hermes.

39/40: χρηματίσα[ι περὶ /τούτων - - Wilh. Hermes.

43/44: [ἐφ' ὑγιε/ίαι Wilh. Hermes.

This inscription records two decrees: the first is a decree of the Demos; the second seems to record the probouleuma which was responsible for the first decree, i.e., the "next ekklesia" mentioned in the second decree would have met on the date of the first decree, the last day (or next to last, if προτέραι is restored) of Elaphebolion. DeLaix lists instances where there is no evidence to show that the Demos had acted on a probouleuma (137 n. 71.; 18 decrees from his list are included in this Corpus). His explanation for this anomaly is the nature of the decrees in his list--since most of them deal with the bestowal of honors, the Athenians may have been less strict in complying with the proper procedure (137/8). I add that the condition of the various stones in question must also be considered: if this decree had been broken off at line 32, it too would have been included in the list. As it is, it is fairly certain that we have the beginning of the probouleuma which led to the first decree, and, although only a small portion of the second decree remains, there is enough to show that the demos did not pass verbatim the probouleuma offered.

Recording the decree (or more exactly, the probouleuma) of the Boule separate from that of the Demos, especially when the Demos made changes, may have been more common than we think because so many texts are fragmentary.

The purpose of this decree is to honor Androkles, the son of Kleinias, from Kerameikos (Henry, 47, records the first 3 lines of this decree and notes that the unique placement of his name "enables the honorand to be included in the prescript rather than isolated in the superscript"). Androkles, elected priest of Asklepios, had taken care of the sanctuary and carried out the other things set down in the laws beautifully and reverently. He is also commended by those elected as epimeletes to maintain order in the theater (εὐκοσμίας) for having been useful to the Demos in that respect as well. Because of these deeds and his virtue and righteousness (δικαιοσύνης), he is to be awarded a gold crown worth a thousand drachmai, pending his euthynai (see #9). The Demos also provides 30 drachmai for a sacrifice and 30 drachmai to have the stele inscribed and then set up in the Asklepieion.

As noted above, not much remains of the probouleuma. Most of what does remain is procedural. The inscription breaks off noting that "the priest of Asklepios" (Androkles' name is not mentioned, cf. DeLaix 123) had contributed to the health and safety of the Boule and Demos. (This phrase, lines 43/4, was restored by Wilhelm: ἐφ' ὑγιείαι σωτηρίαι. If he used II^2 410 as a parallel, it is surprising that Wilhelm would not have continued his restoration of this decree to include "women, children and other possessions" as in the phrase in lines 14-16, II^2 410).

The connection between the priest of Asklepios and the sanctuary of Dionysos is obvious: the Asklepieion was located close to the theater of Dionysos; a sacrifice to Asklepios was performed as part of the Proagon to the City Dionysia (see #63, II ^{2}359, for discussion of this festival). The content of this inscription, however, points to an even closer connection. Androkles was honored at the end of Elaphebolion, the month in which the City Dionysia was held. (The general consensus is that despite the ambiguities in restoring a date for this decree, Elaphebolion is certainly the month; see commentary above.) That it was at least ten days after the festival is not a problem--even if this meeting of the ekklesia was the second one to be held after the festival, the meeting usually held directly after the festival, ἐν Διονύσου, seems to have been an occasion to honor foreigners who might still be in town after the main attraction of the festival--the drama.

The sacrifice and other duties performed so well by Androkles must be connected with the place Asklepios held in the festivities for Dionysos and therefore may be enough to explain why he was honored so soon after the City Dionysia. The inclusion of the fact (lines 15-19) that he had helped to maintain _eukosmia_ (order) in the _theater_, however, suggests that Androkles had not only performed his duties as priest of Asklepios correctly, but also that he had gone above and beyond the call of duty by maintaining _eukosmia_ in the theater (during the festival?) as well. (Hubbe, 184, cites these lines to support his idea that one of the duties of a priest of Asklepios might be to maintain _eukosmia_ in his own sanctuary. Wilhelm, _UDA_ 233, suggests that there may have been a specific reason for Androkles' honors, but acknowledges the fact that with so small a group of decrees honoring priests of Asklepios, it is impossible to tell.)

Although the inscriptions in this Corpus provide an intimate look into the official transactions of the Athenian Demos in the Lykourgan era, they are still involved in dates and formulae and bureaucratic language. They are tantalizing because they are still once removed from the circumstances which led to the enactment of the decrees. Was this decree just a cog in the bureaucratic machinery or had Androkles done something really spectacular to be given such honors?

328/7

55. *DECREE* EM 5283

editor: Kirchner IG II^2 355.

description: This fragment is Pentelic marble. Both sides, the back, and the bottom are broken. The top is smoother--perhaps it is the original surface although the few chisel marks appear to be placed randomly rather than for a surface.

dimensions:
H 0.10 m.
W 0.21 m.
Th 0.24 m.

letters: 0.010 m. Smallest, O, is .007; largest, Y, is .011.

minuscule text:

non stoich.

[Ἐπὶ Εὐθυκ]ρίτου ἄ̣ρ̣χ̣[οντος].

- - - - - Α Ρ̣ - - - -

- - - - - ου Λα̲μ̲π̲τ̲[ρεῦς - -]

commentary: The text is based on Kirchner's. I have dotted the letters at the end of lines 1 and 2; although there are faint traces of strokes, there is not enough to positively identify any of these letters. Kirchner included his reading at the end of line 3: ^^Γ//ʹΓ. I could not find any traces, thus the underlining. The stone is broken on the right where Kirchner read letters. The letters are not in stoichedon order.

Kirchner noted that it was impossible to tell whether this stone records a decree. I think it's very unlikely. The letters are quite large--an average 0.010 m. as opposed to the average of .007 m. usual in Lykourgan decrees. Even if the back of this stone were original, the thickness of 24 cm. suggests a very large stele. It is about 10 cm. more than the usual width, even when the back is preserved.

It is more difficult to say what <u>was</u> recorded on this stone. II^2 370, which records a treaty between the Athenians and Aitolians in 323/2, also has large letters, .013 m. It is only 8 cm. thick, however, and the letters in the other two treaties from the Lykourgan Era, II^2 236 and II^2 329, which record the treaty between Philip and the Greeks, 338/7, and the subsequent renewal by Alexander in 336/5, measure only .005 m., even smaller than the usual .007. Besides, while a treaty in 323/2 (II^2 370) is possible in the historical context of Alexander's death and preparations for the Lamian War (see Mitchel <u>Phoenix</u> 18(1964) 13-17), a treaty much earlier than 323/2 would be an anomaly, considering the provisions in the treaties with Philip and Alexander mentioned above.

A more likely possibility is that this fragment may have been part of a dedicatory base. But I must end this discussion where it began: there is no way to tell. And the seventeen letters seen by Kirchner can not really prove that this fragment was published in the Lykourgan Era, let alone 328/7.

56. *DECREE AND DEDICATION OF THE BOULE* Oropos no. 240

photo: AE (1917) page 41.

editors: Leonardos AE (1917) 40-48 no. 92; Meritt & Traill Councilors 59-60 no. 49.

other bibliography: Lewis BSA 50(1955) 34-36; Oikonomides ΠΛΑΤΩΝ 8(1956) 108-109; Reinmuth Epheb. Inscr. 97.

description: This stele of Pentelic marble is composed of two fragments found built into a house wall near the Amphiaraion. It now stands against a wall in the small museum at the Ampharaion. The molding at the top, 0.072 m. high, is preserved in front; some of it has been chipped away on the sides. There is also a molding at the bottom, 0.045 m. high; it is preserved front and sides. The front and sides are smooth; the back and top are rough-picked.

dimensions:
H 0.96 m. (entire)
0.835 m. (inscribed surface)
W 0.255 m. (top)
0.264 m. (bottom)
Th 0.192 m. (top)
0.225 m. (bottom)

letters: 0.005 m. Smallest, X, is .004; largest, Σ, Φ, are .006.

minuscule text: next two pages.

epigraphical commentary: The stonecutter was not very careful. Alphas do not have cross bars in: line 20; line 32; line 45. Theta is not dotted in: line 41; line 42; line 51. Omitted letters are: tau in line 9; upsilon in line 10; omicron in line 41. Misspellings include: alpha rather than the correct iota, line 24; lambda rather than omega, line 30; eta rather than nu, line 44; alpha rather than delta, gamma rather than delta, line 48; kappa rather than epsilon, line 54.

Meritt and Traill noted that while they could not read a number of letters in the lower right hand portion of Leonardos's transcript, with the use of squeezes in Princeton, they were able to read some letters bracketed by Leonardos. After examining the stone, I was able to read all the letters read by Leonardos. I could not, however, see the new readings offered by Meritt and

Traill with the exception of nu in ’Αντίδοτος, line 26. Meritt & Traill read it as clear; I have dotted it. Underlining designates those letters which Leonardos bracketed and I could not see, but which Meritt and Traill read from the squeeze. This underlining is not meant to dispute the new readings since squeezes do sometimes bring out traces of letters otherwise not apparent. It is merely to designate those letters which I could not see on the stone.

οἵδε ἐπέδοcαν εἰc τὸ ἀνάθημα ὃ ἀνέθηκεν
ἡ βουλὴ ἡ ἐπ' Εὐθυκρίτου ἄρχοντοc   non stoich.
βουλευταί

Φιλόcτρατοc ’Αχαρνε
Εὐθυκράτηc ’Αφιδ[[γ]]ναῖ
Χαιρέcτρατοc ‘Ραμνοῦ
Ο̲ὐ̲λίαc Cτειριεῦ
[Φ]άλανθ̲οc ἐκ Κερα
Εὐκράτηc Λαμπ<τ>ρεῦ
Λυκο<ῦ>ργοc Μελιτε
Καλλιcθένηc Τρινεμ
Εὐετίων Cφήττιο
῞Ενπεδοc Οἰῆθε
Θεοκρίνηc ‘Υβάδηc
Φιλοκράτηc Αἰξωνεῦ
Πρωτοκλῆc Κηφιcιεῦ
Βοῦλιc Θοραιεῦ

Δημήτριοc ’Αφ<ι>δναῖο
’Αμεινίαc ’Αγρυλῆθε
’Αντίδοτοc Cυπαλήττι
Θεόδωροc Παλληνεῦ
’Επιγήθηc ’Εροιάδη
Νίκανδροc Μαραθῶνι
Λυcίθεοc Εὐ<ω>νυμ
ταμίαc
Cωτι<ά>δηc ’Αχαρνεῦ
γραμματεῦc
Cωκράτηc Παιονίδ
Πυθόδηλοc ’Αγνοῦcιο

οἵδε ἐκ τῶν ἄλλων ἐπέδοcαν

Φανόδημοc Θυμαιτά
Δημ<ά>δηc Παιανιεῦ
Πολύε̲υ̲κτοc Cφήττιο
Εὖ[— ca. 6 – Κ]ολλυτε
[Κηφιc]ο̲[φ]ῶν Χολαρ̲γ̲ε

’Αριcτείδηc ῞Ερμ̲[ειοc]
Φείδιπποc Μ[υρρινούcιοc]
Καλλιτέλη̲[c ----]
Καλλικ[------]
’Αριcτίω[ν ----]

vacat 0.022

vacat 0.022

Καλλιcθένηc Χαρ<ο>πίδου Τρινεμεὺc [εἶπεν·] [ἐ]πειδὴ Εὐθυκράτηc Ἀφιδ[ν]αῖοc καὶ Φιλ[όcτρατοc] [Ἀ]χαρνεὺc καὶ Χαιρέcτρατοc Ῥαμνούcι[οc ἀεὶ] [δ]ιατελοῦcιν φιλοτιμούμε<ν>οι πρὸc τὴν βο[υλὴν] [κ]αὶ τοῦ <ἀ>ναθήματοc τοῦ ἐν Ἀνφιαράου τῆ[ι βου]-[λ]εῖ cυνεπεμελήθηcαν καλῶc καὶ φιλοτίμω[c] [δ]εδόχθαι τῆι βουλεῖ ἐπ̣αινέcαι Εὐθυκράτη[ν] Δρακοντί<δ>ου Ἀφι<δ>ναῖον, Φιλόcτρατον Φιλίνο[υ] Ἀχαρνέα, Χαιρέcτρατον Χαιρεδήμου Ῥαμνού-cιον, καὶ cτεφανῶcαι ἕκαcτον αὐτῶν χρυcῶι cτεφάνωι ἀπὸ :𐅅: δραχμῶν ἐπὰν τὰc εὐθύναc δῶcιν ὅπωc ἂν καὶ οἱ ἄλλοι φιλοτιμῶνται πρὸc τὴν βουλὴν εἰδότεc ὅτι χάριταc αὐτοῖc ἡ βουλὴ ἀπο[δ]ώcει τὰc ἀξίαc ἑκάcτωι ὧν ἂν εὐ<ε>ργετή-cωcιν· ἀναγράψαι δὲ τόδε τὸ ψήφιcμα τὸν γραμ-ματέα τῆc βουλῆc ἐν cτήλει λιθίνει καὶ cτῆc[αι] ἐν τῶι ἱερῶι τοῦ Ἀμφιαράου vacat

commentary: The restorations are Leonardos's. Four of his restorations are not included in the text--they are recorded below. Meritt and Traill also did not include them (with no explanation). Lewis (35; not cited by Meritt and Traill) notes of these same four restorations that the one for line 22 "must be abandoned" while those in lines 38, 39, and 40 are respectively "most uncertain," "unwarranted", and "highly speculative". I follow Meritt and Traill who number the two columns as separate lines rather than Leonardos who used one number for each line and then denoted the two columns as a and b (i.e., lines 5 and 25 in this text are denoted 5a and 5b in Leonardos's).

22: Εὖ[καδμοc Κο]λλυτε Leonardos.

38: Καλλιτέλ[ης 'Ερoιάδης] Leonardos.

39: Καλλικ[ράτης Στειριεύς] Leonardos.

40: 'Αριστίω[ν Κολλυτεύς] Leonardos.

This inscription begins with a short statement: those who contributed to the dedication; the Boule from the year of Euthykritos. Lines 4-17, 24-35, list those members of the Boule who contributed; lines 19-23, 36-40, list others who contributed. Then at line 41 begins a decree of the Boule, the reason why this inscription is included in this Corpus. Kallisthenes, son of Charopides, from the deme Trinemeia proposed that Euthykrates of Aphidnai, Philostratos of Acharne and Chairestratos of Ramnous each be crowned with a gold crown worth 500 drachmai because they had contributed liberally to the Boule and had overseen well and emulously the setting up of the dedication in the Amphiaraion for the Boule. The Boule also conferred upon each of those others who contributed so generously the title euergetes (benefactor). The decree is to be engraved on a stele and placed in the Amphiaraion. (The amount to be set aside for this purpose is not recorded as is usual in this formulaic phrase: probably the contributor's generosity was to be taxed further for this task. This may explain the poor workmanship--either they didn't want to spend much money, or they hired a local stonecutter, or both.)

Leonardos's publication includes a thorough study of the prosopography of the men listed. Lewis uses the names of the additional contributors of this decree to help confirm that the governing party under Lykourgos had an "elderly tinge" (35; see #50 for a fuller discussion). Reinmuth has used the name in line 30 of this decree to restore under deme [Εὐ]ωνυμε[ῖς] : [Λυσίθ]ε̣ος Λυσιμέν-ο̣[υς] in an ephebic list of 305/4, II^{2}478 line 48 (his no. 17, line 97). If Reinmuth's identification and his suggestion that the Lysitheos of this decree is the ephebe's grandfather are correct, then we not only have a possible patronymic for our Lysitheos, but also an "elderly tinge" in the Boule of this year.

XII. THE YEAR OF HEGEMON, 327/6

57. *ATHENS BESTOWS PROXENY ON AN ERETRIAN*

EM 2638

editor: Kirchner *IG* II^2 357 (using Wilhelm's text).

supplement: *SEG* 21.287 (Pritchett-Neugebauer, Meritt *Ath.*, Pritchett *AACS*).

other bibliography: Wilhelm *UDA* 231; Meritt *Hesperia* 3 (1934) 4; *Ath.* 98; *GRBS* 17(1976) 151; Pritchett-Neugebauer *Cal.* 53/4; Pritchett *AACS* 378.

description: The fragment of Pentelic marble preserves the upper left hand corner of what had been a stele topped by a pediment. The left side and part of the top of the pediment are original; the back is rough-picked; right side and bottom are broken.

dimensions:	letters: 0.007 m. Smallest,
H 0.23 m. (entire)	O, is .005; largest, K, P, T,
0.12 m. (surface)	are .007. Epsilons and kappas
W 0.122 m.(pediment)	are very square. Theta of
0.11 m. (surface)	ΘΕΟΙ could be .010, only the
Th 0.10 m.	bottom is preserved.

majuscule text:

Π Ρ Ο Ξ Ε Ν Ι .

Τ Ρ Ι Ε Ι Ε Γ .

Α Ι Α Ν Τ . .

Ι Ο Κ Λ Η Σ . .

Υ Ε Ν Ε Ν Η Ι Κ

Ε Ι Α Σ Ε Κ Κ Λ

. . Ε̲ Λ̣ Ρ̲ . . .

epigraphical commentary: Although most of the surface on the horizontal part of the pediment is gone, the bottom part of a circle can be seen, presumably the theta of ΘΕΟΙ. The right hasta of pi at the end of line 3 is now invisible. A very short diagonal stroke remains in the bottom right stoichos for the first letter, line 4. The other 2 sigmas on the stone are faint, but their bottom stroke is horizontal. In line 8, I underline the two letters read by Wilhelm, but now no longer visible.

minuscule text:

stoich. 29

Θ̣ [Ε Ο Ι]
Προξενί[α - - - - - - - - - - Ἐρε]-
τριεῖ. Ἐπ̣[ὶ Ἡγήμονος ἄρχοντος ἐπὶ τῆ]-
ϲ̣ Αἰαντ[ίδος ἕκτης πρυτανείας, ἧι Αὐ]-
τ̣οκλῆς [Αὐτίου Ἀχαρνεὺς ἐγραμμάτε]-
υεν· ἕνηι κ[αὶ νέαι, τρίτηι τῆς πρυταν]-
είας· ἐκκλ[ησία ἐν τῶι θεάτρωι· τῶν π]-
[ροέ]δ̣[ρων ἐπεψήφιζεν - - - - - - -]

commentary: Restorations are Wilhelm's, published by Kirchner; exceptions are noted below. Wilhelm also restored the stoichedon order of 29 letters to the line; the restoration in line 7 requires only 28 letters.

1 restoration: Schwenk, based on new reading of dotted theta.

4 ἕκτης πρυτανείας: Wilh., Ki., Mer. <u>Ath.</u>, <u>GRBS</u>. δεκάτης P.-N., requires ommission of ἧι <u>before secretary's</u> name; in <u>AACS</u> Pritch. acknowledges the irregularity.

4/5 secretary: Mer <u>Hesperia</u> (see #59, commentary). Αὐ]τοκλῆς [Φανίου Ἀχαρνεὺς Wilh., Ki.

6 day in prytany: Mer. <u>Ath.</u>, <u>GRBS</u>. ἐνάτηι Wilh., Ki, P.-N. <u>Cal.</u> (with their restoration in line 4 to produce an intercalary year); if year were ordinary they would restore 1st day of the 6th prytany.

The second and third lines of this decree impart the only information which gives any hint of its content beyond the formulaic prescript: that someone, an Eretrian, if Wilhelm's restoration is accepted, was granted proxeny. Other than that, there is a heavily restored calendric equation (without room for the month). Since Wilhelm's restoration of the archon, Hegemon, no one has questioned the year, 327/6. It is based on the relationship between this decree, $II^2$357 and $II^2$356 (#58); both decrees require the same number of stoichoi for the archon and secretary respectively. The addition of #59 (Hesperia 3[1934] no. 5) confirms the length of the secretary's name as well as the correct patronymic.

I have noted in the discussion for #53 that, due to heavily restored dates, neither 328/7 nor 327/6 can be designated positively as intercalary or ordinary. Since, however, most epigraphists support Meritt's restorations for decrees #53 and #54 which make 328/7 an intercalary year; and restorations for the decrees with dating formulas for this year, #57, #58, #59, present fewer problems if 327/6 is considered to be ordinary. I present the restorations for the dates for these 5 decrees on the assumption that 328/7 was intercalary; 327/6, ordinary. (This decree is relatively rare in that the different restorations do not rely on controversial readings of a letter or letters on the stone. That the disagreement is only over what is within the brackets may explain why the arguments for the nature of the year 327/6 are less heated than those concerned with the "dated" decrees of 328/7.)

This decree affords a good example of the change in attitude toward the lengths of prytanies. When Kirchner published the second edition of the Corpus, it was accepted practice to alter the lengths of prytanies in order to equate the conciliar with the festival year. In his commentary for this decree, Kirchner notes the year as intercalary and the lengths of prytanies as: 40 days for prytanies I-III; 39 days for prytany IV; 38 days for prytanies V, VIII and IX; and 37 days for prytanies VI, VII and X. Pritchett-Neugebauer, in Cal., followed Aristotle's "rule" that in an ordinary year the first four prytanies held 36 days; the last 6 prytanies, 35 days. They carried that over for an intercalary year so that the first four prytanies would have 39 days; the last six, 38 days. In Ath., Meritt agreed in principle with Aristotle's "rule," but thought that, in practice, the Athenians were more flexible (see discussion, #15). For instance, in order to provide workable dating equations for the year 327/6, Meritt assumed that the first six prytanies held 35 days; the next 3 prytanies, 36 days; the last prytany, 37 days (Ath. 99). Since then Meritt has become less "flexible," i.e.: although he still thinks that the four prytanies with one more day than the other six can occur anytime during the year, he now agrees that whatever the sequence, "No prytany during the period of the ten phylai in the fourth century should have had more than 36 days or less than 35 days in an ordinary year" (GRBS 151). In order to keep the same restorations for this decree and #58 of 327/6, Merritt suggests that the sequence of prytanies be 35 days for the first five prytanies, 36 days for the last five prytanies, with a retardation of one day in the festival calendar, in either Gamelion or Anthesterion. This produces a year of 355 days, one more than the usual 354.

Although many scholars, especially Meritt and Pritchett, have contributed to a more thorough understanding of the Athenian calendar since Kirchner published his monumental work, the fragmentary nature of the evidence, especially for this year, 372/6, makes it impossible to know for sure exactly how the Athenians ordered their calendar.

327/6

58. *ATHENS HONORS MEMNON OF RHODES* EM 2662

editor: Kirchner IG II^2 356 (from Wilhelm's & Lolling's transcripts).

supplements: SEG 21.286 (Meritt Hesperia, Ath., Tod, Pritchett-Neugebauer, Pritchett); 23.57 (Tod, Meritt TAPA).

collection: Tod II 199.

other bibliography: Tarn JHS 41(1921) 24; Sauciuc-Saveanu Journ. Sav. (1928) 300; Dinsmoor Archons 371/2; Meritt Hesperia 3(1934) 4; Ath. 98/9; TAPA 95(1964) 225/6; GRBS 17(1976) 151; Wilhelm Att. Urk. V 155; Pritchett-Neugebauer Cal. 52/3; Pritchett AACS 274-276; Henry Prescripts 37 n. 24, 44.

description: This stele of Pentelic marble is very damaged. The molding at the top and just a trace of a diagonal surface in the upper right-hand corner suggest that the stele was topped by a pediment. The right side is preserved, the back is rough-picked; the bottom and left side are broken. Kirchner noted that the middle of the inscribed surface was worn away; "detritus" is now the proper adjective for the entire surface.

dimensions:
H 0.54 m. (entire)
0.452 m. (surface)
W 0.23 m. (entire)
0.268 m. (surface)
Th 0.123 m. (top)
0.126 m. (bottom)

letters: 0.006 m. Smallest, O, is .005; largest, N, T, are .007. Y is .006.

minuscule text: and next page.

stoich. 20

[᾿Επὶ ῾Ηγήμ]ον̣οϲ ἄρχοντο[ϲ ε]-
[πὶ τῆϲ ῾Ιπ]ποθων[τί]δ[οϲ ἐ]β̣[δ]-
[όμηϲ πρυ]τανεία[ϲ, ἧι Αὐτο]-
[κλῆϲ Α]ὐτίου [᾿Αχ]αρ[ν]ε[ὺϲ] ἐ[γ]-
[ραμμ]άτευεν· δευτ[έραι] φθ-
[ίν]οντοϲ, ἕκτει [κ]α[ὶ ε]ἰ[κ]οϲ-
[τῆ]ι τῆ[ϲ π]ρυτανεία[ϲ· ἐκ]κ[λ]-
[ηϲί]α κυρ<ί>α· τῶν προ̣[έ]δ[ρων ἐ]-
[πεψ]ήφιζεν ....8....Η..
...7.... ἔδοξ[ε]ν [τῶι] δήμω-
[ι· ἐπειδ]ὴ Μ[έ]μνω[ν] Τ..Α...
..Η..Ε....7....Β..ΕΙ..
.......14.......Ε.Σ...
..Μ[....9.... π]ρέϲβε..
..Ο....9....ΕΛ.ΛΩΣ ..
..Ε......13.......ΟΥ..
......12......ΕΛΚΩΙ...
..Τ....ΟΙ.ΩΝΚ.ΙΕΥΠΟ.
..ΕΠΙ..5..ΣΤΕ..Ι.Λ..
...ΜΕ.....11.....Σ...
..Ι.ΟΙ....ΓΥΣ.Λ..Ο..
...ΙΛΟ..5..ΑΤ.Ο.Ι.Λ.
...ΑΝ περιτυ[γχ]άνηι [καὶ]
[πρ]ότερον οἱ π[ρ]όγονοι [Φα]-
[ρν]ά[β]αζοϲ καὶ ᾿Αρ[τά]βαζο[ϲ]
[δι]ετέλουν τὸν δῆμον [τὸν]
[᾿Αθ]ηναίων εὐεργετοῦν[τε]-
[ϲ κ]αὶ χρήϲιμοι ὄντεϲ ἐν [τ]-

[ο]ἶϲ πολέμοιϲ τῶι δήμωι [κ]-
[αὶ] ὁ πατὴρ Θυμώνδου Μέ[ντ]-
[ω]ρ τοὺϲ ἐν Αἰγύπτωι ϲτρ[α]-
[τ]ευομένουϲ τῶν Ἑλλήνων
[ἔ]ϲωιϲεν, ὅτε ἧλω [Α]ἴγυπτ̣[ο]-
[ϲ] ὑπὸ Περϲῶν· ἐπαινέϲαι [μ]-
[ὲ]ν αὐτὸν καὶ ϲτεφανῶϲαι [χ]-
[ρ]υϲῶι ϲτε[φ]άν[ωι] αρετη̣..
.ΣΕΝΕΚΑ - - - - - - - - - - -

epigraphical commentary: As noted above, the surface has deteriortated since Kirchner used Wilhelm's and Lolling's transcripts, so much so that their readings must be relied upon almost entirely. It is impossible to fix the few letters that are even faintly visible in any stoichedon order for lines 1-22; and even though a few more letters are visible in lines 23-37, they do not warrant a separate majuscule text. There is, however, a descrepancy between Kirchner's text and what I was able to see in the last two lines. I read:

36 . . Σ Ω Ι Σ Τ
37 . Σ̣ Ε̣ Ν̣ Ε̣ Κ̣ .

while, according to Kirchner's minuscule text, Wilhelm and Lolling read:

36 . Υ Σ Ω Ι Σ Τ Ε . Α Ν . . Α Ρ Ε Τ Η̣ . .
37 Σ Ε Ν Ε Κ Α

Although the sigma in line 37 is at the left-hand edge of the surface of the stone, the stone continues to the left of the inscribed surface another 2 1/2 cm.. Therefore it is impossible that the sigma be the first letter in line 37. Rather than sacrifice the credibility of the entire text, it seems better to assume that somehow (because Kirchner or Wilhelm or Lolling wanted to restore ἀρετῆ/ϲ ?) the letters in line 37 in II^2 356 were shifted one stoichos to the left.

Although he notes that line 36 has only 18 letters, Kirchner gives no indication that the 2 stoichoi at the end of line 36 were vacats; it is now impossible to tell whether these stoichoi were left blank. He records 2 other violations in the stoichedon order. The crowding of 2 letters in one stoichos for his restoration at the end of line 2 is now no longer necessary (see commentary below). I read only a dotted alpha in line 35 st. 9

where Kirchner recorded the alpha and iota of καὶ in st. 9. Since there are 21 letters in line 8, I assume that the iota was omitted by the stonecutter, hence the angled brackets (Kirchner used parentheses and made no comment in his apparatus criticus).

Despite the deterioration of the stone since Kirchner recorded Wilhelm's and Lolling's readings, I record here my reading of the epsilon and iota of ΘΕΟΙ on the base of the pediment.

commentary: The restorations, in a stoichedon order of 20 letters to the line, are Kirchner's based on the work of Wilhelm and Lolling (Kirchner notes in his commentary that for the most part Lolling and Wilhelm agreed). Exceptions and additional restorations are noted below.

2/3 prytany: Dinsmoor; Mer. Ath., TAPA, GRBS. τ]ε[τά/ρ-τηc] Ki., noting that tau and alpha must occupy one stoichos at the end of line 2. [ὀγδόηc v] P.-N. In AACS, Pritch. leaves unrestored. See #57 for discussion of the calendar "problem" for this year.

4 secretary's patronymic: Mer. Hesperia. Φ]ανίου Ki. Although this new restoration requires reading an upsilon for an alpha and a tau for a nu, Wilhelm recorded in Att. Urk. that the letters were difficult to read and accepted Mer's restoration.

11 mid: Henry (44) records lines 10 and 11 from Ki.'s text under the category "Omission of orator." Rather than include the restoration of Memnon, he states: "No name .....]ημ[έ]μνω[ν] seems instanced." The restoration of Memnon, however, would further confirm the omission of the proposer.

18 end: οἰ[κ]ῶν κ[α]ὶ εὖ πο[ι/εῖ Tod.

21 mid: ὁ β̣[α]σ̣[ιλ]εὺc Hiller, recorded by Ki.

23 beg: [οἷc] ἂν who also notes that περιτυγχάνω is a rarer alternative for ἐντυγχάνω.

36/7 ΑΡΕΤΗ../.Ε: my reading of these two lines makes Ki.'s restoration of ἀρετῇ/c impossible (see ep. com. above). Even if the two stoichoi at the end of line 36 were read as vacats, the sigma in line 37 is in st. 2 not, as in Ki.'s text, st.1.

All the epigraphists who have worked with this stone have commented on its condition. Stroud's "absolutely hopeless" (recorded in Pritchett AACS 275) describes most accurately its present state. The lament, however, has been over the inability to provide a secure calendar equation. Even more unfortunate is that the poor condition of the stone continues throughout the text. The middle part was never decipherable, while for the last part we must now rely on what Wilhelm read only with difficulty.

From what is left on the stone, we know that a certain Memnon was honored by the Athenian Demos; we know neither the reasons nor the specific honors awarded except that Memnon is to receive a gold crown. The most intact portion of the decree, lines 23-37, records the various ways that Memnon's ancestors had helped the Athenian Demos in the past. It is the presence of these "ancestors" (πρόγονοι), Pharnabazos (lines 24/5) and Artabazos (line 25) and the relative Mentor (lines 30/1) that identifies the Memnon of this decree as a relative of Memnon I of Rhodes. The honorand of this decree must be Memnon II since the great mercenary leader (Memnon I) died in 333 fighting for Persia against Alexander (and his League of Corinth!). Although the exact relationship can not be ascertained, Tod, who provides a thorough review of the scholarship on this issue, favors Berve's identification of Memnon II as the son of Memnon I, grandson of Artabazos, great-grandson of Pharnabazos, and nephew of Mentor. An alternate indentification, offered by Beloch and followed by Kirchner and Tarn, is that Memnon II is the son of Thymondas, grandson of Mentor, and thus great-nephew of Memnon I.

Tod concludes that, whatever the specific relationship, Memnon II must have been quite young in 327/6, "a fact which may explain the emphasis laid on the achievements of his ancestors and uncle" (282/3). The emphasis, however, is laid on Memnon's relatives only because we do not know what was recorded in lines 10 through 22. The only restoration offered by Kirchner, π]ρέσβε in line 14 is tantalizing because it provokes questions which cannot be answered. If Memnon was honored for something connected with an embassy, then, at the very least, the notion that he was "little more than a boy" (Tod, 282) must be reconsidered (Tarn, JHS makes it clear that the source material precludes any positive identification of the relationships in this family).

What is certain, and accepted by all scholars, is that the Memnon of this decree is somehow related to Memnon of Rhodes and that he was honored by the Athenian Demos. That information, in turn, illuminates another thread in the fabric of Lykourgan Athens--diplomacy. The Athenians may have complied with the terms of their agreements with Philip and Alexander (II^2 236; II^2 329) by not enacting any treaties. This decree, however, indicates that they could still act as an independent state. Tod is certainly a master of understatement when he concludes (284): "It is interesting to find Athens in 327 honoring a member of a family which had rendered such distinguished services to the Persian cause."

327/6

59. *DECREE* Ag. Inv. I 226

photo: Hesperia 3(1934) page 4; Pritchett AACS Plate 21B (latex squeeze of part of fragment).

editor: Meritt Hesperia 3(1934) 3-4 no. 5; SEG 21.288.

supplements: SEG 21.288 (Meritt Hesperia, Pritchett-Neugebauer, Meritt Ath., Pritchett AACS); 23.58 (Meritt TAPA); 25.69 (McGregor, Meritt AE, Pritchett Phoenix).

other bibliography: Pritchett-Neugebauer Cal. 53/54; Meritt Ath. 100-101; TAPA 95 (1964) 223; AE (1968) 107-115; GRBS 17(1976) 152; Pritchett CP 54 (1959) 155; AACS 273/274; Phoenix 23(1969) 166 n. 23; Clement AJA 69(1965) 194; McGregor Phoenix 20 (1966) 214-217; Rhodes Boule 261 (Rhodes lists this decree twice as: Hesperia iii 5, and SEG xxi 288; and describes them as if they were two different decrees); Henry Prescripts 47/48.

description: This fragment of a stele of Pentelic marble was found in the Agora excavations on April 28, 1932. The left side and bottom are broken; although the right side is preserved, some of the surface has broken off. The stele was topped by a pediment.

dimensions:
H 0.25 m. (entire)
0.135 m. (surface)
W 0.25 m. (entire)
0.152 m. (surface)
Th 0.082 m.

letters: 0.006 m. Smallest, Ω, is .004; largest, Φ, is .008. E, K, M, Π, are .005. H is .006.

minuscule text:

stoich. 33

[Ἐφ' Ἡγήμονοϲ ἄρχοντ]οϲ ἐπὶ τῆϲ Οἰνηΐ[δοϲ ἐ]-
[νάτηϲ πρυτανείαϲ] ἧι Αὐτοκλῆϲ Αὐτί[ου Ἀχ]-
[αρνεὺϲ ἐγραμμάτε]υεν· Μουνιχιῶνοϲ ....
.......15....... δεκάτει μετ' εἰκά[δαϲ· τ]-
[ῶν προέδρων ἐπεψή]φιζεν Πάμφιλοϲ Π[αιαν]-
[ιεύϲ· ἔδοξεν τῶι δή]μωι· vacat
........17........ Θριά[ϲ]ιοϲ εἶπ[εν· ἐπε]-
[ιδὴ ....15....... ἐπ]ὶ [Ἡγ]ήμονο[ϲ ἄρχο]-
[ντοϲ ......13...... εἰϲ] τὰϲ ἐπιμ[ελείαϲ]

epigraphical commentary: There is only one line which has provoked controversial readings. I include here what I read in line 4 (before considering the various restorations for this line):

E Y A T E I M E T E I K A

The other readings are best treated in the commentary (below) on the restorations for lines 3/4. There is no violation of the stoichedon order on the stone; the vacat at the end of line 6 is 15 stoichoi.

commentary: The restorations with a stoichedon order of 33 letters to the line are Meritt's. (The demotic, Π[αι-αν/ιεῦς], is restored in lines 5/6 of the Ath. text with no comment; it also appears in the SEG text; the other restorations are from the original publication in Hesperia.)

3/4 restorations: [ἐκκλ/ησία ἐν τῶι θεάτρωι·] ἐνάτει μετ' εἰκά[δας· τ]- Mer. Hesperia; [δευτ/έραι, ἡμερολεγδὸν] δ' ἐνάτει etc. P.-N. Cal.; [πέμπ/τει τῆς πρυτανεία]ς ἐνάτει etc. Mer. Ath.; [ἐνάτ/ει φθίνοντος, νυνὶ] δ' ἐνάτει etc. Mer. AE. In GRBS (152 n. 20) Mer. suggests ὁμῶς rather than νυνί. Henry, who records lines 1-7 (47/8), leaves the 20 stoichoi after Mounichion unrestored and reads: ἐνάτει μετ' εἰκά[δας.

When Mer. originally published this text, he offered no reading for the letter in line 4, st. 16. He was thus able to restore "ekklesia in the theater" between the month, Mounichion, and its date, the 22nd, and assume that the day within the prytany had been omitted. P.-N., using a squeeze, read enough in st. 16 to restore a delta, and then offered their restoration. Mer., in Ath., acknowledged the trace of a letter in st. 16, which made the iota of his Hesperia restoration impossible. He offered the Ath. restoration, which required a dotted sigma in st. 16. Pritch., in AACS, retained the Cal. restoration; added a translation: "on the second day (in the course of the twenties) which is the ninth day in the course of the twenties as one counts days;" and repeated his opinion, already stated in CP, that this restoration was justified by the fact that the nomenclature for this specific date was in transition.

In TAPA, Mer. acknowledged that the letter in st. 16 must be a delta. He also noted that the trace of the letter in st. 18, which had always been read as nu, had not disappeared (as in Pritch. AACS), but rather was enough to confirm the left vertical stoichos of kappa or nu (he saw no trace of a diagonal stroke or either letter). He did not, however, offer a new restoration: "I have no suggestion for the restoration, but believe that it should be made either with ἐνάτει μετ' εἰκά[δας] or with δεκάτει μετ' εἰκά[δας]" (225). Meritt did offer a new restoration in AE. This article is chiefly concerned with a further refutation of Pritchett's use of ἡμερολεγδὸν in the Cal. restoration for this decree (108 n. 3 lists other scholars, including McGregor and Clement, who also disagreed with Pritchett's restoration). Although Meritt withdrew his suggestion of δεκάτει μετ' εἰκά[δας (TAPA), the AE restoration does reflect the transitional nature of the nomenclature for this day, which Pritchett had emphasized since he published Cal. with Neugebauer. In GRBS, Meritt stayed with his AE restoration (offering the slight change recorded above) and noted that there was no calendar equation for this decree, just two ways of naming the 22nd day of the month.

My restoration is based on what I read on the stone in st. 18. I saw no trace of the diagonal or right hand hasta of a nu; I did see a diagonal stroke in the upper right corner of this stoichos, hence, δεκάτει μετ' εἰκά-[δας, 21st day of a full month.

Although the reading of δεκάτει disaffirms the previous restorations, it does suggest some new possiblities. If the restoration, πέμπτει (Mer. Ath.), could be retained as the day in the prytany, the equation, for an ordinary year of the usual 354 days, would be: Mounichion (10) 21 = Prytany [IX] 5 = 287th day. (The two full months in the middle of the year, required for the restoration for #57 and #58, would be offset by two hollow months at the end of the year--30x5+29x4+21 = 287; the sequence of the number of the days in the prytanies would be just the opposite of Aristotle's "rule"--35x6+36x2+5 = 287; see #15 for discussion of the calendar). The sure reading of delta in st. 16, however, leaves only 6 stoichoi for the day in prytany. The restoration of τετράς presents the same problem Meritt faced in Ath. and GRBS--a 355 day year. Even less desirable is that any restoration for a prytany date yields the unusual sequence: prytany; month; day in prytany; day in month.

The other alternative is to assume, as Pritch. and Mer. (AE) did, that the stonecutter recorded two ways of designating the date in the festival year. Both epigraphists were working with ἐνάτει μετ' εἰκάδας, the 22nd day of the month; both noted that the designation for the last decade of the month was in transition (in fact, Mer.'s AE restoration relies on the fact that φθίνοντος was replaced by μετ' εἰκάδας by the end of the 4th century; TAPA 209 n. 27).

Unfortunately, the number of the letter spaces, 19 stoichoi, between Μουνιχιῶνος and δεκάτει makes it impossible to simply replace the number 10 for the number 9 in Meritt's restoration. Fortunately, however, the 21st day of a month had its own special nomenclature. This day was also designated δεκάτη ὑστέρα in opposition to the 20th day--εἰκάς or εἰκάδες. That designation fits: Μουνιχιῶνος [δεκάτει ὑστέρα, ὁμῶς δὲ] δεκάτει μετ' εἰκά-[δας. Perhaps the stonecutter took a bit of poetic license to make sure everyone knew the date in the month; and, in doing so, forgot to include the last element in the usual dating formula--the day in the prytany (Pryt. [IX] [5]).

This fragment of a decree has very little to offer. The only clue to its content is the restoration in line 9, which informs us that some sort of overseeing (ἐπιμ[ε-λίας]) had happened (presumably well enough to merit honors). In addition, the calendric prescript confirms the patronymic for the secretary of 327/6, and allows much speculation as to the date on which this decree was passed (see commentary above).

327/6

60. *ATHENS BESTOWS ISOTELIA* EM 7321

editors: Koehler II 279; II^2 113; Wilhelm Att. Urk. V 154-156.

supplement: Bull. (1942) no. 32 (Wilhelm Att. Urk. V).

other bibliography: Wilhelm Hermes 24(1889) 142; Beitr. 229; Att. Urk. V 154-156; Waszynski Hermes 34 (1899) 566; Dinsmoor Archons 351.

description: This fragment of Pentelic marble was found on the Acropolis. It is broken on all sides and back. The way the stone is broken on the top and the lengths of the first 3 lines suggests that the stele was originally topped by a pediment; there is a trace of diagonal molding on the right side at the end of line 2. Line 4 is inscribed on the fillet above the cymation.

dimensions:
H 0.186 m. (entire)
0.042 m. (above fillet)
0.038 m.(cymation and fillet)
0.077 m. (below cymation)
W 0.16 m.
Th 0.057 m.

letters: 0.008 m. Smallest, O, is .007; largest, Σ, is .009. Letters in lines 2-4 are about .001 m. larger than those in lines 1, 5-6. The main difference is that lines 2-4 were cut deeper.

minuscule text:

stoich. 20

Θεοί
['Ις]οτέλεια
- - - ι καὶ Φανοστρά[τωι]
- - - ίοις αὐτοῖς καὶ [ἐκγόνοις]
['Επὶ 'Ηγήμον]ος ἄρχ[οντος v]
[ἐπὶ τῆς Πανδ]ιον[ίδος ...]
[. ης πρυτανεί]ας ...7...

commentary: The text is based on Wilhelm's, Att. Urk. V. Koehler made the restorations for lines 1-4; his restoration of the tribe in prytany, Πανδ]ιον[ίδος and the 6th prytany, ἕκτης, established a stoichedon order of 19 letters for lines 5-7 (lines 1-4 are not in stoichedon order). Then Wilhelm (in Hermes) recorded Wilamowitz's additional restoration of ['Εφ' 'Ηγήμον]ος at the beginning of line 5 which thus dated II 279 to 327/6. Kirchner, however, pointed out that in the year of Hegemon the 6th prytany was held by the tribe Aiantis, not Pandionis (#57); offered [ἐπὶ Μόλων?]ος and placed II 279 in the year 362/1 as II^2 113. Dinsmoor accepted Kirchner's restoration; Wilhelm did not. In Att. Urk. V, Wilhelm offered the restoration recorded in line 5 of this text. He based this restoration for a stoichedon order of 20 letters on the assumption that ΘΕΟΙ was inscribed in the middle of the stele. If the center of the stele is between the epsilon and omicron of ΘΕΟΙ (line 1), then the center of line 5 (the first in stoichedon order) is between the omicron and sigma at the end of the archon's name. There is no problem, therefore, in assuming that there were 10 stoichoi to the left of the center; 10 stoichoi to the right of center. Concerning the restoration, ἐπὶ rather than ἐφ' is restored for #57 and #58 of the same year and the restoration of the vacat (for which Wilhelm cites parallels) does not seem out of place following four lines which seem to have been self-contained. The advantage of a stoichedon order of 20 letters is that number of the prytany held by Pandionis is not 5 stoichoi long, but 6 stoichoi, which allows the restoration of the numbers first, third or eighth.

Waszynski's restoration of δημοσ]ίοις at the beginning of line 4 was noted only by Wilhelm in his discussion of state slaves in Beitr.

There are only ten letters left of the decree which was recorded on this stele. And those letters fit into the usual calendric formula which precedes the reasons for the decree. Fortunately the stone offers a bit more information as to the content because someone chose to inscribe (or have inscribed?) its essence first: that a man named Phanostratos and [another man?] and [descendants] were granted isotelia, which is the right to pay taxes as citizens do, rather than the special tax on resident aliens. As in #12, this type of grant probably means that Phanostratos was a metic.

327/6

61. *THE TRIBE AIANTIS HONORS TELESKOPAS* Ag. Inv. I 3626

photo: Hesperia 7(1938) page 95.

editor: Meritt Hesperia 7(1938) 94-96 no. 15.

supplement: Bull. (1938) no. 54 (Meritt).

other bibliography: Ferguson Hesperia 7(1938) 1, 15-20.

description: This stele of Pentelic marble is composed of 7 joined fragments. The pediment is well pereserved as are the sides, the bottom, and the rough-picked back.

There is a carved wreath after the last line of the text. The pieces were found in a well during excavations in the Agora, February 27, 1936.

dimensions:
H 1.065 m.
W 0.316 m. (top)
0.365 m. (bottom)
Th 0.07 m.

letters: 0.008 m. Smallest, Ω, is .006; largest, Ψ, is .14. Ε, Ρ, Σ, Τ, Υ, Χ, are .010. Α, Δ, Θ, Μ, are .007.

minuscule text: and next page.

stoich. 16

Θ ε ο ί-
Δημοκράτηc Δημοκλέ
ουc Ἀφιδναῖοc εἶπε·
ἐπειδὴ ὁ θεcμοθέτη-
c ὁ τῆc Αἰαντίδοc ἐπ-
ιμεμέληται τῆc τε κ-
ληρώcεωc τῶν ἀρχῶν
καὶ τῶν δικαcτηρίω-
ν τῆc πληρώcεωc καὶ
τῶν ἄλλων ἁπάντων τ-
ῶν περὶ τὴν Αἰαντίδ-
α φυλήν, ἐπαινέcαι Τ-
ηλέcκοπον Ἀριcτοκ-
ρίτου Ῥαμνούcιον κ-
αὶ cτεφανῶcαι αὐτ[ὸ]-
ν χρυc[ῶ]ι cτεφάνωι ἀ-
πὸ : Χ : δραχμῶν δικα-
ιοcύνηc ἕνεκα καὶ φ-
ιλοτιμίαc τῆc περὶ

τὴν Αἰαντίδα φυλὴν
ὅπωϲ ἂν καὶ οἱ ἄλλοι
θεϲμοθέται οἱ θεϲμ-
οθετοῦντεϲ [φι]λοτι-
μῶνται περὶ [τ]ὴν φυλ-
ὴν εἰδότεϲ ὅτ[ι] χάρι-
ταϲ ἀπολήψονται πα-
ρὰ τῆϲ φυλῆϲ· τὸ δὲ ψή-
φιϲμα τόδε ἀναγράψ-
αι τοὺϲ ἐπιμελητὰϲ
τοὺϲ ἐφ' Ἡγήμονοϲ ἄρ-
χοντοϲ ἐν ϲτήληι λι-
θίνηι καὶ ϲτῆϲαι ἐν
τῶι Εὐρυϲακείωι vv

wreath

commentary: The stoichedon order of 16 letters to the line is violated once: there are 17 letters in line 2: the crowding occurs at the end of the line. Despite the fact that this inscription was found in pieces, the restored stele is very well preserved: only 6 letters need to be restored; that was done by Meritt.

This decree honors Teleskopos, son of Aristokritos of the deme Rhamnous with a gold crown worth a thousand drachmai. He is honored because, as thesmothete he oversaw the election (by lot) of the archons and the filling up of dikasteria (courts) and fulfilled all the other duties of his office with justice and distinction toward the tribe Aiantis. The other thesmothetai; who also served with distinction, are to receive the gratitude of the tribe as well. As this decree shows, the board of thesmothetai was responsible for the annual election of magistrates and the care of the courts (cf. Meritt 95/6). Meritt presumes that Teleskopos had served as thesmothete the year before, that is reasonable. Since there is no mention of the euthynai (see #9) Teleskopos must have already been audited and thus have finished his year in office.

The decree ends with the notice that the epimeletai (there are three, cf. Meritt, 96) are to have the stele inscribed and set up in the Eurysakeion, which was a sanctuary devoted to Eurysakes, the son of Ajax. Eurysakes is discussed at length by Ferguson in his article "The Salaminioi of the Heptaphylai and Sounion" which deals with the two decrees found with #61 at the same time and place (see Ferguson, 1, for specific details). The two decrees, no. 1 from 363/2, no. 2 from about a century later, record the decisions concerning disputes between the two divisions of the genos Salaminioi, the Heptaphylai and the Sounioi. They record as well enough additional information concerning the duties of the Salaminioi and the cults with which they were associated to warrant Ferguson's thorough discussion of this interesting genos.

Besides the obvious mythological ties, a physical connection between the Salaminioi and Eurysakes was already known: II^2 1232 (another decree of the Salaminioi, fin. s. IV) is to be set up in the Eurysakeion. Although Ferguson's two decrees do not record where they are to be set up, #61 does, thus all three were taken for reuse from the Eurysakeion (Ferguson, 1). Not only do these two new decrees confirm that the Eurysakeion was the headquarters of the Salaminioi (Ferguson, 16), no. 1 also records that the Salaminioi provided the priest for

Eurysakes. And this decree, #61, confirms that the Eurysakeion was the headquarters of the tribe Aiantis as well.

The location and description is known from the ancient sources: the Eurysakeion was a temenos with an altar on the Kolonos Agoraios in the deme Melete (Ferguson, 16, who also notes the convenience, both for genos and tribe, of having this sanctuary in the city of Athens).

The honorand, Teleskopos, is listed by Kirchner as _PA_ 13567; Meritt adds that he is the grandfather of an ephebe of the same name (II^2 665 line 55 - 269/8). More is known about the man who proposed the decree, Demokrates, son of Demokles, of the deme Aphidnai (_PA_ 3521; _APF_ 12267IV). Meritt offers a short commentary; Davies, _APF_ goes into a more detailed prosopography of the entire family. Both Meritt and Davies note that the ancient sources describe Demokrates as "old" at the time of Chaironeia. That would make him even older in 327/6. (Davies, 476, estimates an age of 70 at Chaironeia and suggests that Demokrates died soon after proposing this decree.) This information reveals another instance, on the deme level, of an "elderly tinge" to the leadership of Lykourgan Athens (see discussions in #50, #56 for Lewis's hypothesis).

This is the first instance in this corpus of a tribal decree (#65 - II^2 1157 of the tribe Pandionis is the other). The format is similar to that of the deme decrees (see #26 for list of deme decrees in this Corpus): the only notice of the date is at the end of the decree where the officials responsible for erecting the stele are designated by the name of the archon in whose year they officiated. For this decree the officials are the epimeletes of the tribe Aiantis, τοὺς ἐφ' Ἡγήμονος ἄρχοντος.

327/6

62. *DECREE* EM 7169

editors: Pittakis ΕΦ. (1837/39) 83; Rangabé (1855) 421; Velsen & Koehler II 175; II[2] 358; Meritt Hesperia 32 (1963) 435-437 (reprinted in SEG 21.236).

supplements: SEG 21.326 (Dinsmoor; Pritchett-Meritt; Pritchett-Neugebauer; Meritt Ath., Hesperia 32(1963), Hesperia 33(1964); Dow Hesperia, HSCP; Mitchel Phoenix; Bousquet). Bull. (1965) no. 138 (Dow).

other bibliography: Unger Att. Arch. 673; Wilhelm Berl. phil. Woch. (1902) 1097; UDA 231; Dinsmoor Archons 357; Kirchner Gnomen 8(1932) 451; Meritt Hesperia 4(1935) 532; Ath. 84-85; Hesperia 33(1964) 13-15; GRBS 17(1976) 152; Pritchett-Meritt Chron. 6; Pritchett-Neugebauer Cal. 48; Bosquet BCH 81(1957) 492 n. 2; Dow Hesperia 32(1963) 342; HSCP 67(1963) 56-60; Mitchel Phoenix 18 (1964) 14-15 n. 6.

description: This fragment of Pentelic marble was found on the Akropolis, April 2, 1839. Only the right side is preserved. The preservation of a cymation and fillet (upon which the first line is inscribed) suggests that either a pediment or relief topped the stele.

dimensions:
H 0.22 m. (entire)
0.185 m. (surface)
W 0.17 m.
Th 0.075 m.

letters: 0.006 m. Smallest, E, Λ, M, X, are .0055; largest, Σ, T, are .007.

minuscule text: next page.

commentary: The text is based on Meritt's text in Hesperia 32 (1963); which is based on the suggestions and partial restoration by Dow in HSCP. The stoichedon order is 35 letters to the line, except for line 1. Until Dow dated it to 307/6, this decree has always been assumed to be Lykourgan. Although Velsen suggested the year of Aristophanes, 331/0, Koehler did not restore the archon's name. Kirchner based his restoration of Hegemon as archon, 327/6, on Unger's and Wilhelm's work. Dinsmoor dated this "peculiar decree" (p. 357) to the year of Nikokrates, 333/2 (despite some irregularities in the restoration) because of the calendar difficulties in 327/6. Dinsmoor's date was accepted by all the authorities cited above until Dow, HSCP, reviewed the previous scholarship, noted the irregularities, and by careful measurement of the letters and stone found that only the archon and secretary of the year 307/6 fit the required spaces.

stoich. 35

[Ἐπὶ Ἀναξικράτου]ς ἄρχο[ντος],
[ἐπὶ τῆς Ἱπποθωντίδος δεκά]της πρυτανείας ἧι
[Λυσίας Νοθίππου Διομεε]ὺς ἐγραμμάτευεν· Ἐ-
[λαφηβολιῶνος ἕνηι καὶ ν]έαι ἐμβολίμωι, πέμ-
[πτηι καὶ εἰκοστῆι τῆς πρ]υτανείας· ἐκκλησί-
[α· τῶν προέδρων ἐπεψήφιζ]ε[ν] Φανόμαχος Αἰω[ν]-
[ος Κυδαθηναιεὺς· ἔδοξεν] τῶι δήμωι· vacat
..........21........... νος Κυδαθηναιεύ-
[ς εἶπεν· ἐπειδὴ καὶ νῦν καὶ] ἐν τῶι ἔμπροσθεν
[χρόνωι ....8.... καὶ ὁ πατὴ]ρ αὐτοῦ Κυδρίων
[.........20......... το]ῦ δήμου τοῦ Ἀθην-
[αίων ......14....... πράτ]τοντες ἀγαθόν.
[........16....... τὸ κοινὸ]ν τῶν Αἰτωλῶν ὑ-
[..........22.......... κ]αὶ βουλαρχησα-
..........23............θον παρελθεῖν
[..........23........... τ]ετιμήκασιν σ-
- -

(Dow, in his Hesperia article of the same year, showed that the omission of the symproedroi no longer required a date before 318/7). Meritt, after describing Dow's work on this decree as his "most noteworthy achievement"; proceeded to restore the tribe and number of the prytany, albeit by assuming an irregularity in the stoichedon order in line 2 (Hesperia 32 [1963]) and the "major postponement of twelve days in Elaphebolion" which he justifies by noting that in this year the new tribes Antigonis and Demetrias were added to the original ten (Hesperia 33 [1964]). In GRBS, he states again that II^2 358 "is properly assigned to 307/6."

Most of the scholarship of this decree has been concerned with the restoration of the proper date. This decree, however, illustrates the necessity for that type of intricate scholarship discussed in the commentary above because it does provide more information than just the calendric prescript. The information is incomplete but there is notice of an "earlier time;" a father and his son, the presumed honorand, Kydrion; and the Aitolian League.

The decree was still dated to 333/2 when Bosquet discussed the historical context. Mitchel comments on the historical implications which result from the move to 307/6.

XIII. THE YEAR OF CHREMES, 326/5

63. *DECREE* EM 7088

photo: *EΦ.* (1898) Plate 1 (lower right).

editors: Kabbadias *EΦ.* (1898) 7 no. 2; Maltezos *EΦ.* (1908) 315-318 no. 1; *IG* II^2 359.

testimonia: Aischines 3.66-67.

other bibliography: Dinsmoor *Archons* 372; Pritchett-Neugebauer *Cal.* 54; Herz & Pritchett *AJA* 57(1953) 71-83; Meritt *Ath.* 7, 101-102; Rhodes *Boule* 55, 166-167, 227, 231-232, 234; Mikalson *Year* 124-125, 191; Hansen *GRBS* 17 (1976) 115-134; *CP* 74(1979) 43-49; Walsh *ZPE* 41(1981) 107-124.

description: The fragment was found in 1897 in the ruins of a building on the north slope of the Akropolis near the cave of Apollo. Only the left side is preserved. The stone was described by Kabbadias and Kirchner as Pentelic; a more apt description would be "grey" (cf. Herz & Pritchett).

dimensions:	letters: 0.011 m. Smallest,
H 0.16 m.	Λ, is.007; largest, Y, is .013.
W 0.24 m.	O, I, are .008; E, M, X, are
Th 0.11 m.	.009; E, H, K, T, are .010; Σ,
	P, are .011; Y in line 1 is .015.

minuscule text: next page.

commentary: Two letters, no longer clear, are dotted. The stoichedon order of 20 letters to the line was established by Kabbadias when he restored lines 2-3, 7-8. There is one violation--line 6 is restored with 21 letters; the last two, epsilon and iota, were probably crowded into the last stoichos.

Kabbadias read the last letter on the stone in line 5 (st. 12) as a kappa and restored ὀγδόηι κ[αὶ δεκάτηι], the 18th, as the date in the month. Maltezos (who is responsible for the remaining restorations, lines 3, 4, 5) noted that a stoichedon order of 20 letters allowed only the ordinals 5th, 7th, and 10th to be restored in line 3 as the number of the prytany, and that the combination of the 18th of the month with the 30th day in the prytany for either 5th, 7th, or 10th prytanies fit neither an ordinary nor an intercalary year. The problem disappeared when Maltezos read (correctly) an iota rather than a kappa in st. 12 of line 5 and gave the only restoration: ὀγδόηι ἱ[σταμένου], the 8th day of the month. Maltezos' reading is supported by the original photograph, by a squeeze, and by my own observation. The equation is normal for an ordinary year: [Elaphebol]ion 8 = Prytany [VII] 30 = 244th day.

stoich. 20

[Α]ΣΤΥ - - - - -
Ἐ̣πὶ Χρέμητο[ϲ ἄρχοντοϲ ἐ]-
πὶ τῆϲ Ἐρεχθη[ΐδοϲ ἑβδόμ]-
ηϲ πρυτανείαϲ· [Ἐλαφηβολ]-
[ι]ῶνοϲ ὀγ̣δόηι ἱ[ϲταμένου],
[τ]ριακοϲτῆι τῆ[ϲ πρυτανε̣ί]-
[αϲ]· ἐκκληϲία κυ[ρία· τῶν πρ]-
[οέδρω]ν ἐπεψή[φιζε - - - -]

This is the *only* restoration which fits the text remaining on the stone. In fact, Meritt (*Ath.* 7) uses this decree as his "sample" to illustrate the relationship between the festival and conciliar years, and notes that the "restorations are unique for the equation given in lines 4-7."

Mikalson, however, objects to this restoration because Elaphebolion 8 is a festival day, devoted to Asklepios as well as being the Proagon for the City Dionysia. Aischines criticized Demosthenes for having called a meeting of the ekklesia on this festival day in 346/5 (3.66-67). Since Mikalson emphasizes Aischines's contention that such a thing just was not done, he finds the "widespread acceptance of this restoration rather surprising" (citing Dinsmoor, Pritchett-Neugebauer, Meritt; 124). Aischines's protest, on the other hand, is absolute proof that a meeting of the ekklesia *could* coincide with a festival day and more specifically that, at least in 346/5, a meeting _was_ held on Elaphebolion 8 despite its being a festival day. As Mikalson points out (123), if this practice had been illegal, Aischines would have jumped at the chance to accuse Demosthenes of _asebeia_ (impiety) or _paranomia_ (illegality). As it was, Aischines could only protest on the grounds of convention or tradition.

There is nothing, however, to indicate that on Elaphebolion 8, 326/5, there was anything like the crisis which confronted the Demos just twenty years before. Line 1 suggests that routine business was being conducted -- an honorary decree for an individual or perhaps an ambassador. The mason, on the other hand, did record that the meeting was a _kyria ekklesia_ (even if this was an error, see #67, commentary), and this implies that it was a regularly scheduled meeting, perhaps even a well publicized one. Is it possible that the whole of Elaphebolion 8 was not considered a festival day and that, since the festival preliminaries did not begin until the late afternoon or evening, the morning hours were available for meetings?

An affirmative answer is suggested by Deubner's examination of the City Dionysia (138-142, esp. the concluding paragraph). On the evening of the 8th the statue of Dionysos was brought into his temple by the theater from his sanctuary in the Academy by torchlight. This was preceded by the introduction of the poets and actors (the Proagon) and by a sacrifice to Asklepios, whose sanctuary was contiguous with that of Dionysos. The festival proper (das eigentlich Fest) began on the morning of the 9th with the grand procession of _phalloi_, _kanephorai_, and probably the boy's and men's choruses whose competitive performances filled the rest of the day, which ended appropriately in the evening with a _komos_. The 10th was devoted to comedies and the 11th-13th to tragedies. The 14th was again a regular day, open for profane business.

Although Mikalson argues (probably correctly, 125) that the 10th was the first day of the festival, the date for the Proagon is fixed by Aischines to the 8th--whether the "festival proper" runs from the 9th to the 13th or 10th to the 14th. And, at least on the 8th day of Elaphebolion in 346/5 (from Aischines) and 326/5 (from II^2 359), as Hansen so simply states: "We must accordingly assume that one day was sufficient time for a meeting of the assembly, the sacrifice to Asclepius, and the _proagon_ of the Greater Dionysia. The _ecclesia_ cannot have filled more than a part of the day" (_CP_ 44). Hansen is arguing that the evidence shows that meetings of the ekklesia did not have to last all day; I am arguing that the character of the festivities must be taken into account. And both these aspects must be considered before immediately dismissing otherwise reasonable restorations because they conflict with a festival day (see #51 for notice of the seven Lykourgan decrees which Mikalson considers "doubtful").

Thus it is reasonable to assume that the morning of Elaphebolion 8 was not considered a festival day and therefore Demosthenes was not even defying "convention" when he called a meeting for this day. Further tangible support for allowing the accepted date of #63 to stand as it is the simple fact that it is the only restoration which fits the letters on the stone. The only other remote possibility requires reading the clear iota in line 5 st. 12 as a phi in angled brackets. This assumes that the cutter inscribed the upright and went on to the following letters which have straight strokes, intending to return to st. 12 to cut the phi's circle; having failed to do this, he painted the circle, and the paint has completely disappeared. In that case the following restoration would fit what remains on the stone and also give a calendar equation which at first sight seems acceptable:

2 Ἐπὶ Χρέμητο[c ἄρχοντοc ἐ]-
πὶ τῆc Ἐρεχθη[ίδοc δεκάτ]-
ηc πρυτανείαc [Σκιροφορ]-
5 [ι]ῶνοc ὀγδόηι <φ>[θίνοντοc]
[τ]ριακοcτῆι τῆ[c πρυτανεί]-
[αc]·

This restoration, though possible, is nevertheless far from satisfactory and ultimately must be rejected in favor of Maltezos's. First, it is based on the dubious assumption of a stonecutter's error in the case of a clearly surviving letter. Secondly, the calendar equation produces an anomaly for this Corpus: the 30th of Prytany X, even if it ran to 36 days (which it would have to do to fill out the 354 days of the lunar year), demands that Skirophorion be a hollow month; this in turn requires that the ommitted day in the last decade of the hollow month be δευτέρα φθίνοντοc (as in the chart on next page).

In this Corpus it has been assumed throughout (see #15 for full discussion), that the omitted day of the last decade of a hollow month is at the beginning of the 20's, as in ἐνάτηι φθίνοντοc, not at the end, δευτέρα φθίνοντος (Walsh confirms this, see comm., #29). Although the omission of δευτέρα φθίνοντος would fit according to Pritchett's interpretation, the fact that Prytany X would run to 36 days would not. Therefore the alternate restoration should be rejected in favor of Maltezos's, and it should be admitted as fact that there was no legal restriction on meetings of the ekklesia on (the morning of) Elaphebolion 8, neither in 346/5, nor 326/5, nor in any other year.

YEAR	PRYTANY (X)	MONTH (Skirophorion)
348th day	30	23 ὀγδόηι φθίνοντος
349th day	31	24 ἑβδόμηι φθίνοντος
350th day	32	25 ἕκτηι φθίνοντος
351st day	33	26 πέμπτηι φθίνοντος
352nd day	34	27 τετρὰς φθίνοντος
353rd day	35	28 τρίτηι φθίνοντος
354th day	36	29 ἕνηι καὶ νέαι

Nothing remains of the actual content of this decree. It is possible to suggest, however, on the basis of the preserved letters of the heading and the way the stone is broken at the top, that the decree bestowed honors, perhaps proxeny, on a foreigner. The stone is preserved at the back approximately 6 centimeters above the beginning of the text and could have contained at least two more lines of letters the size of ΣΤΥ of the heading, which are twice the size of the letters of the decree and more widely spaced. Kabbadias made the sure restoration [Α]ΣΤΥ- - and pointed out that names beginning with this element are common; PA has ten and eleven more can be gleaned from Bechtel.

Although it is not impossible that the honorand's name appeared singly and in the nominative, it is more common to have name and patronymic, plus demotic or ethnic. Since no demotic begins with ΑΣΤΥ-, one can suggest the ethnic Α]ΣΤΥ[ΠΑΛΑΙΕΥΣ] or Α]ΣΤΥ[ΠΑΛΑΕΩΣ] which would fit nicely the restored space; the first 6 letters end precisely over the space between the 10th and 11th stoichoi of the text, thus leaving equal room for the final six letters of the heading. Astypalaia had probably been at some point a member of the Second Athenian League along with other Doric islands of the southern Aegean: Melos, Kimolos, Pholegandros, Thera and Anaphe (S. Accame, Lega, 82). Thus our hypothetical Astypalaian may have been an ambassador, or perhaps another shipowner who had been prompt and/or generous in bringing grain to Athens during the shortage.

If the date, Elaphebolion 8, is accepted, the inscription is the second example from the Lykourgan period of a meeting of the assembly on what has been recognized as a festival day. Not only that, but it was also a kyria ekklesia, a term which is usually interpreted to designate the most important of the four meetings each prytany, the one for which the citizens received pay at the rate of time and a half. Since #63 records a kyria ekklesia on the 30th day of the [7th] prytany, it poses a special problem for the restoration of #67 (II^2 363) which will be discussed in the commentary on that inscription at the end of 326/5.

326/5

64. *DECREE* EM 2706

photo: Hesperia 32(1963) Plate 84 (stone and squeeze).

editors: Kirchner IG II^2 800; Dow Hesperia 32(1963) 358-363.

supplement: SEG 21.289 (Dow and Dow's text).

description: Only the right side and back of this fragment of Hymettan marble is preserved. The find-spot is unknown. As Dow's photograph shows, the letters are poorly cut.

dimensions:
H 0.18 m.
W 0.109 m.
Th 0.09 m.

letters: 0.006. Letter sizes are not consistent. All of the letters in lines 11 and 12 are smaller than the rest of the text.

minuscule text:

c. 29 non stoich. (1-5)
stoich. (6-12)

[επὶ - - ca. 9 - - - ἄρχοντος ἐπὶ τῆ]c Λεων-
[τίδοc ἕκτηc? πρυτανείαc ἧι Κη]φιcοκλ- v
[ῆc - - - ca. 15 1/2 - - - ἐγρα]μμάτευεν
[- - - - - - - Date: ca. 21 - - - - - - -] ἐκκληcία
[τῶν προέδρων ἐπεψήφιζεν Θε]όπομποc
[- ca. 8?: Demotic: cυνπρόεδροι - ca. 3? -]μένηc Λ[α]-
[μπτρεύc: ca. 9: Name - - Παια]νιεύc: Δημ.
ca. 19
[- - - Demotic: Name - ᾿Ο?]ῆθεν: Θεοκλ-
[ῆc Demotic ca. 14 - Name - Αναφ]λύcτιοc vv
ca. 20
[Name Demotic - - - : - Name - - Σ]φήττιοc ἔ-
[δοξεν τῶι δήμωι Name ca. 8 -]τόρου Συ[$\frac{β}{π}$]-
[ρίδηc / αλήττιοc εἶπεν ἐπειδὴ ca. 6-3]λεωc ...

commentary: The text is based on Dow's. Kirchner published this fragment as II^2 800; dated it to the middle of the third century (when Athens had 12 tribes); and noted that the list of symproedroi was out of order. Dow (359 and n. 3) records mention made of this decree, which chiefly concerns the symproedroi, since its publication. As for [62], Dow's new text is based on careful measurement and consideration of the physical aspects of the stone as well as new readings which I confirm. Differences in readings and thus some restorations between Kirchner's text and Dow's are recorded below.

The photograph of Dow's squeeze with vertical lines drawn in shows that lines 5-12 were inscribed in stoichedon order. Even though the first 4 lines are non-stoichedon, a length of c. 29 letters can be established for them as well and thus the approximate length of the archon's name can be determined. As his dates show, there are a number of possibilities. The year 326/5, with archon Χρέμητος, 8 letters, "is certainly a strong contender" (363).

Kirchner's text ended (in line 12) with the last of the ten recorded symproedroi. Dow's new reading of epsilon at the end of line 10 and the observation that patronymics are never included in the list of symproedroi (τόρου, line 11) led him to assume that the last two lines record the name of the mover and the honorand (?). Thus the listing of only 8 symproedroi would place this decree in the time of the ten tribes, before 307/6. Although Dow has been able to bring a bit more order than in Kirchner's text to the list of symproedroi, the list still cannot be made to conform to the usual order of the tribes. It is this fact that leads Dow to the conclusion: "it seems best at present to admit a preference for 326/5 as the date of I. G., II^2, 800, and to conceive that at this early time, when the practice of listing Symproedroi had only begun, carelessness in the order was more natural than later " (363).

1 end: τῆς] Λεων- Ki.

2 mid: Ki. did not restore number of prytany.
end: Κηφ]ισοκλ- Ki.

3 end: ἐγραμ]μάτ[ευ]εν· Ki.

6 end: Λ- - Ki.

7 end: Εὐξίδημ[ος] Ki.

8 end: ῆθεν· Θεοκλ[ῆς] Ki.

9 end: 'Αναφλ]ύστιος, vacat Ki.

10 end: Σ]φήττιος, Ki.

11/12: τ̣όρου Συ[πα]/λήττιος, - - -] Ki.

As the commentary shows, the date for this decree can not be determined absolutely. Since the stone breaks off at the end of the prescript, there is no content to be dated. However, the likely restoration of the archon Chremes adds further confirmation that listing of symproedroi could occur in the Lykourgan Era and that stonecutters could turn out sloppy work even before Demetrios of Phaleron passed his sumptuary laws at the end of the century.

326/5

65. *THE TRIBE PANDIONIS HONORS THEIR CHOREGOS* EM 7703

editors: Koehler <u>IG</u> II 5.563c; <u>IG</u> II^2 1157.

description: This fragment of Pentelic marble was found on the Akropolis. The left side is preserved although only a part of the surface extends that far. The right side, top and bottom are broken; the back may be original.

dimensions:	letters: 0.006 m. Smallest, Ω, is .004; largest, Φ, is .009. A, Δ, E, Π, are .005; H, Σ, are .006; P is .007.
H 0.185 m.	
W 0.160 m.	
Th 0.081 m.	

majuscule text: next page.

epigraphical commentary: The letters read by Koehler (maj. text) and Kirchner, but no longer visible, are underlined. There are also a number of letters which should be dotted as unclear. Since Koehler included a majuscule text to show what he saw, he bracketed unclear letters in his minuscule text. When Kirchner published this decree as II^2 1157, he took most of the letters for which Koehler had shown only partial strokes (exceptions are st. 10 line 9, st. 12 line 11, st. 5 line 13, st. 7, 9, line 14) out of brackets and read them as clear, i.e., there are no dotted letters in Kirchner's text. Thus, with the exception of letters in st. 8, 9 line 6, st. 3 line 8, st. 10 line 11 (which Koehler read clearly) Koehler would also have dotted the letters which Kirchner printed as clear, but which I have dotted.

. . . . Y̲ K Y Δ A Θ̣ .
. . . . X . P H Γ̣ O Σ .
. . . .$_{\text{H}}$O Σ K A Λ Ω Σ Ḳ
. . . . . Σ E N T H I Π Ạ Ṇ
. . . . N Δ P Ω N E Ψ H Φ .
. . Ạ I Σ E Π Ạ Ị N E Σ A .
. O Δ Ω P O Y K Y Δ A Θ H .
Φ A Ṇ Ω Σ A I̲ X P Y Σ Ω I .
𐅄 : Δ P A X Ṃ Ω N Ạ P E . .
Λ O T I M . . Σ T H Σ . . .
Δ̣ A̲ Φ Y Λ H Ṇ A N̲ Ạ Γ P . .
H Φ I . M A T O Ỵ Σ E Π . .
Π̣ I X . . M . T O Σ A P . .
. Λ̣ I Θ I N̲ Ḥ I Ḳ Ạ I Σ . .
. . . O Y Π A̲ N Δ Ị . . . .
. . Ị . . E ‾ ı . . . . . .

Despite the poor condition of the stone, I was able to add a few new readings. Although both Koehler and Kirchner ended this text at line 15, immediately below that line there is a sure epsilon (visible on the photograph) and traces of 3 other letters.

3 st. 14 new reading.

4 st. 14 new reading.

6 st. 3 new reading.

7 st. 2 new reading.

8 st. 1 Ψ Koe. (maj. text).

9 st. 7 new reading.

11 st. 1 new reading.
st. 12 ı Koe.

14 st. 2 new reading.
st. 7 new reading. ι Koe.
st. 9 new reading. ι Koe.

16 new reading.

minuscule test:

stoich. 25

[..οδῶρο]ụ Κυδαθ[ηναιεὺϲ καταϲ]-
[ταθεὶϲ] χ[ο]ρη̣γὸϲ [ἐπὶ Χρέμητοϲ v]-
[ἄρχοντ]οϲ καλῶϲ κ̣[αὶ φιλοτίμωϲ]
[ἐχορήγ]ηϲεν τῆι Παν̣[διονίδι νική]-
[ϲαϲ ἀ]νδρῶν, ἐψηφ[ίϲθαι τοῖϲ φυλ]-
[έτ]αιϲ ἐπα̣ι̣νέϲα[ι .....11....]
.οδῶρου Κυδαθη[ναιέα καὶ ϲτε- v]
φαν̣ῶϲαι χρυϲῶι [ϲτεφάνωι ἀπὸ v]
ΠΗ : δραχμ̣ῶν ἀ̣ρε[τῆϲ ἕνεκα καὶ φι]-
λοτιμ[ία]ϲ τῆϲ [εἰϲ τὴν Πανδιονί]-
δ̣α̲ φυλὴ̣ν. ἀ̣ν̲αγρ[άψαι δὲ τόδε τὸ ψ]-
ήφι[ϲ]μα τοὺϲ ἐπ[ιμελητὰϲ τοὺϲ ἐ]-
π̣ὶ Χ[ρέ]μ̣[η]τοϲ ἄρ[χοντοϲ ἐν ϲτήλη]-
[ι] λ̣ιθί̣ν̲ηι κ̣α̣ὶ ϲ[τῆϲαι ἐν τῶι ἱερ]-
[ῶι τ]οῦ Πανδ̣ί[ονοϲ].
..Ị..Ε⁻ι........17.........

commentary: The restorations are Koehler's. Koehler also established the stoichedon order of 25 letters to the line. I have printed a vacat at the end of lines 2, 7, and 8 to show that those lines have only 24 letters. Although the restoration in line 4 requires 27 letters, the presence of an eta between lines 3 and 4 led Koehler to presume that the stonecutter had originally omitted the gamma and 2nd eta of ἐχορήγησεν, then added those letters later above line 4. Thus line four had the normal 25 letters.

Although the new readings do not require any changes in Koehler's restorations, they do offer a bit more information. The man honored is now --οδώρου, rather than ---δώρου. And the presence of letters in line 16 suggests either: further directions for the erection of the stele (perhaps who was to pay for it?); or, if a vacat of 11 stoichoi at the end of line 15 were restored, the beginning of an additional decree.

This decree of the tribe Pandionis honors a man from the deme Kydathenaion. He is to be awarded a gold crown worth 500 drachmai because he fulfilled his duties as choregos so well that the men's chorus of Pandionis won. The epimeletai are to have the stele engraved and set up in the sanctuary of Pandion.

There are only 33 tribal decrees listed by Kirchner. They date from 403/2 to the second century B.C. Of the 23 decrees for which the specific tribe is preserved or restored, 10 are from the tribe Pandionis. All 10 were found on or around the Akropolis as were the 6 decrees of the tribe Kekropis and the 4 decrees of the tribe Erechtheis. It can be no coincidence that the eponymous heroes of the three tribes with the most decrees extant were worshipped on the Akropolis, the most thoroughly excavated site in Attica. (The headquarters for the tribe Aiantis is now known--the Eurysakeion, located on the Kolonos Agoraios below the Akropolis [see discussion, #61]. There are, however, only 2 decrees from this tribe extant: II^2 1151 and the only other tribal decree in this Corpus, #61.)

326/5

66. *THE DEME AIXONE HONORS TWO CHOREGOI*

EM 139

editors: Rusopolos <u>BdI</u> (1864) 131; <u>IG</u> II 579; <u>IG</u> II^2 1198.

collection: Michel 151.

other bibliography: Lolling AM 4(1879) 199; Haussoullier Vie Mun. 171,213; Michelhoefer AM 13(1888) 358.

description: The two fragments of Pentelic marble are now joined. Since they were found in the village of Trachones, Michelhoefer was able to establish this place as the site of the ancient deme Aixone. The top, sides, and rough-picked back are preserved; the stele is broken at the bottom.

dimensions:
H 0.51 m.
W 0.315 m.
Th 0.73 m.

letters: 0.008 m. Smallest, Ω, is .005; largest, Φ, is .001. E, N, P, Σ, are .008; M, Π, T, X, are .006.

minuscule text: next page.

commentary: Since the text is virtually complete on the stone, very few restorations were necessary. The only additional restoration since Rusopolos's original minuscule text is the name of the mover in line 1, supplied by Koehler.

There are, however, a number of places where the readings differ. In line 3, only Kirchner included the omitted οι (in parentheses). The amount of drachmai in line 10 takes up only 3 stoichoi, as Rusopolos indicated: ..(; Koehler left the amount blank; Kirchner used Premerstein's reading: Π ι ι////. I can read the pi, st. 11; none of the vertical strokes (which would take up st. 12); and although at first glance, a circular stroke (as in Rusopolos's reading) even appears on the photograph, I read a colon in st. 13. Only Kirchner read the colon at the end of line 16 and the epsilon in line 28; yet he bracketed the omicrons in st. 6 line 19 and st. 9 line 22, which Rusopolos and Koehler read clearly. A sure alpha at the end on line 23 can be read even on the photograph--both Rusopolos and Koehler indicated the stonecutter's error.

This decree of the deme Aixone was proposed by Philoktemon, son of Chremes. It honors the two men, Demokrates son of Euphiletos and Hegesias son of Lysistratos, who performed their duties as choregoi (when Chremes was archon) well and with distinction. They are each to be awarded a gold crown (worth 8 drachmai if Premerstein's reading is correct).

stoich. 19

[Φιλ]οκτήμων Χρέμητο[ϲ]
εἶπεν· ἐπειδὴ οἱ χορηγ-
οὶ (οἱ) ἐπὶ Χρέμητοϲ ἄρχοντ-
οϲ Δημοκράτηϲ Εὐφιλήτ-
ου καὶ Ἡγηϲίαϲ Λυϲιϲτρ-
άτου καλῶϲ καὶ φιλοτίμ-
ωϲ ἐχορήγηϲαν Αἰξωνεῦ-
ϲιν, ἐπαινέϲαι αὐτοὺϲ κ-
αὶ ϲτεφανῶϲαι χρυϲῶι ϲ-
τεφάνωι ἀπὸ Π[III] : δραχμῶ-
ν ἑκάτερον φιλοτιμίαϲ
ἕνεκα καὶ ἐπιμελείαϲ τ-
ῆϲ εἰϲ τοὺϲ δημόταϲ· δοῦ-
ναι δὲ αὐτοῖϲ καὶ εἰϲ θυ-
[ϲ]ίαν τὸν δήμαρχον Δωρό-
[θε]ον καὶ τοὺϲ ταμίαϲ : Δ
[δ]ραχμὰϲ ἀπὸ τῆϲ προϲόδ-
ου τῶν δημοτῶν. ἀναγράψ-
αι δὲ τ[ό]δε τὸ ψήφιϲμα τὸ-
ν δήμαρχον Δωρόθεον εἰ-
ϲ ϲτήλην [λ]ιθίνην καὶ ϲτ-
ῆϲαι εἰϲ τ[ὸ] θέατρον, ὅπω-
ϲ ἂν εἰδῶϲιν οἱ ἀεὶ μέλλ-
οντεϲ χορηγεῖν Αἰξωνε-
ῦϲι ὅτι τιμήϲει αὐτοὺϲ
ὁ δῆμοϲ ὁ Αἰξωνέων τοὺϲ
εἰϲ ἑαυτοὺϲ φιλοτιμου-
[μ]ένουϲ. vacat

vacat

The demarch, Dorotheos, and the treasurer are alloted ten drachmai from the deme's revenues to make a sacrifice. Dorotheos is also to have the stele engraved and set up in the theater so that it is known that the deme Aixone will always honor those choregoi who fulfill their duties with zeal.

This decree marks the second instance of honors bestowed upon choregoi from this year, 326/5. The tribe Pandionis honored their choregos in #65; the deme Aixone honors their choregoi in this decree. Here again is another example of the same type of actions proposed by Lykourgos (and others) on the state level filtering down to the tribal and deme level (see #43 for a parallel in religious matters).

IG II^2 1196 is another decree from the deme Aixone. The first editor, Lolling, based his restoration on the demarch as Δωρ[όθεον (line 4) on lines 15/16 and 20 of this decree and dated II^2 1196 to the same year, 326/5. Kirchner, however, followed Dittenberger and Koehler and dated II^2 1196 to c. 335-330.

326/5 ?

67. *ATHENS HONORS DIONYSIOS (of Herakleia?)* EM 7628, 7626

photos: Hesperia 10(1941) page 48 (the fragments are mislabeled and misplaced; the photo which is labeled fragment a is actually Kirchner's fragment b, the right-hand fragment; and vice versa); AACS Plate 23a (upper part of fragment b); Phoenix 23(1969) Plate 1.

editors: Lolling in Kirchhoff's "Inschriften von der Akropolis" Sitz. Ak. Berlin (1887) 1073 (separate majuscule texts); IG II.5, 492e and II.5, 492f; IG II^2 363 (from Wilhelm's notes); Meritt Hesperia 10(1941) 48-49.

supplements: SEG 12.89 (Oikonomides & Koumanoudis);

21.281 (Meritt Hesperia, Ath., Pritchett-Neugebauer, Pritchett AACS); 23.53 (Pritchett AACS, Meritt TAPA); 25.66 (Pritchett Phoenix).

Bull. (1944) no. 58 (Meritt Hesperia, Dow Prytaneis).

other bibliography: Schweigert Hesperia 8(1939) 33-34; Pritchett-Neugebauer Cal. 54-55; Oikonomides & Koumanoudis ΠΟΛΕΜΟΝ 5(1952/53) 27; Meritt Ath. 88-89; Pritchett AACS 281-283; Meritt TAPA 95(1964) 213-217; McGregor Phoenix 20(1966) 214, n. 4; Pickard-Cambridge Festivals 1-25; Pritchett Phoenix 23(1969) 168-169; Burstein Outpost 72-80; Isager & Hansen Aspects, 200-208; Mikalson Year 190.

description: The two fragments were found on the Akropolis; they are Pentelic marble. Although there is no physical join, Lolling's association of the two fragments has never been questioned. All sides are broken, with the probable exception of a part of the lower right-hand side of Fr. B. The rough-picked back of both fragments is probably original. The surface is corroded. This corrosion is the most likely explanation for the larger than normal size variation of the letters; they could easily have been 0.007 (the usual size for this period) when carved.

dimensions:
Fr. A
H 0.17 m.
W 0.11 m.
Th 0.15 m.
Fr. B
H 0.28 m.
W 0.132 m.
Th 0.15 m.

letters: 0.009 m. Smallest, Δ, Ο, Ω, are .007; H, I, M, are .010; some P's and Σ's have corroded to .011.

majuscule text: next page.

epigraphical commentary: Two letters are underlined; they can not now be read. Any doubtful letters are dotted. There is one new reading: H, line 12 st. 18. The stoichos for the corresponding letter in the minuscule text is in parentheses in the commentary below. In order to make the line designation consistent throughout the commentary, all the texts discussed are numbered to include a restored first line. In spite of surface corrosion and careless cutting, the letters are not difficult to read, except in lines 3 and 4, where the editors have changed their readings to conform to the various dating formulas offered.

Fr. B

. . . . H . . . .
. . . . Λ̣ Γ̣ C̣ . . . . . .
. . . . ı̣ Ọ ı̣ . . . . . .
. . . . Σ Π P Y . . . . .
. . . . P̲ Ọ E Δ P Ω . . . .
. . . . Ẹ Y Σ vacat
Fr. A T Ω I Δ H M Ω . . . . T O Σ Σ Ω Σ . .
H T T I O Σ E . . . . Δ H Δ I O N . .
T E P O N T E . . . . A T O T Ω I . .
Δ Ω Σ E I N Ṭ . . . . Σ M E Δ I M N
I Δ E O I T . . . . Ḥ K E N E N
T E P . . . . Λ̣ Σ Ṭ I
O P Ị . . . . Λ̣ Ẹ .
. Λ̲ . . . .

2 st. 16, 17 (min. st. 22, 23) HỊ Mer. *TAPA*. My own examination of the stone revealed no trace of any letter where Meritt reads the dotted iota.

3 st. 16-18, (min. st. 22-24) ΑΓC Lolling, Koe. ΛΕ Wilh. in II^2 363; ΑΓΟ Mer. *Hesperia*, P.-N.; ΛΕΥ Oik.& Kou.; ΛΕΩ Mer. *Ath*.; ΑΓΟ Mer. *TAPA*.

st. 16 the horizontal mark visible in the photograph should be either the bar of the alpha or a scratch.

st. 17 the middle and lower horizontal strokes of an epsilon, which seem to appear in the photos, could also be scratches; cf. the well preserved epsilon three lines below in the same stoichos.

st. 18 the surface is flaked away at the bottom of this circular letter, but enough of the surface is preserved where the left horizontal stroke of an omega should appear, if that were the letter.

4 st. 16-18 (min. st. 22-24) NOI' Lolling, Koe; NΘE Wilh. NΘ̣Ẹ Mer. *Hesperia*, *Ath.*, *TAPA*; NO[Ψ̣ P.-N. Pritch. has suggested ṂỌỴ in *AACS* or ỊỌ in *Phoenix*.

st. 16 because of its position in the stoichos, to the right of the middle, I do not believe the letter was an iota. It could have been eta, mu, or nu. Although the upright strokes of the mu's and nu's are either vertical or tilt slightly to the right and this stroke has a slight tilt to the left, the nu seen by most of the editors can not be ruled out since the surface is worn and the cutting careless.

st. 17 there are only two choices for this letter: O or Θ̣.

st. 18 there is a stroke on the stone which could be the left-hand vertical hasta of several letters; the main problem is that the stroke seems to begin halfway down its horizontal space, on line with the mid-point of the neighboring omicron, and continues well below the line of the other two letters. Both Meritt and McGregor have stressed the effects of erosion. Since erosion usually follows the incised strokes, the straight vertical now on the stone, which is the result of weathering, suggests one of the letters which have left-hand vertical strokes.

5 st. 16-18 (min. st. 22-24) ΣΠO Lolling.

6 st. 15 (min. st. 21) Ṛ Wilh., Mer. *Hesperia*, P.-N. Mer. in *Ath.* and *TAPA* reads an undotted rho.

st. 18 (min. st. 24) Lolling read an omega.

12 st. 6 (min. st. 12) Γ Lolling, Koe., Wilh. T Mer.; the letter is definitely a tau.

st. 18 (min. st. 24) H new reading.

st. 22, 23 (min. st. 28, 29) .N Lolling.

st. 17-23 (min. st. 23-29) ΔΩKEN. Oik.&Kou. They have read a delta where no one else has seen anything, an omega where I can see two vertical strokes, and they bracket the last two letters--epsilon, nu--which I can read, along with most of the previous editors.

In the text of II^2 363 this line is off one stoichos (cf. #21 for a similar error resulting from Ki.'s dependence on Wilh.'s notes); there should be six letter spaces rather than five before the first letters on the stone, IΔE.

13 st. 1-4 (min. st. 7-10) TEP/ Lolling.

14 end ΛE Lolling. AΓ Wilh.; ΔE Mer.

minuscule text:

stoich. 29

[- - - - - - - - - - - - - - - - -]
..........21..........Η...7....
..........21.........ΑΓ̣Ο̣..5..
..........21..........Ν̣Θ̣Ε̣..5..
[..........19.......... τῆ]ς πρυ[τανε]-
[ίας· ἐκκλησία κυρία· τῶν π[ρ̣οέδρω[ν ἐπ]-
[εψήφιζεν ......13......]εύς vacat
[ἔδοξεν] τῶι δήμω[ι· Πολύευκ]τος Σω[στρ]-
[άτου Σφ]ήττιος ε[ἶπεν· ἐπει]δὴ Διον[ύσ]-
[ιος πρό]τερόν τε [ἐπηγγείλ]ατο τῶι [δή]-
[μωι ἐπι]δώσειν τ[ρισχιλίου]ς μεδίμν-
[ους εἴ τ]ι δέοιτ[ο ....10....]Η̣ΚΕΝ ἐν
[τῆι προ]τέρ[αι σπανοσιτίαι ....]ΛΣΤ̣Ι
....6..ΟΡΙ̣.........17........Δ̣Ε.
...7...Λ - - - - - - - - - - - - - - -

commentary: Wilhelm established the stoichedon order of 29 letters to the line, and offered the first substantial restorations. Schweigert restored the name of the mover, Polyeuktos. The restoration at the beginning of line 12 is Meritt's, Hesperia; Wilhelm's restoration [ους ἔτ]ι δὲ οἱ π and that of Oikonomides and Koumanoudis: [ους εἴ τ]ι δέοιτ[ο καὶ νῦν ἐπέ]δωκεν [ἐν] are both ruled out by readings on the stone (see ep. com., line 12). Oikonomides and Koumanoudis offer two other alternate restorations for line 13 middle, [αι πρυτανείαι; for lines 13/14, τι[μῆς καθ]ορι.

Lines 1-5 have been variously restored to record four different years within the Lykourgan period: 335/4, 331/30, 326/5, 324/3. None of the restorations is without difficulties, hence the omission of a restored dating formula in the text for #67 above. There are, however, very good reasons for keeping this decree in the year of Chremes: it remains the only year in this period for which the secretary is unknown; most important, it fits the well-established date for the grain shortage, 330 to 326. The best way to gain a perspective on the different restorations and their problems is to consider them individually; this is done in the order in which they appeared in print.

lines 2-5, date 324/3

[’Εφ’ ‘Ηγηϲίου ἄρχοντοϲ ἐπὶ τ]ῆ[ϲ ...6..]
..........21..........ΛΕ[.... ‘Ρα]-
[μνούϲιοϲ ἐγραμμάτευεν· ’Α]νθε[ϲτηρι]-
[ῶνοϲ ....15....... τῆ]ϲ πρυ[τανε]-

This is Wilhelm's restoration in II^2 363, restored on the basis of II^2 362 with the suggestion that the patronymic was omitted. The date fits historically, but the dedication, Hesperia 10(1941) 42-49 no. 11, provides the full name of the secretary for 324/3: Εὐφάνηϲ Φ[ρύ-νωνοϲ] ‘Ραμνούσιοϲ. Neither the name nor the patronymic fit any of the various readings of line 3.

lines 1-5, date 326/5

[’Επὶ Χρέμητοϲ ἄρχοντοϲ]
[ἐπὶ τῆϲ ....15.......]η[ϲ πρυταν]-
[είαϲ ἧι ....15.......]αγό[ρου ..]
[...8... ἐγραμμάτευεν· ’Α]νθ̣ε̣[ϲτηρι]-
[ῶνοϲ· ἕκτηι καὶ δεκάτηι τῆ]ϲ πρυ[τανε]-

Meritt, Hesperia 10(1941). Because of the difficulties presented by the secretary's name, Meritt moved II^2 363 to 326/5, a year for which the secretary's name is still unknown and one which is even closer to the historical context of the grain shortage. #17 (Panathenaia decree and law) and #45 (II^2 349) are parallels for the placing of the archon's name as a first line all to itself. The restoration of Anthesterion, however, requires that the concillar date be within the 7th prytany for which the kyria ekklesia on the 30th day is recorded on the stone, #63 (II^2 359). When this discrepancy was pointed out, Meritt offered the text below for 331/30; Pritchett-Neugebauer suggested not another year, but rather the restoration of the month Pyanopsion in lines 4/5:

[...6.. ἐγραμμάτευεν· Πυα]νο̣[ψιῶνοϲ]
[.........19......... τῆ]ϲ πρυ[τανε]-

which would place the date in the 3rd prytany, and thus eliminate the problem of two kyriai ekklesiai in one prytany. The scar, however, in st. 24 (min. text) resulted from erosion of the stroke of a letter (see ep. com.), which could not have been a psi. Another difficulty for this restoration, as well as for Meritt's, is that the day of the month must be omitted, and the only parallels cited by Pritchett-Neugebauer, for omitting the day (II^2 224, 228) omit the month as well.
lines 1-5, date 331/30

[ʼΕπὶ ʼΑριcτοφάνουc ἄρχοντοc]
[ἐπὶ τῆc ....10.... ἑβδόμ]η[c πρυταν]-
[εἴαc ἧι Νικόcτρατοc ʼΑρχέ]λεω̣ [ἐκ Μυρ]-
[ρινούττηc ἐγραμμάτευε· ʼΑ]ν̣θ̣ε[cτηρι]-
[ῶνοc ἑνδεκάτηι, τρίτηι τῆ]c πρυ[τανε]-

Meritt *Ath.* It is difficult to accept the reading of omega in line 3 st. 24, as has been noted in the epigraphical commentary. The nu-movable after ἐγραμμάτευε must be omitted and the name of the secretary is composite rather than attested in any documents (see *Ath.* 89f. for discussion of the name; it was subsequently rejected by Meritt himself, *TAPA*). Although Meritt refers to Dionysios's generous gift of grain during the famine, he leaves unexplained the reference to the "previous shortage" in line 13.
lines 1-5, date 335/4

[..........22.......... ἐπʼ Εὐαιν]-
[ἔτου ἄρχοντοc ἐπὶ τῆc .ι.]ηι̣[δοc πρυ]-
[τανείαc v ἧι Πρόξενοc Πυλ]αγό[ρου ʼΑχ]-
[ερδούcιοc ἐγραμμάτευε· ʼΑ]ν̣θ̣ε[cτηρι]-
[ῶνοc ἑνδεκάτει, τρίτει τῆ]c πρυ[τανε]-

Meritt *TAPA*. Although the secretary for 335/4 does fit the most likely reading on the stone (line 3, ΑΓΟ), there are other difficulties besides the obvious historical one. The vacat in line 3 has parallels, so is not very difficult to accept; but to fit the patronymic, Pylagorou, and the demotic into line 4, either the nu-movable of ἐγραμμάτευε or the upsilon in the patronymic must be sacrificed. Far more disconcerting is the placement of the archon's name, the usual beginning element of the dating formula in this period, 22 stoichoi from the left edge of the stone.

Of the restored dates offered, therefore, only the year 326/5 remains acceptable: 324/3, although historically acceptable, is definitely out; 331/30 and 335/4 are unacceptable both historically and epigraphically.

To facilitate discussion of specific problems, the following composite restoration is offered <u>exempli gratia</u>:

[Ἐπὶ Χρέμητοϲ ἄρχοντοϲ]
[ἐπὶ τῆϲ Ἐρεχθηΐδοϲ ἑβδόμ]η[ϲ πρυταν]-
[εἶαϲ ἧι ....15.......]Α̣Γ̣Ο̣ ..5..
[...8.... ἐγραμμάτευεν· Ἀ]ν̣θ̣ε̣[ϲτηρι]-
[ῶνοϲ ἑνδεκάτηι, τρίτηι τῆ]ϲ πρυ[τανε]-
[ίαϲ· ἐκκληϲία κυρία· τῶν π]ρ̣οέδρω[ν ἐπ]-

On the basis of the seven poorly preserved letters in lines 2-4, the only way to begin to restore a date is to assume (as all previous editors have) that the traces of the three letters in line 4 belong to the name of the month. The observable traces as they are represented in the majuscule text (with commentary), fit only the month Anthesterion. Anthesterion, in turn, the eighth month, suggests the restoration [ἑβδόμ]η[ϲ (seventh) in line 2 to indicate the prytany and leaves two alternatives for the restoration of the dating formula in line 5. First, it may be restored with only the day in the prytany, the 16th (omitting the day of the month as in Meritt <u>Hesperia</u>), but that is very unusual (see epig. comm., P.-N.'s alternate restoration for 326/5); or it may be restored to give both days, the 11th of Anthesterion, 3rd day of the 7th prytany (as in Meritt <u>Ath.</u>, <u>TAPA</u>): Prytany VII 3 = Anthesterion (8) 11 = 217th day.

Despite the fact that this restoration is based on only eleven poorly preserved letters, it is the only one which 1) fits what <u>is</u> left on the stone, which 2) includes all of the normal elements of the dating prescript, in proper sequence, and which 3) is acceptable historically. There are, nevertheless, two objections to this restoration. The first is that there would be two kyriai ekklesiai held in one prytany: #63, dated to the 30th day of the 7th prytany, records ἐκκληϲία κυ[ρία on the stone (line 7); this decree #67, with a date of the 3rd day of the 7th prytany, also records that the meeting was κυρία (line 6) and, although this is completely restored, it fits the 29-letter line and has never been questioned. The objection of two kyria meetings in the same prytany, raised by Pritchett-Neugebauer, led Meritt to reject his restoration for 326/5 (see comm. above). A study of kyria ekklesia, on the other hand, shows that although Aristotle and modern interpreters strongly favor the practice of only one kyria ekklesia per prytany, the sources are, in fact somewhat ambiguous and nowhere is a prohibition against more than one kyria ekklesia per prytany explicitly stated.

Some sort of error is also possible: there are 27 days between the two kyriai ekklesiai--perhaps at the end of the prytany the secretary realized that proper agenda had not been followed on the third, and so the last meeting of the prytany was designated kyria. And, since the decree of the 3rd had already been set up, no one bothered to erase κυρῖα from that stone, #63. There is no rule as to when the kyriai ekklesiai could take place. In fact, a quick examination of decrees with this designation shows: first, they could be any time in the prytany; second, slightly more than half occur after the 17th day of the prytany. And the easy way out, scribal error, cannot be excluded.

The second objection is Mikalson's. This decree (for the year 331/30) is included in his list of doubtful texts (see #35 for list; #51 for fuller discussion). Anthesterion 11 is the first day, the Pithoigia, of the Anthestereia. And since, for this festival, the days start at sunset the day before (Pickard-Cambridge, 1) there is no chance to get in a morning meeting (as in #63) nor is the Anthestereia celebrated by a small number of Athenians (as #51). So, in this case, Mikalson's objection is reasonable.

The most valid reason for rejecting a more specific date for #67 in 326/5 is the same as for any of the other restorations offered: there is so little left on the stone. Restored dates for other inscriptions in this Corpus, however, have been based on as little information, and it is because this restoration provokes still other objections that it must remain a suggested text rather than a certain one. It is because of the number of discrepancies required for the more specific restoration that the minuscule text is offered without restoration of the dating formula and it appears at the end of the decrees of the year of Chremes.

The epigraphical problems in placing this decree in the year of Chremes, 326/5, are less than for any other year in the Lykourgan Era; the historical considerations, on the other hand, are more compelling. The portion of the decree which records the honors bestowed is lost, but some of the reason for bestowing the honors remains; Dionysios had promised earlier that he would donate to the Athenian Demos three thousand medimnoi (of grain) if it should be needed (lines 9-12). Then, in line 13, an "earlier grain shortage" is mentioned, presumably establishing when the promise had been made. It can be assumed that Dionysios is being honored because he performed a service similar to that promised earlier, i.e.: he did something to benefit the Athenians during a "later grain shortage."

Meritt, in his first republication of II^2 363 (for 326/5, Hesperia 48-49), identified the Dionysios of this decree with the tyrant, Dionysios of Herakleia, mentioned in #68II (II^2 360); this latter stele, set up in 325/4 (date from #68I), honors Herakleides of Salamis for his help in securing the grain supply for Athens in 330/29 (line 31, ἐπ' Ἀριστοφῶντος ἄρχοντος). Lines 35-45 record that while transporting grain to Athens, Herakleides had been hindered by the inhabitants of Herakleia. In reaction to this harassment, the Demos voted to elect and send an ambassador to Herakleia to remonstrate with Dionysios about his treatment of ships bound for Athens (especially during a grain shortage!).

When Meritt moved II^2 363 from 326/5 to 331/30, he retained this identification of Dionysios, but, to do so, he had to assume that Dionysios had first been generous in 331/30, but in the very next year had turned around and impeded ships bound for Athens. In neither the _Hesperia_ nor the _Ath._ versions does Meritt mention the all important previous shortage, and in his final version (_TAPA_) he does not discuss the historical circumstances. Burstein (72), although he agrees with Pritchett (_AACS_) that the stone is too badly damaged to allow a restored date (137 n. 39), definitely accepts Meritt's earlier identification of Dionysios but prefers the date 335/4 of Meritt's final (_TAPA_) version for "historical considerations" on the grounds that Dionysios would not be associated with the anti-Macedonian Polyeuktos of Sphettos (the mover, lines 8/9) much later than 334. Burstein's position is weak on two accounts. First, any such strict dichotomy between pro- and anti-Macedonian factions in Lykourgan Athens did not exist (cf. Mitchel _Lyk._, 188-189); secondly, the most important "historical consideration" is the grain shortage (330-326) and the reference in this decree to "a previous shortage." In that context, the year 335/4 just does not fit.

A date _after_ the events of 330/39 however, does fit. In fact, Dionysios's earlier promise, recorded in this decree, could have been the direct result of the Athenian ambassador's visit--recorded in #68II, but undoubtedly using more diplomatic language. On that previous occasion (previous to #68I) he might have had it publicly proclaimed that he would make the donation of grain. The present decree mentions his previous goodwill toward the Demos and undoubtedly went on to mention a more recent benefaction before recording the honors and rights which the Demos would bestow on Dionysios in turn.

Burstein portrays Dionysios as a tyrant adept at diplomatic intrigue, always putting himself and his city first (72-80). Just as Athens maintained diplomatic connections by honoring helpful or potentially helpful foreigners (see discussion, #2), so Dionysios would want to become cordial with potential allies. And by 326/5, when it can be assumed the actual benefaction was given, Lykourgos's program was paying off. Athens was, once again, a factor in Greek politics.

XIV. THE YEAR OF ANTIKLES, 325/4

68. *ATHENS HONORS HERAKLEIDES OF SALAMIS*

EM 7219

photo: Lambrechts Proxenie. Plate 13.

editors: Koehler AM 8(1883) 211-219; IG II 5.179b; IG II^2 360 + Add. p. 660.

supplements: SEG 13.40 (Pritchett-Neugebauer, Peremans); 24.101 (Syll.^{3}, Lambrechts, Pečírka); 26.79 (Marchetti). Bull. (1954) no. 92 (Peremans).

collections: Ditt. Syll.^{2} 152, Syll.^{3} 304; Michel 110.

other bibliography: Drerup Neue Jahrb. (1896) 242; Wilhelm Rh. Mus. 56 (1901) 583; Dinsmoor Archons 372; Kirchner Gnomen 8(1932) 451; Meritt Hesperia 3 (1934) 536; Ath. 102-104; Pritchett-Neugebauer Cal. 55-56; Peremans AC 22 (1953) 94-97; Lambrechts Proxenie. 127, 163; Dow AJA 66(1962) 363; Pritchett AACS 323 n. 40; Pečírka Enktesis 70-72; Rhodes Boule 66-68, 72, 280; DeLaix Proboul. 129-130, 141, 178; Marchetti RBN 122(1976) 51-54.

description: This large stele of Pentelic marble was found on the Akropolis. Despite a number of erasures and subsequent crowding of letters, the text is virtually intact. A molding crowns the top of the stele. The top and back are rough-picked. The sides are preserved. Dow discusses the shape and format of the stele.

dimensions:
H 0.97 m. (entire)
0.927 m. (surface)
W 0.369 m. (top)
0.404 m. (bottom)
Th 0.077 m. (top)
0.112 m. (bottom)

letters: 0.004 m. Smallest, M, O, X, are .003; largest, N, P, Σ, T, Y, are .005. E, I Π, Φ, Ω, are .004.

minuscule text: next three pages.

stoich. 39

θ ε ο [ί]
'Επ' 'Αντικλέουϲ ἄρχοντοϲ ἐπὶ τῆϲ Αἰγεῖδοϲ πέμπτ-
ηϲ πρυτανείαϲ, ἧι 'Αντιφῶν Κοροίβου 'Ελευϲί ἐγρα-
μμάτευεν· ἐνδεκάτηι· τετάρτηι καὶ τριακοϲτῆι τῆϲ πρυταν-
είαϲ· τῶμ προέδρων ἐπεψήφιζεν Φίλυλλοϲ 'Ελευϲί·
Δημοϲθένηϲ Δημοκλέουϲ Λαμπτρεὺϲ εἶπεν· ἐπειδ-
ὴ 'Ηρακλείδηϲ Σαλαμίνιοϲ διατελεῖ φιλοτιμούμ-
ενοϲ πρὸϲ τὸν δῆμον τὸν 'Αθηναίων καὶ ποιῶν ὅτι δ-
ύ̣ναται ἀγαθόν, καὶ πρότερόν τε ἐπέδωκεν ἐν τῆι ϲ-
πανοϲιτίαι :ΧΧΧ: μεδίμνουϲ πυρῶν :Π: δράχμου-
ϲ πρῶτοϲ τῶν καταπλευϲάντων ἐνπόρων· καὶ πάλιν
ὅ̣τε αἱ ἐπιδόϲειϲ ἦϲαν ἐπέδωκε :ΧΧΧ: δραχμὰϲ εἰ-
ϲ ϲιτωνίαν, καὶ τὰ ἄλλα διατελεῖ εὔνουϲ ὢν καὶ φι-
λοτιμούμενοϲ πρὸϲ τὸν δῆμον· δεδόχθαι τῶι δήμω-
ι ἐπαινέϲαι 'Ηρακλείδην Χαρικλείδου Σαλαμίνι-
ον καὶ ϲτεφανῶϲαι χρυϲῶι ϲτεφ̣άνωι εὐνοίαϲ ἕνεκ-
α καὶ φιλοτιμίαϲ τῆϲ πρὸϲ̲ τὸν δῆμον τὸν 'Αθηναίων·
εἶναι δ' αὐτὸν πρόξενον καὶ εὐεργέτην τοῦ δήμου
τοῦ 'Αθηναίων αὐτὸν καὶ ἐγγόνουϲ, εἶναι δ' αὐτοῖϲ
καὶ γῆϲ καὶ οἰκίαϲ ἔγκτηϲιν κατὰ τὸν νόμον καὶ ϲ-
τρατεύεϲθαι αὐτοὺϲ τὰϲ ϲτρατείαϲ καὶ εἰϲφέρε-
ιν τὰϲ εἰϲφορὰϲ μετὰ 'Αθηναίων. ἀναγράψαι δὲ τόδ-
ε τὸ ψήφιϲμα τὸν γραμματέα τὸν κατὰ πρυτανείαν
καὶ τοὺϲ ἄλλουϲ ἐπαίνουϲ τοὺϲ γεγενημένουϲ αὐ-
τῶι ἐν ϲτήληι λιθίνει καὶ ϲτῆϲαι ἐν ἀκροπόλει, ε-
ὶϲ δὲ τὴν ἀναγραφὴν τῆϲ ϲτήληϲ δοῦναι τὸν ταμία-
ν ΔΔΔ δραχμὰϲ ἐκ τῶν εἰϲ τὰ κατὰ ψηφίϲματ' ἀναλιϲ-
κομένων τῶν δήμωι. vacat
Τηλέμαχοϲ Θεαγγέλου 'Αχαρνεὺϲ εἶπεν· ἐπειδὴ 'Ηρ-
ακλείδηϲ Σαλαμίνιοϲ ἐπέδωκεν τὸν ϲῖτον τῶι δή-
μωι πεντέδραχμον πρῶτοϲ τῶν καταπλευϲάντων ἐ-
μπόρων ἐπ' 'Αριϲτοφῶντοϲ ἄρχοντοϲ, ἐψηφίϲαι τῶ-
ι δήμωι ἐπαινέϲαι 'Ηρακλείδην Χαρικλείδου Σαλ-
αμίνιον καὶ ϲτε̣φανῶϲ̣αι αὐτὸν χρυϲῶι ϲτεφάνωι
φιλοτιμίαϲ ἕνεκα τῆϲ εἰϲ τὸν δῆμον τὸν 'Αθηναίω-

ν· ἐπειδὴ δὲ καταχθεὶϲ ὑπὸ Ἡρακλεωτῶν πλέων Ἀθή-
ναζε παρειρ̣έθη τὰ ἱϲτία ὑπ' αὐτῶν, ἑλέϲθαι πρέϲβ-
ευτὴν ἕνα ἄνδρα ἐξ Ἀθηναίων ἁπάντων, ὅϲτιϲ ἀφικόμενοϲ ε-
ἰϲ Ἡράκλειαν ωϲ Διονύϲιον ἀξιώϲει ἀποδοῦναι τ-
ὰ ἱϲτία τὰ Ἡρακλείδου καὶ τὸ λοιπὸν μηδέν' ἀδικε-
ῖν τῶν Ἀθήναζε πλεόντων· καὶ ταῦτα ποιῶν τά τε δί-
καια ποιήϲει καὶ οὐθενὸϲ ἀτυχήϲει τοῦ δήμου τ̲[ο]ῦ Ἀ-
[θηναίων] τῶν δικαίων· δοῦναι δὲ τῶι αἱρεθέντι πρεϲβευ-
τεῖ εἰϲ ἐφόδια τὸν ταμίαν τοῦ δήμου :Π: δραχμὰϲ ἐκ τῶ-
ν κατὰ ψηφίϲματ' ἀναλιϲκομένων τῶι δήμωι. Εἱρέθ-
η πρεϲβευτὴϲ Θηβαγένηϲ Ἐλευϲίνιοϲ. vacat
Τηλέμαχοϲ Θεαγγέλου Ἀχαρ εἶπεν· ἐψηφίϲθαι τῶι
δήμωι τὴν βουλὴν προβουλεύϲαϲαν ἐξενεγκεῖν ε-
ἰϲ τὴν πρώτην ἐκκληϲίαν περὶ Ἡρακλείδου καθότ-
ι εὑρ̣ήϲεται ἄν τι δύνηται ἀγαθὸν παρὰ τοῦ δήμου
τοῦ Ἀθηναίων. vacat
Κηφιϲόδοτοϲ Εὐαρχίδου Ἀχαρνεὺϲ εἶπεν· περὶ ὧν ὁ
δῆμοϲ προϲέταξεν τῆι βουλῆι προβουλεῦϲαι περ-
ὶ Ἡρακλείδου τοῦ Σαλαμινίου, δεδόχθαι τῆι βουλ-
ῆι, ἐπειδὴ Ἡρακλείδηϲ καταπλεύϲαϲ Ἀθήναζε ϲῖτ-
ον ἄγων ἐπέδωκεν τῶι δήμωι τριϲχιλίουϲ μεδίμν-
ουϲ πέντε δραχμῶν ἕκαϲτον, τοὺϲ προέδρουϲ οἳ ἂν λάχωϲι-
ν προεδρεύειν εἰϲ τὴν πρώτην ἐκληϲίαν προϲαγα-
γεῖν, Ἡρακλείδην πρὸϲ τὸν δῆμον καὶ χρηματίϲαι,
γνώμην δὲ ξυμβάλλεϲθαι τῆϲ βουλῆϲ εἰϲ τὸν δῆμο-
ν ὅτι δοκεῖ τῆι βουλεῖ ἐπαινέϲαι Ἡρακλείδην Χα-
ρικλείδου Σαλαμίνιον καὶ ϲτεφανῶϲαι χρ-
υϲῶι ϲτεφάνωι ἀπὸ 𐅅 δραχμῶν· εἶναι δ' αὐτῶι καὶ εὑ-
ρέϲθαι παρὰ τοῦ δ̣ή̣μ̣ο̣υ̣ ὅτι ἂν δύνηται ἀγαθόν, ὅπωϲ ἁ-

ν καὶ οἱ ἄλλοι φιλοτιμῶνται εἰδότες, ὅτι τιμᾶι καὶ στεφανοῖ ἡ βουλὴ τοὺς φ[ι]-
λοτιμουμένους. vacat
Φυλεὺς Παυσανίου Οἰναῖος εἶπεν· ἐπειδὴ Ἡρακλείδης Σαλαμίνιος καταπλεύ-
σας Ἀθήναζε σῖτον ἄγων ἐπ' Ἀριστοφῶντος ἄρχοντος ἐπέδωκεν τῶι δήμωι XXX με-
δίμνους Π δράχμους καὶ διὰ ταῦτα ὁ δῆμος ἐψηφίσατο αὐτῶι τὴν βουλὴν προβου-
λεύσασαν ἐξενεγκεῖν εἰς τὸν δῆμον καθ' ὅτι εὑρήσεται ἄν τι δύνηται ἀγαθὸν παρὰ
τοῦ δήμου τοῦ Ἀθηναίων, καὶ πάλιν ἐπ' Εὐθυκρίτου ἄρχοντος ἐπέδωκεν τῶι (δήμωι) εἰς σιτωνίαν XXX δ-
ραχμάς, δεδόχθαι τῆι βουλῆι τοὺς προέδρους οἳ ἂν λάχωσι προε̣δ̣ρεύειν εἰς τὴν κυρίαν
ἐκκλησίαν προσαγαγεῖν Ἡρακλείδην πρὸς τὸν δῆμον καὶ χρηματίσαι, γνώμην δὲ ξυ-
μβάλλεσθαι τῆς βουλῆς εἰς τὸν δῆμον ὅτι δοκεῖ τῆι βουλῆι ἐπαινέσαι Ἡρακλείδην
Χαρικλείδου Σαλαμίνιον καὶ στεφανῶσαι χρυσῶι στεφάνωι ἀπὸ :Ḟ: δραχμῶν·
εἶναι δ' αὐτῶι καὶ εὑρέσθαι ἀγαθὸ[ν πα]ρὰ τοῦ δήμου ὅτου ἂν δοκεῖ ἄξιος εἶναι, ὅπως
ἂν καὶ οἱ ἄλλοι ἐθέλωσι [ἑτοίμ]ω[ς εὐεργετεῖν τὴν βου]λ̣ῆ̣ν̣ καὶ τὸν δῆ[μ]ο[ν] ὁρῶντες
τοὺς φιλοτιμουμέ[νους - τὸν] δ̣ῆ̣μ̣ο̣ν̣
- π̣ᾶ̣ς̣[α]ς
Α - vacat

in wreath	in wreath	in wreath	in wreath
Ὁ δῆμος	Ὁ δῆμος	Ἡ βουλή	Ἡ βουλή

epigraphical commentary: ΘΕΟΙ, inscribed on the molding,

is not given a line number in either Koehler's or Kirchner's text. Lines 1-64 are inscribed in a stoichedon order of 39 letters to the line (although as Wilhelm points out, there are a number of violations to that order). Lines 66-79 are non-stoichedon with as many as 73 letters crowded into the same width which holds 39 stoichoi above. In most cases, the violations in the stoichedon order are the result of stonecutter's error, i.e., the crowded letters are engraved over an erasure: line 37 has 46 letters with 21 letters crowded into 14 stoichoi (st. 26-39); line 56 has 45 letters with 15 letters crowded into 9 stoichoi (st. 16-24). Lines 41-43 are a combination of an erasure left blank and crowding: in the middle of line 41, 8 letters are crowded into 6 stoichoi (st. 20-25); at the end of line 41 (st. 36-39) and beginning of line 42 (st. 1-7) is an erasure which was not reinscribed (but Y, I, st. 38, 39, are not entirely erased); at the end of line 42, 11 letters are crowded into 6 stoichoi (st. 34-39); and at the beginning of line 43, 11 letters are crowded into 7 stoichoi (st. 1-7).

With the exception of line 3, where 26 letters are crowded into 18 stoichoi (st. 16-33) with no evidence of an erasure, the remaining violations are normal crowding, ΩIE is crowded into st. 28, 29, in line 15; THΣ is crowded into st. 15, 16, in line 16; IΩN is crowded into st. 37, 38 in line 51.

By line 63, the stonecutter must have realized that he could never finish the text with an order of 39 letters. At the end of line 63 (41 letters), he crowded 6 letters into 4 stoichoi (st. 36-39). Line 64 has 61 letters: AIO share st. 3, 4; TIM share st. 15, 16; the last 40 letters are crowded into 21 stoichoi (st. 19-39). The 13 letters in line 65 are crowded into the first 8 stoichoi. And lines 66-79 are crowded into a non-stoichedon order in the same manner as the last half of line 64 and line 65.

In addition to the erasure in lines 41/2 where the stonecutter did not recut letters; st. 35-39 in line 61 was erased and left blank. The erasures in the non-stoichedon part of the text are not as smooth as those above. They occur at the beginning of line 76, between iota and omega (restored in Kirchner's text); at the beginning of line 78 (approximately 10 stoichoi) and between the 2 sigmas at the end of that line; and at the beginning of line 79 after the alpha (approximately 8 stoichoi).

The engraved crowns at the bottom of the stele overlap. I have underlined letters which are no longer visible (the tau in st. 36, line 41, is erased thoroughly, as

Koehler's majuscule text shows); and dotted letters which are unclear. The amount in st. 27, line 43 is 𐅄 (Koehler; Kirchner in Add. p. 660) not Π (Kirchner's text). The alpha in st. 9, line 9, has no cross bar; I read gamma rather than nu in st. 13, line 28, and mu rather than nu in st. 8, line 47.

commentary: The restorations are Koehler's with the exception of the middle of line 76, restored by Dittenberger. Koehler was able to restore what had been erased in line 41/2 from the 2 letters still visible. He could not suggest what the stonecutter had erased at the end of line 61.

This stele records 5 decrees: I (lines 1-27), II (lines 28-45), III (lines 46-50), IV (lines 51-65), and V (lines 66-79). Only Decree I includes a calendric formula, and even that formula omits the month: in the year of Antikles (325/4), the 34th day of the fifth prytany, held by the tribe Aigeis; the 11th day of the month. Since the festival date and the conciliar date do not equate for an ordinary year, Koehler assumed that the 325/4 was intercalary and the omitted month the intercalated Posideon II. Then Kirchner proposed that the stonecutter had engraved πἐμπτηϲ rather than the correct ἐβδδμηϲ to produce an equation for an ordinary year: Elapheboion 11 = Prytany VII 34. Dinsmoor pointed out that the stonecutter could have "no reasonable excuse" in mistaking 5 for 7 (p. 372), and returned to the equation at is is recorded on the stone: (Posideon II) 11 = Prytany V 34 in an intercalary year (this was accepted by Kirchner in *Gnomen*). In order to fit this equation with the equation in #69 (II^2 361), Dinsmoor assumed divergence from Aristotle's "rule" (see #28, #57): 38 days for Prytanies I, VIII-IX; 39 days for Prytanies II-VII; 36 days for Prytany X.

Pritchett and Meritt both accept the date on the stone and the year as intercalary, but differ as to the distribution of the days in the year (again, in order to reconcile with #69). Pritchett-Neugebauer (who conform strictly to Aristotle's "rule"), designate the day as the 190th and assume that the archon intercalated "two or three" extra days in the festival calendar at the beginning of the year (hence the shortening of the last month, Skirophorion, see #69). Meritt (Hesperia) proposed either 36 or 41 days for the tenth prytany. In Ath., however, he objected to the "perpetual irregularity" (104) of Pritchett-Neugebauer's proposal (and his own?) and offered a solution which allowed for a regular sequence of full and hollow months in the festival calendar as well as normal prytany lengths by proposing that extra days were added late in Thargelion, but then immediately corrected: "Thargelion, therefore, had 29 days, 25 of them falling before and including Thargelion 22 and the span from Thargelion 23 to 29 inclusive having only four of them" (104). The equation is Posideon II 11 = Prytany V 34 = 188th day. The distribution of prytanies, 39 days for Prytanies I, II, IX, X; 38 days for Prytanies III-VIII, does not conform to Aristotle's "rule" but does keep to the practise which Meritt now accepts, that there were no more than 39 days, no less than 38 days for a prytany in an intercalary year (see #57).

Despite the disagreement as to the day, the conciliar date and year (and type of year) are established: on the 34th day of the 5th prytany in the year of Antikles, 325/4, the Boule and Demos decided to honor Herakleides of Salamis. Philyllos of Eleusis was the chairman of the proedroi; Demosthenes, son of Demokles, of the deme Lamptrai, was the proposer. Not only had Herakleides been first to deliver 3,000 medimnoi of wheat at five drachmai (Rhodes, 66, says this is a fair price) during the grain shortage, he also contributed 3,000 drachmai toward the purchase of wheat and carried out these actions with benevolence and zeal toward the Demos. For these reasons, the Demos resolved that: Herakleides be crowned with a gold crown; he (and his descendants) be honored with the titles proxenos and benefactor of the Athenians; he be granted enktesis for land and home, according to the laws; and that he serve in the army and pay taxes as an Athenian. This decree ends with the only publication formula on the stele: that 30 drachmai are to be set aside for the secretary to have this decree, and all others commending his deeds, on a stele and set up on the Akropolis.

The next decree, II, gives more background information. Telemachos, son of Theangelos, of the deme Acharnai, the proposer, recalls Herakleides' provision of wheat to Athens first; notes the award of a gold crown; and dates this action of Herakleides to the year of Aristophon, 330/29. Telemachos then goes on to explain that Herakleides had been hindered by the inhabitants of Herakleia on his way to Athens. Therefore Telemachos proposes that an ambassador be elected and provided with 50 drachmai to go to Dionysios of Herakleia and tell him to return Herakleides' sails and inform him that anyone impeding ships bound for Athens will be dealt with. Thebagenes of Eleusis was elected ambassador.

The next decree, III, also proposed by Telemachos, records his motion made in the ekklesia that the Boule issue a probouleuma concerning Herakleides so that he be honored by the Athenians.

Decree IV appears to be the direct result of the call for a probouleuma made by Telemachos in Decree III (Kirchner dates Decrees III and IV to 329/8; DeLaix, 130, notes that III must be earlier than IV; Rhodes, 67, notes "Decree iv declares its dependence on iii"). Kephisodotos, son of Euarchides, of the deme Acharnai, refers to the previous commissioning of the probouleuma; notes Herakleides' action in supplying the wheat; and presents the Boule's probouleuma. That probouleuma proposes that Herakleides be praised and awarded a gold crown worth 500 drachmai; it provides for further benefits the Demos might propose; it ends with the notice that the Boule honors and crowns those who act benevolently and contribute liberally.

Decree V was proposed by Phyleus, son of Pausanias, of the deme Oinaios. Phyleus notes (for the fourth time on the stele) Herakleides' help in 330/29 and that the Demos had commissioned a probouleuma concerning that action. He then dates to the year of Euthykritos, 328/7, Herakleides' contributions of 3,000 drachmai to the grain shortage (mentioned in Decree I). Then follows the probouleuma to be presented to the Demos at the kyria eklesia: that Herakleides be commended and awarded a crown worth 500 drachmai; that the Demos may add furt r benefits; that this is done to award those who help the Demos and Boule of Athens. Below the 5 decrees are 4 wreaths--2 indicate the Demos, 2 the Boule.

The arrangement of the five decrees on the stele is obviously not sequential. The information culled from all 5 decrees, however, does allow for the arrangement of the decrees in the correct chronological order. (Although DeLaix's discussion of the 5 decrees, 129-30, is more difficult to comprehend than Rhodes's listing of the decrees in "logical sequence," 66-67, both DeLaix and Rhodes do agree on the sequence presented below. Kirchner dates II, III, IV, to 329/8; I and, presumably V to 325/4.) The order follows.

1.) Decree III is Telemachos's request for a probouleuma (Rhodes, 66, dates between 330/29 and 328/7). 2.) Decree IV records the probouleuma requested in Decree III. 3.) Decree II records the decree of the Demos which resulted from the probouleuma, Decree IV (DeLaix, 129, implies this relationship; Rhodes, 67, assumes the dependence of II on IV). 4.) Decree V is another probouleuma which includes Herakleides' second act of kindness from 328/7 (DeLaix, 130, places this decree in 328/7; Rhodes, 66, "in or after 328/7"). 5.) Decree I, of the year 325/4, is obviously the last in chronological order; it contains the only instructions for publication and provides for previous decrees. If Decree I is the result of the probouleuma of Decree V as seems likely (Rhodes, 67, agrees), then a date for Decree V closer to 325/4 than the second kindness (328/7) seems more reasonable. Despite the haphazard arrangement of the 5 decrees, Rhodes remarks that "the procedure followed is fairly clear" (66); DeLaix that "this inscription shows the continued working of probouleusis and the constant need for probouleumata" (130).

A few other aspects of this inscription need to be considered. 1.) The appropriation of only 30 drachmai for publication, omission of the month, and errors in the stoichedon order led Drerup to suggest that this stele was set up privately. Lambrechts, (127) agrees; Pečírka (71) notes that the suggestion has been accepted by no subsequent commentators. 2.) Herakleides' status cannot be determined for certain. Pečírka reviews previous suggestions but comments that the "correct solution to this problem seems to depend on correct interpretation of the whole scale of subtle distinctions in the status of foreigners in Athens" (72). Despite the caveat, Pečírka does state the probability that Herakleides was a privileged metic living in Athens. 3.) Although there is still controversy over the date and length of the famine at the end of the 4th century, this inscription provides certain evidence for the years 330/29 and 328/7. Pečírka (71) provides a fuller bibliography (the dates are discussed in his note 2; see also #67).

This inscription is informative in a number of ways. First, it provides a glimpse of the legislative process over a number of years. Second, it provides another instance of the Athenians' pride in bestowing honors on those who benefited Athens. Third, but not least, it shows Athens exercising her diplomatic power with other states by sending an ambassador to remonstrate with Dionysios of Herakleia about his treatment of ships headed for Athens (Decree II, lines 35-45). That the appointed ambassador, Thebagenes, may have established friendlier relations between Dionysios and Athens, in addition to retrieving the sails, is a distinct possibility (see also, discussion, #67).

325/4

69. *DECREE* EM 7174

editors: Pittakis ΕΦ. (1856/61) 3166; Velsen & Koehler IG II 179; IG II^2 361.

supplements: SEG 14.57 (Lewis): 18.15 (Pritchett).

other bibliography: Unger Philol. 39(1880) 418; Att. Arch. 675; Schmidt Gr. Chron. 540, 544, 571; Meritt Hesperia 4(1935) 536; Ath. 104; Pritchett-Neugebauer Cal. 56; Lewis BSA 49(1954) 50; Pritchett CP 54(1959) 155-156; Clement AJA 69(1965) 194; Rhodes Boule 272.

description: This fragment of Pentelic marble was found in the theater of Herodes Atticus in 1857. Enough of the upper right hand corner is preserved to indicate that the stele was topped by a pediment and, as Lewis has pointed out, that the right margin is preserved. The rest of the sides and the back are broken.

dimensions:
H 0.183 m.
0.055 m. (pediment)
0.128 m. (text)
W 0.297 m.
Th 0.075 m.

letters: 0.007 m.
Smallest, O, is .004;
largest, P, Σ, are
The letters are not a consistent size; Π varies by .001

minuscule text: non stoich.

[Ἐπὶ Ἀντι]κλείους ἄρχοντος ἐπὶ τῆς Ἀκαμαν[τ]-
[ίδος δ]εκάτης πρυτανείας, ἧι Ἀντιφ[ῶν] vacat
[Κορ]οίβου Ἐλευσίνιος ἐγραμμάτευεν· θ̣[αργηλι]-
[ῶ]νος ὀγδόηι μετ' εἰκάδας, πέμπτ[ηι τῆς πρυ]-
[ταν]είας· βουλὴ ἐν βουλευτηρίωι· τ[ῶν προέδρων]
[ἐπε]ψήφισεν Ἀρχέστ[ρατ]ος Ἀθ[μονεὺς· - - -]
[- - - - Ἀ]λωπε[κῆθεν εἶπεν· - - - - - - - -]
- - - - - ΨΗΦΙ - - - - -
[- - - - πρε]σβε - - - - -

commentary: The text is based on Lewis's correct observation that the right side of the stone is preserved, not the left, as Kirchner's text suggests. The difference between this text and Kirchner's text is that there are more letters restored at the end of the line in Kirchner's text. Koehler and Velsen restored the archon's name and thus dated the decree to 325/4. They did not restore the secretary's name, but offered Koroibos or Stroibos as the patronymic. After #68 (II^2 360) was found, Kirchner was able to restore the correct name and patronymic (Kirchner also restored ἐπ' rather than ἐπὶ at the beginning of line 1).

As Koehler and Velsen in their majuscule text and Kirchner in his commentary note, only remains of the theta at the end of line 3 (only Pittakis saw a complete theta). The underlined pi in line 7 was seen only by Koehler and Velsen. I include a vacat at the end of line 2: although the surface is broken after the phi, some uninscribed surface remains to the right of the break. This is further confirmation for Lewis's placement of the entire patronymic on the next line (Koehler and Velsen and Kirchner restored Ko- at the end of line 2).

The text is non-stoichedon. With the exception of 30 letters and a vacat in line 2, the length of the 5 fully restored lines varies from 33 to 37 letters.

With the exception of Lewis's observation of the physical characteristics of the stone, all of the scholarship dealing with this inscription deals with the calendar equation. The equation itself is straightforward: the 5th day of the 10th prytany; the 22nd or 23rd day (depending upon whether the month is hollow or full) of Thargelion. And there is no doubt that the year 325/4 is intercalary (the nature of the year and the scholarship before Pritchett and Meritt is discussed in #68). The 5th day of the tenth prytany, however, leaves only 33 days (if one conforms to Aristotle's "rule" (see #28) or, at the most, 34 days (if the last prytany can have 39 days) until the end of the year, a year which, according to the festival calendar, should have at least 37 more days to go; a hollow Skirophorion of 29 days plus 8 days. (Although Pritchett's belief that the omitted day in the last decade of the month is δευτέρα φθῖνοντος would produce only 36 days to go--if Thargelion were hollow--Walsh has shown conclusively that the omitted day occured earlier in the decade, see #29.)

As usual, Pritchett and Meritt have solved the problem in different ways. Since Pritchett abides by Aristotle's "rule", the equation in #68 also presents problems. Therefore, he assumes that the archons intercalated 2 or 3 days at the beginning of the year (before #68) and then subtracted those days in the last month, Skirophorion (after this decree): "Thargelion (IX) 23 = Prytany X 5 = 351st day" (*Cal.* 56). Since Meritt regards Aristotle's "rule" with more flexibility, he finds no inconsistency in the equation for #68. To resolve the inconsistency in this equation, he also presumes an intercalation, but one which happened much later in the year (immediately before this decree) and which was corrected immediately: "Thargelion, therefore, had 29 days, 25 of them falling before and including Thargelion 22 and the span from Thargelion 23 to 29 inclusive having only four of them" (*Ath.* 104). The equation therefore, is: "Thargelion 22 <κατ' ἄρχοντα, 25 κατὰ θέον> = Prytany X 5 = 350th day" (*Ath.* 102; Clement agrees and notes that Lewis's text does not affect Meritt's argument). (Meritt's *Hesperia* article and Pritchett's *CP* article are chiefly involved with the count of days in the last decade of the month. Pritchett used this decree in support of his view that the Athenians only used backward count. Although Meritt was arguing that forward count was possible, he noted that this decree offered no proof either way. In any case, he has subsequently given up the idea of any use by the Athenians of forward count in the last decade. See *Mnemosyne* 30 [1977] 218, especially n. 5.)

Again, once the calendar is discussed, there is little more to add. No one has even argued that the decree was set up privately because the letters are poorly cut and not in stoichedon order (see #16 for other non-stoichedon decrees). Even the phrase, βουλῆ ἐν βουλευτηρίωι (line 5) which is recorded on only two other decrees of the Lykourgan era, #18 (II^2 330+445) and #28 (II^2 338), merits notice by Rhodes only in his Table G with the suggestion that the psephisma was passed by the Boule. This Table G, a list of decrees of the Boule includes only 8 Lykourgan decrees: #18, #27 (II^2 337), #28, #54 (II^2 354), #56 (AE [1917] 40-8 no. 92), #68 (II^2 360), a decree embedded in the naval list II^2 1631 (lines 350-369), and this decree, #69. With the exception of #56, which is a dedication by the Boule and others, and the decree in the naval list, the other 5 inscriptions record psephismata of the Demos as well. It is likely, therefore, that the original stele included not only a decree of the Boule, for which we have most of the prescript, but also at least one other decree, one of the Demos. Otherwise, #69 would be unique for the Lykourgan era. (Enough remains of #69 to show that it was definitely a stele rather than a dedicatory base, as #56.)

325/4

70. *THE DEME ATHMONON HONORS THEIR MERARCHS* EM 7746, 7747

editors: Fr. A Kumanudes ΑΘΗΝΑΙΟΝ 1(1873) 16 no. 5; IG II 580.
Fr. A+B Wilhelm ΕΦ. (1905) 225 no. 5: IG II^2 1203.

testimonia: Pausanias I 31.4; IG I^2 865.

supplement: Bull. (1942) no. 32 (Wilhelm Att. Urk.).

other bibliography: Milchhoefer AM 13(1888) 351; Wilhelm Att. Urk. V 188.

description: The two fragments of Pentelic marble are now joined and restored with plaster to create a stele. Fr. A was found in Marousi. Most of the pediment which tops the stele is preserved, as are both sides of Fr. A and the left side of Fr. B. The sides angle in to the rear (i.e., they are not perpendicular to the front surface). The bottom of Fr. A and top, bottom and right side of Fr. B are broken. The back does not appear to be original.

dimensions:
H 0.70 m. (entire)
0.565 m. (surface)
W 0.423 m. (pediment)
0.395 m. (above)
0.405 m. (below)
Th 0.07 m.

letters: 0.007 m. Smallest, A, is .005; largest, Φ, is .01. E, H, O, T, Ω, are .006; N, Σ, are .007; Π is .008. Letters are poorly cut.

minuscule text: next page.

epigraphical commentary: Although the text is virtually complete, the letters are poorly cut, there are misspellings, and there are discrepancies in the stoichedon order, more, in fact, than Kirchner's commentary implies. Kirchner noted only that line four had 26 letters and lines 17-19 had 27 letters. Line 7, however, also has a violation: the 2nd alpha of μερα̑ρχαϲ occupies 2 stoichoi (st. 18,19). The addition of the epsilon (made by all editors) which was omitted by the stonecutter at the beginning of the line does make 25 letters. But there are only 24 letters on the stone. Lines 17 through 19 present more of a problem which is compounded by the fact that the lower left corner of Fr. A was either broken off before the join or covered by plaster when the two fragments were joined. Consequently, I have underlined letters which were seen by Kumanudes, Koehler, Wilhelm, and apparently Kirchner. There is no doubt that line 17 had 27 letters--enough remains of the first letter, alpha, to show that the stonecutter placed that letter one stoichos to the left of the previous margin and then shifted the letters enough to the left to add the 2nd extra letter so that by the middle of the line, the letters in line 17 are directly below those of line 16. And even though part of line 18 is restored, the same pattern appears: additional letter to the left; crowding to include 2nd letter; regular stoichedon order after the middle of the line. Line 19, however, may have had more than the 27 letters restored by Wilhelm.

stoich. 25

Fr. A θ Ε Ο Ι
θεοδωρίδηϲ εἶπεν· ἐπειδὴ οἱ με-
ράρχαι οἱ ἐπ' Ἀντικλείουϲ ἄρχο-
ντοϲ καλῶϲ̣ καὶ φιλοτίμωϲ τῶν θυ-
ϲιῶν ἐπεμελήθηϲαν καὶ τῶν κοι-
νῶν, δεδόχθαι τοῖϲ δημόταιϲ ϲτ̣-
<ε>φανῶϲαι τοὺϲ μεράρχαϲ τοὺϲ ἐ-
π' Ἀντικλείουϲ ἄρχοντοϲ Χαιρε-
φάνην Χαριά̣δου, Διονυϲοφάνην
Διονυϲο̣δ̣ώ̣ρου, Λυκόφρονα Λυκί-
ϲκου, Ἀντ̣ι̣φ̣ῶντα Ἀρ<ι>ϲτομάχου, v
Λύϲιπ̣π̣ον Λυϲίου, Σμικυθίωνα v
φ[α]λ̣ά̣ν̣θ̣ου χρυϲῶι ϲτεφάνωι ἕκα-
ϲτον αὐτῶν ἀπὸ πεντακοϲίων δρ-
αχμῶν ἀρετῆϲ ἕνεκα καὶ δ̣ικαιο-
ϲύνηϲ τῆϲ εἰϲ τοὺϲ δημόταϲ καὶ
ἀ̣ν̣ειπεῖν Ἀμαρυϲίων τῶι ἀγῶνι. ἀν-
αγράψαι δὲ τό̣[δε τὸ ψήφιϲμ]α [ἐν ϲ]τ<ή>-
Fr. B [λ]ει λ[ιθίνει] καὶ ϲ̣[τῆϲαι ἐν τῶι ἱερ- vv?]
ῶι τὸν δήμ̣α̣ρχον Πο - - - - - - -

in wreath
Σμικυ[θίων]
Φαλάνθ[ου]

in wreath
Λυκόφρων
Λυκίϲκου

in wreath
Χαιρεφάνηϲ
Χαιριάδο[υ]

The majuscule text in EΦ. shows the correct position of the 4 letters that are still legible, ΚΑΙΣ, under ΑΜΑΡ of line 17 (st. 7-10 in text before line 17). Wilhelm's restored text requires that ΚΑΙΣ be farther to the right than it is on the stone: under ΑΡΥΣ of line 17 (st. 9-12 in text before line 17). The correct placement of ΚΑΙΣ would leave at least 2 letter spaces more than are needed to complete the line according to Wilhelm's restoration, even more letter spaces if the letters in the right side of the line were crowded as the ones on the left are. Although I can offer no alternate restoration, line 20 also suggests that the stonecutter was crowding letters at the end of the text. The 15 letters preserved on the stone for line 20 are cut in the space which holds only 10 letters in lines 2-16; 12 letters in lines 17 and 18; and 14 letters in line 19.

In addition to the letters in the lower left corner of Fr. A, two other letters are no longer visible. All dots are mine. Although there would have been enough room to add an extra letter in the left margin before line 17, there is no right margin. In fact, the letters at the end of all the lines are smaller and right at the edge of the stone.

The heading ΘΕΟΙ is cut on the horizontal base of the pediment.

1 st. 19 [Ι] Kum.

4 st. 22, 23 ΤΩΝ.
st. 25 [Υ] Kum.

7 st. 1 Φ. The epsilon was omitted by the stonecutter.
st. 18, 19 Α.

9 st. 10, 11 [ΙΑ] Kum.

10 st. 7-10 [ΟΔΩΡ] Kum.

11 st. 16 Κ. Ki noted in his commentary that the letter was kappa, but dotted the correct letter, iota, as unclear rather than denoting a miscutting.

12 st. 6, 7 new reading. Π[Ο] Kum. [ΠΟ] Koe., Ki.

15 st. 20 Koe. read Α.

18 st. 27 Ε. Again, Ki. merely dotted the correct eta.

19 st. 2-4 EI was read clearly by Kum., Ki.; partially by Koe. Thus these letters were on Fr. A. Wilh. read part of the lambda; Ki. showed it as clear. The rest of the letters in this line, ΚΑΙΣ are on Fr. B.

commentary: Wilhelm (followed by Kirchner) restored the alpha in φ[αλάνθου; Kumanudes restored φ[ι]λάνθου; Koehler did not restore any letter. Kumanudes restored line 18 and the beginning of line 19 ([λ]ει λ[ιθίνει]). Wilhelm restored the rest of line 19 and the names in the crowns. The carved leaves of the three preserved crowns are olive. As Wilhelm noted, there should have been three more crowns.

This decree of the deme Athmonon honors six merarchs. Although these merarchs are designated twice as those who served in the year of Antikles, 325/4 (lines 3, 5), and Antikles is the only archon mentioned on the stone, both Kirchner and Koehler recorded the year 324/3 for this decree without any explanation. It is certainly possible that this decree was passed and published after the merarch's term of office. Since, however, there is no further indication of when the stele was set up, I prefer to include this decree under the only year recorded on the stone: in this case, when the honorable deeds occured. This is the policy for this Corpus. #47, #65, and #66 could have been published later than the years designated in this Corpus because the date on these stones is also given as a modifier for the officials, or official, honored. Since this seems to be Kirchner's policy as well, his designation of 324/3 may be a printer's error. Whenever an eponymous archon's name occurs, Kirchner records on the same line, in the margin, the appropriate date. (The fact that he usually does place the dates for state decrees at the beginning of those decrees can be attributed to the usual practise, at least for the Lykourgan Era, of beginning decrees with the name of the eponymous archon; but see II^2 346 [#37] where he records the date at line 5, where the archon's name occurs, rather than at line 1.) This practice becomes more apparent when one considers Kirchner's treatment of local decrees. The most obvious example is II^2 1184 (#26) where Kirchner prints the date at line 23, the only place where the archon's name occurs. One other decree, already mentioned above as being dated by the designation of the officials honored, is even more pertinent to this discussion. The deme decree, II^2 1198 (#66), honors those choregoi who served in the year of Chremes, 326/5. Chremes' name occurs in line 3, and it is only at line 3 that Kirchner records (in the margin) the Olympiad and then, directly below, the date of Chremes, 326/5. Given his usual practice, therefore, whatever date Kirchner wanted to assign to this decree, the margin at line 3, where the name of the archon Antikles occurs for the first time should have recorded the year in which Antikles held office, 325/4 rather than the date 324/3 which is printed in II^2 1203.

Whether the six merarchs were honored during or after their term of office, we are informed that they oversaw the sacrifices of public moneys well and with distinction. Each of the six merarchs, Chairephanes son of Chariades, Dionysophanes son of Dionysodoros, Lykophron son of Lykiskos, Antiphon son of Aristomachos, Lysippos son of Lysias, and Smikythion son of Phalanthos, is to be crowned with a gold crown worth 500 drachmai because of his excellence and righteousness toward the demesmen, and this is to be proclaimed at the Amarysian games. The demarch is to have the decree engraved on a stele and set up in the sanctuary.

Although the name of the deme is not mentioned in the text, Koehler points out that it has been known for a long time that the Attic deme Athmonon was located in the modern village of Marousi. The testimonia provides further confirmation: I^2 865, found in Marousi, is a boundary stone for the sanctuary of Artemis Amarysia; Pausanias notes that Artemis Amarysia was worshipped in the deme Athmonon.

Before Kumanudes published this decree, the title merarch referred only to a military commander--either of 2,048 men or 32 elephants (Liddell-Scott). Kumanudes noted, however, and Koehler concurred, that a military designation was inappropriate for an official of an Attic deme. The consensus, therefore, is that these merarchs dealt with distribution ("distribution officer of a deme" Liddell-Scott, citing II^2 1203). Wilhelm, in Att. Urk. V, stresses that the title itself plainly shows that the most important function of the merarchs was the distribution of funds, i.e., the merarchs did more than merely supervise sacrifices--they contributed in an even more material way to the welfare of the deme.

The other six dated deme decrees from the Lykourgan era are listed in #26. This decree is a typical example.

XV. THE YEAR OF HEGESIAS, 324/3

71. *DECREE* Ag. Inv. I 4071

photo: Hesperia 10(1941) page 50.

editor: Meritt Hesperia 10(1941) 49-50 no. 12.

supplement: SEG 21.290 (Meritt Hesperia, Ath., Pritchett-Neugebauer.)

other bibliography: Pritchett-Neugebauer Cal. 57; Meritt Ath. 104-105.

description: This fragment of a pedimental stele of Hymettian marble was found in the Agora excavations, April 27, 1936. The top and right side are original; the back, which is very rough-picked, may be original (the preserved thickness also suggests this); the left side and bottom are broken.

dimensions:	letters: 0.007 m.
H 0.21 m. (entire)	Smallest, O, is .005;
0.108 m. (surface)	largest, I, P, Σ, Y,
W 0.147 m. (entire)	are .008. A is
0.095 m. (surface)	.006.
Th 0.104 m.	

minuscule text: next page.

commentary: The text is based on Meritt's Ath. text. In his original text (Hesperia) Meritt restored only: the archon's name; the secretary's name (which established the year and thus the archon's name); the day in the prytany as in the 30's; and the designation, ekklesia. His restoration of ἐγραμμάτευε without the nu-movable in line 4 allowed 11 letters for the month. It was this skimpy restoration which Pritchett-Neugebauer included under the year 324/3 with no comment.

When Meritt returned to this decree in Ath., he decided that although the omission of the nu-movable was possible (in fact #73, II^2 362, has this omission), it was less probable. His addition of the nu-movable narrowed the choice of the month down to two (with only 10 letter-spaces) and allowed him to choose from the three possible tribe and number of prytany combinations he had suggested in <u>Hesperia</u>. The result is the restoration in the text; the equation is: [Posideon 28] = Prytany [V] 3[1] = 175th day in an ordinary year.

stoich. 25

[Ἐπὶ Ἡγηϲίου ἄρχοντοϲ ἐπ]ὶ τῆϲ Α-
[ἰαντίδοϲ πέμπτηϲ πρυτα]νείαϲ
[ἧι Εὐφάνηϲ Φρύνωνοϲ Ῥαμ]ν̣ούϲι-
[οϲ ἐγραμμάτευεν· Ποϲιδε]ῶνοϲ v
[τρίτηι μετ' εἰκάδαϲ, μιᾶι κ]αὶ τρ-
[ιακοϲτῆι τῆϲ πρυτανείαϲ· ἐ]κ̣κλ-
[ηϲία· - - - - - - - - - - - - - -]

The text is in stoichedon order, 25 letters to the line. The dots are Meritt's, with my concurrence.

This is the first of five decrees (#71-#75) whose restoration has benefited from the discovery of the dedicatory base, <u>Hesperia</u> 10(1941) no. 11, which records the name of the secretary for the year of Hegesias, 324/3. Although these five decrees are now dated securely to the Lykourgan Era, they are all fragmentary and none of them contribute any content to the history of this period.

324/3

72. *DECREE* Ag. Inv. I 4224

photo: <u>Hesperia</u> 10(1941) page 51.

editor: Meritt <u>Hesperia</u> 10(1941) 50-52 no. 13.

description: The three fragments of Pentelic marble are noncontiguous. They were all found during the Agora excavations: Fr. B in a well on June 1, 1936; Fr. A and Fr. C in a grave on March 6, 1929. Fr. B and Fr. C are broken on all sides. Fr. A, however, preserves the left side of the sculptured relief and the text as well as the original back. Although he notes that the relief is much battered, Meritt suggests that there were originally three figures: on the left, the preserved figure of "Athena with helmet and spear, facing right, leaning on her shield"; in the center, the half preserved figure of a man; on the right, another figure, now lost.

dimensions:

Fr. A	Fr. B	Fr. C
H 0.56 m.	H 0.17 m.	H 0.076 m.
W 0.26 m.	W 0.13 m.	W 0.162 m.
Th 0.16 m.	Th 0.12 m.	Th 0.15 m.

letters: 0.007 m. Smallest, M, X, are .006; largest, K, P, are .008.

minuscule text:

stoich. 31

[᾿Επ]ὶ ῾Ηγηϲίου ἄρχο[ντοϲ ἐπὶ τῆϲ Πανδιον]-
[ἶδ]οϲ ἕκτηϲ πρυτα[νεῖαϲ ἧι Εὐφάνηϲ Φρύ]-
[νωνο]ϲ ῾Ραμνούϲιο[ϲ ἐγραμμάτευεν ....]

lacuna

- - - - Φ - - -
- - - - ΜẸ - - -
- - - - ΕΚ̣ - - -
- - - - ΝΕ̣ ̣ - -
- - - - ΔΟΣ - -
- - - - ΤΙΚ - -
- - - - Π̣ Ι̣ - -

lacuna

[- - - - - -] χ[ρυϲῶι ϲτεφάνωι]
[ἀπὸ : Χ : δραχμῶν ἀ]ρετῆ[ϲ ἕνεκα καὶ δικα]-
[ιοϲύνηϲ τῆϲ εἰ̣ϲ] τὸν δῆ[μον - - - - - -]

commentary: Restorations are Meritt's. The stoichedon order of 31 letters to the line allows 11 letters for the tribe which held the 6th prytany. Since the tribe Akamantis held the 9th prytany (#73, II^2 362), Pandionis is the only other tribe which fits the restoration.

Although the restorations in Fr. C are based on only 10 preserved letters, they are reasonable, considering that the stele was topped by a sculptured relief--a sure sign that the decree was honorary. This inscription, however, is so uninformative that a specific date cannot be suggested, let alone who was honored with what must have been an impressive stele or why the honors were bestowed.

324/3

73. *DECREE* EM 7176

photo: Hesperia 10(1941) page 46.

editors: Kumanudes <u>EΦ</u>. (1886) 100 no. 7; Wilhelm <u>Hermes</u> 24 (1889) 142-143 no. 18; <u>IG</u> II 5.180c; <u>IG</u> II^2 362.

supplements: <u>SEG</u> 21.291 (Meritt <u>Hesperia</u>, <u>Ath</u>., Pritchett-Neugebauer).
<u>Bull</u>. (1944) no. 58 (Meritt <u>Hesperia</u>).

other bibliography: Sundwall <u>Schaltzyklos</u> 12; Meritt <u>Hesperia</u> 10(1941) 47; <u>Ath</u>. 105; Pritchett-Neugebauer <u>Cal</u>. 56.

description: This fragment of Pentelic marble is broken on the right side and bottom. The left side is preserved. The top has a smooth, medium-picked surface. Although most of it has been broken away, the stele was originally crowned by a molding.

dimensions:
H 0.195 m. (entire)
0.097 m. (surface)
W 0.15 m.
Th 0.08 m.

letters: 0.005 m. Smallest, O, is .003; largest, Γ, H, are .006.

minuscule text: stoich. 28

[᾽Ε]φ᾽ ῾Ηγησίου ἄρχ[οντος ἐπὶ τῆς ᾽Ακαμα]-
[ν]τ̣ίδος ἐνάτης [πρυτανείας ἧι Εὐφά]-
[νη]ς Φρύνωνος ῾Ρ[αμνούσιος ἐγραμμά]-
[τ]ευε· Θαργηλ[ιῶνος ὀγδόηι ἐπὶ δέκα]
[ἐ]νάτηι καὶ ε[ἰκοστῆι τῆς πρυτανεία]-
[ς]· ἐκκλησί[α κυρία· τῶν προέδρων ἐπε]-
[ψ]ήφιζεν̣ - - - - - - - - - - - -

epigraphical commentary: As Meritt noted, the letters on this stone are in stoichedon order and his addition of the correct secretary's name (see #71) allowed him to establish an order of 28 letters to the line, not 27-29 as indicated by Kirchner, following Koehler and Kumanudes. There is one exception to the stoichedon order: in line 5, the final epsilon is to the left of the center of st. 10 (in fact, partly in st. 9). This provides plenty of room for the iota which Meritt restores in st. 10 as well.

The letter in st. 2, line 2, has always been read as episilon (Ξ Kumanudes; E Koehler, Kirchner). The vertical stroke, however, is directly beneath the vertical stroke of the phi above (not to the left, as it should be for an epsilon). Since the lower horizontal stroke could be accidental, a tau is possible. I have added the dot. The last letter, nu, in st. 7 line 7, was dotted by Kirchner and Meritt; Kumanudes and Koehler saw a vertical stroke.

commentary: The text is based on Meritt's from Hesperia (reproduced in Ath.). The basic restorations were made by Kumanudes. Meritt restored the correct secretary's name (see above; Kumanudes suggested Διόγνητο]ς Φρύνωνος [῾Ραμνούσιος]; Koehler and Kirchner left the name unrestored). With the stoichedon order established, Meritt restored ᾽Ακαμαν]τίδος as the tribe in prytany. ᾽Ερεχ/-θ]εῖδος, which was restored by Kumanudes, Koehler and Kirchner, has only 10 letters and is now restored for the 10th prytany (#75). The other tribe with 11 letter spaces, Πανδιονίδος would not work: the letter in st. 2 line 2 could be an epsilon or a tau, but not a nu (Pandionidos is now restored for the 6th prytany, #72).

Although the day in the prytany, the 29th, has not been questioned since Kumanudes, two alternatives have been offered for the day in the month Thargelion, which Kumanudes did not restore. Wilhelm used this decree to counter Unger's determination that 324/3 was an ordinary year (and 325/4 intercalary; see #68, #69 from 325/4) and suggested a date in the 2nd decade in Thargelion. Koehler followed Wilhelm's suggestion and restored ὀγδόηι ἐπὶ δέκα. Kirchner, on the other hand, considered 324/3 intercalary and used Sundwall's restoration: τρίτηι ἐπὶ δέκα. For this year, at least, both Pritchett-Neugebauer and Meritt agree with Dinsmoor's determination that the year 324/3 is ordinary. They present the same equation: Thargelion [18] = Prytany IX 29 = 313th day.

Once the scholarship concerning the date is reviewed, there is nothing left to say about this decree. It must be noted, however, that while the two contemporary experts on the Athenian calendar differ over many aspects of that calendar, the fact that they agree on the restoration for the calendar equations of this year facilitates discussion of the calendar of 324/3 considerably.

324/3

74. *DECREE* EM 7256

editors: Kumanudes <u>ΕΦ.</u> (1886) 103 no. 10; <u>IG</u> II 5.245d; <u>IG</u> II^2 547; Pritchett-Meritt <u>Chron.</u> 2-3.

supplement: <u>SEG</u> 21.292 (Pritchett-Meritt, Meritt <u>Hesperia</u> 10 [1941], <u>Ath.</u>, Pritchett-Neugebauer, Dow).

other bibliography: Koehler <u>Sitz. Ak. Berlin</u> (1891) 936; Meritt <u>Hesperia</u> 4(1935) 536; <u>Hesperia</u> 10(1941) 44 n. 1; <u>Ath.</u> 105-106; Pritchett-Neugebauer <u>Cal.</u> 56; Dow <u>Hesperia</u> 32(1963) 339-40, 351.

description: This fragment of Pentelic marble is broken on all sides. The back, if original, is very rough-picked. There is no way to tell where this fragment stood in relation to the original stele.

dimensions:
H 0.31 m.
W 0.175 m. (entire)
0.138 m. (surface)
Th 0.10 m.

letters: 0.007 m. Smallest, O, is .005; largest, Σ, is.010. H, I, K, P, are .008; Y is .009. Letters are square.

minuscule text:

stoich. 28

[Ἐφ' Ἡγηcίου ἄρχοντος ἐπὶ τῆς Ἐρεχθ]-
[εῖδος δεκάτης πρυτανεία]ς ἡ[ι Εὐφά]-
[νης Φρύνωνος Ῥαμνοῦcι]ος ἐγ[ραμμά]-
[τευεν· Θαργηλιῶνος] δευτέρα[ι μετ' ε]-
[ἰκάδας, πέμπτει τῆς] πρυτανε[ίας· ἐκ]-
[κληςία· τῶν προέδρων] ἐπεψή[φιζεν .]
[......13...... cυμ]πρόεδρ[οι ....]
[......12...... Διον]ύcιος Κ...6...
[......13...... Ἐκαλ]ῆθε[ν, ...7...]
[......15...... Ἀρ]χῖν[ος? ...6...]
.......16.......υς, Επ...8...
.......16.......ς Ἀλω[πεκῆθεν v]
[ἔδοξεν τῶι δήμωι ...]πρ...9...
[...7... εἶπεν ..5..]δρ ...9...
.......17.......ΛΙΛ...8...
.........21.........ιιι..5..
.......19....... προε[δρ...]
.......17....... προγραμ[μ...]
.......17.......ιν καὶ τῆς ε..
.......17.......αι τῆς περὶ ..
[......13...... καθα ο]ὶ νόμοι αὐ[τῶ]-
[ι προσέταττον ....10....]Α!....

epigraphical commentary: A few new or alternate readings need to be noted. Dots are mine unless noted below.

1 st. 22, 23 Σ̣Ḥ only P.-M. read the dotted eta. There is a vertical stroke on the stone. All editors dotted the sigma.

2 st. 19 Kum. read ιι before the omicron.

10 st 18 Χ̣ new reading by Dow (clearly) rather than kappa of the other editors. Although the chi is much more likely, it still should be dotted.

11 st. 17, 20 Υ̣Π̣ new readings by Dow who notes that: the space before the sigma makes omicron unlikely in st. 17; the pi, st. 20, is doubtful. Koe. read only the sigma, st. 18.

12 st. 19 Λ new reading, P.-M.

15 st. 19-21 ΛΙ<u>Λ</u> Dow notes the "fifth" [<u>sic</u>] letter is alpha, delta, or lambda, followed by eta, kappa, or nu." He also notes there is no letter (seen by Kum., Koe., Ki., P.-M.) in st. 21.

16 st. 21 ιι read as dotted by all editors: Dow notes that the letter is more likely nu, the only other choice.
st. 22 new reading Dow, as "one end of a gamma or tau."

commentary: The text is based on Pritchett-Meritt's restorations for the year 324/3 and Dow's subsequent improvements. Although Kumanudes did not date this inscription, Koehler (who made the basic restorations) and subsequently Kirchner assigned it to 318/-308/7, based on the obvious presence of a list of all the proedroi. Pritchett-Meritt, who had the benefit of Dow's work, the correct secretary's name, and #75 (II^2 454; it had already been restored to 324/3) as an example, were able to make a fuller restoration of the calendar prescript and thus assign this decree to 324/3. This restoration adds a new line 1 (so that Kirchner's line 1 is line 2 in this text) and requires a shift in the position of the fragment to the right (i.e., in line 3, Kirchner allowed for only 6 stoichoi before the first letter on the stone, omicron; the new text requires 19 stoichoi).

As for the earlier restorations for the date, Koehler and Kirchner made none before the letters on the stone in line 3. Both restored Πυανοψιῶνος as the month and 29th as the day. Koehler had restored τετάρτηι as the day in the prytany; Kirchner pointed out that the number did not fit the stoichedon order and thus restored πέμπτηι. Working with the previous restoration and adding the number (and tribe) of the prytany, Pritchett-Meritt produced this equation: [Thargelion] [2]9 = Prytany [X 5] = 324th day. It is repeated by Pritchett-Neugebauer in Cal. and Meritt in Ath.

The additional restorations made by Dow are noted below.

8 demotic: K[υδαθηναιεῦc] or K[υθήρριοc] Dow.

9 demotic: Dow.

10 name: Dow, suggested on basis of new reading, st. 18. Καρ?]κῖν[οc Koe., Ki.

14 εἶπεν: P.-M. placed the restoration at the beginning of the line; Dow notes that there should be more space before εἶπεν to allow for the restoration of the spokesman's patronymic.

21 end: Koe., Ki., P.-M. Koe., followed by Ki., also offered αὐ[τοῖc].

This is another decree which has benefited from Dow's work on the symproedroi (see especially his page 339; #31, #53, #75). Pritchett-Meritt's more specific date has not been challenged. As for the content, there is none--only the suggestion made by Koehler long ago that the decree may have recorded honors granted to the proedroi (Sitz. Ak. Berlin).

324/3

75. *DECREE* EM 7253

editors: Pittakis EΦ. (1852/55) 1609; Rangabê (1855) 546; Ussing Inscr. 60; Koehler & Velsen IG II 244; IG II^2 454; Dow Hesperia 32(1963) 350.

supplement: SEG 21.293 (Meritt AJP, Ath., Pritchett-Neugebauer, Dow).

other bibliography: Reusch Hermes 15(1880) 343; Unger Att. Arch. 681; Sundwall De Institut. 11; Meritt AJP 59

(1938) 499; <u>Hesperia</u> 10(1941) 44 n. 1; <u>Ath</u>. 106; Pritchett-Neugebauer <u>Cal</u>. 56.

description: This fragment of Pentelic marble was found on the Akropolis in 1840. The right part of the pediment and the right side are preserved. The back is probably not original: 0.078 m. is not very thick for a stele which has a restored stoichedon order of 38 letters; backs are usually rough picked, this one has a smooth surface.

dimensions:
H 0.23 m. (entire)
0.114 m. (surface)
W 0.132 m.
Th 0.078 m.

letters: 0.005 m. Smallest, Δ, Λ, Ο, Τ, Χ, are .004; largest, Η, Ι, Ρ, Σ, are .006. Letters are not very carefully cut.

minuscule text:

stoich. 38

[Ἐφ' Ἡγησίου ἄρχοντος ἐπὶ τῆς Ἐρε]χ̣θηΐδος[I] δεκάτ-
[ης πρυτανείας ἧι Εὐφάνης Φρύνων]ο̣ς Ῥαμνούσιο-
[ς ἐγραμμάτευεν· Σκιροφοριῶνος ἕκ]τ̣ει μετ' εἰκά-
[δας· ἐκκλησία· τῶν προέδρων ἐπεψήφι]ζ̣εν Χαρίδη-
[μος ------ συμπρόεδροι ------]ος Ἁλαιε-
[ύς[II] ---- ----[III] -----]ς Φρεάρ-
[ριος[IV] --- ---[V] --- Λακ]ιάδης[VI] Ξ
[------ ------ ------] Καλλ
[-- ----- ἔδοξεν τῶι δήμωι ---- -θ?]ηρι̣
36
....................................Ο̣Ι̣
37
....................................Ρ

epigraphical commentary: The surface at the bottom of the stone is broken off. There is no doubt that this small chip is new--the marble is white in comparison to the rest of the stone. Unfortunately, the chip took with it all of the rho in line 11 and most of the iota and omicron in line 10. The break must have occurred after Dow looked at the stone: although he correctly dots a number of letters as unclear, he printed the letters in lines 10 and 11 as clear.

The last letter in line 9 was read as a lambda by Pittakis, Π by Ussing, Γ by Koehler and Kirchner. Although there is a definite vertical stroke to the left of the center of the stoichos, the entire square bounded by that stroke is indented. Thus Dow's suggestion that the letter is a rho corrected to an iota is definitely possible.

commentary: The text is based on the restorations made by Meritt from Dow's suggestion that this decree be moved from 308/7 to 324/3 and have a stoichedon order of 38 letters to the line. The earlier restorations were based on the assumption that the presence of symproedroi required a date between 318/7 and 308/7. Koehler made the basic restorations, including a fully restored line 4 with 38 letters. Reusch (followed by Unger and Sundwall) found that the year 308/7 was the only possible year which combined a short archon's name (Charinos) with a secretary from Rhamnous. Since his restoration of line 1 required a 40 letter line, he restored the festival date as Σκιροφοριῶνος πέμπ]τει μετ' εἰκά/δας . Kirchner combined the restorations made by Koehler and Reusch; corrected the archon's name to Kairimos; and solved the problem of line 4, which was now 2 stoichoi too short, by suggesting vacats before and after ἐκκλησία.

There are no problems once this decree is moved to 324/3: the archon's name, Hegesias, allows for a 38-letter line 1; the correct secretary's name (see Meritt Hesperia) confirms the 38-letter line; the festival date for Skirophorion is now ἕκτει μετ' εἰκάδας (Meritt Ath.); and Kirchner's vacats in line 4 can be eliminated. Dow offered the restoration in line 9 and noted that the "three letters of line 8 [sic] come at or near the place where the patronymic or the name of the Spokesman should fall." He suggests [Θ]ηρι̣[κλέους] or [Θ]ηρι̣[ππίδου] for the end of line 9, beginning of line 10.

Dow's work on the symproedroi has secured another decree for the Lykourgan Era. Unfortunately, this decree offers even less information than #74. Since the day in the prytany was omitted, there is not even a calendar equation, only that the decree was passed in the tenth prytany, the 6th day before the end of Skirophroion.

324/3

76. *DEME DECREE OF PEIRAIEUS* EM 13447, 7719, 13446, + one in British Museum

photo: Stroud CSCA 7(1974) Plate 4.

editors: Fr. A Meritt Hesperia 29(1960) 1 no. 1 (originally Ag. Inv. I 2440, now EM 13447).
Fr. B Wilhelm UDA 235-239 (EM 7719).
Fr. C Conomis Klio 39(1961) 82-83; Meritt Hesperia 32(1963) 12 no. 10 (originally Ag. Inv. I 6439, now EM 13446).
Fr. D Chandler Inscript. no. 109; CIG 1.102; Hicks Brit. Mus. xii; IG II 573; IG II^2 1176 (in Brit. Mus.).
Fr. B+D Wilhelm UDA 235-239; IG II^2 1176.
Fr. A+B+D Meritt Hesperia 29 (1960) 1 no. 1.
Fr. A+B+C+D Stroud CSCA 7(1974) 290-298.

supplements: SEG 19.117 (Meritt Hesperia 1960); 21.521 (Meritt Hesperia 1963).
Bull. (1964) no. 117 (Meritt Hesperia 1963, Conomis).

collections: Michel 143 (Fr. D); Ditt. Syll.^{3} 915 (Fr. D); Behrend Att. Pacht. 30 (Fr. A+B+D), 31 (Fr. C).

description: This inscription consists of four fragments. Frs. A and C were originally in the Agora; they are now in the EM due to Stroud's work which shows that they physcally join Fr. B: the bottom of Fr. A joins the top of Fr. B; the right sides of Frs. A+B join the left side of Fr. C. Fr. D, which does not form a physical join, has been associated with Fr. B since Wilhelm.

The left sides of Frs. A and B, the right side of Fr. C, and the rough-picked back are preserved. Stroud observes that both sides of the joined fragments are not perpendicular to the surface; that this characteristic is more pronounced on the right side, and that it appears to be original (293). He also notes an irregularity in that while the left side is vertical, the right side, both on the joined fragments and on Fr. D, tapers inward (see dimensions below; this also seems to be the case, in reverse, for another deme decree, #42). Indeed, Stroud notes (294) that the fact that the stone cutter had to work with this "rather ragged right edge" accounts for the fact that the lines lengthen from top to bottom.

Stroud also notes that the three fragments that join are bluish-gray and that, while Fr. D was reported as white, McGregor has confirmed that it is bluish-gray as well. The provenance for Frs. B and D was not recorded. Despite the fact the Conomis stated that Fr. C was found near the theater of Dionysos (in Athens), Stroud (291) has shown that Frs. A and C were found in the same grid reference for the Agora excavations, seventeen years apart.

dimensions:
Fr. A+B+C
H 0.174 m.
W 0.208 m. (top)
0.215 m. (bottom)
Th 0.039 m. (top)
0.055 m. (bottom)

letters: 0.006 m. Smallest, O, Ω, are .004; largest, Y, is .008. I, Π, Ξ, are .005; K, Λ, Σ, are .006.

Fr. D
W 0.219 m. (top)
0.229 m. (bottom)

minuscule text: and next two pages. non stoich.

Fr. A Fr. C

[τὴν] ϲκηνὴν προ....αϲι̣...ca. 12...
[ἐ]ὰν τι βο[ύ]λωντ[αι πε]ρὶ τὴν οἰκοδομίαν·
ἐξεῖναι δὲ αὐ[τοῖϲ χ]ρ̣ῆϲθαι λίθοιϲ καὶ
γῆι ἐκ τοῦ τεμ[ένουϲ] τ̣οῦ Διονύϲου, ὅταν δ'
ἐξίωϲιν, παρα..ca. 6.. ἅπαντα ὀρθὰ καὶ ἐ-
ϲτηκότα· ἐ̣ὰ[ν ..ca. 7..]ειψωϲιν πρὸϲ τῆι ϲκη-
νεῖ, κέρα̣̣[μον καὶ ξ]ύ̣λα ἀπίτω λαβὼν πα-
Fr. B |||| [..ca. 5..]ννι.[ὁ δὲ χ]ρόνοϲ ἄρχει τῆϲ μι-
ϲθώϲεω[ϲ] Ἡ̣γηϲίαϲ ἄ̣ρχων· τοὺϲ δὲ δημό-
ταϲ θεωρεῖν ἀργύριο[ν] διδόνταϲ πλὴν ὅ- v
ϲοιϲ οἱ δημόται πρ[οεδρίαν δ]εδώκαϲι·
τούτουϲ δ' ἀπογράψα[ι πρὸϲ τοὺϲ π]ρ̣ια[μέ]-
νουϲ τὸ θέατρον· εἶν[αι δὲ τὴν προεδρίαν]
καὶ τῶι δημάρχωι κα[ὶ ..ca. 9.. καὶ τῶι κή]-
ρυκι καὶ εἴ τῶι ἄλλωι [δεδώκαϲιν οἱ δημόται]
[τὴ]ν π̣ροεδρίαν· ὅϲοι ....ca. 17....
....ca. 13.... ⁄| - - - - - - - - - -

lacuna

Fr. D [- - - τοὺς πριαμένους τὸ θέ]ạτ̣ρ̣[ο]ν πạ[ρέ]-
[χειν τοῖς δημόται]ς ἡδ[ω]λιασμένην τὴν θέαν [κα]-
[τὰ τ]ὰ πάτρια· ἐὰν δὲ μὴ ποήσωσιν κατὰ τὰς συνθ[ή]-
κας τὰς περὶ τὸ θέατρον, οἰκοδομῆσαι μὲν Πειρα-
έας τὰ δεόμενα, τὰ δ' ἀναλώματα τοῖς πριαμένοις
εἶναι· ἐπιτιμητὰς δὲ αἱρεῖσθαι Πειραέας ὅταν πα-
ραδιδῶσι τὸ θέατρον τρεῖς ἄνδρας ἐκ Πειραέων.
ἀναγράψαι δὲ τὸν δήμαρχον καὶ τοὺς ταμίας ἀντί-
γραφα τῶν συνθηκῶν εἰς στήλην λιθίνην καὶ στῆσα-
ι ἐν τῆι ἀγορᾶι τῶν δημοτῶν· παραγράψαι δὲ καὶ τὸ
ὄνομα, παρ' ὧι ἂν κεῖωνται αἱ συνθῆκαι. ὠνηταὶ Ἀρι-
στοφάνης Σμικύθο : 𐅅Η : Μελησίας Ἀριστοκράτο : ΧΗ
Ἀρεθούσιος Ἀριστόλεω Πήληξ : 𐅅 : Οἰνοφῶν Εὐφι-
λήτου Πειραιεύς : ΧΗ
Καλλιάδης εἶπεν· ἐψηφίσθαι Πειραεῦσι· ἐπειδὴ Θεαῖος
φιλοτιμεῖται πρὸς τοὺς δημότας καὶ νῦν καὶ ἐν τῶι

ἔμπροϲθε χρόνωι καὶ πεπόηκεν τριακοϲίαιϲ δραχμαῖϲ πλέον εὑρεῖν τὸ θέατρον, ϲτεφανῶϲαι αὐτὸν θαλλõ ϲτεφάνωι ἀρετῆϲ ἕνεκα καὶ δικαιοϲύνηϲ τῆϲ εἰϲ τοὺϲ δημόταϲ· ϲτεφανῶϲαι δὲ καὶ τοὺϲ πριαμένουϲ τὸ θέατρον Ἀριϲτοφάνην Πειραέα, Μεληϲίαν Λαμπτρέα, Οἰνοφῶντα Πειραιέα, Ἀρεθούϲιον Πήληκα.

commentary: The text is based on Stroud's join of Fr. C to Frs. A and B, already associated by Meritt. Stroud included only the first 4 lines of Fr. D; I have added the rest of Fr. D from Kirchner's text. Even after Wilhelm had associated Fr. B with Fr. A, the significance of the name, Hegesias, was misinterpreted. As Stroud notes, it was Behrend who suggested for Frs. A, B and C that Hegesias denoted the archonship and thus the year, 324/3. Behrend treated Fr. C as a separate document, dated to the middle of the 3rd century on the basis of Meritt's suggestion. (It should be noted that Conomis was closer to the date, since he thought the fragment dealt with construction of the theater of Dionysos in Athens, under Lykourgos's auspices.) With the physical join of Fr. C to Frs. A+B, Stroud was able to substantiate Behrend's suggestion (line 9), show that all 4 fragments belong to the year of Hegesias, and offer better restorations for lines 2 through 16. The restorations for the ends of the lines of Fr. B, that were suggested by Wilhelm are now no longer necessary, since Fr. C provides the ends of the lines. The restorations, therefore, for lines 1-17 are Stroud's; lines 18-33 (Fr. D) are complete.

Stroud has devoted three pages (296-298) to a discussion of this decree from the deme of Peiraieus. He notes that there are two parts. The first part (lines 1-31) deals with a leasing agreement between the demesmen of Peiraieus and the _triamenoi_ of the theater of Dionysos. Stroud (296 n. 33) locates this theater on the Mounichia hill in Peiraieus. The second part (lines 32-40) records a decree proposed by Kalliades honoring Theaios with an olive crown and four of the _triamenoi_:

Aristophanes and Oinophon of Peiraieus, Melesias of Lamptrea, and Arethousios of Peleke.

Stroud considers in detail the various aspects of this particular lease. He does not discuss the nature of the office of the triamenoi, but this name was obviously given to the officials who took care of this particular theater of Dionysos in the Peiraieus. This decree, therefore, represents another instance of the reform and care for detail at the deme level that is so characteristic of Lykourgos at the state level.

324/3

77. *THE SYLLOGEIS HONOR LYSIKLES AND EUTHYKRITOS* Paris — Louvre no. 471

editors: Boeckh CIG 99 (from text of Mueller) and Add. p. 900; Froehner Inscriptions 195-197 no. 99; IG II 607; IG II^2 1257.

other bibliography: Koehler AM 7(1882) 105. Rhodes Boule 129-130.

description: This inscription was found "sans doute" (Froehner) in Athens; it is now in the Choiseul Collection in the Louvre. Apparently only Mueller and Froehner have seen the stone; Kirchner saw a photograph. None of the editors has offered much of a description; only Froehner recorded dimensions, but only height and width.

The inscription is cut on a monument-base, both sides of which are broken (Boeckh). The majuscule texts of Boeckh and Koehler as well as Kirchner's text show that the two decrees, A and B, were inscribed side by side, with the first 2 lines, which record the actual dedication, inscribed above both columns.

dimensions:	letters: Only Kirchner recorded size:
H 0.14 m.	0.006 m. Boeckh noted that letters O,
W 0.28 m.	Θ, Ω are much smaller and that pi
	could be Π or Γ.

minuscule text: next two pages

non stoich.

[Οἱ συλλογεῖς τοῦ δή]μου ἀνέθεσαν Μητρὶ θεῶν ἐπὶ Ἡγησί[ου ἄρχοντος στεφα]-
[νωθέντες ὑπὸ τοῦ δ]ήμου ἀρετῆς ἕνεκα καὶ δικαιοσ[ύνης].

A

[- - - - - - - - - εἶπεν· ἐπειδ]ὴ Εὐθύκριτος
[- - - - τὴν ἀρχὴν ἦρξε μετὰ τῶ]ν συναρχόντων
[καλῶς καὶ δικαίως, καὶ προθύμως ἐπεμελ]ήθη πάντων ὧν αὐ-
[τῶι ἐπέταττον οἱ συνάρχοντες καὶ ἱ]εροποίησεν τῆι Ἀθ-
[ηνᾶι, δεδόχθαι τοῖς τοῦ δήμου συλλογε]ῦσιν, ἐπαινέσαι κα-
[ὶ στεφανῶσαι αὐτὸν χρυσῶι στεφάνωι ἀ]πὸ :Χ: δραχμῶν ἀρε-
[τῆς ἕνεκα καὶ φιλοτιμίας τῆς εἰς τοὺς] συνάρχοντας καὶ δι-
[καιοσυνης τῆς περὶ τὸν δῆμον τὸν Ἀθην]αίων. ἀναγράψαι δὲ
[τόδε τὸ ψήφισμα καὶ τὸν στέφανον ἐπὶ τὸ] ἀνάθημα τὸ κοινὸν
[τῶν συναρχόντων].

B

Ἔδοξεν τοῖς τοῦ δήμου συλλ[ογεῦσιν· - - - εἶπεν]·
ἐπειδὴ Λυσικλῆς Εἰρηνίππ[ου τὴν ἀρχὴν ἦρξε μετὰ τῶν συν-
αρχόντων καλῶς καὶ δικαίως [καὶ ἱεροποίησεν τῶι Διὶ]
τῶι Ὀλυνπίωι καὶ τῶν ἄλλων ἀπά[ντων ὧν αὐτῶι ἐπέταττον οἱ σ]-
υνάρχοντες κατὰ τοὺς νόμους [ἐπεμελήθη καὶ - - - - ὅς]-
ον δύναται ὑπὲρ τῆς ἀρχῆς, ἐπ[αινέσαι καὶ στεφανῶσαι αὐτὸν]
χρυσῶι στεφάνωι ἀπὸ :X: δραχ[μῶν ἀρετῆς καὶ δικαιοσύνης]
ἕνεκα τῆς περὶ τὸν δῆμον τὸν Ἀ[θηναίων καὶ τοὺς συνάρχον]-
τας. ἀναγράψαι δὲ τόδε τὸ ψήφ[ισμα καὶ τὸν στέφανον ἐπὶ τὸ ἀ]-
νάθημα τὸ κοινὸν τῶν συν[αρχόντων].

commentary: Although the two columns, A and B, should be placed along side of each other, I have placed B after A for reasons of space (as did Froehner and Boeckh in his minuscule text). The three elements have been designated in various ways. Froehner designated the dedication as: A (lines 1-2); the first decree as B (lines 3-12); and the second decree as C (lines 1-10). Boeckh designated the three elements as: I (lines 1-2), II (lines 3-12), and III (lines 3-12). Koehler and Kirchner followed

Boeckh's line designations but labelled only the two decrees, A and B. I have followed Koehler and Kirchner in labeling only the decrees, but I have numbered the lines consecutively: dedication, lines 1-2; #77A, lines 3-12; #77B, lines 13-22.

There are a few places where the readings differ. Boeckh read the first letters in line 1 as IOI; he recorded MOY in his addenda. Froehner, Boechkh and Koehler did not read the final sigma in line 2. At the end of line 3, Boeckh recorded ΕΥΟΥΚΑΠΟΣ, in his addendum, ΚΑΙΤΟΣ. In his Addenda, Boeckh also recorded different readings: at the end of line 6, ΤΗΤΑΘ; of line 7, ΣΑΝΤΑ; of line 8, ΑΡΙΣ. Other readings for the end of line 8 are ΑΡΓ, Boeckh (99), and Koehler; Froehner and Kirchner read ΑΡΕ. The first 2 letters in the restoration for line 14, ΟΥ, were read by Froehner and Boeckh (Add.); the omicron only was read by Boeckh (99) and Koehler. Froehner read the kappa in the restoration for line 15; ΜΩ in restoration for line 19 (Koehler read the mu); iota in restoration for line 21. Froehner did not read the final sigma on the stone in line 17. Only Boeckh read a mu rather than nu in Olympioi, line 17.

The differences in restoration reflect not only the different readings, but also show the progress made from the last century in identifying certain set phrases. The restorations are Froehner's unless noted below.

1 beg: Koe, Boe. (Add.), Ki. [Οἱ συλλογεῖϲ τοῦ δή[μου Froe.; Ἀθηνα]ῖοι Boe.

1/2: Koe., Ki. σί[ου ἄρχοντεϲ Λυσικλῆν Εἰρηνίππου καὶ/ Εὔθύκριτον ..6... δ] Froe.; σί[ου ἄρχοντοϲ τοὺϲ συλλογέ-α/ϲ τοῦ δ] Boe.; σί[ου ἄρχοντοϲ στεφανωθέντεϲ ὑπὸ τοῦ δ] Boe. (Add).

2 end: Boe., Koe., Ki. [σύνηστῆϲ περὶ τὸν δῆμον τὸν Ἀθηναίων] Froe.

3 end: Froe., Koe., Ki. Εὐθύ[δημ]οϲ Boe. From Boeckh's two different readings of the letters in ep. com. above, it is obvious that this restoration is only a guess.

4 beg: Boe., Koe., Ki. Froe. added δήμου before τῆν.

6 ἐπέταττον: Koe., Ki. ἐπέταξαν Froe., Boe.

7 beg: Boe., Koe., Ki. [ηνᾶι Πολιάδι σὺν τοῖϲ ἄλλοιϲ συλλογε]ῦσιν Froe.

8/9: Ki. ἀρε/[τῆς τε ἕνεκα τῆς περὶ τοὺς σ] Froe. ἀργ/[υρίου ἀρετῆς τε ἕνεκα τῆς περὶ τοὺς] Boe. ἀργ/[υρί-ου ----ς ἕνεκα τῆς εἰς τοὺς] Koe.

11 beg: Ki. [τόδε τὸ ψήφισμα ἐν στήληι καὶ στῆσαι ὑπὸ τὸ] Froe., Boe.; [τόδε τὸ ψήφισμα ---- ἐπὶ τὸ] Koe.

13 end: Froe., Boe. Koe. and Ki. add εἶπεν at end of line.

14 end: the only difference between Froe.'s restoration and Koe.'s is that Froe. (followed by Boe.) allowed space after the patronymic, presumably for the demotic.

15 end: Boe. (who left a space after καὶ--Koe. and Ki. did not. Froe. restored εὐσεβῶς after καὶ.

16 end: Koe., Ki. ἀπαύ[των ἐπεμελήθη, ὧν αὐτῶι ἐπεταξαν οἱ σ] Froe., Boe., who restored αὐτοὶ instead.

17 end: Koe., Ki. νόμο[ς, ...9..... καὶ ἐθελοντὴς ἀεὶ ὅς] Froe., Boe. did not restore.

18 end: Koe., Ki. ἐπ[οίησε, ἐπαινέσαι αὐτὸν καὶ στεφαν-ῶσαι Froe., Boe.

19 end: Ki., who, in effect used Froe.'s restoration without Froe.'s added τε. μ[ῶν ἀργυρίον, ἀρετῆς καὶ δικαιοσύνης Boe.; [μῶν ἀργυρίου δικαιοσύνης] Koe.

20 end: Koe., Ki. Ἀ[θηναίων καὶ τῆς περὶ τοὺς συνάρ-χον] Froe., Boe.

21 end: Ki. [σμα ἐν στήληι καὶ στῆσαι αὐτὸ τὸ ἀ] Froe., Boe. [ισμα ---- ἐπὶ τὸ ἀ] Koe.

This document was inscribed on a monument base. It consists of a dedication (lines 1, 2) which shows that the base was for a votive offering to the Mother of the Gods by the syllogeis of the Demos. It also notes (if the restoration is correct) that the syllogeis of that year had been crowned by the Demos for their virtue and righteousness. There follow two decrees of the syllogeis concerning two of their group. In #77A (lines 3-12)

Euthykritos, because he has well, justly and zealously carried out his assigned religious duties toward Athena, is to be given a gold crown worth a thousand drachmai, for his virtue and loyalty to his fellow syllogeis and his righteousness to the Demos. The decree and the crown are to be inscribed on the monument dedicated by the syllogeis. Euthykritos's colleague, Lysikles, son of Eirenippos, is to be honored similarly in #77B (lines 13-22). It seems that he has well and justly carried out his duties toward Zeus Olympios as well as the other duties assigned by the synarchontes, according to the laws. He is to receive as well a crown worth a thousand drachmai and both the decree and the crown are to be inscribed on the same dedication.

Obviously the orders recorded at the end of the two decrees were carried out. The votive offering was not only considered, it was set up. Apparently the syllogeis (especially Euthykritos and Lysikles) had gone above and beyond the call of duty in this year.

The exact nature of the syllogeis has been discussed by both Froehner and Boeckh. More recently, Rhodes has discussed the evidence for this board of 30 men composed of 3 bouleutes from each tribe. The syllogeis and Rhodes's discussion have been considered already in #18 (II^2 330) which honors men who were probably not syllogeis. This decree, therefore, offers the most substantial proof (in this Corpus) that the religious duties were, if not an important aspect, at least an honorable aspect of the duties of this "bouleutic sub-committee" (Rhodes, 130).

The non-stoichedon inscriptions in this Corpus are listed in #16. Wilhelm had suggested for one particular one (#80, II^2 366) that it was set up privately. What we have here is a combination of both public and private: a very public group of men--the syllogeis of the Demos--took the initiative to commemorate their year in office, the year of Hegesias, 324/3, to set up a monument to the Mother of the Gods and to honor two of their own--Euthykritos and Lysikles.

324/3

78. *THE EIKADEIS HONOR POLYXENOS* lost

editors: Franz BdI (1835) 209-210 no. 1; Pittakis l'ancienne Athènes (1835) 474-475; Wordsworth Athens^2 (1837) 225-227; Ross Demen (1846) iv; Rangabé (1855) 418; IG II 609; IG II^2 1258.

other bibliography: Loeper AM 7(1892) 397 n. 3; Ziebarth Vereinswesen 182; Klaffenbach AM 51(1926) 24.

description: Koehler and Kirchner noted that the stele was crowned with an aetomata; Rangabé noted as well that the inscription begins in the middle of the stone. Only Koehler noted that the stone was marble. No one has recorded the dimensions; only Kirchner noted the height of the letters.

Although no one seems to know where the stone is now, it was not lost immediately. In 1916, Kirchner noted that the stone was τὴν κυρίαν Πάλη. Before that, Franz, Pittakis, and Rangabé recorded that the stone was in the home of Papariogopoulos, the Russian consul in Athens.

There has been some confusion as to where the stone was found. In order of publication, Franz gave the origin of the stone as Oropos; Pittakis said the coast of Tanagra. Wordsworth was the first to mention Markopolis, the one in the Mesogeia; this designation and location was accepted by Ross, Rangabé, and Koehler. At that point Loeper noted that there were two Markopoleis, one in the Mesogeia, one near Oropos, and that the designations given by the first two publishers fit better with the Markopolis near Oropos. Kirchner accepted Loeper's opinion, without realizing the discrepancies. Not only was Wordsworth the first to mention Markopolis (the one in the Mesogeia) he also noted that he was copying the inscription there. There is no possibility that the stone sat in Markopolis after the Consul's house and before Mrs. Pale's because Rangabé recorded the stone's location as the Consul's house. The explanation must be that, despite the order of publication, Wordsworth copied the inscription in situ (or closer to it than the Consul's house) before it arrived at the home of Paparigopoulos. (The first edition of Wordsworth, 1836, is still later than Franz's article.)

Confirmation of Markopolis in the Mesogeia as the provenance of the stone came with Klaffenbach's publication of a new boundary stone from Koropi (now II^2 2632) and his association of that stone with another boundary stone found near the Markopolis in the Mesogeia. (II^2 2631). As Klaffenbach noted, both stones were not only carved by the same stonecutter, but also their texts are identical. And the texts show that these were boundary stones for land belonging to the koine of the Eikadeis. Klaffenbach states, therefore, that the location for the decree of the Eikadeis (II^2 1258) and consequently the worship of Apollo Parnessos was, in fact, in the neighborhood of the Markopolis in the Mesogeia.

dimensions: not recorded. letters: 0.005 m.

minuscule text: next page.

commentary: The text of this inscription is virtually complete. Although Wordsworth saw all the letters except for the initial epsilon, he did not note that the word ΙΕΡΩΙ in line 24 was actually inscribed ΙΕΡΟΥ; Rangabé, Koehler and Kirchner did note the error. At the beginning of line 2, Wordsworth saw nu, Rangabé recorded N. In addition to the height of the letters, Kirchner included some of the letter forms: ΕΠΡΦΘϐ = Β; Ο = Θ, Ω. These idiosyncracies on the part of the stonecutter explain the spelling discrepancies between various texts.

Since Rangabé did not restore the epsilon at the beginning of line 1, he gave the name of the mover as Pameinon.

This decree, moved by Epameinon, son of Ameinon, commends a certain Polyxenos, son of Diodoros; gives him a gold crown; and provides for the election of three men from the Eikadeis to help Polyxenos in his prosecution of false witnesses against the Eikadeis.

non stoich. 26–32

[Ἐ]παμείνων Ἀμεινίου εἶπεν· ἐπειδή τι-
[ν]ες ἐναντία τῶι ὅρκωι ὃν ὤμοσαν καὶ τε[ῖ]
ἀρᾶι ἣν Εἰκαδεὺς ἐπηράσατο διατελ-
οῦσι πράττοντες καὶ λέγοντες κατὰ Ε-
ἰκαδέων ἐπὶ βλάβει τῶν κοινῶν τῶν
Εἰκαδέων, ἀφ' ὧν τὰ ἱερὰ τοῖς θεοῖς θ-
ύουσιν Εἰκαδέες καὶ τοῖς δικαζομέν-
οις Εἰκαδεῦσιν συνδικοῦσιν ὑπε-
ναντία τοῖς Εἰκαδεῦσιν καὶ μεμαρ-
τυρήκασιν ἐπὶ τοῦ δικαστηρίου ἐ-
πὶ βλάβει τοῦ κοινοῦ τοῦ Εἰκαδέων
ψευδεῖς μαρτυρίας, ἑλέσθαι τρεῖς
ἄνδρας ἤδη ἐξ Εἰκαδέων οἵτινες
συναγωνιοῦνται τῶι ἐπεσκημμέν-
ωι ταῖς μαρτυρίαις Πολυξένωι, ὅπω-
ς ἂν δίκην διδῶσιν οἱ τὰ ψευδῆ μαρτ-
υροῦντες· ἐπαινέσαι δὲ Πολύξενον
Διοδώρου καὶ στεφανῶσαι χρυσῶι στ-
εφάνωι ὅτι δίκαιός ἐστιν περὶ τὰ κοι-
νὰ τὰ Εἰκαδέων καὶ ἐπεσκήψατο τοῖς
μάρτυσιν. ἀναγράψαι δὲ τόδε τὸ ψήφισ-
μα τοὺς ἄρχοντας τοὺς ἐφ' Ἡγησίου ἄρ-
χοντος εἰς στήλην λιθίνην καὶ στῆσ-
αι ἐν τῶι ἱερῶ̣ι̣ τοῦ Ἀπόλλωνος τοῦ Πα-
ρνησσίου.

These false witnesses are apparently members of the koine (association) of the Eikadeis (albeit in bad standing) since they have continued to act and speak against the

Eikadeis despite their oath and the curse given by Eikadeus.

Polyxenos is honored because he has already brought an accusation of perjury against the false witnesses; three more men are to help him because the actions of the false witnesses have affected the property of the Eikadeis and, since the property provides the funds for sacrifices, the Gods.

The text ends with instructions to the archons, serving during the year of the archon Hegesias, to have the stele inscribed and set up in the temple of Apollo Parnessos. The dating of the decree by identifying in which archonship the officials served is typical also of deme and tribe decrees (see #26 for deme decrees, #61 for tribal decrees). According to Rangabê, the text begins in the middle of the stone; no one has recorded the presence of a sculptured wreath; and therefore the representation of the crown received by Polyxenos may have been painted above the text.

The nature of this koine of Eikadeis has been the focal point of discussions by Wordsworth, Ross (and Meier in Ross), and Rangabê. A titular hero named Eikadeus notwithstanding, no one has doubted that the designation has something to do with the number twenty. Wordsworth used Hesychios's definition of triakas to suggest that the eikadeis were analogous to the triakades, i.e., some sort of division within the tribes. M.H.E. Meier decided that they could only be a religious club (θίασος) which came together on the 20th of each month for offerings and feasting. Rangabê, who offered the fullest commentary, rejected the suggestion of a tribal division, agreed that the group met on the 20th (using the Greek Etymology and sources on Epikouros as confirmation), but went further in suggesting that the number twenty came originally from the number of people who had first come together to take care of some sanctuary, probably that of Apollo Parnessos. And with time, the meaning changed from the number of the people to the day of the festival.

Whatever the origin of this group, we do know that by the end of the fourth century, the koine of the Eikadeis swore an oath; it was protected by the hero (God?) Eikadeus (Ross calls him a mythical eponym); it held property (the boundary stones mentioned in the description confirm this); it sacrificed to Gods other than Apollo Parnessos; and the officials of the group were called archons. (Wordsworth offered "magistrates of the Office of Information"; Rangabê, "magistrates.)

Pittakis described this stone as "curious"; the description fits. This inscription allows a glimpse, however incomplete, into Attic society at the local level.

XVI. THE YEAR OF KEPHISODOROS, 323/2

79. *LAPYRIS OF KLEONAI HELPS ATHENS* EM 7178, 7179

editors: Fr. A Pittakis ΕΦ. (1840/42) 404; Rangabé (1855) 520.
Fr. B Pittakis ΕΦ. (1837/39) 301; Rangabé (1885) 818.
Fr. A+B Koehler Hermes 5 (1871) 328-330; Koehler & Velsen IG II 181; IG II^2 365; physical join made by Walbank Contributions 171-175.

supplements: SEG 21.294 (Schweigert, Pritchett-Neugebauer, Meritt); 30.66 (Piérart-Thalmann, Walbank).

other bibliography: Boeckh Epigr. Chronol. Studien 21; Dittenberger Index Schol. Halens (1885/6) x; Wilhelm Arch. Epig. Mitt. 17(1894) 37; Schweigert Hesperia 9 (1940) 338-339; Pritchett-Neugebauer Cal. 57; Meritt Ath. 106; Lambrechts Proxenie. 409-410; Rhodes Boule 43 n. 6; 98-100 n. 1, 132 n. 12; 220 n. 3, 262; DeLaix Proboul. 127, 137; Henry Prescripts 38 n. 26, 42; Piérart-Thalmann BCH Supplement 6(1980) 266-269; Osborne ZPE 41(1981) 153-170; Miller Hesperia Supplement XX (1982) 100-108.

description: As a result of Walbank's examination in 1971, the two fragments of Hymettan marble are joined and form a standing stele in the EM. Kirchner is therefore incorrect in noting of the fragments "non contigua". Fr. A was found on June 20, 1840, east of the Parthenon; the left side and probably the top are original; most of the surface is badly worn and chipped. Fr. B was found on Ocotber 16, 1839 near the Erectheion; the left side, lower right side and bottom are preserved; the surface is in better shape than Fr. A. Although Fr. A is thinner, both backs are rough-picked and therefore may be original. The stele was apparently crowned with a cornice, most of which is now chipped off to make it flush with the inscribed surface.

dimensions:
H 0.952 m.
W 0.289 m. (Fr.A)
0.364 m. (Fr.B mid)
0.371 m. (Fr.B below)
Th 0.076 m. (Fr.A)
0.086 m. (Fr.B)

letters: 0.006 m. Smallest, Δ, Ω, are .004; largest, Y, is .007. A, B, E, I, N, P, T, are .006 m. A number of thetas do not have dots; not all alphas have cross bars.

minuscule text: and next page.

stoich. 32

Fr. A

Ἐπὶ Κηφιcοδώρου ἄρχον[τος ἐπὶ τῆc Ἱππο]-
θωντίδος πρώτης πρυτα[νείας, ἧι Ἀρχίας]
[Π]υθοδώρου ἐγραμμάτευε[ν· Ἑκατομβαιῶν]-
[ο]c ἐνδεκάτει, τῆc πρυτανεί[ας· τῶν προέδ]-
[ρ]ων ἐπεψήφ[ι]ζεν Τιμόcτρα[τ]ο[c ...7.... ἔ]-
[δ]οξεν τῶι δή[μ]ω[ι]· Ἐπιτελ[ης] Σ[ω]ιν[όμου Περ]-
[γ]αcῆθεν εἶπεν· [π]ερὶ ὧν λέγ[ε]ι ὁ ἀ[ρκεθεωρ]-
[ο]c ὁ εἰc τα Ν[έ]μεα κ[α]ι Λάπυ[ριc] ὁ π[ρόξενοc]
τῆc πόλεωc ....Ι δεδόχ[θαι] τ[ῶι δήμωι τ.]
.μὲν ἀρκεθ[εω]ρο - - - - - - - - - - - - - -
.αι εἰc τὸ[ν ......13......]κι - - - - - -
. καὶ Ἀθη[ν]αιοι.ω....8....ω - - - - - - -
.νον μέροc - - - - - - - - - - - - - - - -
.ι αὐτῶι ἀργύ[ριον - - - - - - - - - - - λ]-
αμβάνειν ὑπὲρ[- - - - - - - - - - - - - τ]-
[ο]ὺc προξένου[c - - - - - - - - - - - - -]
.τρια ὁποc - - - - - - - - - - - - - - - -
.νουcια [αὐ]τῶι - - - - - - - - - - - - -
[β]ου[λ]ο[μ]εν.ν Ἀθη[ναι - - - - - - - - -]
[.. τ]ὸν πρ[όξ]εν[ον - - - - - - - - - - -]
....ΤΥΣ....Ο - - - - - - - - - - - - - - -
...\ΓΟ..5..Λ... - - - - - - - - - - - - -

....4.IZH...Γ - - - - - - - - - - - - - - - - - -
.YO..NA[- - - - - - - - - - - - - - - - - - πο]-
[λ]εμ[ί]ο.c ..ο...τωι.Y - - - - - - - - - -
TO...OΣT..6...ΣOΩI - - - - - - - - - - - -
ΣΛ¯Γ...5.O...6..ΣO - - - - - - - - - - - -
..N[- - - - - - - - - - - - - - - - - πρῶτ]-
οιc μετὰ τ[ὰ ἱερὰ] Π - - - - - - - - - - -
.APEK..5..Λ...H - - - - - - - - - - - - - -
.EOIΣ...KOΛ..ΛH - - - - - - - - - - - - -
..AIΓPA.NTA..Λ - - - - - - - - - - - - -

Fr. B

....EIEAI...6..Σ - - - - - - - - - - - -
....Σ καὶ OΣO - - - - - - - - - - - - -
...OE θεωρὸc EI - - - - - - - - - - - -
τὸν θεωρὸν [τ]οῖc προξ[ένοιc - - - - -]
καθὰ Λάπυριc ὁ πρόξενο[c - - - - - -]
τοὺc δὲ ἀποδέκταc μερί[cαι τῶι ἀρκε]-
θεώρωι ὃc ἂν ἀεὶ ἀρκεθεω[ρῆcηι τὸ]
ἀργύριον. vacat

vacat 0.02

ἐπαινέcαι δὲ Λάπυριν Καλλί[ου Κλεωναῖ]-
ον τὸν πρόξενον καὶ καλέcαι [αὐτὸν ἐπὶ δ]-
εῖπνον εἰc τὸ πρυτανεῖον εἰc [αὔριον].
ἀναγράψαι δὲ τόδε τὸ ψήφιcμα [τὸν γραμ]-
ματέα τῆc βουλῆc εἰc τὴν cτήλη[ν τὴν ἐν]
ἀκροπόλει ἐν ἧι γέγραπται Ἐχεν[βρότωι]
Κλεωναίωι τῶι προ<γό>νωι τῶι Λαπύριοc
ἡ προξενία. vacat

vacat

epigraphical commentary: Unless noted below, underlined letters refer to Koehler and Kirchner's readings. Dots denoting unclear letters are mine, unless noted below. Despite the poor conditions of the stone a number of new readings are recorded below. Although Koehler and Kirchner (followed by Miller) have designated lines for the separate fragments, I have followed Walbank in numbering the lines consecutively as is usual when two fragments have been joined to form a stele. I have also followed Walbank in giving the vacat, 8 lines before the end, a line number.

Although Walbank examined this stone before I did, his join and the resulting new text were published after I examined the stone and established my text. The major differences in readings, which occur in lines 10-33, reinforce the fact that the letters are difficult to read. Those differences between Walbank and this text are noted below. (I note that rather than underline letters read previously but no longer visible, Walbank brackets them.) Only Velsen read letters below line 32 and before Fr. B: ⸜_ in st. 14, 15.

Fr. A

1 st. 19 ı Koe. Wal. read st. 1-18 clearly.

2 st. 1-19 Wal. read clearly.

3 st. 2 ˇ Koe. Wal. read st. 2-20 clearly.

4 st. 2 ⸜ Koe. Wal read st. 3-22 clearly.

5 st. 11, 14 new readings.
st. 14-17 ṬIMO Wal., who also records new reading, Ạ, st. 21

6 st. 3 ⊤ Koe.
st. 12 new reading.
st. 22 read by Koe., Ki., Wal.

7 st. 17, 21, 23 Ω, Γ̣, I new readings, Wal.

8 st. 4 ⸦ Koe.
st. 2-4 read by Wal.
st. 11, 18 Ṃ, A new readings, Wal.

9 st. 1 ‾ Koe.
st. 18, 19 ⌒⸜ Koe.
st. 15-19 Δ̣ΕΔ̣Ο̣Χ̣ Wal. (st. 15-new reading).

10 st. 12, 13 PỌ new readings, Wal.

11 [·]AEIΣTON [12]NKA[I 7] Wal., whose text omits iota in st. 3 (obviously a printing error since letters and spaces only add up to 31).

12 st. 8 letter looks like eta.
st. 11, 14, 23 Wal. read clearly.

13 st. 2 ∖ Koe.; ⊣ Vel.; N Lattermann in letter to Ki.
st. 9 Wal. read clearly.

14 st. 2 ⁄| Koe. Ị Ki.
st. 10 new reading, also read by Wal. who dotted only Γ̣Ỵ, st. 10, 11.

15 st. 3 Koe. saw no letter. Ḅ Ki., B Wal.
st. 11 ı Koe. Wal. did not read iota, st. 7.

16 st. 12 new reading, Wal.

17 st. 11-13 INẠ new readings, Wal.

18 st. 1 ı Vel.
st. 2 ı' Koe.
st. 4 ı Koe. Wal. reads clear upsilon.
st. 6-8 EΛΓ Vel.
st. 13 / Koe.

19 st. 4, 6, 19 Λ̣, Ṃ, Ị new readings, Wal., who also dotted upsilon, st. 3.

20 [4.]NΠ̣P̣[OΞ]EN[.]Ṇ[19] Wal.

21 st. 5-7 ‾NΣ Koe., Ki. [...]Λ̣[.]ỊṆ[....]OṂ[19] Wal.

22 [...]ẸṆΣ̣ẸΣ[..]NẠ[20] Wal.

23 st. 5 new reading, also seen by Wal.
st. 1, 2, 8, 19 Λ, H, I, Ḥ new readings, Wal.

24 ΦYOỴ[.]IẠΛ[24] Wal.

25 st. 2 Ẹ Koe., Ki.
st. 6 ·ı/ Koe.
st. 18, 19 Ỵ. Schwenk. ḤṆ Wal., who read letters only in st. 2, 3, 10, 18, 19.

26 st. 17, 18 new readings. Wal. read dotted pi: TO[12]M[.]Π̣[15].

27 st. 17, 18 new reading. ΣΙ[13]ΣΠ̣[15] Wal.

28 st. 2 _ Koe. Δ Vels.
st. 3 I Koe., Vel., Ki. ΣΑΙ[6]Λ̣[.]Α[...]Ị[16] Wal.

29 st. 7 neither Koe. nor Vel. read a letter.
st. 8 | Vel. [..]ΣΙΠ[27] Wal.

30 st. 1 ‾ Vel.
st. 5 new reading, also seen by Wal.
st. 8 N Vel.
st. 11 new Reading, Wal.
st. 14 H Koe., Ki., Vel. I read nothing.
st. 15 Ḥ new reading. Ị Wal.

31 st. 4 Y Vels.
st. 5 Koe. did not read a sigma; Vel., Ki., Lattermann, Wal. did, clearly.
st. 9 new reading, Wal.
st. 10 new reading. _ Vel.
st. 11 new reading, Wal. O Vel.
st. 13–16 ΛΙ.. Koe., Ki.; .HI. Vels; ..ḤṂ Wal.; .ΛΗ. Schwenk.

32 st. 3 new reading, Wal.
st. 5 new reading, Wal. I can see horizontal stroke.
st. 6, 7 both Koe. and Vel. read only upper part of rho and alpha; E[. Wal.
st. 8 Koe. and Vels. read most of nu.
st. 9–11 ṆTẠ Wal. ..T Vels.; .T. Koe., Ki. I read only tau.
st. 13, 14 ΛΙ Koe., Ki.; .Λ Schwenk, Wal.

33 [....]EỊEAỊ[6]Σ Wal. Koe., Ki., read \ in st. 6, I read 2 dotted iotas in st. 6,7.

34 st. 11 / Koe.

35 st. 4 Ḳ Wal.

36 st. 1 new reading, also read by Wal. Koe.
st. 2 new reading, Wal.

39 st. 6 new reading, also read by Wal.
st. 19, 20 new readings, Wal. '/. Koe.; I read only

epsilon, st. 19.

41 st. 9 new reading, also read by Wal.

46 st. 16, 25 new readings, also read by Wal.

47 st. 11 new reading, Wal.

48 st. 16, 17 letters are ΞE on stone; Γ̣Ọ Ki.

commentary: The restorations are Koehler's; exceptions are noted below. The text is in stoichedon order, 32 letters to the line for lines 1-8. Despite the restorations for lines 38-49 of Fr. B which produce line lengths varying from 27 to 32 stoichoi (Walbank designates lines 41-48 "semi-stoichedon"), there are no visible violations of the stoichedon order.

Since lines 9-37 cannot be restored completely, there is no way of knowing when the stonecutter changed from a length of 32 stoichoi to varying lengths. I have followed Kirchner and used dashes rather than a specific number of dots at the ends of these lines as Walbank has done.

Koehler did not restore the name of the secretary; Kirchner restored Εὐκλῆς from II^2 448 (#83). The publication of #85 (Hesperia 9 [1940] no. 42) led Schweigert to restore Ἀρ[χῖας] for the secretary and thus note that Eukles should be corrected to Archias for all the decrees of 323/2. My new reading of the entire name, Ἀρχῖας in line 2 of #83 confirms the name of the secretary.

Kirchner recorded that Lattermann read Ẹ̣Ọ for [Θ]εο[ῖ], presumably before the first line. He must have seen the letters on the little bit of surface which remains of the cornice because the first line of the decree begins directly below what little is left of the projection of the cornice.

The restoration of the calendric formula is straightforward; 11th day of the 1st prytany held by Hippothontis; the month is Hekatombaion. Although Kirchner and Walbank follow Koehler by printing a second ενδεκάτει in parentheses (angled brackets--Walbank) to indicate an omission by the stonecutter, Pritchett noted that the omission of the day in the month does not have to be haplography.

6 patronymic: Ki. PA 4963; see #50, discussion, for Epiteles's career. See also discussion by Wal. (173-174). Σ[ω]ιν[αύτου] Koe.

9 mid [<ἀγαθῆι> τύχηι]: suggested by Wal., but considered "methodologically unsatisfactory," his comm. for line 10.

9/10 [τὸ/ν?] μὲν ἀρκεθέωρο[ν...]: Wal., comm. lines 10-33.

18 mid [αὐ]τῶι: Wal.

25, 29: Hiller von Gaertringen, recorded by Ki. Wal. did not restore.

34 ὅσο [ἄν δέηται ...]: Wal. as an example of the type clause required, comm. line 34.

48 mid: stone reads ΠΡΟΞΕΝΩΙ. The error was noted by Ditt. Although Kirchner recorded προγόνοι, the letters in question are definitely chi and ep̣sịlon. Wal. records in his text the letters as they appear on the stone but notes (175) that Ditt.'s suggestion is preferable.

This decree was passed in the year of Kephisodoros, on the 11th day of the first prytany and Hekatombaion, July 23, 323/2 (Miller, 104). Timostratos was the chairman of the proedroi; Epiteles, son of Soinomos of the deme Pergase, was the mover. Before the text breaks off into scattered bits of information, we learn that the archetheoros (chief ambassador) for the Nemean Games and Lapyris, proxenos of Athens, have reported to the demos. It must be assumed that the lost section of the decree goes into more detail, presumably concerning the two men and what they reported. Miller (104) suggests that they are to receive "some recognition and payments," and that only by line 16 are provisions for the future indicated. Walbank, who believes that "this clause and all that follows it refer to a future occasion" (comm. lines 7-10), elaborates further in his commentary for lines 10-33 (174):

> The fragmentary nature of this document and the absence of parallels make it very hard to

> establish the sense of these lines, let alone to restore them convincingly. From line 10 it is clear that the demos has made at least two decisions: of these, the first concerns the Arketheoros, and the second, I believe, the Proxenoi. Thus, Clause One, [τὸ/ν?] μὲν ἀρχεθέωρο[ν ...], may continue down to line 14, ending with a grant of money, perhaps to the Arketheoros himself, at any rate, to an individual. Clause Two, beginning at line 14, involves receipt [of funds?] in behalf of someone [the theoroi?] by someone else, perhaps the Proxenoi. I suspect that lines 16-18 are an expansion, or explanation, of Clause Two. In lines 18-20 provision seems to be made for any Athenian who wishes to avail himself of the services of the Proxenoi. Lines 21-34 are even more obscure, but, since lines 34ff. seem to be a summary of the whole decree, these lines should probably be regarded as detailed provisions under the heading of Clause Two.

By the beginning of Fr. B, to line 40, provisions are made for a future embassy. After the vacat, Fr. B ends with an invitation to Lapyris, son of Kallias, from Kleonai, to deipnon, a meal, in the prytaneion the next day. The secretary of the Boule is to have the decree recorded on a stele, already on the Akropolis, which records the proxeny of an ancestor, Echembrotos of Kleonai.

The designated stele concerning Echembrotos is extant as II^2 63, dated by Kirchner to before 378/7. Since there is no decree of 323/2 recorded on it, it is obvious that the final directions were not carried out (Miller, 104, suggests "reasons of space"). On the other hand, Walbank points out that since the bottom of II^2 63 is not preserved, the present decree may have been inscribed there as well (175). II^2 63 is also fragmentary, but, as Miller notes (104), the mention of Echembrotos's father indicates that this family had served as proxenoi at

Kleonai for Athens for over a century.

Miller notes that this decree has been "long known but largely ignored" (103). It is unfortunate that the two scholars who have considered this stele recently, Miller and Walbank, were not able to see each other's work since they offer two quite different interpretations. (Miller does mention Walbank's forthcoming re-edition in n. 30, p. 103/4). Since Walbank's interpretation results from a more detailed consideration of the text, I will treat his interpretation first.

Walbank sees this decree as "primarily concerned with Athenian participation in the Nemean festival" (175). His key to his interpretation is his commentary for the very fragmentary lines 10-33 (see above) and especially the use of the plural, proxenoi, in lines 16-36:

> I suggest that these unnamed _Proxenoi_ are religious in function and officials of the Nemean festival itself, appointed to look after the needs of citizens of the various Greek states. It would thus be appropriate for the _Arketheoros_ to introduce to them the members of his delegation of _theoroi_, and the context of this decree may well have been the complications arising out of the failure on the part of the Athenian delegation to take this action at the most recent celebration of the festival. (175)

The problem with this interpretaiton is that Walbank virtually ignores Lapyris, who is not only the only functionary mentioned by name, but also the only one to receive any recorded honor--deipnon in the prytaneion. In addition, I would suggest that, at this point in time, Athens was concerned much more with Macedon than with the Nemean Games.

Miller does stress the historical context by suggesting that this decree indicates "early and tentative successes" in the negotiation of an alliance between Athens and Kleonai. He notes that this decree was passed around the time of the Nemean Games (105, esp. n. 38; Walbank assumes the festival was over, 174 and n. 13) when Alexander's death was rumored but not confirmed (101-102). He reviews the literary evidence, noting especially that not only is there no indication that Kleonai joined the Athenian cause in the Lamian War, but rather the reverse: all indications are that Kleonai remained loyal to Macedon. In this case, the archaeological evidence, which has resulted from Miller's recent excavations at Nemea, substantiates and confirms the literary evidence: the Games returned to Nemea after having been in Argos (probably) from the late 5th century (Miller, 107). Although control of the Games remained with Argos, Miller comments that control "may have carried prestige but proximity to the Games was profitable" (107). The implication that Macedon was responsible for the profitable move (and therefore worthy of loyalty) is derived not only from the fact that Macedon would be the only likely candidate for initiating the shift in the 330's, but also that the Games were moved back to Argos in the first half of the third century, after Macedonian power had dissipated (Miller, 107).

The problems with Miller's interpretation are first, that he really does not take into account that arketheoroi are mentioned throughout the text. Second, he has made it so obvious why Kleonai would remain loyal to Macedon that it becomes difficult to accept this decree as even a tentative alliance with Athens, or that Athens should have been unaware of the situation.

The fragmentary nature of the document allows for either interpretation. Neither interpretation, however, does justice to either Lapyris (Walbank) or Athens (Miller). I would suggest, therefore, that what is on the stone indicates a more general motive on the part of Athens, and it is one that Miller has noted: "The great Panhellenic festival at Nemea would have provided a very appropriate and convenient opportunity for the Athenians to sound out potential allies." (105). Lapyris was in an excellent position to help Athens: his family had served as Athenian proxenoi at Kleonai for at least a century; the games had just recently been moved back to Nemea, only three miles away from where Lapyris lived.

323/2

80. *DECREE* built into a wall on the north slope of the Akropolis

photo: Hesperia 12(1943) 191-267, figure 3 (lower left corner of photo--the square, lighter block), figure 4, figure 8.

editors: Kabbadias EΦ. (1898) 7-10 no. 3; IG II^2 366.

other bibliography: Wilhelm Beitr. 276; Parsons Hesperia 12(1943) 191-267; Meritt Ath. 106-107; Henry Prescripts 38, 43; Osborne ZPE 41(1981) 153-170.

description: This inscription was cut within one of four wreaths engraved on what originally must have been a base. This base of pentelic marble is now on the northwest slope of the Akropolis. It is part of the east wall of a paved court, which Parsons identified as the Pythion. The stone is now upside down, i.e., the wreath with the inscription was originally the farthest to the left; it is now farthest to the right. Deep cuttings for clamps on both sides of the block intrude into the end wreaths. The erasure in the lower left hand part of the inscription is just to the left of the cut on the right hand side, therefore this obliteration may have occurred at the same time that the clamp holes were made. The stone is cracked and worn.

dimensions:
H 0.33 m.
W 1.02 m.
Th 0.98 m.

letters: 0.003 - 0.006 m.
Letters are poorly cut.

minuscule text:

non stoich.

Ἐπὶ Κηφιϲοδώρου
ἄρχοντοϲ ἐπὶ τῆϲ Αἰγ-
ηΐδοϲ δευτέραϲ πρυτα-
νείαϲ· ἕκτηι καὶ δεκά-
τηι τῆϲ πρυτανείαϲ·
τῶν προέδρων
ἐπεψή<φ>ιζ<ε>ν Ἡγ-
ηϲίαϲ Μαραθώνιοϲ·
[ἔδο]ξεν τῶι δή[μ]ωι· Ἀρι-
...6... εἶπεν· ἐπαινέϲαι
- - - - - - - - - κλέουϲ
...7...ον καὶ καλ[έϲαι]
[ἐπὶ] δεῖπνον εἰϲ
[τὸ π]ρυτανεῖον.

commentary: Although the letters are crowded into the wreath and are cut inconsistently, they are still legible, except in the lower left side where they were later erased. The stonecutter obviously made a mistake in line 7: it reads ΕΠΕΨΗΨΙ.ΙΟΝΗΓ. There is now a break in the stone after the iota; it may have been original since there is no trace of a letter. Kabbadias recorded the actual letters in his majuscule text and noted the space; Kirchner recorded: ἐπεψήφιζεν.

This inscription is an abbreviated form of the decree passed in the ekklesia. Only the conciliar date is included: 16th day of the 2nd prytany held by Aigeis.

Only the demotic, Marathon, is supplied for Hegesias, the chairman of the proedroi. Most of the name of the mover (Ari-), the name of the honorand and what must also have been an abbreviated version of why he was honored are lost because of the erasure. The only honor recorded is a meal in the prytaneion (see Osborne's article for a recent discussion of deipnon). Kabbadias noted that although another Kephisodoros held the archonship in 366/5, the inclusion of the prytany date and the name of the chairman of the proedroi pointed to the Kephisodoros of 323/2.

The abbreviated decree, the non-stoichedon order, and the absence of the usual directions for setting up the stele confirmed for Wilhelm that this inscription was set up privately. Kirchner and Henry agree.

It is ironic that in a year when the other five dated decrees record honors to foreigners at what must have been considerable expense (at least two had sculptured reliefs), that the only decree which records honors to a citizen (deipnon pertains only to citizens; see Osborne) had to be set up privately. This seems to be another indication that Athens was concentrating on preparation for what was to become the Lamian War.

323/2

81. *ATHENS HONORS HER AMBASSADOR TO PHOKIS* EM 7180, 2811

photos: AK 19(1976) Plate 14. Relief only: Svoronos ΕΘ. ΜΟΥΣ. plate 213; Speier RM 47(1932) Plate 29.3; Süsserott Plastik Plate 9.3.

editors: Fr. A (relief) Schöll Archaeologische Mittheilungen aus Griechenland I (Frankfurt, 1843) 62 no. 42; Peruanoglu Arch. Zeit (1860) 24 no. 3; Michaelis Parthenon (1871) 280 no. 12; Schöne Gr. Reliefs (1872) 41 no. 75; Sybel

Katalog (1881) no. 6978; Friedrichs-Wolters Gipsabgüsse no. 1171; Le Bas Voyage (1888) 66; Speier RM 47(1932) 63; Süsserott Plastik 64.
Fr. B Pittakis EΦ. (1837/39) 265; (1840/42) 953; Rangabé (1855) 395; Boeckh Epigr. Chronol. Studien (1856) p. 23; IG II 182 (with Velsen's notes); IG II^2 367.
Fr. A+B Schwenk AK 19(1976) 64-66 (based on Walter ÖJ 18[1915] Beiblatt 91); Oikonomides AW 5(1982) 123-127.

supplements: SEG 21.295 (Schweigert, Pritchett-Neugebauer, Meritt); 26.81 (Schwenk).

testimonia: Diodoros xviii 9-11.1.

other bibliography: Binnebössel Studien 15; Schweigert Hesperia 9(1940) 338-339; Pritchett-Neugebauer Cal. 57; Meritt Ath. 107; Raubitschek Hesperia 31(1962) 238-243; Mitchel Phoenix 18(1964) 17; Moretti Iscrizioni no. 1; Schmitt Staatsverträge 24-24; Palagia Hesperia 51(1982) 99-113.

description: These two fragments of Pentelic marble were joined in the Epigraphical Museum as a result of my research for this work (despite Oikonomides's statement on page 23, the fragments were not only separate when I found them in 1974, they were on different floors). The find spot for Fr. A was not recorded. Fr. B was found twice: for number 265, Pittakis records the date found as November 22, 1838; for number 953, he records that it was found in the Erechtheion in 1840. Fr. A (the relief and first line on fillet) and Fr. B (text and three sculptured feet) join at the bottom right of the relief, the top of the text. For Fr. B, only the right side and rough-picked back are original. Although the left 2/3rds of the top frame and the top 2/3rds of the frame on the left side are missing on Fr. A, the four figures are still intact--their heads have suffered the most damage. The surface above the relief was left unfinished; this fact strengthens my argument that the stele was quite impressive (64 n. 70). I estimate the original height to be at least 1.544 m.

The relief contains 4 figures in three sizes. The identity of the tallest (far left) as Athena and the shortest (center right) as the honorand has not been questioned. Since Schöne, the identity of the two figures of middle height, a female (center left) and a male (far right) has been accepted as Boule and Demos (Schwenk 65 n. 11, 12). Their identity as Demokratia and Demos, therefore, is not as straightforward as Oikonomides assumes (123 and n. 5). Palagia who, in her exhaustive attempt to identify a large female torso from the Agora, has shown how ambiguous identifications can be, lists 3 examples (including this relief) of "Boule", one of which, NM 1473, has inscribed above the figure's head ΒΟΛΗ (her list of various possibilities, page 109 n. 58; NM 1473 is Plate 36d); and only one example of Demokratia, the relief of the Law Against Tyranny, #6. Besides the Law Against Tyranny, Oikonomides also cites an unpublished relief in the Akropolis Museum. His description, however, of that relief shows that in both examples Demokratia is crowning Demos rather than joining in the crowning of someone else. It is certain that Demokratia was worshipped in the Agora at this time. Raubitschek's article is concerned with EM 3912 and the now lost II^2 2791 which form a base for a statue of Demokratia (the base is Lykourgan, dated to 333/2 by the presence of archon Nikokrates; in fact, it was when I was inspecting EM 3912 in a storeroom I had not been in before, that I found the relief of this decree--EM 2811). Palagia strongly suggests that the subject of her article, the female torso, S2370, is what remains of that statue. The very fact that Demokratia was worshipped, however, and that the two representations we do have of Demos and Demokratia together confirm an unequal relationship between the two, should discourage their identification in this decree. I prefer, therefore, to keep the identification of the two middle sized figures who are together crowning the figure, described by Walter as "ein Mann in der gewöhnlichen Tracht des Lebens," as Boule and Demos.

dimensions:
H 0.581 m.
W 0.482 m.
Th 0.15 m.

letters: 0.007 m. Smallest, Λ, O, X, Ω, are .006; largest, Σ, is 009. E, P, Y, Φ, are .008.

minuscule text: next page.

commentary: The addition of ΘΕΟΙ as line 1 means that the lines in this text (and Oikonomides') are one numeral higher than texts previous to the publication in Antike Kunst. I add one new reading, Σ in line 14. Pittakis, Rangabé, and Boeckh read a tau at the end of line 2; the vacat read by the rest of the editors (and me) was omitted from the Antike Kunst text--Oikonomides' text retains the error. Pittakis (953) and Boeckh read an omicron at the end of line 5.

stoich. 26

Fr. A Θ E [O I]

[᾿Επὶ Κηφιcοδώρου] ἄρχοντος ἐπὶ ^v Fr. B
[τῆc ...6...ἴδοc τ]ρίτηc πρυτανε-
[ίαc, ἧι ᾿Αρχίαc Πυθ]οδώρου ᾿Αλωπεκ-
[ῆθεν ἐγραμμάτευ]εν· Πυανοψιῶν[ο]-
[c ἐνάτηι ἐπὶ δέκα], ἕκτει καὶ τρια-
[κοcτεῖ τῆc πρυτα]νείαc· ἐκκληcί-
[α κυρία· τῶν προέδ]ρων ἐπεψήφιζε
[......13......ε]ὺc· ἔδοξεν τῶι δ-
[ήμωι ....9....] δώρου Μελιτεὺc
[εἶπεν· ἐπειδὴ ᾿Αc]κληπιόδωρο[c ..]
[...7... πρὸc Φω]κεῖc ἐπρ[έcβευc]-
[εν ἀξιῶν παρὰ τῶ]ν Φωκέ[ων ...6...]
......13......ΣΤΟ - - - - -

The stoichedon order of 26 letters to the line was established by Velsen and is now confirmed by the addition of the relief (Schwenk 64). With the exception of the vacat in line 2, the order is not violated. Restorations are Velsen's with 3 exceptions. The name of the secretary is Archias (see comm. #79). Restorations at the beginning of line 12/end of line 12, and beginning of line 13 are Oikonomides'; Velsen had for lines 11/12: [κα/ὶ ....10.... φω]κεῖc and for lines 12/13: ἐπρ[εσβεῦ ./....11.... τῶ]ν. Oikonomides suggests two possibilities for the name of the ambassador: [᾿Ασ]κληπιόδωρο[c Τι/μάνδρου] and [᾿Ασ]κληπιόδωρο[c ὁ Π/ελλαῖοc]. The date in Pyanopsion, ἐνάτηι ἐπὶ δέκα, is supplied by Meritt. Velsen's restoration of ὀγδόηι ἐπὶ δέκα was based on only two 36-day prytanies out of the first 4; Meritt calculates that the first 3 prytanies had 36 days (see #28 for discussion of Aristotle's "rule").

The disagreement as to the nature of this year--ordinary, Meritt; intercalary, Pritchett--begins to appear in their restorations for the day in the month for this decree. Meritt's restoration gives: Pyanopsion [19] = Prytany III 36 = 108th day of an ordinary year. Pritchett's restoration, Πυανοψιῶν[ος ἕκτει Φθΐνοντος] gives the equation: Pyanopsion [25] = Prytany III 36 = 114th day of an intercalary year. There are two problems. The first is a violation of the stoichedon order: the restoration at the beginning of line 6 is one letter too many. The cutting of the final epsilon and iota in one stoichos is not unusual and would be acceptable if it were not for another problem in this specific instance. Pritchett discusses the other decrees of this year, #82 (II^2 368) and #83 (II^2 448) on pages 57-59 without ever specifically saying how the intercalation took place in this year. It must therefore be presumed that Pritchett had assumed the usual procedure for the creation of an intercalary year; the repetition of the month Posideon, i.e., Posideon I = 6th month; Posideon II = 7th month in a 13 month intercalary year (cf. Meritt, Ath. 3-5; discussion of calendar, #15). Pyanopsion, however, is only the fourth month and nowhere does Pritchett explain where the 6 extra days, making the date the 25th rather than the 19th, came from or for that matter, why. The balance of the evidence, therefore, shows that this year, 323/2, was ordinary. (The next two decrees, #82 and #83, can be restored as well for an ordinary year; see discussion #53, for a similar instance of disagreement as to the nature of the year. In that instance, I stressed the fact that although I follow Meritt, there really is no incontrovertable proof for either interpretation.)

Most of the bibliography recorded above is concerned with the sculptured relief because, although some were been a bit vague in their citations, all of the art historians became immediately aware of Walter's article of 1915 and therefore that this relief was dated to 323/2 (Schwenk 64 n. 4). Epigraphists, on the other hand, have not had that information. (Schwenk 64 n. 5; Oikonomides, 123 n. 2, notes that Charitonides was also aware: Ἡ Μνημειακὴ Διαμόρφωση τῶν Ἐπιγραφῶν, 1956, p. 76). Therefore, the physical join invites a number of comments. First, the join allows for a more accurate measurement of the original width, which confirms Velsen's restoration of a stoichedon order of 26 letters to the line; it also adds a new first line, ΘΕΟΙ.

Second, the content of the relief itself should help in interpreting the very fragmentary text. Since the relief depicts a man being crowned, it can now be confirmed that this is an honorary decree, not a treaty, as suggested by everyone who has treated this decree, with the exception of Mitchel (Schwenk 65 and n. 13). Despite the fact that the relief depicts only one man honored, I continued (AK, 65) to accept Velsen's original restoration for lines 11/12 to the effect that Asklepiodoros and a colleague, both from Phokis, were acting as ambassadors (Oikonomides, 124 n. 6, notes that Ashton in "Aspects of the Lamian War," a 1980 dissertation from the University of Western Australia also accepts Velsen's restoration).

Oikonomides, on the other hand, emphasizes the nature of the dieties in the relief (whether the pair doing the crowning is Boule and Demos or Demokratia and Demos) and correctly concludes that an Athenian citizen is being honored (124). He goes on to associate the fact that only one man is honored in the relief with the beginning of the actual decree, lines 11 through 13 (124), refutes the notion of two ambassadors from Phokis and states: "Instead of ambassadors from Phokis, the relief's scene suggests an Athenian ambassador sent to Phokis" (124). At this point Oikonomides presents an excellent account of the historical situation (124-125), giving special emphasis to the Macedonian ambassadors sent by Antipater to various Greek states to prevent an uprising against Macedon (125, citing Diodotos XVIII 11.1). When Oikonomides returns to the text, he restores lines 11-13 of this decree to reflect the sequence of events: "Asklepiodoros (line 11, cf. our commentary) is the Macedonian ambassador sent to Phokis to ask the Phokians to remain neutral. The Athenians sent immediately also as special ambassador the man honored with this decree" (125). Unfortunately, Oikonomides' restoration requires that the mention of the honorand occur after line 13 in the part of the text which is now lost and thus negates the connection between the relief and lines 11-13, a connection which is the basis for Oikonomides' refutation of two ambassadors from Phokis. (I.e., if the name of the man depicted in the relief as the Athenian honorand is not restored in lines 11-13 but occurs later on in the decree, then what remains of the decree is an historical preamble which could as easily be concerned with two ambassadors from Phokis as a Macedonian ambassador to Phokis.) Specific information explaining the occasion for granting honors is quite often included in honorary decrees--not, however, as a preamble but rather after the honorand has been named. It seems reasonable, therefore, to keep the connection between the relief and lines 11-13 and conclude that the Athenian, Asklepiodoros, is the man depicted in the relief. (Kirchner includes 10 entries for Athenians in PA 2625-2634; an Asklepiodoros--perhaps a metic--was honored in 337/6, #12.)

It has been noted already (see description above) that the stele was quite impressive. The height; the fact that it even had a relief; and the content of that relief all support the conclusion that Asklepiodoros had performed an important service to Athens. That service must have been the conclusion of a treaty with Phokis (cf. Oikonomides, 124). Therefore the date of this decree--Oikonomides gives circa October 27, 323 (124)--

provides a _terminus non post quem_ for the conclusion of the treaty with Phokis. Oikonomides would place that terminus a month earlier (presumably to account for travel time) and the decision in Athens to pursue a treaty with Phokis a month earlier so that: "circa seventy days after Alexander's death, Athens was already on the path of war against the Macedonians" (Oikonomides, 124).

323/2

82. *ATHENS HONORS THEOPHANTOS* EM 7181

photo: Kirchner _Imagines_ Plate 29 no. 63.

editors: Pittakis _EΦ_. (1840/42) 419; (1856/61) 2681; Rangabé (1855) 483; Boeckh _Epigr. Chronol. Studien_ 19 (using Velsen's squeeze); _IG_ II 183; _IG_ II^2 368.

supplements: _SEG_ 3.82 (Kirchner); 12.88 (Oikonomides-Koumanoudes); 21.280 (Schweigert, Oikonomides); 21.296 (Pritchett-Neugebauer, Meritt _Ath_.).

other bibliography: Dittenberger _Sauppio oblata_ 56; Dittmar _Coron_. 80; Wilhelm _ÖJ_ 11(1908) 98; Dinsmoor _Archons_ 373; Schweigert _Hesperia_ 8(1939) 33-34; _Hesperia_ 9(1940) 339; Pritchett-Neugebauer _Cal_. 49, 57-58; Oikonomides-Koumanoudes _ΠΟΛΕΜΩΝ_ 5(1952/55) 27; Lambrechts _Proxenie_. 60, 157; Oikonomides _ΥΠΕΡΕΙΔΟΥ ΛΟΓΟΙ_ I 17 n. 73; Meritt _Ath_. 86; _Hesperia_ 32(1963) 426; Fornara _CJ_ 57 (1961/62) 370-371; Walbank _ZPE_ 48(1982) 264-266.

description: This fragment of Pentelic marble was found on November 29, 1839, on the Akropolis. It is broken on all sides; the rough-picked back is probably original.

dimensions:	letters: 0.006 m. Smallest, O, Ω, are .004; largest, E, H, Π, P, Φ, Ψ, are .008. M, Σ, Y, are .007; A, Δ, are .006.
H 0.335 m.	
W 0.17 m.	
Th 0.09 m.	

minuscule text: next page.

commentary: A number of letters read clearly by Kirchner and partially by Koehler and the other editors should now be underlined. All dots are mine. The letter in st. 16, line 9, which should be the first letter of the patronymic of Theophantos has been read as a diagonal stroke by Velsen, Boeckh, and Koehler; as an upright stroke by Pittakis (2681); as a rho by Oikonomides and Koumanoudes. I can see the bottom of a diagonal stroke: / .

stoich. 33

[Προξενία Θε]οφάντ[ου ....9.... Ἐπὶ Νική]-
[του ἄρχον]τ̣οϲ ἐπὶ τ[ῆϲ ...ντίδοϲ δευτέρα]-
[ϲ πρυτα]νείαϲ, ἧι Ἀρ[ιϲτόνουϲ Ἀριϲτόνου]
[Ἀναγυ]ράϲιοϲ ἐγρα[μμάτευεν· Βοηδρομιῶν]-
[οϲ ἐν]άτει ἱϲταμέν[ου, δευτέραι καὶ τριακ]-
[οϲτ]ῆ̣ι τῆϲ πρυτανε[ίαϲ· ἐκκληϲία κυρία· τῶ]-
[ν πρ]οέδρων ἐπεψήφι[ζεν ....14.......]
[Πολ]ύ̣ευκτοϲ Σωϲτρά̣[του Σφήττιοϲ εἶπεν· v]
[ἐπει]δὴ Θεόφα[ν]τοϲ ....13....., ..5..
...ϲ̣ ἐνδείκνυται τ[ὴν εὔνοιαν πρὸϲ Ἀθην]-
[αίου]ϲ, ἐπαινέϲαι α[ὐτὸν καὶ εἶναι αὐτὸν π]-
[ρόξε]νον καὶ εὐεργ[έτην τοῦ δήμου τοῦ Ἀθη]-
[ναίω]ν. ἀναγράψαι [δὲ τὸ ψήφιϲμα αὐτῶι τὸν]
[γραμ]ματέα τὸν κα[τὰ πρυτανείαν καὶ ϲτῆϲ]-
[αι ἐν] ἀκροπόλει· [εἰϲ δὲ τὴν ἀναγραφὴν τῆϲ]
[ϲτήλη]ϲ δοῦναι τ[ὸν ταμίαν τοῦ δήμου ΔΔ δρ]-
[αχμὰϲ] ἐκ τῶν κα[τὰ ψηφίϲματα ἀναλιϲκομέ]-
[νων].
[Ἐπὶ Κηφι]ϲοδώ[ρου ἄρχοντοϲ ἐπὶ τῆϲ Πανδι]-
[ονίδοϲ πέ]μπ[τηϲ πρυτανείαϲ, ἧι Ἀρχίαϲ Πυ]-
[θοδώρου] Ἀλω[πεκῆθεν ἐγραμμάτευεν· Ποϲι]-
[δεῶνοϲ] δ̣ευτ[έραι ἱϲταμένου ἐμβολίμωι, ὀ]-
[γδόει τῆ]ϲ π[ρυτανείαϲ· τῶν προέδρων ἐπεψ]-
[ήφιζεν.]Ω̣ - - - - - - - - - -

The text consists of 2 decrees, the first, I, passed in 332/1; the second, II, passed in 323/2. Koehler, followed by Kirchner, restored lines 1-4 and the stoichedon order of 33 letters to the line (line 3 has only 23 letters) based on #36 (II^2 345) and #37 (II^2 346). For the rest of the text, Koehler based his restorations on those of the previous editors. Since Kirchner's II^2 368 text: Dittmar restored line 13 to conform to line 19 of #33 (II^2 344, see commentary for #33 for discussion of Walbank's dissociation of #33 from #82I); in place of Koehler's τόδε, Dittmar restored αὐτῶι and brought the line to 33 letters); Schweigert added the demotic to the mover with a vacat after the motion clause to account for the 9 stoichoi allowed (Velsen suggested Λαμπτρεύς). Alternate restorations are: Pittakis's Κηφισοδότου for archon in line 1; Dittenberger's Θεοφάντ[ωι] in line 1; Oikonomides-Koumanoudes's restoration of the ethnic, Ῥοιτειέως from their reading of rho in st. 16, line 19 and the length of 9 stoichoi for the ethnic in line 1. Besides the fact that the majority of editors (including myself) have read a diagonal stroke in st. 16 of line 9, whatever the letter might be, it must surely be the first letter of Theophantos's patronymic rather than his ethnic (in fact Walbank, 264, assumed that Rhoiteieos was a patronymic). With the length of the ethnic established as 9 stoichoi from line 1, it can be determined that the patronymic was 13 stoichoi in line 9.

With the additions and changes which have been made for #82II, not much is left of Koehler's basic restorations. The tribe in prytany (lines 19/20) was added by Kirchner on the basis of #83 (II^2 448). Lolling's restoration of the name Eukles for the secretary is now corrected to Archias (see comm., #83). Since there is controversy over the nature of this year, various restorations for the date have been suggested. Koehler gave the date (lines 21-24) as:

- Ποσι]-
[δεῶνος] δευτ[έραι ἐπὶ δέκα, ἐβδόμηι καὶ δε]-
[κάτηι τῆ]ς π[ρυτανείας· ἐκκλησία κυρία· τῶ]-
[ν προέδρ]ω[ν ἐπεψήφιζεν - - - - - - - - - -

Kirchner restored ὀγδοίηι rather than ἐβδόμηι for II^2 368 from Koehler's addendum, IG II 5 p. 65. Kirchner assumed that the year was ordinary and equated the 12th day of

Posideon with the 18th day of the 5th prytany. There are two problems with this restoration. The first is the use of δευτέραι ἐπὶ δέκα to designate the 12th day of the month (δωδεκάτηι is the only attested form, Pritchett-Neugebauer, 58; also noted by Dinsmoor). The second problem has to do with the relationship between this decree and the first decree of II^2 448 (#83I), which was enacted on the 16th day of Posideon, the 22nd day of the 5th prytany. As Pritchett-Neugebauer point out, (58), both this decree, #82II, and #83I record (restored) ekklesiai kuriai for two dates in the 5th prytany. To resolve the problems, both Dinsmoor and Pritchett-Neugebauer offer restorations for an intercalary year. Dinsmoor suggests: for #82II, δευτ[έρου, ἕκτηι ἱσταμένου, τριακοστῆι τῆ]c, Posideon II (the intercalated month) 6 = Prytany V 30 = 183rd day; and for #83I, ἕκτ[ηι μετ' εἰκάδας, μι]ᾶι καὶ εἰκοστεῖ, Posideon 26 = Prytany V 21 = 174th day. This restoration for #83I would require, however, a vacat somewhere in line 3 and, more damaging, uses forward count in the last decade of the month which is now unacceptable; (see discussion #69). Pritchett-Neugebauer restored: for #82II, δευτ[έραι Φθίνοντος, μιᾶι καὶ εἰκοστῆι τῆ]c, Posideon 29 = Prytany V 21 = 177th day; and for #83I, ἕ[νηι καὶ νέαι ^{v} δευτέραι καὶ εἰκοστεῖ, Posideon 30 = Prytany V 22 = 178th day. They note that the vacat would not be necessary if the spelling, νεΐαι, were used and suggest that either the kyria ekklesia be extended over two days or that the restoration of ἐκκλησία κυρία in line 23 of #82II be corrected to [ἐκκλησία ἐν τῶι Θεάτρωι ^{v} τ]ῶ[ν---] (59).

Pritchett-Neugebauer's restorations, however, depend on a new reading of st. 25 and st. 26 in line 3 of #83. Their restoration of a nu and eta is unacceptable when kappa and tau can be read clearly (see commentary, #83). Thus the restoration in II^2 448 must be retained (lines 3/4): ἕκτ[ηι ἐπὶ δέκα, δευτέρ]/αι καὶ εἰκοστεῖ τῆc πρυτανεί[c·---], and the year 323/2 must be designated ordinary. Meritt gives the equation for #83I: Posideon [1]6 = Prytany V 2[2] = 165th day, and notes that the difficulty in restoration is with this decree, #82II, rather than #83I (Ath. 108). Elimination of ἐκκλησία κυρία (to avoid two in the same prytany) was already suggested by Pritchett-Neugebauer; their alternate restoration (recorded above) is possible, but not necessary because the omega in line 24 is not very clear. I thus record Meritt's suggestion for lines 23/24 (Ath. 107/8).

If the normal sequence of hollow and full months is combined with 36 days for the first 4 prytanies

(Aristotle's "rule"--see #15) then in #83I, both Prytany V 22 and Posideon 16 would be the 166th day. The obvious solution is to be more flexible with Aristotle's "rule" and assume that only 2 of the first 4 prytanies had 36 days which would shorten the number of days to designate Prytany V 22 from 166 to 164. The equation, however, from #81 requires that the first 3 prytanies hold 36 days, so that the day in the conciliar year must be the 165th and further resolution of the equation must take place in the festival calendar. In this text I follow Meritt's solution which indicates that a second Posideon 2 (δευτέραι ἐμβολίμωι) was intercalated on the 8th day of the 5th prytany, [Posideon] 2[+1] = Prytany V [8] = 151st day (Ath. 108/9). The extra day is carried from that point (i.e., the day is the 3rd in Posideon, the 151st in the year; the date is the 2nd), through the month (i.e., for #83A, the day is the 17th in Posideon, the 165th in the year; the date is the 16th) to the end of a full (30 day) Posideon whose dates run: 1, 2, 2, 3-29. Fornara's suggestion, deut[erai <met'> eikadas, o/gdoei kai eikostei te]s requires an omission and the now unacceptable forward count.

This fragment of a stele records two decrees. The first was passed on the 32nd day of the 2nd prytany, the 9th day of Boedromion in the year of the archon Niketes, 332/1. The proposer is Polyeuktos, son of Sostratos, of the deme Sphettos (see #33 for other decrees proposed by this man). The honorand, Theophantos, is to receive proxeny and the title benefactor of the Demos because he has shown good will to the Athenians. Twenty drachmai are appropriated for engraving and setting the stele up on the Akropolis. Only the dating formula remains of the second decree; in the year of Kephisodoros, 323/2, the 2nd day of Posideon, the 8th day of the 5th prytany.

The loss of any text in any year is unfortunate, it is especially so in this year of Alexander's death and preparations for the Lamian War, which have already been mentioned in #79 and #81. Since Theophantos was honored with proxeny and the title euergetes already in 332/1, the occasion for another decree in 323/2 is surely to grant to Theophantos further honors in acknowledgement of further benefits to Athens. Citizenship (which was granted to Euphron in #83) is the obvious choice for the honor; that Theophantos was helpful to Athens in her preparation for the Lamian War (as was Euphron) seems the most likely motive. Further speculation as to Theophantos's country and whether through Theophantos's help that country became a member of the Greek alliance against Macedon--information which would help the historian in the reconstruction of events leading up to the Lamian War--is idle, given what survives of this document.

Consideration, however, of the fact that we have two decrees separated by nine years, on the same stele, may shed some light on the circumstances of its publication. The physical evidence of the fragment shows that it was carved by the same stonecutter at the same time. Thus we are not dealing with a stele set up in 332/1 to which a further decree, concerned with the same honorand, was added in 323/2. Although it is generally assumed that this stele was set up in the year of the second decree, 323/2 (cf. Lambrechts, 60), nothing of the publication formula survives. The year 323/2 is therefore no more than a _terminus non ante_ for the publication date of this stele, #82. In fact, 323/2 seems unlikely since that would mean (presumably) that it was necessary to reinscribe the first decree because it had been destroyed. There is no known circumstance between 332/1 and 323/2 which would account for such action. The historical situation which would allow the destruction of decrees of the Demos is the time after the failure of the Hellenic cause in 321, when an oligarchic regime took over Athens.

The occasion for republication would be the restoration of an ephemeral democracy in 318/7. That government would then, exactly as they did in the case of Euphron, #83, have republished both earlier decrees along with a third one of their own, perhaps on behalf of Theophantos's descendants.

If Wilhelm (see #83) can suggest that #83I was never published, the same could be true of #82II. By this time the Athenians may not have had the time or money to spend on erecting honorary decrees such as they had two prytanies earlier, for #81. (In fact, with so much lost of #81, there is no way to know whether that decree with its carved relief was published when it was passed or is a product of the democracy of 318/7.)

323/2

83. *ATHENS HONORS EUPHRON OF SIKYON* NM 1482

photo: Svoronos ΕΘ. ΜΟΥΣ. Plate 108; relief: Speier RM 47(1932) Plate 29.1; Süsserott Plastik Plate 9.4.

editors: Lolling ΔΕΛΤ. ΑΡΧ. (1892) 56-71; IG II 5.321b (on basis of Lolling's work); IG II^2 448.

collections: Ditt Syll.^{2} 161, 163; Syll.^{3} 310, 317; Michel 111.

testimonia: Demosthenes XVII 16; Xenophon Hellenica VII 1.44-45; Diodoros xviii 11.2; Plutarch Demosthenes 27; Pausanias I 25.4.

supplements: SEG 21.297 (Schweigert, Pritchett-Neugebauer, Meritt Ath.), 21.317 (#83II); 22.95 (#83II); 23.59 (Fornara, Pritchett AACS, Meritt TAPA); 23.61 (#83II); 26.82 (Schwenk).

other bibliography: Wilamowitz Aristot. u. Ath. II 175; Wilhelm AM 22(1897) 198; GGA 160(1898) 221; GGA 165(1903) 784; Binnebössel Studien 15; Speier RM 47(1932) 62, 70, 94; Süsserott Plastik 28, 67; Schweigert Hesperia 9(1940)

338-339; Pritchett-Neugebauer Cal. 57-59; Meritt Ath. 108; TAPA 95(1964) 226-228; Charitonides Hesperia 30 (1961) 33, 53; Fornara CJ 57(1961/62) 370-371; Pritchett AACS 285-286; Clement AJA 69(1965) 194; Dusănić BCH 89 (1965) 128-141; Osborne BSA 66(1971) 305-306; BSA 67 (1972) 141; Vestigia 17(1973) 435; Rhodes Boule 71-72 n. 2, 108 n. 5, 263, 278, 279; Schwenk AK 19(1976) 64-66.

description: This stele of white marble was found in the area of the Stoa of Attalos. It now stands in a gallery in the National Museum in Athens. It is virtually intact and is crowned with a framed relief. ΘΕΟΙ is inscribed on the fillet of the cymation between the relief and the text. The relief depicts from the left, a standing Athena and Zeus, then the honorand, Euphron, approaching the Gods. His horse, which is led by a servant, stands behind Euphron. Koehler identified the Gods as Zeus Sotor and Athena Polias, presumably on the basis of the restorations in lines 27-28.

dimensions:
H 2.35 m. (entire)
0.57 m. (relief)
W 0.675 m. (relief)
0.604 m. (top)
0.657 m. (bottom)
Th 0.268 m. (relief)
0.244 m. (top)
0.279 m. (bottom)

letters: 0.007 m. Smallest, Ο, Ω, are .005 (but can be as large as .007); largest, Φ, is .010 (but can be as small as .006). Most letters vary in size by at least .001.

majuscule text: next two pages.

epigraphical commentary: Since only the first decree (lines 1-34) recorded on this stele of 86 lines, pertains to the Lykourgan Era, I present a text and commentary for only that part, #83I. Although there are letters read by the previous editors which are no longer visible and are thus underlined in the text, with the help of Fordyce Mitchel, I have been able to include a number of new readings. Some confirm the previous readings; others, especially lines 22 and 28, create difficulty in accepting the established restorations. All dots are mine, unless noted otherwise.

2 end new reading (st. 18-23). ..ΚΛ.. Υ Loll.; ..ΚΛ..ΠΥ Ki.

Θ Ε
ΕΠΙΚΗΦΙΣΟΔΩΡΟΥΑΡΧΟΝΤΟΣΕΠΙ.....
ΝΠΤΗΣΠΡΥΤΑΝΕΙΑΣΗΙΑΡ̣ΧΙΑΣΠΥ.....
ΝΕΓΡΑΜΜΑΤΕΥΕΝΠΟΣΙΔΕΩΝΟ.ΕΚΤ....
ΑΙΚΑΙΕΙΚΟΣΤΕΙΤΗΣΠΡΥΤΑΝΕΙΑ.....
ΝΠΡΟΕΔΡΩΝΕ̣ΠΕΨΗΦΙΙ̣ΕΝΕΠΑΜΕΙΝ....
ΤΩΙΔΗΜΩΙ vv ΕΥΦΙΛΗΤ̣ΟΣΕΥΦ̣Ι̣ΛΗ̣Τ̣Ο...
ΝΕΠΕΙΔΗΕΥΦΡΩΝΑΔΕΑΣΙΚΥΩΝΙΟΣΑΝ..
ΘΟΣΩΝΠΕΡΙΤΟΝΔΗΜΟΝΤΟΝΑΘΗΝΑΙ....
ΑΤΟΥΔΗΜΟΥΤΟΥΣΙΚΥΩΝΙΩΝΕΠΑΓΓ....
ΦΙΛΗΝΚΑΙΣΥΜΜΑΧΟΝ...ΑΝ.........
ΙΩΝΤΩΙΔΗΜΩΙΤΩΙΑΘΗΝΑΙΩΝΠΡ̣ΩΤ̣Η̣Ν̣..
ΗΣΩΙΠΟΛΕΩΝΔΕΔΟΧ.Α̣Ι̣Τ̣ΩΙΔΗ.ΩΙΕΠ̣..
ΡΟΝΑΑΔΕΑΣΙΚΥΩΝΙΟΝΑΡ̣.Τ̣ΗΣΕΝ̣Ε̣ΚΑ̣..
ΕΙΣΤΟΝΔΗΜΟΝΤΟΝΑΘΗΝΑΙΩΝ........
ΟΥΣΚΑΙΕΙΝΑΙΑΥΤΩΙΚΥΡΙΑΣ̣ΤΑΣΔΩΡ̣..
ΝΔΕ ΔΟΜ ΕΝ ΑΣ ΠΑΡ Α ΤΟΥ ΔΗΜΟΥΤΟ̣..

ΣΔΑΝΠΑΝΤΕΣΕΙΔΩΣΙΟΤΙΟΔΗΜΟΣ.....
ΣΙΧΑΡΙΤΑΣΤΟΙΣΕΥΕΡΓΕΤΑ........
ΤΩΝΩΝΑΝΕΥΕΡΓΕΤΗΣΕΙ...........
ΝΑΙΟΝΑΥΤΟΝΚΑΙΕΓΓΟΝΟΥΣ........
ΑΙΦΥΛΗΣΚΑΙΔΗΜΟΥΚΑΙΦΡΑΤΡΙΑΣΗΣΑΝ
ΩΝΟΙΝΟΜΟΙΚΕΛΕΥΟΥΣΙΝ v ΚΑΠΑ......
ΝΣΙΚΥΩΝΙΩΝΑΡΕΤΗΣΕΝΕΚΑΚ...Υ....
ΗΜΟΝΤΟΝΑΘΗΝΑΙΩΝΚΑΙΣΤΕΦΑΝΩΣΑΙΧ.
ΙΑΠΟ:Χ:ΔΡΑΧΜΩΝΚΑΙΑΝΕΙΠΕΙΝΑ..ΟΝ..
ΛΩΝΤΩΙΑΓΩΝΙΑΝΑΓΡΑΨΑΙΔΕΤΟΨΗΦΙΣΜ
ΙΘΙΝΑΙΣΚΑΙΣΤΗΣΑΙΤΗΝΜΕΝΜΙΑΝΠΑΡΑ
ΕΤΕΡΑΝΕΝΑΓΟΡΑΙΠΑΡ.ΤΗΝΒΟΥΛΗΝΣ.Κ
ΔΕΤΗΝΑΝΑΓΡΑΘΗΝ..ΝΣΤΗΛΩΝΔ..Ν.Ι.
ΔΗΜΟΥ:Ϝ:ΕΚΤΩΝΚΑΤΑΨΗΦΙΣΜΑΤΑΑΝΑΛΙ.
ΗΜΩΙΤΑΔΕΠΑΝΦΙΛΟΥΤΟΥΕΥΦΙΛΗΤΟΣ..
ΦΟΝΤΩΙΔΗΜΩΙΠΕΡΙΤΗΣΠΟΛΙΤΕΙ.....
ΗΣΠΑΝΔΙΟΝΙΔΟΣΕΙΣΤΗΝΠΡΩΤΗΝΕΚΚΛΗ
ΝΟΜΟΝ *vacat*

3 end E Loll. E.. P.-N.; E followed by kappa or nu Pritch. AACS.

5 st. 25, 26 new readings.

6 end new readings. EYI . Loll.; EYΦ̣Ị.H Ki.

9 st. 10, 24, 25 new readings.

11 st. 13, 23, 25, 27 new readings.

12 st. 12, 15, 17-23, 25-28 new readings.

13 st. 23, 25 new readings.

15 st. 25-28 new readings.

16 st. 28 new reading.

18 st. 21 new reading.

22 st. 20-24 new readings.

23 beg new reading. ΣYKI Loll., Koe., Ki.
st. 11-22, 26 new readings.

28 st. 10-17, 19-28, 30 new readings.

29 st. 17-24, 27, 29 new readings.

31 st. 23 new reading.
st. 28 <Y> Loll.; Ki. read clear upsilon; I read a clear sigma.

32 st. 25 new reading.

33 st. 15 new reading.

minuscule text: next two pages.

commentary: As noted above, only the first decree of this long document is included in this Corpus. The basic restorations and establishment of the stoichedon order of 41 letters to the line are Lolling's, also recorded by Koehler. There are a number of vacats. On the stone, there is a double vacat in line 6; none of the editors noted the vacat in st. 20, line 22, because they only read as far as st. 19.

Θ ε [ο ι] stoich. 41

Ἐπὶ Κηφισοδώρου ἄρχοντος ἐπὶ [τῆς Πανδιονίδος πέ]-
μπτης πρυτανείας ἧι Ἀρχίας Πυ[θοδώρου Ἀλωπεκῆθε]-
ν ἐγραμμάτευεν· Ποσιδεῶνο[ς] ἕκτ[ηι ἐπὶ δέκα, δευτέρ]-
αι καὶ εἰκοστεῖ τῆς πρυτανεία[ς· ἐκκλησία κυρία· τῶ]-
ν προέδρων ἐπεψήφιζεν Ἐπαμείν[ων Ἐρχιεὺς· ? ἔδοξεν]
τῶι δημωι· vv Εὐφίλητος Εὐφιλήτο[υ Κικυννεὺς? εἶπε]-
ν· ἐπειδὴ Εὔφρων Ἀδέα Σικυώνιος ἀν[ὴρ διατελεῖ ἀγα]-
θὸς ὢν περὶ τὸν δῆμον τὸν Ἀθηναί[ων καὶ νῦν ἥκων παρ]-
ὰ τοῦ δήμου τοῦ Σικυωνίων ἐπαγγ[έλλεται τὴν πόλιν]
φίλην καὶ σύμμαχον [οὖς]αν [ἀμυνεῖν? κατὰ τῶν πολεμ]-
ίων τῶι δήμωι τῶι Ἀθηναίων πρώτην [τῶν ἐν Πελοπονν]-
ήσωι πόλεων· δεδόχ[θ]αι τῶι δή[μ]ωι, ἐπ[αινέσαι μὲν Εὔφ]-
ρονα Ἀδέα Σικυώνιον ἀρ[ε]τῆς ἕνεκα [καὶ εὐνοίας τῆς]
εἰς τὸν δῆμον τὸν Ἀθηναίων [καὶ τοὺς ἄλλους συμμάχ]-
ους καὶ εἶναι αὐτῶι κυρίας τὰς δωρ[εὰς τὰς πρότερο]-
ν δεδομένας παρὰ τοῦ δήμου το[ῦ Ἀθηναίων αὐτῶι?· ὅπω]-

c δ' ἂν πάντες εἰδῶc̣ι ὅτι ὁ δῆμος [ὁ Ἀθηναίων ἀποδίδω]-
cι χάριτας̣ τοῖc εὐεργέτα[ιc ἀξίας τῶν εὐεργετημά]-
των ὧν ἂν εὐεργετήcει [ἕκαcτος τὸν δῆμον, εἶναι Ἀθη]-
ναῖον αὐτὸν καὶ ἐγγόνους [καὶ εἶναι αὐτῶι γράψαcθ]-
αι φυλῆc καὶ δήμου καὶ φρατρίας, ἧ̣ς̣ ἂν [βούληται καὶ]
ὧν οἱ νόμοι κελεύουcιν·[v] καὶ <ἐ>π[αινέcαι? τὸν δῆμον τὸ]-
ν Σικυωνίων ἀρετῆc ἕνεκα κ[αὶ ε]ὐ[νοίας τῆc εἰc τὸν δ]-
ῆμον τὸν Ἀθηναίων καὶ cτεφανῶcα̣ι χ[ρυcῶι cτεφάνω]-
ι ἀπὸ : X : δραχμῶν καὶ ἀνειπεῖν α[ὐτ]ὸν [Διονυcίων μεγά]-
λων τῶι ἀγῶνι. ἀναγράψαι δὲ τὸ ψήφιcμ[α ἐν cτήλαιc λ]-
ιθίναιc καὶ cτῆcαι τὴν μὲν μίαν παρὰ [τὸν Δία, τὴν δὲ]
ἑτέραν ἐν ἀγορᾶι παρ[ὰ] τ̣ὴ̣ν̣ β̣ο̣υ̣λὴ̣ν̣ Σ̣.Κ[....9.... εἰc]
δὲ τὴν ἀναγραφὴν [τῶ]ν cτηλῶν δ[οῦ]ν[α]ι̣ τὸν ταμίαν τοῦ]
δήμου : 𐅃 : ἐκ̣ τῶν κατὰ ψηφίcματα ἀναλι[cκομένων τῶι δ]-
ήμωι. τάδε Πανφίλου τοῦ Εὐφιλ̣ήτο<υ>· [δοῦναι δὲ τὴν ψῆ]-
φον τῶι δήμωι περὶ τῆc πολιτεί[ας τοὺc πρυτάνειc τ]-
ῆc Πανδιονίδος εἰc τὴν πρώτην ἐκκλη[cίαν κατὰ τὸν]
νόμον.

The restoration in line 10 requires only 40 letters. Neither Koehler in his majuscule text nor Kirchner in his commentary have noted that the letters in line 16 are not in stoichedon order: the 24 letters on the stone occupy 28 stoichoi.

Since ΘΕΟΙ is inscribed on the fillet of the cymation, it has not been give a line designation. Additions and alternatives to Lolling's text are recorded below.

1 Πανδιονίδος: Ki. Ἀκαμαντίδος Loll., Koe.

2 Ἀρχίας: Schw. from #85 (Hesperia 9[1940] 335/43 no. 43). My reading confirms this restoration. [Εὐ]κλ[ῆς] Loll., Koe., Ki. and PA 5716, listing this decree and #'s 79, 81, 82.

3/4 date: Loll., Koe., Ki., Mer. Since alternate restorations must be treated in relationship to #82II, those restorations by Dins., P.-N. to conform to an intercalary year, for this decree, #83I, have been recorded with an explanation of the restoration used in this decree, in the commentary for #82. Fornara suggests this restoration to allow for the kappa in st. 25 and keep the year intercalary: Posideonos ek[tei met' eikadas, deuter]ai kai eikostei tes prytaneia[s. Pritchett, in AACS, reexamines the stone and notes that "the traces seem very elusive" and that therefore the nature of this year cannot be determined by the (restored) date of this decree.

5 end demotic: Wilam., using PA 4766; Ki. added the question mark.

6 end demotic: Charitonides, who suggests that the proposer may be the same man who is listed (line 325) as a bouleutes from Κικυννῆς in the bouleutai list which he published and dated to 336/5. Κηφισιεύς Loll., as a suggestion; Ki. included this demotic without a question mark, referring to PA 6068.

8 end: Loll., Ki. Koe. left this blank.

9 end: Loll., Ki. Koe. left blank.

10 end: Loll., Ki. added question mark; Koe. left blank.

16: This line is not in stoichedon order. As noted above, 24 letters on the stone occupy 28 stoichoi. Although by st. 22 the spacing seems more regular, even if the regularity were maintained to the end of the line, there would be only 13 stoichoi left for a restoration which requires 17 letters. If we keep Loll.'s restoration, it must be kept in mind that the final 17 letters would be crowded. The alternative is to assume that αὐτῶι was either omitted or never part of the text and that only 36 letters occupied this line.

19 mid: Koe., Ki.

22 end: The new reading of 3 letters and a vacat presents a problem. As can be seen in the majuscule test, there is no place for the epsilon of ἐπαινέσαι and the iota of καὶ is placed above the pi. Retention of Lolling's restoration (with an omitted epsilon) leave the line one letter short.

28: Lolling's reading of only the first 9 letters (followed by Koe., Ki.) enabled him to restore ἐν ἀ[κροπόλει παρὰ τὸν νεὼ τῆς Πολιάδος, εἰς], presumably to correspond with the presence of Athena Polias in the relief. The new reading makes that restoration impossible. The presence of the sigma and kappa at the end of the line suggests that the second location was to be in Sikyon. F. Mitchel suggests Σ̣[ι]κ[υωνιάσιν v εἰς].

31 end restoration: Koe., who noted that this usage was unusual. This is noted by Ki. as well. Πάμφιλος Εὐφιλήτου εἶπεν· τὰ μὲν ἄλλα καθάπερ Εὐφίλητος is suggested in Syll.[3] as more appropriate. My new reading of Εὐφίλητος suggests that the stonecutter may have added a superfluous τοῦ and omitted the entire phrase. Given the errors in lines 16 and 22, that is an acceptable possiblity.

This stele records two decrees. The first, #83I, from 323/2, honors Euphron, son of Adea, of Sikyon with citizenship; the second, #83II, from 318/7, renews the honor granted to Euphron as well as the reasons, accepts Euphron's child, and gives the order for the publication of both decrees (Wilhelm, AM, n. 2, suggests that #83I had not been published). Much of the literature on this inscription deals with the information which #83II adds to the historical situation in 318/7. Most of the remaining literature deals with the restoration of the dates of the two decrees, especially #83I. The date of #83I has been discussed above (and in comm. for #82); discussion of #83II lies outside the chronological framework of this work. We now turn, therefore, to a discussion of #83I, which provides the most clear-cut and substantial epigraphical confirmation for the historical situation in 323/2, already established by the literary sources.

The decree opens with the usual preamble: when Kephisodoros was archon, when the tribe Pandionis held the 5th prytany; Archias, son of Pythodoros of the deme Alopeke was secretary; the *date* (see above) is the 16th of Posideon, the 22nd day of the prytany. The meeting is a kyria ekklesia; the chairman of the proedroi is Epameinon, possibly of the deme Erchia; the mover is Euphiletos, son of Euphiletos of the deme Kephisia. The occasion of the decree is that Euphron, already distinguished as a good man by the Athenians, has now come from Sikyon to announce that that state (the first Peloponnesian state to do so) offers friendship and alliance to the Athenians. As a result, the Demos resolves to commend Euphron because of his virtue and good will toward the Athenians and the other allies and because he was first to bring this critical alliance to the Athenians. So that all see that the Athenians return their gratitude with a benefaction of like value, Euphron (and his descendants) is to be granted citizenship and to be recorded in the tribe, deme, and phratry, as he chooses, as the laws allow (Osborne, *BSA* 1972 p. 133, notes that this decree, line 22, records the only use of ὧν οἱ νόμοι κελεύσιν). Euphron is also to be given a gold crown worth a thousand drachmai and he is to be announced at the games of the Greater Dionysia. The stele is to be engraved and one is to be placed by the sanctuary of Zeus. The second location cannot be ascertained. I suggest, however, that the "agora," which can be read clearly on the stone, is in Sikyon rather than Athens. Fifty drachmai are appropriated for the publication. The last four lines are concerned with the _psephos_, or second, confirming vote, to be made at the next ekklesia. Osborne does not refer to the suggestion made in _Syll._[3] (see comm. above) which would substantiate his observation that this is a rider added by Panphilos, son of Euphiletos, the mover (_BSA_ 1971 p. 306; on page 305, Osborne notes that the psephon became an essential element in grants of citizenship in the fourth century; c.f. also, _BSA_ 1972 p. 149).

Koehler notes that this decree confirms the statements made in Diodoros and Pausanias that the Peloponnesian states joined the Hellenic cause after the battle of Thermopylae. Dittenberger (_Syll._[2] 163) noted pseudo-Demosthenes's reference to the installment of a tyrant in Sikyon by the Macedonians shortly before the Lamian War. Koehler then suggested that the tyrant was responsible for Euphron's death. It appears, therefore, that despite this grand monument erected after the fact to commemorate a grand alliance, Euphron was not able to deliver that which he had promised.

The existence of this stele brings us full circle to where this Corpus began 15 years earlier. The Lykourgan Era begins with expression of thanks to friends and allies who had helped Athens at Chaironeia. This era of relative peace ends with the Lamian War or as the Athenians called it--the Hellenic War (#83II line 44). And as soon as possible--the restored democracy of 318/7--we find the Athenians again acknowledging their indebtedness to one who had contributed to the Hellenic cause. (Kirchner, in his commentary, says about the same thing: "Monumentum insigne ad illustrandum rerum statum, qui ante et post bellum Lamiense in Graecia fuit.")

323/2

84. *ATHENS HONORS APOLLONIDES OF SIDON*

EM 7165

editors: Fr. A Pittakis ΕΦ. (1852/55) 1362; Rangabé (1855) 2291.
Fr. B Pittakis ΕΦ. (1840/42) 473; Rangabé (1855) 501.
Fr. A+B Koehler IG II 171; IG II^2 343 + Add. p. 659.

supplements: SEG 24.103 (Schweigert, Lambrechts, Pečírka). Bull. (1944) no. 65 (Schweigert).

other bibliography: Dittmar Coron. 66-68; Johnson CP 9 (1914) 425; Leonardos ΑΔ 1(1915) 213; Dinsmoor Archons 373; Schweigert Hesperia 9(1940) 342-343; Pritchett-Neugebauer Cal. 58-59; Lambrechts Proxenie. 60-61, 89, 93, 157; Meritt Ath. 108-109; Charitonides Hesperia 3(1961) 53; Pritchett AACS 285-286; Pečírka Enktesis 63-69.

description: This fragment of Pentelic marble is composed of 2 smaller fragments. Fr. A, on the left, was found on the Akropolis on December 20, 1848. The only preserved side, on the left, is not well preserved; other sides and back are broken. The right side of Fr. A joins the left side of Fr. B which was also found on the Akropolis, September 20, 1840. The bottom right side is preserved on Fr. B; the surface, however, is broken away before that preserved right side.

dimensions:
H 0.20 m.
W 0.305 m.(surface)
0.33 m.(entire)
Th 0.065 m.

letters: 0.005. Smallest, Λ, Ο, Χ, Ω, are .004; largest, Κ, Σ, are .006. Some alphas do not have crossbars; some thetas do not have center dots. Upsilon looks like psi.

majuscule text:

.ΝΕΠΑ̣Μ̣Ε̣Ι̣...............Η̣Σ̣Η̣.......
.ΝΑΓΥΡΑΣΙΟ̣....Ε.........Ε̣Μ̣ΠΟΡ̣Ο̣....
ΥΚΛΗ̣ΡΟΙΑΠ̣ΟΦΑΙΝΟΥΣΙ...Ο..ΩΝΙΔΗΝ....
ΙΟΥ̣ΣΙΔΩΝΙΟ..Ι...ΑΝ̣Δ̣...ΑΓΑΘ̣ΟΝ v Κ....
.ΝΤΩΙΔΗΜΩΙΤΩΙΛΟΗ̣Ν̣Α̣Ι̣.Ν̣..ΔΟΧΘ̣ΑΙΤΩ̣...
.ΠΑΙΝ/⁝ΣΑΙΛΠΟΛ̣ΛΩΝ̣ΙΔΗΝΔ̣..Η̣ΤΡΙΟΥΣΙ...
.ΑΙΣΤΕΦΑΝΩΣΑΙΛΥΤΟΝ v ΧΡΥ.ΩΙΣΤΕΦΑΝΩ..
.ΙΛΙΩΝΔΡΑΧΜΩΝΑΡΕΤΗΣΕΝΕΚΑΚΑΙΕΥ̣ΝΟΙΑ̣.
.ΕΙΣΤΟ̣ΝΔΗΜΟΝΤΟΝΑΘΗΝΑΙΩΝΚΑΙΕΙΝΑΙΑΥ̣.
.Ρ̣ΟΞΕΝΟΝΚΑΙΕΥΕΡΓΕΤΗΝΤΟΥΔ̣Η̣ΜΟΥΤΟΥΑΘ̣.
..ΑΥΤΩΝΚΑΙΕΓΓΟΝΟΥΣΕΙΝΑΙΔΕ̣Α̣ΥΤΩ̣ΙΚΑΙ.
.Α̣ΙΟΙΚΙΑΣΕΓΚΤΗΣΙΝΚΑΤΑΤΟΝΝΟΜΩΝΑΝΑΓ̣Ρ
ΔΕΤΟΔΕΤΟΨΗΦΙΣΜΑΤΟΝΓ.ΑΜΜΑΤΕΑΤΗΣΒΟΥΛ̣
ΕΝΣΤΗ̣ΛΕΙ̣...Ι̣Ν̣Ε̣ΙΚ̣Α̣Ι̣ΣΤΗΣΑΙ̣ΕΝΑΚΡΟΠΟ..
ΕΙΣΔΕΤΗ...........ΤΗ ΣΣΤ̣ΗΛΗΣΔΟΥΝ...
ΤΑΜΙΑΝΤ..........Δ ΡΑΧ ΜΑ...Τ Ω Ν....
.ΑΙΨΗΦΙΣ ΜΑ̣..........ΟΜ Ε ΝΩΝΤΩΙ. Η Μ̣....

epigraphical commentary: The line numbers coincide with the minuscule text, based on Schweigert's restoration which adds 4 restored lines. Therefore line 6 of this text is line 1 in Koehler's majuscule text, line 2 in Kirchner's text. Schweigert included only lines 1-10 in Hesperia. Since he offered a number of new readings, the underlined letters for these lines refer to his readings, unless noted below; underlined letters in lines 10-22 indicate letters read by Koehler and Kirchner. All dots are mine.

6 end neither Koe. nor Ki. read anything; HΣI Leonardos, supported by Pec. who does not agree with Schw.'s readings: KEPΔH[Σ ? (st. 23-27).

7 st. 24, 28, 29 not read by Koe., Ki. Pec. confirms Schw.'s readings.

8 mid Schw. read st. 10-17; Koe. and Ki. read sigma, st. 16 and iota, st. 17 (which Schw. did not read); omicron, st. 22, is clear (not read by Koe., Ki.).

9 st. 17-19 Λ.O Koe., Ki.; A.. Leon.; AΠA Schw. Letter in st. 18 could be eta, but not pi; Pec. notes Schw.'s reading as far from clear.
st. 29 vacat also seen by Leon. I Koe.; E Schw., which Pec. notes as "very suspect".

10 st. 21 new reading.
st. 29 I seen by Koe., Ki., Schw.

11 st. 21 new reading.

14 st. 23 new reading.

16 st. 6 although Ki. noted the letter as omega, he printed O.
st. 12 K Koe., Ki. Letter is a gamma as Pec. also notes.

17 st. 34 new reading, seen also by Pec.

18 st. 34 new reading.

19 st. 12 new reading.

20 st. 18-20 tau is actually between iota and sigma above; eta is between sigma and tau.

21 mid Again, order is disturbed. Delta is in st. 17, not st. 18 as in Koe., Ki. This disturbance continues to the end of the line--omega is between st. 28 and st. 29.

22 beg Since these crowded letters are inscribed over a rasura, the second letter, iota, may have been left from the original, incorrect cutting. Pec suggests for the original either [T]A[[ΦI]]ΣMATA or [[Ψ]HΦI]]ΣMATA.

The stoichedon order is completely disturbed. Ki did not mention this, possibly because without a majuscule text it is impossible to explain. Although Koe. showed some disturbance at the beginning of the line, his majuscule text has AΨHΦIΣMA occupying 9 stoichoi whereas these letters actually occupy only 7 stoichoi. At the middle of the line, OMEN occupies st. 17-21; my new reading of HM with a restored delta would occupy 4 stoichoi, st. 27-3ὀ (this new reading is apparently confirmed by Pec., 66, who reads the delta as well). Pec. devotes most of pages 65 and 66 to a discussion of the irregularities of the line lengths. On page 66, he includes a diagram of the letters in the middle of lines 19-22 and considers various explanations. His conclusion is that the "stonecutter was certainly both inconsistent and careless, but I think there can be no doubt about his tendency to end the lines with complete words, which may perhaps explain the <u>vacat</u> in l. 12 and the violation of the <u>stoichedon</u> order in l. 20."

minuscule text: next two pages.

commentary: The text is based on Schweigert's addition of the dating preamble to Kirchner's text. Schweigert restored the first 3 1/2 lines on the assumption that Epameinon, the chairman of the proedroi in #83I (II^2 448) is the same Epameinon in this decree (line 6), and therefore, that #83I and this decree, #84, were passed on the same day. The rest of the restorations are Koehler's, unless noted below. Kirchner's restorations of ειπε in the middle of line 7 and ἀποφαίνουσι in line 8 would require the placement of the pi at the end of line 7 and the iota at the end of line 8 in st. 26. Since these letters are in fact in st. 27, there is room for the numovable restored correctly by Koehler, Leonardos, and Schweigert. Pečírka also notes this error which ends with line 9 where the theta which Kirchner places in st. 25 is actually in st. 26. Koehler's restorations for lines 20-22 fit despite the violations of stoichedon order. Because the delta of δραχμάς is in st. 17 rather than st. 18, as in Koehler's majuscule text, I indicate only 2 stoichoi for the amount rather than the 3 allowed by Koehler and Kirchner (Pečírka confirms this by suggesting that the amount was probably only 20 drachmai).

stoich. 36

[Ἐπὶ Κηφισοδώρου ἄρχοντος ἐπὶ τῆς Πανδιονί]-
[δος πέμπτης πρυτανείας ἧι Ἀρχίας Πυθοδώρο]-
[υ Ἀλωπεκῆθεν ἐγραμμάτευεν· Ποσιδεῶνος ἕκτ]-
[ηι ἐπὶ δέκα, δευτέραι καὶ εἰκοστῆι τῆς πρυταν]-
[είας· ἐκκλησία κυρία· τῶν προέδρων ἐπεψήφιζ]-
Fr. A [ε]ν Ἐπαμεί[νων ......13......]Η̣Σ̣Η̣....9?....
Ἀναγυράσιο[ς εἶπ]ε[ν· ἐπειδὴ οἱ] ἔμπορο[ι καὶ να]- Fr. B
ύκληροι ἀποφαίνουσ[ιν Ἀπ]ο[λλ]ωνίδην [Δημητρ]-
ίου Σιδώνιο[ν ε]ἶ[ναι] ἄ[νδρα ᵛ ἀγα]θὸν ᵛ κ[αὶ εὔνο]-
[ω]ν τῶι δήμωι τῶι Ἀθηναί[ων, δε]δόχθαι τῶ[ι δήμωι]
[ἐ]παινέσαι Ἀπολλωνίδην [Δημ]ητρίου Σι[δώνιον]
[κ]αὶ στεφανῶσαι αὐτὸν ᵛ χρυ[σ]ῶι στεφάνω[ι ἀπὸ]
[χ]ιλίων δραχμῶν ἀρετῆς ἕνεκα καὶ εὐνοία[ς τῆ]-
[ς] εἰς τὸν δῆμον τὸν Ἀθηαίω[ν]· καὶ εἶναι αὐ[τὸν]

[π]ρόξενον καὶ εὐεργέτην τοῦ δήμου τοῦ Ἀθ[ηναί]-[ων] αὐτ<ὸ>ν καὶ ἐγγόνους· εἶναι δὲ αὐτῶι καὶ [γῆς] [κ]αὶ οἰκίας ἔγκτησιν κατὰ τὸν νόμον. ἀναγ[ράψαι] δὲ τόδε τὸ ψήφισμα τὸν γ[ρ]αμματέα τῆς βου[λῆς] ἐν στήλει [λιθί]νει καὶ στῆσαι ἐν ἀκροπό[λει], εἰς δὲ τὴ[ν ἀναγραφὴν] τῆς στήλης δοῦν[αι τὸν] ταμίαν τ[οῦ δήμου ..] δραχμὰ[ς ἐκ] τῶν [εἰς τὰ κα]-[τ]ὰ ψηφίσμα[τα ἀναλισκ]ομένων τῶι [δήμωι].

vacat 0.03

Although the stoichedon order is not violated on the stone (with the exception of lines 20-22) the restored line lengths vary from 35 to 38 letters. Schweigert suggests that the stonecutter was observing syllabic divisions, but also notes that even that was not consistent. Pečírka agrees with Schweigert that the order was 36 letters to the line with exceptions; his conclusion is cited above (ep. com. line 22). There are 2 vacats on the stone, one more in Leonardos's restoration for line 9.

4 date: Loll., Koe., Ki., Mer. for #83, lines 3/4 (see comm. #83). ἕκτηι μετ' εἰκάδας, μιαῖ καὶ εἰκοστῆι Schw., who used Dins.'s restoration for II^2 448 (#83). This restoration was subsequently accepted by neither P.-N. nor Mer. Although Dins.'s restoration requires a vacat (which Schw. dropped to obtain a 36-letter line 4 in this decree) the restoration in lines 3/4 in #83 now conforms to its stoichedon order. Thus the same restoration in line 4 of this decree now requires a line length of 37 letters. Since the line lengths do vary in this decree, this presents no problem. Pec. records Schw.'s restoration (lines 1-10) verbatim and discusses the various restorations offered for the date of #83I, especially noting the one-letter discrepancy. Although he does not make a decision as to the correct restoration, he does note that the discrepancy of one letter is acceptable and in that case, that the disturbance in the stoichedon order would be more likely in this decree, #84, "probably" (65).

9/10 restoration: Leon. ιου Σιδώνιο[νε]ι[στὰ ἅπα[ντα] ἀγαθὸν ἐκ [τῶν ἰδί/ω]ν Schw. My reading of NΔ in st. 18, 19 and vacat in st. 29 supports Leon. and makes Schw.'s restoration difficult to accept (see also Pec. in ep. com. line 9).

This decree records honors bestowed upon Apollonides, son of Demetrias, of Sidon. Since the merchants reported that he had shown himself to be a good and benevolent man, the Demos votes that Apollonides be crowned with a gold wreath worth a thousand drachmai and that he and his descendants be called proxenos and benefactor of the Athenians. He is also to be granted enktesis for both land and home, according to the laws. (Probably) 20 drachmai are to be designated for the engraving and setting up of the stele on the Akropolis.

The date, according to Schweigert, is the same as that of the first decree of #83. Pritchett and Meritt have noted Schweigert's restoration in their discussions for #83I to the effect that those restorations do fit this decree. Pečírka points out that while the one-letter discrepancy in the lengths of the 2 restorations is not a serious obstacle, the name, Epameinon, is common; the length of his demotic cannot be determined for this decree; and that the same Epameinon may have been chairman in two different years (67). So, although Pečírka acknowledges that a date in 323/2 would fit epigraphically was well as historically, he finds it "necessary to mark Schweigert's date with a query" and to point out that "any other date in the second half of the fourth century is equally possible" (67). Kirchner did not restore a specific date, but assigned this decree and II^2 342 to "ante a. 332/1(?)" to associate both decrees with the fall of Tyre. Walbank, who has recently joined a new fragment to II^2 342, notes that since the men honored in both II^2 342 and II^2 343 (this decree) could have been metics living in Athens, there would be no problem bringing II^2 342 down to the 320's as well (per ep.).

In contrast to many of the decrees in this Corpus for which the date can be restored but not the content, the text of this decree is virtually intact. Yet even this complete text is laconic. Since neither the status of Apollonides nor the specific services which he rendered are included, Pečírka can infer that Apollonides was not a metic because lines 7 and 9 imply that the help given to the Athenian shippers was outside Attica (67); Lambrechts can state that Apollonides was honored for economic reasons (60). All that we know, however, is that Apollonides was honored by the Athenian Demos with the titles of proxenos and benefactor and the right to own land in Attica (for enktesis, see #1; see above for the suggestion that he may have been a metic).

Although the date for this decree is somewhat tenuous, the next decree, #85, provides an example of a person (or persons) being honored for their help with the grain supply (an economic reason) in this year of the Lamian War.

85. *ATHENS GRANTS HONORS* Ag. Inv. I 4935e (A), EM 7333 (B), I 4935b (C)+EM 12572 (J), I 4935 (D), I 4935c (E), I 4935d (F), I 5496 (G), I 4935f (H), I 2752 (I), EM 7332 (K).

photos: Hesperia 8(1930) p. 28 (Fr. A-F); Hesperia 9 (1940) p. 337 (Fr. I, C+J, G, H, K).

editors: Fr. K Pittakis ΕΦ. (1852/55) 1445; Rangabê (1855) 2316; IG II 290.
Fr. J, K IG II^2 414c,b (II^2 414a is now disjoined--see #25).
Fr. B IG II^2 369 (with Wilhelm's text).
Fr. A-F Schweigert Hesperia 8(1939) 27-30 no. 7.
Fr. A-K Schweigert Hesperia 9(1940) 335-343 no. 42.

supplements: SEG 21.298 (text; Schweigert Hesperia 1939, 1940; Rostovseff, Brashinsky 1959; Robert Bull. 1962); 24.102 (Brashinsky 1967).
Bull. (1944) no. 65 (Schweigert Hesperia 1940); (1962) no. 108 (Brashinsky 1959).

other bibliography: Rostovseff Soc. Econ. Hist. III 1627 note 189; Brashinsky KSIIMK 74(1959) 1-8; KSIA 109(1967) 49-51; Acta (1967) 119.

description: Of these 11 fragments of Pentelic marble, 8 were found in the Agora excavations. The other 3 (now in the EM) were found below the Akropolis: Fr. B and Fr. J on the north slope; Fr. K near the cave of Pan. With the exception of the preserved back and right side of Fr. H and the right side of Fr. I, all other fragments are broken on all sides and back.

The first section, lines 1-5, consists of frs. A,B and I. Although they do not form a physical join, each preserves one leter of ΘΕΟΙ, as well as the molding which served as the bottom frame of a scupltured relief. Fr. B preserves the full molding, 0.073 m., and a sculptured foot. The next section, lines 6-13, consists of Frs. C and J, the only physical join of the inscription (although the photo shows that these two fragments join, they are still separate--C in the Agora, J in the EM). The rest of the fragments follow as discrete elements: D, E, F, G, H, K.

dimensions:

Fr. A
H 0.11 m. (entire)
0.064 m. (surface)
W 0.09 m.
Th 0.04 m.

Fr. B
H 0.17 m. (entire)
0.063 m. (surface)
W 0.115 m.
Th 0.10 m.

Fr. I
H 0.088 m. (entire)
0.064 m. (surface)
W 0.063 m.
Th 0.056 m.

Fr. D
H 0.14 m. (entire)
0.035 m. (surface)
W 0.105 m.
Th 0.075 m.

Fr. F
H 0.127 m. (entire)
0.105 m. (surface)
W 0.085 m.
Th 0.06 m.

Fr. H
H 0.21 m. (entire)
0.11 m. (surface)
W 0.11 m.
Th 0.145 m.

letters: 0.008 m. Smallest, O, Ω, are .006; largest, B, is .10. Most letters vary by .001 m., i.e., E can be .007 or .008; P, Σ, can be .008 or .009. Nu is distinctive throughout: N.

Fr. C
H 0.125 m.
W 0.08 m.
Th 0.08 m.

Fr. J
H 0.13 m.
W 0.088 m.
Th 0.055 m.

Fr. E
H 0.09 m. (entire)
0.075 m. (surface)
W 0.042 m.
Th 0.068 m.

Fr. G
H 0.20 m. (entire)
0.09 m. (surface)
W 0.054 m.
Th 0.075 m.

Fr. K
H 0.22 m.
W 0.155 m. (entire)
0.13 m. (surface)
Th 0.135 m.

minuscule text: next three pages. stoich. 28

Fr. B

Fr. A θ ε [ο] ἷ Fr. I

Ἐ̣πὶ Κη[φιcοδ]ώρου [ἄρχοντος ἐπὶ] τῆς
[Ο]ἰ̣νεΐ̣[δος ὀγ]δόης [πρυτανείας ἧ]ι Ἀρ-
[χίας Πυθοδώρου Ἀλωπεκῆθεν ἐγρ]α̲[μ]-
[μάτευεν - - - - - - - - - - - - - - -]

lacuna

Fr. C [....10.... Ἀθ]η̣ν̲[αί]ων κα[....8....]
[.....11.....] ὅτι δ[ύ]ναντ̣[αι ἀγαθὸν] Fr. J
[δημοςίαι τε κ]αὶ ἰδ[ί]αι τ[οῖς τε ἀφικ]-
[νουμένοις εἰ]ς Βόςπορο[ν, ἐπαινέςα]-
[ι δὲ καὶ ..5.. κ]αὶ Ἀςτυμ....9....
[καὶ ....9....] Πολ[υ]ςθέν̣[ην ...6...]
[...7... καὶ ςτ]εφ[αν]ῶ̣[ςαι ἑκάςτους]
[τούτων χρυςῶι] ς[τεφάνωι - - - - - -]

lacuna

Fr. D [.. ἐπιδέδω]κ̣εν τ̣ῶ[ι δήμωι XXX μεδίμ]-
[νους πυρῶν ?] κ̣αὶ νῦν [ἐπιδέδωκεν εἰς]
[τὸν πόλεμον] τῶι δή[μωι ....10....]
[δεδόχθαι τῶι] δήμω[ι ἐπαινέςαι ...]
[...7... Δημη]τηίο[υ εὐνοίας ἕνεκα]
[καὶ φιλοτιμί]ας τ[ῆς εἰς τὸν δῆμον τ]-
[ὸν Ἀθηναίων κ]αὶ ςτ[εφανῶςαι αὐτὸν]
[χρυςῶι ςτεφά]ν̣ω̣ι̣ [ἀπὸ - - - δραχμῶν]

lacuna

Fr. E .... Ⱶ - - - - - - - - - - - - - -
....ΕΠ - - - - - - - - - - - - - -
....ΤΕ - - - - - - - - - - - - - -
....ΛΕ - - - - - - - - - - - - - -

lacuna

Fr F [............27.............. δ]-
[οῦναι]δ̣[ὲ περὶ αὐτοῦ τὴν ψῆφον τοὺς]
[πρυτ]ά̣νει[ς τῆς Οἰνεΐδος εἰς τὴν πρ]-
[ώτην] ἐκκλ[ησίαν .....15........]
...α̣ιος ε̣[ἶπεν? στῆσαι δε καὶ παρὰ τ]-
οὺς] προγ[όνους Σάτυρον καὶ Λεύκων]-
[α εἰκ]ονα̣ [αὐτοῦ χαλκῆν ἐν τῆι ἀγόραι]

lacuna

Fr. G - - - -Ι- - -
- - -ΕΣΤ- - - -
- - - -ΟΥ- - - -
- - - vacat - - - -
- - - -Ρ- - - -

lacuna

Fr. H - - - - - - - -Η...
- - - - - - -Α̣ΙΕΙ..
[- - - - - α]ὐτῶν.
[- - - - - - - - σ]τρατ
[- - - - - - - ὅ]πως ἀ-
[ν - - - - - - - τ]ὴν ἐ-
[κκλησίαν - - - - -]Ο̣Λ̣

Fr. K lacuna

[.... Ἀ]θ̣ηναι.......18.........
[..κεχ]ειροτο[νημέν ....11..... Ἀ]-
[θηναί]ων εἰδό[τες ὅτι ....11.....]
[.. τὰς] δωρεὰς κ.......16.........
..5..ου ἐκ τῶν ....16.........
..5..αι αὐτοὶ ....16.......

[.. δημ]όσιον αν.........16.........
[. γρα]φομένας ....17.........
...5..α καὶ το.........17.........
...5..ας τῆς ....18.........
[.... τῶ]ι δή[μωι ....16.........]

commentary: The text is based on Schweigert's. Many letters which Schweigert read as clear are barely visible; they are dotted. A number of letters which Schweigert dotted must be underlined. Letters dotted by Schweigert are: H, st. 13, line 6; N st. 20, line 11; K st. 10, line 14; NΩI st. 12-14, line 21; A, E st. 4, 7, line 30; A st. 23, line 39. In Fr. E, line 22, Schweigert read a clear omega. In Fr. F: there is a lower horizontal stroke above the nu in line 28; in line 32, Schweigert read a clear alpha, I had recorded a dotted delta. In Fr. K: nu st. 12, line 51 is clear (because of the distinct way nu's are cut in this inscription)--it is dotted by Koehler, Kirchner and Schweigert; phi, st. 5, line 52 is dotted by both editors before Schweigert--I can see nothing; alpha st. 6, line 54 was seen by everyone but me.

The restorations are Schweigert's. Of the previously published fragments, B and J are "joined" to other fragments from the Agora (which changes previous restorations); Schweigert's changes for Fr. K are chiefly to conform to a 28 letter line rather than the stoichedon order of 21 letters in II^2 414 (because of the shorter line, Kirchner had actually included a bit more restoration). Schweigert's association of Fr. I with Fr. A and Fr. B allowed him to correct the name of the secretary for the year from Eukles to Archias--the last two letters in line 3 of Fr. I are AP not EY.

Brashinsky (KSIIMK) offers the restoration for lines 30-32 (Schweigert offered no restoration here). I have added ε[ἶπεν]? to fill the 4-letter space before Brashinsky's restoration. Since the restoration is tentative, I have kept the final iota in line 32 (which makes a 29-letter line) to avoid changing the numeration of the subsequent lines. Brashinsky's alternate restoration: εἰ-κ]όν[ας αὐτῶν χαλκᾶς would definitely require an 8th line for Fr. F.

If Schweigert's association of the various fragments is correct, then we are dealing with a large stele topped by a relief. Unfortunately, it is very fragmented and thus what should be a very informative document is not. In fact, even the fragmentary information which can be gleaned is the result of heavy restoration.

The dating formula gives only the year, that of Kephisodoros, 323/2, and the prytany, the 8th, held by the tribe, Oineis. The next section (C+J) gives the most substantial information: it gives a locale, the Bosporos, and substantiates the fact that we are dealing with an honorary decree, i.e., an undetermined number of persons are to be honored with gold crowns. Rostovseff suggests that they are residents who helped "those who were coming to the Bosporos (line 8ff)"; Brashinsky (KSIA) suggests that the honorands are merchants.

The next section (D) records that a gift of grain had been bestowed and that now something else has been given for the war. The donor, (presumably) a son of Demetrias, is to be honored as well with a gold crown. Schweigert's restoration at the beginning of Fr. F indicates that someone is to be honored with citizenship. The psephon as an essential element in citizenship grants is discussed in #83. Brashinsky continues that line of thought by offering names for two honorands and suggesting that a statue or statues of bronze were to be set up in the Agora. The rest of the fragments do not contribute to the content of the document.

Only Schweigert (in both articles) places this document in its historical context. He not only mentions the earlier grain shortage of 330-326 (Hesperia 1940; Rostovseff designates the year of this decree, 323/2, as the end of the famine) but Schweigert also connects this inscription to the most important event of the time--the Lamian War (_Hesperia_ 1940 p. 337, 1939 p. 30) with the implication that the maintenance of the grain supply is as important during a war as it is during a famine.

XVII. THE YEAR OF PHILOKLES, 322/1

86. *DECREE* EM 7183, 2754

photo: Pečírka Enktesis Plate 11.

editors: Fr. A Pittakis EΦ. (1840/42) 1026; (1856/61) 2702; Rangabé (1855) 537, 541; IG II 185 (Velsen); IG II^2 371.
Fr. B Kirchner IG II^2 308.
Fr. A+B Wilhelm SEG 3.82; publication in Att. Urk. V pages 159-160 no. LX.

supplements: SEG 3.82 (Wilhelm).
Bull. (1942) no. 32 (Wilhelm Att. Urk. V).

other bibliography: Dinsmoor Archons 373; Pritchett-Neugebauer Cal. 59; Pečírka Enktesis 58-59.

description: The two fragments of Pentelic marble were found on the Akropolis. Pittakis records that Fr. A was found east of the Erechtheion, November 22, 1839; Kirchner recorded only "in arce". Fr. A, which is broken on all sides, is topped with a molding. Since the bit of marble above the molding shows no traces of sculpture, the stele was probably topped with a pediment rather than a relief--Pěcírka allows for either possibility. Only the right side of Fr. B is original; the surface is very worn.

dimensions:
Fr. A
H 0.17 m. (entire)
0.10 m. (surface)
W 0.112 m.
Th 0.09 m.
Fr. B
H 0.115 m.
W 0.19 m.
Th 0.085 m.

letters: 0.008. Smallest, O, is .006; largest, Σ, is .010. B, Γ, N, Y, are .009.

minuscule text: next page.

stoich. 22

Fr. A ['Επὶ φιλοκλέου]c ἄρχον[τοc ἐ]-
[πὶ τῆc 'Ακαμαντ]ίδοc ἑβ[δόμη]-
[c πρυτανείαc ἧι] Εὐθυγ[ένηc]
['Ηφαιστοδήμου Κ]η̣φιc[ιεὺc ἐ]-
[γραμμάτευεν· 'Ανθ]εcτ[ηριῶν]-
[οc - - - - - - - - - - -]

Fr. B [.......8.... πρόξε]νον καὶ ε[ὐε]-
[ργέτην τοῦ δή[μου τοῦ 'Αθην[α]-
[ίων καὶ αὐτὸ]ν καὶ ἐκγ<όν>ουc κα̣-
[ὶ εἶναι αὐτῶ]ι ἔγκτηcιν γ[ῆc]
[καὶ οἰκίαc καθάπε]ρ [τ]οῖc ἄλ-
[λοιc προξένοιc· ἀναγ]ράψ[αι]
δὲ τόδε τὸ ψήφιc]μα ἐν cτή[λη]-
[ι λιθίνηι - - - - - - - - - - -]

epigraphical commentary: The text is based on Wilhelm's publication of the two fragments as belonging to the same stele. For Fr. A, the letters are still legible; only one letter now needs to be dotted as unclear. This is not the case with Fr. B, which is badly worn, even more so now than when either Wilhelm or Pečírka saw it. I could read only lines 1 and 2, the beginning of line 3 (KAIE), the omicron in line 5 and rho in line 6. Since Pečírka accepts Wilhelm's readings (with some reservation, the new ones in lines 3, 4 and 5) and even reads eta at the end of line 4 and "perhaps" ΠΕ at the middle of line 5 (st. 14, 15), I record Wilhelm's readings with the caveat that due to the condition of the stone it is now impossible to confirm those readings. Pečírka also had access to the squeezes in the Berlin Academy which do confirm Wilhelm's readings--squeezing may be the reason why the stone can no longer do so.

The same caveat applies to a discussion of whether the two fragments were, indeed, part of the same stele. Pečírka was able to see enough letters in Fr. B to observe that the letters in Fr. A were taller and broader, to measure the stoichedon pattern, and to conclude that the "difference between the measurements of the stoichedon pattern and the letters exclude, I think, the connection of the two fragments" (59).

commentary: The restorations for Fr. A with the stoichedon order of 22 letters to the line are Velsen's. Wilhelm was able to add the tribe in prytany, Akamantis, because the only other tribe which takes up 11 stoichoi, Pandionis, is designated as holding the tenth prytany in #89 (II^2 375). Kirchner, the first editor of Fr. B, noted only that the text was stoichedon, and restored the first two lines and the middle of lines 6 and 7. By associating Fr. B with Fr. A and thus establishing the stoichedon order, by noting that the right side was original, and by reading new letters in lines 3 and 4, Wilhelm was able to restore the rest of Fr. B. As noted above, the letters are now illegible. As Pečírka has accepted Wilhelm's readings, he also accepts Wilhelm's restorations but notes that the clause, [καθά]περ [τ]οῖϲ ἄλ-[λοιϲ προξένοιϲ] is unusual.

This decree does not provide much information, even less so if the two fragments must be dissociated, as Pečírka wants. Fr. A tells us only that: there was a decree moved in the year of Philokles, 322/1, when the tribe Akamantis held the 7th prytany, in the month Anthesterion.

If Fr. B does belong to Fr. A, then the decree dealt with a grant of the titles proxenos and benefactor of the Athenian Demos to someone and his descendants as well as enktesis for land and home, just as with the other proxenoi.

The present condition of Fr. B precludes either confirmation or denial of its association with Fr. A. If the fragments must be dissociated, then Fr. B, with its unusual clause in reference to enktesis, can be dated only to the 2nd half of the 4th century--Kirchner offered "ante a. 336/5." If, however, Fr. B is associated with

Fr. A, then the unusual clause may reflect the conditions of the time. The "Hellenic War" was over, and there may have been a number of people appealing to Athen's kindness--τοῖς ἄλλοις προξένοις.

In any case, it is interesting to note that the first extant decree (Fr. A) dated to this year comes in the seventh prytany, after the conclusion of the war.

322/1

87. *DEMADES PROPOSES HONORS* EM 7184

photos: Hesperia 8(1939) p. 174; LF 89(1966) Plate 1.

editors: Kumanudis ΕΦ. (1886) p. 101 no. 8; Wilhelm Hermes 24(1889) 145; IG II 5.185b; IG II² 372; Schweigert Hesperia 8(1939) 173-175 no. 4, joined II² 372 with II² 289; Oikonomides ΠΛΑΤΩΝ 8(1956) 116; Pečírka LF 89(1966) 262-266 disjoined II² 372 and II² 289.

supplements: SEG 21.300 (Schweigert, Pritchett-Neugebauer, Oikonomides, Meritt); 23.60 (Pečírka LF, Enktesis). Bull. (1968) no. 213 (Pečírka LF).

other bibliography: Reusch De diebus cont. 11; Unger Philol. 38 (1879) 427; Att. Arch. 677; Ditmar Coron. 111; Leonardos ΑΔ (1916) 216; Pritchett-Neugebauer Cal. 59-60; Meritt Ath. 110-111; Pečírka LF 89(1966) 262-266; Enktesis 57-58; Rhodes Boule 72 n. 2, 262, 269; DeLaix Proboul. 139 n. 78; Lewis CR 91(1977) 215-216.

description: This fragment was designated "Hymettian" by Koehler and Kirchner. Although Schweigert's association of this fragment with II² 289 (designated as "Pentelic") has been refuted, Pečírka does accept that the fragments are of the same marble. He does not, however, specify which type of marble and thus "marble" might be a more appropriate designation. The fragment is broken on all sides and the back.

dimensions:
H 0.12 m.
W 0.10 m.
Th 0.081 m.

letters: 0.005 m. Smallest, O, is .004 largest, H, K, Y, are .0055. Δ, E, M, are .005. E's are square; middle strokes in M are as long as outside strokes.

minuscule test: stoich. 27

[Ἐπὶ Φιλοκλέους ἄρχοντος ἐπὶ τῆς]
[...ντίδος ὀγ]δό[ης πρυτανείας ἧι]
[Εὐθυγένης Ἡφ]αισ[τοδήμου Κηφισι]-
[εὺς ἐγραμμάτ]ευε[ν· Ἐλαφηβολιῶνο]-
[ς ἐνάτηι ἐπ]ὶ̣ δέκα, [ἐνάτηι τῆς πρυτ]-
[ανέας· ἐκκ]λ̣ησία ἐ̣[ν Διονύσου· τῶν π]-
[ροέδρων ἐ]πεψήφ[ιζεν .....10.....]
...7....ς· ἔδοξ[εν τῶι δήμωι· vacat]
[Δημάδη]ς Δημέ[ου Παιανιεὺς εἶπεν·]
...7...ΥΚΟ̣ - - - - - - - - - - -

epigraphical commentary: There has never been any controversy over the reading of the letters on the stone. All editors have read the same letters except that Kumanudes did not read the sigma in line 2 and the delta in line 4. For line 6, both Kumanudes and Koehler (in majuscule texts) and my reading show strokes that could be a dotted lambda and a dotted epsilon; I have therefore taken these letters out of brackets. Kumanudes's reading of the last letter in line 10 suggests rho; omicron (which Kirchner printed without a dot) is more likely. I add one new reading: a dotted iota in line 5.

commentary: Wilhelm made the basic restorations and established the stoichedon order of 27 letters to the line. Koehler noted Wilhelm's restoration of Demades (line 9) but did not include it in his text because the full name was too short to fit the stoichedon order. Kirchner solved the problem by assuming a vacat of 5 spaces at the end of line 8. For line 10, Koehler suggested το]ῦ κ[οινοῦ; Kirchner suggested "perhaps" [Ἐπειδὴ Ε]ὔκο[μος]; [ἐπειδὴ Λ]υκο̣[-- was suggested by Schweigert and recorded by Meritt. As Kirchner noted, the spelling, πρυτανέας, can be found in #88 (II[2] 373, line 17).

The date used in the text (lines 5/6) was first suggested by Pritchett-Neugebauer but rejected because the date would make this year intercalary instead of ordinary and because the 13th of Elaphebolion would conflict with the Greater Dionysia. Pritchett-Neugebauer thus returned to the restoration proposed by Leonardos and followed by Dinsmoor and Schweigert: 'Ελαφηβολιῶνος ἐνάτηι ἐπὶ] δέκα, [ἕκτηι τῆς πρυτανείας; Elaphebolion 19 = Prytany VIII 6 = 255th day of an ordinary year. Koehler, Kirchner, and Oikonomides, however, follow Wilhelm who assumed that the year was ordinary. Wilhelm's restoration requires a stonecutter's error: ἐνάτηι ἐπὶ δέκα, ἐνάτηι <καὶ δεκάτηι> τῆς πρυτανέας. Meritt agreed that the year was ordinary (because he designated 323/2 as intercalary--see commentaries for that year) but proposed instead Pritchett-Neugebauer's first restoration, which eliminates a stonecutter's error. If one follows Meritt's conclusion that 323/2 was ordinary rather than intercalary (as I have--again, see especially commentary, #83) then this year, 322/1, should be ordinary. The equation is: [Elaphebolion] 1[3] = Prytany VIII [8] = 278th day of an intercalary year. The conflict with the Dionysia will be discussed below.

Rather than bemoan the fragmented state of this document, is is perhaps more constructive to realize how fortunate we are to have any documents from the year which saw the imposition of a Macedonian garrison in Munychia at its beginning and the remodeling of the constitution to make Athens more oligarchic at its end. We cannot assume that Athens was experiencing business as usual and this may be reflected in the problems with the calendar restorations for all of the decrees of this year.

In addition to the conciliar calendar, which may have been affected, the festivals also may have been altered in some way to accomodate a new regime. That may explain the discrepancy of a meeting of the ekklesia during the Dionysia in the restoration of this particular decree; Lewis points out that the festival was shortened during the Peloponnesian War and notes of the problems of the calendar of 319/18 that "the period is one of major political disturbance" (216). The fact that the particular festival in question is the Dionysia further supports the acceptance of a date, Elaphebolion 13, which apparently conflicts with the usual course of the festival from Elphebolion 10 to 14 (see comm. #63, which records a meeting on Elaphebolion 8 which is known to be the date for the Proagon to the Greater Dionysia). Despite Mikalson's work which supports the conclusion that meetings of the ekklesia were not held on festival days, the specific nature of the Dionysia in relation to those meetings is still not clear. As Lewis points out, Mikalson's "treatment of Elaphebolion in general and the Dionysia in particular is unsatisfactory" (216). Although the first day of the festival is now accepted as the 10th (see comm. #63) the fact that there is evidence for meetings on the 12th, 13th and 14th suggests that the length of the festival as well as the length of the program for each day could vary. I.e., there is the possiblity that either the festival could be shortened or that during the course of the festival the program of plays for one of the days might be short enough so that a meeting of the ekklesia could be accomodated. Elaphebolion 10 "is the only necessary day of the ἑορτῆ; the rest is the ἀγῶν of variable length" (Lewis, 216). Therefore, given the nature of the year and the nature of the festival, the restoration of a meeting of the ekklesia on Elaphebolion 13 is definitely possible.

Although what little remains on the stone does not confirm its date, at least it does not refute it. The restoration ἐν Διονύσου has never been questioned. Demades was not only still alive (in contrast to many other leaders from the Lykourgan Era), he was quite active in this year. It is the presence of Demades as mover that makes the loss of the rest of this document so unfortunate. Even if II^2 289 were still associated, that fragment would offer very little additional information. As it is, recovery of the entire stele may have provided valuable new insight as to how Athens was reacting to this eventful year.

322/1

88. *ATHENS HONORS THE DOCTOR EUENOR* EM 7186

editors: Pittakis EΦ. (1840/42) 371; Rangabé (1855) 377; Velsen & Koehler IG II 186; IG II^2 373.

collection: Michel 112.

supplements: SEG 21.301 (Pritchett-Neugebauer, Meritt, IG IX^2); 24.105 (Lambrechts, Pečírka).

testimonia: IG IX^2 I, fasc. 2, xviii, 79-80.

other bibliography: Hartel Studien 215-217; Wilamowitz Hermes 22(1887) 240 n. 1; Dittmar Coron. 68-72, 79; Wilhelm WS 29(1907) 1; Att. Urk. V 59-60; Nachmanson Beitr. 70; Dinsmoor Archons 373-74; Pritchett-Neugebauer Cal. 41; Lambrechts Proxenie. 67; Meritt Ath. 111-112; Pečírka Enktesis 72-74; Rhodes Boule 72 n. 1, 250, 278, 279; DeLaix Proboul. 122, 124, 141; Mikalson Cal. 151; Henry Prescripts 48-49.

description: This fragment of Pentelic marble was found on the Akropolis on April 21, 1840. Although the surface is worn away at the edges, both sides are preserved. The back is very rough-picked but probably original.

dimensions:
H 0.40 m. (entire)
0.34 m. (surface)
W 0.36 m.
Th 0.136 m.

letters: 0.006 m. Smallest, O, X, Ω, are .004; largest, Φ, is .009. B, Σ, Y, Ψ, are .007. E, H, are .006; I, M, N, T, are .005. Letters from line 16 on are not as well cut and slightly smaller.

minuscule text: next two pages.

stoich. 33

[- - - - - - προςαγα]γεῖν Εὐήνορα [πρ]-
[ὸς τὸν δῆμον, γνῶ]μ[ην] δὲ ξυμβάλλεςθαι τῆ[ς]
[βουλῆς εἰς τὸν] δῆμον ὅτι δοκεῖ τῆι βουλ[ῆ]-
[ι], ἐ[πειδ]ὴ Εὐή[νωρ] Ἀκαρνὰν πρόθυμός ἐςτι[ν]
περὶ τὸν δῆμον τὸν Ἀθηναίων καὶ ποεῖ ὅτ[ι]
δύναται ἀγαθόν, εἶναι δὲ αὐτὸν πρόξενο[ν]
καὶ εὐεργέτην τοῦ δήμου τοῦ Ἀθηναίων κα-
ὶ αὐτὸν καὶ ἐκγόνους καὶ εἶναι αὐτῶι καθ-
άπερ τοῖς ἄλλοις εὐεργέταις καὶ ἀναγρ[ά]-
ψαι τόδε τὸ ψήφιςμα ἐν cτήληι λιθίνηι τὸ-
ν γραμματέα τῆς βουλῆς καὶ cτῆςαι ἐν ἀκρ-
[ο]πόλει, εἰς δὲ τὴν ἀναγραφὴν τῆς cτήλης [δ]-
[οῦ]ναι τὸν ταμίαν τοῦ δήμου :ΔΔ: δραχμὰς ἐ[κ]
[τῶ]ν κατὰ ψηφίςματα ἀναλιςκομένων τῶι [δ]-
[ήμ]ωι.

stoich. 39

[Ἐπ]ὶ Φιλοκλέους ἄρχοντος ἐπὶ τῆς Οἰνεῖδος ἐνά[τ]-
[ης] πρυτανέας, ἧι Εὐθυγένης Ἡφαιςτοδήμου Κηφι[ς]-

[ιε]ὺϲ ἐγραμμάτευεν· Θαργηλιῶνοϲ δευτέραι ἱϲτα̣-
[μέ]ν̲ου, τρίτει καὶ εἰκοϲτεῖ τῆϲ πρυτανείαϲ· ἐ̣κκ[λ]-
[ηϲ]ία· τῶν προέδρων ἐπεψήφιζεν Εὔαλκοϲ Φαληρε[ύ]-
[ϲ· ἔ]δοξεν τῶι δήμωι· Διόφαντοϲ Φραϲικλείδου Μυ̣[ρ]-
[ρι]νούϲιοϲ εἶπεν· τὰ μὲν ἄλλα καθάπερ τῆι βουλεῖ·
[ἐπ]ειδὴ δὲ Εὐήνωρ Εὐηπίου δι' <ε>ὐεργεϲίαν πρόξεν-
[ο]ϲ̣ ἐγένετο τοῦ δήμου τοῦ Ἀθηναίων καὶ ἅπαντα ὅϲ-
[α] προϲέταξεν αὐτῶι ὁ δῆμοϲ ὁ̲ Ἀ̲θηναίων καὶ ἰδίαι
καὶ κοινεῖ ἐπιμέλεται· ἀγαθ[εῖ] τύχει ἐψηφί̣ϲ̲[θαι]
τῶι δήμωι ἐπαινέϲα<ι> μὲν Εὐήνορα Εὐηπίου κα̣[ὶ ϲτε]-
φανῶϲαι θαλλοῦ ϲτεφάνωι φιλοτιμίαϲ ἕνε[κα καὶ]
[ἐ]πιμελείαϲ. εἶναι δὲ αὐτῶι καὶ ἐγγόνο[ιϲ γῆϲ καὶ]
[οἰ]κίαϲ̲ ἔγκτηϲιν ἀπέχον̣τι τῶν [κ]ο̣ι̣[νῶν καὶ τῶν ἱε]-
[ρῶν·] ἐπι̲μέλεϲθαι δὲ α̣ὐ̣τ̲ο̣ῦ̲ [τὴν τε βουλὴν τὴν ἀεὶ β]-
[ουλεύο]υϲαν καὶ το̣ὺ[ϲ ϲτρατηγοὺϲ τοὺϲ ἀεὶ ὄνταϲ·]
[ἀναγράψ]αι δὲ τ- - - - - - - - - - - - -
- -

epigraphical commentary: Letters in lines 1-15 (#88I) are inscribed in a stoichedon order of 33 letters to the line. Although the letters from line 16 on (#88II) are crowded into the same width and not as well cut, they are inscribed in stoichedon order as well; 39 letters to the line. Pečírka assumes that the letters after line 15 are cut in another hand. It is very possible, however, that the same stonecutter inscribed the entire stone: despite the crowding and sloppier appearance of the letters in #88II, the letters are very similar in both parts; omicron and chi, in particular, are unusually small compared to the other letters on both parts of the stone. I would suggest, therefore, that whenever #88I was passed and erected; in 322/1, the same stonecutter was called in to inscribe #88II on that stone which was already erect and in situ.

With the exception of line 25 (st. 19, 20) and lines 30, 31 (st. 6) which also may be new breaks, the letters which I have underlined as no longer visible or dotted as unclear are all on the periphery of the stone and thus the condition may be the result of chipping (or squeezing?) after the stone was examined by Kirchner, who has no dotted letters in his text. (Although Kirchner offered no new readings, he did print a number of letters as clear which Koehler had shown as partially visible in his majuscule text, but bracketed in his minuscule text. There is one instance, line 5, st. 5, where Kirchner bracketed a letter which Koehler had not bracketed and which I would dot.) Underlined or dotted letters read clearly by Kirchner and unbracketed by Koehler are: line 1 st. 23,27; line 2 st. 14,32; line 3 st. 13,14,32; line 4 st. 2,9; line 5 st. 11,12; line 7 st. 32,33; line 8 st. 33; line 9 st. 32; line 10 st. 32; line 11 st. 32,33; line 12 st. 2; line 14 st. 32; line 19 st. 3; line 24 st. 2,37; line 25 st. 19,20; line 26 st. 36; line 27 st. 25; line 30 st. 6, 20; line 31 st. 6,18-21. Those letters which Koehler bracketed but Kirchner read as clear are: line 1 st. 21, 26; line 2 st. 32; line 3 st. 32; line 4 st. 10,14; line 6 st. 1; line 18 st. 39; line 21 st. 38; line 30 st. 27,28; line 32 st. 16. The letter in st. 24, line 23 is eta on the stone. There is one mistake in Koehler's majuscule text; in line 15, ΩΙ is placed one stoichos to the right of where it is on the stone. Koehler's minuscule text continues the error: since he puts all of the restoration for δήμωι on line 15, line 14 has only 32 letters.

For line 30 st. 25-28, Koehler, Kirchner and Wilhelm (in II^2 373, Att. Urk. V) read: N.OI. Velsen read N:OI.

In WS, Wilhelm agreed with Premerstein's reading, N.PI. What little is left of the letters in st. 27 and 28 supports Pečírka's conclusion: "In my opinion ỌỊ is more likely but P̣Ị is not impossible" (73).

commentary: The restorations are Koehler's (with Velsen). The stoichedon order, also established by Koehler, is 33 letters to the line for lines 1-12; 39 letters to the line for lines 16-33. Although #88II is not neatly inscribed, there is no violation of the order on the stone. Pečírka (73 n. 5) offered the restoration, τοὺϲ στρατηγοὺϲ for the middle of line 32 because the formula is more common in this period and because Koehler's restoration, τοὺϲ πρυτάνειϲ (used also by Kirchner) requires a 38-letter line. Pečírka's restoration maintains the stoichedon order.

Various restorations have been offered for the end of line 30, beginning of line 31. Wilhelm, in WS, used Premerstein's reading in st. 27, 28, to restore τῶν ὀρίων τῆϲ Ἀττι/κῆϲ] assuming stonecutter's error to account for a 37-letter line 30. Kirchner returned to Koehler's restoration (recorded in this text) but substituted ὀρίων (ascribing that to Wilhelm) for ἱερῶν: τῶν [κ]ọị[νῶν καὶ τῶν ὀρ/ίων (the omission of the right bracket after the nu in line 31 is obviously a printer's error in Kirchner's text). Pečírka notes that Wilhelm's restoration which implies that land in the border regions was exempt from enktesis has been accepted by later scholars (73) and has some ancient support (74). Since Pečírka, however, does not come to a conclusion as to which restoration is correct and Wilhelm returned to Koehler's restoration in Att. Urk. V, I have used Koehler's restoration in this text for these lines.

Although Kirchner explained the date on the stone--Thargelion 2 = Prytany IX 23--by assuming that prytanies 1-8 had 38 days (for an intercalary year), that arrangement of prytanies is no longer acceptable. The nature of the mistake in transcription, however, has varied. Dinsmoor suggested that the stonecutter mistakenly cut δευτέραι ἱσταμένου instead of δευτέραι ἐπὶ δέκα, or Thargelion 12 = Prytany IX 23 of an ordinary year. Although Pritchett-Neugebauer consider 322/1 to be ordinary, they are noncommittal as to the specific date. They suggest either an error in the festival date: Thargelion <1>2 = Prytany IX 23 = 307th day; or in the prytany date: Thargelion 2 = Prytany IX <1>3 = 297th day. Meritt, who considers 322/1 to be intercalary, suggests that rather than having 23 mistakenly written for 13, the stonecutter wrote 23 rather than 18 ("ΔΔIII, possibly, for ΔΠIII" p. 112). The calendar equation would then be: Thargelion 2 = Prytany IX <18> = 326th day of an intercalary year. Although an error of 23 written for 13 is more understandable, everyone since Kirchner has assumed some sort of stonecutter error. That assumption, in addition to the fact that the cutting in #88II is of poor quality (for whatever reason--see ep. com. above) makes Meritt's explanation of the error possible. Mikalson notes that the 2nd day of every month was devoted to the Agathos Daimon. He does not delegate this decree to the "doubtfuls" (see #35) because both Dinsmoor and Pritchett-Neugebauer offer interpretations which do not require the meeting to take place on Thargelion 2. It should be noted, however, that the nature of the festival should be taken into account (as in #63) and that for this year in particular there are extenuating circumstances (see #87). Further indication that the stonecutter was not above error occurs in line 6 which is in the better cut section. Koehler, followed by Kirchner, assumed that the stonecutter inserted an unnecessary <ΔE>. Although he notes that δὲ comes unusually late in the sentence, Nachmanson (following Dittmar and Michel) retains the δὲ and suggests that that rather than cutting a superfluous word, the stonecutter omitted a word: δὲ <ἀποδοτικόν>. Hartel's (217) suggestion that the phrase, ὁ δῆμοc ἐψηφῖσατα, was omitted, would solve the problem of a probouleumata without a sanction by the ekklesia being published as a separate document (see below). Henry records lines 16-22 (#88II) and describes them, appropriately, as "an example of the degree of perfection in design achieved by the end of this period." Although Henry's primary concern is the formulaic prescripts of decrees, he does include discussion of various dating restorations when appropriate. It is surprising, therefore, that he makes no mention of the problem with the date for this decree.

This fragment records the end of one decree (#88I) and the beginning of a second decree (#88II), which is dated to the year of Philokles. Both are concerned with honors granted to Euenor, son of Euepios of Akarnania. II^2 374, a decree which grants Euenor citizenship, informs us that he was from Argos in Arkarnania. Although the use of the words ἐπιμέλται (line 26) and ἐπιμελεῖαc (line 29) in this decree indicates that Euenor is a doctor, II^2 374 also confirms his profession: ἰ[ατρός (line 4). In #88I, all that remains is a probouleuma (resolution of the Boule) to the effect that Euenor has acted zealously toward the Athenian Demos, doing what good he could. For that the Boule suggests that Euenor be honored with the title of proxenos and benefactor, both he and his descendants. Pečírka notes that the placement of δὲ in line 8 reflects either an unaccustomed formula for the granting of further privileges or that the formula was not completely inscribed; Nachmanson's and Hartel's suggestions are recorded in the commentary; #88I ends with publication instructions: 20 drachmai are to be alloted; the stele is to be set up on the Akropolis.

#88II begins with a full prescript and dating formula; the date is discussed in the commentary above. The chairman of the proedroi is Eualkos of Phaleron; the mover is Diophantos, son of Phrasikleides of the deme Myrrinous. After acknowledging the Boule's gnome, Diophantos proposes that since Euenor became proxenos because of his benefaction and carried out the duties assigned to him by the Demos, both publicly and privately, that the Demos should award him an olive crown because of his patriotism and diligence; and that he and his descendants be granted enktesis for both land and house with the exception of public and sacred areas, and protection of the Boule and the strategoi (generals). The text breaks off at the beginning of the publication formula.

There is no question that Euenor is a foreigner. Whether he is a metic or not cannot be ascertained. Wilamowitz decided that Euenor could not be a metic because he was granted proxeny, an honor reserved for foreigners. On the other hand, as Pečírka points out: "it is certain that Euenor practised his profession more or less permanently in Athens" (74 and n. 7). Therefore Euenor's status can only be asertained when it is known "whether continuous residence in Athens for a longer period necessarily meant that a foreigner became a metic" (Pečírka, 74).

The relationship between the two decrees has also provoked discussion. The stone, in its present condition records a probouleuma, apparently published as a discrete document, to which a decree of the Demos was added at a later time--both the inclusion of the full prescript with complete dating formula and the crowded and careless cutting confirm that #88II is a discrete document.

Placing two decrees which deal with the same subject on the same stone is not unusual. What is unusual is that while the full prescript with dating formula in #88II should indicate a discrete document, the presence of the phrase, τὰ μὲν ἄλλα καθάπερ τῆι βουλεῖ, indicates that #88II is a rider to the probouleuma above (DeLaix uses the term "amendment"). In that case, a full prescript and date should not be necessary because riders were usually added on the same day the probouleuma was presented to and passed by the ekklesia. Rhodes's suggestion (72 n. 1; which does explain the complete date), that #88II was passed when an adjourned assembly was reconvened, only works if it allows time for #88I to have been at least cut, if not erected (see ep. com.). DeLaix considers this decree "another example of the ecclesia accepting a probouleuma in toto but adding further stipulations" (124). He sees no problem, however, because he follows Hartel, who assumed that the indication that the ekklesia had sanctioned the probouleuma had been omitted when the stonecutter inscribed #88I (see comm. above). Dittmar's elaborate explanation (68-72, paraphrased by Pečírka, 72-73 n. 2) is unnecessary as long as Hartel's contention that the Boule was not acting on its own is accepted. There is no indication, however, of what the stonecutter may or may not have omitted in line 6. What we have is two documents which share more than a common subject; since they are integrally related, they should have been published at the same time--but they were not.

Although DeLaix and Rhodes (as well as previous scholars) basically agree on the content, i.e., that #88II is a rider to an earlier probouleuma in #88I, neither offers an adequate explanation as to why the two documents were not published at the same time. The reason may be that they did not consider the year recorded on the stone. I have noted for the earlier decrees of this year, #86 and #87, and already in the commentary above for this document, that 322/1 was not a normal year in Athenian history. That in itself could explain the apparent departure from the normal legislative process. The nature of that departure, however, might be even more significant. Whether the Boule acted on its own (an indication of oligarchic tendencies) or not, the Demos, at some later date, amended the original probouleuma by granting further honors to Euenor. Although amendments or riders from the ekklesia are not unusual, adorning them with a complete prescript with full dating formula is unusual. I suggest that the Demos was making a statement of its sovereignty at a time when that sovereignty must already have been threatened.

89. *DECREE* lost

photo: none; drawing in Vischer Kleine Schriften II(1878) Plate VII.3.

editors: Vischer Kleine Schriften II(1878) 93-100 no. 71; IG II 188; IG II^2 375.

supplement: 21.302 (Pritchett-Neugebauer, Meritt).

other bibliography: Reusch De diebus cont. 133; Unger Philol. 38(1879) 427; Dinsmoor Archons 373; Pritchett-Neugebauer Cal. 60; Meritt Ath. 111-112.

description: This stone is now lost and apparently only Vischer saw it. He records only that it was found in Oropos, that he thought the marble was Pentelic, and that the letters were difficult to read. Since Vischer recorded the text in the home of Paparrhigopolis, the exact find spot cannot now be ascertained.

dimensions: none recorded letters: 0.008 m. (Vischer)

minuscule text: next page.

commentary: Since I was not able to examine the stone, I have taken the text verbatim from Kirchner's edition. Vischer (98) noted that the letters were difficult to read and that, for example, episilon could be eta, or eta be nu, or omicron could be theta (no central dot) or that lambda could be alpha (no cross bars). Koehler acknowledged those problems in his majuscule text. Kirchner noted only the places where different readings could support different restorations: he noted that the first two letters in line 2 could be ΘΗ or ON; that line 8 read ΕΝ.ΙΔ.ΤΟ..ΡΙ; and that the end line of 9 read Η ΗΜΟΡ.

The restorations and stoichedon order of 25 letters to the line are Vischer's. Vischer suggested either Ἐρεχ]θηΐδος or Πανδι]ονΐδος as the tribe in prytany. Koehler chose Erechtheis (following Vischer's min. text), which meant line 1 had only 24 letters; Kirchner chose Pandionis, which allows for 25 letters in both line 1 and 2. Koehler ended his minuscule text with the beginning of line 8, noting that the rest of the readings were too ambiguous to obtain any accurate restorations.

stoich. 25

[Ἐπὶ Φι]λοκ[λέουϲ ἄρχοντοϲ ἐπὶ τ]-
[ῆϲ Πανδι]ον̣ίδοϲ δεκάτηϲ [πρυτα]-
[νεία]ϲ ἧι Εὐθυγένηϲ Ἡφαιϲ[τοδή]-
[μο]υ Κ[ηφ]ιϲιεὺϲ ἐγρα[μ]μάτε[υεν· Θ]-
[αρ]γηλιῶνοϲ ἕνηι καὶ ν[έ]αι, ...
[... κ]αὶ τριακοϲτῆι [τ]ῆ[ϲ] πρ[υταν]-
[είαϲ· ἐκκ]λ[η]ϲί[α]· τῶν [π]ροέδ[ρων ἐπ]-
[εψήφιζεν Ἀ?]ν[τ]ίδ[ο]το[ϲ Θ]ρι[άϲιοϲ?]·
[ἔδοξεν τῶι] δή[μ]ω[ι]· Ἡγήμ[ων? ..5..]
.....10.....Ε..ϹII - - - - - - -
.....13......ΛΕΣ - - - - - -
........16........T - - - - -
........16.......ΣΛΛ - - - - -
[......12......πρ]ΑΤΤΩΝ - - -

The name of the chairman of the proedroi was suggested by Vischer. Kirchner included that name in his text with Vischer's first choice for the demotic (although Vischer suggested three other alternative demotics, Kirchner recorded only Ἐρικεεύϲ in his commentary).

Since Vischer (who had Boeckh's help with the calendar restoration), everyone has accepted that the month must be Skirophorion rather than Thargelion, which was obviously cut on the stone. But even when that error is acknowledged, what remains of the dating formula still presents problems. Vischer offered for the prytany date (lines 5/6): [ἐνάτηι κα]ὶ τριακοστῆι. Unger was able to restore [ὀγδο/ίηι κ]αὶ... on the assumption that prytanies I through VIII and X had 38 days (this was to account for #87 and #88, but is now no longer acceptable; see comm., #88). Pritchett-Neugebauer restored [πέμπ/τηι κ]αὶ...; the equation is <Skirophorion> 29/30 = Prytany X 3[5] = 354th day of an ordinary year. (Dinsmoor, 373, rejected Unger's restoration, but suggested either 35 or 37 as the day in the prytany for an ordinary year). Meritt, who considers 322/1 to be intercalary (see comm. for #87, #88), restores [ἑβδό/μηι κ]αὶ..., which gives the equation: <Skirophorion> 29 = Prytany X 3[7] = 383rd day (this assumes that Skirophorion had 30 days, the 30th designated ἕνη καὶ νέα ἐμβόλιμος). Although I follow Meritt, who designates 323/2 ordinary and 322/1 intercalary (again, see commentaries for #87, #88) I prefer in this case to follow Kirchner who, in turn, followed Reusch who commented that even after substituting Skirophorion for the definite Thargelion on the stone, the day in prytany cannot be ascertained.

All that is left of this decree is the formulaic prescript. And, although at first glance that prescript seems normal, the discussion (above), concerned with calendar, shows that it is not. In addition, as Koehler pointed out, and Kirchner reiterated, by this time the territory of Oropos should not have been a part of Athenian territory. It should be noted, however, that Vischer examined this stone in someone's *home* in Oropos. On the other hand, the prescript of this decree indicates that it is an Athenian decree rather than a deme decree. Such decrees are usually found either in Athens or in a state sanctuary, such as the Amphiaraion. This decree, therefore, presents another anomaly for the year 322/1.

322/1

90. *DECREE* EM 88

editor: Kirchner *IG* II^2 376.

other bibliography: Meritt *Ath.* 110.

description: This fragment of Hymettian marble was found in the theater of Dionysos. All sides and back are broken. One (horse?) hoof remains of what must have been a sculptured relief above the text.

dimensions:
H 0.18 m. (entire)
0.07 m. (surface)
W 0.014 m.
Th 0.095 m.

letters: 0.007 m. Smallest, H, O, T, X, are .005; largest, Y, is .008. Π is .006. Letters are poorly cut.

stoich. 31

minuscule text:

[᾿Επὶ Φιλοκλέο]υϲ ἄρχοντοϲ [ἐπὶ τῆϲ ....]
[....11.....η]ϲ πρυτανε̣[ίαϲ, ἧι Εὐθυγέ]-
[νηϲ ῾Ηφαιϲτοδήμ]ο̣υ̣ Κηφι[ϲιεὺϲ ἐγραμμά]-
[τευεν· Ποϲιδεῶν / Γαμηλιῶν]οϲ ἕνη[ι καὶ νέαι ..5..]

commentary: I record two new readings: sigma at the end of line 1; omicron at the beginning of line 4. Dots are mine. Restorations and stoichedon order of 31 letters to the line are Kirchner's, apparently based on the name of the secretary for this year.

What remains of the text of this document offers no information. The physical evidence, however, substantiates the restoration of either Posideon or Gamelion as the month in which this decree was passed and presumably erected. Despite the poor letter cutting, this stele was crowned with a sculptured relief, an indication that originally, this was not a run-of-the-mill document. A date in the middle of the year, before any of the more completely dated decrees of this year, fits better historically.

322/1

91. *DECREE* lost

editors: Koehler & Velsen <u>IG</u> II 189; <u>IG</u> II^2 377.

description: This fragment was found on the Akropolis; it is now lost. (Although I was allowed to go through the list of inscriptions still on the Akropolis, this decree was not included in the inventory.) The stone was not described by Velsen and Koehler. Since he includes no dimensions, apparently the stone was already lost by the time Kirchner edited this decree.

dimensions: no measurements letters: no measurements

minuscule text:

........17........M - - - - - - -
[....10..... τῶι] δ[ῆμ]ωι τῶι ['Αθηναίων -]
[......14.......c]θαι εἰc - - - - - - - -
........17........ΟΣΚΟ - - - - - - -
.......14....... τοῦ δήμο[υ - - - - -]
.......14...... τοῖc ἰδί[οιc - - - - -]
[... ἐπὶ Φ]ιλοκλέουc ἄρχο[ντοc - - -]
....8....I//ΟΥ κατεcκευ[α - - - - -]
[ἐνδεικν]ύμενοc τὴν ε[ὔνοιαν - - - - -]
....9.....ΤΕΠΙΤ - - - - - - - - - - -
....9.....ΤΙ - - - - - - - - - - -
....9.....Η - - - - - - - - - - - -

commentary: Koehler recorded in his commentary a number of letters read by Velsen but not included in the majuscule text for II 189: ΥΜΙΟ, line 1; Ν˥ΣΚΟ line 4; Ο...˥ΟΤΟ, line 5; Ν.ΤΟΙΣ, line 6; ΑΤΙ, line 11. The restorations are Koehler's, with the exception of the restoration at the end of line 2, and the addition of ἐν τδ δεικν]ύμενοc at the beginning of line 9, made by Kirchner. Koehler (or Velsen?) made one restoration at the end of line 6, ἰδί[οιc ἀναλώμαcι], which Kirchner did not include. Unless Kirchner saw the stone, and noted that the left hand side (but not the surface) was intact, there is no explanation for his establishing a left hand margin, especially since his schema would place the date, ἐπὶ Φ]ιλοκλέουc 4 stoichoi to the left of that left-hand margin. Although Kirchner printed exact numbers of letters for the unrestored (or non-existent?) part to the left of the recorded letters, and the letters in Koehler's majuscule text are printed in stoichedon, neither editor stated that the letters on the stone were cut in stoichedon.

This text is as laconic as the comments made by the editors. The only information that can be gleaned is that either something happened or someone served during the archonship of Philokleos. Thus this document serves as an appropriate finale to an era which began with war and ended with war.

APPENDIX
INSCRIPTIONS OF THE LYKOURGAN ERA DATED TO A SPECIFIC YEAR

Included are: date; Corpus number (for decrees); most recent edition; latest citation in SEG or Bull. (where applicable); short description. AD = ΑΔ; B = Bull. (number after date refers to citation, not page); H = Hesperia; PPA = ΠΡΑΓ. ΑΚΑΔ. ΑΘΗΝ.

338/7

#1	II^2 237	SEG 24.95	Honors to Akarnanians
#2	II^2 238	SEG 17.25	Honors to two Andrians
#3	II^2 244	SEG 19.57	Law and instructions for Peiraieus fortifications
	II^2 236	SEG 17.23 B(1953)54	Treaty between Philip and the Greek cities
	II^2 3023		Dedication by gymnasiarch
	II^2 5226	SEG 27.24	Monument to Chaironeia dead
	H 19(1950) 263/7 no. 20	SEG 22.136	Mining records

337/6

#4	II^2 239	SEG 21.267	Honors to Alkimachos
#5	H 9(1940) 325/7 no. 35		Lemnos decree

#6	H 21(1952) 355/9 no. 5	SEG 24.96 B(1959)129	Law against tyranny
#7	II^2 240		Athens bestows proxeny
#8	II^2 241		Decree
#9	H 7(1938) 292/4 no. 19	B(1939)59	Honors to Chairestratos
#10	II^2 242		Honorary decree
#11	II^2 243		Honors to Kaliteles
#12	II^2 276	B(1944)65	Honors to Asklepiodoros
#13	II^2 1255		Honors to hieropoioi
#14	II^2 304+604	SEG 18.11 B(1960)132	Honors to two doctors
	II^2 2834		Dedication
	II^2 4594	SEG 12.165	Dedication to Artemis
	H 12(1943) 52/5 no. 12	B(1944)57	Choregic monument
336/5			
#15	II^2 328	SEG 21.268	Lykourgos proposes honors
#16	H 26(1957) 207/8 no. 54	SEG 17.27	Decree
	II^2 329		Renewal of treaty by Alexander
	II^2 4392		Dedication
	H 30(1961) 30-59	SEG 23.85 B(1963)84	Bouleutai list

336/5 or 335/4		
#17 II^2 334+ H 28(1950) 239-247	SEG 25.65 B(1966)279	Law and regulations concerning the Lesser Panathenaia
335/4		
#18 II^2 330+445	B(1942)32	Honors to Phyleus
#19 H 9(1940) 327/8 no. 36		Decree
[20] II^2 332		Decree
#21 II^2 333	SEG 21.271	Lykourgos proposes a law to deal with religious reforms
#22 II^2 331	SEG 21.270	Decree
II^2 1700		Bouleutai list
II^2 3042	SEG 21.690	Lysikrates monument
334/3		
#23 II^2 335+ H 4(1935) 169-170	SEG 21.274 B(1944)65	Demades proposes a decree
#24 II^2 405	SEG 21.275	Citizenship to Amyntor
#25 II^2 414a	SEG 21.276	Honors to Diotimos
#26 II^2 1184	B(1942)32	Decree from deme Cholargos
II^2 1156	SEG 15.109	Ephebic monument
II^2 1189		Ephebic monument
II^2 1493, 1495, 1494	SEG 22.133 B(1966)133	Accounts by treas-surers and priests of Athena
II^2 1750		Prytany list
II^2 2970	SEG 22.148	Ephebic dedication

H 29(1960) 39/40 no. 49	SEG 19.196	Choregic dedication
333/2		
#27 II^2 337	SEG 25.67	Enktesis for Kitians
#28 II^2 338		Honors to Pythias
#29 II^2 339a	SEG 26.75 B(1958)189	Proxeny to a Chian
#30 II^2 340		Decree
#31 II^2 336	SEG 21.273,278 B(1942)32	Citizenship to Archippos
#32 PAA 13(1948) 5-23	SEG 24.203 B(1950)72a	Lease of a garden by orgeones of the Hero Iatros
II^2 2791	SEG 21.679 B(1963)78	Dedication by Boule
II^2 2976	SEG 21.682 B(1942)31	Ephebic dedication
H 9(1940) 59/66 no. 8	SEG 21.513	Ephebic monument
AM 76(1961) 143/6	SEG 21.680 B(1964)133	Ephebic dedication
AM 76(1961) 147/8	SEG 21.681	Ephebic dedication
Praktika (1954) 70/1 no. 68	SEG 16.106	Ephebic monument (not full publication)
332/1		
#33 II^2 344	SEG 21.279	Athens grants proxeny
#34 H 5(1936) 413/4 no. 11		Decree
#35 II^2 420	SEG 22.93	Decree

#36	II^{2} 345		Plataians honored
#37	II^{2} 346		Honors to son of Aristeides
#38	II^{2} 347	SEG 14.55	Honors to Amphis
#39	H 8(1939) 26/7 no. 6		Proxeny for an Abderite
#40	VII 4252		Gold crown to Amphiaraos
#41	VII 4253		Honors to Phanodemos
#42	AD 25(1970) 204-214		Decree from Eitea
#43	REG 91(1978) 289-306		Eleusis honors Philokomos
	II^{2} 2792		Dedication
331/30			
#44	II^{2} 348	SEG 26.76	Honors to an actor
#45	II^{2} 349		Honors to Rheboulas
#46	II^{2} 1181		Deme decree
	II^{2} 4594a	SEG 12.165	Ephebic dedication
	H 37(1968) 374/80 no. 51	SEG 25.177 B(1971)250	Dedication by phialai
331/30 or 330/29			
#47	H 31(1962) 401/3 no. 3	SEG 21.520 B(1967)226	Teithrasians honor their councilors
330/29			
#48	II^{2} 351+624	SEG 24.99	Honors to Eudemos
#49	II^{2} 352		Decree
	II^{2} 1924+ 2409	SEG 16.136,145 B(1958)189	Diaitetai list

II^2 3103	B(1930)190	Dedication by gymnasiarch
329/8		
#50 VII 4254		Honors to Demades and friends
#51 II^2 353		Honors to a Larisaian
#52 II^2 1256	B(1942)44a	Honors to Bendis epimelites
II^2 1672	SEG 19.147 B(1959)130	Accounts of epistates and treasurers in Eleusis
II^2 1925		Diaitetai list
II^2 2836		Dedication
II^2 2837		Dedication
328/7		
#53 II^2 452	SEG 25.68	Decree
#54 II^2 354	SEG 23.56 B(1960)132	Honors to Androkles, priest of Asklepios
#55 II^2 355		Decree
#56 AE (1917) 40/8 no. 92		Bouletai list and dedication
II^2 3052	SEG 21.691	Choregic monument
II^2 4595		Dedication
327/6		
#57 II^2 357	SEG 21.287	Proxeny to an Eretrian
#58 II^2 356	SEG 23.57	Honors to Memnon
#59 H 3(1934) 3/4 no.5	SEG 25.69	Honors to someone
#60 II^2 113	B(1942)32	Athens bestows isotelia

#61	H 7(1938) 94/6 no.15	B(1938)54	Honors to Teleskopas
[62]	II^2 358	SEG 21.326 B(1965)138	Decree
	H Suppl. I (1937)no.1	SEG 17.45 B(1938)82	Prytany list
	H 16(1947) 184 no.90	B(1948)44	Dedication by prytanes
	AD 18B(1963) 18	SEG 23.104	Choregic dedication
326/5			
#63	II^2 359		Decree
#64	II^2 800	SEG 21.289	Decree
#65	II^2 1157		Decree of Pandionis
#66	II^2 1198		Aixonians honor their choregoi
#67	II^2 363	SEG 25.66 B(1944)58	Honors to Dionysos
325/4			
#68	II^2 360	SEG 26.79 B(1954)92	Honors to Herakleides
#69	II^2 361	SEG 18.15	Decree
#70	II^2 1203	B(1942)32	Decree from Athmones
	II^2 1926		Diaitetai list
	II^2 2838		Dedication
	II^2 4371	SEG 17.80	Dedication to Asklepios
	II^2 4428		Dedication
	H 17(1948) 39 no.25		Dedication

324/3

#	Inscription	Reference	Description
#71	H 10(1941) 49/50 no.12	SEG 21.290	Decree
#72	H 10(1941) 50/2 no.13		Decree
#73	II^2 362	SEG 21.291 B(1944)58	Decree
#74	II^2 547	SEG 21.292	Decree c. symproedroi
#75	II^2 454	SEG 21.293	Decree
#76	II^2 1176	SEG 21.521 B(1964)117	Decree from Peiraieus
#77	II^2 1257		Decree
#78	II^2 1258		Decree by Eikadeis
	II^2 2935		Dedication
	H 10(1941) 42/8 no.11	SEG 21.290	Dedicatory base
	AE (1918) 73/6 no.95	B(1969)152	Ephebic list
	AE (1974) 175/188	B(1976)177	Dedication by poletai

323/2

#	Inscription	Reference	Description
#79	II^2 365	SEG 21.294	Honors to Lapyros
#80	II^2 366		Decree
#81	II^2 367	SEG 26.815	Athens honors Asklepiodoros
#82	II^2 368	SEG 21.296,280	Proxeny for Theophantos
#83	II^2 448	SEG 26.82	Honors to Euphron
#84	II^2 343	SEG 24.103 B(1944)65	Honors to Apollonides

#85	H 9(1940) 335/43 no.42	SEG 24.102 B(1944)65	Honorary decree
	II^2 370	SEG 25.70 B(1965)141	Treaty between Athens and Aitolia
	II^2 3025		Choregic dedication
	II^2 3054		Choregic dedication
322/1			
#86	II^2 371+308	SEG 3.82 B(1942)32	Decree
#87	II^2 372	SEG 23.60 B(1968)213	Honorary decree
#88	II^2 373	SEG 24.105	Honors to Euenor
#89	II^2 375	SEG 21.302	Decree
#90	II^2 376		Decree
#91	II^2 377		Decree
	II^2 2839		Dedication

ABBREVIATIONS

AC L'Antiquité Classique. Louvain.

ΑΔ 'Αρχαιολογικὸν Δελτίον. Athens, Archaeological Service.

AE 'Αρχαιολογικὴ 'Εφημερίς. Athens, Archaeological Society.

AJA American Journal of Archaeology. Archaeological Institute of America.

AJP American Journal of Philology. American Philological Association.

AK Antike Kunst. Vereinigung der Freunde antiker Kunst. Basel.

AM Mitteilungen des Deutschen Archäologischen Instituts (Athenische Abteilung). German Archaeological Institute.

Anc. Soc. Ancient Society. Catholic University, Louvain.

APF Archiv für Papyrusforschung und verwandte Gebiete. Leipzig.

Arch. Epig. Mitt. Archaeologisch-epigraphische mittheilungen aus Osterreich-Ungarn. Vienna. (Superseded by ÖJ.)

Arch. Zeit. Archaeologische Zeitung. Berlin. (Superseded by JDAI.)

Archaeology Archaeology. Archaeological Institute of America.

ΑΘΗΝΑΙΟΝ 'Αθήναιον. Σύγγραμμα περιοδικὸν κατὰ διμηνίαν ἐκδιδόμενον συμπράξει πολλῶν λογίων. Athens.

AW The Ancient World. Chicago.

BCH Bulletin de Correspondance Hellênique. Paris.

BdI Bulletino dell'Instituto di Corrispondenza Archeologica. Rome.

Berl. Phil. Woch. Berliner Philogische Wochenschrift. (Superseded by Philologische Wochenschrift.)

BSA Annual of the British School at Athens. London.

CJ The Classical Journal. Athens, University of Georgia.

CP Classical Philology. Chicago, University of Chicago.

CRAI Comptes Rendus de l'Académie des Inscriptions et Belles-Lettres. Paris.

CSCA California Studies in Classical Antiquity. Berkeley.

ΔΕΛΤ., ΑΡΧ. Δελτῖον Ἀρχαιολογικὸν, ἐκδιδόμενον ὑπὸ τοῦ Γενικοῦ ἐφόρου τῶν ἀρχαιοτήτων καὶ μουσεῖων. Athens. (Earlier title of ΑΔ.)

ΕΛΛΗΝΙΚΑ Ἑλληνικά. Φιλολογικὸν, ἱστορικὸν καὶ λαογραφικὸν Περιοδικόν. Σύγγραμμα τῆς Ἑταιρεῖας Μακεδονικῶν Σπουδῶν. Thessaloniki.

ΕΦ. Ἐφημερὶς Ἀρχαιολογική. Athens, Archaeological Society. 1832-1909. (Earlier title of AE.)

Epigraphica Epigraphica. Revista italiana di Epigrafia. Milan.

GGA Göttingische Gelehrte Anzeigen. Göttingen.

GRBS Greek, Roman and Byzantine Studies. Duke University, Durham, North Carolina.

Hermes Hermes. Zeitschrift für klassische Philologie. Wiesbaden.

Hesperia Hesperia. Journal of the American School of Classical Studies at Athens. Athens, American School.

HLB Harvard Library Bulletin. Cambridge, Mass., Harvard College Library.

HSCP Harvard Studies in Classical Philology. Cambridge, Mass., Harvard University.

HThR Harvard Theological Review. Cambridge, Mass., Harvard University.

Index Schol. Halens Index Scholarum in Universitate litteraria Fridericiana Helensi cum vitebergensi consociata. Wittenberg.

Jahrb. Jahrbücher für classische philologie. Leipzig. (Superseded by Neue Jahrb.)

JDAI Jahrbuch des Deutschen Archäologischen Instituts. Berlin, German Archaeological Institute.

JHS Journal of Hellenic Studies. London, Society for the Promotion of Hellenic Studies.

Journ. Sav. Journal des Savants. Paris.

Klio Klio. Beiträge zur alten Geschichte. Berlin, Akademie-Verlag.

KSIA. Kratkie soobshchenia Instituta archeologii. USSR, Akademii Navk.

KSIIMK. Kratikie soobshschenia Instituta istorii materialnoi kultury. USSR.

LF Listy Filologické. Praque, Naklad. Čs. Akad.

Mnemosyne. Mnemosyne. Bibliotheca Classica Batava. Leiden.

Monatsber. Berl. Monatsberichte der preussischen Akademie Berlin. Berlin, Prussian Academy.

Musée belge Le Musée belge. Revue de philologie classique. Liége.

ΝΕΑ ΕΣΤΙΑ Νέα ʽΕστία. Athens.

Neue Jahrb. Neue Jahrbücher für Philologie und Paedagogik. Leipzig.

ÖJ Jahreshefte des Österreichischen Archäologischen Instituts. Vienna, Austrian Archaeological Institute.

Opus. Arch. Opuscula archaeologica. Skrifter utg. av Svenska institutet i Rom. Lund, Swedish Institute at Rome. (Superseded by Opuscula romana.)

Philol. Philologus. Zeitschrift für klassische Philologie. Berlin, Berlin Academy.

Phoenix Phoenix. The Journal of the Classical Association of Canada. Toronto, University of Toronto.

ΠΛΑΤΩΝ Πλάτων. Δελτίον τῆς 'Εταιρείας 'Ελλήνων Φιλολόγων. Athens, Greek Philological Society.

ΠΟΛΕΜΩΝ Πολέμων. 'Αρχαιολογικὸν περιοδικόν. Athens.

ΠΡΑΓ. ΑΚΑΔ. ΑΘΗΝ. Πραγματεῖαι τῆς 'Ακαδημίας 'Αθηνῶν. Athens, Athens Academy.

RBN Revue Belge de Numismatique. Brussels.

REA Revue des Études Anciennes. Paris, Les Belles Lettres.

REG Revue des Études Grecques. Paris, Les Belles Lettres.

Rev. Arch. Revue Archéologique. Paris, University of Paris.

Rev. Crit. Revue Critique d'histoire et de litteratures.

Rh. Mus. Rheinische Museum. Frankfurt.

RM Mitteilungen des Deutschen Archäologischen Instituts (Römische Abteilung). Mainz, German Archaeological Institute.

Sitz. Ak. Berlin Sitzungsberichte der Deutschen Akademie der Wissenschaften zu Berlin, Klasse für Philosophie, Geschichte, Staats-, Rechts- und Wirtschaftswissenschaften. Berlin, Berlin Academy.

Sitz. Ak. Münch. Sitzungsberichte der Bayerischen Akademie der Wissenschaften, Philosophische-Historische Klasse. Munich, Bavarian Academy.

Sitz. Ak. Wien Sitzungsberichte der Österreichischen Akademie der Wissenschaft in Wien, Philosophische-Historische Klasse. Vienna, Austrian Academy.

TAPA Transactions and Proceedings of the American Philological Association. American Philological Association.

WS Wiener Studien. Zeitschrift für klassische Philogie und Patristik. Vienna.

ZPE Zeitschrift für Papyrologie und Epigraphik. Bonn.

BIBLIOGRAPHY

Arndt, Paul. La Glyptotèque Ny-Carlsburg. Munich: Bruckmann, 1896-1912.

Behrend, Diedrich. Attische Pacturkunden. Munich: Beck, 1970.

Beule, Charles Ernest. L'Acropole d'Athenes. Paris: Firmin Didot freres, fils et c[ie], 1862.

Binnebössel, Rosemarie. Studien zu den attischen Urkundenreliefs des 5. & 4. Jahrhunderts. Kalendkirchen (Rhineland): T. Meeuws, 1932.

Boeckh, August. Corpus inscriptionum graecarum. Berlin: G. Reimer, 1828-1877.

__________. Epigraphisch-chronologische Studien. Jahrbücher für Classische Philologie Supplement II (1856/57).

Bournouf, Emile. "Inscriptions trouvees a l'acropole d'Athenes." Rev. Arch. 28(1974) 315-319.

Braccessi, L. "Il decreto ateniese del 337-6 contro gli attentati alla democrazia." Epigraphica 27(1965) 110-126.

Brashinsky, J. B. "Epigraphical Evidence on Athen's Relations with the North Pontic Greek States." Acta of the Fifth Epigraphic Congress. Oxford: Blackwell, 1971.

Broneer, Oscar. "Excavations on the North Slope of the Acropolis in Athens, 1933-1934." Hesperia 4(1935) 109-188.

Buermann, H. "Animadversiones de titulis Atticis quibus civitatis alicui confertur sine redintegratur." Jahrb. Supplement X 1878/9, 343-362.

Burstein, Stanley M. Outpost of Hellenism: The Emergence of Heraclea on the Black Sea. (University of California Publications in Classical Studies, Vol.14) Berkeley: University of California Press, 1974.

Chandler, Richard. Inscriptiones Antiquae, 2nd. ed. Oxford: Clarendon Press, 1774.

Cohn-Haft, Louis. The Public Physicians of Ancient Greece. (Smith College Studies in History, XLII) Northhampton, Mass.: Department of History of Smith College, 1956.

Conomis, N. C. "Lykourgos c. Leocr. § § 124-127, The Decree of Demophantus and the Law of Eukrates." Hellenika 16(1958) 6-13.

__________. Lycurgi Oratio in Leocratem cum Ceterarum Lycurgi Orationem Fragmentis. Leipzig: Teubner, 1970.

Coumanudis, S. and Gofas, D. "Deux dêcrets d'Éleusis." REG 91(1978) 289-306.

Daux, Georges. Fouilles de Delphes, fasc. 3 part 2: Inscriptions depuis le tresor des Atheniens jusqu'aux bases de Gelon. (French School in Athens) Paris: de Boccard, 1943.

Davis, John Kenyon. Athenian Propertied Families. Oxford: Clarendon Press, 1971.

DeLaix, Roger Alain. Probouleusis at Athens. (University of California Publications in History, Vol. 83) Berkeley: University of California Press, 1973.

Deubner, Ludwig August. Attische Feste. Berlin: H. Keller, 1932.

Diepolder. Die Attischen Grabreliefs. Berlin: H. Keller, 1931.

Dinsmoor, William B. The Archons of Athens in the Hellenistic Age. Cambridge: Harvard University Press, 1931.

Dittenberger, Wilhelm. "De Menelai Pelagon istitulis," Satura philologa Sauppio oblata. Berlin: Weidmann, 1879.

__________. Sylloge inscriptionum graecarum. Leipzig: S. Hirzel, 1883. Second edition, 1898. Third edition, 1915-1924, edited by Kirchner.

Dittmar, Armin Maximilian. De Athensium more exteros coronis publice ornandi quaestiones epigraphicae. Leipzig: Leipziger Studien zur classischen Philologie, 1890.

Dow, Sterling. "The Athenian Anagrapheis." HSCP 67(1963) 38-54.

__________. "The Preambles of Athenian Decrees." Hesperia 32 (1963) 335-365.

__________. "The Purported Decree of Themistokles." AJA 66(1962) 353-368.

Dragatsis. "Psephisma from Pireaus." AE (1900) 91-102.

Drerup, Engelbert. "Inscriptions Attiques." Musée Belge 9(1905) 390-393.

Ferguson, William Scott. The Athenian Secretaries. (Cornell Studies in Classical Philology, VII) New York: Macmillan for Cornell University, 1898.

__________. "The Attic Orgeones." HThR 37(1944) 61-140.

__________. "Orgeonika." Commemorative Studies in Honor of Theodore Leslie Shear. Hesperia Supplement VIII 1949, 130-163.

Foucart, Paul François. Des Associations Religieuses chez les Grecs. Paris: Klincksieck, 1873.

__________. "Décret Athénien de l'an 333." REG 6(1893) 1-7.

__________. "Une Loi athénienne du IV° Siècle." Journ. Sav. (1902) 177-193, 233-245.

__________. "Le Culte de Bendisen Attique," Melanages Perrot. (Recueil de Mémoires concernant L'archéologie Classique) Paris: Thorin et fils, 1903.

Frickenhaus, August Heinrich. Athens Mauern im IV Jahrhundert v. Chr. Bonn: C. Georgi, 1905.

Friederichs, Karl und Wolters, Paul. Gipsabgüsse antiker Bildwerke. Berlin: W. Spemann, 1885.

Froehner, W. Musee National du Louvre: Les incriptions grecques. Paris: C. de Mourques, 1865.

Ghiron-Bistagne, Paulette. Recherches sur les Acteurs dans la Grèce Antique. Paris: Sociêtê d'êdition "Les Belles Lettres," 1976.

Gilbert, Gustav. "Erste und zweite Lesung in der athenischen Volksversamlung." Neue Jahrb. (1879) 225-240, (1880) 529-538.

Hansen, Mogens Herman. "ΟΙ ΠΡΟΕΔΡΟΙ ΤΩΝ ΝΟΜΟΘΕΤΩΝ: A Note on IG II^2 222, 41-52." ZPE 30(1978) 151-157.

Hartel, Wilhelm August. Studien über Attisches Staatsrecht und Urkundenwesen. Vienna: K. Gerold and Son, 1878.

Hartwig, Paul. Bendis; eine archaeologische Untersuchung. Leipzig, Berlin: Giesecke & Devrient, 1897.

Hausmann, Ulrich. Griechische Weihreliefs. Berlin: D. Gruyter, 1960.

Hausoullier, Bernard. La Vie Municipal en Attique. (Biblioteque des Écoles françaises d'Athènes et de Rome, fasc. 38) Paris: Ernest Thorin, 1884.

Henry, Alan S. The Prescripts of Athenian Decrees. (Mnemosyne Supplement 49) Leyden: E. J. Brill, 1977.

Herington, C. J. Athena Parthenos and Athena Polias. (Publications of the Faculty of Arts of the University of Manchester, 7) Manchester, England: University Press, 1955.

Hicks, Edward Lee. The Collection of Ancient Greek Inscriptions in the British Museum I. Oxford: Clarendon Press, 1874.

Hicks, Edward Lee, and Hill, G. F. A Manual of Greek Historical Inscriptions, 2nd edition. Oxford: Clarendon Press, 1901.

Hoeck. "Das Odrysenreich in Thrakien." Hermes 26(1891) 89-116.

Hubbe, R. O. "Decrees of the Precinct of Asklepios." Hesperia 28(1959) 159-201.

Isager, Signe and Hansen, Mogens Herman. Aspects of Athenian Society in the Fourth Century B.C. Odense: Odense University Press, 1975.

Jacoby, Felix. Die Fragmente der griechischen Historiker. Vols. III B: Fragmenta; III B Suppl.: Commentary; III B Suppl.: Commentary and Notes. Oxford: Clarendon Press, 1950-1954.

Kahrstedt, Ulrich. Staatsgebiet und Staatsangehörige in Athen. Stuttgart-Berlin: W. Kohlhammer, 1934.

Kalogeropoulou, Athena G. "Ψῆφιcμα ἐξ Εἰτέαc Ἀττικῆc." ΑΔ 35(1970) 204-214.

Kirchhoff, A. "Inschriften von der Akropolis." Sitz. Ak. Berlin (1887) 1059-1074.

Kirchner, Johannes Ernst. Imagines Inscriptionum Atticarum, 2nd edition. Edited by G. Klaffenbach. Berlin: Gebr. Mann, 1948.

__________. Prosopographia Attica, 2nd edition. Berlin: G. Reimer, 1930.

Koehler, Ulrich. "Aus den attischen Inschriften." AM 7(1882) 96-111.

__________. "Ein Neues Aktenstück aus der Finanzverwaltung des Lykurgos." Hermes 1(1886) 312-322.

__________. "Studien zu attischen Psephismen." Hermes 5(1871) 1-20, 328-353.

Kougeas, S. B. "Ὁ ὑπὲρ τῆc δημοκρατίαc Νόμοc τοῦ Εὐκράτουc" ΝΕΑ ΕΣΤΙΑ 52(1952) 836-839.

Koumanoudes and Oikonomides. "Ἐπιγραφικὰ Σύμμεικτα." ΠΟΛΕΜΩΝ 5(1952/5) 22-30.

Kumanudes, Stephanos A. "Ἀττικα Ψηφίcματα." ΑΘΗΝΑΙΟΝ 5(1876) 102-103, 184-186.

__________. "'Επιγραφαὶ ἐκ τῶν περὶ τὸ 'Ασκληπιεῖον τόπων." ΑΘΗΝΑΙΟΝ 6(1877) 127-148.

Lambrechts, A. Texst en Uitzicht van de Atheense Proxeniendecreten tot 323 v.C. (K.V.Ac. Wetenschapper, Klasse der Lettern, Vol. 32) Brussels: Paleis der Academiën, 1958.

Larsen, J. A. O. "The Judgement of Antiquity on Democracy." CP 49(1954) 1-14.

Lattermann, Heinrich Wilhelm Albert. "Griechische Bauinschriften." Dissertation, Strassburg, 1908.

Le Bas, Phillipe. Voyage archéologique en Grèce et en Asie Mineure. Paris: Firmin-Didot et cie., 1888.

Lenz, Emil. Das Synedrion der Bundesgenossen im zweiten athenischen Bunde. Königsburg: Elbing, 1880.

Leonardos, Basile. "'Αττικὸν Ψήφισμα τοῦ 320/9." ΑΔ 1(1915) 194-224.

Lewis, D. M. "Dedications of Phialai at Athens." Hesperia 37(1968) 368-380.

__________. "Law on the Lesser Panathenaia." Hesperia 28(1959) 239-247.

__________. "Notes on Attic Inscriptions." BSA 49(1954) 17-50.

__________. "Notes on Attic Inscriptions II." BSA 50(1955) 1-36.

Linders, Tullia. Studies in the Treasure Records of Artemis Brauronia found in Athens. (Svenska institutet i Athen Skrifter, 40/9) Lund: P. Aström, 1972.

Lippold, George. Antike Skulpturen der Glyptotek Ny Carlsberg. Leipzig: E. Schwabe, 1924.

Lolling, H. J. "'Επιγραφαὶ ἐκ τῆς 'Ακροπόλεως." ΔΕΛΤ. ΑΡΧ. (1889) 86-94.

Lord, George D. "An Attic Lease Inscription." AJA 3(1899) 44-53.

Maier, Franz Georg. Griechische Mauerbauinschriften. Heidelberg: Quelle & Meyer, 1959-1961.

Meier, Moritz Hermann Eduard. Commentatio epigraphica II. Halle: Pfeffer, 1854.

Meisterhans, Konrad. Grammatik der attischen Inschriften, 3rd edition. Edited by E. Schwyzer. Berlin: Weidmann, 1900.

Meritt, Benjamin D. The Athenian Year. (Sather Classical Lectures, Vol. 32) Berkeley: University of California Press, 1961.

__________. "The Entrance to the Areopagus." Hesperia 22(1953) 129.

__________. "Greek Inscriptions." Hesperia 4(1935) 525-590.

__________. "Greek Inscriptions." Hesperia 5(1936) 353-441.

__________. "Greek Inscriptions." Hesperia 8(1939) 48-82.

__________. "Greek Inscriptions." Hesperia 21(1952) 340-410.

__________. "Greek Inscriptions." Hesperia 26(1957) 198-221.

__________. "The Hollow Month at Athens." Mnemosyne 30(1977) 217-242.

__________. "Of Athenian Dates and Days." AE (1968) 107-115.

__________. "A Suggested Text for I.G., II^2, 420." AJP 85(1964) 304-306.

__________. "The Year of Archippos at Athens (318/7 B.C.)." Hesperia 45(1976) 173.

__________. "The Year of Neaichmos (320/19 B.C.)." Hesperia 32(1963) 425-438.

Meritt, B. D., and Traill, John S. The Athenian Agora, Vol. XV: Inscriptions. The Athenian Councilors. Princeton: American School of Classical Studies in Athens, 1974.

Michaelis, Adolf. Der Parthenon. Leipzig: Breitkopf und Härtel, 1870-1871.

Michel, Charles. Recueil d'inscriptions grecques. Brussels: H. Lamertin, 1900. Supplement, 1912-1927.

Mikalson, Jon D. The Sacred and Civil Calendars of the Athenian Year. Princeton: Princeton University Press, 1975.

Miller, H. A. E. O. De decretis atticis quaestiones epigraphicae. Breslau: Grass, Barth, 1885.

Mitchel, Fordyce W. "Demades of Paeania and IG II^2. 1493, 1494, 1495." TAPA 93(1962) 213-229. Corrigenda, AJA 70(1966) 66.

__________. Lykourgan Athens: 338-322. Lectures in Memory of Louise Taft Semple. (University of Cincinnati Classical Studies, Vol. II) Norman: University of Oklahoma Press, 1973.

Mitsos, Markellos Th. "Inscriptions from Athens." Hesperia 16(1947) 262-266.

Mommsen, August. Feste der Stadt Athen im Altertum. Leipzig: Teubner, 1898.

Moretti, Luigi. Iscrizioni storiche ellenistiche. Florence: La nvova Italia, 1967.

Nachmanson, E. Beiträge zur Kenntnis der altgrieshischen Volkssprache. Uppsala: C.J. Lundström, 1910.

__________. Historische Attische Inschriften. Bonn: A. Marcus und E. Weber, 1913.

Nouveau choix d'inscriptions grecques. (Institut Fernand-Courby de Lyon) Paris: Societe d'Edition "Les Belles Lettres," 1971.

Oikonomides, A. N. "Δημάδου τοῦ Παιανέως Ψηφίσματα, καὶ Ἐπιγραφικαὶ περὶ τοῦ Βίου Πηγαί." ΠΛΑΤΩΝ 8(1956) 105-129.

__________. ΥΠΕΡΕΙΔΟΥ ΛΟΓΟΙ I. Athens, 1958.

__________. "Κριτικὰ καὶ Ἑρμηνευτικὰ εἰς τὸν Νόμον τοῦ Εὐκράτους." ΠΟΛΕΜΩΝ 6(1956/7) summeikta 28-36.

Osborne, Michael J. "Athens and Orontes." BSA 66(1971) 297-321.

__________. "Attic Citizenship Decrees: A Note" BSA 67(1972) 129-158.

__________. "Attic Grants of Citizenship," Akten des VI Internationalen Kongresses für Griechische und Lateinische Epigraphik (Vestigia, 17). Munich, 1973.

__________. "Entertainment in the Prytaneion at Athens." ZPE 41(1981) 153-170.

Ostwald, Martin. "Athenian Legislation against Tyranny." TAPA 86(1955) 103-128.

Papagiannopoulos-Palaios. "'Επίμετρον." ΠΟΛΕΜΩΝ 3(1947/48) 128.

Pečírka, Jan. The Formula for the Grant of Enktesis in Attic Inscriptions. (Acta Universitatis Carolinae Philosophica et Historica Monographica XV) Prague: Department of Publications at the Charles University, 1966.

Peek, Werner. "Attische Inschriften." AM 67(1942) 1-217.

Pfuhl, Ernst. De Atheniensum Pompis Sacris. Berlin: Weidmann, 1900.

Pickard-Cambridge, A. W. The Dramatic Festivals of Athens, 2nd. ed. Revised by John Gould and D. M. Lewis. Oxford: Clarendon Press, 1968.

__________. The Theater of Dionysos at Athens. Oxford: Clarendon Press, 1946.

Pittakis, Kyriakos S. L'ancienne Athènes. Athens: E. Antoniades, 1835.

Pleket, H. W. Epigraphica. 2 Volumes. Leiden: E.J. Brill, 1964, 1969.

Pouilloux, Jean. Choix d'inscriptions grecques. Paris: Société d'Edition "Les Belles Lettres," 1960.

__________. Recherches sur l'histoire et les cultes de Thasos I. École français d'Athènes. Études thasiennes 3,5) Paris: E. de Boccard, 1954-58.

Pritchett, W. Kendrick. Ancient Athenian Calendars on Stone. (University of California Publications in Classical Archaeology, iv. 4) Berkeley: University of California Press, 1963.

__________. "The Athenian Count of Days." CSCA 9(1976) 181-195.

__________. "The Intercalary Month at Athens." CP 63 (1968) 53-54.

Pritchett, W. K., and Meritt, B. D. The Chronology of Hellenistic Athens. Cambridge, Mass.: Harvard University Press, 1940.

Pritchett, and Neugebauer, O. The Calendars of Athens. Cambridge, Mass: Harvard University Press, 1947.

Prott, H. von, and Ziehen, L. Leges Graecorum Sacrae e Titulis collectae. Volume II. Leipzig: Teubner, 1906.

Rangabé, Alexandros Rizos. Antiquités Helléniques. Athens: Typographie et lithographie royales, 1842-1855.

Reinmuth, O. The Ephebic Inscriptions of the 4th c. B.C. Leiden: Brill, 1971

Reusch, Adam. "De diebus contionum ordinarium apud Athenienses." Dissertation, Strassburg, 1879.

__________. "Zum Corpus Inscr. Att. II." Hermes 15 (1880) 337-347.

Rhodes, P. J. The Athenian Boule. Oxford: Clarendon Press, 1972.

Robert, Louis. "Sur une loi d'Athènes relative aux Petites Panathênées." Hellenica 11-12(1960) 189-203.

Ross. Die Demen von Attica und ihre Vertheilung unter die Phylen nach Inschrifen. Halle: 1846.

Rostovseff, Mikhail. Social and Economic History of the Hellenistic World III. Oxford: Clarendon Press, 1941.

Samuel, Alan E. Greek and Roman Chronology. Munich: Beck, 1972.

Sauppe, Hermann. De proxenis. Göttingen: G. F. Kaestner, 1877.

Schaefer, Arnold D. Demosthenes und Seine Zeit. Volume III, in two parts. Leipzig: Teubner, 1885-1887. (Raised number after the volume number indicates the part.

Schmidt, Adolf. Handbuch der Griechischen Chronologie. Jena: 1888.

Schmitt, Hatto Herbert. Die Verträge der griechisch-romischen Welt von 338 bis 200 v. Chr. (Die Staatsverträge des Altertums, Vol. 3) München: Beck, 1969.

Schöll, R. "Uber attische Gesetzgebung." Sitz. Ak. Münch. (1886) 83-139.

Schöne, Richard. Griechische Reliefs aus athenischen Samnlungen. Leipzig: Breitkopf und Härtel, 1872.

Schubert, J. G. De proxenia Attica. Dissertation, Leipzig, 1881.

Schweigert, Eugene. "Greek Inscriptions." Hesperia 8(1939) 1-47.

__________. "Greek Inscriptions." Hesperia 9(1940) 309-357.

__________. "Inscriptions from the North Slope of the Acropolis." Hesperia 7(1938) 264-310.

Scranton, Robert Lorentz. Greek Walls. Cambridge, Mass.: Harvard University Press, 1941.

Sealey, R. "On Penalizing Areopagites." AJP 79(1958) 71-73.

Sololowski, Franciszek. Lois Sacrés des citées grecques. (Ecole française d'Athenes: Travaux et Memoires, xi.) Paris: E. de Boccard, 1969.

Speier, Hermine. "Zweifiguren-Gruppen im fünften und vierten Jahrhundert vor Christus." RM 47(1932) 1-94.

Stroud, Ronald. "An Athenian Law on Silver Coinage." Hesperia 43(1974) 157-188.

Sundwall, I. De institutis reipublicae Atheiensium post Aristotelis aetatem commutatis. Helsingfors: ex Officina typographica Societatis litterariae fennicae, 1907.

__________. Zur frage von dem neunzehn jährigen schaltcyklus in Athen. (öfversigtaf Finska vetenskapssocietetens Fördhandlingar. LII) Helsingfors: 1909-1910.

Süsserott, Hans Karl. Griechische Plastik des 4. Jahr. v.C. Frankfurt am Main: V. Klostermann, 1938.

Svoronos, I. N. ΤΟ ΕΝ ΑΘΗΝΑΙΣ ΕΘΝΙΚΟΝ ΜΟΥΣΕΙΟΝ. Athens: Beck & Barth, 1903-1911.

Swoboda, H. "Seuthes III." Paulys Real-Encyclopädie der classischen Altertumswissenschaft. II A. Stuttgart: Metzgersche Verlagsbuchhandlung, 1923.

Sybel, Ludwig von. Katalog der Sculpturen zu Athen. Marburg: Elwert, 1881.

Thumser, Victor. De civium Atheniensium muneribus eorumque immunitate. Vienna: C. Gerold sons, 1880.

Tod, Marcus Niebuhr. Greek Historical Inscriptions. Volume II. Oxford: Clarendon Press, 1948.

Traill, John S. The Political Organization of Attica. Hesperia Supplement XIV 1975.

Travlos, John. Pictoral Dictionary of Ancient Athens. London: Thames and Hudson, 1971.

Tréheux, Jacques. "L'Inventaire des Clērouques." BCH 80 (1956) 462-479.

Trendelenburg, Adolf. "Das Bendis relief in Kopenhagen." Wissenschaftliche Beilage zum Jahresbericht des Askansschen Gymnasiums zu Berlin (1898).

Unger, G. F. "Attische Archonten." Philol. Supplement V 1889. Pages 627-714, especially 667-678.

________. "Der attischen Schaltkreis." Philol. 39(1880) 473-526.

Usener, H. "Chronologische Beiträge." Rh. Mus. 34(1879) 388-441.

Ussing, Johan Ludvig. Inscriptiones Graecae ineditae. Copenhagen: Reitzel, 1847.

Vallindas, P. G., and Pantazopoulos, N. I. "Συμβολὴ εἰς τὰ περὶ μισθώσεως κατὰ τὸ ἀρχαῖον Ἑλληνικὸν δίκαιον." ΠΡΑΓ. ΑΚΑΔ. ΑΘ. 13 fasc. 2(1948) 5-23.

Vanderpool, Eugene. "Some Attic Inscriptions." Hesperia 31(1962) 399-403.

________. "The Apostle Paul in Athens." Archaeology 3(1950) 34-37.

________. "Two Attic Demes of Eitea." ΑΔ 25(1970) 215-216.

Vischer, Wilhelm. Kleine Schriften II. Leipzig: S. Hirzel, 1878.

Walbank, Michael B. "The Decree for Lapyris of Kleonai (IG 2.^{2} 365)," Classical Contributions. Studies presented to M. F. McGregor. Locust Valley, N.Y.: J. J. Augustini, 1981.

Wilamowitz-Moellendorff, Ulrich von. Aristoteles und Athen II. Berlin: Weidmann, 1893.

Wilhelm, Adolf. "Attische Psephismen." Hermes 24(1889) 108-152.

________. Attische Urkunden I. Sitz. Ak. Wien (1911).

__________. Attische Urkunden V. Sitz. Ak. Wien (1942).

__________. Beiträge zur griechischen Inschriftenkunde. (Sonderschriften des Österr. Archäol. Institutes Wien, Volume VII) Vienna: A. Holder, 1909.

__________. "Bemerkungen zu Griechischen Inschriften." Arch. Epig. Mitt. 15(1892) 1-12.

__________. "Ein Beschluss der Athener," Mélanges Nicole. Recueil de mémoires de philologie classique et d'archeologie offerts à Jules Nicole. Geneva: Imp. W. Kündig & fils, 1905.

__________. "Beschluss der Athener aus dem Jahre 338/7 v. C." ÖJ 10 (1907) 32-35.

__________. "Inschriften aus dem Peiraieus." ÖJ 5(1902) 127-139.

__________. "Psephisma für den Komödiendicter Amphis." AM 15 (1890) 219-222.

__________. Urkunden dramatischer Aufführungen in Athen. (Sonderschriften des Österr. Archäol. Institutes Wien, Volume VI) Vienna: A. Holder, 1906.

Woodward, A. M. "Treasure-Records from the Athenian Agora." Hesperia 25 (1956) 79-121.

Wycherly, R. E. The Athenian Agora, Vol. III: Literary and Epigraphical Testimonia. Princeton: American School of Classical Studies in Athens, 1957.

__________. "Two Notes on Athenian Topography." JHS 75(1955) 118-121.

Ziebarth, Erich G. L. Das griechische vereinswesen. Leipzig: S. Hirzel, 1896.

ATHENIAN EPONYMOUS ARCHONS FROM THE LYKOURGAN ERA, 338/7 — 322/1

338/7	Χαιρώνδας
337/6	Φρύνιχος
336/5	Πυθόδηλος
335/4	Εὐαίνετος
334/3	Κτησικλῆς
333/2	Νικοκράτης
332/1	Νικήτης
331/30	Ἀριστοφάνης
330/29	Ἀριστοφῶν
329/8	Κηφισοφῶν
328/7	Εὐθύκριτος
327/6	Ἡγήμων
326/5	Χρέμης
325/4	Ἀντικλῆς
324/3	Ἡγησίας
323/2	Κηφισόδωρος
322/1	Φιλοκλῆς

ANCIENT AUTHORS CITED

AISCHINES
On the False Embassy
II.73: 63
Against Ktesiphon
III.9-12: 101
III.24: 17
III.27,97-98: 1, 12
III.27,236: 18, 24, 25
III.66-67: 308, 309, 310
III.164-167: 223, 226

ANDOKIDES
On the Mysteries
I.80,96: 33

ARISTOTLE
Athenaion Politeia
AP 43: 1, 75, 146, 149, 240
AP 45.4: 78
AP 54.6: 67

ARRIAN
Anabasis
I.18.1: 27
VI.28.4: 27, 29

CURTIUS
XI.45: 223, 226

DEINARCHOS
Against Demosthenes
I.34-36: 223, 227
I.45: 63
I.62-63: 33, 37, 40

DEMOSTHENES
Third Olynthiac
III.10: 33, 39
On the Treaty with Alexander
XVII.11.2: 407, 417
On the Crown
XVIII.20-23: 38, 39
XVIII.132-134: 33, 37
XVIII.248: 18, 20
Against Aristokrates
XXIII.20-23: 38
XXIII.118: 223, 225
Against Timokrates
XXIV.20-23: 18, 24, 25

DIODORUS SICULUS
xvii 3.3: 1, 12
xvii 62-63: 223
xviii 9-11.1: 395
xviii 11.2: 407, 417

HARPOKRATION
"Alkimachos": 27, 29, 30, 47

HYPEREIDES
In Defense of Euxenippos
III.16: 85, 91

ISAIOS
?On the Estate of Pyrrhos
III.80: 137, 139
On the Estate of Kiron
VIII.19,20: 137, 139

LYKOURGOS
Against Leokrates
I.42: 13, 17
I.44: 18, 24
I.52-53,127: 33, 37

LYSIAS
On the Property of Aristophanes
XIX.46: 66

PAUSANIAS
I.25.4: 407, 417
I.26.5: 93
I.31.4: 348, 354

PLATO
Republic 354A: 256

PLUTARCH
Demosthenes 14.4: 33, 37
24.1: 223
27: 407
Phokion 16.1-3: 33

[PLUTARCH]
Lives of the Ten Orators
844a: 134, 136
852b: 108, 120, 125

XENOPHON
Hellenika
VII.1.44-45: 407

LIST OF ENTRIES BY PREVIOUS OR ORIGINAL PUBLICATION

(See Appendix or Abbreviations for abbreviations used in this list.)

PUBLICATION	SEG	Schwenk
AΔ 25(1970) 204-214		#42
AE (1917) 40-48 no. 92		#56
Hesperia		
3(1934) 3-4 no.5	21.288, 23.58 25.69	#59
4(1935) 69-70	21.274	#23, with $II^2$335
5(1936) 413-4 no. 11		#34
7(1938) 94-6 no. 15		#61
7(1938) 292-4 no. 19		#9
8(1939) 173-5 no. 4		see #87
8(1939) 26-7 no. 6		#39
9(1940) 325-7 no. 35		#5
9(1940) 327-8 no. 36		#19
9(1940) 335-43 no. 42	21.298, 24.102	#85
10(1941) 49-50 no. 72	21.290	#71
10(1941) 50-2 no. 13		#72
21(1952) 355/9 no. 5	12.87, 15.95, 17.26, 18.12, 24.96	#6
26(1957) 207-8 no. 54	17.27	#16

PUBLICATION	SEG	Schwenk
28(1959) 239-47	18.13, 21.269, 25.65	#17, with $II^2$334
31(1962) 401-3 no. 3	21.520	#47
<u>IG</u> II^2		
113 (II 279)		#60
237 (II 121)	17.24, 21.266, 24.95	#1
238	17.25	#2
239 (II 123)	21.267	#4
240 (II 124)		#7
241 (II 127)		#8
242 (II 125)		#10
243 (II 126)		#11
244	19.57	#3
276		#12
289		[was with II^2 372, #87]
304 (II Add.159b)	18.11	#14, with $II^2$604
308		#86, with $II^2$371
328 (II 180)	21.268	#15
330 (II 5.128b)		#18
331 (II 342)	21.270	#22
332 (II 132)		[#20]
333 (II 162)	15.96, 16.53, 21.271	#21
334 (II 163)	18.13, 21.269, 25.65	#17, with H28 (59)239-247
335 (II 5.163b)	21.274	#23, with H4 (35)169-170
336 (II 230)	15.97, 21.273, 21.278, 28.50	#31
337 (II 168)	24.98, 25.67	#27
338 (VII 3499)		#28
339a (II 169)	16.54, 21.277, 26.75	#29
340 (II 492)		#30
343 (II 171)	24.103	#84
344 (II 210)	3.84, 12.88, 21.279	#33
345 (II 173)		#36
346 (II 174)		#37
347 (II 5.173b)	14.55	#38

PUBLICATION	SEG	Schwenk
348 (II Add.208b)	21.282, 23.54, 26.76	#44
349 (II Add.175b)		#45
350		[see Intro.]
351 (II 176)	21.283, 24.99	#48, with $II^2$624
352 (II 177)		#49
353 (II 178)		#51
354 (II 5.178b)	18.14, 21.285, 23.56	#54
355		#55
356	21.286, 23.57	#58
357	21.287	#57
358 (II 175)	21.326	[#62]
359		#63
360 (II 5.179b)	13.40, 26.79	#68
361 (II 179)	14.57, 18.15	#69
362 (II 5.180c)	21.291	#73
363 (II 5,492e,f)	12.89, 21.281, 23.53	#67
365 (II 181)	21.294, 30.66	#79
366		#80
367 (II 182)	21.295, 26.81	#81
368 (II 183)	3.82, 12.88, 21.296	#82
371 (II 185)	3.82	#86, with $II^2$308
372 (II 5.185b)	21.300, 23.60	#87
373 (II 186)	21.301, 24.105	#88
375 (II 188)	21.302	#89
376		#90
377 (II 189)		#91
405 (II 5.193b)	21.275	#24
414a (II Add.180b)	21.276	#25
414b,c (II 290)	21.298, 24.102	#85, with H9 (40)335-343
420 (II 5.493b)	21.322, 22.93	#35
445 (II 219)		#18, with $II^2$330
448 (II 5.321b)	21.297, 21.317, 22.95, 23.59, 23.61, 26.82	#83
452 (II 236)	14.56, 21.284, 23.55, 24.100, 25.68	#53
454 (II 244)	21.293	#75

PUBLICATION	SEG	Schwenk
547 (II 5.245d)	21.292	#74
604		#14, with II^{2}304
624		#48, with II^{2}351
800	21.289	#64
1157 (II 5.563c)		#65
1176 (II 573)	19.117, 21.521	#76
1181		#46
1184		#26
1198 (II 579)		#66
1203 (II 580)		#70
1255		#13
1256 (II.5 Add.573b)		#52
1257 (II 607)		#77
1258 (II 609)		#78
IG VII		
4252		#40
4253		#41
4254		#50
PPA 13(1948) 5-23	24.203	#32
REG 91(1978) 289-306		#43
Tod *GHI* II		
178		#1
180		#4
181		#7
189		#27
193		#45
198		#48
199		#58

INDEX

I. *INSCRIPTIONS CITED*

(Bold numbers indicate entries in this Corpus; see Appendix or Abbreviations for abbreviations used.)

AE (1917)40-48 no. 92(#56): 80, 204, 246, 248, 263, 264, 266, 274, **280-284**, 304, 348.
AE (1937) 808-823: 257.
AE (1965) 134-136: 132.

AD 25(1970) 204-214(#42): 34, 137, 140, **205-212**, 229, 366.

AM 25(1900) 72: 254.
AM 49(1924) 1-13: 231.
AM 97(1982) 171-184: 248.

EM 3912: 396.
EM 13067: 118, 127, 128.

HESPERIA 3(1934) 3-4 no. 5 (#59): 154, 286, 287, **294-298**.
HESPERIA 4(1935) 169-170 no. 32(#23): 32, 46, **129-132**, 134, 135, 154, 163, 192, 250. See also II^{2}335, H 9(40) 339-340.
HESPERIA 5(1936) 413-414 no. 11(#34): **181-183**, 188.
HESPERIA 7(1938) 94-96 no. 15(#61): **300-305**, 319, 379.
292-294 no. 19(#9): 48, **49-51**, 53, 54, 61, 148, 276, 303.
HESPERIA 8(1939) 26-27 no. 6(#39): 183, 188, 189, 193, **195-198**.
27-30 no. 7. See H 9(40) 335-343 no. 42.
HESPERIA 9(1940) 66 no. 9: 26. See also II^{2}463.
HESPERIA 9(1940) 325-327 no. 35(#5): 28, 29, **30-33**, 46, 47, 54, 131, 187, 250, 251.
327-328 no. 36(#19): **105-106**, 118.
335-343 no. 42(#85): 134, 387, 414, **426-432**. See also II^{2}414c,d.
339-340 (#23): 32, 46, **129-132**, 134, 135, 154, 163, 192, 250. See also II^{2}335, H4 (35) 169-170 no. 32.
HESPERIA 10(1941) 42-49 no. 11: 327, 356.
49-50 no. 12(#71): **355-356**, 359.
50-52 no. 13(#72): **356-358**, 359.
288 no. 78: 211.
HESPERIA 21(1952) 355-359 no. 5(#6): 25, **33-41**, 51, 91, 102, 122, 207, 247, 396.
HESPERIA 26(1957) 207-208 no. 54(#16): **79-80**, 128, 140, 348, 375.
HESPERIA 28(1959) 169-171 no. 1(#14): **68-71**.
239-247 (#17): **81-94**, 109, 121, 123, 151, 218, 248, 327. See also II^{2}334.
HESPERIA 29(1960) 1 no. 1 (#76): 80, 140, **366-370**. See also II^{2}1176, H 32(63) 12 no. 10.
39-40 no. 49: 132.
HESPERIA 30(1961) 30-57:

241, 245.
HESPERIA 31(1962) 401-403 no. 3(#47): 137, 140, **228-231**, 352.
HESPERIA 32(1963) 12 no. 10 (#76): 80, 140, **366-370**. See also II^{2}1176, H 29(60) 1 no. 1.
HESPERIA 35(1966) 281-282 no. 8: 229, 231.
HESPERIA 43(1974) 151-188: 33, 38, 39.
321-324 no. 3: 79.

IG I^2
242: 211
243: 211
324: 211

IG II^2
24: 168
25: 168
33: 168
43: 17
63: 389
113(#60): 45, **298-300**.
123: 17
210: 177
222: 39, 102, 172.
223: 204
224: 328
228: 328
236: 279, 294.
237(#1): **1-12**, 17, 143, 170, 193, 426.
238(#2): 6, **13-17**, 79, 333.
239(#4): **27-30**, 32, 46, 55, 131, 187, 250, 251.
240(#7): 28, 29, **41-47**, 48, 54, 131, 190, 192, 235, 250.
241(#8): 29, 46, **47-49**, 54, 131, 235, 250.
242(#10): 48, **51-55**, 56, 61.
243(#11): 48, 51, 54, **55-56**, 61, 78.
244(#3): **18-26**, 39, 92, 102, 109, 122, 123, 134, 247.
276(#12): 48, 51, 53, 54, 56,

IG II^2 (continued)
57-63, 113, 300.
285: 134. See also II^{2}414d.
289: 436, 440.
304(#14): **68-71**. See also II^{2}604, H28(59)169-71no.1.
308(#86): **433-436**, 448. See also II^{2}371.
328(#15): 10, **72-79**, 80, 92, 101, 125, 149, 154, 183, 190, 237, 244, 251, 258, 266, 288, 297, 311, 398, 405.
329: 279, 294.
330(#18): 51, 76, **95-105**, 118, 127, 148, 192, 247, 348, 375. See also II^{2}445.
331(#22): 80, 98, 118, **126-128**, 222.
332[#20]: **106-108**, 118.
333(#21): 26, 57, 78, 90, 92, 107, **108-126**, 131, 145, 218, 259.
334(#17): **81-94**, 109, 121, 123, 151, 218, 248, 327. See also H 28(59) 239-247.
335(#23): 32, 46, **129-132**, 134, 135, 154, 163, 192, 250. See also H4(35) 169-170 no. 32, H9(40) 339-340.
336(#31): 11, 39, 102, 131, **159-172**, 185, 264, 363.
337(#27): 67, 78, **141-146**, 153, 192, 348.
338(#28): **146-151**, 153, 155, 158, 183, 248, 339, 346, 348, 397.
339a(#29): 74, 75, 149, **151-157**, 312, 346.
339b: 152, 153, 157.
340(#30): **157-158**.
342: 425
343(#84): **418-426**.
344(#33): **177-181**, 403, 405.
345(#36): 78, 183, **187-190**, 192, 195, 222, 403.
346(#37): 183, 188, 189, **190-192**, 353, 403.
347(#38): 183, 188, 189, **192-195**, 198.

IG II^2 (continued)
348(#44): **220-223.**
349(#45): **223-227,** 238, 258, 327.
350: 180
351(#48): 78, 187, **232-238,** 239, 251. See also II^{2}624.
352(#49): 236, **238-240.**
353(#51): 131, 134, 187, **248-252,** 311, 330.
354(#54): 263, 265, **266-278,** 287, 348.
355(#55): **278-279.**
356(#58): 287, 288, **289-294,** 297, 300.
357(#57): 265, **285-289,** 292, 297, 299, 300, 339, 340.
358[#62]:**305-307,** 314.
359(#63): 187, 251, 252, 277, **308-313,** 327, 329, 330, 439, 445.
360(#68): 16, 98, 331, 332, **334-344,** 345-348 passim, 360.
361(#69): 80, 339, 340, **344-348,** 360, 404.
362(#73): 355, 356, **358-360.**
363(#67): 180, 187, 222, 236, 251, 252, 310, 313, **322-333,** 344.
365(#79): 245, **381-392,** 397, 405, 414.
366(#80): 80, 376, **392-394.**
367(#81): 193, **394-401,** 405, 407, 414.
368(#82): 177-181 passim, 398, **401-407,** 414, 416.
369: See H9(40) 335-343 no. 42.
370: 279
371(#86): **433-436,** 448. See also II^{2}308.
372(#87): 131, 250, **436-440,** 445, 448, 450, 451.
373(#88): 216, 437, **440-448,** 450, 451.
374: 445, 446.
375(#89): 435, **449-451.**
376(#90): **451-452.**
377(#91): **452-454.**
405(#24): 129-131 passim, **132-134,** 170, 250.
410: 222, 276.
414a(#25): 78, 79, 129-131 passim, **134-136,** 163, 426, 430.
414c,d(#85): 134, 387, 414, **426-432.** See also H9(40) 335-343 no. 42.
414d: 134. See also II^{2}285.
417: 62.
420(#35): 28, **183-187,** 236, 251, 330, 445.
445(#18): 51, 76, **95-105,** 118, 127, 148, 192, 247, 348, 375. See also II^{2}330.
448(#83): 387, 398, 403-406 passim, **407-418,** 421, 424, 425, 431, 438.
452(#53): 79, **260-266,** 274, 287, 363, 398.
454(#75): 356, 359, 362, **363-365.**
463: 26. See also H9(40) 66 no. 9.
467: 209
478: 284
483: 70
493: 209
522: 70
547(#74): 356, **360-363,** 365.
587: 10
604(#14): **68-71.** See also II^2 304, H28(59)169-171 no. 1.
624(#48): 78, 187, **232-238,** 239, 251. See also II^{2}351.
641: 70
657: 223
665: 304
800(#64): **313-316.**
839: 175
840: 175
865: 348, 354.
911: 185
1151: 319
1156: 132
1157(#65): 304, **316-319,** 322, 352.
1176 (#76): 80, 140, **366-370.**

IG II^2 (continued)
See also H 29(60)1 no. 1, H 32(63) 12 no. 10.
1180: 228
1181(#46): 80, 140, **227-228**.
1184(#26): 80, **136-140**, 209, 216, 218, 228, 229, 304, 353, 354, 379.
1189: 132
1193: 209
1196: 322
1198(#66): 140, **319-322**, 352, 353.
1203(#70): 140, 230, **348-354**.
1232: 303
1255(#13): **63-67**, 104, 175, 256, 258.
1256(#52): 67, **252-259**.
1257(#77): 80, 103, **370-376**.
1258(#78): **376-380**.
1283: 255, 257.
1324: 66, 254, 258.
1361: 258
1425: 103
1441: 17
1493,1494,1495: 131, 150.
1496: 122, 150, 258.
1596: 124
1620: 231
1622: 62
1623: 79, 134, 136.
1629: 245
1631: 348
1672: 79
1700: 98
1749: 103
1750: 98, 132.
1924+2409: 246
2498: 11
2499: 176
2631: 377
2632: 377
2791: 396
2821: 103
2970: 132
5804: 70
6007: 211
7020: 245

IG II^2 (continued)
7062: 63
7879: 61

IG VII
4252(#40): 183, **198-201**, 203, 204, 222, 241, 244, 248, 249.
4253(#41): 183, 200, **201-205**, 241, 244, 246, 248.
4254(#50): 102, 204, **241-248**, 283, 304, 387.

IG IX^{2}I, fasc. 2 xviii 79-80: 440

PAA 13 fasc. 2 (1948) 5-23 (#32): **173-176**, 218.

REG 91(1978) 289-306(#43): 140, **212-219**, 322.

SEG III
82: 401, 433 (#82, #86)
84: 177 (#33)
759: 254, 258.

SEG X
64b: 257

SEG XII
87: 33 (#6)
88: 177, 401 (#33, #82)
89: 322 (#67)

SEG XIII
40: 334 (#68)

SEG XIV
55:193 (#38)
56: 260 (#53)
57: 344 (#69)

SEG XV
95: 33 (#6)
96: 108 (#21)
97: 159 (#31)

SEG XVI
53: 108 (#21)
54: 151 (#29)

SEG XVII
24: 1 (#1)
25: 13 (#2)
26: 33 (#6)
27: 80 (#16)

SEG XVIII
11: 68 (#14)
12: 33 (#6)
13: 81 (#17)
14: 267 (#54)
15: 344 (#69)

SEG XIX
57: 18 (#3)
117: 366 (#76)

SEG XXI
266: 1 (#1)
267: 27 (#4)
268: 72 (#15)
269: 81 (#17)
270: 126 (#22)
271: 108 (#21)
272: 127, 128.
273: 159 (#31)
274: 129 (#23)
275: 132 (#24)
276: 135 (#25)
277: 151 (#29)
278: 159 (#31)
279: 177 (#33)
280: 401 (#82)
281: 323 (#67)
282: 220 (#44)
283: 232 (#48)
284: 260 (#53)
285: 267 (#54)
286: 289 (#58)
287: 285 (#57)
288: 295 (#59)
289: 313 (#64)
290: 355 (#71)
291: 358 (#73)

SEG XXI (continued)
292: 360 (#74)
293: 363 (#75)
294: 381 (#79)
295: 395 (#81)
296: 401 (#82)
297: 407 (#83)
298: 426 (#85)
300: 436 (#87)
301: 440 (#88)
302: 449 (#89)
317: 407 (#83)
322: 183 (#35)
326: 305 [#62]
520: 229 (#47)
521: 366 (#76)

SEG XXII
93: 183 (#35)
95: 407 (#83)

SEG XXIII
53: 323 (#67)
54: 220 (#44)
55: 260 (#53)
56: 267 (#54)
57: 289 (#58)
58: 295 (#59)
59: 407 (#83)
60: 436 (#87)
61: 407 (#83)

SEG XXIV
95: 1 (#1)
96: 33 (#6)
98: 141 (#27)
99: 232 (#48)
100: 260 (#53)
101: 334 (#68)
102: 426 (#85)
103: 418 (#84)
105: 440 (#88)
203: 173 (#32)

SEG XXV
65: 81 (#17)
66: 323 (#67)
67: 141 (#27)

SEG XXV (continued)
68: 260 (#53)
69: 295 (#59)

SEG XXVI
75: 151 (#29)
76: 220 (#44)
79: 334 (#68)
81: 395 (#81)
82: 407 (#83)

SEG XXVIII
50: 159 (#31)
66: 381 (#79)

Syll.[3] 296: 246

II. *PROPER NAMES*

A. Athenians

ΑΓΑΣΙΑΣ 96, 99, 101
ΑΓΩΝΟΧΑΡΗΣ 243, 245
ΑΙΩΝ 306
ΑΜΕΙΝΙΑΣ 28, 30, 32, 35, 36, 44, 48, 50, 53, 56, 281, 377, 378
ΑΝΑΞΙΚΡΑΤΗΣ 306
ΑΝΔΡΟΚΛΗΣ 266, 272, 276-278 passim
ΑΝΤΙΓΕΝΗΣ 221
ΑΝΤΙΔΟΤΟΣ 142, 281, 450
ΑΝΤΙΔΩΡΟΣ 233, 235, 239
ΑΝΤΙΚΛΗΣ 334, 335, 339, 340, 345, 350, 352, 353
ΑΝΤΙΝΟΥΣ 233, 239
ΑΝΤΙΣΘΕΝΗΣ 65, 66
ΑΝΤΙΦΑΝΗΣ 44, 48, 65, 66, 96, 215, 217, 233, 235
ΑΝΤΙΦΗΜΟΣ 7, 13
ΑΝΤΙΦΩΝ 10, 335, 345, 350, 353
ΑΠΟΛΛΟΔΩΡΟΣ 142
ΑΡΕΘΟΥΣΙΟΣ 368, 369
ΑΡΙΣΤΑΡΧΟΣ 162
ΑΡΙΣΤΕΙΔΗΣ 281
ΑΡΙΣΤΙΩΝ 281, 283
ΑΡΙΣΤΟΚΡΑΤΗΣ 107, 368
ΑΡΙΣΤΟΚΡΙΤΟΣ 301, 302
ΑΡΙΣΤΟΛΕΩΣ 368
ΑΡΙΣΤΟΜΑΧΟΣ 350, 353
ΑΡΙΣΤΟΜΕΝΗΣ 65, 66
ΑΡΙΣΤΟΝΙΚΟΣ 82, 91
ΑΡΙΣΤΟΝΟΥΣ 178, 182, 184, 189, 191, 194, 197, 199, 210, 402
ΑΡΙΣΤΟΞΕΝΟΣ 194, 195
ΑΡΙΣΤΟΤΕΛΗΣ 82, 91, 242, 244
ΑΡΙΣΤΟΤΙΜΟΣ 35, 36
ΑΡΙΣΤΟΦΑΝΗΣ 220-222 passim, 224, 225, 228, 229, 235, 305, 328, 368, 369
ΑΡΙΣΤΟΦΩΝ 229, 232, 233, 239, 240, 331, 335, 337, 341
ΑΡΧΕΛΑΣ 147, 152, 158, 162, 165
ΑΡΧΕΛΕΩΣ 222, 328
ΑΡΧΕΣΤΡΑΤΟΣ 345
ΑΡΧΙΑΣ 382, 387, 402, 403, 412, 414, 416, 422, 428, 430
ΑΡΧΙΝΟΣ 361
ΑΣΚΛΗΠΙΟΔΩΡΟΣ 349, 397, 400
ΑΥΤΙΑΣ 286, 290, 295
ΑΥΤΟΚΛΕΙΔΗΣ 273
ΑΥΤΟΚΛΗΣ 21, 286, 290, 295

ΒΛΕΠΥΡΟΣ 230, 231
ΒΟΥΛΙΣ 263, 264, 281

ΔΑΙΠΠΟΣ 249
ΔΕΞΙΟΣ 253, 255, 256
ΔΗΜΑΔΗΣ 29, 30, 32, 44, 46-48 passim, 54, 91, 130-134 passim, 189-192 passim, 204, 242, 244-246, 248-250, 281, 436, 437, 439
ΔΗΜΕΑΣ 30, 44, 48, 130, 133, 191, 192, 242, 244, 249, 250, 437
ΔΗΜΗΤΡΙΟΣ 202, 203, 281
ΔΗΜΟΚΛΗΣ 210, 242, 244, 301, 304, 335, 340
ΔΗΜΟΚΡΑΤΗΣ 136, 301, 304, 320, 321
ΔΗΜΟΣΘΕΝΗΣ 25, 37, 41, 91, 101, 131, 226, 227, 242, 244, 309, 311, 335, 340
ΔΗΜΟΧΑΡΗΣ 242, 244
ΔΙΟΓΝΗΤΟΣ 359

ΔΙΟΔΩΡΟΣ 21, 377, 378
ΔΙΟΜΝΗΣΤΟΣ 185
ΔΙΟΝΥΣΙΟΣ 361
ΔΙΟΝΥΣΟΔΩΡΟΣ 350, 353
ΔΙΟΝΥΣΟΦΑΝΗΣ 350, 353
ΔΙΟΤΙΜΟΣ 21, 79, 134-136 passim
ΔΙΟΦΑΝΤΟΣ 53, 54, 56, 442, 446
ΔΙΥΛΛΟΣ 199-201 passim, 203, 242, 244
ΔΡΑΚΟΝΤΙΔΗΣ 282
ΔΩΡΟΘΕΟΣ 107, 224, 321, 322

ΕΙΡΗΝΙΠΠΟΣ 372, 373, 375
ΕΝΠΕΔΟΣ 281
ΕΠΑΜΕΙΝΩΝ 377, 378, 412, 416, 421, 422, 425
ΕΠΙΓΕΝΗΣ 213
ΕΠΙΓΗΘΗΣ 281
ΕΠΙΤΕΛΗΣ 242-244 passim, 382, 387, 388
ΕΠΙΧΑΡΗΣ 199, 202, 243, 245
ΕΥΑΙΝΕΤΟΣ 84, 95, 96, 105, 107, 115, 118, 122, 127, 128, 328
ΕΥΑΛΚΟΣ 442, 446
ΕΥΑΡΧΙΔΗΣ 336, 342
ΕΥΒΟΙΟΣ 196, 197
ΕΥΔΥΔΗΜΟΣ 213, 217
ΕΥΕΤΙΩΝ 273, 281
ΕΥΘΥΓΕΝΗΣ 434, 437, 441, 450, 452
ΕΥΘΥΔΗΜΟΣ 373
ΕΥΘΥΚΡΑΤΗΣ 53, 54, 56, 60, 184, 281-283 passim
ΕΥΘΥΚΡΙΤΟΣ 260, 263, 264, 272, 278, 281, 283, 337, 342, 370, 371, 373, 375, 376
ΕΥΚΑΔΜΟΣ 282
ΕΥΚΛΗΣ 387, 403, 414, 430
ΕΥΚΟΜΟΣ 437
ΕΥΚΡΑΤΗΣ 35, 35, 40, 91, 281
ΕΥΚΤΗΜΩΝ 202, 203
ΕΥΞΙΔΗΜΟΣ 315
ΕΥΡΥΚΡΑΤΗΣ 185
ΕΥΦΑΝΗΣ 327, 356, 357, 359, 361, 363
ΕΥΦΙΛΗΤΟΣ 320, 321, 368, 412, 413, 415-417 passim
ΕΥΦΥΗΣ 253, 255, 256
ΕΦΙΠΠΟΣ 249
ΕΧΦΑΝΤΟΣ 242, 244, 249

ΗΓΗΜΩΝ 285-287 passim, 290, 295, 299, 302, 305
ΗΓΗΣΙΑΣ 71, 320, 321, 327, 355-357 passim, 359, 361, 363, 365, 367, 369, 371, 376, 378, 379, 393, 394
ΗΓΗΣΙΠΠΟΣ 7
ΗΦΑΙΣΤΟΔΗΜΟΣ 434, 437, 441, 450, 452

ΘΑΛΛΟΣ 65, 66
ΘΑΡΡΙΑΔΗΣ 228
ΘΑΡΡΙΑΣ 228
ΘΕΑΓΓΕΛΟΣ 335, 336, 341
ΘΕΑΙΟΣ 368
ΘΕΑΝΓΕΛΟΣ 335, 336, 341
ΘΕΙΟΦΑΝΗΣ 70
ΘΕΟΔΩΡΙΔΗΣ 350
ΘΕΟΔΩΡΟΣ 96, 281
ΘΕΟΚΛΗΣ 314
ΘΕΟΚΡΙΝΗΣ 281
ΘΕΟΜΝΗΣΤΟΣ 184
ΘΕΟΠΟΜΠΟΣ 314
ΘΕΟΦΑΝΗΣ 69, 70
ΘΕΟΦΑΝΤΟΣ 403
ΘΕΟΦΙΛΟΣ 142
ΘΕΟΦΡΑΣΤΟΣ 263, 264
ΘΕΟΦΩΝ 242, 244
ΘΕΟΧΑΡΗΣ 62
ΘΗΒΑΓΕΝΗΣ 336, 341, 344
ΘΗΡΙΚΛΗΣ 365
ΘΗΡΙΠΠΙΔΗΣ 365
ΘΟΥΔΗΜΟΣ 107
ΘΡΑΣΥΒΟΥΛΟΣ 174-176 passim
ΘΡΑΣΥΛΕΩΝ 242, 244
ΘΥΜΟΧΑΡΗΣ 162, 243, 245, 246

ΙΠΠΟΚΛΗΣ 206, 207, 209-211 passim
ΙΠΠΟΧΑΡΗΣ 96, 97, 101

ΚΑΛΙΤΕΛΗΣ 55, 56, 281, 283
ΚΑΛΛΙΑΔΗΣ 368, 369
ΚΑΛΛΙΒΙΟΣ 60-62 passim
ΚΑΛΛΙΚΡΑΤΗΣ 283

ΚΑΛΛΙΣΘΕΝΗΣ 281-283 passim
ΚΑΡΚΙΝΟΣ 363
ΚΕΦΑΛΙΩΝ 19
ΚΗΦΙΣΟΔΟΤΟΣ 194, 336, 342, 403
ΚΗΦΟΣΟΔΩΡΟΣ 381, 382, 388, 393, 394, 397, 402, 405, 412, 416, 422, 428, 431
ΚΗΦΙΣΟΚΛΗΣ 314
ΚΗΦΙΣΟΦΩΝ 19, 25, 60-63 passim, 241-246 passim, 249, 255, 281
ΚΛΕΙΝΙΑΣ 272, 276
ΚΟΡΟΙΒΟΣ 335, 345
ΚΟΤΥΟΣ 224, 225
ΚΡΑΤΙΣΤΟΛΕΩΣ 196
ΚΤΗΣΙΚΛΗΣ 129-131 passim, 133, 135, 137, 138, 150, 161, 163, 164, 166

ΛΥΚΙΣΚΟΣ 350, 353
ΛΥΚΟΥΡΓΟΣ 67, 72, 73, 77-79, 91, 108, 115, 120-122, 125, 126, 131, 134-136 passim, 141, 143-145, 187, 189, 190, 204, 205, 218, 219, 232, 233, 237, 238, 242, 244, 246, 252, 259, 263, 265, 266, 281, 283, 322, 333
ΛΥΚΟΦΡΩΝ 73, 77, 115, 122, 135, 143, 189, 233, 242, 244, 263, 350, 353
ΛΥΣΑΝΙΑΣ 147
ΛΥΣΙΑΣ 224, 306, 350, 353
ΛΥΣΙΘΕΟΣ 281, 284
ΛΥΣΙΚΛΗΣ 370, 373, 375, 376
ΛΥΣΙΜΕΝΗΣ 248
ΛΥΣΙΠΠΟΣ 350, 353
ΛΥΣΙΣΤΡΑΤΟΣ 320, 321
ΛΥΣΙΦΩΝ 243, 245

ΜΑΝΤΙΚΛΗΣ 230, 231
ΜΕΛΗΣΙΑΣ 368, 369
ΜΕΝΕΣΤΡΑΤΟΣ 35, 36
ΜΝΗΣΙΦΙΛΟΣ 130, 133, 135, 161, 164, 165
ΜΝΗΣΩΝ 130, 133, 135, 161
ΜΟΙΡΟΚΛΗΣ 213, 217
ΜΟΛΩΝ 299

ΝΑΥΣΙΝΙΚΟΣ 65, 66
ΝΑΥΣΙΦΙΛΟΣ 65, 66
ΝΙΚΑΝΔΡΟΣ 281
ΝΙΚΗΡΑΤΟΣ 243, 245, 246
ΝΙΚΗΤΗΣ 84, 177, 178, 180, 182, 184, 186, 188, 189, 191, 192, 194, 197, 199, 201, 210, 214-218 passim, 402
ΝΙΚΙΑΣ 243, 245
ΝΙΚΟΚΛΗΣ 105, 106
ΝΙΚΟΚΡΑΤΗΣ 29, 141-144 passim, 147, 149, 152, 153, 158, 165-167 passim, 174, 176, 306, 396
ΝΙΚΟΣΤΡΑΤΟΣ 189, 191, 194, 197, 221, 222, 328
ΝΟΘΙΠΠΟΣ 224, 306

ΟΙΝΟΦΩΝ 368, 369
ΟΛΥΜΠΙΟΔΟΡΟΣ 65
ΟΥΛΙΑΣ 281

ΠΑΜΦΙΛΟΣ 263, 295
ΠΑΝΤΑΛΕΩΝ 272
ΠΑΝΦΙΛΟΣ 413, 417
ΠΑΥΣΑΝΙΑΣ 96-98 passim, 100-102, 104, 337, 342
ΠΟΛΥΕΥΚΤΟΣ 178, 180, 281, 326, 332, 402, 405
ΠΟΛΥΞΕΝΟΣ 376, 378, 379
ΠΡΟΚΛΕΙΔΗΣ 272
ΠΡΟΞΕΝΟΣ 96, 105, 107, 127, 128, 328
ΠΡΩΤΟΚΛΗΣ 281
ΠΥΘΕΑΣ 146-150
ΠΥΘΟΔΗΛΟΣ 72, 73, 79, 80, 84, 96, 97, 263, 272, 281
ΠΥΘΟΔΩΡΟΣ 382, 402, 412, 416, 422, 428
ΠΥΛΑΓΟΡΑΣ 96, 105, 127, 128, 328

ΡΗΒΟΥΛΑΣ 223-226

ΣΜΙΚΥΘΙΩΝ 350, 353
ΣΜΙΚΥΘΟΣ 368
ΣΩΙΝΑΥΤΗΣ 387
ΣΩΙΝΟΜΟΣ 243, 245, 382, 388
ΣΩΚΡΑΤΗΣ 281
ΣΩΣΙΔΗΜΟΣ 147, 148
ΣΩΣΤΡΑΤΙΔΗΣ 242, 244, 249

ΣΩΣΤΡΑΤΟΣ 178, 180, 326, 402, 405
ΣΩΤΙΑΔΗΣ 281
ΣΩΦΙΛΟΣ 242, 244, 245

ΤΗΛΕΜΑΧΟΣ 335, 336, 341-343 passim
ΤΗΛΕΣΚΟΠΟΣ 300-304
ΤΙΜΟΚΛΗΣ 209-211 passim
ΤΙΜΟΚΡΑΤΗΣ 209-211 passim
ΤΙΜΟΣΤΡΑΤΟΣ 382, 388
ΤΙΜΩΝΙΔΗΣ 21

ΦΑΙΔΡΟΣ 243, 245
ΦΑΛΑΝΘΙΔΗΣ 213, 214, 216
ΦΑΛΑΝΘΟΣ 281, 350
ΦΑΝΙΑΣ 286
ΦΑΝΟΔΗΜΟΣ 199-201 passim, 202-205, 242, 244, 246, 281
ΦΑΝΟΜΑΧΟΣ 306
ΦΑΝΟΣΤΡΑΤΟΣ 143
ΦΕΙΔΙΠΠΟΣ 281
ΦΙΛΑΝΘΗΣ 352
ΦΙΛΕΑΣ 221
ΦΙΛΙΝΟΣ 282
ΦΙΛΙΠΠΟΣ 7, 13, 15
ΦΙΛΟΔΗΜΟΣ 21
ΦΙΛΟΚΗΔΗΣ 107
ΦΙΛΟΚΛΗΣ 433-435 passim, 437, 441, 445, 450, 452-454 passim
ΦΙΛΟΚΡΑΤΗΣ 255, 256, 281
ΦΙΛΟΚΤΗΜΩΝ 320, 321
ΦΙΛΟΚΩΜΟΣ 212-214 passim, 216, 217
ΦΙΛΟΣΤΡΑΤΟΣ 281-283 passim
ΦΙΛΥΛΛΟΣ 335, 340
ΦΡΑΣΙΚΛΕΙΔΗΣ 53, 54, 56, 442, 446
ΦΡΥΝΙΧΟΣ 25-28 passim, 30, 32, 35, 36, 44, 48, 50, 53-56 passim, 60, 65, 84
ΦΡΥΝΩΝ 327, 356, 357, 359, 361, 363
ΦΥΛΕΙΔΗΣ 230, 231
ΦΥΛΕΥΣ 95-104 passim, 337, 342

ΧΑΙΡΕΔΗΜΟΣ 282
ΧΑΙΡΕΣΤΡΑΤΟΣ 28, 30, 32, 35, 36, 44, 48-50 passim, 53, 54, 56, 60, 281-283 passim
ΧΑΙΡΕΦΑΝΗΣ 350, 353
ΧΑΙΡΙΑΣ 147, 152, 158
ΧΑΙΡΙΓΕΝΗΣ 96, 99
ΧΑΙΡΙΩΝΙΔΗΣ 147
ΧΑΙΡΩΝΔΑΣ 7, 13, 25, 26
ΧΑΡΗΣ 60-63 passim
ΧΑΡΙΑΔΗΣ 350, 353
ΧΑΡΙΔΗΜΟΣ 37, 97, 100-102, 364
ΧΑΡΟΠΙΔΗΣ 282, 283
ΧΑΡΟΨ 163
ΧΡΕΜΗΣ 308, 309, 311, 315, 316, 318, 320, 321, 326, 327, 329, 330, 331, 353

II.A (Athenian names which do not appear in Greek)

AISCHINES 37, 101, 226, 227, 238, 310
ARISTOTLE 150
CHARINOS 365
DEINARCHOS 238
DEMETRIOS (Phaleron) 266, 316
EUBOULOS 25
HYPEREIDES 37, 91
KAIRIMOS 365
KTESIPHON 101
LYKOURGOS ("Ibis") 144, 145
PERIKLES 126
PHOKION 37
SAMAKION 211
STROIBOS 345
SOKRATES 256

II.B Non-Athenians

ΑΔΕΑ 412, 415
ΑΛΚΙΜΑΧΟΣ 27-29 passim, 46
ΑΜΥΝΤΩΡ 132-134 passim
ΑΜΦΙΣ (ΑΝΦΙΣ) 192-195 passim
ΑΝΤΙΠΑΤΡΟΣ 28, 29, 46
ΑΠΠΟΛΛΩΝΙΔΗΣ 418, 422, 424-426 passim
ΑΡΙΣΤΕΙΔΗΣ 191, 192
ΑΡΤΑΒΑΖΟΣ 290, 293
ΑΡΧΙΠΠΟΣ 159, 161, 162, 166-169 passim
ΑΣΚΛΗΠΙΟΔΩΡΟΣ 54, 57, 60-62 passim, 397, 399, 400

ΔΗΜΗΤΡΙΟΣ 133, 134, 422, 424, 428, 431
ΔΙΟΝΥΣΙΟΣ 322, 326, 328, 331-333 passim, 341-344 passim
ΔΡΑΚΟΝΤΙΔΗΣ 13, 14, 16, 17

ΕΥΔΗΜΟΣ 78, 232-234 passim, 237, 238
ΕΥΗΝΩΡ 440-442 passim, 445-448 passim
ΕΥΗΠΙΟΣ 442, 445
ΕΥΦΡΙΛΛΟΣ 162, 168
ΕΥΦΡΩΝ 406-408 passim, 412, 415-417 passim
ΕΧΕΝΒΡΟΤΟΣ 383, 389

ΗΓΗΣΙΑΣ 13, 14, 16, 17
ΗΡΑΚΛΕΙΔΗΣ 98, 331, 334-337, 340, 341, 344

ΘΕΟΦΑΝΤΟΣ 180, 181, 401-403, 405-407 passim
ΘΥΜΩΝΔΑΣ 291, 293

ΚΑΛΛΙΑΣ 383, 389
ΚΑΡΦΙΝΑΣ 7-9 passim, 11, 12
ΚΟΙΡΟΣ 250
ΚΟΤΥΟΣ 224, 225
ΚΥΔΡΙΩΝ 306, 307

ΛΑΠΥΡΙΣ 381-383 passim, 388-390, 392
ΛΕΥΚΩΝ 429
ΛΥΚΟΣ 153

ΜΕΜΝΩΝ 289, 290, 293, 294
ΜΕΝΤΩΡ 291, 293

ΟΝΟΜΑΡΧΟΣ 196, 197

ΠΑΝΧΑΡΗΣ 168
ΠΟΛΥΣΘΕΝΗΣ 288

ΡΗΒΟΥΛΑΣ 223-226 passim, 258

ΣΑΤΥΡΟΣ 429
ΣΕΥΘΗΣ 224-226 passim

ΤΙΜΑΝΔΡΟΣ 397

ΦΑΝΟΣΤΡΑΤΟΣ 299, 300
ΦΑΡΝΑΒΑΖΟΣ 290, 293
ΦΙΛΙΠΠΟΣ 12, 41, 44, 46, 47, 49, 90, 136, 151, 169, 205, 223, 238, 279, 294
ΦΙΛΟΥΡΓΟΣ 234
ΦΙΛΩΝ 61
ΦΟΡΜΙΩΝ 7-9 passim, 11, 12
ΧΑΡΙΚΛΕΙΔΗΣ 335, 336, 337
ΧΟΙΡΟΣ 249, 250

II.B (Non-Athenian names which do not appear in Greek)

AGATHOKLES 69
AGIS III 225, 226
ALEXANDER 225, 279, 293, 294, 391, 401, 405
ANTIPATER 225, 399
HARPALOS 63
HIPPARCHOS 168
LYSIMACHOS 223
MEMNON (of Thrace) 225, 226
NEOPTOLEMOS 223
PHILIPPIDES 223
SITALKES 258

II.C Incomplete Names

By first letter

Α------ 263
ΑΙ------ 152
ΑΝ------ 230
ΑΡ...7... 235
ΑΡΙ...6.. 393
[Α]ΣΤΥ--- 312
ΑΣΤΥΜ--- 428
Γ------ 263
ΔΗΜ------ 314
ΔΗΜΟΚΡ...Σ 130, 133, 135
Ε------ 162
ΕΥ--c.6-- 281
ΕΥΞΕΝ--- 162
ΕΥΠΟΡ--- 73, 74
Θ------ 263
ΚΑΛΛΙΚ--- 281
ΚΗΦΙΣΟΚΛ-- 315
ΛΥΚΟ---- 437
ΜΑΝΤ--c.5-- 231
ΜΟΣΧ---- 65, 66
ΝΙΚΙ---- 162
ΠΕ------ 221

By first letter at end

---ΑΓΟΡΟΥ 327
...7...ΑΝΗΣ 230
----ΗΜΟΥ 189
---ΙΝΙΑΔΗΣ 230
---ΚΛΕΟΥΣ 393, 394
[..4.KR]ΑΤΗΣ 211
-c.6-3- ΛΕΩΣ 314
-c.3?-ΜΕΝΗΣ 314
....8...Ν 197
---ΟΔΩΡΟΥ 318
---ΟΘΕΡΣ 161
....9....Ο[Σ] 191
------ΟΣ 162
---ΟΦΡΟΝΟΣ 161
.3.ΠΠΟΣ 249
..5..Σ 73, 74
----ΤΟΡΟΥ 314

III. *GEOGRAPHICAL*

A. Attica

ΑΓΓΕΛΗΘΕΝ 62, 224, 225
ΑΓΝΟΥΣΙΟΣ 199, 202, 263, 264, 272, 281
ΑΓΡΥΛΗΘΕΝ 281
ΑΘΜΟΝΕΥΣ 140, 345, 348, 352, 354
ΑΙΞΩΝΕΥΣ 35, 36, 60-62 passim, 140, 319-322 passim
ΑΛΑΙΕΥΣ 21, 224, 263, 364
ΑΛΩΠΕΚΗΘΕΝ 96, 147, 148, 174, 175, 345, 361, 397, 402, 412, 416, 422, 428
ΑΝΑΓΥΡΑΣΙΟΣ 178, 182, 184, 189, 191, 194, 196, 197, 199, 201, 402, 422
ΑΝΑΦΛΥΣΤΙΟΣ 314, 315
ΑΦΙΔΝΑΙΟΣ 19, 53, 54, 56, 60, 202, 203, 281-283 passim, 301, 304

ΑΧΑΡΝΕΥΣ 28, 30, 32, 35, 36, 44, 48, 50, 53, 54, 56, 60, 69, 70, 242, 244, 281-283 passim, 286, 290, 295, 335, 336, 341, 342
ΑΧΕΡΔΟΥΣΙΟΣ 96, 105, 107, 127, 128, 328
ΒΟΥΤΑΔΗΣ 73, 77, 79, 115, 122, 135, 143, 189, 233, 242, 244, 263

ΔΙΟΜΕΙΕΥΣ 224, 306

ΕΙΡΕΣΙΔΗΣ 7, 13
ΕΙΤΕΑΙΟΣ 10, 34, 140, 209-212 passim
ΕΚΑΛΗΘΕΝ 361
ΕΛΕΥΣΙΝΙΟΣ 79, 119, 139, 140, 162, 212-214 passim, 216, 217, 335, 336, 340, 341, 345
ΕΡΙΚΕΕΥΣ 450
ΕΡΜΕΙΟΣ 281
ΕΡΟΙΑΔΗΣ 21, 272, 281, 283
ΕΡΧΙΕΥΣ 7, 228, 412, 416
ΕΥΠΥΡΙΔΗΣ 242, 244, 249
ΕΥΩΝΥΜΕΥΣ 44, 48, 233, 281, 284

ΗΤΙΩΝΕΙΑ 19, 20

ΘΗΜΑΚΕΙΕΥΣ 147
ΘΟΡΑΙΕΥΣ 263, 281
ΘΡΙΑΣΙΟΣ 295, 450
ΘΥΜΑΙΤΑΔΗΣ 199, 200, 202, 203, 242, 244, 281

ΙΚΑΡΙΕΥΣ 96, 99

ΚΕΡΑΜΕΙΚΟΣ 87, 94
ΕΚ ΚΕΡΑΜΩΝ 272, 276, 281
ΚΕΦΑΛΗΘΕΝ 65, 66, 162
ΚΗΦΙΣΙΕΥΣ 281, 414, 416, 434, 437, 441/2, 450, 452
ΚΙΚΥΝΝΕΥΣ 164, 412, 414
ΚΟΛΛΥΕΥΣ 281-283 passim
ΚΟΠΡΕΙΟΣ 189, 191, 194, 197
ΚΥΔΑ 161
ΚΥΔΑΘΗΝΑΙΕΥΣ 162, 172, 306, 318, 319, 363
ΚΥΔΑΝΤΙΔΗΣ 56, 243, 245
ΚΥΘΗΡΡΙΟΣ 65, 66, 363

ΛΑΚΙΑΔΗΣ 161, 364
ΛΑΜΠΤΡΕΥΣ 242, 244, 278, 281, 314, 335, 340, 369, 370, 403

ΜΑΡΑΘΩΝΙΟΣ 82, 91, 212, 281, 393, 394
ΜΕΛΙΤΕΥΣ 263, 281, 304, 397
ΜΟΥΝΙΧΙΑ 21, 24, 26, 369, 438
ΜΟΥΝΙΧΙΑΣΙ 2¿,24
ΜΥΡΡΙΝΟΥΣΙΟΣ 53-56 passim, 281, 442, 446
ΕΚ ΜΥΡΡΙΝΟΥΤΤΗΣ 222, 328

ΝΕΑ 82-85 passim, 90

ΟΙΗΘΕΝ 281, 314
ΟΙΝΑΙΟΣ 96, 97, 99, 100, 263, 337, 342

ΠΑΙΑΝΙΕΥΣ 30, 44, 48, 60, 61, 105, 130, 131, 133, 135, 191, 192, 233, 239, 242-245 passim, 249, 250, 281, 295, 296, 314, 437
ΠΑΙΟΝΙΔΗΣ 221, 281
ΠΑΛΛΗΝΕΥΣ 107, 147, 152, 158, 162, 165, 281
ΠΕΙΡΑΙΕΥΣ 19, 20, 67, 102, 140, 143-146 passim, 188, 255, 256, 366, 368
ΠΕΙΡΑΙΕΥΣ (demotic) 35, 36
ΕΚ ΠΕΙΡΑΕΩΝ 368-370 passim
ΠΕΡΓΑΣΗΘΕΝ 243, 245, 382, 388
ΠΗΛΗΞ 368-370 passim
ΠΟΤΑΜΙΟΣ 60

ΡΑΜΝΟΥΣΙΟΣ 105, 212, 281-283 passim, 301, 302, 327, 356, 357, 359, 361, 364, 365

ΣΟΥΝΙΕΥΣ 7, 140, 228, 303
ΣΤΕΙΡΙΕΥΣ 281, 283
ΣΥΒΡΙΔΗΣ 314
ΣΥΠΑΛΗΤΤΙΟΣ 142, 281, 314, 315
ΣΦΗΤΤΙΟΣ 178, 180, 243, 245, 273, 281, 314, 315, 326, 332, 402, 405
ΤΕΙΘΡΑΣΙΟΣ 140, 162, 229-231 passim

ΤΡΙΝΕΜΕΥΣ 281-283 passim

ΥΒΑΔΗΣ 281

ΦΑΛΗΡΕΥΣ 130, 133, 135, 161, 174, 266, 316, 442, 446
ΦΗΓΟΥΣΙΟΣ 142, 263
ΦΙΛΑΙΔΗΣ 143
ΦΛΥΕΥΣ 147, 158, 242, 244
ΦΡΕΑΡΡΙΟΣ 364
ΦΥΛΑΣΙΟΣ 242, 244

ΧΟΛΑΡΓΕΥΣ 136-140 passim, 218, 243, 245, 281
ΧΟΛΛΕΙΔΗΣ 263

ΩΑΘΕΝ 249

(Incomplete demes)

Φ..^{7}.... 162
..^{6}...ΕΥΣ 194

III.A (Athenian places which do not appear in Greek)

BRAURON 125
EPAKRIA 212
MT. PENTELIKON 212
NEW PHALERON 211
SEMACHIDAI 212

III.B Non-attica

ΑΒΔΗΡΙΤΗΣ 195, 196
ΑΙΓΥΠΤΙΟΣ 143-145 passim
ΑΙΓΥΠΤΟΣ 145, 291
ΑΙΤΩΛΟΙ 279, 306
ΑΚΑΡΝΑΝ 1, 6-9 passim, 11, 12, 441, 445
ΑΝΔΡΙΟΣ 13, 16, 17, 192, 194, 195
ΑΠΟΛΛΩΝΙΑΤΗΣ 29
ΑΣΤΥΠΑΛΑΙΕΥΣ 13

ΒΟΣΠΟΡΟΣ 428, 431

ΕΡΕΤΡΙΕΥΣ 285-287 passim

ΗΡΑΚΛΕΙΑ 322, 331, 336, 341 344

ΚΙΤΙΕΥΣ 78, 141-146 passim
ΚΛΕΩΝΑΙΟΣ 381, 389-392 passim
ΚΡΗΣ 45

ΛΑΡΙΣΑΙΟΣ 248, 249, 250
ΛΕΜΝΟΣ 30-32 passim, 47, 54

ΜΑΚΕΔΩΝ 17, 45, 46, 54, 134, 151, 169, 223, 225, 250, 332, 390, 391, 399-401 passim, 406, 438

ΠΕΛΛΑΙΟΣ 29, 397
ΠΕΛΟΠΟΝΝΗΣΟΣ 190, 412, 416, 417
ΠΕΡΣΗΣ 291, 293, 294
ΠΛΑΤΑΙΕΥΣ 78, 187, 190, 232-234 passim, 237
ΠΥΤΝΑΙΩΣ 152, 157

ΡΟΙΤΕΙΕΥΣ 403

ΣΑΛΑΜΙΝΙΟΣ 331, 334-337 passim, 340
ΣΑΜΟΣ 19, 254
ΣΙΔΩΝΙΟΣ 418, 422, 424
ΣΙΚΥΩΝΙΟΣ 407, 415-417 passim

ΦΩΚΕΥΣ 397, 399-401 passim

ΧΙΟΣ 45, 151-153 passim, 157

III.B (Non-Athenian places which do not appear in Greek)

ANAPHE 313
ARGOS 391
ARGOS (in Akarnania) 445
BOIOTIA 91
DELPHI 205, 245
DODONA 257
EPIDAUROS 17
EUBOIA 258
IKOS 205
KEOS 17
KIMOLOS 313
KYPROS 143, 145
MELOS 313
NEMEA 391, 392
ODRYSIA 223, 225–227 passim, 258
OLYNTHOS 39
OROPOS 84, 90, 91, 124, 146, 151, 198, 201, 248, 451
PAROS 258
PHOLEGANDROS 313
RHODES 289, 293, 294
THASOS 168, 169
THERA 313
THESSALY 250
THRACE 66, 225, 226, 256, 258, 259
TROIZEN 17
TYRE 425

IV. *DIETIES, FESTIVALS, SACRED SITES, RELIGIOUS OFFICIALS AND GROUPS*

ΑΓΑΘΗΙ ΤΥΧΗ 116, 123
ΑΓΩΝ ΑΜΑΡΥΣΙΩΝ 350, 353
ΑΓΩΝ ΔΙΟΝΥΣΙΩΝ 413, 417
ΑΘΗΝΑ 86, 93, 94, 120, 371, 395
ΑΘΗΝΑ ΙΤΩΝΙΑ 116, 123
ΑΘΗΝΑ ΝΙΚΗ 87, 94
ΑΘΗΝΑ ΠΟΛΙΑΣ 87, 373, 408
ΑΘΗΝΑ ΥΓΙΕΙΑ 86, 93
ΑΚΡΙΣ 213, 217
ΑΜΦΙΑΡΑΟΣ 116, 124, 151, 198, 199–201 passim, 203, 242, 244
ΑΠΟΛΛΩΝ ΠΑΡΝΗΣΣΙΟΣ 337–380 passim
ΑΡΕΙΟΣ ΠΑΓΟΣ 34–36 passim, 40, 89, 93
ΑΡΚΕΘΕΩΡΟΣ 382, 383, 388–390 passim
ΑΡΤΕΜΙΣ ΒΡΑΥΡΩΝΙΑ 116, 124, 125, 151
ΑΡΧΑΙΟΣ ΙΕΡΟΝ 89, 93
ΑΡΧΑΙΟΣ ΝΕΩΣ 86, 89, 93
ΑΡΧΗΓΕΤΙΣ 89, 93
ΑΡΧΟΥΣΑΙ 138, 140
ΑΣΚΛΗΠΙΕΙΟΝ 69–71 passim, 193, 255, 267, 272, 273, 276
ΑΣΚΛΗΠΙΟΣ 70, 116, 124, 253, 254, 266, 272, 273, 277, 278, 309, 310
ΑΦΡΟΔΙΤΗ (Kitian) 142, 143

ΒΩΜΟΣ, ΤΗΣ ΑΘΗΝΑΣ 87, 94

ΔΗΜΗΤΗΡ 117, 124, 139
ΔΙΟΝΥΣΟΣ 116, 123, 221, 254 277, 310

ΕΙΚΑΔΕΙΣ 376–380 passim
ΕΙΚΑΔΕΥΣ 378–380 passim
ΕΠΙΜΕΛΗΤΑΙ ΤΗΣ ΕΥΚΟΣΜΙΑΣ 272, 276
ΕΥΡΥΣΑΚΕΙΟΝ 302–304 passim, 319

ΖΕΥΣ ΟΛΥΜΠΙΟΣ 116, 123, 372, 375
ΖΕΥΣ ΣΩΤΗΡ 116, 123, 408

ΗΡΑΚΛΕΙΑ 213, 217, 219
ΗΡΑΚΛΗΣ ΕΝ ΑΚΡΙΔΙ 214–217 passim, 219
ΘΕΑΤΡΟΝ (ΕΝ ΔΙΟΝΥΣΟΥ) 188, 189, 197, 221, 222, 238, 267, 272, 276, 277, 286, 321, 367, 369, 437, 439

ΘΕΑΤΡΟΝ ΤΟΥ ΔΙΟΝΥΣΟΥ (Peiraieus) 368-370 passim
ΘΕΑΤΡΟΝ ΤΟΥ ΠΑΝΑΘΗΝΑΙΚΟΥ 233, 237, 238
ΘΕΣΜΟΦΟΡΙΑ 136-140 passim, 218
ΘΕΩΡΙΑ 115
ΘΕΩΡΟΣ 383, 390
ΘΗΣΕΙΟΝ 214

ΙΕΡΕΥΣ 69, 272, 273, 276-278 passim
ΙΕΡΟΝ 442
ΙΕΡΟΝ ΤΟΥ ΑΜΜΩΝΟΣ 147-150 passim
ΙΕΡΟΝ ΤΟΥ ΑΜΦΙΑΡΑΟΥ 146-149 passim, 151, 198-200 passim, 202-204 passim, 243, 244, 246, 248, 282, 283, 451
ΙΕΡΟΝ (ΤΗΣ ΑΡΤΕΜΙΔΟΣ ΑΜΑΡΥΣΙΩΝ?) 350, 353
ΙΕΡΟΝ ΤΗΣ ΑΦΡΟΔΙΤΗΣ 143, 144
ΙΕΡΟΝ ΤΗΣ ΒΑΣΙΛΗΣ 210
ΙΕΡΟΝ ΤΗΣ ΒΕΝΔΙΔΗΣ 65, 66, 255
ΙΕΡΟΝ ΤΟΥ ΔΙΟΣ 413, 417
ΙΕΡΟΝ ΤΟΥ ΗΡΑΚΛΕΩΣ ΕΝ ΑΚΡΙΔΙ 215, 217
ΙΕΡΟΝ (of Heros Iatros?) 174-176 passim
ΙΕΡΟΝ ΤΗΣ ΙΣΙΔΟΣ 143, 145
ΙΕΡΟΝ ΤΟΥ ΠΑΝΔΙΟΝΟΣ 318, 319
ΙΕΡΟΠΟΙΟΣ 63, 65-67 passim, 82, 83, 86-88passim, 93, 95-104passim

ΚΑΝΗΦΟΡΟΙ 87, 94, 116, 120, 123, 310
ΚΟΡΗ 117, 124

ΜΗΤΗΡ ΘΕΩΝ 371, 374, 376

ΝΑΟΠΟΙΟΣ 245
ΤΑ ΝΕΜΕΑ 245, 382, 388, 390 391
ΝΕΩΣ ΤΗΣ ΠΟΛΙΑΔΟΣ 415

ΟΡΓΕΩΝ 63, 65-67 passim, 173-175 passim, 252, 255, 256, 258

ΠΑΝΑΘΗΝΑΙΑ 88, 91, 92, 116, 123, 149, 150, 233/4, 237
ΠΑΝΑΘΗΝΑΙΑ, ΜΙΚΡΑ 81-83 passim, 85, 91, 94, 218
ΠΑΝΝΥΧΙΣ 88, 94
ΠΟΜΠΕΥΣ ΑΘΗΝΑΙΟΣ 86, 93
ΠΥΘΙΟΝ 138, 140

ΣΤΑΔΙΟΝ ΤΟΥ ΠΑΝΑΘΗΝΑΙΚΟΥ 79, 233, 237

ΤΑΜΙΑΣ ΤΗΣ ΘΕΟ 17, 20, 150
ΤΑΜΙΑΣ ΤΟΥ ΘΕΟΥ 86, 93, 116, 131
ΤΕΜΕΝΟΣ ΤΟΥ ΔΙΟΝΥΣΟΥ 367

ΧΟΡΗΓΟΣ 316, 318-332, 353

IV. (Items which do not appear in Greek)

ACHELOOS 254
AGATHOS DAIMON 445
AGLAUROS 126
AJAX 303
AMMON 150
AMPHIARAIA 204
ANTHESTERIA 330
APOLLO 28, 32, 124, 205, 246
ARTEMIS AMARYSIA 354
ATHENA PARTHENOS 126

BASILE 206, 209, 211
BENDIDEIA 67, 258
BENDIS 63, 65-67 passim, 252-254 passim, 256-259 passim
BOULE 396, 399

CHALKEIA 251, 252

DELOPTES 254
DEMOKRATIA 396, 399
DEMOS 396, 399
DIONYSIA 188, 222, 223, 238 277, 309, 310, 437-439 passim

ECHELOS 211
ERECHTHEION 93, 177, 395
EURYSAKES 303

HADES 254
HEPHAISTEION 36, 37
HEPHAISTOS 204
HERMES 254
HEROS IATROS 173, 175, 218

ISIS 144

KEKROPS 205
KEPHISOS 211
KODROS 211
KOLONOS AGORAIOS 304, 319

NELEUS 211
NYMPHAION 255
NYMPHS 254

PAN 254
PITHOIGIA 330
PROAGON 277, 309, 310, 439
PYTHAIS 205, 246

SALAMINIOI 303
SYNOIKIA 185

TELESTERION 217

GENERAL INDEX

Aitolian League 306, 307
Amphiktiony 37
asebeia 310
atimos 35, 36

Basileus (Persian king) 292
Bouleuterion 34-36 passim, 148

CALENDAR
conciliar year 74-76 passim, 166, 250, 288, 327, 339, 340, 393, 405, 438
count of days in last decade of month 74, 76, 77, 154, 155, 250, 297, 311, 347
distribution of days into 10 prytanies ("Aristotle's Rule") 75-77 passim, 149, 182, 183, 237, 250, 251, 287, 288, 297, 312, 339, 340, 346, 346, 397, 405
festival year 74, 76, 156, 166, 250, 251, 288, 339, 340, 346, 405, 444
full month 74-77 passim, 154, 155, 166, 251, 297, 340, 346, 404
hollow month 75-77 passim, 155, 157, 166, 251, 259, 311, 340, 346, 404
intercalary year 74-77 passim, 149, 165, 166, 264-266, 274, 286-288 passim, 309, 339, 340, 346, 347, 360, 397, 398, 404, 405, 414, 437, 438, 444, 445, 450, 451

Chaironeia (battle) 12, 17, 25, 37, 71, 90, 151, 237, 304, 417
Corinthian War 168

DECREES
Mikalson's "doubtfuls" 187 (list); #4, #5, #35, #48, #51, #63, #67
moved by Demades 131(list); #4, #5, #7, #8, #23, #24, #51, #87
moved by a deme 140(list); #26, #42, #43, #46, #47, #66, #70, #76
moved by Lykourgos 78-79 (list); #15, #21, #25, #27, #36, #48, #53
moved by a tribe 319(list); #61, #65
non-stoichedon 80(list); #16, #22, #26, #46, #56, #69, #76, #77, #80

Delian League 17
demosios (public slave) 115, 121, 300
dikasterion (court) 20, 301, 302
dokimasia 161, 167

ephebe 106, 126
ephebeia 132
epimeleia (supervision) 295, 298
eukoșmia (order) 272, 277
eutaxia (discipline) 62, 243, 247
euthyna (audit) 50, 51, 97, 101, 102, 104, 147, 148, 150, 215, 272, 276, 282, 303
exetasis (examination) 115, 121, 122

Gaugamela 226
grain shortage 313, 326-328 passim, 331, 332, 335, 337, 341, 344, 431, 432

Hellenic League 17, 41, 136, 293
Hellenic War See Lamian War.

HONORS
ateles (exemption from metic's tax) 8, 10-12 passim
citizenship 8, 11, 29, 132-134 passim, 159, 161, 163, 165, 167, 169-172 passim, 195, 225, 226, 406, 413, 415-417 passim, 431, 445
crown 56
deipnon (dinner in the Prytaneion) 162, 164, 383, 389, 390, 393, 394
eisphora (to be taxed as an Athenian) 8, 12, 234, 335, 341
enktesis (right to own land) 8, 12, 141, 143-145 passim, 234, 237, 335, 341, 423, 424, 426, 434, 435, 442, 446
gold crown 7, 50, 65, 66, 69, 70, 96, 97, 100-102 passim, 147, 148, 161, 166, 196-200 passim, 202, 203, 209, 210, 230, 243, 247, 255, 256, 272, 276, 282, 283, 291, 293, 301, 302, 318-321 passim, 335-337 passim, 341, 342, 350, 357, 371, 372, 375, 378, 413, 422, 424, 428, 431
isoteleia (equality in taxes) 60, 61, 298-300 passim
ivy crown 194, 195
oak crown 66
olive crown 14, 16, 60, 61, 66, 213, 217, 234, 369, 442
prosodos (leave to approach or speak) 14, 16, 79
proxenia 28, 41, 44, 46, 151-153 passim, 177, 178, 180, 181, 195, 196, 245, 250, 285-287 passim, 312, 383, 402, 405
proxenos 14, 16, 29, 44, 178, 194, 197, 335, 341, 382, 383, 388-390 passim, 392, 402, 423, 424, 426, 434-436 passim, 441, 442, 446, 447
zenia (entertainment in the Prytaneion) 14, 16, 60, 191, 192

HONORARY TERMS
andragathia (uprightness) 14, 16, 60, 163, 166
arete (goodness) 7, 97, 147, 194, 195, 209, 210, 213, 217, 272, 273, 318, 350, 353, 357, 369, 371-374 passim, 412, 413, 416, 422, 424
epieikes 194, 195
euergetes (benefactor) 14, 16, 44-46 passim, 72, 178, 181, 194-197 passim, 234, 237, 282, 283, 335, 337, 341, 402, 405, 413, 423, 424, 426, 434, 435, 441, 442, 446
eunoia (good will) 7, 14, 16, 50, 69, 70, 133, 134, 178, 179, 181, 213, 217, 234, 335, 402, 405, 412, 413, 416, 422, 424, 428, 453
eunous (benevolent) 45, 191, 192, 195, 207, 209, 210, 335, 341, 422
eusebos (piously) 272, 276
dikaios (justly) 50, 96, 97, 99, 371, 372, 375
dikaiosyne (righteousness) 50, 97, 147, 194, 195, 209, 210, 243, 247, 255, 256, 272, 276, 301, 302, 350, 353, 357, 369, 371, 372, 374, 375
philotimia (zealous conduct) 65, 69, 70, 96, 99, 104, 147, 148, 202, 203, 243, 247, 301, 302, 318, 321, 335, 337, 341, 371, 375, 428, 442
philotimos (generously) 50, 65, 66, 147, 202, 221, 230, 242, 244, 255, 256, 282, 283, 318,

320, 321, 350
prothymos (eager) 441

hosios (innocent) 34-36 passim

King's Peace 168

Lamian War 259, 279, 391, 394, 405, 406, 417, 418, 426, 432, 436
Law of Eukrates 33-41 (#6)
Law on Silver Coinage See H 43(1974) 151-188.
League of Corinth See Hellenic League.

LEGISLATIVE TERMS
aprobouleutic measure 78, 92
gnome 56, 73, 78, 97, 142, 202, 204, 273, 336, 337, 441, 446
kyria ekklesia 236, 239, 240, 326-330 passim, 342, 359, 402-404 passim, 412, 416
open clause 101
open probouleuma 144, 192
probouleuma 56, 78, 92, 148, 192, 203, 204, 225, 274-276 passim, 336, 341-343 passim, 445-448 passim
psephon 167, 172, 413, 417, 429, 431

metic (resident foreigner) 12, 20, 54, 62, 66, 67, 145, 300, 344, 400, 425, 426, 446, 447

MONTHS
Anthesterion 182, 236, 288, 327-330 passim, 434, 435
Boedromion 131, 178, 180, 402, 405
Gamelion 28, 32, 184-186 passim, 263-265 passim, 274, 288, 452
Elaphebolion 30, 32, 76, 107, 162, 166, 167, 188, 189, 191, 194, 197, 222, 274, 275, 277, 306, 309-311 passim, 313, 339, 437-439 passim
Hekatombaion 92, 150, 155, 184-186 passim, 382, 387
Maimakterion 73, 74, 76, 77, 158, 161, 221
Metageitnion 72, 77, 147, 148, 152, 153, 155, 156, 214, 216, 218
Mounichion 130, 133, 135, 295-298 passim
Posideion 74, 76, 105, 106, 182, 339, 340, 356, 403-405 passim, 412, 414, 416, 422, 452
Pyanopsion 242, 244, 249-252 passim, 327, 397, 398
Skirophorion 25, 26, 50, 51, 53, 54, 60, 115, 122, 128, 182, 224, 225, 274, 311, 312, 340, 346, 347, 364, 365, 450, 451
Thargelion 7, 10, 25, 174, 175, 200, 202, 233, 236, 239, 340, 345-347 passim, 359-361 passim, 442, 444, 445, 450

nomothesia 39, 102, 122, 247
nomos (law) 18-20 passim, 24-26 passim, 33, 35-40 passim, 44, 50, 51, 81, 91, 92, 94, 96, 97, 102, 108, 109, 115, 120-122 passim, 132-134 passim, 162, 167, 169-172 passim, 243, 272, 273, 335, 361, 413, 416, 423, 424

OFFICIAL BOARDS
agonothetai 32
apodektai 39, 383
Boule of the Areios Pagos 35-38 passim, 40, 41
diaitetai 246
dokimastai 39
epimeletai (of Bendis) 252, 255, 256, 258
epimeletai (of the Amphiaraic games) 204, 241-243 passim, 247
nomothetai 19, 25, 35-40 passim, 82, 91, 96, 101, 102, 105, 115, 118, 122, 205, 243, 247
proedroi (presiding officers) 73, 78, 96, 97, 142, 202, 203, 224, 273, 336, 337, 367

prytaneis 93, 96
strategoi 7, 9, 12, 37, 44, 46, 78, 79, 86, 93, 135, 150, 186, 187, 189, 442, 446
syllogeis of the Demos 103, 104, 370-376 passim
symproedroi 162, 164, 165, 168, 172, 185, 263, 264, 266, 314-316 passim, 361, 363-365 passim
synarchontes 97, 103, 104, 371, 375
thesmothetai 20, 30-33 passim, 53, 54, 161, 167
thesmothetai of tribe Aiantis 301-303 passim
triamenoi 368-370 passim

OFFICIALS
Curator of the Naval Yards 231
demarch 214-217 passim, 321, 322, 350, 353, 367, 368
epimeletes (superintendent) 66, 199, 200, 266, 302, 303, 305, 318, 319
epimeletes of the fountains 147, 149, 150
epimeletes of wall-building fund 20, 25
epistates (chairman) 238
epistates of the proedroi 7, 20, 30, 32, 35, 44, 48, 50, 53, 54, 60, 61, 73, 77, 78, 96, 97, 105, 107, 115, 116, 122, 123, 127, 130, 131, 133, 135, 136, 142, 143, 147, 158, 161, 162, 172, 178, 182, 184, 189, 191, 194, 197, 199, 202, 221, 224, 233, 235, 236, 239, 242, 243, 249, 263, 272, 286, 290, 295, 306, 309, 314, 326, 329, 335, 340, 345, 359, 361, 364, 382, 393, 397, 402, 403, 412, 416, 421, 425, 437, 442, 450
director of Theoric Fund 149, 150
grammateus (secretary) 65, 281
grammateus of the Boule 9, 14, 16, 35, 36, 69, 234, 243, 282, 423, 441
grammateus of the prytanies 7, 10, 13, 15, 19, 28, 30, 32, 35, 36, 44, 48, 50, 51, 53, 56, 60, 73, 80, 96, 98, 105, 107, 122, 127, 130, 133 135, 147, 148, 152, 153, 158, 161-165 passim, 178, 182, 184-186 passim, 189, 191, 194, 196, 197, 199-201 passim, 204, 221, 222, 226, 233, 236, 239, 242, 243, 247, 249, 263-266 passim, 272-274 passim, 286, 290, 292, 295, 298, 306, 314, 315, 327-329 passim, 335, 341, 345, 355-357 passim, 359, 361, 364, 365, 382, 387, 397, 402, 403, 412, 416, 422, 428, 430, 434, 437, 442, 450, 452
herald of the Demos 199, 200, 367
merarch 348-350 passim, 352-354 passim
nomothete 202, 203, 205
poletes 82, 91/92
presbeutes (ambassador) 336, 341, 344, 345, 397, 399, 400
tamias (treasurer) 14, 20, 44, 83, 137, 209, 210, 281, 321, 322, 335
tamias of the Demos 9, 35, 60, 69, 96, 97, 99, 100, 116, 121, 123, 148, 178, 197, 234, 243, 247, 272, 273, 336, 402, 413, 423, 441
tamias of the stratiotic fund 100, 131, 149, 150, 199, 200, 244
tamias of the wall-building fund 20/21, 25
taxiarch (commander of a tribal contingent) 86, 93
teichopoioi (wall-repair officers) 20
trierarch 62, 63

paranomia (illegality) 310

Peloponnesian War 126, 258, 259, 438

Second Athenian League 17
Social War 17

Thermopylae (battle) 417

TRIBES
Aiantis 301-302 passim, 304, 305, 319
Akamantis 211
Antiochis 132, 211
Erechtheis 319
Kekropis 319
Pandionis 304, 316, 318, 319, 322

TRIBES (in prytany)
Aiantis 185, 286, 356
Aigeis 142, 147, 163, 249, 250, 335, 339, 393
Akamantis 28, 32, 73, 74, 105, 130, 133, 135, 221, 263-265 passim, 345, 359, 414, 434, 435
Antiochis 32, 98, 115, 122, 127, 128, 188, 189, 191, 194, 197, 272
Erechtheis 32, 107, 199, 200, 201, 309, 311, 329, 359, 361, 364, 449
Hippothontis 163, 242, 244, 290, 306, 382, 387
Kekropis 32, 182, 224
Leontis 35, 185, 233, 239, 314
Oineis 163, 295, 428, 429, 431, 441
Pandionis 6, 7, 13, 44, 48, 50, 53, 54, 56, 60, 143, 152, 299, 357, 359, 402, 412-414 passim, 416, 422, 435, 449, 450

"War" 233, 237, 412, 428, 431
War against Philip 205
War against Sparta 162, 168